The World of Fatwas

Scholar, author, former editor and minister, Arun Shourie is one of the most prominent voices in our country's public life and discourse.

By the same author:

Are We Deceiving Ourselves Again?
Where Will All This Take Us?
The Parliamentary System
Will the Iron Fence Save a Tree Hollowed by Termites?
Governance, and the Sclerosis that Has Set In
Courts and Their Judgments
Harvesting Our Souls
Eminent Historians
Worshipping False Gods
A Secular Agenda
Missionaries in India
Indian Controversies
'The Only Fatherland'
The State as Charade
These Lethal, Inexorable Laws
Individuals, Institutions, Processes
Religion in Politics
Mrs. Gandhi's Second Reign
Institutions in the Janata Phase
Symptoms of Fascism
Hinduism: Essence and Consequence
Does He know a mother's heart?: How Suffering Refutes Religion

The World of Fatwas

or the Shariah in Action

ARUN SHOURIE

HarperCollins *Publishers* India

First published in 1995
First published in Rupa Paperback in 2002

This edition published in 2012 by
HarperCollins *Publishers* India

HarperCollins Publishers India, Cyber City, Building 10-A, Gurugram,
Haryana-122002, India

www.harpercollins.co.in

P-ISBN : 978-93-5029-342-3
E-ISBN : 978-93-5029-540-3

14

Typeset in Palatino Linotype 11/14
InoSoft Systems Noida

Printed and bound at
MicroPrints India, New Delhi

MIX
Paper
FSC FSC® C218906

This product is made of FSC®-certified and other controlled material.

HarperCollins Publishers, Macken House, 39/40 Mayor Street
Upper, Dublin 1, D01 C9W8, Ireland

For
reformers
of all traditions

Contents

Introduction

A fatwa is a decree, a ruling. The usual sequence is that a Muslim puts an issue before an authority, and the latter rules on the matter. The authorities that can issue a fatwa are well recognized. They can be individuals, they can be institutions—an institution like the Dar al-Ulum at Deoband has a special department for just this purpose. Of course the authority may take up a matter *suo motu* also.

The fatwas accumulate. From time to time they are compiled. These compilations become both the high literature of the community as well as the Islamic version of *Supreme Court Reports.* They are read by, and read out to the faithful. The conduct, and even more so the mind of the community is set by them—directly in some matters, indirectly in even more. In particular, the local maulvi, to whom the average Muslim is liable to turn when he is in doubt about some point of conduct or when he is entangled in a dispute with another person, will turn to what some authority has decreed in its fatwa on the matter. Problems of life, belief and law which confront the believer are thus answered by the fatwas, explains the twelve-volume collection of fatwas issued by the Dar al-Ulum, Deoband, as there is no question about human life, it explains, for which the Mufti cannot obtain the answer by looking up the Book of Allah, the Sunna of the Prophet and the law books. Moreover, it explains, the fatwas have saved the ordinary Muslim 'the travails of inquiry' in regard to the Book, the Sunna and the rulings of the jurists of the schools of Islamic law. Issuing fatwas is an art, it explains, by which answers to day-to-day problems are obtained. One cannot obtain these answers from any other source, it declares. And, as will become apparent when we consider the content and range of the subjects which the fatwas tackle, there can be no doubt that the mufti issuing fatwas has to have encyclopaedic knowledge—for he will be required to pronounce on matters that range from personal hygiene, to marital relations, to the fine points of the law on inheritance, to whether the earth moves around the sun or the sun moves around the earth, to the way a Muslim should live in and the extent of allegiance he should owe to a country like India.

In the bookshops in the Muslim areas of our cities—for instance in the bookshops around the Jama Masjid in Delhi—the collections of fatwas fill shelves after shelves. They are put together with great care, the sort of care one associates with sacred literature. The pages are well laid out. The calligraphy is often a work of art. The volumes are beautifully bound—ever so often with gilded embossing on the covers.

In a word, fatwas are the shariah in action. Now, we are being continually told that the shariah is sacred, that it cannot be touched, that it is of the essence of Islam, that touching it would be nothing short of an assault on Islam. One would therefore expect that there would be studies upon studies of these volumes of fatwas. At the least one would expect that those who regard continuing separate personal laws for the Muslims to be an eternal commitment, one would expect at least them to have devoted some time to studying these volumes—after all, they are asking that something be continued; surely there would be some curiosity to find out what it is that they are urging be continued.

The other point relates to the ulema. While there is no clergy or Church in Islam, the ulema exercise decisive influence over the community. The fatwas are their most accessible output. They reveal the mindset of the ulema. They reveal the mindset which the ulema seek to instil and perpetuate in the community. In fact, because of the way most fatwas come to be given—that is, by a layperson asking the authority for a ruling on a matter—and because of the way the volumes are organized—they first set out the question which the querist has sent, and then give the ruling—the volumes are an excellent prism through which one can glean the mind of the community as well, a prism through which one can glimpse the concerns of the community as well as the presuppositions which the community has internalized.

For all these reasons one would expect a host of studies on fatwas. But then one would reckon without our intellectuals. It is yet more proof of the fact that our intellectuals have seceded from our country; that there is hardly a study in either English or Urdu on the fatwas. During the months that I worked on the subject I came across just two solitary essays on it. The poor things could hardly be called studies: they were inadequate, in fact they were timorous.

The reason for this inattention is not that some inquiry has led our intellectuals to conclude that the fatwas are unimportant. The reasons are less estimable.

First, our scholars have not spared time for this vital material for the same reason on account of which they have not spared time for other things vital to our existence as a country. Most of the intellectual work in India consists in writing footnotes to work being done in the West—this has been so in the case of Marxist intellectuals even more than it is in the case of the others. And when our intellectuals are not engaged in writing these footnotes, they are busy following the fashion of the day in Western circles, busy 'applying', as the phrase goes, to Indian material the notion or 'thesis' which has become fashionable in the West. In a word, our scholarly work is derivative. So the first reason there has been no substantial study of the fatwas in India is that they have not yet caught the eye of the West.

The second reason is that analysing the fatwas would expose that which neither the secularist nor the liberal Muslim wants exposed. The liberal Muslim has internalized the notion that to bring the truth about the shariah to light, to put in the open facts about those who are the public face of the community, is to 'help the enemies of Islam'. The secularist is even more reluctant to have these facts put to public view. He has established his credentials of secularism by espousing the very positions which the ulema and fundamentalist Muslim politicians have advocated. Once the facts about the ulema, about the law they lay down, about the norms they prescribe become common knowledge the secularist would be out of the very thing he has made the proof of his secularism.

The third reason is just plain funk. Bringing the truth about the ulema and their fatwas out into the open is certain to call upon one the wrath of the ulema. The secularist naturally does not want that to happen: quite the contrary, he is ever anxious to be in the good books of the ulema—their certificates are invaluable in establishing his credentials; being invited to their gatherings is what gives him an edge over other secularists. And the liberal Muslim doesn't want to tangle with the ulema for the very reason that they have the power to issue fatwas.

Yet the subject is of manifest importance: the shariah is a vital public issue in India today, and the fatwas are the shariah in action; no group exercises greater influence over the average Muslim than the ulema; and nothing reveals the mindset of the ulema as do the collections of their fatwas.

Hence this study.

I have taken up five collections of fatwas for analysis. These are:

- *Fatawa-i-Rizvia,* Volumes I to XII;
- *Kifayat-ul Mufti, Mufti Kifayatullah ke Fatawi,* Volumes I to IX;
- *Fatawa-i-Ulema Dar al-Ulum, Deoband,* Volumes I to XII;
- *Fatawa-i-Ahl-i-Hadis,* Volumes I to IV;
- *Fatawa-i-Rahimiyyah,* Volumes I to III.

A word about these collections.

Most Indian Muslims are Sunnis, some say almost 85 to 90 per cent are Sunnis. Most Indian Sunnis are Barelvis, some would say two-thirds of them are, in particular those living in the countryside. The *Fatawa-i-Rizvia* is the most important collection of fatwas of the Barelvis. It consists of the fatwas issued by the most influential figure among them—Maulana Ahmad Riza Khan. He was a prolific issuer of fatwas, a formidable polemicist, often an abusive one, an indefatigable campaigner, in a word a pugilist. Few dared to cross swords with him, indeed few dared to even stand in his way. He lived from 1856 to 1921, and came to exercise a mesmeric hold over vast numbers.

Some of the practices which he allowed, indeed prescribed, were ones which others condemned as vestiges of paganism and polytheism—for instance, celebrating the *urs* or observing the anniversaries of pirs and 'saints'. At the same time he was most emphatic in denouncing anyone who joined hands with the kafirs even for attaining strictly Islamic objectives. Thus, for instance, he heaped abuse and scorn at those who had agreed to work under the leadership of Gandhiji even though it had been with the object of restoring the greatest of Islamic institutions, the Caliphate. You have agreed to work under a kafir, he railed. You have made Muslims the slaves of a kafir, he railed. I have used the twelve-volume set of his fatwas published in August 1994.

Mufti Kifayatullah was the mufti of Delhi, he was in fact often addressed as the *Mufti-i-Azam*, the Grand Mufti. His mastery of the Hadis literature was said to be unequalled. Born in 1872, he lived till 1952. He was devoted to *Tabligh* work. He founded the Jamiat-ul-Ulama-i-Hind, and remained its president from 1919 to 1942. He participated vigorously in the Khilafat and Civil Disobedience movements, and was twice imprisoned during the latter. He became a member of the Congress Working Committee in 1930. As the demand for Pakistan gathered momentum, he was one of its principal opponents among the Muslim ulema. In a word, a nationalist among the ulema. Quite apart from that, he was an astute, one is tempted to say a judicious man. Often his formulations are a pleasure to read—he doesn't give a black or white answer; often he clears a path in between the contending positions. Often his advice is sagacious. The *Kifayat ul Mufti, Mufti Kifayatullah ke Fatawi* is the nine-volume collection of his fatwas. I have used the set published between 1982 and 1987.

The Dar al-Ulum is of course well known. Started in 1866, it is often referred to as the Al-Azhar of India. From its beginning it was profoundly anti-West, it was anti-modern. Accordingly, many persons associated with it exerted themselves to undermine the British. That opposition was an aspect of its commitment to orthodoxy. Lauding this commitment to orthodoxy as one of the hallmarks of the Dar al-Ulum, a Government of India publication, *Centres of Islamic Learning in India*, says,

> One of the main objects of the Darul Ulum was to provide the Indian Muslims with a direct access to the original sources of

> Islamic Learning, produce learned men with missionary zeal to work among the Muslim masses to create a truly religious awakening towards classical Islam, ridding the prevalent one in India of innovation and unorthodox practices, observances and beliefs that have crept into it and to impart instruction in classical religion.
>
> The Darul Ulum has achieved this aim to a great extent, having been undoubtedly the greatest source of orthodox Islam in India, fighting, on the one hand, religious innovation (bid'at) and, on the other, cultural and religious apostasy under Western or local influences. It has succeeded in instilling in its alumni the spirit of classical Islamic ideology which has been its motto. As a matter of fact, Deoband has established itself as a school of religious thought—a large number of religious *madrasahs* were founded on its lines throughout the country by those who graduated from it, thus bringing classic religious instruction to large sections of Muslim masses. Some of these schools and colleges have in their right become renowned centres of learning....

That praise for re-establishing orthodoxy in Islam, for purging it of *bid'at,* a condemnatory word for heretical 'innovation', for purging it of 'religious apostasy' which the study says had crept into it 'under Western or local influences', that approbation is from a publication of our secular government! But at the moment I am on the institution's fatwas.

Ordinary people began to approach the Dar al-Ulum very early on for rulings on all sorts of matters. Soon enough the demand became so considerable that it could not be handled on an ad hoc basis. In 1892 a separate department was set up for issuing fatwas. By now literally a few lakh matters have been settled by the institution's fatwas. Initially the fatwa would be issued, and that would be the end of the matter. No copy of the fatwa would be kept, no record would remain. Eventually, copies began to be kept. For decades these were stored merely by the date on which the fatwa had been issued. On a visit to the institution soon after Independence, Maulana Azad, then the country's education minister and one of the most important figures in Pandit Nehru's government, himself commended the work which the institution had been doing in this field—it is a great religious service, he said, by which the difficulties of the people are being removed. He urged that a collection of them be published. Grouping the fatwas by subject, weeding out the repetitions, and selecting the ones that settled the more general principles of law on the matter took many years of painstaking effort. It was in 1962 that the Dar al-Ulum began publishing the fatwas in volumes organized around subjects. The set comprises twelve volumes. It has been through several reprints. I have used the set which was published between 1981 and 1985.

The Ahl-i-Hadis have been an influential reform movement, one is almost tempted to say a self-righteous movement except for the fact that that expression would be true of almost all the other groups too—who could have excelled Maulana Ahmad Riza Khan in being certain that he alone was right? The Ahl-i-Hadis did not capture the masses, but their influence far exceeded the numbers who professed adherence to them. And there were good reasons for this: they had a large number of followers among the 'aristocracy', they had great influence at courts such as that of Bhopal; more important, they came in a sense to set the norms. This was because of their basic position: they taught that instead of going by the rulings of any of the law schools one should regulate one's life by the Sunna of the Prophet, that is by what the Prophet himself had said, by the way he himself had acted. As the sayings and deeds of the Prophet are set out in the Hadis, they styled themselves as the Ahl-i-Hadis. They were also known as the Muhammadis and the Wahabis. They proclaimed that the world was about to end soon, in particular any time from 1884 as the fourteenth century of the Islamic era had begun that year and the Prophet had declared that the world would end in that century. This lent an urgency to their mission. They held that going back to the Hadis was the way to bring the Muslims together—for one could thereby vault over the feuds that had arisen among the law schools. They also introduced innovations in the manner of saying the namaz: some of these would appear trivial to the observer—should one lean on one knee or both, should one say *Amin* audibly or softly; but, as we shall see, these are exactly the sorts of things over which sects break each other's heads; moreover, other changes which they decreed were not just in ritual—they taught, for instance, that nothing was to be gained by observing the urs etc., of pirs, that nothing was to be gained by namaz for the dead. Campaigns were always afoot, therefore, to prevent them from praying in mosques used by other Muslims.

They inveighed against all syncretistic practices, condemning all these as vestiges of paganism and polytheism. They denounced the Barelvis for advocating observances of special days connected with 'saints' and the like; they denounced the Deobandis for basing their prescriptions on the jurists rather than on the Quran and the Sunna of the Prophet. As happens with all purist groups, while they succeeded in influencing other sects, a sub-sect grew from within which maintained that they were not pure enough: the Ahl-i-Hadis had argued that the others had departed from the true path by going by the rulings of sundry law schools rather than by regulating life in accordance with what the Prophet had said and done. From within them grew the Ahl-i-Quran who declared that the Ahl-i-Hadis had gone just as grievously wrong by putting all the stress on the Hadis. 'What about the Quran?' they asked. Allah, not the Prophet should be the Guide, His word should be the determinant. The Ahl-i-

Hadis had set out to unite the Muslims. They became another sect, indeed a sect on account of which there were many contentions. The four-volume set, *Fatawa-i-Ahl-i-Hadis,* was published between 1981 and 1989.

As is well known, a number of Islamic institutions came to be set up in western India. Rander in Gujarat in particular became an important centre of such institutions. As a number of Indians from these areas went and settled in East and South Africa, institutions and religious functionaries from places like Rander were the ones that came to exercise influence among Indian Muslims in those countries. The three-volume *Fatawa-i-Rahimiyyah* is a collection of the fatwas of Mufti Sayyid Abdur Rahim Qadri of Rander. Among the sets which have been used it is the only set which is available in English. It has been highly commended by several authorities. For instance, commenting on the set, the most influential figure in Islamic discourse in India today, Maulana Abul Hasan Ali Nadwi, rector of the Nadwat al-Ulama, Lucknow, and chairman of the All India Muslim Personal Law Board, writes:

> Books on *Fiqh* and *Fatawa* are being frequently published in our country and this is but natural, because *fatwas* and jurisprudential questions are a daily necessity of the Muslims; new problems arising every now and then call for immediate religious guidance. But this requires profound proficiency in *Fiqh,* extensive and intensive knowledge of its ingredients and a masterly aptitude for the principles of *Fiqh.* Over and above this, piety and prudence, fear of God, sense of responsibility and conformity with the predecessors' pattern are also necessary. Those who know the difficulties of this path and possess a consummate understanding of the Hanafite *Fiqh,* they alone can truly estimate the academic and practical value and worth of the *Fatawa-e-Rahimiyyah*; and also testify to the fact that Allah the Most High has fully blessed the learned author with

> these capabilities, which are the prerequisite in this age for the discharge of this delicate duty. May Allah the Most High bestow upon the Mufti Sahib a goodly reward, and health and strength in order to complete this beneficial series!

The three-volume set I have used was published between 1975 and 1982.

Even by itself this is a vast amount of primary material the forty volumes comprise over 18,000 pages. I could not have gone through the material but for the help of Mr Yashpal Bandhu, Mr Sita Ram Goel, and two friends who happen to be Muslim: at their request I have to withhold their names, such are the apprehensions under which even scholars like them have to live. Together the four were literally my eyes in the matter. They interrupted their own work to lead me through the volumes, often putting themselves to considerable personal inconvenience. I am most grateful to them. In addition, Mr Sita Ram Goel has taken the trouble to go through the manuscript with a toothcomb. To him accoSSSSSrdingly, I am doubly grateful.

So as to show the continuity of the tradition I have in addition referred to the three most widely used texts on Sunni law—the *Fatawa-i-Alamgiri,* the compilation which was put together at the instance of Emperor Aurangzeb; the *Hidayah* of Sheikh Burhanu'd-din Ali (d. AD 1198); and the *Fatawa-i-Qazi Khan* of Imam Fakhruddin Hasan bin Mansur al-Uzjandi al-Farghani (d. AD 1196). The way in which the tradition has remained locked in a straitjacket will become apparent in the chapter on women and talaq in which I have illustrated the point by using, not primarily the volumes of fatwas listed above but the twelfth-century *Fatawa-i-Qazi Khan*—an unconscionable and totally indefensible practice like 'conditional divorce' continues unchanged and unchallenged as one of Allah's boons to men from the twelfth-century

Fatawa-i-Qazi Khan, through the volumes *of* fatwas that we are primarily concerned with, to the rulings of our courts in present-day India.

There is one final extension. A vital part of my argument is that, while many of the things we read in the fatwas seem strange to us, they accurately reflect what has been set out in the Quran and the Hadis. This fact that what they are enforcing is what the Quran and the Prophet prescribed is also one of the sources of the strength of the ulema: in the end they can always cite the Quran and the Hadis, and no Muslim can find an answer around those ultimate authorities. Therefore, after setting out what the fatwas have to say, I have taken some of the themes which occurred most frequently and set out what the Quran and Hadis have to say on those matters. It is possible that the reader will feel embarrassed or angered by what is said in the fatwas, as well as in the primary sources. But he must remember that that is what the texts actually say, and that both the collections of fatwas which I have used and of course the Quran and the collections of Hadis are available in bookshops throughout our country. Indeed, they are the high literature of the community. They constitute the texts which students learn and memorize at the 'centers of Islamic learning' that we are forever being told are among the prides of India. Instead of being embarrassed or angered by what he reads now, he should ask himself:

- Why has he not encountered the material earlier?
- Why is he embarrassed at reading it? Is it because it punctures the image of Islam that he has been maintaining in his social circle? Is it because it knocks out the premises—'Islam is the religion of tolerance'—on which he has rested his 'secularism'?

And more pertinently, in a sense anticipating what he may feel on reading what follows, he should ask:

- When the material is freely available, when it is in the widest possible circulation in the very language in which the more impressionable masses have ready access to it, when this is what they are being constantly urged to read and indeed to live by, when this is the material which is taught and internalized in the 'centers of Islamic learning', when it forms the staple of those who control the mind and reactions of the community, when in fact it constitutes the very device through which they control and direct the community, when it is the high literature of the community, when it is the material on which the learned of the community are weaned, when it constitutes the most authoritative out-turn of those who are the most highly respected and the most influential personages in the community, when these are the norms and decrees by 'which the community is to regulate its life, why should the material not be available in English also, why should it not be scrutinized?

I would therefore hope that instead of doing the usual thing, that is expending their energies in pasting motives, the ones who are angered or embarrassed at encountering this material will turn to the material in the original, that they will read it, analyse it, and broadcast their findings. That way they will be devoting themselves to something useful, indeed to something lofty—they will be helping free Muslims from the thrall of the ulema, they will be helping in their liberation. And this initial study would have been taken a step further.

Their Sway

1

Their ways, their power

The Ali Brothers—Maulana Mohammed Ali and Maulana Shaukat Ali—had had little to do with the Congress. It was only in 1919 that for the first time they attended the Congress session as delegates: they had just been released from jail, and had come straight to the session.

At the urging of several Muslim leaders Gandhiji had taken up the Khilafat question. By then the Khilafat was a bankrupt and discredited institution. But Gandhiji concluded that as Muslims in India felt so strongly about it, all Indians—in particular the Hindus, even more particularly he, personally—must make the issue their own. Nothing should be expected of the Muslims or Muslim leaders, he insisted, our support for the issue must be unilateral, it must be absolutely unconditional. Many felt that as a reciprocal gesture Muslim leaders should at least have Muslims give up slaughtering cows. Gandhiji was adamant: there must be no bargaining, he maintained; if as a result of our espousing the issue of Khilafat, Muslim hearts melt and they of their own decide to give up slaughtering cows, that would be a consummation, but we must not make support for Khilafat conditional upon anything. Others maintained that Muslim leaders must give up the demand the British had engineered them to make—that of separate electorates. Again Gandhiji was adamant: he saw of course the

British design to divide the two communities; he saw too that this device—separate electorates—was the poisoned seed which would eventually tear them apart; but his answer to that was that everyone must take up an issue dear to the Muslims and thereby wean them from the designs of the British. Not just Lala Lajpat Rai, Swami Shraddhananda, Pandit Madan Mohan Malviya, but even the young Jawaharlal—the sentence occurs in the context of the Angora Deputation—felt that Mohammed Ali 'wanted to use Hindus simply as pawns'.[1] But Gandhiji was adamant: he would rather be deceived a thousand times, he maintained, than not trust.

In the event, in the following two years the Ali Brothers toured India and addressed meetings jointly with Gandhiji. Their names became household words. 'Shaukat has me in his pocket'—became Gandhiji's refrain. 'I shall go wherever *sircar* (meaning Gandhiji) asks me to go'—that became Shaukat Ali's refrain.

In 1923 Maulana Mohammed Ali was chosen the president of the Congress. His presidential address at Kakinada covered a lot of ground. Turning to the advent of Gandhiji on to the Indian scene he declaimed:

> Many have compared the Mahatma's teachings, and latterly his personal sufferings, to those of Jesus (on whom be peace).... When Jesus contemplated the world at the outset of his ministry he was called upon to make his choice of the weapons of reform.... The idea of being all-powerful by suffering and resignation, and of triumphing over force by purity of heart, is as old as the days of Abel and Cain, the first progeny of man....
>
> Be that as it may, it was just as peculiar to Mahatma Gandhi also; but it was reserved for a Christian Government to treat as a felon the most Christ-like man of our times (*Shame, Shame*)

1. Mahadev H. Desai, *Day-to-Day with Gandhi*, Volume IV, *28 January to 8 November 1924*, Sarva Seva Sangh Prakashan, Varanasi, 1969, p. 22.

> and to penalize as a disturber of the public peace the one man engaged in public affairs who comes nearest to the Prince of Peace. The political conditions of India just before the advent of the Mahatma resembled those of Judea on the eve of the advent of Jesus, and the prescription that he offered to those in search of a remedy for the ills of India was the same that Jesus had dispensed before in Judea. Self-purification through suffering; a moral preparation for the responsibilities of Government; self-discipline as the condition precedent of *Swaraj*— this was Mahatma's creed and conviction; and those of us who have been privileged to have lived in the glorious year that culminated in the Congress session at Ahmedabad have seen what a remarkable and rapid change he wrought in the thoughts, feelings and actions of such large masses of mankind.

At the culmination and conclusion of his address too Maulana Mohammed Ali proclaimed:

> In 1921 we gave a year to ourselves and the same period to the Government; but our part of the contract was not fulfilled, and we could not demand *Swaraj* as the price of our unfinished work. Let us go back to Nagpur, and with trust in our Maker and a prayer addressed to Him to give us courage, fortitude, perseverance and wisdom begin the great work once more that our great leader has outlined for us. If only we do not prove unworthy of him we shall win back our lost liberty, and it will not be as a prayer for success, but as the declaration of the announcement of victory won, that we shall then raise the old, old cry:
>
> MAHATMA GANDHI KI JAI.

Gandhiji was in Yeravda Jail at the time. Within the month his health had completely collapsed. On 12 January 1924 the pain had become so intense, his condition was so alarming that the civil surgeon, Colonel Cecil Maddock removed him to the Sasoon Hospital for an immediate operation. As chloroform was being administered, electricity failed. The operation was performed with the help of kerosene lamps.

The recovery was painfully slow. Leaders from all over came to pay their respects, explain their position, give assurances for the future.

'By that time Shaukat Ali's army came up,' writes Mahadev Desai interrupting his narrative of Pandit Motilal Nehru's visit on 27 January 1924. 'After some casual chat, Shaukat Ali talked about his activities. It was a moving sight to see him uncover Bapu's feet and kiss them at the time of his departure.'[2]

A few days later Hakim Ajmal Khan, Mohammed Ali and Shaukat Ali came together. 'The meeting with Hakimji, Mohammed Ali and Shaukat Ali,' writes Mahadev Desai,

> was also as touching as that with Shaukat Ali alone. Mohammed Ali also kissed Bapu's feet, but with the covering kept intact. Bapu himself was the first to greet Hakimji with joined palms and then they shook hands. Hakimji asked Bapu, 'You must have undergone a lot of suffering?' 'O, it was a torture.' 'What brought about this disease?' 'I must have committed an offence,' replied Bapu, 'God is giving me the fruit.' Mohammed Ali was simply sitting silent. Tears were streaming down his cheeks in profusion....[3]

The AICC met at Ahmedabad in June 1924. Gandhiji was pained to tears by the proceedings. He saw how much ground had been lost in the preceding two years. He wanted to leave, but was not able to make himself do so. Maulana Azad insisted he give the message he had promised. 'I complied,' wrote Gandhiji that evening for *Young India,* in an article entitled 'Defeated and Humbled', 'and in a short speech in Hindustani laid bare my heart and let them see the

---

2. Mahadev H.Desai, *Day-to-Day with Gandhi,* Volume III, *October 1920 to January 1924,* Sarva Seva Sangh, Varanasi, 1968, pp. 315–16.

3. *Day-to-Day with Gandhi,* Volume IV, op.cit., p. 21.

blood oozing out of it. It takes much to make me weep. I try to suppress tears even when there is occasion for them. But in spite of all my efforts to be brave, I broke down utterly. The audience was visibly affected. I took them through the various stages I had passed and told them that it was Shaukat Ali who stood in the way of my flight....'[4]

Though Gandhiji had named just one member as the one whose speech had driven a dagger through his heart, writes Mahadev Desai, 'It was not he alone but the whole All India Congress Committee that had done so; and, as if specially to beg Gandhiji's pardon on behalf of the whole Committee, it was Maulana Mohammed Ali, the President, who again rose at the end of Gandhiji's heart-rending statement and, with eyes flowing with tears, fell at Gandhiji's feet.'[5]

A few weeks later, Gandhiji sets off for Delhi. It is the first time he is proceeding on tour since his release. The platform at Delhi is packed. It takes a long time for Gandhiji and his companions to wade through it. Tension too is in the air: Hindus and Muslims have been at each other again. There have been communal riots in Delhi and Nagpur in July.

They take the tonga to Maulana Mohammed Ali's house in the city. 'The Maulana had a boil on his leg,' writes Mahadev Desai.

> It burst out, but hardly was he free from that trouble, when two new boils sprang up, which are still painful. When he came to the station, he was limping all the while, but immediately on reaching home he sat down to spin. The spindle was a little out of order and the thread drawn out snapped, frequently; the Maulana, however, would not give up spinning. I thought he would give up the wheel in an hour or so, but he plied the wheel all through his leisure time. After Bhai Devdas repaired the spindle, his zeal increased all the more. He was working

---

4. Mahatma Gandhi, *Collected Works*, Volume XXIV, pp. 334–40.
5. Mahadev H. Desai, *Day-to-Day with Gandhi*, Volume IV, op. cit., p. 96.

> away at the wheel all through the time Gandhiji was talking with Mussulman brothers. He must have thus spun as many as 500 yards before night time.[6]

Gandhiji returns to Ahmedabad after ten days. On 9 September another Hindu-Muslim riot breaks out, this time at Kohat in the North West Frontier Province. Gandhiji is back in Delhi. He again chooses to stay at the house of Maulana Mohammed Ali. The latest riot, the continuing animosity between the communities pains him, it makes him feel utterly helpless. Suddenly, and, as was his wont in these matters, without consulting anyone, he announces that he shall go on a fast for twenty-one days for Hindu-Muslim unity. There is consternation all round, specially because Gandhiji is still feeble from the previous illness. Mahadev writes:

> The reader is aware that on the first day I was asked peremptorily not to discuss the fast. But can the Maulana be ordered so? So he was told, 'Don't cry like that. Have patience.' The Maulana's plea was put forth with all the resentment that love generates and backed up with tears gushing in his eyes. 'What is this Bapu? Is this the kind of *mohabbat* (love) you have for us? You have simply cheated us. You will take every step only after consultation with us—that was our understanding. Has it evaporated?'
>
> 'But can there not be some things about which I have to render my account to *Khuda* first and last?'
>
> 'But you have made *Khuda* the witness between you and us.'
>
> 'No, we are both *Khuda's* bondsmen. Both of us are pledged to Him. It is with Him that I hold converse today. This thing (fasting at the call of God) is, by its very nature, such as forbids consultation with others. It is bred in my bones. My whole life has been built upon its basis. All my former fasts had been undertaken without anybody's previous consultation.'

6. Ibid., p. 141.

'But may it not be a hasty step when it is taken so suddenly? You simply laugh it out, you don't worry at all but have you thought of what may happen to us?'

'Everything will go well with you. And why do you take it for granted that I shall die?'

'And why do you take it for certain that you will live on? Playing these pranks with health and imagining that nothing is going to happen!'

'Oh, come now. Take my word for it. Calm yourself. You must not give way to tears. I will explain further tomorrow.'....[7]

As the months pass, however, at one public meeting after another Gandhiji is saying how sorry he is that the Ali Brothers are not with him on the platform. He is reading out telegram after telegram from them—Maulana Shaukat Ali is busy with some other engagement, Maulana Mohammed Ali is busy with the new printing press....

Soon enough the same Maulana Mohammed Ali who had been kissing Gandhiji's feet, who had been falling at his feet, who had been shedding tears in such profusion, who had hailed him as 'the most Christ-like man of our times', declares at Aligarh and again at Ajmer:

However pure Mr Gandhi's character may be, he must appear to me from the point of view of religion inferior to any Mussalman though he be without character.

Ambedkar, who was to narrate this about-turn with much relish in support of his thesis that Muslims cannot coexist with non-Muslims, recorded the sequel. 'The statement created a great stir,' he wrote.

Many did not believe that Mr Mohammed Ali who testified to so much veneration for Mr Gandhi was capable of entertaining

7. Ibid., pp. 192–93.

such ungenerous and contemptuous sentiments about him. When Mr Mohammed Ali was speaking at a meeting held at Aminabad Park in Lucknow he was asked whether the sentiments attributed to him were true. Mr Mohammed Ali without any hesitation or compunction replied:

> 'Yes, according to my religion and creed, I do hold an adulterous and a fallen Mussalman to be better than Mr Gandhi.'[8]

What explained this about-turn? Had Maulana Mohammed Ali's gestures of veneration been mere pretence? Had all those tears been sham? Had the brothers concluded that they had sucked all the 'use' they could out of 'the old man', as they now began to dub Gandhiji, and that he was no further use to them or to Islam?

As the controversy swelled, Maulana Mohammed Ali gave his version of the reason for his statement. In a letter to Swami Shraddhananda he wrote:

> The fact is as I had stated verbally to you. Even then some Mussalman friends have been constantly flinging at me the charge of being a worshipper of Hindus and a Gandhi-worshipper. The real object of these gentlemen was to alienate from me the Mussalman community, the Khilafat Committee and the Congress, by representing that I had become a follower of Mahatma Gandhi in my religious principles. I had, therefore, on several occasions plainly declared that in the matter of religion, I professed the same belief as any other true Mussalman, and as such I claimed to be a follower of the Prophet Mohammed (on him be peace) and not of Gandhiji. And further that since I hold Islam to be the highest gift of God, therefore, I was impelled by the love I bear towards Mahatmaji to pray to God that He might illumine his soul with the true light of Islam. I wish, however, to emphatically declare that I hold that today neither the

---

8. B.R. Ambedkar, *Thoughts on Pakistan*, Thacker & Co., Bombay, 1941, p. 302.

> representatives of Islam nor of the Hindu, Jewish, Nazarene or Parsi faith can present another instance of such high character and moral worth as Gandhiji and that is the reason why I hold him in such high reverence and affection. I deeply revere my own mother, and if contentment and gratefulness under all circumstances be the true meaning of Islam, I claim there is no person, howsoever well-versed in religion, who has understood it better than she. Similarly, I regard Maulana Abdul Bari as my religious guide. His loving kindness holds me in bondage. I deeply admire his sincerity of heart. But in spite of all this, I make bold to say that I have not yet found any person who in actual character is entitled to a higher place than Mahatma Gandhi.
>
> But between belief and actual character there is a wide difference. As a follower of Islam I am bound to regard the creed of Islam as superior to that professed by the followers of any non-Islamic religion. And in this sense the creed of even a fallen and degraded Mussalman is entitled to a higher place than that of any other non-Muslim irrespective of his high character even though the person in question be Mahatma Gandhi himself.[9]

In a letter to the *Tej* he put the point even more sharply, saying, '...to consider one's creed as superior to that of every non-Muslim is the duty of a Mussalman.' The Maulana wrote:

> There was one sentence in Swamiji Maharaj's letter which is liable to give the impression that I do not consider right action as essential for salvation. That is not at all my belief nor that of any other Mussalman. The essential conditions for salvation are faith, purity of action, persuading others to do good and to warn them against evil and to submit to all consequences of your actions with patience. I hold that a non-Moslem is perfectly

9. Mahatma Gandhi, *Collected Works,* Volume XXIII, Appendix 13, pp. 567–69.

entitled to reward for his good actions even as a Mussalman is liable to be punished for his evil deeds.[10]

The point at issue was not at all as to the essential conditions for salvation, but only regarding the distinction between Belief and Conduct. That is the reason why I gave to Mahatmaji the highest place among all the Mussalmans that I know of so far as actual character was concerned. But to consider one's creed as superior to that of every non-Muslim is the duty of a Mussalman. By stating this I refuted the charge of Gandhi-worship levelled against me and that was precisely my object and not to hurt the feelings of my Hindu brethren or to revile Mahatma Gandhi. If anyone can have reason to complain, it is my own co-religionists, none of whom I considered to be worthy of being ranked with Mahatma Gandhi in excellence of character.[11]

Gandhiji's reaction of course was typical. To a correspondent in Patna who sought his view he wrote:

Dear Friend,

I kept your letter by me all this time. I can see nothing to except in Maulana Mohammed Ali's statement. May not a man seven feet tall say of another five feet in height that the former is superior to the latter in height, although the latter is superior to the former in every other respect? May not the Maulana truthfully say that he is superior to the so-called greatest man in the world in so far at least the Maulana believes a religion which in his opinion is the best of all? I think the Maulana has legitimately drawn the contrast.

Yours sincerely,

M.K. GANDHI[12]

---

10. On this proposition see the fatwas cited in Chapter 4 below, as well as the verses from the Quran and the Hadis cited in Chapter 10 below.

11. Mahatma Gandhi, *Collected Works*, Volume XXIII, Appendix 13, p. 569.

12. Ibid., Volume XXVI, p. 214.

The Kohat matter also took an ugly turn. Muslims were the overwhelming proportion of the population. Hindus and Sikhs had been set upon and driven out. They had been thrashed, killed, forced to undergo conversions.

But to the astonishment of all, in December 1924 at the session in Bombay of the Muslim League (of all things), the till-recently president of the Congress, Maulana Mohammed Ali, moved an embellishment to what, even to begin with, was a partisan resolution. The resolution maintained that 'the sufferings of the Hindus of Kohat are not unprovoked, but that, on the contrary, the facts brought to light make it clear that gross provocation was offered to the religious sentiments of the Mussalmans, and the Hindus were the first to resort to violence; and further that, though their sufferings were very great, and they are deserving of the sympathy of all Mussalmans, it was not they alone that suffered....'[13]

'M. Mohammad Ali's resolution on Kohat at the Muslim League Session created a great stir in the friends' circle,' wrote Mahadev Desai in his *Diary*. 'Bapu complained, "Nothing could be a greater eye-opener than this !"'[14]

Gandhiji too was in Bombay. He wrote to Mohammad Ali:

> My dear Friend and Brother,
>
> Never do anything in a hurry. The resolution of Zafarali Khan is really better than yours. You have meant well but you have done badly. Your resolution reads as if Hindus richly deserved what they got. You state as facts that provocation was from Hindus, that violence too was commenced by them. You state that the Hindu suffering was great, (but) the Hindus were

---

13. For Maulvi Zafar Ali's resolution and the embellishment by Maulana Mohammad Ali, see Syed Shariffuddin Pirzada, *Foundations of Pakistan, All-India Muslim League Documents, 1906-1947*, National Publishing House, Karachi, 1970, Volume I, pp. 28–29.

14. Mahadev Desai, *Day-to-Day with Gandhi*, Volume V, 1970, p. 111.

not the only ones to suffer, meaning thereby that both suffered almost equally or if not equally, certainly not so much as to call for any special mention. The resolution, after recording its emphatic findings on the main facts, asks the public to suspend its judgment on the details of the allegations of the Government. Does it not follow that the Government version being true on the main facts, their finding on the details is likely to be true? If all parties are agreed on the main facts, is it worthwhile asking for a Commission on details? You make the League ask the Mussalmans to invite the Hindus to go to Kohat and to settle their differences with the Mussalmans honourably and amicably. This means that the Hindus are the offenders in the main. But if such is your opinion, then again why a Commission? You then proceed to invite the Hindus not to provoke and ask the Mussalmans not to resort to violence. This means that there was extraordinary provocation by the Hindus. The fact is that the kind of language used in the vile verses has become the normal condition of the Punjab. You might have said that such language was unpardonable for Kohat. Your condemnation of the Government coming at the end and in the language it is couched has no force whatsoever and you have made no case for condemnation either.

Zafarali Khan's resolution is in every way much superior to yours, and far less offensive. You have erred grievously in that you have made no mention of the destruction of temples. How I wish you had remained silent: I have read the resolution again and again and the more I read it the more I dislike it. Yet you must hold on to it, if you don't feel that it is wrong. What I want to do is to act on your heart and thereon (on) your head. I am not going to desert you whilst I have faith in you. The resolution is a revelation of the working of your mind. However crude the language, it shows your belief. I must, therefore, put forth greater effort still and see if I cannot bring you to a correcter perspective. You should not be ignorant of Hindu opinion on these matters. You must not say that Hindus even denied provocation and initial violence. They may be wrong in so believing, but seeing that they believe so, you should not have stated what you have. If you could not have the resolution like the Congress one, you might have protested and voted against it without dividing the League. With deep sympathy and love,

Yours,

M.K. Gandhi

'Bapu at first would not let me take down a copy of this letter,' Mahadev recorded, but agreed afterwards. 'When I talked of Shaukat Ali's shamelessness, Bapu said: "The cat will be out of the bag by the end of the year." "Rather by the end of two or three months, Bapu !," I said. "Still better then," Bapu returned.'[15]

It was soon out. Maulana Shaukat Ali accompanied Gandhiji to Rawalpindi to meet the refugees from Kohat. The two issued separate statements on what they had learnt about the riots.[16] Worse emerged. The sequel is recorded by Mahadev Desai:

Left Delhi on the 3rd morning. Kohat was the only subject discussed at Hakimji's residence right up to 10.30 p.m. on the preceding night. Dr Ansari and Hakimji (Ajmal Khan) held the view that the separate inquiry reports were best left unpublished. But Motilalji Nehru strongly opposed. 'That's impossible. The public was certain to expect the publication of the Inquiry Committee's findings and it is incumbent upon us to satisfy it.' It was at last decided to publish the reports, but with some changes. Shaukat Ali accompanied us in the train up to Sawai Madhopur on the 3rd morning to make them. Bapu first revised Shaukat Ali's report. He kept his every view intact, but cancelled only unnecessary repetitions. Shaukat Ali accepted

15. Mahadev Desai, *Day-to-Day with Gandhi,* Volume V, 1970, pp. 111–12.

16. Mahadev Desai, *Day-to-Day with Gandhi,* Volume VI, 1970, p. 49.

> the deletions. His last paragraph was a little clumsy and Bapu re-wrote it for him. Bapu then began to amend his own report. Shaukat Ali vehemently insisted that Bapu must drop the comparison with (Gen.) Dyer, the paragraph showing Bapu's reasons for his blaming Muslims and the sentence that it was, by and large, not the Muslim community that had suffered but the Hindus. Bapu slashed all that. I protested, though not strongly, against all those incisions and said that that mind itself was vitiated which could not bear the statement of even bare facts. 'But what else can be done?,' Bapu rejoined, 'that is the only way to change his attitude. Moreover, he too has conceded much.'[17]

It became even more evident in the following months that the two Maulanas had no further use for 'the old man'.

Gandhiji was all too aware of what had happened but continued to maintain that he would rather be deceived a thousand times than not trust others, he continued to teach that when comrades leave us we should not harbour ill will at their leaving us, rather we should be thankful that they had stayed the course with us up to that point.....

What ethic is it that validates 'using' others, 'using' even a person like Mahatma Gandhi?

Is it really the case that a Muslim, however low his character, is better 'in a religious sense' than a non-Muslim even if the latter has a character like that of Gandhiji? In what way is that 'using a man', in what sense is that relative estimate of believers and non-believers 'religious'?

When Shaukat Ali refused to sign the report which pinpointed the responsibility on Muslims of Kohat, was he being merely, and routinely partisan? Or was he obeying a higher religious command?

The answers will become apparent as we proceed.

---

17. Ibid., Volume VI, p. 49.

'With care and due circumspection'

'al-Salam Alikam, My Lord, I have received your letter just now. Allah be praised that all is well,' wrote Iqbal to his friend, the historian Akbar Shah Najibabadi on 12 April 1925.

> You have rightly observed that the influence of professional theologians (*maulwis*) had declined steeply as a result of Sir Syed Ahmad Khan's movement but that the Khilafat Committee has re-established their prestige among Indian Muslims due to the Committee's need for political *fatwas.* This was a grave mistake which has perhaps not been realized by anyone till now.

He continued,

> I have had an experience of this (mistake) recently. Some days ago I had written an essay in English on the subject of *Ijtihad.* It was read at a conference held here. Allah willing it will be published also. But some people have pronounced me a *Kafir.* In any case, I will talk to you about all this in detail when you come to Lahore. In India, these days in particular, we haye to move with care and due circumspection.[18]

Ijtihad, as is well known, is the right to interpret the texts. It had been one of the devices by which Muslim society had tried to loosen the straitjacket. But barely 200 years after the Prophet's death, the ulema decreed that 'the doors of *Ijtihad* have been closed.' This was being done, they said, because there were no pious Muslims left who could give reliable interpretations. Literal adherence shall be the rule henceforth, they decreed. As we know from his *Lectures,* which we shall take up in a moment, Iqbal believed that there was absolutely no basis for this embargo, and he held it to have been responsible for the subsequent stultification of Islamic

18. *Kalliyat-i-Makatib-i-Iqbal,* edited by Syed Muzaffar Hussain Burney, Urdu Academy, Delhi, 1991, Volume II, pp. 584–85.

society. But, as he wrote, he was dubbed a kafir for espousing that view. And he, with all the robustness he counselled to the world, chose to be careful and circumspect. The paper was not published.

Three years later the Muslim Association at Madras invited him to deliver lectures on modernizing Islamic thought. He organized the theme in six lectures which he delivered at Madras, Mysore, Hyderabad and Aligarh during 1929. He added a seventh lecture later. The collection was published by the Oxford University Press in 1934.

At one level *The Reconstruction of Religious Thought in Islam* is a powerful plea to break out of the straitjacket of *taqlid*, of slavishly following the rulings and doctrines of the past. He exhorted Muslims to see that the Quran 'embodies an essentially dynamic outlook on life', and to make that outlook their own, rather than 'the false reverence of the past'.

He traced the ossification of Muslim society to the fact that, ever since the acutest minds gravitated to Sufism, 'the Muslim State was.... left in the hands of intellectual mediocrities, and the unthinking masses of Islam, having no personalities of a higher calibre to guide them, found their security only in blindly following the schools.'

There was a point to the efforts of the conservative thinkers in striving to organize affairs, he said, 'because organization does to a certain extent counteract the forces of decay'. But in the process they had smothered creativity and initiative, and thereby themselves caused the stagnation they would have liked to ward off. '....They did not see, and our modern *Ulema* do not see,' Iqbal wrote, 'that the ultimate fate of a people does not depend so much on organization as on the worth and power of individual men. In an over-organized society the individual is altogether crushed out of existence. He gains the whole wealth of social thought around him and loses his own soul. Thus a false reverence for past history and its artificial resurrection constitute no remedy for a people's decay. "The verdict of history", as a modern writer has happily put it, "is that worn out ideas have never risen to power among a people who have worn them out"...'

Far from leaving no room for human thought and legislative activity, Iqbal said, 'the intensive breadth of the principles' enunciated in the Quran 'virtually acts as an awakener of human thought.' The schools and systems of law which the Islamic jurists had founded, their rulings and those of the subsequent commentators—which the propaganda of Islamic fundamentalism in India today would have us regard as unchangeable—'are after all individual interpretations, and as such cannot claim any finality'. 'Did the founders of our schools ever claim finality for their reasonings and interpretations?' Iqbal asked, and answered, 'Never'. He therefore declared himself in favour of 'a complete *Ijtihad*'—of the right to a complete interpretation on one's own. 'The teaching of the Quran that life is a process of progressive creation,' he declared, 'necessitates that each generation, guided but unhampered by the work of its predecessors, should be permitted to solve its problems.' He lamented the fact that 'In view of the intense conservatism of the Muslims of India Indian judges cannot but stick to what are called standard works,' and nailed the consequence: 'The result,' he wrote, 'is that while the peoples are moving the law remains stationary.' To bring the point home Iqbal drew attention to what had been done to Abu Hanifa. The example is telling as the overwhelming proportion of Muslims in India are Sunnis, and the overwhelming proportion of Sunnis are Hanafites—that is, they claim to settle their matters in accordance with the school of law Abu Hanifa founded. Abu Hanifa was known for his innovativeness, he strove against the tendency of other jurists to 'eternalise the decisions given on concrete cases'. But the modern Hanafi legist, Iqbal pointed out, had done just that to the interpretations of Abu Hanifa and his immediate followers—he had 'eternalised' the rulings which these persons had given in reference to very specific situations and circumstances.

As we saw, within but a few generations of the Prophet's death, 'the doors of *Ijtihad*' were closed, the right to arrive at interpretations of the original injunctions, that is, was taken away on the ground that no Muslims were left who had the piety to exercise the right.

Iqbal traced much of the ossification of Muslim society to this decision and raised a powerful voice against it. 'The closing of the door of *Ijtihad* is pure fiction,' he wrote, 'suggested partly by the crystallization of legal thought in Islam, and partly by that intellectual laziness which, specially in the period of spiritual decay, turns great thinkers into idols. If some of the later doctors have upheld this fiction, modern Islam is not bound by this voluntary surrender of intellectual independence....'

But then, remember, 'in India, these days in particular, one must proceed with care and due circumspection.' And so we see that in the same *Lectures* in which he hailed 'the dynamic outlook of the Quran,' Iqbal cautioned, 'Only we should not forget that life is not change, pure and simple. It has within it elements of conservation also,' and that therefore, 'in any view of social change the value and function of the forces of conservatism cannot be lost sight of.'

'It is with this organic insight into the essential teaching of the Quran that modern Rationalism ought to approach our existing institutions,' he wrote. 'No people can afford to reject their past entirely; for it is their past that has made their personal identity.' In Islam, he said, the task of reforming institutions is even more delicate as it's character is non-territorial, as 'mutually repellent races' have adopted it. Hence, he declared in words which echo admonitions we shall soon encounter, 'In the evolution of such a society even the immutability of socially harmless rules relating to eating and drinking, purity or impurity, has a life of its own, inasmuch as it tends to give such society a specific inwardness, and further secures that external and internal uniformity which counteracts the forces of heterogeneity always latent in a society of a composite character....'

On the one hand he hailed the changes in Turkey—it 'alone has shaken off its dogmatic slumber,' he wrote, 'and attained to self-consciousness,' on the one hand he charged Muslim countries with 'mechanically repeating old values.' But on the other hand, on the very page he advocated 'healthy conservative criticism' 'as a check on the rapid movement of liberalism in the world of Islam.'

'We heartily welcome the liberal movement in Islam,' he wrote. Only to add,

> but it must also be admitted that the appearance of liberal ideas in Islam constitutes also the most critical moment in the history of Islam. Liberalism has a tendency to act as a force of disintegration, and the race-idea which appears to be working in modern Islam with greater force than ever may ultimately wipe off the broad human outlook which Muslim people have imbibed from their religion. Further, our religious and political reformers in their zeal for liberalism may overstep the proper limits of reform in the absence of a check on their youthful fervour. We are today passing through a period similar to that of the Protestant revolution in Europe, and the lesson which the rise and outcome of Luther's movement teaches should not be lost on us. A careful reading of history shows that the Reformation was essentially a political movement, and the net result of it in Europe was a gradual displacement of the universal ethics of Christianity by systems of national ethics. The result of this tendency we have seen with our own eyes in the

> Great European War which, far from bringing any workable synthesis of the two opposing systems of ethics; has made the European situation still more intolerable. It is the duty of the leaders of the world of Islam today to understand the real meaning of what has happened in Europe, and then to move forward with self-control and a clear insight into the ultimate aims of Islam as a social policy.

What then is the ultimate message of the *Lectures*? Professor Mujeeb sums it up with his usual acuity: 'Finally, the challenge thrown out (in the *Lectures*) to the Muslims to reconstruct their life in accordance with the ideals of Islam is reduced to a hesitant and formal admission that some change might be made somewhere, but caution is more necessary than courage....'[19]

Was it prudence which had dictated this ambivalence—the 'care and due circumspection' Iqbal had spoken of in his letter to Akbar Shah? Or conviction?

One telling clue is that the lectures were delivered in English—a language in which they were less liable to have an impact on the broad mass of Muslims or even the Muslim literati, but also the language in which they were less liable to provoke the ire of the ulema. The Urdu translation of the lectures was never published during Iqbal's lifetime.

The *Lectures* were eventually published in Urdu only in *1958*—the poet having been safely dead for twenty years.

And to this day the *Ulema* exclaim how much better it would have been had the *Lectures* never been published.[20]

A Taubah-nama

Joseph Hell was a German orientalist. He wrote a book

---

19. M. Mujeeb, *The Indian Muslims*, George Alien and Unwin, London, 1969, p. 456.

20. See, for instance, Maulana Abul Hasan Ali Nadwi, *Nuqsh-e-Iqbal*, Majlis-e-Tehqiqat, Lucknow, pp. 39–40.

on the Arabs and Islam in German. The English translation was published as *The Arab Civilization* by the well-known firm Heffer and Sons of Cambridge, England, in 1926. The translation had been done by Salauddin Khuda Baksh, the son of Khan Bahadur Khuda Baksh, the bibliophile who founded the famous library in Patna which still bears his name. The book was translated into Urdu by Nazir Niyazi and published by Jamia Millia in 1927.

(The entire episode has been set out methodically in Shaista Khan, *Akabar ke Taubah-name*, 'Apologies of the VVIPs', so to say. The book furnishes the texts of the strictures and responses. The following account merely summarizes Shaista Khan's introductory essay. The book was composed and printed in 1993 by Maktaba Jamia. For much of 1992 and 1993 the Jamia Millia itself was convulsed by strikes and demonstrations over the Mushirul Hasan affair. In the event, *Akabar ke Taubah-name* has not been released to this day!)

In addition to describing Arab civilization, the book had criticized it also on some points. The translator had added many footnotes 'correcting' Hell's narrative at several points or, to put it more precisely, furnishing the Islamic version of those points.

Rumbling started. Objections were first taken to the footnotes: they did not go far enough in presenting the Islamic refutation of the criticisms, it was charged. Soon exception was taken to the book having been published at all, in particular to its having been published by an educational institution such as Jamia Millia.

The footnotes do not go far enough, the editor of *Maaraf*, Riyasat Ali Nadwi, charged in a seventeen-page critique in the journal's issue of May 1929. Mistakes survive in the volume, the editor said: it wrongly asserts that congregational prayers started not in Mecca but in Medina; it errs in its account of the *hukum* on *zakat*, of the introduction of the *mimbar*, the pulpit; it is wrong in saying that luxurious living started in the days of Usman....

Not earth-shaking matters, in any case matters which ought to be settled by evidence. But in fact, as happens invariably—in fact, as is invariably made to happen—these details soon became questions about fidelity to the Faith. The critique was enough to shake the translator: he wrote a detailed reply which the Jamia magazine carried in its issue of June 1929. He distanced himself from the book: the book is just a simple, straightforward account, he wrote, it is not some deep investigation. Yet, he added, scholarship cannot be divided between Eastern and Western, scholars should benefit from whoever says wherever he says it. Niyazi also gave detailed replies to each of the individual points of criticism.

A much more formidable figure took up the cudgels—Maulana Abdul Majid Dariyabadi: editor of *Sach* and *Sidque*, well-known Urdu journals of the time devoted to religion and social reform.

He said he had *not* read the book, but that it was clear that by publishing such a book Jamia had served neither the *millat* nor Islam—a statement with which all will be familiar who followed the barrage that was let loose against Rushdie or Mushirul Hasan or Abid Reza Bedar sixty years later: I do not have to wade through filth to know that it is filth, was Shahabuddin's justification for asking for the ban on Rushdie's book without reading it.

Next, a fatwa-issuing, theological seminary entered the fray—the Amarat-i-Shariah – the very organization which was in the news three years ago with its fatwa declaring the director of the Khuda Baksh Library, Abid Reza Bedar, to be a kafir. In its journal *Amarat*, Maulwi Mahmud Sher let loose strong strictures on the book as well as the translator. The strictures had started from details. They had already roped in the decision of Jamia Millia to publish the translation. They now raised the question of Faith: 'Why has he (the translator) brought this load of torment on his head by draping the garment of Urdu on the work of an enemy of Islam?' asked the Maulwi. We did not expect, the Maulwi declared, an establishment like the Jamia to produce a book which hurts one's sentiments—a standard refrain, as we shall see as we proceed. We had many expectations of this organization, Maulwi Mahmud Sher continued. What is most regrettable is that this book was published with the permission of and in consultation with a man as capable and zealous as Dr Zakir Hussain Sahib: the target was thus made specific—first some details in one book; then the translator; next the organization which had been so perfidious as to publish it; and finally the man running that institution.

Remember that the Jamia had been the object of the ire of the fundamentalists from the very beginning. It had been set up with the specific and declared object of nurturing citizens who, being devout Muslims, would dedicate themselves to the nationalist cause. Aligarh had already fallen to the fundamentalists: Jamia had been set up to counter the Aligarh ideology; it was therefore in the line of fire. Dr Zakir Hussain in particular was known for his efforts to widen the minds of the students and to give the institution a catholic character. The zeroing-in thus was not without a purpose. But to proceed.

The Maulwi wrote that he had read many books on the civilization of Arabia but that this book totally lacked sympathy with Arabia—another typical refrain: the focus is not on specifics, the motives of the author are questioned. In fact the book does not deserve either attention or answer, declared the Maulwi even as he focussed attention on it! Dr Abid

Husain and Dr Zakir Hussain, both of whom know German, should have written a rejoinder to it in German, declared the Maulwi who had just declared that the book did not deserve an answer! In other words, the enemy should have been countered on his soil rather than being enabled to bring his attack on Islam into India through a translation. We hope, the Maulwi concluded, that he—Dr Zakir Hussain—will cancel the publication of this book.

The charge had thus been raised to zero in on Dr Zakir Hussain; and what he had to do had been specified: provide a refutation, have it put out in German, withdraw the book from circulation.

By October 1929, Shaista Khan writes, Maulana Abdul Majid Dariyabadi had declared a virtual war on the book: this is an important technique—to harness all the forces one can drum up on one point, so that the targets just *have* to do something on the matter; their concession then becomes the proclamation of victory of the fundamentalists, and a warning to all for the future.

Dariyabadi repeated the charges that Riyasat Ali Nadwi had made, and added a few more—the author was wrong in saying that luxurious living had started during the Caliphate of Umar itself and increased during that of Usman...., he had been wrong in maintaining that Usman had favoured his family....

Jamia was by now unnerved. It devoted a four-page editorial to the matter: so as to make available to readers here the results of work done elsewhere, the Academy had decided to publish translations of works of orientalists, it explained; it had decided that wherever these scholars made mistakes, these were best ignored for those gentlemen too were human and they could well err; it was difficult for these scholars to gain full understanding of foreign cultures and foreign languages, the editorial bent backward to say; in fact, a service could be rendered to Urdu-speaking people by pinpointing and correcting the mistakes made in these books, the editorial explained—as if to say that its purpose in publishing the translation had been to bring the book's mistakes to the attention of Urdu readers; it acknowledged that there was merit in some of the points *Maaraf* had raised, and said that the author of the critique deserved thanks.

A typical liberal's editorial! One premised on the hope that by conceding some merit to the assaulters, that by being conciliatory, the fire would be quenched.

Dariyabadi smelled timorousness, he launched almost a movement against the book, reports Shaista Khan.

Apart from pressing his attack in the journal, he wrote to several notables and began publishing their opinions.

Napaak German chatter, wrote one. I had seen the book in German, wrote another, and had never thought it would be considered worthwhile enough to be translated into Urdu.

I saw a few pages of the book, wrote Mushir Hussain Kidwai, the lawyer, I could not bring myself to wading through more of it. An educational institution which produces graduates like the translator, he thundered, should be dug up from the foundations and converted into plough-fields.

Ghulam Bhik Nairang, who was to later become the deputy leader of the Muslim League in the Central legislature, wrote that the book ought to be consigned to fire.

Hakim Mohammed Jamil Khan declared: I have not read this book thus far, nor can I read it. I am astonished how such a napaak thing got published by the Jamia. That must have come as a real blow—for Hakim Mohammed Jamil Khan was the son—the only son—of none other than Hakim Ajmal Khan, one of the founders and principal patrons of the Jamia Millia.

Alas, sighed another, such reprobate material—*mada fasiq*—is being put out in Urdu, and that too by an educational establishment like the Jamia.

After reading what you have written, wrote the editor of *Khilafat* to Dariyabadi, every Muslim hangs his head in shame.

The 'Islamic achievements' of Jamia have become known by your review, wrote Al Amir Ahmed Alvi Kakorvi, and make me feel very sad; I apprehend that this book will greatly harm the Muslims.

To publish such a contemptible book is proof of going out of the *jamiat*, the community of Muslims, declared the editor of *Kashaf*.

The editor of *Al-Jamiat* wrote: by translating such a heart-searing and false book into Urdu, the translator has served neither history nor Islam and the Muslims; we regret, he added, that in spite of this Jamia is shielding this book. The editor of *Congress* thundered: from beginning to end the impugned book is a heap of ignorance and sin.

A relative of Dr Zakir Hussain wrote: your issue is an arrow which has pierced my heart; Dr Zakir Hussain Khan is my relative and a native of this place; I pray to Allah that He may further your enterprise and organization so that others can be brought to the right path.

The editor of *Medina* wrote: Sir, you have lived up to your love of the Prophet; I will pay my compliments to you in *Medina* after reading your review (!).

The last communication in the series was from Maulana Azad, who, as we shall see, was himself to be given the treatment soon enough. This book has not passed under my eyes, he wrote, but the extracts you have presented indicate that the author does not know the history of Islam. But the Maulana added: I do not understand why you have looked upon it—the book and translation—as an act of the Jamia. If a professor of Jamia selected a wrong book for translation, or if he fell short of a proper exposition, that is his individual failing. You should have addressed him as a translator. The question of bringing in the management does not arise.

The campaign had by now created considerable consternation at the Jamia. Maulana Mohammed Ali, whom we have encountered, was approached for advice. On his advice the translator, Nazir Niyazi, addressed a long letter to the journal *Sach*.

He sought to distance himself, and even more so the management of Jamia from the contents of the book, saying that neither he nor they were responsible for 'certain baseless ideas expressed in the book about the Prophet', nor did they seek to encourage such ideas. His responsibility was strictly limited to that of translation, Niyazi wrote, and as translator all he could do was to correct some mistakes of the author in footnotes. This is what he had done. I also find objectionable those portions of the book to which you have raised objections, he wrote. That is what I have made clear to Maulana Mohammed Ali when he mentioned to me your letter and the other writings on the book, he wrote.

Under the circumstances to spread the notion that the management of Jamia or the translator do not care for the prestige of the Prophet is very regrettable, Niyazi complained. Maulana Mohammed Ali has assured me that I should trust in your honesty, and I hope, said Niyazi, that you will not form a wrong opinion about my *iman*, faith, and *aqayad*, beliefs. He ended with the plea that the editor would clarify in the journal that the translator has not accepted the wrong descriptions given by Dr Hell, and that he has not sought to hurt the sentiments of Muslims.

The campaigners had him where they wanted him. Naturally, they gave a final twist to the dagger, for the translator was hardly the one who had to be brought to his knees.

There could not have been a stranger apology, the journal, *Sach*, commented. Instead of himself apologizing, he wants *us* to whitewash him. Where the poor man had sought to fortify his letter by recording that it was being written on the advice of Maulana Mohammed Ali, the journal turned this round: it is evident, it wrote, that he has not written the letter on his own, but because of Maulana Mohammed Ali.

His inner intentions are known only to Allah, it wrote, dismissing the translator's protestations, we have to go only by his words and their fruit. But now his intention is becoming clear.... He has taken us and our readers to be simpletons... What concerns us is that a despicable person is maligning the Prophet and another man is publishing those assertions—when there was no need to do so—with a few so-called corrections. We hold the second person to be equally guilty of the crime....

Today he is saying that Hell has made baseless statements. But, the journal noted, earlier this is what he had written: 'There is no book in our language which contains a detailed description of Arab Civilization. This book of Professor Hell will not only fulfil this commonly felt need, but also prove to be a guide to students of the history of Islam.'

Are such felt-needs met by baseless assertions?, the journal asked.

Those running Jamia realized that the matter could not be put to rest at the level of the translator. In November 1929 the Jamia magazine itself put out an announcement.

Last month numerous national newspapers and magazines have objected to the publication of *The Arab Civilization,* the announcement said. We have consulted Maulana Mohammed Ali, Maulana Azad and Allama Iqbal. All three have expressed the opinion that the footnotes written by the translator for correcting the misunderstandings and mistakes of the author are neither sufficiently lucid nor well argued. A deeper criticism is needed. The vice chancellor of Jamia is at present in Hyderabad, the statement continued. He has been requested to look into the matter. He has promised to return very soon, and to try his best to remove the misgivings of the well-wishers of Jamia.

The beleaguered management went further. It promised that the announcement of what is done will be published by newspapers before it is carried by this magazine.

Victory was almost complete. It was soon complete altogether.

The vice chancellor, Dr Zakir Hussain, wrote to the editor of *Sach* on 13 December 1929. When the Jamia Millia published this book it did so with good intentions, he wrote, believing that in doing so it was doing a service to Islam and scholarship. Some responsible persons had also been consulted in this regard, he said. But now a complaint has arisen that some portions of this book are likely to misguide the ordinary Muslim in matters of religion as well as scholarship.

Persons at Jamia Millia do not think that they or those they have consulted cannot make mistakes, Doctor Sahib wrote with characteristic modesty. They are prepared to review their actions at the invitation of anyone. Hence, Maulana Azad and Maulana Mohammed Ali and Dr Mohammed Iqbal have been consulted in this matter.

Now comes the operational part: the conditions which the Jamia had to agree to would do credit to the 'Self-criticisms' the cadre had to write during the 'Rectification Campaigns' of the Chinese Communist Party.

The translator has been requested, Dr Zakir Hussain wrote, that he should consult these high personages and other members of the world of scholarship (the reference was quite clearly to the ulema) and write a detailed essay on the objectionable portions of this book in accordance with the advice received from these people.

Notice the two points: (i) the translator—the 'transgressor' would be the word more appropriate in view of what the Jamia was agreeing to—should himself write the essay; (ii) he should do so after consulting those who had pronounced adversely on the book, and he should write in accordance with the advice they give.

Not just that. This essay, wrote Dr Zakir Hussain, is to be published in the form of a volume and made available to all those who have already purchased the book. And a German translation is to be made available to Dr Hell.

But even that was not all. In future, Dr Zakir Hussain, the *Sheikh-ul-Jamia,* assured, whenever the Jamia Millia publishes a book regarding Islamic Civilization it will consult these high personages and others in the world of scholarship.

The editor of *Sach* who had led the campaign was condescension itself. Dr Zakir Hussain is a God-fearing and simple man, he wrote in response. But instead of making a straightforward confession like a true Muslim of the mistakes he has made, it seems that his statement has been drafted by persons in some government office. But at least there is an acknowledgment that a mistake has been made. The gain is that an essay will be written and distributed, and before publishing books in the future there will be consultations.[21]

Notice the progress of the campaign: a few details about facts are swiftly raised to matters of Faith, to one's fidelity to the Prophet.

Notice the technique of whipping up a chorus.

---

21. As noted earlier, the full texts are given in *Akabar ke Taubah-name,* op. cit. The foregoing is merely a summary of the introductory essay of the writer and compiler, Shaista Khan.

Notice that those who lend their voices to the chorus do so often without reading the book, indeed in one case without even reading the 'review' of the book written by the leader of the campaign.

Notice the role of the Urdu newspapers and journals.

Notice the role of the notables.

Notice the presumption of the liberals that by bending they would save their skin, and thus be able to continue their 'main work'.

But see what the terms are which they have to agree to in the end as repentance.

Each one of these features is repeated again and again in the assaults the ulema have launched since.

The clamour for banning Rushdie's book without reading it.

Rushdie's hope at one stage that by getting 're-converted' to Islam he would deflect the campaign.

The misrepresentations of what Mushirul Hasan and Abid Reza Bedar had said.

The virulent role of the Urdu press in the campaigns against them.

The equivocal report of the committee which was appointed to go into the Mushirul Hasan affair....[22]

But how could you have thought I meant....?

Maulana Azad was universally respected for his erudition. His speeches swayed the audience, his writings fired readers. He was also among the most prominent nationalist Muslim leaders: his journals were successively closed down by the British, he spent nine years in their jails, he became the

---

22. Some details of the episodes involving Mushirul Hasan and A.R. Bedar will be found in my *Indian Controversies, Essays on Religion in Politics*, ASA Publications, New Delhi, 1993, pp. 363–86, and 387–97.

president of the Congress and represented it during the vital negotiations with the Cripps Mission.

It is widely accepted that in recent times few have brought to bear on the study of the Quran the learning that Maulana Azad marshalled for the purpose. The *Tarjuman al-Quran* is his major work. It has acquired the status of a classic.

The rendering and commentary are a product of the times. They seek to go beyond, or obscure, the externals on which Islam, the ulema in particular, lay so much stress. Instead they emphasize 'the essence'. Moreover, while Islam, and the ulema in particular, have always insisted on the sharpest possible distinction between believers and non-believers, while they have insisted in fact on the ceaseless and eternal hostility between the two, Maulana Azad maintained that the essential message of the Quran was tolerance, he focussed on the essential humanity that was common to both believers and non-believers.

'The Quran,' he wrote, 'points out that the teaching of a religion is two-fold. One constitutes its spirit; the other its outward manifestation. The former is primary in importance, the latter secondary. The first is called *Din*: the second *Sbar'a* or *Minhaj* and *Nusk*. *Shar'a* and *Minhaj* mean the path; and *Nusk* merely the form of devotion or worship.'

'The Quran,' he continued, 'states that the differences which exist between one religion and another are not differences in *Din*, the basic provision, but in the manner of giving effect to it, or in the *Shar'a* and *Minhaj*, not in the spirit of religion, but in its outward form.' 'The difference was but natural,' he emphasized. 'The essential purpose of religion is the progress and well-being of humanity. But the condition and circumstance of man have not been the same in every clime and at all time. Intellectual and social aptitudes have varied from time to time and from country to country necessitating variations in *Shar'a* and *Minhaj*. That explains the differences noticeable between one *Shar'a* and another.' And in support of this he called attention to what the Quran (22.67) proclaims:

> To every people have We appointed observances which they observe. Therefore, let them not dispute this matter with thee, but bid them to their Lord (the basic provision) for thou art on the right way.

To bring the point home, Maulana Azad recalled the telling instance. 'When the Prophet gave up his practice of turning towards Jerusalem in prayer and chose to turn towards Kaba in Mecca instead, the change was displeasing to the Jews and Christians,' he recalled. 'So great was the importance attached to the outward form ! The ceremonial was with them the criterion of right and wrong and truth and untruth! The Quran made a different approach to the subject. It did not regard the outward form by any means the criterion of inward truth or the basis of religion. Every religion has had to evolve its own ritual as demanded by its environment.' Hence his central point: 'The thing that matters is devotion to God and righteous living. So, he who is anxious to practice truth in life, has primarily to concentrate on the essential and make that the test of everything or the criterion by which he should distinguish right from wrong or truth from untruth.' See what the Quran (II.148) proclaims, he pointed out:

> And for every one a side to turn to (for prayer).
> Better therefore, vie one with another in good works.
> God will gather you all together, for God hath power over all things.

And what constitutes true religion is spelled out in the Quran (2.177) itself, the Maulana stressed:

> Righteousness is not that you turn your faces (in prayer) towards the east or the west; but righteousness is this, that one

> believeth in God, in the Last Day, in the angels, in the Books and in the Prophets, and for the love of God given of his wealth to his kindred and to the orphans and to the needy and to the way-farer, and to those who ask and to effect the freedom of the slave, and observeth prayer and payeth the poor-one and is of those who are faithful to their engagements when they have engaged in them, and endureth with fortitude poverty, distress, and moments of peril—these are they who are true in their faith and these are they who are truly righteous.

In the chapter *Maida* (Surah V of the Quran), Maulana Azad pointed out, reference is made to the different religious social dispensations. After referring successively to Moses, Jesus and the Prophet of Islam, the Quran (5.48), Maulana Azad pointed out, states:

> To each among you have We prescribed a law and an open way. If God had so willed, He would have made you all of one pattern; but He would test you by what He hath given to each. Be emulous then, in good deeds.

'Read the above passage carefully and ponder over every word of it,' Maulana Azad admonished. 'When the Quran was delivered, the followers of the prevailing religions took the outward forms of religion for religion itself, and all enthusiasm for religion therefore was spent on ritual. Every group denied salvation to every other merely on the basis of ritual. But ritual was not religion, said the Quran, nor the criterion of truth. It was merely an outward aspect of religion. The spirit was something superior to it, and that alone was *Din* or religion.' '*Din*,' he continued, 'in reality was devotion to God through righteous living, and was no exclusive heritage of any single group of people. On the other hand, it was the common heritage of all mankind, and knew no change. Actions and customs are but secondary to it. They have changed and are liable to change from time to time and vary from country to country under the exigencies of time and circumstance. Whatever differences one may notice between one religion and another, they relate particularly to this sphere of life.'

'Look at the phrase, "To each among you (your groups) have We prescribed a law (*Shar'd*) and an open way (*Minhajy*),"' Maulana Azad wrote. 'Mark that the term used here is not *Din* which should be the same for every one. That admits of no variation. *Shar'a* and *Minhaj* could not have been from the very nature of things uniformly the same for one and all. It was therefore inevitable that they should be different for different countries and different times. The differences of this type are not really differences in the basis of religion. They are so only in things subsidiary to it.'

'It is this truth,' Maulana Azad stressed, 'which the Quran aims to emphasize whenever it states: "Had God so wished, He would have made you all of but one pattern." The statement takes cognizance of the differences in disposition of different sections of making a living in different countries, resulting in differences in manners, customs and ways of living. But differences of this character are incidental to the nature of man and should not form the criteria of truth and untruth, and result in mutual dislikes and hostilities. Only the basis of religion should not be disturbed *viz.*, devotion to one God and righteous living. That is why the Quran lays such great stress on the need for tolerance....' *Din* consisting solely of devotion to God through righteous living—that alone is the core, that is the essence which is not to be violated, which is not to be changed. The shariah, the regulations, the *Minhaj*, the precise road one is to traverse, that depends on time, place, circumstance—it is as liable to be varied as time and circumstance vary. That was the central theme of Maulana Azad's *Tarjuman al-Quran*.

In a word, the *Sirat al-Mustaqim* – the straight path, as the opening of the Quran, the *Surah-ul-Fatiha* christens it – is: 'Believe and act righteously.'

The original work was issued in two volumes—the first came out in 1930, the second in 1936. Maulana Azad had laboured hard and long, in jail and outside, on the work. In particular, as Dr Syed Mahmud remarked in his introduction to the English version, 'Maulana Azad had, as I know, set great store by his commentary on the opening chapter of the Quran (the *Surah-ul-Fatiha* of seven verses) wherein he had surveyed its entire ideology. Indeed he regarded his achievement as a distinct landmark in the field of Islamic thought....'

It was this very exposition of his of the *Surah-ul-Fatiha* which became the butt of the ulema's propaganda.[23]

From the time the first volume of the *Tarjuman al-Quran* was published, for over a decade the commentary and the Maulana continued to be attacked—by the ulema to whom its ecumenism was anathema, as well as by those who were opposed to the Maulana's politics: for them the book was a handy occasion for discrediting the man in the eyes of Muslims, the book's ecumenism was the hatchet by which this could be best accomplished.

The Maulana was accused of wanting to start another Brahmo Samaj with its delusions of universalism. But everyone who has set out to forge a universal system has ended up creating just another sect, warned Ghulam Ahmed Parwez, who was to become later an important religious philosopher in Pakistan. He held up to the Maulana the latter's own words—'No one can enter the circle of Islam,' the Maulana had written, 'till he accepts obedience to Prophet of Allah as much as he accepts the unity of Allah.' In this confession of faith, Parwez pointed out, obedience to

23. The sequence and the supporting texts are meticulously set out in Qumarastan Khan, *Sirat al-Mustaqim*, Khuda Bakhsh Oriental Public Library, Patna, 1992, on which the following is based.

the Prophet of Allah and belief in the finality of his prophethood had been made as integral a part of the Faith as belief in the unity of Allah. Is there some difference in what the Maulana used to write in 1912 and what he has written in the commentary, Parwez asked, and which of the two does he believe now? The thesis that the Maulana has propounded, Parwez said, leads to the following conclusions:

- It is not necessary to believe in that Islam which in common parlance is known as *Din-i-Muhammadi*;
- Whoever is a believer in God and a doer of good deeds will attain salvation, whether or not he accepts the prophethood of Muhammad, whether or not he accepts the Muslim way of worship, whether or not he lives in accordance with the shariah.

How can these practical inferences be squared with Islam?, Parwez charged.

Hafiz Mohammed Ibrahim Sialkoti was more pungent. There is enough material in the Maulana's book, he wrote, to enable all to claim vindication, including the Qadiyanis and the non-Muslims. The fact of the matter is that the Maulana wants to set up an Islami Brahmo Samaj, Ibrahim Sialkoti charged. Just as Raja Ram Mohan Roy presented a scheme of reforms while remaining in the fold of the Hindu nationality, so also the Maulana wants to bring about reforms of the same sort while remaining in the fold of Islam, he said. What is so terrible about that?, you might ask. There is a difference between the two situations that is as vast as the distance between heaven and earth, Sialkoti declared. Raja Ram Mohan Roy was trying to reform a corrupt society, he was trying to lift it out of its *jahliyat*, its ignorance, namely its idol worship, etc. And in advocating those reforms, Sialkoti claimed, the Raja had been influenced by the Quran. But the Maulana is wanting to do this after the Din has been perfected, he is wanting to do this after the Quran has been revealed and its meaning has been made secure, Sialkoti charged. If the Maulana claims that he is not introducing reform, Sialkoti asked, how is it that what he is advocating never occurred in 1,350 years to any of the Companions, to any of the Companions of the Companions, to any imam, to any *mujtahid,* to any *muhaddis,* to any *faqih....* If what he is advocating is manifest, then it would have been within the knowledge of all Muslims. On the other hand, if it is very subtle, Sialkoti taunted, then it is a reflection on all these great men of Islam that not one of them ever had the insight to discern it.

The Maulana has only seen the letter of the shariah, Sialkoti declared, he has missed its spirit. The shariah can be changed or reformed only by Allah, and that work is reserved only for a prophet. It cannot be done by common folk going by their own subjective opinions.

Yes, it is right to say, 'Believe and live righteously,' Sialkoti allowed, but remember, he added, only that form of belief, only those deeds, which have been revealed through the Prophet of Allah, only those are permissible, only those earn merit.

While the Maulana had made much of the fact that Islam recognizes the earlier prophets, and while even today apologists of Islam draw attention to the same fact to establish their claim that Islam is a tolerant creed, these critics put that concession in perspective. One could have followed the earlier prophets till Allah sent down the Seal of Prophets, Mohammed, and completed the Message through him, they said. That having been done, it is now wholly impermissible to follow any of the earlier prophets.

With due respect to the Maulana, Sialkoti taunted Azad, we must know from the Maulana that if the Jews, or the Christians, or the Brahmos and Aryas, or Gandhiji and his followers, though staying away from the Quran, try to become righteous, will Allah accept their good deeds, and accord them merit for these deeds? Will they be entitled to salvation according to Allah's promise? We shall soon see how devastating, indeed conclusive an objection that was to the Maulana's attempt to read ecumenism into Islam. If they can attain salvation without living in accordance with the Quran, the critics pointed out, then the door is closed to the *dawat* of the Quran.

They scoffed at the entire endeavour on which the Maulana had expended so many years and such toil. He has translated the Quran into the Hindi language (i.e., Urdu), Sialkoti said, and done well by Hindi also, but what has been gained? This that the followers of different religions have been allowed to follow the prophets of their own times—and this when the shariahs of those times are not known, instead they have been asked to find what those shariahs were and follow them. They have been asked to do so even though those shariahs were incomplete (that is why the Prophet had to be sent down to complete them), even though several of the commandments of those shariahs have been abrogated. In spite of this being the situation, the Maulana has assured them that if they follow their own prophets they will attain salvation. After this permission, the critics asked, why should the Quran be followed? What had been needed, they said, was that by his *Tarjuman* the Maulana should have imprinted on the hearts of men the belief that without following the path of Muhammad, the *Sirat al-Mustaqim* is not available. But the result of the Maulana's efforts has been the opposite: there is now no need to be specifically attached to the Prophet.

What a marvel!, exclaimed Sialkoti. He who says the way of the Prophet alone is the way of the Quran is not the follower of the Quran, and he who says that the essence of the Vedas, of the Torah, of the Bible.... is the way of the Quran, *he* is the follower of the Quran!

This doctrine is beyond our feeble understanding, Sialkoti exclaimed, let this understanding adorn the Maulana alone....

And so on.

As is well known, Maulana Azad was not one to be easily persuaded. He was convinced of his own worth, and standing as a scholar. He could not but have looked with some condescension, indeed some disdain on some of those who were campaigning against his work. Even so he sought to explain himself, or let himself be persuaded to do so. But the explanations he offered in fact explain away his entire thesis, so much so that in surveying the controversy half a century later the editor of *Sirat al-Mustaqim* has thought it necessary to reproduce facsimiles of the letters which Maulana Azad wrote at that time.

This is being done, the editor writes, because the reader of *Tarjuman al-Quran* will scarcely believe that the author of that work also wrote these letters.

The Maulana now maintained that when he had said that the essence of the Quran and of Islam is 'Believe and act righteously', he meant exactly the things which the critics were alleging he had omitted. When a Muslim talks of '*iman*', belief, the Maulana said, he means not just monotheism, not just belief in Allah. He includes in the word belief in the Prophet of Allah—to believe in Allah without believing in His Prophet is no belief in the Quran. Not just belief in Allah, not just belief in Allah and His Prophet, but also belief in the entire chain of Prophets set out in the Quran, belief in the angels, in the Book, in the Hereafter, in the Last Day,—that is, the Maulana was now saying, when I used the word 'Believe' I meant each and all of the elements of Belief which have been enumerated in the Quran and by the Prophet. The commentary mentions, he emphasized, that the denial of anyone link in the chain is denial of the whole. In particular to deny the

Prophet is *kufr.* Anyone who foregoes belief in anyone of these elements shuts the door to salvation. Similarly when I talk of *amal,* deeds, when I talk of living righteously, he said, what else could I mean except to do those deeds which have been called *aimal salah,* the meritorious deeds by the Quran.

Where the reader might have thought that the Maulana had charted a new, humanist course, the Maulana now declared that he had only said that which had been the unanimous belief of all Muslims for 1,300 years.

Where the reader would have thought that the Maulana was making a vital distinction between Din and shariah, and thereby opening an aperture for liberating Muslim society, he now claimed that sort of distinction applied only to the past, to the times before the Revelation. As for the future, with the Revelation, the Message having been completed—and this completed message included the shariah and Minhaj—no change was now possible. The shariah and Minhaj had been set out to prevail over, they supersede all the other shariahs, the Maulana declared.

Where the reader would have thought that the Maulana had deliberately turned the emphasis away from external observances—keeping fasts, etc.—he now maintained that these observances were essential, that the only reason they had not been set out in his commentary on the *Surah-ul-Fatiha,* the very commentary which he had regarded as his distinctive, landmark contribution, was that he was only dealing with one aspect of the matter, that he was not writing a comprehensive book on beliefs and law.

Where the reader would have thought that the Maulana had attempted an opening to ecumenism by not insisting that Muhammad was the final Prophet, he now explained that the only reason he had not done so was that he was not setting out all the elements of Belief, that he was writing a commentary only on the seven-verse *Surah-ul-Fatiha.*

'In any case,' he now wrote, 'the answer to your question is that to Believe one should believe in Allah, in the Prophets of Allah, in the Hereafter, in the Last Day and in the Quran and those learned in the Quran. And to act righteously means to do those deeds which the Quran has declared to be meritorious deeds.'

Moreover he now declared, 'The Quran declares that the teaching of all the past Prophets has also been the same (as that contained in the Quran). If a Jew would like to act on the true teaching of Hazrat Moses, if a Christian would like to act on the true teaching of Hazrat Jesus, then he would have to adopt exactly the path which the Quran has set out.' 'No other path is possible except this,' declared Maulana Azad. 'This is the reality,' he now claimed, 'which is made clear at places in the *Tarjuman al-Quran*.'[24]

How effective the attack had been!

What is left of the ecumenism of the Maulana's commentary? When 'Belief' means every element of 'Belief' spelled out in the Quran—including belief in those who are learned in the Quran, that is the ulema!—when 'living righteously' means doing all that, and that alone which the Quran terms meritorious, when one follows another Prophet only when one treads the *Sirat al-Mustaqim* prescribed by the Quran—what is left of that broad-minded tolerance, what is left of the ecumenism which the original commentary of the Maulana had led us to believe was the essence of the Quran, and discerning which the Maulana had regarded as his distinctive, his landmark contribution?

Where is the aperture he was opening for modernizing law and mores by distinguishing between the essential and the accidental?

---

24. For the foregoing see letters of Maulana Azad to Ghulam Rasul Mehr dated 15 January 1936, and to Hakim Saadullah Gayavi dated 14 May 1936, reproduced in Qumarastan Khan's informative *Sirat al-Mustaqim*, op. cit., pp. 210–16.

The group which was not to be

To whom did each of these reformers feel compelled to bend? Why?

As those who portray Islam as being inherently democratic always note, there is no clergy or church in Islam. The mullah or imam in a mosque is just one who leads a ritual, he is not supposed to have any authority beyond that. The word 'ulema' which we hear so often, and with such awe, is the plural of *'alim'*—the man of learning. By definition, anyone can acquire the requisite learning. But what is the position in practice?

The Sufis were free-wheeling spirits. Like our mystics they emphasized direct perception, darshan. They had no time for rules and ritual, certainly none for intermediaries like the present-day ulema. What happened? They were set upon as heretics and disrupters, to the point that they came to talk in only the elliptical phrase, and be secretive at all times. Shah Waliullah was as fundamentalist as anyone can be, and as authoritarian in insisting on the enforcement of Islam as anyone can be. But seeing the fossilization which had gripped Islamic society, he advocated that 'the doors of *Ijtihad*' be opened again, that the revelations of the Quran and the deeds and enunciations of the Prophet ought to be reinterpreted. Seeing that few in eighteenth-century India understood Arabic, he translated the Quran into Persian. What happened? 'The publication of a Persian translation of the Quran, which he had undertaken in the belief that it would help considerably in disseminating knowledge of the Holy Book,' writes Professor Mujeeb in *The Indian Muslims*, 'brought him into unpleasant prominence. The conservative *Ulema* accused him of innovation, strong opposition was aroused and once some people even went to the extent of hiring ruffians to beat him up....' Sir Syed Ahmed Khan became the most dogged champion and rationalizer of British rule in India. He enunciated the two-nation theory—his words and propositions presaged to the dot what Jinnah was to proclaim in the 1930s and 1940s. But there was the other side to him: he argued vigorously against slavish adherence to precedents, he urged reinterpretation and reformulation of Islamic dogma. What happened? He was abused and reviled by the ulema. He was threatened with death. A fatwa declaring him guilty of kufr was obtained from the ulema at Mecca. From Iqbal to Maulana Azad to Dr Zakir Hussain, each was reduced to temporizing. It was not just that the particular reform he was urging was thereby foreclosed. What befell him, and the way he had to bend became a warning that deterred others.

In a word, there is intimidation, and it works.

And there has been the other way. 'Indeed, in all great Muslim thinkers up to and including the eighteenth-century Shah Waliy Allah of Delhi, there is no dearth of revolutionary statements,' writes Fazlur Rahman, the Pakistani modernist, in his *Islam and Modernity*. 'But orthodoxy had developed an amazing shock-absorbing capacity: all these thinkers were held in high esteem by orthodox circles as great representatives of Islam, but such statements of theirs as had some radical import were invariably dismissed as "isolated" (*shaadhdh*) or idiosyncratic and were quietly buried.'[25]

But it is not mere stratagems, it is actual power which has enabled the ulema to bury every reformist impulse. To start with, there was the pattern that was set during the Prophet's own life: from the time he acquired control of Medina, Islam became indissolubly linked with the state. Subsequently, states far and wide came to be captured in the name of

---

25. Fazlur Rahman, *Islam and Modernity, Transformation of an Intellectual Tradition*, University of Chicago, 1984, p. 30.

Islam. The rulers—often dissolute, often tyrannical—needed the ulema to provide rationalizations for their rulership. Often there was friction of course: Alauddin Khilji's remark is oft-quoted—'I do not know whether such commands are permitted or not by the *Shari'ah.* I command what I consider to be of benefit to my country and what appears to me opportune under the circumstances. I do not know what God will do with me on the Day of Judgement;' and the occasional monarch—Mohammed Tughlaq—even lashed out at the ulema. But such enunciations and actions had to do with cutting the ulema to size, with not allowing a rival centre of authority. As agents and allies and rationalizers, they continued to have a key role, and, from that role to acquire great power. The ulema for instance came to have great say in applying the law: they assessed evidence, they decided which rule of law was applicable, they decided whether the accused was guilty or not, they decreed what punishment was to be inflicted on the guilty. Such power over the daily life of the individual, naturally gave them great power over the community, as distinct from merely the court, in the countryside as distinct from merely the capital.

Moreover, they are the ones who presided over and conducted the rites of passage: they or their trainees solemnized marriages, among a myriad things, they certified divorces. They are the ones who cited, interpreted, procured, issued, and to this day issue fatwas. In a word, they had, and to this day have, a decisive say in the day-to-day life of an ordinary Muslim. This hold has been tightened by the premise which has been dinned into every Muslim—that Islam does not concern merely the matters of the spirit, that it encompasses every detail of life. This is the claim of every totalitarian ideology—of Nazism, of Marxism-Leninism for instance—the claim namely that it has the right to regulate the totality of life. Just as this premise delivered total control to the party in Nazi and communist societies, it has been the doctrinal foundation of the vice-like hold which the ulema have acquired over Muslims.

This totalitarian premise, and Islam becoming the state religion, set the stage. The lethal edge to the power of the ulema came from two further features. The state of which Islam became the state religion, and in which the ulema became wielders of vast authority was—and remained—medieval. Eighth-century Arabia became not just the model, it became the mould. The state which the ulema could and would bring down on anyone who dared to disregard them was ferocious. In addition, there was the tradition of medieval, tribal societies from Arabia to Afghanistan—of enforcement through parastatal terrorism. To this day, no Muslim who speaks out against the ulema can afford to forget this lethal potential.

Next, there are the networks. The ulema control the mosques, they control the madrasahs and *maktab*s.

They control every seminary: it is not just that they thereby control the mindset of those who will control the community in different geographical areas; the contacts and bonding, the 'Old Boy Networks' which are formed among course-mates at the seminaries give the ulema an unequalled capacity to ignite the entire community. Moreover, the ulema directly or indirectly control every single one of the organizations which are taken to speak in the name of Islam—the Jamaat-e-Islami, the Majlis-e-Mushawarat, the Tamir-e-Millat, the All India Shia Conference, etc. The Muslim who sets out to urge a new, liberal view has nothing even remotely comparable to these networks. Indeed, the organizations which had originally been set up to impart a different perspective have slid back into the grip of elements who are in awe of the ulema:

the Aligarh Muslim University was to have provided modern education and a modern perspective to its wards; it fell to reactionary elements long ago, indeed during Sir Syed's time itself—he scoffed at the fatwa when it was issued but soon, to keep the institution going, he had to agree to a compromise with the obscurantists: even his own interpretations of the texts, to say nothing of those of other innovators would be kept out of the classrooms, religious studies would be handed over to the traditionalists, to the very persons whose notions and perspectives Sir Syed held responsible for the stagnation of Muslim society. Similarly, the Jamia Millia Islamia was to have imparted a nationalist perspective, yet today its functionaries have to always be watchful lest someone charge them with not being Islamic enough.

Next comes the Urdu press. It has been one of the most potent allies of, in some ways the instrument of the ulema, as we saw in reviewing the campaigns against Dr Zakir Hussain and Maulana Azad. We saw the same role and the same potency in the campaigns in 1992 against Mushirul Hasan, pro-vice-chancellor of Jamia Millia in Delhi, and Abid Reza Bedar, director of the Khuda Bakhsh Library in Patna. A shrill tone, wholesale distortions, creating echoes upon echoes of their allegations, fomenting an extreme insecurity and then presenting everything as an assault on Islam—these are its hallmarks. And they invariably end up being deployed to fortify the world view which the ulema want the community to retain.

And then there is the effect of patronage. Funds from Saudi Arabia, or Iran, or Iraq, or other 'Islamic' sources go to the ulema, to elements and organizations controlled by or beholden to them. The funds are almost never channelled to liberals. The Indian state is of course worse. As the ulema control the community, it is to the ulema, and to those who speak their language that the state genuflects. As the state has got weaker, the ulema have been able to press their campaigns with greater and greater ease. And in turn they have been able to fortify their hold over the community by demonstrating that it is to them that the state bends—on Shah Bano for instance; that it dare not step in their way: look at the audacity of their current campaign to set up a parallel structure of courts—the shariah courts—outside the legal system of the country.

Now, the power of such an establishment rests on the flock being distanced from the rest, it rests on the followers being separate. And, secondly, on their being in a state of anxiety, in fact fear—the fear in particular that they are in imminent danger of being swallowed up by the surrounding mass.

The life and outlook of the people of India have been syncretistic, they have been inclusive. And even within Islam, and in the state even under Islamic rule there have been exponents and promoters of that line—Akbar and Dara Shikoh down to the ones we saw attacked, Maulana Azad and Zakir Hussain. But the line which has prevailed has been the other one, the ideology of separateness.

The problem is not the particular issue which erupts—whether a prosperous Muslim lawyer should pay Rs 125 to the seventy-five-year-old woman who he has kicked out after having been married to her for forty-three years and after she has borne four children; the problem is not 'Triple talaq'. The problem is that the Muslim community remains in thrall of the ulema, that the ulema need, and are therefore insistent on an ideology of separateness; and that they have the means to enforce this ideology.

Taken as a class, politicians are less dogmatic than theologians. They are also more attuned to the world of today than the graduates of, say, the Islamic seminaries at Deoband, Saharanpur or Lucknow are liable to be, conditioned as the minds of the latter are by archaic syllabi. But these factors notwithstanding, the politicians—both 'national' politicians and politicians who set themselves up as Muslims first—have been reinforcing that same ideology of separateness which is the stock-in-trade of the ulema. The 'national' politicians have sought to woo the Muslims not through the reformist elements among them but Ali Mian, Imam Bukhari, Shahabuddin, etc. On every issue—Shah Bano, the infiltration from Bangladesh, altering the Waqf Act, whatever—they have eventually adopted the line which the ulema, with their ideology of separateness espoused.

The contribution of Muslim politicians has been even more direct. Since Sir Syed's time, exceptions like Maulana Azad and in the Shah Bano case Arif Mohammed Khan apart, these politicians have depended on that same ideology of separateness: always making externals to be of the very essence of Islam, always frightening the poor and lay and ignorant Muslim that Islam, and hence his existence is in danger. If we acquiesce to the Supreme Court order on maintenance, to the high court's order on talaq, shariah will be next; if shariah goes, Islam goes—their chant has been no different, it has only been louder than that of the ulema. Their campaigns and rhetoric, and their victories in particular have all ended up fortifying the ulema on the one hand, and the most reactionary elements within the political leadership on the other: for the issue which has been taken up in these campaigns has been a 'religious' one; often the ulema have been brought centre stage during the campaign—from Khilafat to the campaign for reversing the Shah Bano verdict; the networks which have been relied upon, and which as a result of the campaign acquired even wider reach and further sinews have been the ones in the control of the ulema.

Hence the problem: as Asaf Fyzee noted, Iqbal and Abdur Rahim and others in India have rebelled against the straitjacket 'and yet none ventures to face the wrath of the *Ulema*'.[26]

The liberals add their mite.

The liberals' contribution

The liberal who happens to be a Hindu is so apologetic, he has internalized sham secularism so much, he is in any case so innocent of the texts—of Islam, of Hinduism, of our laws and our Constitution—and he has internalized double standards to such an extent that he has made silence on all matters Islamic, indeed toeing the fundamentalists' line proof of secularism. The 'secularists' of the English press are a ready example. They will refer to Ali Mian as 'the moderate, universally respected Muslim leader', without bothering to read anything he has written. They will refer to sundry muftis and maulwis as 'Muslim divines'. They will shut their eyes tight to what organizations like the All India Muslim Personal Law Board or the All India Milli Council are doing; and will jump in to shout and scream should any agency of the state take a step to uncover their activities. Worst of all, they will, by a Pavlovian reflex, weigh in on the same side as the ulema on issues, and insist that anyone who opposes that side is 'communal', 'fascist', 'revanchist'.

The effect of such shouting is not limited to poisoning the air of discourse. Weak rulers are swayed by that air. And so public policy bends to the ulema. The latter are thus twice strengthened.

Like his Hindu counterpart, the Muslim liberal is innocent of the canonical texts of the tradition: as a result when the ulema or some politicians shout, 'But that is against the shariah,' as they do at every turn, the liberal is not equipped

---

26. A.A.A Fyzee, *A Modern Approach to Islam*, Oxford University Press, Delhi, 1981, Reprint, p. 105.

to answer. Quite the contrary: he has gone along and convinced himself that the ulema are right on one thing, that the texts are too arcane and complex for him to discern their meaning. But that is what all priestly classes have always said—that unless one knows Latin,....—and the assertion is as much without warrant in the case of Islam as it is in other cases: the Quranic verses in question, the Hadis in question deal with mundane, day-to-day matters using ordinary, day-to-day words and expressions, often words so earthy, expressions so explicit as to be embarrassing by today's standards. Taking the assertion of the ulema about the meaning being deep and difficult to discern is just a rationalization for not bothering to study the texts, it is a rationalization for avoiding the trouble that would ensue if one joined issue.

The consequence is inevitable: the Muslim liberal is apologetic and defensive vis-à-vis the very ones because of whom he has no place in Islam. 'The Doors of *Ijtihad* must be reopened,' that has been the plea of every modernizer for a hundred years—we encountered it in the case of Iqbal a while ago. But why should there be that plea at all? After all, there is said to be no church in Islam. There is no Pope upon whom Muslims must wait to call a Vatican II. Why not just study the texts, formulate the new interpretation and broadcast it? But the liberal lacks the self-confidence to even make a beginning. He waits, he appeals, he hopes—that the very ones whose shop would shut if 'the doors of *Ijtihad*' were opened will indeed open them.

He appeals to them for a 'dialogue'. The Resolution which the Muslim Intelligentsia Meet passed on Triple talaq in 1993 illustrates how deeply ingrained, and in the end how futile, is the old habit. Instead of seeing, and presenting, the 'Triple talaq' matter as a symptom of the larger problem, the intellectuals put the issue at its narrowest. 'The point at issue in the current controversy is neither reform of Muslim Personal Law nor reinterpretation of the Shari'at,' they resolved. The dispute is between the different schools of Islamic jurisprudence, they said, and, as the practice is contrary to the provisions of the Quran, 'the point involved is the reiteration of the authority of the Quran and the Tradition (*hadis*).' Accordingly, the Intellectuals Meet appealed to the Muslim Personal Law Board 'to convene a representative conference of Islamic jurists, Muslim clerics and intellectuals in India and provide an authentic interpretation on the issue keeping in mind the social realities on the ground.'

The object therefore is to have an authentic interpretation of the Quran. This is to be provided by the Muslim Personal Law Board. To aid it in doing so a meeting is to be convened. By the Muslim Personal Law Board.

Months and months passed after that Resolution was passed and duly sent to the Board. Reminders were sent. The Muslim Personal Law Board did not deign to respond. The intellectuals kept waiting.

It is as if Martin Luther were to appeal to the Pope to convene a conference to examine the very doctrine which gave Rome, in particular the Pope their authority.

But why should the ulema enter into a dialogue? They would then be recognizing the modernizing liberals as their equal. Indeed, the ulema would then be the lawyers for the defence, while the liberals are lawyers for the prosecution. The ulema therefore spurn such overtures, and instead take the position, 'You state what you have in mind, and we will tell you whether that is right or wrong'—that way they are not one of two lawyers, they are the judge. This is their unvarying response. But the liberal does not have the confidence to leave them alone and proceed to formulate and broadcast the reforms, he doesn't have the wherewithal either. Spurned, his reflex is to renew his petitions for dialogue.

Moreover, the liberal Muslim is as distant from the Muslim community as he is from the texts. Indeed, as he is in relation to the ulema, and the texts, he is not just distant, he is defensive. Far from showing that the way he has adopted—of acquiring the new learning and skills, of succeeding in professions—is the way, he feels guilty about having succeeded, as a person might be who has run away from the slum and made it but is constantly weighed down by the knowledge that his family is still wasting away in that ghetto.

Distant, defensive, with neither resources nor organization, the liberal is easily frightened away by the minatory ranting of the fundamentalists. He seldom speaks out on 'Islamic' issues—he is not equipped to do so, in any case to be concerned about them, to work at them isn't the thing that a secular, modern person should be seen doing. On the rare occasion he speaks, he does not speak the whole truth—'Showing up the terror to which the power to pronounce talaq subjects Muslim women will only help the enemies of Islam,' inveigh the fundamentalists, and he subsides. When one Muslim country after another was modernizing Islamic personal law, the ulema here inveighed, 'But they can do so as they are Islamic countries; here that cannot be allowed because this is not a Muslim country,' and the liberal resigned himself to their assertion. As over the last five years some of the 'Islamic' countries fell into the hands of fundamentalists and started reverting to the older, iniquitous laws, the fundamentalists began asserting, 'When Islamic countries are reintroducing the shariah, how can it be allowed to be undermined here?,' and again the liberal resigned himself to their assertion.

Throughout, the fundamentalists have foreclosed all possibilities of any foundational critique of Islam by a standard 'heads I win, tails you lose' accusation: if the critique has been from a Muslim, they have dismissed it, maintaining, 'But he is a *murtad*, an apostate; there is no reason to listen to him;' if it has been from a non-Muslim, they have ruled it out of court, maintaining, 'But he is a kafir, why should he be listened to?'

Of course the liberal doesn't share that dodge. But his defensiveness vis-à-vis the ulema leads him to a position the practical consequences of which are exactly the same. He does not examine the texts himself, he does not himself confront the assertions of the ulema. When someone else does so, he wails, 'For heaven's sake, don't you see you are making our task difficult? Now they say, "You are saying the same thing which that enemy of Islam is saying."' A person less defensive would let them go on saying what they will, and instead urge the community to assess the substance of the points irrespective of who was urging them.

Just as destructive is the misplaced 'loyalty' he has internalized. He does not speak the whole truth—neither about the texts, nor about Muslim society and its controllers—on the premise that to do so would 'help the enemies of Islam'. That premise has been dinned into the community by the ulema, for it is enough by itself to foreclose any challenge to their authority, it is enough to foreclose examination of texts on which that authority rests. It is also enough to shut off inquiry from the other side: it could have been the case, for instance, that reformers would look at the backwardness of Muslim society, trace it back to its roots—the texts, the mindset, the social mores—and urge reforms in these; but when talking the truth about the texts, about the social mores becomes 'helping the enemies of Islam', that door to improvement is closed. And the power of the ulema remains intact.

For ever so long Indian Muslims, and therefore Indians in general have suffered because of this timorousness of the Muslim liberal. For a brief moment it seemed that Ayodhya would spell a change. On the one hand, the Muslim community was brought face to face with the costs of the politics of Shahabuddin, Imam Bukhari and the rest: it seemed more willing to listen to the liberal voices within it. On the other, the Muslim liberal was reminded that it was not enough for him to be liberal. If the community continued to follow obscurantist leaders, there *would* be a reaction, and all, including the Muslim liberal would be sucked down in its tow.

Several Muslim liberals therefore began taking a lead in defining what ought to be done on issues which had become the preserve of the obscurantists. On 'Triple talaq' itself, as we saw, several months before Justice Tilhari gave his judgment, the Muslim Intelligentsia Meet had passed a resolution condemning the practice as being in violation of the Quran and Hadis. It had drawn attention to the 'extreme hardship and harshness' to which the practice exposes women. So, there was an aperture of opportunity.

But the moment passed: soon enough Ali Mian, the All India Milli Council and the rest were once again in the forefront; the Muslim liberal was once again back in his cubbyhole.

Each of these factors contributes to the power of the ulema. But, as we shall see, the central explanation is different.

It is the ideology of Islam itself: it is totalitarian, and it is millenarian.

It lays claim to regulate the totality of life. Hence it delivers to those who set themselves up to enforce the claim, control over every aspect of life.

Second, it claims that the moment Islam prevails the millennium shall dawn. It follows that the one who does not surrender to it is thwarting that millennium, he is standing in the way of Allah—exactly as the one who did not surrender to communism was thwarting *that* millennium, exactly as he was standing in the way of history. Therefore, all means are not just permissible, not just justified, all means needed to put him out of harm's way are mandated—they are mandated by the very one who mandated the Way, that is by Allah Himself; indeed, the mandate for them is implicit in, it is a necessary element of the mandate for the Way itself.

This is the mindset that delivers power to the ulema. And the ulema ensure that that mindset persists.

And the reason they prevail over the reformers is that the propositions they articulate, the mindset they seek to perpetuate are indeed the propositions and the mindset which the founts of Islam—the Quran and the Sunna of the Prophet—prescribe.

It is not just ignorance of the texts which defeats the liberal. It is that ulema are faithful to the texts.

What is the mindset of the ulema?

What is the mindset they instil and perpetuate in the community?

2

All of Life

'If only a part of the '*supari*' enters the woman, has the woman to bathe?' 'If only the forepart of the man enters the *sharamgah,* the vagina, is a bath obligatory? Even if there is no discharge of semen?' 'If both the man and the woman have clothes on during the act, is a bath necessary?' 'What is the hukum according to shariah: must one bathe immediately after intercourse when there is an apprehension that doing so will precipitate an illness?' 'If semen is emitted while one is awake, is a bath required?' 'If one-fourth to one-third part of the man's organ enters the sharamgah, the vagina, and the gushing semen enters the vagina, is a bath necessary for the woman?' 'For the last few days I am not sleeping well. And it has also become a habit that I stop night discharge. Sometimes no drop emits. And sometimes I have the suspicion that the drop has (kood kar) gushed out upon excitation. And sometimes I think it has not (kood kar) gushed as a result of any excitation. Sometimes the drop is of the size of a *chuvanni* (the old four-anna piece), sometimes it is slightly larger, sometimes a little smaller. Sometimes it also happens that after stopping the discharge, and though there is no excitation, a drop or two comes out. In this condition is a bath necessary?' 'Why does a bath become necessary when one has intercourse with a thick cloth tied around one's organ? And is such an action jaiz or not according to the Sunna?'

'If a woman has a discharge like men upon excitation, is a bath necessary?' 'If a woman discharges without co-habitation, is a bath necessary?' 'If a man knowingly inserts a finger in the vagina of a woman, is a bath due upon the woman or not?' 'If to put some medicine or to examine some problem, or even otherwise a woman inserts a finger in the vagina of a woman, is a bath obligatory?' 'If a minor boy has intercourse with a woman who is a major, or a major man has intercourse with a girl who is a minor, then on whom is the bath due?' 'A man's semen is thin; he urinates, bathes after that, and then the remaining semen emits, is the bath due or not?'

'A minor girl is raped; is a bath necessary for her?' 'A man had intercourse with his wife; in the morning she menstruated; is a bath incumbent upon her?' 'Is a bath due or proper after sodomy, after adultery, after prostitution?' 'If a person has intercourse many times during a night, will it be enough for him to have a bath once in the morning?' 'If a woman puts her finger in her vagina twice or thrice to put some medicine, is a bath necessary?' 'If she puts a finger in the vagina without being excited, is a bath required? And if she does so while she has kept the *roza,* will there be any effect on the roza?'

'Upon waking up a person notices that there is some moisture at the mouth of the organ. He is certain that there has been no discharge, or he does not remember it. And he does not remember whether it is the fluid before the discharge of semen or semen itself. And there is no effect of the semen on the clothes or the body. Should he bathe?' 'Zaid had intercourse with a woman in a dream. But before discharge had taken place, he woke up. When he got up to urinate, a few white drops discharged. Is a bath required?' 'Umar is suffering from a disease of quick discharge of semen. If he imagines a woman in his thoughts or in a dream or while he is awake, his organ is disturbed, and a few white drops are discharged from his organ. And sometimes it so happens that a few white, thin drops are discharged even without a dream or his imagining anything. Is a bath mandatory in all these conditions?'....

Not quite the stuff of fatwas, you would expect. But those are the matters on which the ulema of the Dar al-Ulum, Deoband, have been asked to give and have with great piety delivered fatwas.[1]

The volumes of fatwas devote pages and pages to an even more exotic subject—namely, what the believer should do with an animal which has been used for intercourse. 'What is the hukum about the animal with which a man has had sexual intercourse—what is the hukum about the animal and the man?', asks the querist, and after due deliberation the ulema of this great 'centre of Islamic learning' issue a fatwa. The other matters which call forth fatwas are just as earth-shaking.

'Is a pregnant goat which has been used for intercourse halal or haram? Has one to wait for her to deliver or should she be killed and buried without waiting?' 'Zaid has had intercourse with a goat. What is the law in respect of her? Can we eat her flesh or drink her milk? And what is the law for him who has had the intercourse?' 'What is the punishment for having intercourse with a minor child or a goat?' 'Zaid decided to have intercourse with an animal which is halal such as a cow or a goat. He approached the animal and inserted his male member into its vagina. But there was no ejaculation. Should Zaid or other Muslims regard as halal the

---

1. See, *Fatawa Dar al-Ulum, Deoband,* Volume I, pp. 162–71.

meat or milk of that animal? Has Zaid to do penance for this offence?' 'Zaid had intercourse with a cow, and then sold it. How should that money be spent? Can it be used for *sadqah*? And what is the punishment fo Zaid?' 'What is the punishment for one who has intercourse with a mare? What should be done with that mare?' A fatwa on one and each of these matters.

And the answers are not always predictable, often they turn on subtle differences. It is enough for the believer who has had intercourse with an animal to do *taubah*, decree these men of learning, but in the usual case the animal must be killed and burnt. In the usual case, that is, its meat should not be eaten. However, to take one instance, 'If there is no ejaculation (inside the animal) its meat and milk are halal, without question,' rule the ulema of Dar al-Ulum, Deoband. 'But if there is ejaculation, it is better to kill the animal and bury its flesh. No one should eat it, though it is not haram to eat it.' And so on.[2]

'What do the noble ulema say regarding the following proposition?' asks the anxious querist. 'A man has built a modern-type latrine (with flush) in his house in such a way that when one sits in it for easing nature, one's back faces the Qiblah. His tenant insists that this method is wrong and therefore the direction of sitting should be changed. Hence it is submitted that if it is legally improper, kindly oblige us if there is any scope for it. Please reply and Allah will reward you !' Maulana Mufti Hafiz Qari, to give his full title, cogitates over the matter, and gives a categorial fatwa. He rules: 'The tenant's insistence is correct; the direction of the latrine must be changed.' It is not just that believers think it necessary to refer a matter such as this to a religious authority, it is that

2. For fatwas on these and other matters see, *Fatawa Dar al-Ulum, Deoband*, Volume XII, pp. 221–66.

that authority in turn sees the matter as an entirely religious question. The Mufti deems it necessary to consult and invoke the highest authorities of Islam to settle the matter. 'The Holy Prophet (*Sallallaho alaihe wa sallam*!) has instructed: When you go to the latrine (and sit for easing nature), sit neither facing the Qiblah nor with your back towards it (*Bukhari* and *Muslim*). Hence the eminent jurisconsults have declared that it is a near-prohibited abomination (*Makruh-e-tahrimt*). to face the Qiblah or have one's back towards it while passing urine or defecating, whether one is outside a habitation or within the habitation and a building (*Nural-Ezah*, p. 30; *Al-Durr e-Mukhtar Ma*'s *Shami*, Vol. I, p. 316). In the inquired case therefore one should sit a little obliquely so long as the direction of the latrine is not set right. Finis.'[3]

Maulana Ahmad Riza Khan too has a fatwa on the same matter. In addition to reiterating the 'neither face nor back' position, it contains a premise about adjudging Muslims which we shall encounter again in a much more important context. 'What is the hukum,' asks the agitated querist, 'when in spite of the exhortations of the ulema, the people of the neighbourhood do not make the effort to alter the urinals of the mosque when these face the east or the west? Is the *imamat* proper of one who urinates in them?' 'Neither the face nor the back should face the Qiblah while urinating,' declares the *Fatawa-i-Rizvia*. 'Those who do so are the wrong-doers. It is proper for the managers of the mosque or the people of the neighbourhood to alter the direction northwards or southwards. And till this is done it is incumbent on those urinating to sit in the altered direction.' But as the matter involves believers, Maulana Ahmad Riza Khan makes the sort of allowance which we will see it is incumbent upon every Muslim to make when what is in question is the conduct

3. *Fatawa-i-Rahimiyyah*, Volume III, pp. 10–11.

of a fellow Muslim: 'It may be that the ones who know are already doing so (that is, they are already sitting at the desired angle while urinating in the mosque's urinals). One should retain the favourable presumption about Mussalmans. Their *imamat* cannot be said to be improper just for this reason.'[4]

May a mother spread paper on the floor so that the child may defecate on it rather than soil the floor, and so that the excreta may be thrown away that much more easily? Not quite a religious question, you would think. But that is only because we have not yet grasped the basic claim of Islam, nor have we got to know the ulema. The question is duly deliberated over by Mufti Sayyid Abdur Rahim Qadri, and pronounced upon by invoking one of the highest authorities in shariah, namely *Shami*?[5]

May one sleep with one leg resting on the other knee? Again not a momentous question exactly, not quite the question one would think of as a religious one. But guidance on it is sought from the religious authorities in Rander. Mufti Sayyid Abdur Rahim Qadri urges a slight latitude in the matter in view of the fact that the dress worn by men now is less liable to expose 'the unseen'. But common sense is not sufficient even in such a matter. The Mufti therefore feels compelled to record that the Companions had seen the Prophet reclining in the mosque with one leg resting on the other.[6]

And would you consider the interval at which one should remove one's pubic hair to be a religious question? But it most certainly is, both in the eyes of the believers and in those of the ulema. 'After how many days should one remove pubic hair, etc.? What is the Sunna method and what

4. *Fatawa-i-Rizvia*, Volume II, p. 154.
5. *Fatawa-i-Rahimiyyah*, Volume III, p. 12.
6. Ibid., Volume I, p. 85.

is better?,' asks the querist. Notice that he considers that even on such a matter he should seek a ruling from a religious authority; not just that, notice his request about the Sunna—the believer has internalized the notion that even on this question he should regulate his conduct in accordance with the practice of the Prophet. The Mufti fortifies him in both premises by treating this to be a matter of the shariah, and by setting out the practice of the Prophet on the matter to nail the intervals he is prescribing. 'The excellent course,' the Mufti rules, 'is that cleanliness should be acquired every week, particularly on every Friday; i.e.,one should pare the nails, prune the hair of moustache and shave off the arm-pit and pubic hair and then take a bath. If the arm-pit and pubic hair cannot be shaved off every week, they should be removed after at least fifteen or twenty days. The maximum period is of forty days. If one does not acquire cleanliness after forty days, one will be extremely guilty (*Shami*, Vol. V, p. 358).' 'It is also reported in a tradition that the Holy Prophet (*Sallallaho alaihe wa sallam*) used to pare his nails and clip his moustache every Friday, shave off pubic hair after every twenty days and arm-pit hair every forty days (*Al-Taliq al-Sabeeh*, Vol. IV, p.405). Finis.'[7]

But where there is a general principle, there are always the specific occasions to consider. Hence to the foregoing there is the related question: What about the period between sighting of the crescent moon of *Zil Hajj* and the slaughtering of the animal, can one pare one's nails and cut the hair during this period also? If not, why not? Notice first the feature which we shall encounter again and again: one question leads to another, all of them remain religious questions, the categories and subcategories never end. Notice next the reason the Mufti gives for his ruling: it gives us a first glimpse of the

---

7. *Fatawa-i-Rahimiyyah*, Volume III, p. 184.

mindset, of the universe of reasoning and perception which we shall encounter throughout. 'It is praiseworthy,' rules the Mufti, 'for a man intending to make a sacrifice to refrain, after sighting the *Zil Hajj* crescent, from cutting hair from his body and paring his nails till he has slaughtered the animal because he is making a sacrifice in lieu of the sacrifice of his own life—each part of the sacrificial animal is in lieu of each part of the body of the man who is sacrificing; the Holy Prophet (pbuh.!) has given this order so that no part of his body may be absent at the time of the descent of divine mercy. But if more than forty days have passed one should not be idle in removing the unwanted hair, nails etc., to save oneself from abomination (*karaahat*).'[8]

Can one poison an adulteress? Can one pick one's nose in front of others? What should be the length of one's beard? Can one eat fowl which was killed by a Muslim, but whose entrails were removed and which was then put into boiling water so that its feathers may be removed? Are turmeric pieces boiled in bovine urine or dung, then cleansed with dust and dried, clean or not? Can one eat a hen which has been recovered from the mouth of a cat—the hen was slaughtered immediately after being retrieved from the cat's mouth; blood did come out but no motion was felt in the hen? These and hosts of similar questions are put to these religious authorities. And they settle them as matters that are integral to the shariah. They feel compelled to settle even these matters by looking up the hightest authorities of shariah.[9]

Often the ruling turns on quantitative distinctions, often on qualitative ones. 'A cat attacked a hen and broke its head,' reports the querist, 'but the hen is alive and writhing.

---

8. *Fatawa-i-Rahimiyyah,* Volume II, p. 73.

9. For examples in this paragraph see, for instance, *Fatawa-i-Rahimiyyah,* Volume II, pp. 80–81; Volume III, pp. 185–86.

Is it proper to slaughter it and cook it for eating?' The ruling turns on the extent of the head or the neck which is wrenched, and whether the cat has totally severed it or not. As the Mufti declares: 'In the inquired case, if the hen is alive and so much portion of her neck has remained in tact that it can be slaughtered, it is correct to eat it after slaughtering and cooking. But it is not proper to eat the wrenched head. If, however, the whole neck has been broken along with the head and no portion of the neck is in tact for slaughtering, then there is no way of slaughtering it and it is unlawful (*haram*) to eat it (*Sbamf*).'[10]

And where the earlier authorities have not settled the matter explicitly, the ulema settle it by deploying that hoary 'principle' of shariah, namely *qiyas*, reasoning by analogy. Notice how the *Fatawa-i-Rahimiyyah* settles that question about the hen which was retrieved from the mouth of the cat: The hen can be eaten, it rules; and the reason is that 'It is stated in *Durr-ul-Mukhtar* (Vol. V, p. 262) "A sick goat was slaughtered. If it moved or blood came out of it, it is lawful (for eating), otherwise not."'[11]

Notice that the Mufti has not thought it fit to settle the matter by suggesting some clinical signs that the person may look for in the hen at hand, he has thought fit to go looking for the answer in a book of shariah, the *Durr-ul-Mukhtar.* The book in question happens to have been written in the seventeenth century. As even that great fount of authority did not have a direct edict on a hen, specially a hen obtained from the mouth of a cat, an analogy is sought. It is found in the case of a sick goat. And that is how this question gets settled.

Marriage and divorce are of course the warp and woof of the shariah, and we will have occasion to take up the fatwas

---

10. *Fatawa-i-Rahimiyyah*, Volume II, p. 80.

11. Ibid., Volume III, p. 201.

on them in some detail later on. Here we may only note that the farthest permutations and combinations are dealt with by the fatwas, and again the categories and subcategories never end.

Often the answers are predictable, but not always. 'How is it if a Muslim marries a non-Muslim woman in an Arya Samaj mandir, and if one attends such a marriage?' asks the querist. 'To marry a non-Muslim woman (infidel and polytheist) is unlawful (*haram*) and a grave sin,' decrees the Mufti. 'The Holy Quran says: "Wed not idolatresses till they believe" (II. 221). Hence to attend such a marriage function is also not permissible. If one marries considering it a lawful act, it is infidelity (*kufr*). It is necessary for such a man to renew his faith (*iman*) openly and in public.' A predictable answer.

But the answers are not always predictable. Recall the stern stance of the *Fatawa-i-Rahimiyyah* on the question of paring one's nails and cutting one's hair. One would expect the authority to be equally stern on matters that impinge on others much more directly, matters in which another is liable to be hurt much more. But that is because we have not yet got acquainted with either the shariah or the ulema. May one marry the stepmother of one's wife and keep them both in one house?, the querist asks. Yes, rules the *Fatawa-i-Rahimiyyah,* it is permissible to marry one's stepmother-in-law and to have both in one's house at one and the same time. Will one's wife become unlawful for one if one commits adultery with her sister, that is one's sister-in-law?, asks the querist. 'In the inquired case,' rules the *Fatawa-i-Rahimiyyah,* 'she will not be unlawful forever, but some jurisconsults have ruled that he should not have carnal connection with his wife till his sister-in-law has experienced one monthly course.'[12]

If a dog falls into the well, what is the hukum for the

12. For the preceding three rulings, *Fatawa-i-Rahimiyya,* Volume II, pp. 86–87.

water in the well? If a man dies in the well...? If a shoe falls in the well...? If the beeth of a crow falls into the well...? Is *kute ka jutha,* something licked by a dog, *paak* or not? If a dog puts its mouth in ghee/ in milk/in a pitcher full of sugar-cane juice, does the thing remain paak or not? If the one that puts its mouth in these things is not a dog but a cat? If it is a mouse? Each of these cases and sub-cases is dealt with separately, and occasions separate fatwas.

If the *belna* by which juice is extracted from sugar cane is licked by a dog, what is the hukum? Is the jutha of a cat paak or not, in what way and for what reason does it differ from something which has been licked by a dog? Is the urine of a cow or a camel paak or not? What is the hukum regarding the urine of that animal whose meat is halal? Is the skin of an animal which has been killed by *jhatka* paak or not? Is a bath mandatory if some drops of urine fall on one? Is the water of a hookah paak or not? Is it jaiz to make a drum out of the skin of a dead mare? Can one Muslim smoke a hookah used by another? Can one use the fat of an animal which is haram? How can one make paak a spoon which has been licked by a dog? Is it permissible to urinate while standing? Can one use toilet paper after defecation? There are several fatwas on the use of toothpicks.[13]

Similar subjects are dealt with in great earnestness in the *Fatawa-i-Rizvia.* Must a woman untie her *chotie* while bathing? What is the hukum if something is sticking to the teeth? How much must one wash one's mouth and nose? How much water may one take into the nose? Is the namaz one observes valid if one washes oneself at less than twenty-two places? If there is some discharge after one has had a bath, is the namaz valid? What if the discharge is not of semen but

13. For *fatwas* on the topics listed in the last two paragraphs see *Fatawa Ahl-i-Hadis,* Volume I.

of urine? Is rainwater flowing from drains paak? Does the water in a tank of dimensions X by Y by Z get polluted by urine? If a person with socks or bandages puts his feet in the water, does the water remain paak? Does eating fish fulfil one's oath of eating meat? What if Zaid had taken a vow to drink water but the water he drank had *zaufran* in it? Is it haram or is it merely detestable to eat the meat of a *khachar* whose mother is a mare? Can the meat be eaten of a kid whose father or mother is haram? Can one wipe one's mouth with paper after eating? Can one do *talawat* by putting one's head in the lap of one's wife when she is menstruating? Each of these, and scores upon scores of similar subjects, occasion a fatwa.

But matters of day-to-day living are not the only ones on which the believers seek and the ulema issue fatwas. Alongside matters such as the ones listed in the foregoing paragraphs, a collection like the *Fatawa-i-Rizvia* contains fatwas on esoteric questions. Can Satan—as ever present an entity in the world of fatwas as in that of the Quran and the Hadis—take on the appearance of the Prophet? In what condition will the dead rise, in particular will they be clad or will they rise naked? How much time is left for the Day of Judgement? Will the sun which will rise on the Day of Judgement, and which will be one-and-a-half *neza* be the same as the sun that rises and sets ordinarily or will it be some other sun? Will the angels Munkir and Nakir be present? How shall the *shahid* be interrogated in the grave? On the Day of Judgement also will everyone rise naked or will one be covered by a shroud? Do angels take possession of the souls of men and Allah that of the souls of animals? Similarly, the geography of Heaven, its meteorology, the boons that await the believer in it are the subjects of earnest exposition.

Mufti Kifayatullah devotes his very considerable learning to determining whether it is permissible to watch wrestling or kabaddi—as is his wont, he gives a qualified ruling: to see wrestling in such a way that private parts come to be seen is *najaiz*, he declares; to determining whether one may work as a butcher, as a writer of deeds—the decree is naturally qualified: one may write deeds, but not deeds of transactions involving the payment and receipt of interest, as a broker—of property, yes, but not as that of stocks and shares; to determining whether the believer may pay *pugdi*, whether he may mate a horse with a she-donkey, whether he may keep a dog as a pet— as usual, Mufti Kifayatullah's answer is not a simple 'Yes' or 'No', one may keep a dog for the protection of crops in the field or for that of grain in the storage bins, but one must not keep a dog as a pet; scholarship is also devoted to determining whether it is only the saliva of the dog or its body also which is napaak, and whether the saliva of a cat as distinct from that of a dog is paak.

We have already seen the ulema of the Al-Azhar of India expend their time and energy on sifting out the circumstances which entail a bath. They also devote their scholarship to determining whether the water of a tank remains pure if a man bathing in it has an erection, or if a woman discharges in the tank some menstrual blood or the blood that follows the delivery of a child; whether the water remains paak if a dog, if a pig falls into it, whether it remains paak if either dies in it; whether the water is rendered napaak by the beeth of a fish; whether the water in the *wuzu* tank of a mosque remains paak if a *chhipkali* falls in it and dies; whether it is jaiz to do *ivuzu* with the water which remains after doing *istinja*, that is after cleaning oneself after defecation; whether the water remains paak if a bird falls in it, dies and swells; whether it remains paak if the beeth of a bird which is itself haram falls into the well; whether the water of that well can be used by Muslims which is used regularly by the *bhangis*, by those who clean up excreta, etc., or from which the polytheists take out water; and if in the latter case Muslims can use that well then what is the significance of the Quran calling the polytheists najas, that is unclean; whether one may eat food which was cooked with water from a well in which soon after a dead cock was found; whether one may use water from a well into which a snake has fallen, into which a napaak bhangi has fallen, into which a frog has fallen, has swollen, and a stench has risen but the frog has not as yet burst, into which a dog has fallen and died but which has been discovered only one-and-a-half months after it fell in, into which the beeth of an eagle, of a crow falls, into which a cloth ball used by children falls, into which a chick which is a day or two old but which was stillborn falls, from which a frog has been seen coming out but when we do not know whether it is one that lives on land or in water, nor whether it is *dam-e-sayal* or not, into which a goat or dog has fallen and then urinated in it, in which a tortoise has died, in which a pig fell and which was then killed with spears, etc., in the well itself. They determine whether water may be taken from a well from which Hindus also draw water, from a well into which a kafir has fallen and died, in which a Hindu has taken a dip, in which the *mengnis* of a goat are found—if these are whole and if they have shredded—into which a menstruating woman has fallen, into which a shoe, a bird which cannot be taken out, a horse has fallen.... In instances where this is necessary or feasible the ulema also labour to prescribe how the tank or well may be made paak once again.

The ulema look up authorities, and in turn give their verdicts on whether the kafirs having been pronounced najas, that is unclean by Allah, a believer may eat food cooked by them; whether the beeth of a *kabutar* is najas or not; whether cloth from which semen drops have been washed but on which stains still remain is paak or not; whether the root of a hair is paak or not; whether the water or milk into which a crow or hen has put its beak or into which the urine of either has fallen is paak or not. They devote their years of scholarship to answering the querist who asks, '*Us pani ka jis mein chuhe ki mengni gir jaye kya hukum hai?*'; to determining how soup into which a dog has put its mouth, how a bottle of honey into which a mouse has fallen, a jar of *gulkand* in which mice have died, ghee in which a dog has put its mouth is to be made paak....

The ulema of this famous institution of Islamic learning expend their time and energy to debate and determine whether clothes which have been soiled during summer by sweat at the time of excitation are paak or not; whether the hair of a dog is paak or not; whether utensils from which Christians have eaten pork can be made paak by washing or not; whether discharge from the vagina at the time of sexual intercourse is najas or not; whether water can make the polytheists paak or not; whether the hide of a dog which has been butchered after reciting *Bismillah* is paak or not; whether water into which a hand which has touched the mud balls which the believer uses for cleaning himself after defecation has been put is paak or not. They settle what the hukum is to be 'when there is suspicion of *nadi*, the liquid that is discharged before semen'. They lay down what is to be done in the following predicament: 'Because of excessive sexual indulgence, upon the least excitement nadi appears on Zaid. At night he changes his cloth. But then the suspicion remains that the nadi may have touched the thigh or feet. In this condition should namaz be read after washing the entire body or after just changing the clothes?'[14]

---

14. For *fatwas* of the Dar al-Ulum on these and related matters see *Fatawa Dar al-Ulum, Deoband*, Volume I, pp. 173–361.

Each of the authorities expends a great deal of time, energy and scholarship on laying down the law in regard to women who are menstruating.

As a woman having her periods is not to touch the Quran, the querist asks the venerable Mufti Kifayatullah, can she touch a book which has ten or twelve verses of the Quran cited in it? The Mufti gives the matter his anxious consideration and decrees: she may handle the book but she must not touch the pages on which the *ayat*s are reproduced.

He has then to settle the following question: A woman used to menstruate in the last week of every month; she was married in the second week of the month, but she started menstruating on the nuptial night itself when her husband had sexual intercourse with her; however, the husband did not know this, and he had sexual intercourse with her a second time; under the circumstances has either of them committed a sin; if so, what is the penance?

The Mufti-e-Azam has next to direct his scholarship to an even more complex problem. As is well known, great significance is attached to the exact dates on which the menstrual period has begun and on which it has ended—as we shall see when we take up the fatwas on talaq, points of law too turn on whether a pronouncement was made within or outside these dates. The anxiety of the querist in obtaining a fatwa in regard to the following conundrum is therefore understandable: A woman menstruated for thirty-six days, after that there was purity for three days, then there is bleeding for one day, then there were three dry days, then ten days in which there was bleeding, followed by one dry day, and then one day with bleeding, followed by nine dry days, which were followed by nine days with bleeding; since then there has been no flow of blood; earlier she used to have a flow for eight days, but she does not remember the dates; if, *Khuda nakhwasta,* God forbid, she continues in this disturbed condition, how should we reckon the days of flow and of purity? [15]

Maulana Ahmad Riza Khan applies his mind and learning to deciding similar issues. 'What do the *Ulema-i-Din* say on this matter?' asks the querist. 'A woman has a white emission and then eight days of menstruation; is it proper to have sexual intercourse with her before she has taken her bath?' The Maulana's answer comes to depend on at least three sets of classifications: the normal length of her cycle, and whether this one is of exceptional duration; whether water, etc., are available for her to have a bath and whether there is any other difficulty, for instance, some ailment in her having a bath; whether she is a Muslim or she is Jew or Christian.

The next ruling also turns on an esoteric distinction. When one's wife is menstruating, the Maulana is asked, is it proper to use her thighs or belly for ejaculation? It is proper to use her belly, the Maulana pronounces, not her thighs. 'The principle,' declares the Maulana, 'is that every part of her body above the navel can be used but none below it.' The question is repeated five pages later, but with a note of urgency added: while the wife is menstruating, is it proper for the husband to rub his organ against her thighs or belly to secure ejaculation? The husband, the querist writes, is a highly passionate person, and the fear is that he may commit adultery. The Maulana reiterates his previous ruling.

Next the Maulana turns to unravel another conundrum. What do the *Ulema-i-Din* say on this matter, asks the querist: A menstrual cycle lasts for forty days; if menstrual blood stops in eight days, and after namaz, roza and sexual intercourse, blood flow starts again—what is the hukum?

'What do the *Ulema-i-Din* say on the following matter?'

---

15. On these and related questions, *Mufti Kifayatullah ke Fatawi*, Volume II, pp. 282–86.

asks the querist. 'Can one eat food cooked by a woman in menses, can one have her eat with us; what is the hukum if she dies during that period?'

'What do the *Ulema-i-Din* say about the following?' asks the next querist. 'A woman gave birth to a son and the flow stopped in eight days; can she do roza and namaz, can she wear bangles of silver and glass, has the house and bed she used remained paak or should they be kept off-limits for forty days?'

How long after giving birth to a child is the woman napaak? At nikah the girl is made to recite the *Kalima* five times; if she is menstruating can she recite it? Umar is in a state of impurity due to nocturnal emission; he meets Zaid, who says 'Salam'; should he reply or not? Can he repeat some beneficent invocation in his heart without uttering anything?....

The querists ask these and other questions as questions of religion. They seek answers to them from a religious authority. The religious authority, Maulana Ahmad Riza Khan, in turn treats them as religious questions and fortifies his answers where necessary with citations from other religious authorities.[16]

If a man has intercourse with his wife who is in a state of menstruation, or wetness, asks the querist, what is the penance?—one dinar, rules the Maulana, if he has the intercourse at the beginning of the menstrual period, and half a dinar if it is towards the end of the period; if she has bathed then...., if she has not bathed then.... The ruling, with citations from authorities and the rest takes two-and-a-half closely calligraphed quarto-size pages.

That sort of ruling—that one can get by with paying half a dinar—leads a querist to ask, 'I read a Hadis which states that the Prophet (pbuh.!) has said that if a man copulates with his wife during her menses, he should give half a dinar

16. On the foregoing, *Fatawa-i-Rizvia,* Volume II, pp. 34–41.

in charity (*Mishkat*). This proves that if a man wants to have sexual congress during his wife's menstrual period, he can do so by giving half a dinar in charity. Kindly elucidate this point and oblige me.'

Mufti Sayyid Abdur Rahim Qadri comes down heavily on that sort of a construction being put. He declares in the *Fatawa-i-Rahimiyyah*:

> What you have understood from the *hadith* that one can copulate with his wife during her menstrual period by giving half a *dinar* in charity, is absolutely wrong. The giving of half a *dinar* is not payment of fee but it is by way of a fine and penalty, and is purported to save oneself from divine wrath. It is mentioned in books of jurisprudence (*fiqh*) that penitence (*kaffara*) is binding upon one who copulates with his wife during the state of fasting in the month of Ramzan. It does not mean that if one wants to have sexual intercourse during the state of fasting, one can do so by making the atonement (*kaffara*). It is common knowledge that coition during menses is *haram* (unlawful); that it is dirty and unclean, and a work of gross sin. Its unlawfulness is proven from the Quran: 'They question thee (O Muhammad) concerning menstruation. Say: It is an illness, so let women alone at such times and go not in unto them till they are cleansed' (*Sura* II, *Baquarah*: 222). A severe prohibition has been reported in the *hadith*. It is stated in the holy *Mishkat* that the Prophet (pbuh.!) said: He who goes in unto a woman during her menstruation or unto her anus or visits an oracle, he is a repudiator of Muhammad's religion (p. 56).
>
> The books of *fiqh* report explicit unlawfulness concerning this. Read the following words of *Mala Bud Minho*: 'Coition during menstrual and post-children periods is *haram*' (p. 17). Not only this, it is not proper to touch or see the menstruating wife's body from the knee to the navel, and jurisprudents have made it explicit that 'to copulate, considering it *halal* (lawful) is *kufr* (unbelief)' (*Fath u'l Qadir*, vol. i, p. 15). If some unfortunate person

commits this major sin, it is incumbent upon him to repent, and vow not to repeat it, with humility and a sincere heart, before Allah. Over and above that, he should give alms in accordance with his capacity, because infringement of law and committing of major sin stirs divine wrath but it passes by alms-giving. One *hadith* says: If this act happens when the blood is red (i.e., in the beginning), the doer should give one *dinar* in charity and if it happens when the blood has become pale, he should give half a *dinar* (*Tirmizi*, vol. i, p. 20).[17]

Notice how the question is looked upon as a purely religious question, and is settled by invoking the Quran, the Hadis, and the authorities on shariah.

The ulema of Dar al-Ulum too devote their earnest consideration to ruling on matters such as the following: whether intercourse is permissible with a wife who is menstruating, whether penance is mandatory in such a case; how long one must wait if there is a doubt as to whether the menstruation has ended or not; how is the following to be reckoned—there was blood flow for forty days, then for one week there was no flow, then blood began to flow again; how is menses to be counted if the woman bleeds continuously for three months; is penance mandatory if one has intercourse with the wife after she has completed her menstruation but before she has had her bath; can a woman do her beads when she is menstruating?....[18]

And so do the ulema of Ahl-i-Hadis.

Each of the collections devotes several fatwas to problems connected with istinja, namely on cleaning oneself after passing urine or after defecation. They insist that cleaning oneself with stones or lumps of soil (and in either case these should be an odd number) and then using water is a matter of

17. *Fatawa-i-Rahimiyyah,* Volume I, pp. 52–53.

18. *Fatawa Dar al-Ulum, Deoband,* Volume I, pp. 278–84.

religion. The highest authorities, including the practice of the Prophet are invoked on this question with as much fervour as on any other. There are the usual dissections of categories and subcategories: should the soil and water be used simultaneously or one after the other, and, if the latter, in which order; if stones are not handy, can dried bone be used instead; differences are set out between *chhota* istinja and *bada* istinja; is the hukum in regard to istinja for women the same as it is for men; can one use the same lumps that have been used for cleaning oneself after defecation for cleaning oneself after urination?....

There are differences between the schools of Islamic jurisprudence, and, as we shall see, the controversies over even these matters take on fierce tones. The Ahl-i-Hadis are asked, 'What is the injunction regarding cleaning excreta with the help of paper? Is it equivalent to the use of water? Can namaz be said after having cleaned oneself in this manner?' The Ahl-i-Hadis weigh the matter and decree: 'Yes, it is permissible to clean the excreta with the help of paper. Besides every solid and dry thing is permissible. Cleaning with the help of stone, wood, cloth and soil is permissible. However, cleaning with the help of bone, cow dung and the droppings of animals is not permissible....'[19]

The Barelvis pour scorn on this position. May one use paper for istinja, the querist asks, specially if one has to ease oneself in a train where lumps of soil or stones are not liable to be available? 'To do istinja with paper is detestable and prohibited,' thunders Maulana Ahmad Riza Khan, 'and it is the practice of Christians. Respect for paper is ordained, even if it is blank, and if it has something written on it then it is worthy of great respect—so it is stated in *Durr-ul-Mukhtar.* As for the excuse of the train, why does it occur to Zaid alone

19. *Fatawa Ahl-i-Hadis,* Volume I, p. 45.

and not to other Mussalmans? Can they not keep *dhela*s and old cloth with them?' 'Yes,' scoffs the Maulana, 'if the practice of Christians alone is acceptable then it is a disease of the heart. Medication is needed.'[20]

The question comes up again, and the Maulana is equally stern. What is the hukum about doing istinja with blotting paper of the English type?, asks the querist. 'To do istinja with paper is a Christian practice, and it is prohibited by Shariah.' When the paper is capable of being written on or is valuable, and even when it is not so, using it for istinja is prohibited, for it is worthy of respect, the Maulana rules. And he gives a second reason: 'It is very necessary to save oneself from the practices of Christians, unless one has no alternative.....' he declares.[21]

As happened in relation to questions we encountered earlier, often the decree turns on quantitative measures. 'After urination, *kalukh* was taken,' reports the anxious querist, 'but water was not used. After that namaz was observed. During the namaz he remembered that water had not been used. In these circumstances is the namaz efficacious or not?' 'If the urine had not spread over a surface exceeding a rupee then a *dhela* is enough for cleansing,' rules the *Fatawa-i-Rizvia*. '*Namaz* is done. If it had spread over a surface exceeding a rupee then cleansing cannot be done with a *dhela*. It is necessary to wash with water. If one remembers during the *namaz* that water was not used, one should at once step aside and do the *istinja*. And it is desirable that he should do the *wuzu* also again, and observe the *namaz* also again. If one remembers after the *namaz*, then one should do the *istinja* and observe the *namaz* again.'[22]

---

20. *Fatawa-i-Rizvia*, Volume II, p. 153.
21. Ibid., Volume II, p. 156.
22. Ibid., Volume II, pp. 153–54.

Some of the decrees prescribe practices or countenance practices which are manifestly unhygienic. How is it to use the same dhela for doing istinja again?, asks the querist. The ulema of Deoband have recourse to a venerable authority to settle even this matter: they rule, 'According to *Kashf al-Durr al-Mukhtar* to do so is detestable (as distinct from being prohibited). But if it is necessary because of being on a journey etc., then using it (the mud-ball) a second, third or even more times is not objectionable after it is dry and after rubbing its surface.'[23] Similarly while enumerating which solids one may use for wiping oneself clean as part of istinja, the *Fatawa-i-Rizvia* lists the earth and walls.[24]

The examples can be multiplied manifold. But even the few which have been given will be sufficient to establish a few preliminary points.

Some preliminary points

We are conditioned to thinking of fatwas as being decrees to execute or excommunicate someone. The vast range of subjects which the volumes actually deal with will put the fatwas in perspective. They are commands and decrees not just on matters in the public domain, they aim to regulate the most private of private domains too.

Second, the questions by themselves show that the faithful have certainly internalized the notion that even such matters are religious matters, and that answers to them also have to be sought from religious authorities. This is a vital point. For when the believers have accepted the fact that even on such matters which are, so to say, wholly private they must go by what religious authorities say, they are fully

23. *Fatawa Dar al-Ulum, Deoband,* Volume I, p. 376.

24. *Fatawa-i-Rizvia,* for instance Volume II, pp. 143, 156.

conditioned to follow the decrees of those authorities on matters that are in the public domain.

Third, as far as the religious authorities are concerned, of course, these questions are religious questions, indeed, as they never cease to emphasize, in Islam all questions are religious questions. Islam is unique, they insist, it provides a complete code, a code that regulates every aspect of life. As we shall see, this is a major pillar of their power, and they are most emphatic in making both the believers and other entities—like the state in India—internalize this claim.

Finally, while others may be a bit squeamish in discussing such questions, and a little surprised at encountering them in 'religious' books, the ulema have no qualms about discussing such matters and laying down the law on them as much as on any other matter. They regard it as one of their functions to do so. The point is set at rest by Maulana Mufti Abdur Rahim Qadri.

It transpires that a maulvi, styling himself as Hazrat Shaykh al-Islam Maulana Maulvi, published two pamphlets attacking the Hanafite jurists for holding that intercourse with an animal does not vitiate a fast, even if ejaculation takes place. He cited the great authorities of Hanafite law—*Shami* and the *Durr-ul-Mukhtar*—as having decreed this. He also chided the learned ulema for filling religious books with discussions of such topics. The writings of the maulvi were referred to Mufti Abdur Rahim Qadri for opinion. The Mufti's elucidation takes up ten printed pages of the *Fatawa-i-Rahimiyyah.* On the substance of the question, the decision turns on whether the ejaculation took place upon intromission into the animal—in which case the fast is rendered void—or it took place by the man merely touching the animal's genitals with his hands or kissing it, without using his sexual organ—in which case the fast is not vitiated. The Mufti cites authorities to nail the distinction, and he argues that the maulvi who had made the charge against the Hanafite jurists had misrepresented their rulings on the matter.

He then turns to the charge that Hanafite jurists have filled religious books with discussions about such matters. He says that such incidents do take place, and therefore it is necessary to set out the law on them. He draws pointed attention to the fact that the Prophet and the Companions did not shy away from discussing such matters, that in fact they did so in a forthright and frank manner. By taking up such matters and specifying the rules of Shariah in regard to them, declares the Mufti, the ulema are doing a real service. On the other hand, in his feigned prudery the Maulvi who has made those charges against the Hanafite ulema is just imitating the Jews and polytheists of Medina. It is this exposition which is of interest to us at the moment. The Mufti writes:

> Even as physicians and doctors, in connection with medical treatment, have to examine, without bashfulness and modesty, the private parts of human beings and animals (both male and female), the spiritual physicians too (the Prophet of Islam and his successors—the religious doctors, jurisprudents and traditionists) have described and explained in detail all the directives and propositions (*masa'il*) concerning devotions, social affairs and ritual cleanliness (*tahara*); e.g., cleanliness and uncleanliness, urine, faeces, water, dust, menses and puerperium (*nifas*), bathing and *tayammum*, sitting and getting up, etc. Indeed there are among these also propositions the frank mention of which looks contrary to bashfulness and modesty, but if one practises prudery, what other way is there of knowing these problems? In the verification of such propositions there is no scope for prudery. In such matters even a father did not hesitate to ask for information from his daughter. Hazrat 'Umar felt about a woman that she was restless due to the long separation of her husband who was away at *jihad*. He, therefore, asked his daughter, Hazrat Hafsa, as to how long a wife could

remain away from her husband. She replied that a wife could live away for not more than four months. Immediately, Hazrat 'Umar, as Caliph, issued an order that no soldier should remain away from home for more than four months (*Al-Farouq*, Vol. ii, p. 96).

It is stated in the Holy Quran: 'And she, in whose house he was, asked of him an evil act. She bolted the doors and said: Come! He said: I seek refuge in Allah!' (XII: 22).

It is also stated in the same Holy Quran: 'Must ye needs lust after men instead of women' (XXVII: 55).

Fatawa -i- Rahimiyyah

And Again: 'They question thee (O' Muhammad) concerning menstruation. Say: It is an illness, so let women alone at such times and go not in unto them till they are cleansed. And when they have purified themselves, then go in unto them as Allah hath enjoined upon you. Truly Allah loveth those who turn unto Him, and loveth those who have a care for cleanness. Your women are a tilth for you (to cultivate): go to your tilth as ye will' (II: 222–23).

The description of the occasions of the revelation of these is still more forthright. As regards the above verse, it has been reported by Hazrat Abd Allah ibn Abbas as follows:

Hazrat Ibn Abbas says that the people of Madina who came to be known with the title of Ansars were formerly polytheists. The Jews were their neighbours. Since the Jews had a heavenly Book (the Torah), these polytheists thought that the Jews were superior to them in knowledge and hence in many things they used to adopt the Jewish mores and manners. For coition, the Jews always adopted the anterior position, with the female partner lying supine, because they thought it was more conducive to feminine modesty; and the Ansars also followed this method. Contrary to this, the Quraysh enjoyed coitus with different postures—anterior, posterior, lying on the sides, squatting etc. When the Emigrants (*Muhajir*) came to Madina, one of them married an Ansari woman and tried to copulate with her in his own manner and wont (using different positions), but the woman disliked it and said that it was done only in the supine position. She would not allow the man to take any other posture. When this disagreement prolonged and it was reported to the Holy Prophet, God revealed the aforesaid verse: 'Your wives are your tillage: go in unto your tillage in what manner soever you will' (II. 223).

That is, you may have coitus in any posture you like, but the intromission must take place in the place from where the child is born (*Abu D.*, Vol. i, p. 301).

Fatawa -i- Rahimiyyah

It is stated in a *hadith* that Hazrat Umm-e-Saleem came to the Holy Prophet (pbuh.!) and said: 'O Prophet of Allah ! Allah is not ashamed of saying the truth. Is bathing necessary if a woman experiences nocturnal emission?' 'Yes,' he said, 'if she marks water (semen).' Umm-e-Saleem blushingly covered her face and asked: 'O Prophet of Allah ! Does a woman too have nocturnal emission (emission of semen)?' 'Yes,' he said, 'may your hands be besmeared with dust! How otherwise could the child resemble its mother? The man's water is thick and white whereas the woman's is thin and pale; whichever of the two waters precedes or dominates, the child resembles the master of that water' (*Mishkat*, vol. i, p. 48, *Matba-e-Mujtabai*).

Hazrat Ayesha reports:

Rafa'ah's wife came to the Holy Prophet (pbuh.!) and told him that Rafa'ah had pronounced irrevocable divorce thrice (*talaq-e ba'ina*). Then she married Abd al-Rahman but he had something like tassel of cloth (i.e., he was impotent). The Prophet said: 'Perhaps you want to remarry Rafa'ah.' (In her heart she wanted to say 'yes'). The Prophet, perceiving her intention, said: 'No, not so long as he (another husband) may taste you and you taste him.' (That is, the *halalah*—a woman's marrying her first divorcer after being divorced by the second husband will not be correct as long as the second husband has not consummated the marriage.)

The Holy Prophet (pbuh.!) asked Jabir (when the latter returned from a journey): 'Did you marry a virgin or a non-virgin?' Jabir said: 'A widow.' The Prophet said: 'Why didn't you marry a virgin so that she would have dallied and caressed with you and you would have fondled with her?' Then, having reached Madina, the Holy Prophet (pbuh.!) said: 'Let us wait here till Isha so that the women may tidy their hair and also remove the pubes' (Abridged from *Bukhari*, vol. ii, p. 789).

Fatawa -i- Rahimiyyah

Though many more could be adduced, only seven *hadiths* have been cited here, because the Holy Prophet (pbuh.!) and his revered Companions were unaccustomed to and unacquainted with that false sense of modesty which seems to be the characteristic feature of Samrodi Sahib (the Maulvi who had written those two pamphlets). When a large portion of the religion concerns women, only that narrow-minded and short-sighted man who wants to keep the religious teaching incomplete and tolerate suppression in it can indulge in sham modesty. When God Himself declares that He is not ashamed of saying the truth, His honest and virtuous slaves too do not feel any shame or guilt in telling the truth. But Samrodi Sahib is not concerned with truth and honesty; to him truth is only this that he may exultantly throw mud at the Hanafite rite and leave no stone unturned to insult and disparage—by taunting and twitting, jeering and sneering at—the distinguished jurisprudents. With great concern and anxiety he says:

'O dear brothers-in-religion! Wake up from your sleep of negligence. How long will you be asleep? What startling things have been written in our religious books! Our *Ulema* have petted us into sleep by explaining to us that our jurisprudence is the very kernel and gist of the Quran and the *Hadith*.'

He further writes: 'Could such books be called religious books in which the writers derive sensual delight by writing such strange and obscene things?'

At another place he says:

'It is worth mulling over. Let *ghairat* (jealousy, in the sense of being jealous for the service of religion) come near you and make use of your intelligence and sagacity. Other people have taken exception to and decried such things.'

And again:

Fatawa -i- Rahimiyyah

'Could the religion of Islam be such that they write such things in books? Such things should be in the books of the Arya Samaj; not in our books, not at all.' Then he adds: 'I have written these few problems by way of sample only because my heart becomes restless and my pen trembles at writing the other problems.'

I am your well-wiser,
Abd al-Jalil Samrodi
Dated 21-8-50.

At another place he sarcastically writes against the Hanafite *mazhab* thus:

'Why should not a *mazhab* which has such pleasing qualities be popular in the world? Where can one find such things in the Divine Word and the Prophet's *hadiths*?'

This Samrodi Sahib's scoffing is meant merely to malign the honourable jurisconsults and to instigate the ignorant, otherwise it is quite evident from the Quranic verses and the holy *hadiths* cited above that neither Allah the Most High nor the Holy Prophet nor the venerated Companions feel any such false modesty and bashfulness in teaching the propositions of religion.

Samrodi Sahib does not conform to the 'striving Imams' (*A'imma-e mujtahidin*); he rather has the dubious distinction of following the Jews and polytheists of Madina. From the two traditions given below it will become evident as to whom he, though being a *ghair-muquallid*, is following:

Fatawa -i- Rahimiyyah

(1) A polytheist derisively told Hazrat Salman Farsi: 'Your Companion (the Holy Prophet) teaches you the manners of even relieving (urination and defecation) yourselves?' Salman replied: 'He is affectionate to us like a father. He has taught us that while relieving ourselves we should not sit facing the Qiblah, we should not use our right hand for cleansing and be not content with less than three clods; that we should use three clods and should not use dung or bones' (Narrator, *Muslim*).

The Holy Prophet (pbuh.!) said (to his Companions): 'I am unto you as a father is unto his children. I teach you that when you go to answer the call of nature you should not sit facing the Qiblah nor with your back towards it. Use three clods of earth for cleansing and do not use dried dung or bone and your right hand for cleansing' (*Mishkat*, p. 42).

The religious divines and jurisprudents are the true heirs of the Holy Prophet (pbuh.!) and the prophets and the real religious leaders; they have endeavoured to compile in detail all the propositions in the light of the Quran, the Prophet's sayings and the Companions' practice for the benefit of the followers of Islam that will be born till the Doomsday in order that they have no difficulty in finding the solution of any problem that may beset them. We should rather be grateful to them than deride and make light of these men of light and learning and smirch their reputation insolently....[25]

* * *

---

25. *Fatawa-i-Rahimiyyah*, Volume II, p. 19–23.

The reader will judge how adequate the explanation is. But for us two points are of significance: as is evident from the defence, it is the considered view of the ulema that taking up such questions is an important function which they have to perform as religious authorities, and that in coming to this view of their functions they have before them the final authority in such matters, that is the practice of the Prophet himself. Several consequences follow, and they shall become evident as we proceed. At the moment we need note just one lemma that follows ineluctably from the premise that laying down the law on these matters too is a religious function and hence a duty of the religious authorities, in the present instance the ulema. Such a view naturally determines the direction in which the training and scholarship of these authorities are going to get oriented. The fact that for centuries the largest proportion of the best minds of Islam has remained preoccupied with such questions, with these externals, with these trivia has turned Islam even further away from the inner-directed search than would in any event have been the case, given its basic doctrine.

But the principal consequence is different. For the fact that the ulema devote so much of their time to such matters is not fortuitous. The claim of the ulema, indeed of Islam that it shall regulate all of life is of the very essence of the religion. The claim is: Islam, in practice that means the ulema shall regulate the totality of life; there is no aspect of the life of the believer which shall be outside the jurisdiction of the ideology; the believer shall have no sphere of autonomy vis-à-vis either Islam or the ulema. It is this claim and its enforcement which make Islam a totalitarian ideology, the claim that it has the right and the duty to regulate the totality of life. Once this claim of an ideology has been internalized by the followers, the hold of those who have or who usurp the responsibility to enforce the claim is ensured. For if the followers submit to be governed even in these private matters by the dictates of the enforcers—the party in Marxism-Leninism, the ulema in Islam—then they are all the more ready to follow the directives of that authority on public issues.

Believers and Kafirs

3

Identity: from distinctiveness to assertiveness to aggressiveness

From its earliest beginnings, and certainly from the Prophet's years at Medina, the core of Islam has not been some inner-directed search—as it is in the teaching of the Buddha, for instance—but the founding, consolidation, expansion of a state. The religion has been an instrument for this—an ideology to define and weld a group, an ideology to rationalize the conquest and conversion and subjugation of others.

In addition, there has been quite obviously an anxiety about the revelations, and the doctrines which flowed from them: from the earliest days therefore there has been the strictest embargo on examining the revelations and the doctrines—whether they be the cosmology or theology, or doctrines about any other matter, like marriage and divorce—which flowed from the revelations. This prohibition in turn has reflected two distinct apprehensions. First, there has been the anxiety that the doctrines would not withstand scrutiny. They are strictly dated in that they reflect the state of knowledge of seventh-century Arabia, but they have been projected as, they have *had to* be projected as eternal verities. This anxiety has naturally intensified with each advance of scientific knowledge, but not just of scientific knowledge. For, as we just saw, the claim of Islam has been that it provides and constitutes a blueprint for the totality of man's life and his relationships: the result is that progress in every sphere—for instance, the progressive democratization of governance, the progressive humanization of laws, the more egalitarian and humane ways of viewing the weak: women or minorities—each of these has exacerbated the anxiety as it has called in question some part of the revelation and doctrine. The very claims—the claim that Islam has a blueprint for the totality of life and the claim that the blueprint is a seamless whole not one thread of which can be replaced—have thus boomeranged.

There has been an even more fundamental apprehension. The revelations—and the doctrines and blueprint which flowed from them—were totally intertwined with the Prophet himself. Thus, when knowledge advanced on a particular point, or when the new laws regarding evidence or divorce were so obviously more rational and more just, they called into question not just one cosmological theory or law, they called into question the authority of the Prophet himself. He might have said—as he is reported to have done in connection with the date palms incident—that on affairs of the world his knowledge was like that of any other man, and that it was only in regard to matters relating to Din that his word ought to be treated as final. But clearly that kind of a distinction could not be held up by the heirs of his state and legacy. For one thing, divorce, alimony, estates..... the state itself were all just 'affairs of the world'. For another, once the habit of questioning his word got afoot in this sphere—and that too a sphere so vast as to encompass 'affairs of the world'—what was there to stop it from taking apart and examining what the Prophet had said on affairs of things other than the world? Where would that leave the religion?

The anxieties could be kept at bay in one way and one way alone—by ensuring that nothing but nothing was examined. Accordingly, this has been the hallmark of faith.

That the quest has not been an inner-directed one and that there have been all these apprehensions have led to one predictable result: the entire emphasis has been on externals, on the uniform to be worn, so to say. Here too several factors have combined to convert this emphasis into a fixation, and to give it a peculiarity. In the doctrinal sphere from the beginning there had been the charge of *Israeliyat*—the charge, namely, that the revelations were just regurgitations of Jewish and Christian legends.[1] Accordingly, from the days of the Prophet himself there has been the anxiety to always make sure that they are different, to *show* that they are different, to *insist* that they are different. In the world of affairs and men too the same anxiety surfaced, and from the very beginning. Islam was a latecomer, the people already professed some creed or the other, they belonged to and in fact were strongly rooted in some community or the other—in Mecca and Medina at the time of the Prophet, and in every land it conquered later on. Therefore, there has been the anxiety, indeed the compulsion to *make* them different. No sooner did his power get consolidated in Medina that the Prophet began ensuring that the believers did things differently—the Qiblah was changed from Jerusalem to the Kaba, the festivals and holidays were altered.

The earlier factors—that the quest was not inner-directed, and the apprehensions about the doctrines—had led to focusing on externals. This need to separate the doctrine and the community from the pool from which they had been taken gave the focus a particular edge: an insistence not just

---

1. See, G.H.A. Jyunbol, *The Authenticity of the Tradition Literature*, Khayats, Beirut, 1966.

on externals but on those externals which would set the community apart from the others.

These twin features—the fixation on externals, and the insistence on those externals which separate believers from the others—have continued through the centuries, and are a hallmark of the fatwas.

But the sequence does not end there. There are two further steps: from externals, to externals which separate one, to flaunting those particular externals aggressively, to making being aggressive the external which sets the community apart. And this last feature is quite the hallmark of the image of the community which the fatwas insist must be imprinted on the minds of all—of the believers, and specially of the non-believers.

The first step—the fixation on externals—will become evident from considering activities which come closest to the inner-directed search: fasting, the ablutions before prayer, the prayer itself. The second step—of doing a thing in the way which is the opposite of the way the others do it—will be evident from what the fatwas say regarding the dress a Muslim ought to wear. And the third step—of being aggressive being made the hallmark of the community—will become evident from considering the insistence of the ulema on slaughtering cows.

Externals

When we study the discourses of the Buddha or what Gandhiji has to say on, say, fasting, the content is all about looking within, about self-purification. But even when they deal with purely religious subjects the fatwas are all about the form to which the believer must adhere. They resemble instructions a drill sergeant gives to cadets for a parade.

Consider fasting. With Gandhiji it is a means of quietening the senses, an occasion for looking within, for calming the mind so that it is more receptive to the silent, still, inner voice, exactly as is, say, the abstaining from speech on a day of silence. But in the fatwas observing the fast, even during the holy month of Ramzan, is another device for identifying with the chimerical ummah, it is yet another device for regimentation. The whole discussion is about the externals that attend the abstention from intake. A person who has been weaned on Buddhist texts on meditation, on Gandhiji's writings about fasting will be startled at the subjects which the fatwas on observing the roza fasts deal with—at the points these authorities think it worthwhile to stress and dilate upon, at the things which preoccupy the querists.

Full forty-three pages of Volume VI of the *Fatawa Dar al-Ulum, Deoband* are devoted to considering what breaks the roza fast and what does not, what breaks the roza fast and makes repetition mandatory but entails no punishment, and what breaks the fast and entails both repetition as well as expatiation by undergoing a penalty.

Does using a *datun* break the fast? Does using toothpaste? Does putting oil on one's head, for some of it is bound to enter the pores of one's scalp? Does leaving the *paan* in one's mouth and falling asleep break it? Does putting snuff in one's nose?—this weighty question being pronounced on more than once. Does nose-bleed? Does putting tilak, or someone else putting tilak on one break it? Does putting medicine in one's eyes?—for clearly there is 'intake'. Does an injection? Sand or dust flies into a man's mouth, he spits it out; is the fast broken? Do bleeding gums break it? Does the fast break if a woman puts dry medicine in her vagina? What is the hukum if one swallows the saliva which forms on one's lips? What is the hukum if one breaks wind while one is in a tank during roza? Does the fast break if one puts ointment on one's piles? If one puts *surma* in the eyes? Does it break by kissing and cuddling? The ulema devote earnest consideration to each of these situations and after diligent inquiry pronounce that none of these break the roza fast.

Does the fast break if the bath which is enjoined after sexual intercourse is taken after daybreak? If blood from the gums is swallowed? If saliva admixed with paan is swallowed? By smoking the hookah? By putting medicine in the nostrils? By insertion in the vagina? By masturbation? By kissing and cuddling, leading to discharge of semen? By putting oil in one's ears? By taking snuff? By eating and intercourse? By semen being discharged upon merely lying next to one's wife? By discharge of semen while one is asleep? If semen is discharged by merely sitting next to the wife, pray what is the hukum? If one did not sight the moon on the twenty-ninth day but learnt later that it had in fact appeared? If someone burns incense near a person who is observing the fast? If the woman begins her menstruation? And so on. Earnest consideration. Diligent looking up of authorities. Minute analysis based on analogical reasoning.... Each of these situations is pronounced to necessitate a repetition of the fast though none of them entails punishment.

Does intercourse break the fast even if there is no ejaculation? Does taking water because of intense thirst? Does sighting the moon on the last day and taking food? If one thinks the sun has set and breaks the fast, and the sun appears again? Does the fast of the wife, who is keeping rozas, break upon her husband, who is not keeping rozas, having intercourse with her? Does it break if one has intercourse with a prostitute? What is the hukum if one drinks milk in the morning? What is the hukum if, without knowing it, one has intercourse with one's wife during *Ramzan* or masturbates?

Does eating raw meat and rice break it? How is it to have intercourse with one's wife during Ramzan? And till what hour of the night can one do so? If upon awaking one has intercourse with one's wife and then learns that the day has dawned—what is the hukum? May one on whom punishment is mandatory expiate it by paying a price? What is the hukum if because of a fire in the house the roza is broken? If out of ignorance one eats after the *azan*? And so on.[2]

What the ulema shall hold after their study is not always easy to foresee, for, as we saw earlier, the rulings are often based on subtle distinctions. Thus, for instance, the consequences of the discharge of semen depend on whether this happened involuntarily or voluntarily; in the latter case too there are several subdivisions: masturbation voids the fast but it does not entail any punishment, but intercourse entails repentance also; when the non-fasting husband has intercourse with the wife who is observing the fast, repentance is ordained for *her*; intercourse during the day in the month of Ramzan is declared to be 'a great sin', voiding the fast as well as entailing punishment, but intercourse at night is pronounced to be 'proper', though the bath consequent upon the intercourse can be postponed till after daybreak.... And so on.[3]

The *Fatawa-i-Rahimiyyah* also devotes itself to the solemn consideration of the same sorts of questions and in it also the decrees turn on fine distinctions. Thus medicine or oil dropped in the ears or oil rubbed on the scalp is declared to render the fast infructuous because in these cases the substance is said to reach the brain and affect it; on the other hand, medicine or collyrium applied to the eyes is declared

2. On the above see *Fatawa Dar al-Ulum, Deoband,* Volume VI, pp. 403–46.

3. Ibid., pages 155, 156, 161, 171.

not to vitiate it as there is said to be no passage between the eyes and the brain, and between the eyes and the stomach.[4]

Whether blood from the teeth will void the fast is declared to turn on whether the taste of blood predominates or that of saliva (in the former case it voids the fast, in the latter case it does not).[5] Ejaculation resulting from intromission and coition with an animal is declared to vitiate the fast, and entail both—bathing as well as making good the fast. But, as we saw, ejaculation which has occurred without the man having 'used his organ' and instead by his having merely 'touched the animal's with his hand or kissed the animal' is declared not to vitiate the fast—though a bath is recommended. And in turn these verdicts turn not on hygiene or medical knowledge, but on the proper interpretation of *Shami*, a text of the eighteenth and nineteenth century, and *Durr-ul-Mukhtar*, a text of the seventeenth century.[6]

Consider next the wuzu, the ritual washing before the prayer. If the Buddha were speaking on it or Gandhiji were writing on it, he would take it for granted that the devotee was keeping himself clean. The ritual washing, they would emphasize, is symbolic—washing your hands as you enter the place of prayer ought really to be washing out unwholesome thoughts you have been carrying around, they would say, much as ringing the bell suspended at the entrance to the temple or striking the gong placed there is done not to alert the deity but to nudge the mind of the devotee into shedding the cares and chatter it has been embroiled in outside, to empty it so that it may receive.

Contrast this with so many of the preoccupations of the querists and the ulema in the fatwas on wuzu. Here is one

4. *Fatawa-i-Rahimiyyah*, Volume II, pp. 14–15.

5. Ibid., Volume III, p. 96.

6. Ibid., Volume II, pp. 16–26.

string of questions on which the learned of Dar al-Ulum, Deoband, the Al-Azhar of India as it is so often called, expend their time and scholarship.

If the droplet (of urine) doe's not come out, stays in the 'mouth' (of the penis) but can be seen, is the wuzu broken or not? (The wuzu remains intact till the droplet comes at the 'mouth'.) If the knee or thigh gets exposed, will the wuzu remain intact? (Yes.) If the droplet of urine does not come out because one has inserted cotton wool in the 'mouth' of the penis, does the wuzu break? (It does not break till the moisture comes out on the outer side of the cotton wool.) How is it to touch a woman, with no cloth intervening, after wuzu? (If the parts touched are hands and feet wuzu does not break; if the private parts are touched it breaks.) If after wuzu one sees a woman and is excited, what is the hukum? (That seeing which leads to erection but does not lead to the discharge of nadi on the outer part, does not break the wuzu.) Does emission of sputum break wuzu? (No.) If one does an improper act with a minor does wuzu break? (No, not if nadi or semen is not emitted by penetration.) If a person stops his wind from being discharged during wuzu or namaz, do these remain in tact? (Yes.) If one passes wind but there is neither sound nor odour, is wuzu broken? (Yes, if wind has escaped, whether or not there is noise or odour, wuzu is void and must be repeated.) If one accidentally sees the private parts of another man, is the wuzu void? (No.)[7] And so on.

The *Fatawa-i-Rizvia* too takes up for analysis whether, among other things, wuzu is void and has to be repeated if some mehndi remains on the hands, if surma remains in a corner of the eyes, if some polish remains on the nails, if there is blood in the saliva, if one's nose flows, if there is

7. *Fatawa Dar al-Ulum, Deoband,* Volume I, pp. 135–50.

phlegm.... It specifies how much of the beard must be washed....[8]

Verses of the Quran, the Hadis, principles of Islamic jurisprudence like qiyas, reasoning by analogy, are all brought to bear on matters such as these, and the verdict turns on what these texts say, on what can be said on the basis of these principles of jurisprudence: if the thigh gets exposed by the breeze unfurling the dhoti or lungi or undergarment, is the wuzu void? The wuzu remains intact, pronounce the Ahl-i-Hadis ulema, because it is stated in a Hadis in *Sahih al-Bukhari* that upon buttocks having got exposed once the wuzu was pronounced not to have broken, and so, when exposure of buttocks does not void wuzu, naturally the exposure of a thigh cannot be held to void it....[9] And, as always, every question leads to categories and subcategories: if you break wind during namaz, and you suffer from flatulence, Allah shall pardon the transgression, and the namaz shall have taken place; but for the next namaz you should do wuzu again....[10] So, the question is whether the person can be held to suffer from chronic flatulence.

Wuzu completed, the fatwas on the actual prayer, namaz, take up pages after pages—running into hundreds. But again the preoccupation is with externals: the distance between the imam—the one leading the prayer—and the others, the way the rows ought to be formed, the way the shoes ought to be kept, the sequencing of the movements and genuflections, the way the phrases have to be pronounced, the language in which they may be pronounced.... And of course the familiar questions turn up again for erudite examination.

Who can lead the congregation, that is who can be the

8. *Fatawa-t-Rizvia,* Volume I, pp. 6–94

9. *Fatawa Ahl-i-Hadis,* Volume I, p. 74.

10. Ibid., Volume I, p. 74.

imam? The basic position is straightforward—any devout Muslim can be the imam—and it is often taken to illustrate the democratic ethos of Islam as well as the proposition that there is no clergy or church in Islam.

But naturally in the hands of jurists, the matter becomes one that requires complex analysis, reference to texts, and much cogitation. For while it is simple enough to say 'any devout Muslim can lead the congregation,' one has to decide who is 'a devout Muslim'.

Can one who writes out loan or interest papers be an imam? Can a woman? Can one who is in love with a Shia? Can Deobandis, can Shafi'ites, can Barelvis? Can one who beats his mother or father? Can one who has taken money for his sister's wedding? Can one who helps his brother-in-law who in turn has abducted a girl?.... These and other criteria are pronounced upon by the ulema of Ahl-i-Hadis.[11]

Can an adulterer lead the prayer? One who is guilty of sodomy? A man whose wife does not observe the purdah? A bearded man who says he is better than another man simply because the latter does not have a beard?..... These and other criteria are pronounced upon by Mufti Kifayatullah—his answers are as always well modulated: if the wife does not observe the purdah in spite of the husband asking her to do so, he is not at fault, and it is all right to have him as imam, rules Kifayatullah; that a man says to another, 'I am better than you because I have a beard,' does not prove that he is arrogant, he is merely stating a fact, and so it is all right to have him as imam, rules Kifayatullah....[12]

Can one who calls another '*haramzada*' lead the prayer? One who is an adulterer and smokes bidis? One who plays chess? One who has piles? One who swoons? One

11. *Fatawa Ahl-i-Hadis,* Volume II, pp. 149–223.

12. *Mufti Kifayatullah ke Fatawi,* Volume HI, pp. 37–112.

who serves drinks and whose wife does not keep veiled? One who keeps his hair long? One who dines at the place of an apostate woman? One who wears his pyjama reaching down below the ankles?—the latter question is taken up twice. One who does istinja with water only?—the question is pronounced upon thrice. One who uses black hair dye? One who wears a pyjama of six *girahas*' width? One who has himself photographed? One who gets a girl married to a Qadiani? One who supports innovation and polytheism? One who is wearing a dhoti? One who wears a topi? One who participates in the funeral of a Hindu? One who does not cut his pubic hair? One who plucks his white hair? One who is wearing dentures? One who cuts his beard?—a matter which engages all the jurists, in this collection it is found necessary to pronounce on it thrice. One who adopts Hindu cultural mores? One who eats fish? One who takes interest and maintains relations with Shias? One who speaks and acts against the beard? One whose wife wears a sari? One who plays cards? One who adopts innovations (in religious matters)? One who does not stop his women from playing the dholak and singing songs at weddings?.... Such are the questions on which the ulema of Deoband expend over 200 pages.[13]

Their verdicts are orthodoxy itself. Even apart from the time of namaz, to wear a pyjama reaching below the ankles is haram and prohibited, they pronounce, and the said imam should not do so. Wearing a pyjama of this kind is a ground for disqualifying a man from being an imam and to observe the namaz behind him is detestable. One should persuade him to change or one should change him, but if one nonetheless observes the namaz in the congregation behind him one shall obtain the benefit of observing namaz

13. *Fatawa Dar al-Ulum, Deoband,* Volume III, pp. 99–333.

in the congregation.... Similarly, they pronounce one who acquires Hindu mores to be a fasiq—a bad character, a sinner—and a *sakht gunahgar*, a great sinner; they decree that one who approves of such ways is also a fasiq, and that such a person is not qualified to be an imam. To play chess, the ulema declare, is detestable according to Imam Abu Hanifa, and a man habituated to it is not qualified to be imam.... And how could they rule otherwise? Had the Prophet not said, 'He who plays chess is like one who dyes his hand with the flesh and blood of swine?'....[14] So, the answers are orthodoxy itself.

But obviously not orthodox enough. For, as we shall see elsewhere, the *Fatawa-i-Rizvia* decrees that to observe namaz behind a Deobandi, or even behind one who has been to madrasahs run by Deobandis is detestable, prohibited and infructuous !

Now, it is not just fortuitous that the ulema should devote so much scholarship and time to settling such questions. For remember the criterion was that any pious Muslim can be an imam. But as Islam's basic claim is, in the eyes of the ulema its distinguishing feature is that it provides a complete code, a code covering every aspect of life, it is natural to see that the man who is to be selected to lead the prayer abides by the code in every particular.

Selecting the one who is to lead the prayer is of course just one step. The person selected, the fatwas go on to specify scores and scores of things he must do or he must refrain from doing while leading the prayer.

Can he lead the prayer wearing a cap? Can he do so standing a foot higher than the congregation? Can he do so with his sleeves rolled up?..... The topics are endless, and

---

14. On the three examples see *Fatawa Dar al-Ulum, Deoband,* Volume III, pp. 117 and 263, 240, and 120 respectively. On the Hadis about chess, see *Sahih Muslim,* Volume IV, p. 1222, Hadis 5612.

there are several shades of emphasis. On the reckoning of the ulema of the Ahl-i-Hadis a man wearing a shirt with sleeves rolled up can lead the prayers provided the shirt covers the shoulders. The usually moderate Mufti Kifayatullah is much stricter on the point: to read the *khutba* or namaz in a half-sleeved shirt, he decrees, is detestable and contentious for this is not the dress for prayers for Muslims....[15]

The same sorts of matters continue with reference to members of the congregation: what if a dog passes between the imam and the congregation?.... And of course the matters that come up in every context. What if there is discharge during the prayer? What if during namaz one remembers that after urinating one had taken kalukh but not used water? What if while cleaning oneself after defecation or passing urine a drop or two falls on oneself or on one's clothing, can namaz be done in that clothing?.... And as always the decrees entail categories and quanta: the jurist distinguishes between two situations in which water used for cleaning oneself after defecation may have fallen on one's attire: (i) the situation in which water falls in the midst of or immediately after cleaning; and (ii) the situation in which the water which falls on one from the lota or hand has not mixed with the water covered by the first circumstance; the latter is declared to be paak, and no remedial action is required; in the former circumstance, the corrective required turns on the quantum of water—if the cloth has got wet over an area less than that of a dirham then, while a bath is not required, it is preferable to bathe again, if the area exceeds that one can bathe.... Similarly, the jurists rule that if the dog which passed in front of the congregation was red-brown the namaz is not

---

15. Compare *Fatawa Ahl-i-Hadis,* Volume I, p. 197, and *Mufti Kifayatullah ke Fatawi,* Volume III, p. 71.

broken but that if it was black then it is broken, as it is if a donkey or woman passes in front....[16]

The inner-directed search in the Buddha's discourses on meditation, in Gandhiji's writings on prayer and fasting, and the preoccupations here.... And notice both sides of the transaction: the laity have manifestly internalized the doctrine that in regard to even prayer such questions are vital—that is why they keep querying the ulema on these matters; and on the other side the ulema regard these questions to be so vital that they expend so much scholarship and time on them.

Sacrifice of animals for Allah's glory

The fatwas on sacrifice are of the same kind, except that most of us would feel a bit nauseous at reading, and in religious books at that, details of how living things are to be slaughtered.

From the Buddha's *Discourses* to Gandhiji's *Anasakti Yoga* we are taught that what has to be sacrificed is our ego, our base instincts, our hankering after the fruit of action. But here the position is completely the opposite: sacrifice refers to the physical slaughter of a living animal.

And even on that the concern of the fatwas is wholly with externals: their concern is just with the mechanics of slaughtering the poor animal.

The direction of the animal to be slaughtered should be towards the Kaba, the fatwas reiterate. Does that mean its eyes, nose, forehead should point that way, or what? The ulema set the matter out in detail: the head of the animal to

16. The examples can be multiplied many times over. For the three which have been given see, *Fatawa Ahl-i-Hadis*, Volume III, p. 75; *Fatawa-i-Rizvia*, Volume II, pp. 153–54; and *Mufti Kifayatullah ke Fatawi*, Volume II, pp. 281–82.

be slaughtered should be to the south, it should be lying on its left side, its back should be to the east.... The man who slaughters the animal should also face the Qiblah....

The concerns of the faithful are also only with these practical details. May a sickle be used to slaughter the animal? (There is a difference of opinion among the learned: Shami says, 'Yes'; Ahmad Riza Khan says, 'No', as using it is akin to using a blunt knife; but then he relents: one may use a sickle if one is doing so out of necessity.) Which leg of the animal should be placed near its neck? If no part of the *ghundi* is joined to the head, can the animal be slaughtered still? (Don't go by the *ghundi,* the fatwa declares; if three of the four arteries which connect the neck to the head are severed, it is halal; if only one or two are cut below the ghundi, it is not halal; if all four or three are cut above the ghundi....)

What if a blunt knife is used and the animal dies before three arteries are severed, is it halal? (There is a difference of opinion among the learned on this matter too.)

If the hand of the sacrificer is weak, may another hold the knife with him? If so, must both of them recite the *takbir*? (A fierce difference of opinion on that among the Barelvis and Deobandis.)

Is an animal sacrificed by a Shia, a Deobandi, an Ahl-i-Hadis polluted? Is meat sent by a Deobandi polluted even if it has been brought by a Muslim? A most emphatic, 'Yes', to each question in the *Fatawa-i-Rizvia,*...[17]

Is it correct to combine the missed sacrifice with the current year's sacrifice? If one is sacrificing for deceased persons, is it necessary to keep separate portions for each deceased person or can all be combined in one? ('It is necessary to keep a separate portion for each. One portion is not sufficient for more than one deceased person.... If one can

17. On the foregoing, *Fatawa-i-Rizvia,* Volume VIII, pp. 316–32.

afford it, sacrifice should be made on behalf of the deceased as it is a very meritorious work from which the deceased benefit very much.') Is it permissible to sacrifice a barren goat or not? ('It is permissible, not forbidden.... The barrenness of a sacrificial animal is not a defect even as castration and inability to mate are no disqualifications for sacrifice. A barren animal is often very meaty and fatty and its meat is also very delicious....') Is it permissible or not to use the milk and hair of a sacrificial animal? What about its hide? Is it incumbent on one to sacrifice on behalf of his minor children? On behalf of one's wife? Why may nails not be pared or hair cut between sighting the crescent of Al Hajj and slaughtering the animal?

Can one sacrifice an animal whose tail has been chopped off? (Not if more than one-third of it has been chopped off, but according to one authority one can sacrifice an animal if a little less than half its tail is intact.) Can one sacrifice an animal which has a tumour on its body? (Yes.) If the sheath of the horn has been cast off? (Yes, but not if the horn has been uprooted.) An animal without ears? A castrated goat? An animal which has been used for copulation? An animal which has reached the prescribed age but has not yet cut its teeth?....[18]

The prescriptions are so clinical that they cannot but foment cruelty. 'What is the regulation if a live kid or calf comes out from the womb of the slaughtered animal?,' asks the querist. The *Fatawa-i-Rahimiyyah* declares: 'If the offspring is alive, it too should be slaughtered; if dead, it cannot be used'—and that on the authority of *Shami* ![19] Is it justifiable to sacrifice a cow whose calf is still dependent on it for

---

18. On the foregoing, *Fatawa-i-Rahimiyya,* Volume II, pp. 66–75; Volume III, pp. 162–69.

19. *Fatawa-i-Rahimiyya,* Volume II, p. 69.

milk?, asks the querist, and adds that the calf is four to five months old. There is no objection in sacrificing such a cow, decrees Mufti Kifayatullah. If the calf is so young that it does not as yet eat anything, then slaughter the calf also, he decrees. But that shall not be a sacrifice of the calf, he cautions, it will be justifiable to eat its flesh '*vaise hi*', 'just like that'. And if it is not that young then it is not necessary to slaughter it. When it is that small, and the cow is sacrificed but it is not, the sacrifice will be complete, but this—sacrificing the cow but not killing the calf—is not desirable....[20]

The externals that will set one apart

The fixation on externals is the first step. Next, the ulema insist that the believers adhere to those externals which will set them apart from the non-believers, that they do things in ways which are the opposite of—and visibly the opposite of—the way the non-believers do them, that they flaunt these differentiating externals. An innocuous thing like dress becomes an instrument for what would today be called strong political statements.

In shariah it is haram to wear clothes which obscure the difference between kafirs and Muslims, declares the *Fatawa-i-Rizvia*. True religion, it declares, is that to wear the dress of the form which the *firangi*s use is kufr. Quoting authorities, it pronounces that even to *say* that what one is wearing is the same as the dress or item of dress which is associated with kafirs—even to *say* so, when manifestly that is not the case in fact, is kufr: thus it pronounces the woman who said of the rope which she had tied around her waist, 'It is *zunnar*' (the sacred thread worn by Hindus), has become a kafir. For that reason, declares the *Fatawa-i-Rizvia*, clothes of an

20. *Mufti Kifayatullah ke Fatawi*, Volume VIII, pp. 203–4.

anglicized form are detestable, they are *'haram, sakht haram, ashad haram'*—forbidden, strictly forbidden, absolutely forbidden—and anyone doing namaz in them is a sinner, a sinner who deserves punishment. A Muslim is prohibited from even stitching clothes which are associated with another qaum—like trousers, the English cap, jacket etc.[21]

Even the more circumspect Mufti Kifayatullah lays emphasis on clothes being used to set the believers apart. He says that strictly speaking Shariah prescribes no special design or shape for the dress a believer must wear—except that men are forbidden from wearing a few things (silken garments, clothes having zari) and dress which resembles the dress worn either by some kafir qaum or by women. One's Islam is dependent on one's beliefs and deeds, he says. Dress does not bear on the basics of Islam but, he stresses, it is necessary for Muslims to maintain the Islamic form and appearance. There are distinguishing features by which every qaum and class is recognized. In the same way the beard and dress are the Islamic hallmarks of Muslims. He who erases these cultural marks does not erase Islam but, the Mufti holds, he does erase Islamic distinctiveness.

From this general position follows a touchstone: if a form of dress or an item is generally associated with some other qaum then Muslims must shun it; if the form or item has come into such general use among a people or in an area that it is no longer associated with any particular non-Muslim group, then a Muslim too may use it. It is on this touchstone that Kifayatullah decrees whether Muslims may wear particular things. About the suit and 'English style hair', he says that thus far in India they are detestable and condemnable as they resemble what Kafirs wear and do. Either of the two—a hat

---

21. *Fatawa-i-Rizvia*, Volume III, pp. 422–3; Volume IX, Book II, pp. 90–91, 190.

or English-style hair—is by itself enough to cause suspicion about the qaum to which one belongs, he rules. But a definite hukum can only be given if a person looking at the subject comes to doubt the qaum of the latter—if, for instance, the person wearing a hat is taken to be a Christian. If things come to be used commonly by others—boots, coat, trousers—then 'the suspicion becomes weak and the detestableness become less'—for then there is less apprehension that the person using that item will be taken to belong to some non-Muslim qaum. For that reason a Muslim should not, for instance, wear a dhoti as it shall approximate the dhoti non-Muslims wear; similarly, where only non-Muslim women wear a sari, for Muslim women to wear it is detestable, but where it is customary for Muslim women to wear a sari it is all right for a Muslim woman to wear it.[22]

The volumes of fatwas are replete with statements to this effect. The most cogent statement of the general position that I found is contained in Maulana Maududi's *Libas ka Masla.*[23] It will pay us to recall both the arguments he uses and the tenor he employs—the believers are kept different as much by the former as by the heavy sarcasm and minatory rhetoric of the latter.

If dress is divorced from culture, its only purposes are to cover specific parts of the anatomy and to shield one against the weather, he writes. If these were the only purposes, dress would be common to peoples, differing only according to the requirements of the climate, for anatomy is the same everywhere. And yet we find that it differs, and that as culture, history, laws, mores evolved, dress also changed.

The dress of each people, Maududi says, is the qaum*i*-

---

22. *Mufti Kifayatullah ke Fatawi,* Volume IX, pp. 153, 154, 158–61.

23. Maulana Abul Ala Maududi, *Libas ka Masla,* Darul Ishat, Nishat-e-Saania, Hyderabad, Deccan, 1947.

tongue through which it manifests its *qaumiyat* and acquaints the world with it. Apart from geographical factors the other factors that affect the dress which a people wear—culture and religion of the qaum, its social mores, its economic condition, its morals and customs, the external influences on it—keep changing. These factors affect aspects of life other than dress also just as they affect the dress. The dress evolves on its own in response. No need is felt to change it by fiat.

In responding to those factors a qaum assimilates them, it transforms them to its own nature—as a tree grows, he says, and changes; it takes nourishment from the earth, from air, but it transforms them to its own nature, while assimilating them the tree retains its *imli-ness*, its mango-ness.

He comes down heavily on those who are urging Muslims to give up their distinctive, traditional dress and adopt the Western dress: they are misleading Muslims into erasing their identity, he says, and as far as progress is concerned they are catching the wrong end of the stick.

Those advocating a change of dress say that discarding the dress which was associated with the qaum lying prostrate leads to change and improvement, that by doing so the qaum will progress like the qaum whose dress it adopts. But this is a very narrow way of viewing the question, the Maulana says, it is bereft of thought. If dress alone is changed and not the way of life, great discord is bound to follow. The qaum itself should advance, the dress will then change on its own. Nothing is gained by jumping from one condition to another just as nothing is gained by feeding potions to a minor to suddenly make him a major. On the contrary, if a qaum tries to have a dress which is not in consonance with its economic capacity, ruin is bound to follow.

More important, dress, Maududi says, is part of the culture of a people like its language and script. If these are given up, the qaum melts away into the general mass. In fact for a qaum to adopt the dress of another qaum is a reflection of an inferiority complex. It means that the qaum considers itself base, downtrodden and backward, that it believes it has nothing of which it can be proud, that its forbears were not capable of leaving anything which it could retain without feeling ashamed. It shows that the nature of the qaum has fallen so low, that its social mind is so counterfeit, that it is so bereft of constructive thought that it cannot forge a better life for itself; that to show itself to be cultured it borrows everything from others, and without any shame it announces to the world that culture, civilization, etiquette, beauty, lustre—whatever is worthwhile is only in the life of others; and that whatever is with others is the standard of all progress; and that we have spent all the thousands of years of our qaumi life in a *jungli* condition, that we could not produce anything which was worthwhile and worthy of respect.

It is evident, Maududi says, that any qaum which has any self-respect cannot accept the ways of others in this way. History is a witness to the fact which we are seeing in our own times with our own eyes that a qaum accepts these fallen ways only in two circumstances. Either when it has been defeated and beaten on all fronts by other qaums and accepts defeat and lays down arms—as has happened in Hindustan, Turkey, Iran, etc. Or when it has neither history nor traditions to back it, when it has not had any culture or civilization, when it does not have any distinguishing constructive power, or when in the world it has the position of an upstart like Japan.

If there is something which is worth taking from another qaum, Maududi says, it is the knowledge which it has acquired and what has been gained from it, the practical ways by which it has acquired success in the world. And if there is any useful lesson in its history, in its ways of organization, and its mores then that should certainly be adopted—after thorough examination. Such things are the common heritage of mankind. Not to respect them, to be niggardly in partaking of them out of national pride is gross ignorance.

But, he continues, leaving these things aside, to adopt from the other qaum its dress, its ways of living, its foods, and to take these to be the means to progress is just a symptom of deficient comprehension and nothing else. Can any intelligent person imagine for even a moment that Europe has progressed because of trousers, coat and tie or because it eats with knife and fork, or that its items of cosmetics—powder, lipstick, etc.—have carried it to the skies of progress? If that is not so—and it is obvious that it is not—then, after all, why is it that the first thing the counsellors of progress leap towards are these things? Why don't they see, Maududi asks, that this glitter that we see in the life of Europe is the culmination of centuries of hard work? Any qaum which works as hard can attain the same heights.

It is obvious from these arguments, Maududi concludes, that for a qaum to adopt the dress and culture of another qaum is against its nature, that it is illogical, that it does not stand to reason from any standpoint. In normal circumstances no qaum would even think of deserting the ways it has followed for centuries. It is only in abnormal circumstances that it thinks of such things—as some women, when they are pregnant, start eating mud, or when, having some abnormality in the eye, one starts seeing everything as crooked.

Maududi turns next to consider the question from the point of view of shariah.

Islam is the law of nature, he says. In every matter it adopts the rule which conforms to intelligence and nature. Once you take off your coloured spectacles and see things in their true light, you will come to the same conclusions as

Islam does. It does not specify any particular dress or way of life for man, says Maududi—he starts thus from the same acknowledgment which we encountered in the *Mufti Kifayatullah ke Fatawi,* and from that catholic starting point he reaches the same conclusion of doing things differently by the same route as Mufti-e-Azam Kifayatullah! Islam does not specify any particular dress or way of life. On the contrary, it adopts the ways as it finds them. But—and here we see the aperture being opened—it lays down some principles and requires that every qaum change its ways of life, etc., in accordance with those principles, says Maududi.

Foremost among these are the limits regarding the region between the knees and the navel. It is necessary that this region must be covered whatever the qaum, and all women wherever they live must cover all parts of their body other than the face and hands. Second, men should leave wearing silken clothes and ornaments of gold and silver. And both men and women should refrain from wearing clothes which suggest pride, insolence, unnecessary exhibitionism and lavishness—things which drape down to the ground and by wearing which a person shows off his superiority in comparison with others, these are condemnable in the eyes of Islam. Shed these, Maududi says. Then whatever is the customary dress of your country is acceptable to Islam.

But then there is the third principle: Islam, Maududi reminds the believers, requires that things which polytheism and idolatry have made their symbols be banished from your dress—for instance, the (sacred) thread, the cross, pictures, or similar things which are customary with non-Muslims.

And Islam also requires, stresses Maududi, that there must be something in the dress of Muslims by which they can be distinguished and recognized, something which keeps them from getting lost among non-Muslims, something by which Muslims can recognize one of their own so that social life among them is strengthened.

What this something is to be Islam has not particularized, says Maududi, and gives a telling example. At the time of the Prophet all used to wear the Arab dress. To distinguish the believers he specified that they should wear the *amama* (turban) *and* the topi because the Arabs used to wear either the amama *or* the topi. But when all of Arabia had become Muslim there was no longer any need for this—because by then the Arab dress had itself become the Muslim dress. The same sequence was repeated in lands like Turkey and Iran which Islam conquered. Therefore, Maududi counsels, in a land where most of the people are non-Muslims, every Muslim should incorporate some such insignia which sets him apart.

He goes on to elaborate and reiterate his arguments—pronouncing those who adopt the ways of others to be bats. And he recalls that the Prophet had said that a Muslim should be able to recognize a Muslim and thereby deal with him as a Muslim. Maududi stresses that the Prophet had also said that he—the Prophet—shall not be responsible for a Muslim who merges himself with non-Muslims: that is, if in an engagement the Muslims kill him taking him to be a non-Muslim then he himself will be to blame for his killing. And Maududi quotes the Hadis, which as we shall see soon is oft-quoted by the ulema in their fatwas: One who lives like another qaum, the Prophet had said, shall be taken to be of that qaum, and shall be dealt with accordingly.

This is the general perspective. It is the leitmotif which runs through the fatwas on a thing like dress. And from it follows a host of specific injunctions, even as the general proposition is acknowledged by the ulema that shariah prescribes no specific dress.

Among the reasons why a Muslim must not use toilet

paper instead of stones or lumps of earth, why he must not urinate while standing is that these are things the Christians do, that they are filthy 'habits' of Christians.[24] The angarkha was not worn in the time or country of the Prophet, the ulema tell us. But it is worn in India now. As the kafirs wear the angarkha with '*ulta purdah*'—i.e., with the buttons being affixed on the right side and the buttonholes on the left side—it is right for Muslims to wear it with '*seedha purdah*'—i.e., with buttons on the left and buttonholes on the right sides respectively: to abandon the 'seedah purdah' and start wearing the 'ulta purdah' is haram for Muslims, they decree.[25] To wear the hat Christians wear is kufr,[26] to wear trousers is detestable.[27]

In general, the *Fatawa-i-Rizvia* informs the faithful, the dhoti is a mark of the Hindus, and therefore wearing it is prohibited. If a Muslim wears a dhoti with the intention of being like the kafirs, then he is guilty of kufr: That is, he is automatically out of Islam, and his wife is automatically out of his nikah—to restore the status quo ante he must embrace Islam again, and go through the nikah again. Even if he does not wear the dhoti with the intention of being like the kafirs, his doing so is detestable, for by wearing it he will look like them nonetheless. The general position thus is that when a mark or dress is distinctive to a religious group other than Muslims, for a Muslim to wear it on him is kufr. When a mark or dress is by custom associated with a religious group other than Islam then it is detestable, and it is incumbent for a Muslim to shun it. In the former category are the tilak, zunnar, chotie; in the latter are trousers, the English cap or hat, jacket, and the 'ulta purdah'. Even to stitch such

---

24. *Fatawa-i-Rizvia*, Volume II, pp. 146–153, 156.
25. Ibid., Volume VIII, p. 444.
26. Ibid., Volume IX, Book II, p. 178.
27. Ibid., Volume III, p. 419.

clothes is haram for a Muslim. The essence of the matter is to be visibly different from non-Muslims.

By itself there is nothing wrong with the dhoti from the point of view of shariah, the *Fatawa-i-Rizvia* states. In fact in rural areas it is the common dress of Hindus and Muslims, it says, but it is prohibited because wearing it makes a Muslim look like the kafirs. Muslims in cities already do not wear it, though they refrain from doing so not because they see it as the dress of kafirs but because they see it as being contrary to civilized etiquette. The point is that, and the *Fatawa-i-Rizvia* cites authorities to drive the injunction home, if Muslims of an area regard it as the attire of kafirs, then it ought to be shunned. In particular, a dhoti or sari tied at the rear is to be shunned as that is the way the kafirs tie it, and so observing namaz while wearing a dhoti or sari tied in this way is detestable.[28]

As usual there are some variations in the degree of emphasis, but only in the degree. The fatwa volumes display almost a paranoia about the tilak. Mufti Kifayatullah's general position is that it is the mark of kufr, but he relents to the extent that he makes the outcome depend on intention and circumstance. Hindus and Muslims are in a procession together; supporters of the cause put *chandan* tilaks on the participants, including some Muslims: are the Muslims guilty of kufr?, he is asked. Is their nikah with their wives terminated? One should not cross the physical, moral, legal and religious limits of moderation in any circumstances, rules Kifayatullah. Unity is a very good thing, and its fruits are definitely pleasant. But, says the Mufti, who, as we shall see, argued long and hard for united action alongside Hindus, to give up one's form and shape, one's moral spirit, one's national character, one's religious dignity, and to think doing so

28. *Fatawa-i-Rizvia,* Volume IX, Book I, pp. 90–92, and Volume III, p. 424.

to be 'unity' is to exceed the limits of moderation. To put chandan and marks on the forehead is the special national and religious characteristic of the Hindus, he says. It was obligatory for those Muslims, he rules, to abstain from this. But, he adds with his usual moderation in regard to specific transgressors, because we do not know whether the chandan was put on those Muslims with their willing approval, one cannot decree that those on whom chandan was put are apostates or kafirs or that their nikah has become void. However, he concludes, they should do taubah and abstain from such actions in the future.[29]

The Barelvis are predictably much more stern. As we shall see when we discuss the disputes which arose among the ulema over the Khilafat movement, the Barelvis taunted Mufti Kifayatullah, Maulana Abdul Bari of Firangi Mahal and the Deobandis in general on the ground, among others, that by involving Muslims into a campaign in which they were embroiled in such practices—proclaiming the '*jai*' of a kafir, namely Mahatma Gandhi, participating in processions in which books like the Gita and the Ramayana were shown as much respect as the Quran, in which kafirs put tilak and chandan on the foreheads of the believers—these ulema (though Ahmad Riza Khan would never use such a respectable expression for them) had deliberately ensnared Muslims in kufr. Tilak, the *Fatawa-i-Rizvia* declares, is a way of worshipping Mahadev and is kufr. And, it declares with great emphasis, to acquiesce in kufr even for a second is as much kufr as it is to consent to kufr for a hundred years. By wiping off the tilak the kufr which has taken place is not erased: you must embrace Islam again, you must do nikah again; the reason for this is that a person who having bowed

29. *Mufti Kifayatullah ke Fatawi*, Volume IX, p. 319.

to Mahadev raises his head is in the same position as a person who lies prostrate before Mahadev all day long.[30]

Just as there is a paranoia about chandan, tilak, zunnar, the cross etc.—things which are associated with kafirs—there is a corresponding obsession with the beard.

To trim the beard to less than fist-length is forbidden, haram, declares the *Fatawa-i-Rahimiyyah.* To shave off the beard is abominable, it declares—a person who does so is a fasiq: there is near-prohibition against his leading the prayer, his evidence may be rejected, azan and iqamat shouted by such a man—a man whose deviation and unrighteousness are manifest—is abominable, declares *Fatawa-i-Rahimiyyah* citing authorities, and therefore it is abominable and impermissible to appoint such a man for shouting the azan and iqamat. It is also haram, it declares, citing authorities again, for a man to cut the beard of another.[31]

Mufti Kifayatullah is just as emphatic. To cut the beard is haram, he declares. One who cuts it, like the one who does not observe the namaz is a fasiq, and a sinner. He clubs the man who shaves his beard with the one who goes to cinemas and enjoys pictures, with the one who has his photograph taken, and declares that such a person is not fit to be an imam?[32]

The ulema of Deoband decree the same: it is clear from the Hadis, they rule, that to trim or shave the beard is haram; the imamat of one who even speaks against the beard, let alone of one who trims or shaves it, is detestable as he is a sinner.[33]

---

30. *Fatawa-i-Rizvia,* Volume VI, pp. 150,151. See also for instance p. 50 to the same effect.

31. *Fatawa-i-Rahimiyya,* Volume II, p. 195; Volume III, pp. 14–15.

32. *Mufti Kifayatullah ke Fatawi,* Volume IX, pp. 95, 264–65, 329–30. That is his general position. But in one instance he relents a bit: the imamat of a man who shaves his beard is destestable, he declares, but, he adds with the practicality so characteristic of him, if everyone in the congregation also shaves his beard then such a person can be imam; Volume III, pp. 62. 64. For fatwas dealing specifically with hair and beards see Volume IX, pp. 161–73.

33. *Fatawa Dar al-Ulum, Deoband,* Volume III, pp. 289–90.

The *Fatawa-i-Rizvia* is replete with fatwas to the same effect. To shave one's beard is haram, it decrees, and to say that to do so is within my rights is to insist on sin, though it is not kufr, strictly speaking. However, to mock the beard is kufr, to say 'Those who shave their beards are better than those -who keep beards' is kufr: the ones guilty of such denigration are out of Islam and their wives are out of their nikah—to restore the status quo ante the guilty ones must embrace Islam again and they must do the nikah again.[34]

These examples can be multiplied many times over—for ensuring that Muslims keep the beard is a major preoccupation of the ulema. Instead of multiplying these we should consider the reason for this emphasis and, although doing so will anticipate a point which is the subject matter of a subsequent chapter, we should see what the *basis* is for their insistence. The *Fatawa-i-Rizvia* provides us answers to both.

We know from *Sahih al-Bukhari*, the *Fatawa-i-Rizvia* reminds us, that the Prophet said, 'Erase the moustache and grow the beards.' We know from *Sahih Muslim* and *Jama-i-Tirmizi* that the Prophet said, 'Make the moustache very short and leave the beard alone.' It is in *Imam Jafar*, 'Make the moustache very small, and let grow the beard, and do not make your appearance like that of the Jews.' The Prophet says, 'Let the beards grow full and trim the moustache, do the opposite of Jews and Christians.' He has told us to cut the moustache very short and to keep the beards long and spread out, to act contrary to the polytheists (*mushrikon ke khilaf karo*).[35]

The reason for the decrees thus is that as non-Muslims keep (or used to keep) the moustache and shave the beard, Muslims must keep the beard and shave the moustache —

34. *Fatawa-i-Rizvia*, Volume VI, pp. 168, 182; Volume IX, Book I, pp. 30, 218.

35. Ibid., Volume IX, Book I, p. 127.

exactly the reason we have been encountering all through the decrees on dress and appearance. This is the premise, this is the attitude from which secularists and do-gooders turn their eyes. But it is a foundational, a basic premise, it is an attitude which dictates an entire approach: the obsession with 'identity', and the insistence in defining this identity as the '*not* the other'. In the face of this to go on chanting, 'We are all one,' and to think that the chant will make us one is to be the fool.

The second point to notice is the ultimate authority for the attitude, as well as for the specific decrees on the beard: the authority is the Prophet himself. '... I hope that after me you shall live long,' the Prophet is quoted in *Nasai* as telling a Companion, recalls the *Fatawa-i-Rizvia*, 'then inform the people that he who ties his beard, or he who hangs the *kaman ka chilha* around his neck, or does *istinja* with the excreta or bones of any animals—then without doubt the Prophet is disgusted with them.' Two men with moustaches came in sight of the Prophet, recalls the *Fatawa-i-Rizvia* from another Hadis. Upon seeing them the Prophet felt disgust and asked, 'Who told you to keep it?' 'Our emperor,' they said. 'But my Allah has told me to cut the moustache and keep the beard,' the Prophet remarked. Muslims should remember this Hadis, the *Fatawa-i-Rizvia* declares—that the Prophet felt disgust at seeing them; those Muslims who keep an appearance contrary to his command shall cause disgust in Allah and the Prophet, it warns. The fatwa further reminds the faithful that the Prophet also said that on the Day of Judgement man wakes up in the same condition in which he dies. Therefore remember, when Allah and the Prophet see you looking like the Magians how disgusted they will feel. And remember, when on the Day of Judgement the Prophet is disgusted at seeing you, you shall have no one to support you....[36]

36. Ibid., Volume IX, Book I, p. 128.

Now, to anticipate the point which shall come out sharply later, when the Prophet himself has commanded a thing, by what authority can it be discarded? Second, when the Prophet himself has declared that the reason that Muslims should do one thing is that it is the opposite of what non-Muslims—the Jews, Christians, polytheists—do—in this particular instance that they must keep the beard and cut the moustache *because* the non-Muslims keep the moustache and cut the beard—then how can that reason not be the governing principle for the ulema in determining what Muslims should do? How do the platitudes which our secularists keep repeating stand in the face of this?

Is it any surprise that when in the *bhai-bhai* days of the Khilafat movement some Muslims began wearing the Gandhi cap, an avalanche descended? Maulana Ahmad Riza Khan accused them of 'burning the mark of Islam', the Turkish cap, and donning the headdress of a kafir. As usual his denunciation was fulsome: 'Even if the burning of Turkish caps entails only the loss of goods,' he thundered, 'it is *haram.* And even if to wear Gandhi caps is just to incline towards the polytheists, it would be even more strictly *haram.*' But in fact the situation was worse, he decreed. 'Those who used to wear Turkish caps knowing them to be the mark of Islam, those very persons have now burnt them and made the wearing of Gandhi caps their hallmark. By doing so, having defiled the mark of Islam, they have consented to become the disciples of a *Kafir....*'[37]

Mufti Kifayatullah was among those who had urged Muslims to join hands with Gandhiji over the Khilafat issue. He had to explain his position in regard to the Gandhi cap repeatedly. The explanations he gave, the terms in which he had to defend the fact of some Muslims wearing it tell the

37. Ibid., Volume VI, p. 11

tale: they point to the general problem. We shall see that it is exactly those sorts of terms and constructions that the Mufti as well as others like the ulema of Deoband had to use in regard to the general question—of joining hands with Gandhiji and other kafirs in the struggle to free India from the British. The Gandhi cap, the Mufti opined, is actually an old Muslim cap which has been worn in the United Provinces for long. All that has happened is that it is now being made out of khaddar, but that is being done only to make it cheap so that no one may be hard put to wear it. Stung by charges and fatwas to the contrary, the Mufti in turn declared that those who are saying that wearing it is contrary to the shariah are grave sinners.[38]

From assertiveness to aggressiveness

What begins as a fixation on externals thus becomes an insistence on those externals which are manifestly the opposite of what the kafirs do. The next step is the natural progression: the ulema insist next that Muslims have a right to, indeed that it is their duty to do the thing which will put the kafirs down, the thing doing which will put the kafirs out.

Just as Muslims were to define their identify by doing things in ways contrary to the ways of the kafirs, the latter were to do those things which would put them, their sacred places in particular, at the mercy of Muslims. They were to do things which would mark their inferiority, the equivalent of Jews being asked by the Nazis to wear the Star of David. The ulema urged the Muslim rulers most persistently that such regulations be adopted, and enforced. To take one instance, Saiyid Ali Hamadani urged that the following 'covenant' be imposed on the Hindus:

38. *Mufti Kifayatullah ke Fatawi*, Volume IX, pp. 149–50, 158, 160, 269.

- They (the Hindus) will not build new idol temples.
- They will not rebuild any existing temple which may have fallen into disrepair.
- Muslim travellers will not be prevented from staying in temples.
- Muslim travellers will be provided hospitality by *zimmis* in their own houses for three days.
- Zimmis will neither act as spies nor give spies shelter in their houses.
- If any relation of a zimmi is inclined towards Islam, he should not be prevented from doing so.
- Zimmis will respect Muslims.
- Zimmis will courteously receive a Muslim wishing to attend their meetings.
- Zimmis will not dress like Muslims.
- They will not take Muslim names.
- They will not ride horses with saddle and bridle.
- They will not possess swords, bows or arrows.
- They will not wear signet rings.
- They will not openly sell or drink intoxicating liquor.
- They will not abandon their traditional dress, which is a sign of their ignorance, in order that they may be distinguished from Muslims.
- They will not openly practise their traditional customs amongst Muslims.
- They will not build their houses in the neighbourhood of Muslims.
- They will not carry or bury their dead near Muslim graveyards.
- They will not mourn their dead loudly.
- They will not buy Muslim slaves.

Setting out this 'covenant', S.A.A. Rizvi writes:

In emphasizing such a covenant, Saiyid 'Ali was acting as an *'alim* and not as a sufi. Sultan Qutub'd-Din adopted Persian dress and divorced one of his wives whom he had illegally married earlier. Occasionally he attended congregational prayers led by the Saiyid on a platform built at the site of the Kali Mandir, which he himself had helped to destroy. The demolition of the temple contravened the covenant; probably the Brahmans had not allowed Saiyid 'Ali's followers to stay in the temple and the infringement was used as a pretext and later a precedent set by the Saiyid in Kashmir.[39]

Truly, an alim! Hamadani (AD 1314–85) was a famous Sufi and is regarded as their patron saint by Muslims in Kashmir. His renowned dargah in Srinagar stands on the site of a Kali temple which he helped destroy.

As the Muslim invaders saw the veneration in which the gentle cow was held by the Hindus they made a special point of slaughtering cows en masse. To rub it in, when they destroyed a temple they slaughtered cows at the very spot at which the idol had stood, they broke the idol to smithereens, had the pieces buried under the steps of some Jama Masjid so that the faithful tread over it as they came for prayers, they put the pieces of the idols and pieces of the flesh of cows which had been slaughtered in sacks, and sent them off to be strewn in the streets of Mecca so that the faithful on their holy pilgrimage tread on them.

We thus read in *Alberuni's India*:

> .....When Muhammad Ibn Alkasim Ibn Almunabih conquered Multan, he inquired how the town had become so very flourishing and so many treasures had there been accumulated, and then he found out that this idol was the cause, for there came pilgrims from all sides to visit it. Therefore, he thought it best to have the idol where it was, but he hung a piece of cow's flesh on its neck by way of mockery. On the same place a mosque was built.

39. On the foregoing, S.A.A. Rizvi, *A History of Sufism in India*, Munshiram Manoharlal, Delhi, 1978, Volume I, pp. 295–96.

> When the Karmatians occupied Multan, Jalam Ibn Shaiban, the usurper, broke the idol into pieces and killed its priests....

The acclaimed Muslim historian Firishta informs us:

> From thence the King (the 'gentle' Feroze Shah Tughlaq, honoured to this day in Delhi) marched toward the mountains of Nagrakote, where he was overtaken by a storm of hail and snow. The Raja of Nagrakote, after sustaining some loss, submitted, but was restored to his dominions. The name of Nagrakote was, on this occasion, changed to that of Mahomedabad, in honour of the late king.... Some historians state that Feroze, on this occasion, broke the idols of Nagrakote, and mixing the fragments with pieces of cow's flesh, filled bags with them, and caused them to be tied round the necks of Brahmins, who were then paraded through the camp. It is said, also, that he sent the image of Nowshaba to Mecca, to be thrown on the road, that it might be trodden under foot by the pilgrims, and that he also remitted the sum of 100,000 *tunkas*, to be distributed among the devotees and servants of the temple (that is, the Kaba).

In the *Muntkhab-ut-Tawarikh* we are told:

> The temple of Nagarkot, which is outside the city, was taken at the very outset.... On this occasion many mountainers became food for the flashing sword. And that golden umbrella, which was erected on top of the cupola of the temple, they riddled with arrows .... And black cows, to the number of 200, to which they pay boundless respect, and actually worship, and present to the temple, which they look upon as an asylum, and let loose there, were killed by the Mussalmans. And, while arrows and bullets, were continually falling like drops of rain, through their zeal and excessive hatred of idolatry they filled their shoes full of blood and threw them on doors and walls of the temple.... The army of Husain Quli Khan was suffering great hardships. For these reasons he concluded a treaty with them.... and having put all things straight he built the cupola of a lofty mosque over the gateway of Raja Jai Chand.

In the *Maasir-i-Alamgiri* we are told:

> During this month of Ramzan abounding in miracles, the Emperor as the promoter of justice and overthrower of mischief.... and the reviver of the faith of the Prophet, issued orders for the demolition of the temple situated in Mathura.... Praised be the august God of the faith of Islam, that in the auspicious reign of this destroyer of infidelity and turbulence, such a wonderful and seemingly impossible task was successfully accomplished.... The idols, large and small, set with costly jewels, which had been set up in the temple, were brought to Agra, and buried under the steps of the mosque of the Begum Sahiba, in order to be continually trodden upon. The name of Mathura was changed to Islamabad....

We read in the *Akhbarat* of Aurangzeb:

> The Emperor, summoning Muhammad Khalil and Khidmat Rai, the *darogha* of hatchet men..., ordered them to demolish the temple of the camp there and slaughter cows in the temple.... It was done.[40]

Now, the Quran does not require cows to be sacrificed, it does not even say that Allah is specially pleased by a devotee sacrificing a cow.[41]

There was one brief moment when at least two or three

---

40. For detailed citations from Islamic historians on these and hundreds of other instances see, Sita Ram Goel, *Hindu Temples: What Happened to Them, The Islamic Evidence*, Voice of India, New Delhi, 1993.

41. Even as impassioned an advocate of cow sacrifice as Maulana Ahmad Riza Khan is hard put to finding a Hadis to support his repeated exhortations. The cow is permissible, that much is ancient shariah he says, and alludes to the narration in the Quran of a roasted calf having been served to the guests of Abraham. He recalls a Hadis in which the Prophet is reported to have sacrificed a cow for his wives and to have then said that it be eaten but there is no reliable Hadis within our sight at present, adds Ahmad Riza Khan, about whether or not he—the Prophet—himself ate it. However, he stresses, there are thousands of worldly blessings of which the Prophet did not partake. And, therefore, he concludes, the Hadis cited against beef is not correct. On all this, *Fatawa-i-Rizvia*, Volume VIII, pp. 369–70, 451.

of the ulema spoke up against this practice. The moment was the Khilafat movement, and it is captured in the letter of Maulana Abdul Bari of Firangi Mahal to Gandhiji. He wrote:

> I thank you for the success of the day of prayer for Khilafat appointed for promoting unity between Hindus and Muslims. The stand you have taken in this matter has made a deep impression on the Muslims, especially on those among them who are religious-minded. Some *Ulema* have particularly asked me in their letters to convey their congratulations to you. One of them is Maulana Suleman Saheb of Fulwari. He writes to say that he has decided not to kill cows in future and to dissuade others likewise from doing so. If people like you go on working for unity, the country will progress the sooner and the causes of discord will disappear.

Several persons had been writing to Gandhiji that if Hindus are to fight for the Khilafat—a cause dear to the Muslims—Muslims too should do something that would show that they have regard for Hindu sentiments, they ought to give up slaughtering cows. Gandhiji alluded to these suggestions, only to reject them firmly. 'There can be no zest or point in giving help in expectation of a return,' he wrote. Publishing Maulana Abdul Bari's letter Gandhiji wrote, 'Our Muslim brethren have not sought our help on the issue of Khilafat. If, however, we want their friendship, if we regard them as our brethren, it is our duty to help them. If, as a result, they stop cow-slaughter, it will be a different matter. That will not be surprising. But we cannot offer them our help on condition that they stop cow-slaughter. Duty seeks no reward. But it is the obvious duty of those who are eager to protect cows to give all possible help to the Muslims on the Khilafat issue...'

There was a jam-packed meeting in Delhi a few days later. Gandhiji was in the chair. At the very commencement of his speech he took up the point. He said:

> I am grateful for the resolution passed yesterday thanking the Hindus in general and me in particular. I wish also to say that whatever help the Hindus and others have rendered in connection with the Khilafat is no more than their duty. Duty is a kind of debt. There can be no return for its payment. Mr Asaf Ali has, in the notices he sent about this meeting, mentioned the subject of cow-protection. My humble opinion is that the issue of cow-protection may not be raised on this occasion by the Hindus. If we are one people, if we regard one another as brothers then Hindus, Parsis, Christians and Jews born in India have the clear duty of helping the Muslims, their fellow-countrymen, in their suffering. That help which demands a return is mercenary and can never be a symbol of brotherhood. Just as adulterated cement cannot hold bricks together, so mercenary help cannot make for brotherhood. The noble traditions of the Hindus require that they help their Muslim brethren. If the Muslims feel themselves bound in honour to spare the feelings of Hindus, then, whether we help in the matter of the Khilafat or not, they may stop the slaughter of cows. Though, therefore, I yield to none in my reverence for the cow, I do not wish to make my help in the Khilafat conditional on anything. On the contrary, I feel, that there is greater protection for cows in help given unconditionally. Only if we serve one another without laying down conditions can affection and fraternal love grow amongst us and the path to cow-protection be cleared. I, therefore, hope that all Hindus will make the Khilafat cause their own without insisting on any conditions....

At the close of the meeting Maulana Abdul Bari rose to thank the chair. He said:

> Mahatma Gandhi may say what he pleases with regard to keeping the subject of cow-protection out of the matter in hand. It is to his credit and to that of our Hindu brethren. Should the Muslims, however, forget the assistance rendered

> by their Hindu brethren, they will have forgotten their noble traditions. I say that, whether they help us in the Khilafat issue or not, we and they are of one land and, therefore, it behoves us to stop the slaughter of cows. As a Maulwi, I say that, in refraining from cow-slaughter of our own free will, we in no way go against our faith. Nothing else has created so real a spirit of brotherhood between us as the magnanimity shown by the Hindus on the Khilafat issue. I pray that God may preserve for ever this friendship between the two communities.

Reporting the proceedings to his readers Gandhiji felt vindicated: 'Maulana Abdul Bari Sahib has shown us,' he wrote, 'that this (selfless help, doing our duty on a cause dear to Muslims) is a far simpler and easier way to ensure the protection of cows than to spend huge sums and quarrel with the Muslims for the purpose.'[42]

The views Maulana Abdul Bari enunciated at that time show what every reader of the Quran and Hadis knows—that killing cows is not mandatory. But it was a fleeting moment, and even at that moment voices such as those of Maulana Abdul Bari were in a minority. That moment passed. Voices such as those of Abdul Bari were soon forgotten.

The contrary view, the view which represented a continuation of the attitudes which had determined the conduct of Muslim invaders, the view which prevailed, and which, as we shall see, prevails to this day is reiterated dozens of times in volumes such as the *Fatawa-i-Rizvia.*

Sacrificing cows is definitely in accordance with the requirements of shariah, rules the *Fatawa-i-Rizvia.* It cites an ayat from the Quran which does not have a word about the cows, saying that it says, 'We have set the sacrifice of the cow and the camel among the marks of the *Din* of Allah.'

---

42. On the preceding see *The Collected Works of Mahatma Gandhi,* Publications Division, Navjivan Press, Ahmedabad, 1965, Volume XVI, pp. 305–06, 319–20, 323–24.

And this, the fatwa says, is known to Abdul Bari. It goes on to quote several ulema to the effect that slaughtering cows is an essential and long-standing practice of Islam. If Hindus object to the killing of cows on 'communal grounds'—the grounds of the Hindus, note, are 'communal', the grounds of Muslims are spiritual obedience to Allah!—then it is not right for Muslims to refrain from killing cows. In fact, decrees the fatwa, on every occasion Muslims should keep up what has been prevalent in Islam for so long. If they stop it, they shall be sinners.

The fatwa goes on reiterating this point, and returns to emphasize again that if the Hindu asks that cow-killing be stopped on account of his religious point of view, then it is *not* right for Muslims to stop killing the cows. And if the Hindu cites his false faith to have it stopped, then the Muslims must *not* stop it. And, warns the fatwa, the Islam of those who agree to do what they, the Hindus, are saying is counterfeit. For if you agree to their proposition you will be strengthening their false religion and doing so is not permissible in shariah.

The fatwa proceeds to quote the fatwas which had been issued earlier by the ancestors of Abdul Bari and by Abdul Bari himself: that if someone restrains us from sacrificing a cow, then it becomes obligatory to sacrifice it, because we cannot give up our religious work under duress.

Those who advocate the contrary to please the polytheists, the fatwa declares, are out to undermine Islam. They are great sinners, they are *mufsid*, they are *amr-bil-haram,* they are the enemies of Islam, they are the dacoits of Muslims, they are brothers of the Devil—*Shaitan ke bhai,* the workers for the Devil—*Iblis ke karinde,* the enemies of truth, the heirs of the hypocrites. Quoting the Quran, the fatwa declares that they shall be consigned to Hell for ever.

So much for persons—like Maulana Abdul Bari—who advocate that Muslims give up slaughtering cows. As for anyone who leaves the sacrifice of cows under their influence, the fatwa declares that he too is the enemy of Allah, the worker for Satan, the abandoner of that which is obligatory, and one fit for the fires of Hell.[43]

The continuation of the sacrifice of cows and the prohibition against participation in the meetings of Hindus, declares the *Fatawa-i-Rizvia* a little later, are both among the necessities of religion. He who declares the former haram and the latter halal— as Maulana Abdul Bari was doing, and as, in regard to meetings, Mufti Kifayatullah was doing—is calumnizing Allah and the Prophet. By the ordinances of the Holy Quran, declares the fatwa, his abode is *Jahannum*, Hell, and it is incumbent to apply the injunction of kufr upon him.[44]

And again: to stop sacrificing cows for the sake of Hindus is haram, declares *Fatawa-i-Rizvia,* citing as authority the *Durr-ul-Mukhtar.* And he who does what is haram, it pronounces, sets himself up for the torture of Jahannum, of Hell. He who is guilty of that which is kufr in *Fiqh* is out of Islam, his wives have become haram for him: he must embrace Islam again, he must go through the nikah again if he wants the status quo ante to be restored.[45]

And again: it is proper to continue sacrificing cows. To stop doing so out of consideration for Hindus is haram. Unity with Hindus is haram. And the ones who are advocating this unity (it was in the name of unity and, worse, as an expression of gratefulness that Abdul Bari, etc., were advocating that Muslims give up killing cows) 'are by their own admission sacrificing the entire life of the Quran and Hadis on idolatry'.[46]

The examples can be multiplied many times over from

---

43. *Fatawa-i-Rizvia,* Volume VI, pp. 18–19.
44. Ibid., Volume VI, p. 101.
45. Ibid., Volume VI, pp. 149–50.
46. Ibid., Volume VI, pp. 169.

this set[47] as well as from other collections of fatwas. Instead of going on multiplying examples, it will be better to peruse any one fatwa in some detail.

Pages 443 to 457 of densely packed text printed in quarto size of Volume VIII of the *Fatawa-i-Rizvia* are devoted exclusively to exhorting Muslims to continue slaughtering cows. Perusing them will give us a glimpse of the premises and the lines of argumentation of these ulema, and even more of the insistence, the presumptuousness, the peculiar variety of malevolence which underlies those premises and lines of argumentation.

We shall also see another feature which too is germane to the way the ulema advance from position to position. Recall that the fatwas on dress had always to begin by acknowledging that strictly speaking shariah prescribes no particular dress. But within paragraphs by well-practised steps the ulema were insisting that Muslims wear dresses of a specific sort. The position on slaughtering cows is the same. The Quran does not attach any special merit to it. The Hadis as we have seen are just as ambiguous. Even the indefatigable Maulana Ahmad Riza Khan has to acknowledge that he has not 'as yet' been able to sight any reliable Hadis which reports the Prophet himself as having eaten the meat of the sacrificed cow. The Maulana's retort, as we have seen, is that 'there are thousands of worldly blessings of which the Prophet did not partake,' and so the absence of the Hadis, he concludes, is no argument for Muslims to *not* eat beef. The point works to the opposite effect just as well: as there are scores and scores of things which the Prophet made mandatory which Muslims do *not* follow—charging and paying interest for instance—why must they insist on doing something which neither Allah nor the Prophet has even commended, to say nothing of commanded?

47. For instance, *Fatawa-i-Rizvia*, Volume IX, Book II, p. 271.

That is the position as far as the canonical authorities are concerned. Now notice the steps by which from this position the killing of cows is made a religious duty incumbent upon every Muslim.

The ordinances of shariah, says the *Fatawa-i-Rizvia*, are the ones which are appropriate, opportune and beneficial for the given time and place. For instance, at the time of the Prophet women used to come to the mosque for all the five namaz and were not required to observe purdah. But later the Caliphs decreed that women should wear the veil, and they stopped young women from going to mosques. When disturbances spread, the ulema stopped all women, old as well as young, from going to mosques. While the Prophet had said, 'When your woman asks for permission to go to the mosque do not stop her ....,' while he had said, 'Do not stop Allah's women from going to Allah's mosque,' the fatwa notes, later authorities decreed the contrary. Yet the ordinances of the Caliphs and of the ulema do not stand contrary to the Hadis. In fact, they were declared to be consistent with shariah. Citing several authorities the fatwa shows that in the same way gradually the ordinances came from shariah and from 'wise leaders' for purdah and made veils mandatory, though they had not been so earlier. There are hundreds of such ordinances in our shariah, it declares.

There are two kinds of justifications and condemnations in shariah, the fatwa explains. First there are the deeds which gratify the personal (the inner?) senses; among these for instance are the commendation of the prayer of Allah and the prohibition of idolatry. Then there are the deeds which are considered in view of their external effects: for instance the commendations of Arabia and the prohibition of opium and *bhang*. And it gives as an example an instance which we have encountered earlier: the angarkha was not worn in the time or country of the Prophet; now it is worn here in India; as the kafirs wear it with the ulta purdah, it is right for Muslims to wear it with the seedha purdah; to abandon the seedah purdah and wear the ulta purdah is haram.

The authorities of shariah, notes the fatwa, looking at the external effects which things have, enjoin things which enhance the glory of Islam, and condemn those that bring honour to kafirs.

Eating cow meat is not recommended because it is beneficial for personal reasons, and not having it is also not sinful. And shariah does not make eating anything specific mandatory, nor does it make not eating it sinful. But from these considerations, the fatwa holds, all that is proved is that to continue cow slaughter is not necessary for personal reasons.

But, and here comes the turn, our religious ordinances do not depend only on this criterion. On the contrary, declares the fatwa, deeds which are commended for their external effects are also absolutely necessary. To give in to compulsion and abstain from things which are by no means harmful to us Muslims—in that lies our religious degradation. Now, our shariah certainly does not want our degradation, nor is it expected that the present rulers should honour one side and dishonour the other.

After all, the fatwa continues, there must be some reason for stopping a practice from which there are thousands of benefits to Muslims. There is no reason to do so except to fulfil the insistence of Hindus. To do so is to keep us from that food to which our natures are inclined, and from meat which Allah has called the best of all foods—here and in the Hereafter.

Moreover, all cannot afford goat meat, the poor cannot subsist without beef. And there is evidence in medical books to the effect that there are many advantages in meat for our bodies, for increasing the strength of the body. These advantages cannot be obtained from foods other than meat. And then there are thousands of profits which are obtained from the hides of cows—profits in reaping which the Hindus also participate with us.

Moreover, cow slaughter is specially justified in Din, in the Quran. Allah says that he has made camels and cows for you. It is clear that in this country camels cannot be used for sacrifice. And if we stop eating cows and turn to camels, the prices of camel meat will shoot up. The poor will not be able to eat it. The alternative, goat meat, is available only to a few.

There is justification in our shariah for slaughtering the cow. Citing an ayat from the Quran (which has not a word about the cow) the fatwa translates its import as follows: 'Without doubt Allah commands you: slaughter the cow.'

Next, says the fatwa, there is no prohibition against killing the cow in the real religion of the Hindus. They have unnecessarily taken the honouring of it upon their heads. In fact, there is evidence in the books of the Hindus that leaders of Hindus did not deprive themselves of tasting the pleasure of cows.

Hindus object, saying killing is involved. But killing is involved in everything: in goat, fish, etc. When from their own books it is established that Ram, Lakshman, Krishna were hunters, what is the cure for that killing?

There are some sects among Hindus which consider all killing as reprehensible—to the extent that some of them tie cloth across their mouths so that a fly or an insect should not die. And there are others who eat chicken, goat, fish with relish. When this is their own condition, how can a fatwa prohibiting cow slaughter be issued to meet their religious standards?

And when a cow dies they use the hide, etc. And they use and abuse the bail, the ox, in every way—they beat it, they work it to exhaustion. Thus the bail is not honoured. Then why don't they give permission happily to Muslims to slaughter bails?

This—the demand for stopping the killing of cows—is just their insistence.

As for disturbance being caused by the killing of the cow—where cow slaughter is banned by law, the responsibility for the disturbance shall fall upon Muslims; and this will bring opprobrium upon Islam; and so Muslims should not do so. But where there is no prohibition, the cause for the disturbance are the Hindus—that even when there is no prohibition they would that we abandon our religious practices. In that event they shall be punished. For if the shariah were to prohibit us from doing a thing because the Hindus may cause a disturbance, they shall find an easy way to restrain us from every religious ceremony they want us to give up—they will just create a disturbance. By acting this way Islam will be denigrated, it will be lowered.

The fatwa goes on reiterating these arguments, the citations, the assertions—paragraph after paragraph, page after page. From our heavenly Book and from the ordinances of our true Prophet, the permission for cow slaughter is well proved.... from these ayats it is clear that Allah has ordained the sacrifice of camel, cow, goat—all.... And so on.

In Hindustan, it continues, cow slaughter is an act that greatly glorifies Islam. By our fatwas we have proven that here the sacrifice of cows is proper and to abandon it out of regard for Hindus is improper.

The fatwa strongly condemns those who say that it should be given up—they are guilty of *gunah kabira,* it declares. It goes on to quote the fatwas issued by Abdul Wahab, by his ustad, Abdul Hai, and by other ulema of Firangi Mahal—pointing out that these are fatwas which have been included in the compilations of Abdul Hai in which he himself declares that to stop cow slaughter out of regard for Hindus is improper, that to continue it is proper.

Cow slaughter is the glory of Islam, the fatwa declares,

and the unity which is being observed with Hindus is haram, prohibited, it is *qatai* haram, wholly prohibited.

Cow slaughter is the religious right of a Mussalman, it declares, and a right at that which particularly glorifies Islam. To stop it because of polytheists is to glorify the polytheists, while the sacrificing of cows is the glorification of Islam.

This theme is reiterated repeatedly.

And the Quran says you should make Allah and the Prophet happy—they have a better right that you appease them than the polytheists have .... unity with the Hindus is haram and to stop cow slaughter because of it is haram...,[48]

Even this precis of the fatwa is sufficient to show the steps by which something for which there was at best a permission is transformed by the ulema into a religious duty, the steps by which doing the one thing that hurts another the most becomes a matter of principle, a religious right, an Allah- and Prophet-ordained duty. To give it up would be to give up that which is a long-standing practice in Islam. If we yield on this, they will force on us anything. It would be to strengthen the false religion of the polytheists. It would be to abandon religious work under duress. It would be to do that which we are prohibited from doing—namely to honour kafirs. It will be to degrade Islam. On the other hand, to kill cows is to do the thing which particularly glorifies Islam.

And—a point to which we shall return—notice how the Quran and the Hadis are used by these 'learned men'.

To this day

And the ecumenism of the Khilafat days on this issue also went the same way as Maulana Mohammed Ali's copious tear-shedding.

---

48. On the foregoing, *Fatawa-i-Rizvia*, Volume VIII, pp. 443–59.

In the important work, *Separatism Among Indian Muslims*, Francis Robinson ascribes Maulana Abdul Bari's protestations on cows, etc., to an altogether less estimable reason. There had been talk, the book recounts, of a *Shaikh-ul-Islam*, the leader or head of Islam for all of India. Maulana Abdul Bari coveted this post, and it was to bag it that he offered Gandhiji a bargain. Citing records of the Home Department, Robinson writes that in early 1919, 'Abdul Bari is said to have arranged to call a conference of *Ulema* and Muslims at the height of the Mahatma's Rowlatt Satyagraha at which he would be elected *Shaikh-ul-Islam* and Muslim demands regarding Khilafat would be formulated. Gandhi and the Hindus would support these demands and Abdul Bari in turn would use his new-found position to ban cow-slaughter. The deal, however, came to nothing.'

The boost which the Khilafat agitation gave to the ulema, their increasingly aggressive role, the continuing conversions by force, fraud and allurement gave an urgency to the *Hindu Sangathan* movement. 'Abdul Bari, the erstwhile apostle of Hindu-Muslim unity, came to the fore again,' writes Robinson. 'Now he spoke the language of the zealot. He urged Muslims to sacrifice cows without regard for Hindu feelings....'[49]

Only one word needs to be added. And that is this: the same attitude, the same premises, the same malevolence, the very words continue to this day. Maulana Abul Hasan Ali Nadwi, popularly known as Ali Mian, is today the most influential Muslim leader and scholar. Head of the *Nadwatul Ulema* at Lucknow, chairman of the All India Muslim Personal Law Board, one of the founding members of the Saudi Arabian King's *Rabita-e Alam-e Islami*, Ali Mian is invariably referred to by our press as the universally respected scholar, the moderate Muslim leader. Here is what he said on the

---

49. Francis Robinson, *Separatism Among Indian Muslims, The Politics of the United Province' Muslims, 1860–1923*, Cambridge South Asian Studies, Vikas, 1975, pp. 329, 339.

subject of cow slaughter while addressing Indian and Pakistani pilgrims in Jeddah on 3 April 1986:

> Cow slaughter in India is a great Islamic practice—(said) Mujaddid Alaf Saani II. This was his far-sightedness that he described cow slaughter in India as a great Islamic practice. It may not be so in other places. But it is definitely a great Islamic act in India because the cow is worshipped in India. If the Muslims give up cow slaughter here then the danger is that in times to come the coming generations will get convinced of the piety of the cow.[50]

The very words, the very malevolence of the fatwas. Yet, when the fatwas are cited the retort is: 'But who reads them?'

This basic attitude, this malevolent way of establishing one's identity—by insisting on doing that one thing which hurts the feelings of the other—has led 'the leaders of the community' to twist what is in their own law books, to insist on disregarding what the Constitution and laws say, to conjure up 'religious' arguments if these will work, and 'secular' arguments if these are necessary, and to go on doing so with a persistence which will surprise anyone who is not conversant with the fatwas, and the premises which underlie them.

The *Hidayah* says:

> It is the duty of every free Muslim arrived at the age of maturity to offer a sacrifice, on the '*Idu'l-Azha*', or 'Festival of the Sacrifice', provided he be then possessed of a *Nisab* (i.e., sufficient property), and be not a traveller. This is the opinion of Abu Hanifah, Muhammad, Zufar, and Hasan, and likewise of Abu Yusuf, according to one tradition. According to ash-Shafi'i, sacrifice is not an indispensable duty, but only laudable. At-Tahawi

---

50. Maulana Abul Hasan All Nadwi, *Zimmedarian aur Ahl-e-watan ke Haquq*, Majlis Tehqiqaat o' Nashrat Islam, Lucknow, 1986.

reports that, in the opinion of Abu Hanifah, it is indispensable, whilst the disciples hold it to be in a strong degree laudable. The offering of a sacrifice is incumbent on a man on account of himself, and on account of his infant child. This is the opinion of Abu Hanifah in one tradition. In another he has said that it is not incumbent on a man to offer a sacrifice for his child....

There is manifestly a difference of opinion about whether a sacrifice is at all mandatory. Assuming that an animal *has* to be killed, whether this animal should be a goat, a camel or a cow is left to the believer. That there is a choice in the matter is evident from what the *Hidayah* proceeds to say:

> *The sacrifice established for one person is a goat; and that for seven, a cow or a camel. If* a cow be sacrificed for any number of people fewer than seven, it is lawful; but it is otherwise *if* sacrificed on account of eight. *If* for a party of seven people the contribution of anyone of them should be less than a seventh share, the sacrifice is not valid on the part of anyone of them. *If* a camel that is jointly and in an equal degree the property of two men should be sacrificed by them on their own account, it is lawful; and in this case they must divide the flesh by weight, as flesh is an article of weight. *If*, on the contrary, they distribute it from conjectural estimation, it is not lawful, unless they add to each share of the flesh part of the head, neck and joints. *If* a person purchases a cow, with an intent to sacrifice it on his own account, and he afterwards admit six others to join with him in the sacrifice, it is lawful. It is, however, most advisable that he associate with the others at the time of purchase, in order that the sacrifice may be valid in the opinion of all doctors, as otherwise there is a difference of opinion. It is related from Abu Hanifah that it is abominable to admit others to share in a sacrifice after purchasing the animal, for, as the purchase was made with a view to devotion, the sale of it is therefore an abomination....[50a]

Now, Article 48 of our Constitution directs the state: 'The State shall...., in particular, take steps for preserving and

50a. See, e.g., T.P. Hughes, Dictionary of Islam, 1885, Rupa, 2007, pp. 552–53.

improving the breeds, and *prohibiting the slaughter, of cows and calves and other milch and draught cattle.'*

On the one hand we have the books of Muslim law: assuming that they make it obligatory for a Muslim to kill animals, they clearly give him an option—he may kill a goat, *or* a cow, *or* a camel to satisfy Allah. On the other, we have the Constitution: in regard to one set of animals—'cows and calves and other milch and draught cattle'—it directs the state to, among other things, prohibit their slaughter. There is no difficulty in harmonizing the two: Muslims are free to go on killing animals other than the ones mentioned in Article 48.

That would no doubt fulfil what is written in their law books. But it would fall short of that very special way of defining their identity—of doing that which puts the kafirs down, of doing that which puts them out. Therefore, their 'leaders' have been insisting that it is the cow which they must slaughter.

In 1956 Bihar enacted the Preservation and Improvement of Animals Act. The Act banned the slaughter of cows. Writs were filed against it on behalf of Muslims. The Act runs afoul of the freedom which Article 25 guarantees to us to profess, practise and propagate our religion, it was argued. A Constitution bench of the Supreme Court had eventually to consider the matter. It recalled what is stated in books such as the *Hidayah*—that slaughtering a cow is not the only course mandated for a Muslim; it is one of the options held out for him. Hence, the bench concluded, cow slaughter is not a practice which is essential to the practice of Islam. And hence banning the slaughter of cows does not violate Article 25 of the Constitution, the Supreme Court held.

As it could not be established that killing the cow alone would meet the requirement of their religion, the petitioners pressed an 'economic' argument: A person with seven members in his family, it was argued, would in the alternate have to sacrifice seven goats—and he may not be able to afford that many goats. Hence, while there may not be a 'religious compulsion' to sacrifice a cow, there would be an 'economic compulsion' to do so. The Supreme Court rejected this by recalling that several Muslim rulers had themselves prohibited the slaughter of cows, and they would not have done so if Islam had made the sacrifice of cows mandatory. The Court held therefore that a total ban on cow slaughter does not violate Article 25 of the Constitution.[51]

A Constitution bench of the Supreme Court having pronounced on the matter, and there being in addition the directive to the state in Article 48, the issue should have been settled. But no.

Since 1950 there had been in operation the West Bengal Animal Slaughter Control Act. The Preamble of the Act stated that it was being enacted to control the slaughter of certain animals as it was expedient to do so with a view to increase the supply of milk and to avoid the wastage of animal power necessary for improvement of agriculture. Section 2 and the Schedule of the Act specified that its provisions would apply to bulls, bullocks, cows, calves, and castrated buffaloes. Section 4 provided that notwithstanding anything in any other law which may be in force or in any other usage to the contrary, no person shall slaughter any animal listed in the Schedule unless he had obtained in regard to that animal under the relevant sections of the Act a certificate from the competent authority certifying that the animal was over fourteen years of age and was unfit for breeding or that the animal had become permanently incapacitated from work or breeding because of age, injury, deformity or an incurable disease. In the case of cows for instance these provisions entailed that

51. On all this see *Mohammed Hanif Quareshi and others vs State of Bihar*, AIR 1958 SC 731.

healthy cows which are not fit to be slaughtered in terms of the provisions of the Act were not to be slaughtered at all. Section 12 of the Act permitted the state government to exempt from the operation of the Act the slaughter of any animal for any religious, medicinal or research purpose.

Acting in the name of Muslims their leaders pressurized the state government, or persuaded it if you will, to exempt cows from the Act and allow their slaughter on Bakr Id.

The Hindus appealed to the Calcutta high court against the exemption. First, their locus standi was questioned: it was a matter between the state which had granted the exemption and Muslims to whom the exemption had been granted, the argument went. How do these others come in?, it was argued. The high court held that the petitioners had a right to approach the Court on behalf of the Hindu community which had felt aggrieved by the exemption which the state government had granted. Next, the same argument which had been rejected so unambiguously by the Constitution bench of the Supreme Court was urged again on behalf of Muslims: namely, that slaughtering cows is a requirement of their religion, and as Article 25 guarantees them freedom of religion, they have a right to slaughter cows on Bakr Id. The high court rejected the contentions, and upheld the appeal of the Hindus on the principles set out by the Supreme Court in Quareshi's case. The Act envisaged a total ban on the slaughter of healthy animals, it recalled. This was the very object of the Act. Hence Section 12 which allowed an exemption had to be strictly construed: an exemption could be allowed only if it could be shown to be *necessary* for the purposes mentioned in the Act—that is, religious, medicinal or research. As sacrificing cows was not a practice essential to the practice of Islam, the exemption was untenable. The judgment was delivered in August 1982.

The matter was thereupon brought to the Supreme Court. The same contention was repeated. The Supreme Court has therefore had to reiterate what it had held earlier. Article 25 protects practices which are essential to the practice of a religion. Sacrificing a cow is one of the options available to a Muslim, and is therefore not an essential practice. An exemption to the central purpose of a law has to be strictly construed. As the very purpose of enacting the 1950 Act was to prohibit the slaughter of healthy animals, exemption under Section 12 can be given only if it can be shown that their slaughter is strictly necessary for purposes of religion, medicine or research. As this cannot be shown to be the case in the matter of slaughtering cows which are healthy, the Calcutta High Court was entirely correct in striking down the exemption, the Supreme Court has held. That being obvious from what the Supreme Court had itself held in the past, a new and fantastic plea was urged. While Article 25 of the Constitution gives protection only to practices which are essential to a religion, it was urged, Section 12 of the Act must be taken to allow exemptions for any religious practice: the Supreme Court has rejected this line of argumentation summarily.[52]

The object thus is to continue to kill cows one way or another—by arguing that doing so is an essential requirement of Islam; if that cannot be maintained, then by arguing that it is in any case one of the practices of Islam; if that too does not work, then by arguing that there is an economic compulsion to kill them....

To the ordinary observer the doggedness, the insistence would be scarcely comprehensible. But that is because he is innocent of the fatwas and the psychology which lies behind them. The point is to do the one thing which will show the

52. *State of West Bengal etc. vs Ashutosh Lahiri and others*, JT 1994 (7) SC 697.

kafirs down, which will put the kafirs out—for in doing so, as the fatwas state again and again, lies the glorification of Islam.

At least now the matter should have ended. But then how would identity be defined, how would kafirs be put down?

And so Bakr Id had but to come and the Muslims of Bengal insisted on butchering cows.

As the *Fatawa-i-Rizvia* says, to stop cow slaughter because of polytheists is to glorify the polytheists, to slaughter cows—specially when doing so hurts the polytheists—is to glorify Islam.

That is the basic, the foundational rule in defining identity. And yet unless you acknowledge that Islam is the reli-gion of peace, of tolerance, of brotherhood, you are a Hindu chauvinist.

The Quran too is put to use

Recall how the journey began: from wanting to be different. And see where it has ended: in doing that which will put the others down, in doing that which will put them out. As we have seen, along the way every argument has been put to use.

The Quran—in the name of which all this is done—is not spared either.

In Chapter 10 we shall consider in detail the vital verses which deal with sacrificing animals for the glory of Allah—verses 22.34 to 37. In verse 34 Allah declares that for every nation He has appointed a sacred rite, so that all may glorify His name by invoking it while sacrificing an animal to Him. In verse 35 He urges the believers to give the meat in charity. In verse 37 He says that it is not the meat or blood of the sacrificed animal which will reach Him, it is the piety of the devotee. None of these three verses names any particular animal which must be sacrificed. The only verse in which a particular animal is named is verse 22.36. Here is Yusuf Ali's rendering of this verse:

> The sacrificial camels
> We have made for you
> As among the Symbols from
> Allah: in them is (much)
> Good for you: then pronounce
> The name of Allah over them
> As they line up (for sacrifice):
> When they are down
> On their sides (after slaughter),
> Eat ye thereof, and feed
> Such as (beg not but)
> Live in contentment,
> And such as beg
> With due humility: *thus have*
> *We made animals subject*
> *To you, that ye*
> *May be grateful.*

Notice the words I have italicized, the reference there is to '*animals*'.

Now, here is how the verse is rendered in Maulana Azad's *Tarjuman al-Quran*:

And the camels, have We allowed you to offer (for sacrifice) as marks of devotion to God; these marks bode much good to you. So whenever (you offer them as sacrifice) do it, in the name of God, as they stand in a row; and when they fall over on their sides, use them for food, (both for your own selves and also for) him who is content (and asketh not), and him who asketh. *Thus have We made them (the cattle) serve your purposes to the intent you should be thankful.*

Notice the words I have italicized. What is rendered as

'animals' in Yusuf Ali becomes 'the cattle'. In a country where cow slaughter is a cause of such tension, Yusuf Ali's rendering leaves a clear way out: Allah is not saying that the believers must sacrifice cattle in particular. But the rendering attributed to Maulana Azad implies that Allah does have cattle in mind. A difference of consequence, therefore.[53]

Maulana Ahmad Riza Khan goes the whole hog. The *Fatawa-i-Rizvia* presents the Quran as saying: 'We have set the sacrifice of the cow and the camel among the marks of the *Din* of Allah!'[54] And a moment later that becomes: 'Without doubt Allah commands you: slaughter the cow!' Store this rendering, one in which Maulana Ahmad Riza Khan adds words to the Word of Allah so freely, and recall it when we come to Chapter 8—there you will see how vehemently the Maulana comes down on a querist who suggests a possible construction by which the Quran's assertion that the Sun moves around the Earth may be reconciled with what has become known since then.

Surely this is nemesis of a kind: the zeal to do down the *kafirs* has superseded the Revelation in the name of which the *kafirs* are to be done in!

---

53. I say 'rendering attributed to Maulana Azad', because the Urdu version of his *Tarjuman al-Quran* does not have the words 'the cattle': Contrast Maulana Abul Kalam Azad, *Tarjuman al-Quran*, Sahitya Academy, New Delhi, 4th Reprint, 1989, Volume IV, p. 820; and Maulana Abul Kalam Azad, *Tarjuman al-Quran*, Syed Abdul Latif (tr.), Syed Abdul Latif Trust for Quranic and other Cultural Studies, Hyderabad, Volume III, 1978, pp. 466–67.

54. *Fatawa-i-Rizvia*, Volume VI, p. 18.

4

'Worse than All Creation'

'The word *Kafir* is also used as a term of abuse,' states the *Fatawa-i-Rizvia*, 'but in Shariah it is a legal term. According to Shariah he who is not a Muslim is a *Kafir*.'[1]

The candour is characteristic of Maulana Ahmad Riza Khan, but there is a redundancy. In differentiating the term as a term of abuse from its meaning in law, the Maulana makes a superfluous distinction: as we shall see, the position which is accorded to a kafir in law leaves no room for anything but abuse. And not just verbal abuse—but abuse in the basic sense: the wrong use, to put it mildly, of another human being.

But first, the definition in shariah.

The Hindus of course are 'absolutely *Kafirs*' and he who does not regard them as kafirs, the ulema declare, is himself a kafir. They are definitely idolaters and polytheists, the fatwas declare. They certainly bow before idols in worship. But supposing this is not so, they emphasize, the order of kufr certainly applies on one who even respects idols. Even to regard idols as intercessors, to want intercession from them—these too are kufr. So there is no doubt in Hindus being kafirs.[2]

---

1. *Fatawa-i-Rizvia*, Volume VI, p. 122.

2. Ibid., at several places. For instance, Volume IX, Book I, pp. 139, 209, 216–17.

'Are Christians kafirs?' the querist asks. In shariah every non-Muslim is a kafir, the fatwas state, be he Jew or Christian, Magian or polytheist. And, they declare, he who does not know the *Ahl-i-Kitab*, the People of the Book, to be kafirs is himself a kafir. For Allah says, Doubtless all those who are kafirs, *kitabi*s or polytheists, are in the Fire of Hell, and shall always remain in it. And also: Doubtless they are kafirs who take the Prophet, the son of Mariam, to be Khuda. Jews and Christians are kafirs and shall remain kafirs until they declare faith in Allah and the Prophet.[3]

Kafirs are to be distinguished from zimmis. The latter too are kafirs in that they are non-Muslims, but they are ones who have submitted themselves to Islamic power, to the Islamic state in particular, who, as acknowledgment of their subjecthood pay the *jazia* and live in 'absolute obedience'. In recompense they are granted some minimal rights: the rights are of course the barest minimum, in a sense they codify forever—for as long as Islamic power lasts in any case—their servile status; and their actual condition has been much worse than even the nominal rights would suggest.[4] But these are rights which flow from the grace, so to say, of Islamic power and the Islamic state. And they are accorded—even in nominal terms—solely in view of their accepting and submitting themselves to the suzerainty of Islam. Kafirs as such have not even these minimal, nominal rights. There is no covenant between Muslims and them.[5]

---

3. Ibid., at several places. For instance, Volume VI, pp. 55, 166; Volume IX, Book II, p. 190.

4. Evidence from primary sources is set out in, for instance, Bat Ye'or, *The Dhimmi, Jews and Christians under Islam*, Associated University Presses, London, 1985.

5. For instance, see *Fatawa Dar al-Ulum, Deoband*, Volume XII, pp. 273–74; *Fatawa-i-Rizvia*, Volume VI, pp. 529–30.

Evil by Design of Allah

The kafirs are not what they are because of some fortuitous circumstance. They are so by the design and decree of Allah Himself. 'If God please,' says Allah speaking of Himself in the Quran, 'He would surely bring them, one and all, to the guidance' (6.35–36). 'If thou art anxious for their guidance,' Allah counsels His messenger, 'know that God will not guide him whom He would lead astray, neither shall they have any helpers' (16.37). Do not waste your breath on them, Allah counsels: 'Just now is Our sentence against most of them; therefore, they shall not believe. On their necks have We placed chains which reach the chin, and forced up are their heads. Before them have We set a barrier and behind them a barrier, and We have shrouded them in a veil, so that they shall not see. Alike is it to them if thou warn them or warn them not; they will not believe' (36.6–10).

In fact, Allah tells the Prophet, leave them to their torment, waste no grief on them: 'And what has been sent down to thee from the Lord will surely increase many of them in insolence and unbelief; so grieve not for the people of the unbelievers' (5.72).

Allah is the author of everything, of every person's deed, fortune, misfortune, whatever. He creates man. He determines his growth, his fortune, the things that will help and those that will hinder him (56.57–74). He is the author of every act, whatever it be: 'It is God who has created you and all that you have done' (37.96). 'And that unto the Lord is the term of all things. And that it is He who causeth to laugh and to weep, and that He causeth to die and maketh alive....' (53.43–55). He has created the soul, its sense of proportion and of right and wrong (91.7–8).

'No leaf falls but He knows it,' we are told, 'There is no seed in the darkness of the earth, no green shoot or dry but it is inscribed in the perspicuous Book' (6.59). 'No female conceives or brings forth,' we are reminded, 'without His knowledge' (35.11). 'He well knew you when He produced you out of the earth,' we are told, 'and when you were embryos in your mother's womb' (53.32). Allah knows 'that which his [i.e. man's] soul suggests to him, Allah is closer to him than the jugular vein' (50.16). So, He decrees everything, He knows what is happening as well as what is to happen. And He is all powerful to make it happen or to stop it from happening.

In particular, it is Allah Himself who decides and ensures that some will not believe, that they will sin. 'Seeth thou not,' He asks, 'that We send the Satans against the infidels to urge them to sin?' (19.83). It is because of this decision of Allah that the errors, lapses, sins occur. 'Verily,' we are told again and again, 'they against whom the decree of the Lord is pronounced shall not believe, even though every kind of sign comes to them, till they behold the dolorous treatment....' (10.96–99). It is only because Allah has so willed that they persist in their unbelief and then suffer for it. To continue the preceding verse, 'But if thy Lord had pleased, verily all who are in the earth would have believed together. What! Wilt thou compel men to become believers? No soul can believe but by the permission of Allah: and He shall lay His wrath on those who will not understand.'

When in spite of the true Faith being put to them the kafirs refuse to embrace it, therefore, they do so by the decree and design of Allah Himself. When so basic a thing—their unbelief—has been put into them by Allah Himself, and has been put there so unalterably, the other traits of the kafirs—which, after all, flow from their basic corruption—too have been implanted by Allah. They too are accordingly inherent in them. From their bodies to their beliefs to their very souls—everything is thus coloured in corruption. The results are predictable.

The punishment for a sin committed by a Muslim is not permanent, say the fatwas, the torture of a kafir is *permanent.*[6] The souls of believers are free to go where they will—they can return to their own house or go elsewhere, the fatwas say, and it is proven, they say, that they can return to help their acquaintances; but the souls of the kafirs are imprisoned....[7]

Their good is of no account

As Allah Himself has instilled evil in the kafirs, as He has Himself led them astray, we are told, it is unlikely, indeed it is unimaginable that they shall do any good. Even if they do some little good it shall be of no account in the Hereafter, it shall not be accepted by Allah. All the boons of the Day of Judgement are only for Muslims, kafirs are wholly excluded from them, declares the *Fatawa-i-Rizvia* in response to a specific question. The questioner cites several verses from the Quran and asks the Maulana to specify their import: There is no doubt in this, Allah says, that whoever is Muslim and Jew and Sabian and Christian, of these whoever believes in Allah and the Day of Judgement and also does good deeds, on the Day of Judgement such men shall have nothing to fear and shall not be sad in their hearts. O', dear one, Allah tells the Prophet, say to these Jews and Christians that you, the Ahl-i-Kitab are wholly in the wrong so long as you do not maintain the Torah and Bible in the original form in which they had descended to you from your *Rab*; and, O', dear one, without doubt the defiance and kufr of many of them shall increase by this Quran, therefore do not grieve for these kafirs. Whoever believed in the Prophet, Allah declares,

6. *Fatawa-i-Rizvia,* Volume XI, p. 55.

7. Ibid., Volume XII, p. 202.

and helped him follow the light which descended with him, such persons would benefit. O', dear one, Allah tells the Prophet, say, O' you people, I have been sent to you men by Allah, because His is the sovereignty on earth and in heaven, none else is to be worshipped, it is He who gives life and death—so believe in Allah and His Prophet because he believes in Allah and His word, follow him so that you may be guided. Without doubt, declares Allah, those who deny Allah and his prophets and desire to create a difference between Allah and His prophets and say that we will believe in some and want to find a way between believing in all and denying all, those are wholly kafirs. And we have prepared torment and disgrace for kafirs. He who believes in Allah and all the prophets and does not deny some and believe in others, Allah will benefit him soon; Allah is the pardoner, and kind. Without doubt this is Islam with Allah, declares Allah; the Jews and Christians wilfully rebelled and he who denies the verses of Allah should know that Allah shall take him to account soon; if they dispute with you, Allah tells the Prophet, then say, I and my followers all believe in Allah, and say to the Jews and Christians and polytheists—if you become Muslim and believe then you shall find the way; and if they turn away then you are only to convey the message, Allah is seeing the believers. He who desires a faith other than Islam, Allah declares, it will not be accepted, and he will be in loss on the Day of Judgement. The Jews and Christians recognize Muhammad as they recognize their sons and one sect among them wilfully hides the truth, Allah points out drawing attention to their perfidy—in that they clearly recognize Muhammad as the Seal of Prophets and yet deny the truth; those who do not believe the Prophet whom they have recognized, they put their lives in loss; prior to this they used to desire victory over the kafirs through this Prophet, and when the recognized one came they denied him; the curse of Allah on the kafirs..... And so on.

Reproducing these, the *Fatawa-i-Rizvia* says that the essence of these *ayatsis* that even if a kafir apparently does some good deed—for instance, if he exercises patience—he is recompensed for it in this world only. There is nothing for it in the end, he shall get nothing for it there. The food of Paradise is haram for kafirs, it declares. Pious livelihood and elegance are confined exclusively to Muslims. Allah destroys and pulverizes the things of the kafirs—what happens is akin to what happens when light comes through the window: you see specks, but when you take them in hand they are nothing. Their things—the good things the kafirs may do—are as ash blown away by the wind, so that even the specks are not visible now.[8]

The attitude to kafirs

Such being the division which Allah has Himself created between believers and kafirs, such being the evil which He has instilled in the latter, how should Muslims deal with kafirs? That is the question which comes up again and again in the volumes of fatwas.

For the Muslims the basic relationship has naturally to be one of unremitting hostility, the believer has to be forever on the alert. But what he should do in a given time and circumstance, the fatwas declare, is to be assessed with reference to that time and that circumstance. There are two touchstones: what type of attitude towards them, what type of relationship with them will strengthen me in my faith; and, second, what shall advance the collective strength and position of Islam?

8. *Fatawa-i-Rizvia,* Volume VI, pp. 162–66. See also, ibid., Volume IX, Book I, p. 65 where the same point is reiterated—that no good deed of a kafir and polytheist is acceptable to Allah.

Both strands of the answer—of unremitting hostility and unrelenting alertness towards the non-believers on the one hand, and the tactical adjustment on the other—are rooted in the Quran itself.

Allah repeatedly delineates the basic character of the non-believers and just as often prescribes the basic attitude that every Muslim must maintain towards them. 'Let not the believers take for friends or helpers unbelievers rather than believers,' Allah warns, 'If they do that in nothing will there be help from Allah...' (3.28). And again: 'O, ye who believe:

Take not into your intimacy
Those outside your ranks:
They will not fail
To corrupt you. They
Only desire your ruin:
Rank hatred has already
Appeared from their mouths:
What their hearts conceal
Is far worse.
We have made plain
To you the Signs,
If ye have wisdom.
Ah! ye are those
Who love them,
But they love you not,
Though ye believe
In the whole of the Book,
When they meet you,
They say, 'We believe':
But when they are alone,
They bite off the very tips
Of their fingers at you
In their rage. Say:
'Perish in your rage;

Allah knoweth well
All the secrets of the heart.'
If aught that is good
Befalls you, it grieves them;
But if some misfortune
Overtakes you, they rejoice
At it. But if ye are constant
And do right,
Not the least harm
Will their cunning
Do to you; for God
Compasseth round about
All that they do.

(Quran, 3.118–20)

That, then, is the assessment—by Allah Himself—of the basic character of the non-believers, and that is the basic attitude which Allah Himself has decreed the believer have towards them. But what precisely should be done at a particular place and time depends on what will help Din at that place and time. Allah's counsel accordingly changes as the situation changes.

In the early Meccan surahs Allah tells the Prophet to hold on to his faith, to see of course that the non-believers do not transgress upon him in his faith but to leave them alone (for instance, Quran, Surah 109). He counsels waiting: 'As for them, they are but plotting a scheme, And I am plotting a scheme. Therefore, grant a delay to the unbelievers: give respite to them gently (for a while)' (86.15–17). As time and circumstance change, Allah is assuring the Prophet that He Himself has made the unbelievers deny the true faith: ' ... Verily Allah misleadeth whom He will, and guideth whom He will'; and, therefore, Allah tells him, 'Spend not thy soul in sighs for them: Allah knows their doings' (Quran, 35.8); 'Leave them to their forging' (Quran, 6.137). But once the Prophet's power is consolidated, Allah declares, 'They demand thee to hasten the chastisement that Allah has decreed' (Quran, 22.45–46), and commands that when they persist in their unbelief, and they fight against you, observing proper limits, 'Kill them wherever ye shall find them and eject them from whatever place they have ejected you' (Quran, 2.190–93). Fight them 'and let them find in you a harshness' (Quran, 9.123), make sure that 'wheresoever they are come upon they are slaughtered all' (Quran, 23.60–64). When and wherever you encounter them, slay them till they are completely vanquished. This is a test God has devised for you (47.4); a duty even though you may demur (2.216–17); 5.36; 8.38–39, 59–60). Strike terror in their hearts (8.60). Take no prisoners till they are fully vanquished (8.67). (See also, 4.76, 89.)

The first lemma is that the believer must shun relationships of friendship, intimacy and trust with the non-believers. This point is reiterated by the fatwas again and again—on the strength of verses such as 3.28, 118–20 cited above. Sometimes, as we shall see, fierce disagreements arise over whether for instance acting jointly with the kafirs—even though the believers and kafirs may be pursuing different objectives—does not amount to violating the command of Allah, and does not willy-nilly encoil the believers into friendship, intimacy and trust with the kafirs.

The second rule is: limit your dealings with kafirs to the minimum which is necessary, let there be no relationship which is not strictly enjoined by necessity. Jews and Christians are Ahl-i-Kitab, true, rules Mufti Kifayatullah. If per chance one eats with them then there is no harm. But to keep up relations with them beyond necessity and to establish relations of eating-drinking is not correct. For there is the apprehension of injury to *Din*.[9] The Quran does not say that one must not have any relations with kafirs, Kifayatullah rules stretching the

9. *Mufti Kifayatullah ke Fatawi*, Volume IX, p. 327.

point to accommodate the times, just that one should not associate with them to the harm of Islam. The Prophet himself once inquired if the gift from the goat which had been sacrificed had been sent to the Jewish neighbour; he bought and sold from kafirs who stayed in *Dar-ul-harb*.... The essence of the matter, Kifayatullah says, is that to maintain friendship and love with them so far as the liking for their religion is concerned—that is haram. And what is jaiz is only that kind of meeting with them, only those kinds of commercial relations with them which are required for living as neighbours or to fulfil social and cultural necessities....[10] These rulings may sound a bit severe to us but in fact they are the most moderate of the rulings.

Quoting ayats of the Quran and Hadis, *Fatawa-i-Rizvia* declares: the polytheists are unclean, a kafir howsoever noble the qaum to which he may belong, howsoever noble his family cannot be better than even a slave Muslim. The *nasab* of Muslims and kafirs is rent asunder, it declares, no relationship between them survives. Without a doubt, it declares, all kafirs—kitabis as well as polytheists—are in the Fire of Hell, and there they shall remain eternally. They are worse than all creation. Without a doubt he who believes in the Faith—that is, Islam—and does good deeds is better than the whole world.[11]

The kafirs are the enemies of Allah, and to befriend the enemies of Allah is to invite His wrath, declares the *Fatawa-i-Rizvia*. It recalls the Prophet's warning that Allah shall raise the friends of each qaum in that group. It recalls his warning: Beware of bad companions that you shall be counted with them. And therefore it declares: Do not sit with them; Do not let them sit near you; Do not be the first to greet them; Do not drink water with them, nor eat food with them, nor of course marry among them. For, association with the

10. *Mufti Kifayatullah ke Fatawi*, Volume IX, pp. 330–31.

11. *Fatawa-i-Rizvia*, Volume XI, pp. 155, 160.

bad is fatal poison. To befriend them is to befriend the enemies of Allah. It reminds the faithful of the admonition in the Quran: You shall not find among the believers those who shall make friends with the enemies of Allah and His *Rasul*, be they their brothers....[12]

But merely refraining from befriending and associating with kafirs is not enough. Enmity against the enemies of Allah and the Prophet is a duty incumbent upon every Muslim, declare the ulema.[13] In the *Fatawa-i-Rizvia* the fatwas on kafirs are grouped under the heading, *'Nafrat ke Ahkam'*—the *'Ordinances of Hatred.'* Anyone to whom the struggle between Islam and kufr is 'just a quarrel between clerics' is himself a kafir: he is out of Islam, his wives are out of his nikah, declare the fatwas.[14]

There must be no circumlocution or mealy-mouthedness towards the kafir, the fatwas declare. A kafir shall be called a kafir, for Allah has commanded that a kafir be called a kafir. A believer who does not do so—that is, who does not call a kafir a kafir— should be made to understand, and if still he does not do so, all connections with him must be severed. The only small distinction is that if for some opportune reason—when that opportune reason is not for the needs of Din, and when it is not confined to the extent required by that need alone—a person, knowing some persons to be kafirs evades calling them kafirs, in that circumstance he is a sinner but not a kafir himself; however, if he actually thinks that calling a kafir a kafir is wrong and contrary to civilized etiquette, then

---

12. *Fatawa-i-Rizvia,* Volume VI, p. 187; Volume IX, Book I, pp. 13, 78, 140.

13. Ibid., Volume IX, Book I, pp. 313–14. Here, as we shall see, Maulana Ahmad Riza Khan is applying this general proposition with his customary force to the ulema of Deoband, declaring that as they are the worst of kafirs enmity towards them is incumbent.

14. *Fatawa-i-Rizvia,* Volume VI, p. 80.

he puts a blemish on the Holy Quran, and to put a blemish on the Holy Quran is kufr.[15]

Not one word implying respect

The third rule can come as no surprise: do not accord a kafir any position of respect. A simple query—Can a kafir be given a position to look after a mosque?—thus becomes the occasion for a fusillade.

Allah has commanded, declares the fatwa, that we should not make non-believers even writers of accounts. When He has said that we should not make them even writers, when doing even this much is a violation of the Quran, to put them in charge of a mosque is necessarily, absolutely haram.... The Holy Quran stands witness, the fatwa reminds the faithful, that in any affair of Muslims a non-Muslim shall not be a well-wisher of Muslims. Allah says, O believers, do not take any non-believer to be your confidant; they shall spare no effort to harm you; it is their heartfelt desire to get you into trouble; enmity is evident from their faces, and that which is hidden in their hearts is even greater; We have clearly set the signs before you, if you have sense.... The fatwa recalls that the *Durr-ul-Mukhtar* has declared it to be strictly wrong to appoint a kafir to the post of even a *tahsil-i-ashar* because the Quran has said that no kafir can be allowed to acquire authority over any believer. A man is appointed to collect *ashar* from the traders and to safeguard the pathways—for instance, the *moharrar* of the octroi post and the policeman at the chowki on the way. When it is basically not right to appoint them to even these puny duties,

15. *Fatawa-i-Rizvia,* Volume VI, pp. 138–39; Volume IX, Book I, pp. 313–14. As we shall see, Maulana Ahmad Riza Khan stresses these points to their limit in regard to the Deobandis and the Ahl-i-Hadis.

the fatwa asks, how can they be appointed to perform such important religious functions?

Citing *Durr-ul-Mukhtar*, citing *Shami* and other authorities, the fatwa declares that to make him even a moharrar is to put the kafir in a position of respect, and to respect a kafir is haram.[16]

This being the norm, we can imagine what ferocious controversies broke out when persons like Maulana Abdul Bari of Firangi Mahal and Mufti Kifayatullah nonetheless agreed to have Muslims conduct campaigns jointly with kafirs in 1918. Even though these were in defence of a purely Islamic institution, the Khilafat, several of the ulema denounced the campaigns saying that by joining them Muslims would willy-nilly have to accord a position of respect to a kafir, Mahatma Gandhi, they would indeed have to function with him as their leader—so instructive is that singular episode that we will return to it soon.

Far from according a kafir a position of respect, the fatwas prohibit Muslims from even using words of respect towards a kafir, they forbid even gestures of salutations which by the custom of that place amount to showing one's respect for another.

A Muslim must refrain from saying things like, 'The non-Muslims are better than Muslims,' warns the *Fatawa-i Rahimiyyah*, as there is apprehension of kufr in such words. And it quotes *Sirat-i-Zakhira*'s observations on blasphemy to the effect that one who says, for instance, 'The Jews are better than the Muslims for they discharge the rights of their children's teacher fully' becomes an infidel by uttering the words.[17] Mufti Kifayatullah is his succinct self: 'A *Kafir*,' he rules, 'cannot be

---

16. *Fatawa-i-Rizvia*, Volume VI, pp, 529–30.
17. *Fatawa-i-Rahimiyyah*, Volume III, p. 8.

better than a Muslim under any circumstances. A Muslim is better than *Kafirs* in all circumstances.'[18]

Maulana Ahmad Riza Khan is of course his explicit self in this as on other matters.

To praise any act or deed of a kafir, declares the *Fatawa-i-Rizvia,* is kufr. To respect a kafir is kufr, it declares citing the *Durr-ul-Mukhtar,* those who utter such words of respect are out of Islam, their wives are out of their wedlock; to restore the status quo ante they must embrace Islam again and go through their nikah again. Even if it be in a poem, it declares, not to call a kafir bad, not to call a believer good is wholly kufr.[19]

This being the position in law, who but those ignorant of the fatwas, who but those who deliberately shut their eyes to the premises of Islam would have been surprised at the about-turn of Maulana Mohammed Ali which we saw in the opening chapter?

Not even at his death

There must be no slackening of the rule even upon the man's death. When our leader or ruler who happens not to have been a Muslim dies, asks the querist, can we read the *Kalima-i-Ilabi* for him and secure some benefit for his soul? Can we at least beg pardon for his sins or not? It is not proper to pray for his benefit nor to seek pardon for a kafir, rules even the moderate Mufti Kifayatullah.[20] The Lokmanya dies. Members of the Khilafat Committee publish a poster condoling his death. On the tenth day there are gatherings in some mosques at which prayers are said for the departed

---

18. *Mufti Kifayatullah ke Fatawi,* Volume I, p. 41. For the way in which Mufti Kifayatullah tries to get over the rule he has himself reiterated, see below the discussion of choosing between the leadership of a kafir, Gandhiji, and of a non-practising Muslim, a Shia at that, Jinnah.

19. *Fatawa-i-Rizvia,* Volume VI, pp. 126, 191, 194–95.

20. *Mufti Kifayatullah ke Fatawi,* Volume IX, pp. 341–42.

leader. What is the hukum in regard to those who published the poster and in regard to those who organized the prayers and participated in them?, the querist asks Maulana Ahmad Riza Khan. It is haram to join such gatherings, he declares. He who joins them deserves condemnation, he is not qualified to lead prayers. It is a duty to beware of the enemies of the Faith. To ask *dua* for a polytheist, to read the *janaza* namaz and the *fatiha* for him is wholly kufr, it is to go contrary to the Quran.

And on top of all this, the Maulana rages, the extreme cruelty: that these persons bared their heads in the mosque, and converted the House of Allah's prayer into a place of mourning for a polytheist! The Muslims who did these things, he declares, have become oxen to the cart of the polytheists. And this had to be so, he pronounces, for when they left Islam (in Ahmad Riza Khan's view the Deobandis, Ahl-i-Hadis, etc., had all become kafirs') common humanity—*insaniyat*—had also naturally to desert them. Now, he who wants can be an ox, the Maulana declares of these Muslims, he who wants can be a donkey.... He who has honoured a non-Muslim, he declares, has helped demolish Islam.... Recalling ayats from the Quran of the kind we have noted earlier, he reiterates that unity and cooperation with kafirs and polytheists is wholly haram. Accordingly, he concludes, those who published the poster have become apostates, they are out of Islam, their wives are out of their nikah.[21] And all this because they have merely prayed for the soul of a kafir, because they have accorded the man respect, albeit upon his death, and though the man in question was the Lokmanya.

Mahatma Gandhi keeps a twenty-one-day fast for Hindu-Muslim unity. He nearly dies. At the conclusion of his fast, says the querist, Hindus all over the country held meetings to

21. *Fatawa-i-Rizvia,* Volume IX, Book II, pp. 270–71.

celebrate its conclusion and success. Muslims abstained from participating in these, the querist reports, but, he says, the Pesh imam of a mosque has participated in, even presided over such meetings. Does this act of the Pesh imam not support kufr and polytheism?, the querist asks. Remember that the person who has undertaken that ordeal is no less than Mahatma Gandhi, remember that the purpose of the fast has been to promote unity among Hindus and Muslims. Remember that the fast has been undertaken at the house of Maulana Mohammed Ali. Recall all that copious shedding of tears. And remember that the question is being asked of Mufti Kifayatullah—that is, not only of a moderate among the ulema but of one who has been, and is going to continue for three decades to be a supporter of joint action with the Hindus, specifically under the leadership of Mahatma Gandhi. How does even such a person respond? He lets off the Pesh imam, but the ground on which he does so itself nails the point. Kifayatullah does not say that it is right or even permissible to pray for Gandhiji because of his nobility and spirit of service, nor because he is leading a movement which is in the interests of the country, nor even because Gandhiji has put himself through that scorching ordeal for the sake of Hindu-Muslim unity. Kifayatullah decrees that it is jaiz to pray for the long life of a non-Muslim with the intention that perhaps Allah may guide him, and that during the rest of his life that non-Muslim may be lit by Islamic enlightenment. That is why it is not right for the people to taunt the Pesh imam for participating in and presiding over the meeting, rules Kifayatullah.[22]

Maulana Ahmad Riza Khan is as always more candid. Talking of non-believers in general and in particular about

22. *Mufti Kifayatullah he Fatawi,* Volume IX, pp. 35–36; the point is reiterated at pp. 321–22.

those he declares to be the scum among non-believers—that is, the Maulanas of Deoband—he admonishes the believers: remember the Hadis of the Prophet in which he warned the faithful that if the non-believers are ill do not visit them, if they die do not participate in their funeral. The Maulana quotes Hadis after Hadis of the Prophet: Stay away from them, keep them away from you, lest they lead you astray, lest they cast you in tumult; If they fall ill do not go to inquire after them, if they die do not join the funeral; When you meet them, do not greet them; Do not sit near them, do not drink water with them, do not intermarry with them; Do not read namaz at their death; When you see anyone of the wrong faith (*bad-mazhab*), be bitter and harsh towards him, Allah considers every one of the wrong faith to be his enemy; He who honours one of the wrong faith helps in demolishing Islam; None of them shall be able to cross the bridge of *Sirat*, and will instead be torn to pieces and fall into the Fire as flies and spiders do.... And there are other Hadis to the same effect, the Maulana points out. His special wrath, as we shall see, was always reserved for the Deobandis, Wahabis, etc. But the Hadis he cites apply to non-believers in general, and the Maulana never hesitates to invoke them in spelling out what attitude believers should have towards kafirs: Ahmad Riza Khan's wrath against the Deobandis, etc., was not because they were Deobandis, he hurled these Hadis at them not because they were Deobandis but because, in his reckoning, Deobandis, etc., had become kafirs.

Allah, the Prophet and his mother

That a prayer cannot be said for a person like the Lokmanya, that thanks cannot be given for the fact that a person such as Gandhiji has survived a searing ordeal nor can prayers be said for him would seem strange to us. But only because we have kept our eyes so tightly shut to the facts. In this the ulema are adhering strictly to the practice and edicts of the Prophet himself: Hadis from him have already been alluded to; there is also the famous incident involving a person no less than his own mother.

As is well known, the Prophet's, mother, Amina, died when he was a child of six: she had taken him to Medina; after staying there a month she and the child were on their way back to Mecca; but about halfway, at Al-Abwa, she fell sick, and soon died; she was buried there. As the revelations were yet to descend, technically speaking she died a non-believer. Later in life, when the Prophet was proceeding from Al-Hodaibiya to Medina he visited his mother's tomb which was on the way. He 'wept and moved others around him to tears', the Hadis narrates. On being asked what had happened, he explained, 'I asked my Lord's permission to pray for forgiveness for her, but I was not allowed. I then asked His permission to visit her grave, and I was allowed....'[23]

The editors and commentators of the traditions explain the significance of Allah forbidding the Prophet from seeking forgiveness for his mother. While setting out the Hadis in *Sunan Nasai Sharif* Allama Wahid al-Zaman comments: 'The permission to pray was not granted because Allah will not forgive the idolaters. Why should the Prophet pray for them?'[24] Correspondingly, while setting out the Hadis in *Sahih Muslim,* Abdul Hamid Siddiqui explains: 'There are different reasons for it. The one obvious reason is that the

---

23. *Sunan Abu Dawud,* Ahmad Hasan (tr.), Kitab Bhavan, New Delhi, 1993, Volume II, p. 919; also *Sahih Muslim,* Abdul Hamid Siddiqui (tr.), Kitab Bhavan, 1978, Volume II, p. 463; *Sunan Nasai Sharif,* Allama Wahid Al-Zaman (tr.) Aitqad Publishing House, Suiwalan, Delhi, 1986, Volume I, p. 658.

24. *Sunan Nasai Sharif,* op. cit., Volume I, p. 658.

mother of Hazrat Muhammad (may peace be upon him) was not a believer in the technical sense of the term. She had lived in the intermittent period (the period in which the teachings of the previous prophets were blurred and no new prophet was raised). Her status in religion is thus known best to God. The Holy Prophet (may peace be upon him) was, therefore, forbidden to seek forgiveness for her, since her position as a believer was not explicit. If the Holy Prophet had been allowed to do this, it could lead to misgiving among the people and they would believe that forgiveness could be sought even for a non-Muslim.'[25]

The case of Abu Talib, the Prophet's uncle and guardian, the father of Hazrat Ali is just as conclusive. For forty years he served and protected the Prophet and was his friend. But he did not accept Islam even on his deathbed, even though urged by the Prophet himself to do so at least at that penultimate moment. Thus he lived and died an unbeliever. *Sunan Nasai Sharif* sets out what happened at that moment and subsequently:

> Said bin al-Matib heard his father saying that when Abu Talib was about to die he (the father) went to visit him. Abu Jahl and Abdullah bin Umiah were sitting there. The Prophet said, 'O my Uncle! say, "There is no god but Allah". On account of this utterance (by you), I will intervene in your favour with Allah the Almighty.' Abu Jahl and Abdullah bin Umiah said, "O Abu Talib ! Do you hate the religion of Abd al-Mattlab?" Then they went on talking to him, so that, at the end, Abu Talib said, 'I am steadfast in Abd al-Mattlab's religion.' The Prophet observed, 'I will pray for you till I am forbidden.' The following revelation came at that time, 'The Prophet and the others who believe should not pray for idolaters.' It was also revealed,

---

25. *Ṣahih Muslim,* Volume II, pp. 463–64.

'You cannot guide whomsoever you want.'[26]

Nasai furnishes another equally telling Hadis:

Ali relates, I heard that a man prayed for his parents who were idolaters. I said to him, 'Do you pray for them even though they were idolaters?' He replied, 'Abraham prayed for his father although the father was an idolater.' So I went to the Prophet and told him. Then this revelation came, 'The prayer which Abraham offered for his father was on account of a promise which Abraham had made. When he heard that he (the father) was an enemy of Allah, he (Abraham) turned against him (the father).[27]

When even the Prophet is forbidden from saying a prayer, and when he is forbidden from doing so even for his mother, when he refrains from doing so for a man who has served and protected him and been his zealous guardian for forty years, the ulema are only enforcing the law when they proclaim the ones to be kafirs who upon the death of the Lokmanya pray for him or who offer thanks and pray for the long life of Gandhiji upon his surviving that terrible ordeal of a fast. And when persons like Mahatma Gandhi and the Lokmanya do not deserve a prayer, where does the ordinary kafir stand?

Not even a respectful greeting

In what words should one return the greetings of kafirs,

---

26. *Sunan Nasai Sharif,* Volume I, pp. 658–59. See also *Sunan Abu Dawud,* Volume II, p. 914: Abu Talib died; the son, Hazrat Ali, reported the death to the Prophet: 'Your old and astray uncle has died.' The Prophet said, 'Go and bury your father, and then do not do anything until you come to me.' So Ali went and buried him, and returned to the Prophet. The Prophet ordered him to take a bath, and when Ali had done so the Prophet prayed for Ali.

27. Ibid., p. 659.

the querist asks, and how should one greet them? To greet a kafir first unless it be in necessity, declares the *Fatawa-i-Rizvia*, is improper. In Hindustan, it adds, according to the etiquette which is in vogue, even in necessity it is not required in shariah to greet them—for instance, it is enough to say, 'Lala Sahib', 'Babu Sahib', 'Munshi Sahib', or to put one's hand to one's head without using the words from one's side, then the sorts of words which are customary are enough. If he does salam using the words also, then, the ulema say, in reply the Muslim should say *'Wa alaiq'*. But, cautions the *Fatawa-i-Rizvia*, this expression is taken as being associated with Muslims only; therefore the kafir will not take it to be a response to his salam, and will in fact take it to be a sign of discrimination. In such a circumstance, relents the *Fatawa-i-Rizvia* in a rare show of consideration, use whichever word seems appropriate, you may use 'salam' in return for *salami*.[28]

In particular, the ulema repeat again and again, nothing must be done out of regard for the false religion of kafirs or out of regard for their religious sentiments—for that would be to strengthen their faith in their false religion, it would therefore be to strike at Islam.

To say anything which shows regard for the religious sentiments of non-Muslims and respect for their *devta*s and their leaders, declares the *Fatawa-i-Rizvia*, is wholly kufr.[29]

In fact, where it helps the cause of Din—by establishing its 'glory', that is its dominance, by reminding the kafir that a thing of his is being spurned *because* he is a kafir, and where this is going to incline him to adopt Islam—the things which will show the kafirs down, which will put them out ought to be done. We have already seen the application of this norm in the stress the ulema lay on slaughtering cows

28. *Fatawa-i-Rizvia*, Volume IX, Book I, pp. 65–66.
29. Ibid., Volume VI, p. 125.

—their proposition being that, while it may not be a matter of consequence in other countries, slaughtering cows is 'a great Islamic act' in India *because* the cow is worshipped in India. We find the same criterion at work even in so innocuous a gesture as accepting a gift.

When to accept, when to spurn a gift

Hindus send us puris, etc., from their homes or purchased out of their income from the bazar, the querist reports, and asks whether these should be accepted. The Prophet accepted gifts from kafirs on some occasions and also refused them on others, recalls the *Fatawa-i-Rizvia.* There is the Hadis: Allah does not forbid good conduct towards those kafirs who do not oppose you in the Faith. On another occasion the Prophet said: Accept their gifts and let them come home. But there are also instances to the contrary, it recalls. When a person who had not become a Muslim till then came to give a gift, the Prophet said: I have been stopped from accepting things given by kafirs. On another occasion he said: I do not accept any gift from any polytheist. On still another occasion he said: We do not accept anything from the polytheists. And so on.

What should be done, Maulana Ahmad Riza Khan says, depends on whether, in the given time and situation, it is opportune to accept or refuse; it depends on who is bringing the gift and who is accepting it. If the believer feels that by accepting the gift he will turn the other person towards Islam, then the gift should be accepted. On the other hand, if things are such that refusal to accept the gift will pain the person bringing it and this will cause him to become disgusted with his own false religion—that is, if, by realizing that you have refused the gift because of his polytheism, he is liable to turn away from polytheism—then under no circumstances should you accept it.

And one must also watch the effect of the gift on one's own adherence to the Faith. If there is the apprehension that by accepting the gift one shall in any way be inclined towards that person or that by doing so one will go soft in regard to adhering to the requirements of the Faith, then know that gift to be fire. And remember, declares the fatwa, that without doubt gifts have a great effect in promoting inclination and affection. The Prophet has warned, the Maulana emphasizes, a gift makes one blind, deaf and besotted (*diwana*); he has said, a gift blinds the eye of the wise man.[30]

In any case, one must not accept any gift which is associated with the false beliefs and religious practices of the kafirs. Thus, for instance, as we shall see later, Mufti Kifayatullah holds that to occasionally eat food which has been cooked or touched by a kafir is permissible. But even he stresses that gifts which are connected with ceremonies of their religious festivals—such as sweets which the kafirs offer as gifts on Diwali—should not be taken.[31] Maulana Ahmad Riza Khan of course expresses the matter with much greater emphasis. Some Hindus sacrifice animals to their idols; not having a butcher of their own, they call in a Muslim butcher; the latter sacrifices the animals with the mandatory Islamic invocations—'*Bismillah*', etc.; it is detestable for Muslims to assist in this manner, the fatwa declares, and, although the animal having been slaughtered in the proper manner the meat has become halal, when that meat is distributed later on, the Muslim must not take it—for to do so is to assist in consummating the kafirs' false purpose (their *maqsad batil*, that is their purpose of venerating the idol), to take the meat is to take sacrificial meat, that is meat which

30. *Fatawa-i-Rizvia*, Volume IX, Book, I, pp. 93–94.

31. *Mufti Kifayatullah ke Fatawi*, Volume IX, p. 328.

has been sacrificed to false idols. It is haram to eat such meat. The *Fatawa-i-Rizvia* drives home the point with a contrast. To take sweets or meat which have been offered out of respect to idols is to fulfil the intention of the kafirs, there is also degradation (*zillat*) in doing so. Contrast it with the case of an animal (for instance, an ox) which they may have freed in the name of an idol, says the fatwa. *That* animal *can* be used for sacrifice in the name of Allah, and the meat eaten. Because, says the Maulana, eating it is against the kafirs and it degrades them. There is no harm in doing so.The condition is that doing so should not cause a disturbance, for to save oneself from disturbance is incumbent.[32]

Never assist them in their kufr

That last instance—shunning gifts which are associated with the religious ceremonies and festivals of kafirs—carries us to the general rule: a Muslim, the fatwas declare again and again, must never assist, he must never participate in, he must not even view as a bystander any ceremony or procession of the kafirs connected in any way with their false religion—even persons who happened to have merely viewed a religious procession of the Hindus as it went by are pronounced by the ulema to have sinned, in some instances to have even foregone their Islam. The Muslim must actively dissociate himself from all such occasions, ceremonies, processions, etc. He must feel an abhorrence and repugnance towards them.

Is it undesirable or haram for Muslims in the interests of Hindu-Muslim unity to participate in any way—for instance by contributing towards the expenses, by helping with the arrangements—in the festivals of the Hindus?, Mufti Kifayatullah is asked. Recall that he has been a proponent of

32. *Fatawa-i-Rizvia,* Volume VIII, pp. 337–38; also p. 363.

joint political action with the Hindus. Recall that his is the voice of moderation—when questions come up, for instance about conflicting timings of *aarati* and namaz, about routes which processions are to take, he counsels that the matter be settled by negotiation, by mutual accommodation. But on the question at hand—about helping in a religious function, be it ever so indirectly, even he is a purist. It is haram to participate in the religious gatherings of kafirs and polytheists in which there are manifestations of kufr and polytheism, in which idols are worshipped or honoured, he declares. To go to such gatherings even with the intention of amusement, even for *sair-tamasha,* even to establish unity with them, or to add to the *raunaq,* or for any work which comes within the definition of kufr, and to contribute towards the expenses of such gatherings is haram. As for helping with the arrangements alone or doing so for the promotion of peace, it is permissible to do so—provided the help is rendered in a form that one is far away from all manifestations of kufr, provided enjoyment and amusement are not the motives, and provided also that there is some compulsion to participate in the joint arrangements.[33]

It is haram for Muslims to participate in a religious procession of Hindus, the Mufti rules again a little later, in particular in a procession in which polytheism and idolatry are manifested. To put marks on the forehead—as is done by well-wishers and organizers at such processions—is permanently haram; in fact, there is the apprehension of kufr in doing so. One who does such things becomes a fasiq, a sinner, and must do taubah.[34]

---

33. *Mufti Kifayatullah he Fatawi,* Volume IX, p. 35. In the particular circumstances in which the question was asked, the Mufti ruled that the movements of Hindu Sangathan and Mahabir Dal, and their consequences had not left any compulsion in place, and hence participation even in making arrangements was no longer justifiable.

34. Ibid., Volume IX, p. 45.

But what if one goes to the festivals or *melas* of non-Muslims to sell *qandil* or to set up shop?, the Mufti is asked. To participate in religious gatherings of kafirs where such rites and ceremonies are performed by which kufr and polytheism are manifested amounts to enhancing the raunaq of such gatherings, and to increasing the blessings they—the kafirs—seek. Therefore participation in such gatherings is condemnable. To go to such fairs for trade is *karahat tanzihi*, to go to them for watching the tamasha is *karahat tahrimi.*[35]

What if one merely sets up a *sabil* or distributes *paan* at a Hindu religious festival?, the Mufti is asked. As the atmosphere is a bit more relaxed at the time when his opinion has been sought, the Mufti is a little less stern, but only a little. If such a thing is done to enhance respect for their festival then it amounts to kufr, he rules. If it has been done not for honouring their religious deeds but to maintain peace and as reciprocity, and if it is done at some place other than where the festival is being held, then it is desirable. If it is done at the place itself, even for the purposes of maintaining peace and as reciprocity it is *makruh*, that is detestable, and haram, prohibited. It is not kufr. However, it is kufr when those (the Muslims) who do the thing think it good and when their conduct indicates that they admire and applaud such practices.[36]

Observing the form but watching one's heart—that distinction, and doing the former also only when this is necessary, is emphasized again and again even by this moderate and civil Mufti. The Jagadguru of the Hindus came to our town, was it right to honour him?, asks the querist. On the coming of any Hindu leader to join in welcoming him in accordance with the requirements of reciprocity, rules the Mufti, and to garland him is not kufr— provided the Hindus

35. Ibid., Volume IX, pp. 54–55.

36. Ibid., Volume IX, pp. 338–39.

also deal in the same way with Muslim religious leaders. In this, the Mufti emphasizes, there is no respect for polytheism and kufr. Instead, it is to abide by civility and morality.[37]

A little later his emphasis tilts to the critical edge. Islam has stopped you from denigrating the leaders of other religions, he declares, adding, it has not commanded that you show respect for them. Especially that sort of respect which touches the bounds of worship—that cannot be proper by any means. Ever the practical man, the Mufti concedes with one hand: especially where both Muslims and non-Muslims live or where non-Muslims are in a majority, he says, in such a place conciliation, to live in peace, and to participate with them in trade, agriculture, industry and in politics is proper, and in certain circumstances justifiable. And then by characteristic circumlocution he introduces the limits which must be observed, and the warning: in any case, he continues, it is necessary that Muslims should remain true to their religious injunctions, that they should maintain intact their religious character, honour and respect—otherwise it shall be incumbent upon Muslims to defend their religion, its respect and honour.[38] In a word: conciliation and peace to the extent that religious injunctions and the character, respect and honour of the religion are maintained to their satisfaction.

And that is the moderate formulation of the moderate one among the ulema.

Maulana Ahmad Riza Khan predictably is not satisfied with reciprocity. He does not countenance consideration being shown even formally for the religious sentiments of the non-believers—active dissociation, hostile spurning are enjoined, that is his tenor.

When a procession bearing idols is brought to or passes

37. Ibid., Volume IX, pp. 329–30.

38. Ibid., Volume IX, p. 336.

their house and the persons thank the processionists, when they allow the processionists to put a tilak mark on them, when they join the Hindus in shouting 'jai' to the false god—all of them and all those who joined such a procession are close to kufr, declares the *Fatawa-i-Rizvia*. More specifically, those who had the tilak put on them, those who joined Hindus in saying that 'jai' have become kafirs, it declares. Their women are out of their nikah. Those who did not do these things but joined the procession have come close to kufr.[39] The places of worship of the kafirs, it declares, are places of the Devil. To join in the prayers of kafirs, to go to their places of worship is kufr. And to think lightly of kufr is also kufr.[40] To participate in Dussehra has been declared to be kufr *by* the *Fuqah*, it pronounces. To place flowers on idols, to blow the conch are certainly kufr, it declares. To call out the 'jai' of a kafir is the way of kafirs, it declares. To stop sacrifices of cows for the sake of Hindus is haram, it says citing the *Durr-ul-Mukhtar.* And he who does what is haram deserves the torture of Hell, it warns. And he who is guilty of that which is kufr in *Fiqh*—for instance one who is guilty of doing the things listed above: participating in a religious festival of non-believers like Dussehra, placing flowers on idols, blowing the conch—is out of Islam; he must embrace Islam again, he must do nikah again.[41]

Joining a procession in which books like the Ramayana are carried with respect is kufr, it declares, and the same consequences follow for any Muslim who does so.[42] To continue to sacrifice cows and the prohibition against participating in meeting of Hindus, it declares, are both among the necessities of

39. *Fatawa-i-Rizvia,* Volume VI, p. 50.

40. Ibid., Volume VI, p. 53.

41. Ibid., Volume VI, p. 149.

42. Ibid., Volume IX, Book II, p. 316.

religion. He who declares the former haram and the latter halal is calumnizing Allah and the Prophet. And by the ordinances of the Quran his abode is Jahannum, Hell. And pronouncing the injunction of kufr upon him is incumbent, rules the *Fatawa-i-Rizvia.*[43] Notice that already Maulana Ahmad Riza Khan is moving beyond the prohibition of participating in any gathering, procession, ceremony that has to do with the religion of the Hindus; participating in any meeting of Hindus—for instance, a meeting held as part of a political movement—is prohibited, he declares, and this prohibition, he emphasizes, is among the necessities of Islam.

The singular exception Kifayatullah and Ahmad Riza Khan allow is that a Muslim may go to the fairs of non-believers for trade—but, as we have seen, even in doing this much he is warned to take all the precautions which have been listed above: manifestations of kufr and polytheism are invariably the central features, the very purposes of these fairs; the Muslim must ensure that no respect for these creeps into his heart; as far as possible he must set up his business far away from places where these manifestations are on display, etc.[44]

Just as one must stay away from any function, procession, ceremony, thing—recall the case of sweets distributed after Diwali—or mark—recall the dreaded tilak—which is associated with the religion of the kafirs, one must never in any way assist them in any matter which relates to their religion.

Can we help any Hindu religious activity by giving a contribution, the Ahl-i-Hadis are asked, for instance by contributing towards the construction of a temple? They (the Hindus) demand contributions, the querist says, and if we do not give anything there is the danger that they may misbehave with

43. Ibid., Volume VI, p. 101; also p. 150.

44. For instance, *Mufti Kifayatullah ke Fatawi,* Volume IX, pp. 54–55, 338–39 referred to above; *Fatawa-i-Rizvia,* Volume IX, Book I, p. 38.

us. The religious activities of Hindus are *sharkiya* or *kufriya,* rules the fatwa of Ahl-i-Hadis. Therefore it is not proper to help in any of their religious activities by giving *chanda,* etc. To help in the construction of a temple is to support idolatry and infidelity, it is strictly forbidden. As for the nuisance they may be as a consequence, remember what Allah says in the Quran... Faith is dear, and you believers are perfect; therefore do not be unnerved by these dangers.[45]

What of a Muslim who has assisted not in constructing a temple, but just the house of a Hindu which has in it, among other things, a temple? Mufti Kifayatullah rules that if the person helped out of his own volition—that is, if he did so even though there was no compulsion upon him to do so—and if he had a liking for what was going to be done there, then his commitment to Islam is in doubt. He has to embrace Islam again. Even if he helped make such a house out of some compulsion, his help, though it does not make him a kafir, is still not free of sin. He must therefore do taubah.[46]

A camel dies. A person who was devoted to it has a statue of it made. People start making offerings to it and the camel becomes well known as Mian Milu. A Muslim breaks it, and clears the ground. What is the hukum of the ulema?, Kifayatullah is asked. To make a statue or sculpture, to worship it, to make offerings there are all clear violations of shariah and of Islamic injunctions, they are polytheism and idolatry, the Mufti rules. If there had been Islamic rule both the one who got the statue made and the one who made it would have been punished, and the one who broke it would have been rewarded, he rules.[47]

Thus, one must not assist or participate—not even

---

45. *Fatawa Ahl-i-Hadis,* Volume II, pp. 39–40.

46. *Mufti Kifayatullah ke Fatawi,* Volume IX, p. 20.

47. Ibid., Volume IX, pp. 237–38.

indirectly—in any activity which is associated with the false faith of the kafirs. One must in fact actively dissociate oneself from it. It must generate detestation in one, just as such things did in the Prophet. Not only that, one must not countenance anything that puts the false faith of the kafirs and the true Faith—Islam—at par, even symbolically, even formally.

While our leaders and the Supreme Court keep chanting, 'All religions are one'; while they keep recalling the Vedic pronouncement, 'Truth is one, only the sages call it by different names'; while they keep recalling Ashoka's rock edict, 'One who reveres one's own religion and disparages that of another, due to devotion to one's own religion and to glorify it over all others, does injure one's own religion certainly',[48] the ulema proclaim the very opposite set of values, the truly Islamic values to be fair to the ulema. Thus we have Maulana Ahmad Riza Khan descend as an avalanche on persons who countenance processions in which books like the Gita and Quran are carried with equal respect; he declares that for a Muslim to even say, 'Hindus should live by the Vedas, Muslims should live by the Quran,' is kufr; a temple is the abode of Satans, he says, a Muslim is forbidden from going into it; to describe the Holy Quran as being like the Veda is kufr; to say that Hindus should live by the Veda is

48. For instance, the Supreme Court's verdict on the Ayodhya Reference: *The Ayodhya Reference*, Voice of India, New Delhi, 1995, pp.31–33, and my comment at pp. 171–74. For representative chants of our politicians, see pp. 31–33 where the Court reproduces passages from the Dr Zakir Husain Memorial Lecture of the president, Dr Shankar Dayal Sharma; for their invoking Ashoka's edict, see Dr Sharma's inaugural Address to the Seminar on Indic Religions organized by the Khuda Bakhsh Oriental Public Library at the National Museum, New Delhi, 24 December 1993, p. 3.

to ask people to follow kufr, and to ask people to follow kufr is kufr....[49]

A man delivers a sermon before an assembly in which non-Muslims such as Hindus are present, the querist informs the ulema of Dar al-Ulum, Deoband; the man says that there is no difference between Hindus and Muslims, and that we create differences because of our foolish doctrines; he says that the idol house as well as the Kaba are both made of stone and that there is no difference between blowing the conch and calling out the azan; he compares the scriptures of the Hindus and the Holy Quran, and says that the two decree the same things—all staples, if I may add, of the speeches of our leaders, of the writings of our secularists, of the panegyrics to secularism in the judgments of our courts. What is the law in regard to such a person?, asks the querist of the ulema of Deoband.

These are utterances of kufr, they declare. A person who has such beliefs and teaches such beliefs is not a Muslim but an infidel and an apostate, they declare. He is a reprobate and a heretical inventor, in fact an infidel and an apostate, they repeat. Muslims should keep away from him rather than listen to his infidel utterances.[50]

Yet, whenever our courts and leaders recall those *Sarva Dharma Samabhava* passages they address them to the Hindus, asking them to live up to these ideals. They never address the

---

49. For instance, *Fatawa-i-Rizvia,* Volume IX, Book II, pp. 298–99. The eleven questions which provide the occasion for the fatwa are themselves worth reading: A Hindu is made to sit on a chair while Muslims sit on the ground; to consider a matter among Muslims a panchayat *is* constituted with a Hindu as its head; he exhorts us to stop eating beef out of consideration for the feeling of Hindu brothers; he goes to a temple where he says, 'Hindus should live by the Vedas, Muslims should live by the Quran'.... What is the law regarding such a person? Maulana Ahmad Riza Khan of course comes down heavily on each such deed and expression.

50. *Fatawa Dar al-Ulum, Deoband,* Volume XII, p. 370.

passages to the ulema who staunchly and openly denounce the ideals, who proclaim from housetops that to countenance such parity—even for the sake of form, even nominally and verbally—is to be out of Islam!

Far from saying 'Vedas and the Quran are all holy books'; far from saying, 'Hindus should live by the Vedas, Muslims should live by the Quran'; far from participating in a procession in which other books like the Gita and Ramayana are carried like the Quran equally with respect—that is, far from saying or doing anything which puts Islam and other religions at par, the Prophet and other prophets (named though they are in the Quran as prophets who had been sent earlier by Allah) at par, the Quran and other holy books at par; far from doing or saying anything which entails any of these effects, a Muslim who says anything which even obscures the distinction between the ordinary Muslim—even himself—and kafirs is guilty of kufr and thereby out of Islam. He is a kafir and out of Islam if he utters words having this effect even in exasperation or jest.

A Muslim who says, 'All right, all right, hell for me'; a Muslim who when asked about a rope tied around his or her waist says, 'It is zunnar'; a Muslim who says, 'All right, I will meet the same end as Hindus'—each and every one of them is guilty of kufr, and out of Islam, declare the ulema.[51]

In the preceding chapter we saw the insistence of the ulema that Muslims must dress in a manner and generally do things in a manner which is the opposite of the way kafirs do them. We saw their insistence that Muslims shun doing some particular thing, be it ever so trivial—using toilet paper, urinating while standing—because, among other reasons, that is

51. For instance, *Fatawa Dar al-Ulum, Deoband,* Volume XII, pp. 370, 434, 437; *Fatawa-i-Rizvia,* Volume VI, pp. 52–57, 72–73, 76, 80, 125, 126, 149, 150–51, 191; Volume IX, Book II, pp. 298–99.

what or how Christians and other kafirs do. There is the counterpart to these rules in matters connected with purely religious rituals.

It is *bid'at* to inform people of the hour after azan by striking the gong or bell, one may keep an alarm clock instead, rules Kifayatullah.[52] It is bid'at and undesirable to greet each other and shake hands after Id, he rules. Among the reasons on account of which doing so is undesirable? That it is comparable to Hindus embracing each other on the day of Holi.[53]

Physically detestable too

In matters touching upon religion thus the watchwords are: conquer, suppress, convert, detest, shun. In principle the norms in regard to day-to-day matters cannot be very different, for, as the ulema are forever reminding the faithful, Islam makes no distinction between matters of religion and matters of day-to-day life. In practice the fact that in India the Muslims have to live amidst a majority which is non-Muslim has led the ulema to make some relaxations. The watchwords here are: unless absolutely necessary, avoid the kafirs; when absolutely unavoidable, do the minimum that you just have to. Not much of an improvement, but still a difference at least. However, as we shall see, the relaxations which are made and the niggardly way in which they are made end up reinforcing the central rule—that one must keep oneself apart from the kafirs.

The Quran, as we know, has pronounced the kafirs to be unclean. It has warned the believers not to be friends with them, not to take any among them to be a confidant. This judgment and this command of Allah are elaborated upon, and repeatedly reiterated, and applied with great vigour in the fatwas.

---

52. *Mufti Kifayatullah ke Fataivi*, Volume III, p. 10.

53. Ibid., Volume IX, pp. 21–23.

Kafir*s* are portrayed as filthy as well as untrustworthy.

Most of the ulema begin by saying that the impurity which the Quran ascribes to the kafir*s* relates to their beliefs, and not to their bodies. Therefore, on the question of food cooked or handled by them, for instance, the ulema hold that unless some impurity is manifest on the food a Muslim may take it (with the exception of meat, to which we shall soon come). However, that is just the position in principle, so to say. Having stated this, the *Fatawa-i-Rizvia* proceeds to observe, 'But there is no doubt in this that the Hindus, rather all the *Kafirs* in general, remain dirty and filthy. In fact, most things which are filthy are, in their eyes, pure. Indeed, in the eyes of the Hindus some of the filthy things are ones that purify.' 'Therefore,' it declares, 'as long as one is not in difficulty, to save oneself from them is best....piety lies in saving oneself....' It portrays Hindus as ones who make sweets from *kadhai*s which are licked by dogs all evening, which they—the Hindus—wash with their filthy water in the mornings, and which they then wipe with the *angochha* they have had draped around themselves for a year and which would have at any moment a *chhatank* of urine in it... All Hindus, it declares, remain thoroughly filthy, water and utensils used by them are repugnant in the extreme. It is necessary to save oneself from them. People among whom *gobar* is taken as purifying, what have they to do with piety, asks the *Fatawa-i-Rizvia,* and declares, it is better to keep away from drinking and eating with the people who do not keep to piety.[54]

Other kafirs, for instance Christians, fare no better. Apart from menstrual blood, nothing—like liquor, urine, excrement—is actually impure in the religion of the Christians,

---

54. *Fatawa-i-Rizvia,* Volume II, pp. 135, 137; Volume IX, Book I, p. 224; Volume XI, p. 155.

the *Fatwa-i-Rizvia* pronounces. The Christians, according to it, think it laughable to save oneself from such things and they think it contrary to their self-formed culture (*apni sakhta tehzib*)—as distinct from Islam, that is, which is Allah-given. Therefore, their condition is manifestly mired in filth.... The Mussalman people, it says, know by reason that it is undesirable to be in contact with urine, excrement and blood. The Christians laugh at them on this matter. Therefore, it is wholly detestable in shariah and undesirable to use any moist (non-dry) thing which has been touched by them—for instance, a paan which may have been prepared entirely by a Muslim but has then passed through the hands of a Christian. Apart from hygiene, the fatwa elaborates, there is another consideration which implicates both non-dry as well as dry things touched by Christians in detestability. In shariah, just as it is a duty to save oneself from sin, so also it is necessary to save oneself from imputations. Similarly, to open oneself to taunts without reason is improper in shariah. Moreover, Muslims have been prohibited from involving themselves in things which embroil them in infamy and trouble. Just as bad is it for them to cause hatred towards themselves. Now, to take things like paan which have been touched by Christians, to accept sweets from them leads other Muslims to hate and defame one, it invites trouble, it opens the doors to discords. In every way, therefore, it embroils a Muslim in things from which the shariah enjoins that he save himself.[55]

Mufti Kifayatullah also states that when the Quran speaks of the impurity of kafirs it is referring to the impurity of their beliefs, not their bodies. The body of a human being per se is paak, except to the extent that there is some impurity manifest on it—some filth, some sore, etc. Therefore, he

---

55. *Fatawa-i-Rizvia,* Volume II, pp. 126–27.

rules that it is permissible for Muslims to use water from a well used by Hindus, that, once the other person has cleaned his hands, etc., a Muslim may eat in the same plate as another, be the latter *chamar* or bhangi—from the point of view of *tabligh,* he says, the ones who ate food served by untouchables are worthy of appreciation.[56]

Having set out the general principle, he says: Now comes the question—why does the Muslim eat with the non-Muslim? If there is some necessity on account of which he eats with the non-Muslim then, rules the Mufti, no *ilzam,* no charge shall lie against him. But if there is no necessity, the Mufti states, there shall be the charge of eating and drinking with non-Muslims, though not the charge of eating that which is impure or forbidden.[57] From the point of view of the non-Muslim that is little consolation.

The *Fatawa-i-Rahimiyyah*'s position is about the same. Is it permissible or not to dine with an infidel?, the querist asks. 'One can dine betimes but to make it a regular habit is abominable,' the fatwa declares, and quotes in support what is stated in *Nafa al-Mufti wal Sa'il*: 'To dine with him once or twice for the sake of pleasing him (recall Mufti Kifayatullah saying that those who ate food served by untouchables were worthy of appreciation from the point of view of *tabligh*) is proper but to do so always is abominable. The Holy Prophet (pbuh.!) has dined with an infidel once.'[58]

Meat of course stands on an altogether different footing. All the authorities stress, and repeatedly, that a Muslim must buy or eat the meat only of that animal which has been slaughtered by a Muslim, or meat which, from the time the

---

56. For instance, *Mufti Kifayatullah ke Fatawi,* Volume II, pp. 99, 277, 278, 286, 287, 288–89, 290–91; Volume IX, pp. 319–21, 331–32.

57. Ibid., Volume II, p. 287.

58. *Fatawa-i-Rahimiyyah,* Volume II, p. 191.

animal was slaughtered to the time the meat is given to him, has been in the sight of a Muslim.[59]

The general principle thus is: the body of a non-Muslim is paak, therefore eating with him or eating food touched or cooked by him is permissible. But one should do this only on the rare occasion when one is impelled by necessity, and not make a habit of this.

For that caveat there are three reasons. First, though their bodies have been made intrinsically paak by Allah, non-believers do not observe the rules of hygiene, they live mired in filth. Second, eating with them will open one to the charge of associating with them. The third reason is the general risk which is stressed again and again in the context of kafirs—the risk that associating with them will contaminate one spiritually and mentally.

Maulana Ahmad Riza Khan presents the contrary argument as put forth by an author—that by the saying of the Prophet and the rulings of the ulema it is permissible to eat food prepared by heathens unless the impurity and pollution are evident from the food itself. But the manner in which the instances relating to Hindus, for instance, are presented would itself create aversion enough in the believer to desist from taking such food. And, the Maulana says, all that the ulema have held is that it is permissible to eat food prepared by heathens. There is no compulsion, he says, to stand by the verdict of the ulema; one can employ his own common sense in determining the purity of an impure thing; if it is declared to be pure by a religious head, one is free to accept it or to not accept it.

In arguing that Muslims have been permitted to partake of things handled by or made by kafirs, unless the impurity is manifest, the scholar whose argument the Maulana is reviewing

---

59. For instance, *Mufti Kifayatullah ke Fatawi*, Volume VIII, p. 259.

had given seven sorts of situations in which the Prophet and the ulema have pronounced such items to be permissible. For the present context what is of interest is the way kafirs are pictured by the author and by Maulana Ahmad Riza Khan while discussing the propositions.

First there is the instance of the well, we are told. Pagans, non-believers, ignorant and foolish children who have no sense of piety, as well as careless and impure women—that is, women in their menstrual courses—and all sorts of people draw water from the well. Yet the water is held to be pure both for ablutions and drinking till the impurity is visible or has been logically inferred.

The second, third and fourth instances concern situations in which a shoe falls in a well or pond, where children put some limb in the water, or where rats, mice, insects, small animals or reptiles sip or fall into oil kept in a vessel for making soap, etc.—the shoe may have had filth, the rats etc. may be filthy but, the argument goes, in each instance the ulema have held that, unless the filth is manifest, the water and oil remain pure.

The fifth, sixth and seventh cases relate directly to kafirs.

There is the matter of food and sweets prepared by Hindus and other non-believers. These persons are not only careless in preparing them, they are, we are told, themselves very dirty and full of filth and pollution. Every eatable item prepared by them is feared and apprehended to have some admixture of unclean matter like cow dung, etc. in it, we are informed. We know, the Maulana points out, that for them the dung of cows and bullocks as well as the urine of female calves are holy and pure. Nothing is more holy and sanctified for them than this urine and dung. The ulema hold eating or drinking these to be forbidden. Yet they permit us to take sweets and foods—it matters little that they have been prepared by Hindus.

Sixth, it is seen that the pots and utensils of the worst of non-believers and polytheists are dirty, the Maulana summarizes. We know it well that these pots are not free of filth. They drink wine, they eat pork and other kinds of forbidden meat from their pots. Yet the code of Islamic doctrine says that the use of their pots is not forbidden. They are pure till the filth is manifest. Even the Prophet allowed their use. The pots of kafirs and non-believers seized in war were frequently used by Muslims in front of the Prophet and he never forbade them from using these.

The final case concerns persons who are doubly repugnant: non-believers who are drunkards. They are never clean. Their clothes, specially their trousers, we are informed, are full of filth and impurities of all kinds. They have no idea of istinja, their clothes are wet with wine and urine. Yet the ulema hold that by themselves these clothes are pure. Mussalmans wear these clothes without washing them, and attend namaz in them, the Maulana summarizes: doing so is not bad in the eyes of Islamic law unless the filth is manifest. It has been acknowledged since the days of the Prophet that saying prayers, namaz in clothes of non-believers seized in war is permissible. Mussalmans have been doing so, the author says, and have never entertained any suspicion or presumption in taking the clothes to be pure and clean.

In short, says the author, it is not correct to pass a verdict of impurity merely on presupposition or presumption. If cows, goats and other animals fall into a well and come out alive, the cleanliness and purity of the well are not affected. Admittedly the legs and thighs of these animals are dirty with urine and dung. Yet the ulema hold that given the quantity and flow of water through which they may have passed, it is probable that the filth from their bodies would have been washed away. Under the circumstances the water from the well is to be regarded as clean and worthy of use.

The condescension, the picture which is drawn of Hindus and other non-believers, their being clubbed with animals and vermin—any text doing this in the case of Muslims would call forth howls of denunciation. From the secularists as much as from Muslims.

That is one point. The other comes out in the Maulana's summing up of and his deduction from the arguments. His point is that what the ulema have done is merely to permit that one may eat or drink such things. But there is no compulsion to stand by the verdict of the ulema. One can employ common sense in determining whether or not a thing which is permitted is pure. A person may or may not accept a thing which has been declared pure by a religious person. The touchstone here is one's own psychological reaction to the thing. If the apprehension that a thing is impure assails one's mind with particular force, the presumption should not be overlooked altogether. If one is mentally not satisfied about the purity of an object, it should be taken to be impure.[60]

Together the two things can have only one result: on the one hand a picture is painted of Hindus, etc., as ones who remain mired in filth; and on the other stress is laid on one's psychological or mental reactions to a thing. Together they can only mean that, while in theory the body of a kafir is paak, in practice it is best to save oneself from things cooked or handled by him.

By contrast a Muslim is not just pictured as being always pure, he is held to be pure by virtue of the fact that he is a Muslim. He is declared to be pure when alive, and his corpse is said to be pure when he dies. The ulema cite Hadis of the Prophet, and also the sayings of Companions to this effect. In *Sahih al-Bukhari* when the discussion turns to the sweat of a person in a state of impurity, we find it declared that a Muslim is always pure. In another incident, also narrated in *Sahih*

60. *Fatawa-t-Rizvia*, Volume II, pp. 93–97.

al-Bukhari, Abu Huraira says that once he came upon the Prophet when he—Abu Huraira—was in a state of impurity; he says he slipped away, had a bath, and returned to the Prophet's presence. The Prophet asked him, 'Abu Huraira, where have you been?' Abu Huraira told him that he had been in a state of impurity, that he had felt that it was hateful to meet the Prophet in that state and so he had gone to have a bath. The Prophet remarked, '*Subhan Allah,* a Muslim is never defiled.' Incidents involving the Companions of the Prophet to the same effect are narrated in connection with an assembly that has gathered around a corpse to mourn the death of a Muslim, about the man who washes the corpse. These persons are not required to bathe, unlike Ali who was ordered by the Prophet to bathe when he returned after burying his father, Abu Talib, as the latter had lived and died a non-believer.

This declaration of purity is next extended from the body of a living Muslim to the corpse of a Muslim who has died though it is reported that some later jurists—including Abu Hanifa and Malik—demur at this and consider the corpse of a Muslim to be impure. Authorities are cited to the effect that even the hair or other organs which may be removed from the corpse of a Muslim remain pure.[61]

They are untrustworthy

Just as the kafirs are filthy, just as they are intrinsically,

---

61. These and other authorities are recalled while pronouncing that a well has remained pure into which a Muslim girl had drowned and from which the corpse had been taken out an hour and a half later. The fatwa does not counsel determining the state in which the body was; that the quantum of water in the well was more than sufficient also comes in as an incidental point at the very end; the fatwa declares the well to continue to be pure on the ground that the girl was a Muslim, and a Muslim, alive or dead, is pure: see, *Fatawa Ahl-i-Hadis,* Volume I, pp. 14–18.

inherently filthy, the kafirs are intrinsically, inherently, incorrigibly untrustworthy, declare the fatwas again and again.

By definition the kafir does not adhere to the principles and norms of the one and only true Faith. He is not likely to even know them. His guidance, help, judgement are therefore liable to be coloured. Coloured by his ignorance: he may give a verdict asking a Muslim to do 'X' not knowing that 'X' is haram. And coloured by his perfidy too: for, as Allah has Himself warned, the kafirs are always out to beguile the believer into practices which will implicate him in kufr.

It is entirely understandable that for these reasons no non-believer can be asked to handle a religious function—other religions too would not countenance his doing so in their case. But as Islam sets out to regulate the totality of life, mundane activities also, as we have seen, become religious activities. To have a kafir decide for one or guide one even on mundane activities entails the believer in the risk of being led—wittingly or unwittingly—to do things which violate the Islamic code, and thus embroil him in sin.

For many drinking or not drinking liquor, for instance, is a 'secular' decision, in that it has nothing to do with religion. But that cannot obviously be the case for a Muslim—the prohibition of liquor is for him, and most emphatically for the ulema a religious matter. What about taking allopathic medicines? Most allopathic medicines have liquor, say the fatwas. Taking them will therefore involve taking liquor and that is a grave sin. This must not be done until one is in extreme necessity, that is until there is no other alternative to taking that medicine. Even if one assumes about a particular kafir doctor that, being an exception to the general rule, he individually is not evil-minded enough to want to embroil his Muslim patients in sin, he is not liable to think imbibing or not imbibing liquor to be a matter of any great significance. He is, therefore, liable to prescribe liquor-based or liquor-using medicines even when these are not absolutely necessary. This being the case, decrees Mufti Kifayatullah, if a Muslim doctor says that the patient can be saved only by taking alcohol one may take it, but not if a non-Muslim doctor says so.[62] For the same reason when, for instance, the husband has deserted the wife, the marriage can be dissolved by approaching a Muslim judge; if it has been dissolved by the order of a non-Muslim judge, then the dissolution should be done by a panchayat of Muslims also; only then will the woman be free.[63] On matters involving Muslims, the ulema often strike down decisions of panchayats which had among their members some non-Muslims also. As they hold kafirs to be untrustworthy, they rule that the evidence of a kafir is not to be taken into account.[64]

What holds for a thing like medicine applies a fortiori for more substantial questions like property, inheritance, and of course marriage. The reading of the nature and malevolence of the kafirs having been presented for centuries as springing from the Quran itself, the premises and the rules which follow from it have been at the root of the demands and campaigns of the ulema throughout. They form the basis of a vital plank of their platform today.

As the confidence of fundamentalists has gathered strength in the last few years, the ulema have declared their determination to set up 'shariah courts'—outside and parallel

---

62. *Mufti Kifayatullah ke Fatawi,* Volume II, p. 211.

63. Ibid., Volume VI, pp. 134, 134–35.

64. For instance, a husband pronounces talaq; the only witness is a woman who happens to be a kafir; has the divorce taken place?, asks the querist. 'He (the husband) should search his heart,' decrees the fatwa, 'and ask whether he gave it. For Allah knows what is in the heart'—this is standard for, as we see elsewhere, everything is made to turn on the ex post facto statement of the husband. The fatwa adds, 'The word of the *Kafir* is by its very basis not reliable.' *Fatawa-i-Rizvia,* Volume III, p. 621.

to the normal system of courts which administers the law of the land. Only one who is not acquainted with the fatwas, with the world view and psychology underlying them, only one who is ignorant of the conviction which permeates them—about the untrustworthiness and unfitness of non-believers—will be surprised at the current campaign of the ulema. For the campaign is not fortuitous: it is a continuation of course of the politics of separateness; but it is more, it is a reflection of, a translation into practice of, a device to further reinforce the psychology which the fatwas have dinned into the community over the centuries. It is this psychology, not just etymology which leads the *Standard Twentieth Century Dictionary, Urdu into English*, to set out the meaning of *Hunood* as: 'Hindu: Slave Thief Adj. Black'; and of *Hindustani* as, inter alia, 'Basic Urdu....bastard form of Urdu written for Sanskrit script'.[65]

But it would be, to risk a malapropism, sacrilegious for a secularist to see any of this.

One final inference before we proceed.

Double standards

As the non-believers have been misled by Allah Himself, a corollary follows necessarily: it is but right that believers and non-believers should be treated unequally. Allah Himself says in the Quran (35.9):

> Shall he, the evil of whose deeds are so tricked out to him that he deemeth them good, be treated like him who seeth things aright? Verily, Allah misleadeth whom He will, and guideth whom He will. Spend not thy soul in sighs for them; Allah knoweth their doings.

---

65. *Standard Twentieth Century Dictionary, Urdu into English*, compiled by Professor Bashir Ahmed Qureshi, revised and enlarged by Dr Abdul Haq, Educational Publishing House, Delhi, 1995, p. 678.

The fatwas reflect this belief in double standards.

The differential attitude to conversion and apostasy illustrates this vividly. Islam regards it as a right and duty to convert persons from other religions. The ulema vehemently insist on it. Now, when a man converts to Islam, he is renouncing his original religion; from the point of view of his original religion, therefore, he is an apostate. But no Muslim cleric would countenance even for a moment the proposition that the authorities of that other religion have any right to punish the convert. On the other hand, if a Muslim converts back to his original religion, the ulema insist that the punishment is death—where they cannot enforce this penalty because the state is not under Islamic rule they insist that all Muslims must completely severe all connection with him.[66]

Exactly the same position holds in regard to doing something or refraining from doing something out of regard for the other person's religious sentiments. If we read the Urdu papers, at every turn they declare that such and such measure or statement must be taken back, that an apology must be tendered because the measure or statement has hurt the *mazhabi jazbat* of the Muslims. By contrast, as we have seen, the fatwas declare again and again that to do anything out of regard for the religious sentiments of non-believers, or to refrain from doing something—for instance, slaughtering cows—out of regard for the religious sentiments of kafirs is kufr, it is to strengthen the kafirs in their kufr, it is to help 'demolish Islam'.

In exactly the same way to help in any way whatsoever in constructing a temple for instance—by making a donation, by

66. For the verdict that the apostate ought to be killed, *Fatawa Dar al-Ulum, Deoband,* Volume XII, p. 438; for the verdict that the apostate would be killed but for the fact that India is not an Islamic state, *Mufti Kifayatullah ke Fatawi,* Volume IX, pp. 359–61; for the verdict that Muslims must not maintain any contact with him, *Fatawa Dar al-Ulum,* Volume XII, p. 342; also *Fatawa-i-Rizvia,* Volume VI, p. 487.

making a sculpture, by contributing materials—is, as we have seen, kufr. But if a Hindu contributes money or materials or land towards the construction of a mosque, the aid can be taken. There are caveats of course, but they further substantiate the point about double standards. The question of whether or not one may accept contributions or material for a mosque from a Hindu is ever so often considered together with whether or not one may accept contributions from a prostitute, whether or not a mosque constructed by either becomes a mosque. Often the fatwas urge that wherever possible one should do without the contribution of Hindus: the reasons are practical, not, as they were in regard to the prohibition against helping construct a temple, religious. In the latter case the reason is that one would be furthering kufr. But in regard to avoiding the help offered by a Hindu, even where it is voluntarily offered and offered out of a feeling of brotherhood, the reason given is that people might say that Muslims do not have even this much devotion for their religion that they are not able to raise enough from among themselves even for a mosque; second, that accepting that help may lead to disputes about ownership; third, that while a mosque is a place of worship of Allah, the money may have been earned and the materials acquired in a way which is haram. Devices are therefore suggested: for instance, if it is thought necessary to accept the contribution it would be better if the Hindu were to assign the money or materials to a Muslim, and the Muslim were to give it for the construction of a mosque.[67]

An even more vivid instance is the stance in regard to the continuation of religious practices. It is the right and duty of a Muslim to carry on his religious rituals. Where the state is an

67. The subject is often pronounced upon, a number of eamples can be given. See, for instance, *Fatawa Ahl-i-Hadis*, Volume II, pp. 37–40, 46–49; *Mufti Kifayatullah ke Fatawi*, Volume VII, pp. 72–81; *Fatawa-i-Rizvia*, Volume VI, pp. 396, 460, 479.

Islamic one, to enable Muslims, and to get them to observe these rituals is, in the eyes of the ulema, one of its primary duties. Where the state is not an Islamic one, they do not countenance the slightest restriction being placed on Muslims observing any of their rituals: till just fifty or sixty years ago, for instance, there was a ferocious controversy among the ulema over whether or not a loudspeaker could be used in a mosque—for the azan, for the prayers, for the khutba; that there was such an intense controversy and till so recently shows that the practice of using loudspeakers is not a practice essential to the practice of Islam, no more than it is an essential practice for a religious procession to traverse a particular route in a crowded city; but the slightest attempt to regulate these in the interests of peace—of mind or body—is bound to be denounced as an intolerable interference in the practice of Islam. But the same ulema think it entirely natural that in an Islamic state adherents of other faiths should not be allowed to carry on their practices.

Under no circumstances can the Islamic ruler give permission to kafirs to continue their religious rites, declares the *Fatawa-i-Rizvia,* and asks: shall he permit them to practise their kufr and thereby himself become a kafir? Shall the ruler not even raise an objection to their doing things which are forbidden by Islam, to say nothing of his saying, 'Yes, do such things'?[68]

---

68. *Fatawa-i-Rizvia,* Volume VI, p. 4. What holds for states holds for homes too. A Hindu servant is working in the house of a Muslim. The servant says his prayers and during the ritual blows the conch. Is the Muslim who allows this to be done a kafir? Not a kafir but certainly a sinner, says the *Fatawa-i-Rizvia,* because to put down deniers is a duty incumbent upon Muslims. The duty has to be discharged according to one's capacity: if the Muslim cannot stop his servant from blowing the conch, he can at least dismiss the servant from his service, declares the fatwa. And to keep such a person who carries on his idolatry in a Muslim's house!, it exclaims. Curse upon him who gives shelter to a person who is a sinner in shariah, it pronounces: *Fatawa-i-Rizvia,* Volume IX, Book I, p. 169.

It adds that there are several Hadis to the effect that no non-Muslim should remain in the Arab island. And the purpose of the Hadis and the ordinances of shariah is that no non-Muslim should stay or stay for long in the Arab island, it says without any compunction. If someone comes for trade or special work, he should finish that and leave. Manifestly no one shall be allowed to stay for up to one year. And again it cites the *Durr-ul-Mukhtar....*[69]

So, no non-Muslim shall be allowed to stay in the Arab island, but if a Bangladeshi who has entered India illegally is asked to leave, that is an assault on Islam!

Similarly, even today in no Islamic state can teachers in a school impart religious education of their faith to non-Muslim children—and this is but a particular application of the principle enunciated above, namely that to allow teachers to impart to Hindu students learning from the Upanishads or Gita would be to promote kufr, it would be to wean the students on the wrong faith, to fortify them on the road of error. The converse—that for the same reason a non-Muslim state may put restrictions on imparting Quranic education to students—is rejected with force and vehemence as intolerable.

No restriction can be tolerated on teaching of the Quran and on religious instruction, declares Kifayatullah. The query related to a move to have teachers fill in bonds to the effect that they would not impart Quranic or religious instruction without the permission of government; if they did so, the bond would be forfeited. No non-Muslim state has the power that it should be able to stop Muslims from receiving religious instruction, Kifayatullah rules. It is wrong to stop religious instruction because of such an ordinance, the Mufti declares. The teacher who accepts this order and does not express his indignation against it is not fit to be imam or

69. *Fatawa-i-Rizvia,* Volume VI, p. 5.

guide of Muslims. To seek permission for fulfilling one's duty is unprincipled, says the Mufti. Were such a thing to be done, tomorrow permission will have to be sought for namaz also.[70] The next step is but the logical sequel: a Muslim may do vis-à-vis a non-Muslim what he may not do vis-à-vis a Muslim. This extends even to day-to-day commercial transactions. The kafirs of Hindustan, declares the *Fatawa-i-Rizvia,* are not zimmis. Zimmis are those kafirs who live in an Islamic state by submitting to Islam, and who pay jazia. Commercial relations with the real kafirs are proper, in fact even those transactional relationships which are improper when entered into with Muslims and zimmis, it declares, are proper when done with real kafirs and non-zimmis—with the caveat that they should not entail a breach of promise, for that is absolutely haram in all circumstances. The fact that the kafirs of Hindustan are not zimmis, far from entailing a prohibition against commercial relations with them, is a facilitation, says the *Fatawa-i-Rizvia*[71]—that is, it gives one all the more latitude in entering into such dealings as yield an advantage to the community.

It is well known that Muslims are strictly prohibited from taking interest. Insurance also has been prohibited—it has been held to be a form of *jua, of* gambling; and to take insurance has been held to reflect lack of faith in Allah.

But even as much of a purist as Mufti Kifayatullah holds that while a Muslim may never charge interest from a Muslim, as India is Dar-ul-harb, it is proper for Muslims to charge interest from kafirs though, as some ulema feel that India is not Dar-ul-harb, one must 'exercise caution' while taking interest; that while it is proper to take interest from kafirs, it would be best to give the proceeds to the poor and to students. On some occasions the thing that makes a difference is that the ones from

70. *Mufti Kifayatullah ke Fatawi,* Volume IX, p. 316.

71. *Fatawa-i-Rizvia,* Volume VI, pp. 5–6.

whom it is being charged are kafirs; on others that the country is not under Islamic rule; on still others the argument is pragmatic: as the British are in power at the time, Kifayatullah adds the further argument that leaving the interest in the banks or post offices, for instance, enables the government to reap huge profits, and these, says Kifayatullah, it distributes to missionaries who in turn use it to the detriment of Muslims and Islam.[72]

Similarly, the Mufti condemns insurance as jua. But as India is Dar-ul-harb, he rules, if the insurance company is owned wholly by *Harbi* kafirs—that is kafirs who stay in the Dar-ul-harb—and if Muslims can reap advantage from taking insurance from it, insurance can be permissible. In reality, life insurance is najaiz, improper, the Mufti reiterates, but on the principle that this is Dar-ul-harb, to reap any profit or advantage from a Harbi Kafir is permissible. That to take out insurance is to gamble is stated again and again by the Mufti, but in a Dar-ul-harb, he declares, it is permissible for Muslims to obtain advantage from kafirs even by gambling. Therefore if Muslims gain some advantage from kafirs through insurance, there is no objection. Not only may Muslims take out insurance as individuals, if by forming an insurance company Muslims gain some advantage—that is, they gain some amount from kafirs—then that too will be jaiz, rules the Mufti. In the same way, he says, one may take commission from an insurance company of kafirs.[73]

---

72. *Mufti Kifayatullah ke Fatawi,* Volume I, pp. 21–22; Volume VIII, pp. 48–49, 50,51, 54, 59, 60–61, 62–63; Volume IX, p. 328. Some of these rulings are taken up in the following chapter.

73. Ibid., Volume VIII, pp. 67, 69–72. When querists ask—What are the rules of shariah by which you have justified insurance?—Kifayatullah quickly retraces his steps, and asserts that in fact he has *not* justified insurance, that all he has said is that those ulema who hold India to be Dar-ul-harb have scope for justifying it! Of course he glosses over the fact that he

And yet if we were to go by secularist discourse there is no religion which has abolished distinctions as Islam has, there is no religion which treats all equally as Islam does!

has himself been pronouncing India to be Dar-ul-harb: see *Mufti Kifayatullah ke Fatawi*, Volume VIII, pp. 72–73.

5

Khilafat, Independence, and After

The overriding commitment to Islam, to aggrandizing Muslim power, the implications that flow from the inherent superiority of believers, the inherent impurity of kafirs, their inherent untrustworthiness, their sole and perpetual aim of doing the believers in—all these remained the pivots of fierce controversies throughout the country's struggle for freedom.

Several of the ulema had intense hatred of the British. They looked upon the British as usurpers, as the ones who had demolished and then replaced Islamic rule in India. Worse, the British were seen as the harbingers of 'westernization' and 'modernization' which were enticing the faithful away from Islamic ways and mores. Many of the ulema were therefore active in igniting the people against the British in the nineteenth century.[1]

Sir Syed and others thought this policy to be ruinous for Muslims. Three years after the 1857 uprising, Sir Syed published his famous tract, *The Loyal Mohammedans of India*. He sought to establish in it that Muslims had in fact stood by the British rulers. When the evidence is examined, he wrote, 'then will one glorious fact stand out in prominent relief and

1. I.H. Qureshi, *Ulema in Politics*, Karachi, 1972, Renaissance Publishing House, Delhi, 1985, is a fulsome account of their activities in this regard.

become patent to the universe'—namely that 'if in Hindustan there was one class of people above any other, who from the principles of their religion, from habits and associations, and from kindred disposition, were fast bound with Christians, in their dread hour of trial and danger, in the bonds of amity and friendship, those people were the Mohammedans, and they alone....' 'I really do not see that any class besides the Mohammedans displayed so much single-minded and earnest devotion to the interests of government or so willingly sacrificed reputation and status, life and property, in their cause....' '.... It is to the Mohammedans alone that the credit belongs of having stood as the staunch and unshaken friends of the government amidst that fearful tornado that devastated the country, and shook the Empire to its centre; and who were ever ready, heart in hand, to render their aid to the utmost extremity, or cheerfully to perish in the attempt, regardless of home and kindred, of life and its enjoyments....'

Yes, a few *badmash*es had joined the general madness, he acknowledged. Sir Syed was unequivocal in denouncing them, in declaring that they were neither representative of Muslim sentiment nor indeed men of religion:

> Be it known however that I am no advocate of those Mohammedans who behaved undutifully, and joined in the Rebellion: on the contrary I hold their conduct in utter abhorrence, as being in the highest degree criminal, and wholly inexcusable; because at that momentous crisis it was imperatively their duty, a duty enjoined by the precepts of our religion, to identify themselves heartily with the Christians and to espouse their cause; seeing that they have, like ourselves, been favoured with a revelation from Heaven, and believe in the Prophets, and hold sacred the word of God in His holy book, which is also an object of faith with us. It was therefore needful and proper, that where the blood of Christians was spilt, there

> should also have mingled with it that of Mohammedans; and those who shrunk from manifesting such devotedness, and sided with the rebels wilfully disobeyed the injunctions of religion, besides proving themselves ungrateful to their salt, and thereby incurring the severe displeasure of Government, a fact that is patent to every peasant....

Those who aroused the people by virtue of being maulvis, he wrote, were not men of religion at all:

> Among the scum of the people who were upheaved to the surface amidst the convulsions into which the country was thrown, it is remarkable how many there were who were styled Moulvies; and yet they were merely ignorant and besotted scoundrels, who had no just claim to the appellation, which may have been given to them by courtesy only, because some of their ancestors may have been Moulvies. The fellows were alluded to in the public prints as really what they professed to be, and, having assumed high-sounding and inflated names to give themselves the prestige of learned Moulvies and holy Fuqeers, it was natural that the authorities should be misled into the belief that men of note and influence were implicated in the rebellion, as its promoters and leaders. The fact is, however, that not one of these individuals was looked up to as a Pastor or spiritual guide; on the contrary, they were of no repute whatever, and were heartily despised by all good Mohammedans, who had penetrated the character of these lowbred pseudo-Moulvies. Those who were really learned and pious Moulvies and Durveshes kept aloof, and did not pollute themselves by the smallest degree of complicity in the rebellion, which they utterly denounced and condemned as infamous and criminal in the extreme. With one solitary exception I do not find that any learned and influential Moulvie took any part in the rebellion. I know not what possessed him to act in the way he did, but

> his understanding must have been warped; and we know that 'to err is human'.....[2]

Inculcating loyalty to the British was accordingly one of the declared objectives of the Anglo-Oriental College which Sir Syed set up, strengthening the foundations of British rule was the central objective of the Indian Patriotic Association which he set up. He vehemently opposed the nascent Congress and poured sarcasm at persons like Justice Faiz Badruddin Tyabji for encouraging Muslims to participate in its sessions. He stoutly opposed every demand for democratization as well as for freedom from British rule on the ground that both of these would cause Muslims to drown in the sea of Hindus.

This dissonance between the two approaches continued right up to the exit of the British—with one addition, and that was the attitude of different sections of the ulema to the demand for Pakistan.

All were agreed that there could be only one legitimate objective: furtherance of the interests of Islam as a religion and of Muslims as a community. Differences arose because of different assessments about which course would best subserve the interests of Islam and of Muslims: the continuance of British rule felt some, driving out the British declared others; formation of an out-and-out Islamic country in one part of the subcontinent felt some, keeping the subcontinent united and re-extending the sway of Islam over the whole of it felt others. There were further subdivisions: those who agreed among themselves that the British ought to be driven out disagreed over the way this ought to be done—Muslims should strive

2. For these and other representative passages see 'The Gloss-over School', in Arun Shourie, *Indian Controversies, Essays on Religion in Politics*, ASA Publications, New Delhi, 1993, pp. 103–45.

alone to do so felt some, there is no alternative to joining hands with kafirs for the purpose felt others.

The debates were indeed intense. And the way they are presented today depends a great deal on the scholar's vantage point: I.H. Qureshi writing from Pakistan focuses on the ulema whose activities, exhortations and religious arguments strengthened the movement for partitioning the country; Muslim scholars like Mushirul Hasan writing in India are at pains to focus attention on ulema associated with Jamiat-ul-Ulama-i-Hind, etc., who joined the general struggle for Independence for a united India. It is a fascinating story, but pursuing it will take us too far afield. For purposes of our present concern its interest is twofold. First, as the reference points for the debate among the ulema were 'religious', the debate helps us see what 'religious' arguments each side mustered to fortify its position. The second point is even more specific, and in view of the theme of this chapter that is the one we will focus on here.

The point arose from a fortuitous circumstance: the main struggle for Independence for a united India was being led by Mahatma Gandhi, a kafir, indeed one who was devoutly steeped in and doggedly sticking to kufr. When the movement for creating a separate Islamic state—Pakistan—gathered momentum, that movement was being led by Mohammed Ali Jinnah, a Shia. In the reckoning of ulema like Mufti Kifayatullah, Shias, though thoroughly misguided, were still an Islamic group. The trouble however was that Jinnah was not even adhering to Shi'ite norms—indeed he was quite ostentatious in parading his disregard for what in the eyes of the ulema were essentials of Islam. On the other hand, several of the ulema— all the Barelvis, for instance—had declared time and again that Shias were no longer Muslims at all. The choice thus became between following an out-and-out kafir—Mahatma Gandhi—and following one who was in the reckoning of many a murtad, an apostate, and, even in the reckoning of others, one who was only nominally a Muslim.

The fatwas which the Muftis and Maulanas hurled at each other help explicate the general principles we have been considering. The attitude to kafirs, the circumstances in which and the purposes for which Muslims may work with them—all these questions are discussed threadbare. The picture which emerges is far from reassuring: even those ulema, for instance, who exhorted Muslims to join hands with Hindus did so on grounds which reinforce the apprehensions that emerge from studying the foregoing material.

Mufti Kifayatullah

Mufti Kifayatullah was among the staunchest advocates of joining hands with Hindus to throw the British out. He supported the Khilafat movement as well as several other campaigns. Maulana Ahmad Riza Khan, on the other hand, opposed every activity in which believers would willy-nilly have to join hands with kafirs, in which they would—even for a moment and even for attaining an Islamic objective—have to accept the leadership of a kafir. A few representative fatwas of the two will therefore give us glimpses of both sets of positions.

If someone follows Gandhi, is he a kafir'?, Mufti Kifayatullah is asked. To call a Muslim a 'kafir' on political grounds is very wrong, the Mufti rules. If someone is with Gandhiji in a political programme, and keeps his religion and beliefs in tact then there is no violation of shariah. The Muslim who accuses another Muslim of being a kafir and says that your fate shall be the same as the fate of Gandhi—as Maulana Ahmad Riza Khan was incessantly doing in regard to any Muslim who even associated with kafirs—it is about his own iman that such a person should worry. Of course if one believes in Islam but does not affirm it publicly, then he is not a Muslim.[3]

But he—Gandhi—says he conducts his politics in accordance with an 'inner voice', and this 'voice' is not Islam, the critics pointed out; he is giving a particular religious colour to politics, they pointed out. Gandhi can try to colour those who are from his religion in his own colour, Kifayatullah explains, non-Hindus are not influenced by those beliefs. Not for a second is non-violence obeyed by or acceptable to Muslims as a religious injunction or belief, he declares. It has been accepted for the time being in these times of helplessness as a provisional policy, and there is no prohibition in shariah against doing so, the Mufti rules. As for Gandhi keeping fasts, as for his keeping fasts of silence, and the claim that he is in touch with Khuda, these, Kifayatullah explains, are his personal actions. Muslims have nothing to do with such actions of his. One can have joint action with an individual or organization for the political objective of throwing out an alien power. One can have joint action with an individual or organization that is acquainted with the strategies for attaining this political objective, only to the extent of the political requirements of that objective. The person or organization does not have any significance other than this, Kifayatullah—the advocate of working with and under the leadership of Gandhi—explains. To cooperate with Hindus, he explains alluding to the Quranic prohibition, is not to take them into confidence. It is just akin to Hindus and Muslims of a *mohalla* joining hands to throw out thieves. As for Gandhi's spirituality, after Islam, Kifayatullah writes, and apart from Islam there can be no other spiritual or religious

---

3. *Mufti Kifayatullah ke Fatawi,* Volume I, pp. 61–62.

movement from the point of view of Muslims, nor can there be any other movement for the eventual betterment of Muslims. Kifayatullah repeatedly draws attention to the example of the Prophet himself: on occasions he took the help of kafirs—the Jews—on others he refused it and instead destroyed them; on other occasions still the Prophet took the help of one set of kafirs to destroy another group of kafirs. His decision thus varied with time and circumstances.[4]

That is the essential point: our sole objective is to advance the interests of Islam and of Muslims; today, Kifayatullah stresses, the principal danger to them comes from the foreign power; unfortunately Muslims cannot drive it out acting by themselves; therefore, as a temporary expedient Muslims should engage in joint action with Hindus; of course, such cooperation does not mean, it should not mean that we take them into our confidence, nor that we befriend them. Kifayatullah sees and presents Gandhiji as a leader who knows what strategies to adopt in the given circumstances. Of course, Gandhi is in religious terms a kafir, he acknowledges, and shall remain so until he embraces Islam.

His objections to Jinnah and the Muslim League were also strictly strategic. Jinnah and the League are not the instruments for furthering the interests of Muslims, he stresses repeatedly, drawing oblique attention to the waywardness of Jinnah. And his objection to the demand for Pakistan was not that India is one and ought not be partitioned: his objection, as we shall see, was that by creating Pakistan its advocates would be confining the sway of Islam to a corner of the subcontinent and thus foreclosing the opportunities for acquiring hegemony over the whole of the subcontinent.

The freedom movement of Hindustan, he declares, is a

---

4. The points are reiterated many times. For instance, *Mufti Kifayatullah ke Fatawi*, Volume IX, pp. 407–11.

patriotic movement. It is incumbent upon every patriotic Hindustani to join it.[5]

In Hindustan a foreign (British) government is reigning, he writes. It has inflicted limitless harm on Hindustanis in general and Muslims in particular. When the residents of this land struggle to secure Independence from this foreign government, it becomes a duty incumbent on Muslims as much as on non-Muslims to join the movement. And till the entire population of Hindustan joins this movement for Independence, success is not likely. Therefore, he says, it is necessary for Muslims to work along with the qaumi *majlis*, Congress, in political matters. A Muslim can remain pious even by being in the Congress, he writes. The Jamiat-ul-Ulama-i-Hind has worked on this principle, he explains. But along with doing so, he continues, for their own qaumi and religious life it is necessary for Muslims to strive to strengthen their own internal organization and collective strength. And for these purposes the Jamiat-ul-Ulama-i-Hind is available.[6]

Again and again querists and critics confronted the Mufti with the ayats of the Quran in which believers are prohibited from befriending the kafirs, in which they are warned that kafirs wish nothing but harm to the faithful. The purport of the ayat, the Mufti explained, is that it is not right to strike friendship with kafirs with the object of gaining honour in this world. But if the object is to safeguard Din, and that object can be secured only by joint action with kafirs—as distinct from friendship with or affection for them—then such joint action is not covered by the prohibition in the ayat. It is another thing, rules Kifayatullah using the sort of sleight of terms so typical of the subtle, if by the nature of that joint action worldly advantage may also be attained.

5. Ibid., Volume IX, p. 382.

6. Ibid., Volume IX, p. 382, 387–88.

When Muslims have the power to confront and defend themselves in the face of the enemy then, the moderate Kifayatullah declares, without doubt it is not proper to take the help of kafirs. However, at a time when a non-Muslim power is out to destroy Muslims, it is not a hukum of shariah that you should allow yourself to be destroyed but not save yourself through joint action with kafirs.

Religion is wholly politics of shariah, and politics of shariah is wholly religion, Kifayatullah goes on to say. Changes in the politics of shariah will be in accordance with religion and to the extent that the Quran and Hadis permit... There is no prohibition in shariah against joining non-Muslims to fight for Independence.... If a village is attacked by dacoits, Muslims can certainly protect themselves and others through joint action with non-Muslims.

Moreover, as Hindustan is the country of Muslims also, occupation of it by the British is not right even by Muslims. Thus when a struggle for Independence is launched it becomes a duty incumbent upon Muslims also to join it: that Hindus should struggle to make their land free and Muslims should leave their land in the occupation of a foreign power should be a matter of shame and humiliation for Muslims, Kifayatullah declares.

But even if this be the case, the critics and querists asked, why should Muslims not join and work through the Muslim League? Why should they cooperate with, much less join the Congress? If it is the object of the Muslim League also, Kifayatullah explains, that it shall sacrifice life and property to free Hindustan, then the object is very correct and right. And if men of wisdom and sound opinion conclude that the League alone can secure Independence then, without doubt, it is incumbent upon Muslims to join the League and not cooperate with the Congress. But then a question will come up before

Muslims: if Muslims, who in numbers and education and wealth are weak and just one-third of Hindus can remove the English alone, then why cannot the twenty-four crore Hindus—who are thrice the number of Muslims, and much stronger than even that much in education and wealth—banish the British on their own?

Hence, Kifayatullah concludes, cooperation with Hindus is for reaching our own destination, it is for the attainment of our own objective. In fighting for Independence the other communities are also discharging their obligation towards the country.[7]

In Muslim affairs it is not right to accept the leadership of a non-Muslim, Kifayatullah declares. However, out of some necessity to accept the leadership of a non-Muslim, or to work in association with non-Muslims in political or economic matters is not forbidden, he writes. He cites the sorts of situations in which this is unavoidable: to accept a non-Muslim as the chairman of a municipality or council, to accept the leadership of a non-Muslim officer in the police or armed forces, or the partnership of a non-Muslim in a shop, to obey the British government and its laws, to act on the advice of a non-Muslim doctor or hakim. In the same way, he says, it is right for Muslims to cooperate with others to banish British rule, to end the harm it is heaping on the Islamic world and on Islamic nations. For the protection of Islamic rights one can also join the Congress, he rules, as it is acting in the national interest and working to rid the country of foreign rule.[8]

Congress is a political party, he stresses in the face of fatwas asking Muslims to shun it, not a religious institution. And the Constitution which prevails and, in the view of the progressive, will prevail in Hindustan will be democratic. In it each qaum will get a share proportionate to its population. Either Muslims should not participate in the struggle for freedom and

---

7. *Mufti Kifayatullah ke Fatawi*, Volume IX, pp. 389–91, 391–92, 397.

8. Ibid., Volume IX, pp. 393–94.

declare that the subordination or slavery of British rule is acceptable to them, or they should declare that they shall by their own efforts set up a permanent Islamic state, or they should participate in the Congress assuming a befitting share of the work. They can do so as individuals or as a collectivity, the latter would be better. In either case participation should be wholehearted, Kifayatullah says. It should not be that at the time of doing things they sit away, and then for seeking their share they put out their hands.[9]

Can one follow Jinnah, a Shia, or Gandhi, a Hindu?, Kifayatullah is asked. Shias are a sect of Islam, he says. Several sects of the Shias are out of Islam, he acknowledges, but even so they are counted to be within Islam. Their status is like that of the other Ahl-i-Kitab, the People of the Book—namely Jews and Christians. The leader or guide of Muslims should be a follower of the shariah and of the injunctions of Islam—which Jinnah was manifestly not. But if, adds the ever-practical Kifayatullah, by misfortune such a person is not around, or by their misfortune Muslims do not recognize him or cannot make him their leader, then the leadership of some political leader is permissible, whether Jinnah or Gandhi, provided the political guidance of such a leader is useful and sound.[10]

Muslim League has no practical programme for the attainment of Freedom, Kifayatullah explains. If only one could have expected some useful and effective action from the Muslim League, he writes, then certainly the advice would have been to join it. Congress is an active organization, and if Muslims join it in sufficient numbers they will be able to protect their rights also.[11]

9. Ibid., Volume IX, pp. 395–96.

10. Ibid., Volume IX, p. 398.

11. Ibid., Volume IX, pp. 397, 399.

The controversy continued throughout the freedom struggle. At each turn it would flare up. Posters would appear taunting Kifayatullah, Abdul Bari and others—their fatwas would be lampooned, and contrasted with the plain and manifest meaning of the ayats of the Quran. Kifayatullah's fatwas in response to the often hostile and acerbic questioning of the League's supporters take up over a hundred pages of closely packed text. He held on to his position.

Many of the fatwas merely keep reiterating a few basic points. Even so it will be well worth our while to follow them for a while—the questions which are asked, the terms in which he justifies his position, what he says about the Congress, about the Muslim League, about Gandhiji and Jinnah is most instructive. Each of these—the questions, the answers, and the arguments—gives us a glimpse of the mindset of the community, of the notions which had been drilled into it, notions which it had internalized. They also enable us to see the values and objectives of the moderate, the 'nationalist' among the ulema.

Why does the Jamiat-ul-Ulama-i-Hind object to the Muslim League when the latter is trying to unite and organise Muslims and when it has also—this is in 1939—declared itself for complete Independence?, Kifayatullah is asked in a typical question. The majority of Muslim Leaguers consider British rule to be the shadow of Khuda's beneficence, Kifayatullah opines, and they want to take shelter in the cloak of the British. They support the British Empire and they strengthen the foundations of British power. They do not only support capitalism, they want to establish capitalism as the permanent system. They do no concrete work for the qaum. In fact they make office in and membership of the Muslim League an instrument of prestige and glory, and through these they acquire lofty decorations from the rulers. True, the League has proclaimed complete Independence to be its goal. It has also admitted that Muslims cannot attain complete Independence alone. In spite of this it does not adopt the way to freedom: viz, Hindu-Muslim unity. In these circumstances, what should we take their declaration for Independence to be except a fraud?, asks Kifayatullah.[12]

But can the Jamiat-ul-Ulama-i-Hind not clean up the Muslim League by joining it?, the Mufti is asked. Experience has proven, Kifayatullah responds, that it is impossible to cleanse the Muslim League of deniers (munkirs of Islam) by joining it. Today, according to the League 90 per cent Muslims are in the League. Have these 90 per cent Muslims been able to remove even one munkir from the League? It is said that 80 per cent of the ulema are also with the League. But do these 80 per cent of ulema have any influence on the League? If they have then it is that from the platforms of the League there is a mighty effort to destroy the influence of ulema and to humiliate and denigrate them. Instead, the faithful are asked to follow an individual, Kifayatullah declares.

The Congress is a composite organization. Remaining steadfast on their religion, Muslims can join Congress. Alluding to Jinnah with the indirectness so typical of him, Kifayatullah says that many among non-Congressi Muslims are indifferent to Islam and are lovers of Western education and European civilization. By being Congressi the Congressi-Muslims are not distancing themselves from Islam as the lovers of European civilization non-Congressi Muslims are.[13]

But does it not happen that differences between the Muslim League and the Jamiat divide and harm Muslims?, Kifayatullah is asked. Yes, it happens, it certainly happens, he replies. But on whom can the responsibility be fixed? On

12. Ibid., Volume IX, p. 405.

13. Ibid., Volume IX, p. 405.

the Muslim League alone. Because generally it incites Muslim masses against the ulema, it rakes up *fasads* of various kinds, it sets one against the other, and specifically against the Congressi-Muslims. Just recently papers have carried the statement of Mr Jinnah by which he has prohibited Muslim Leaguers from joining meetings of the Jamiat-ul-Ulama-i-Hind. From this statement you can get an idea of the mentality of the League's Qaid-i-Azam—of how in the name of unity he is creating differences and disruption among Muslims.[14]

When he is asked why Muslims should join the struggle for freedom which will give rulership to the majority, Kifayatullah asks in return: but is Muslim League striving to establish a pure Islamic state? It too has accepted the principle of joint rule in the Government of India Act of 1935 passed after the Round Table Conference. If the Hindus do not want to throw out the British then the Jamiat-ul-Ulama-i-Hind shall not undertake any joint action with them. This joint action is limited only to the purpose of weakening British power and to liberating Hindustan from Britishers.[15]

While Gandhiji was the problem for some, the progressive and secularist leaders in the Congress were a problem for others. What is the guarantee that Independence attained under the Congress will protect the rights and religion of Muslims, the querist asks, when its leaders think it reactionary even to take the name of religion, when they call it 'communalism'? Muslims can protect their religious and political rights by their own power and sacrifice, Kifayatullah writes, not by the pledges of the Congress or of the British.[16]

A non-Muslim says: disobey laws—so as to establish Ram Raj; a non-Muslim says wear khaddar, and a Muslim

14. Ibid., Volume IX, p. 406.
15. Ibid., Volume IX, p. 407.
16. Ibid., Volume IX, p. 407–17.

obeys him and feels proud of doing so, and asks other Muslims to do so and hates those who do not do so; a non-Muslim says do not pay tax on salt.... Is this how Muslims ought to conduct themselves?, the critic asks Kifayatullah.

The question should have been asked directly, admonishes Kifayatullah. That a foreign power has come from afar and conquered our country; it is exploiting and draining away its wealth; and all want to banish it...and a non-Muslim is showing the way to fight it and inspiring the people to battle... should such a person be followed? In Hindustan both nations live in accordance with their religious principles. Their first duty is to free their land from the forcible occupation of a foreign power. We should join hands with all to throw out this alien race from thousands of miles away. The responsibility for the oppression that follows is of the government, and not of the leader or group fighting for its rights. True, there are risks and dangers, but there is no other way. And those who die in this struggle shall be martyrs; to dub them suicides is strictly contrary to shariah, it is to spread ignorance.

He—Gandhi—has not given the advice of wearing khaddar out of his religious beliefs, but as a device to weaken the foreign power and strengthen the people. This is far more worthy of being adhered to than the orders which are obtained from non-Muslim rulers and courts, and which are implemented. In fact I feel, Kifayatullah goes on to say, that for Muslims khaddar is indeed the best clothing. Moreover, when the intention of the one who wears it is to benefit his brothers, then it is to kill two birds with one stone, and the rewards will be double. To dub this to be the conduct of the Gandhi-worshipping sect is beyond my comprehension, Kifayatullah writes. In fact, to call a Muslim who wears khaddar a Gandhi-worshipper is itself a great cruelty—because they are Muslims and the thought of worshipping any one but Khuda does not enter even their imagination. They are worshippers of Allah, not of even the Prophet. In spite of this to call them Gandhi-worshippers—what great audacity and arrogance it is, exclaims Kifayatullah.

Kifayatullah goes on to explain that while it is true that, not being a Muslim, Gandhi does not give his advice so as to implement the shariah, but every Muslim can also see that that advice is not contrary to the shariah—for example, when he says, 'Do not drink', he does not say it to implement shariah, but clearly what he is saying is in accord with shariah, and every Muslim should heed it.[17]

There had been much controversy among the ulema over whether Muslims, in particular the ulema themselves should join the Assemblies. Various arguments were pressed by those who opposed doing so—upon joining the Assemblies Muslim members will per force have to associate with kafirs, it was argued, in particular Muslim women members will have to associate with kafir males and Mussalmans with kafir women. Kifayatullah ruled that Muslims, in particular the ulema and shaikhs ought to join the Assemblies: it is necessary to see that the resolutions which are passed in these bodies accord with the shariah, he said. Accordingly he issued a fatwa to this effect. The fatwa is of particular interest as in it Kifayatullah explains the reason on account of which he and the Jamiat-ul-Ulama-i-Hind are opposed to the demand for Pakistan. In our view the demand for Pakistan is dangerous for Muslims, he declares, because neither is a real Pakistan being asked for nor is there any hope of getting it. What those who are asking for Pakistan are demanding amounts only to erasing the glory of Islam from all of Hindustan and confining it to a small part of it. And even in this part, he points out, a contrary national party—presumably,

17. Ibid., Volume IX, pp. 413–18.

Hindus—is present. Moreover, it also means cutting off the hands and feet of crores of Muslims in the remaining part, and, having done so, deserting them. For such a thing to happen is dangerous, Kifayatullah says, it is certainly dangerous.[18]

Another querist-cum-critic elicits an equally telling clarification. There are eighty-one sects among Muslims of India, the querist writes. If members of one of them desert and join hands with the enemies of Islam or create trouble for Muslims, then on the Day of Judgement will they be raised as Muslims or with the enemies of Muslims? On one side is Wardha, says the querist, and on the other is Kaba. To which side should Muslims go?

It is well known that he who befriends the enemies of Islam shall be one of them, begins Kifayatullah. But if to attain one's interest and object on some occasion he joins with the enemies of Islam—that will not be counted. Therefore, if there are two enemies, and to save oneself from the powerful one he derives strength from the weaker one, that also will not be counted.

In regard to the present movement, rules Kifayatullah, the analogy of Wardha and Kaba is not appropriate. It is a wrong accusation to say that Muslims are supporting Wardha. They are fighting for their own rights. Muslims on the one side desirous of rights are joining hands with another community desirous of rights. Muslims on the other side are, according to their claim, working separately. They too are not going to Kaba. The destination and object of both is the same, the paths differ.[19]

Neither Hindus nor the British are friends of Islam, Kifayatullah says, and between these two he who is more powerful is more harmful for Muslims[20]—a position which

18. Ibid., Volume IX, p. 422.
19. Ibid., Volume IX, pp. 422–23.
20. Ibid., Volume IX, pp. 423–24.

had one operational consequence in the situation prevailing before 1947, and has the opposite consequence today.

But according to shariah, the Mufti is asked, should the Muslim majority—the reference is to the Muslim League and its followers—join the Muslim minority—an euphemism for the Jamiat-ul-Ulama-i-Hind—or should the Muslim minority join the Muslim majority? The Mufti, who was confronted with questions of this sort continually, answers with the indirectness and skill for which he was so well known. The question of 'majority' or 'minority' depends on the strength of the argument, he says. If in the world the majority consists of polytheists, it will not be proper for Muslims to join them. And if the majority of even Muslims departs from truth, it shall be the duty of the minority which is on truth to continue to adhere to truth.[21]

Mr Jinnah is a Shia, a querist notes and asks: Is he a Muslim? Second, being a Muslim, can he protect the rights of Muslims better or Mr Gandhi, or the Congress president, or the Congressi-Hindus who are in a majority in the Congress Working Committee? Third, if Mr Mohammed All Jinnah says that I am a Muslim first and then a Hindustani, is this right, or is one first a Hindustani and then a Mussalman? Fourth, is Mr Jinnah an expert in the politics of Hind and law? The point of the last question was obviously the same as of the preceding ones: if Jinnah too is an expert on the politics of Hindustan and on law, why should he not be followed rather than that other expert—Gandhi?

Kifayatullah's answers are as telling as they are precise: (1) Generally, he says, I know that Mr Jinnah is a Shia, and Shias are a sect of Islam; (2) Compared to a Muslim, a non-Muslim cannot be acknowledged to be a defender of Muslim rights; (3) It is true that a Muslim is first a Muslim, and then a

21. Ibid., Volume IX, pp. 423–24.

Hindustani; (4) He—Jinnah—is an expert of politics and law.[22] But in the very next pronouncement Kifayatullah fastens caveats to the first and fourth answers.

What the real thoughts of Mr Jinnah are, I do not know in reality, Kifayatullah says as he is pressed again on the point. But that his apparent conduct is not like Islamic conduct is more evident than the sun. His being from the sect of Shias is also evident. He is an educated person, Kifayatullah acknowledges, only to add, his education and make-up are that of European education and civilization. His being apart from Islamic education and civilization is an open secret.

It is true that non-Muslims cannot be acknowledged to be defenders of Muslim interests, Kifayatullah affirms, only to ask: but which Muslim has proclaimed them to be so? In the Congress Muslims will protect the interests of Muslims by their own efforts. They do not want Hindus to protect Islamic rights.

He reiterates, it is true that a Muslim is first a Muslim and only then a Congressi—and adds—or a Muslim Leaguer, or anyone else.

Mr Jinnah is an expert in law, Kifayatullah acknowledges, only to add, but of English law, not of Islamic law. And of British politics, not Islamic politics. He has not even acquired elementary acquaintance with them, Kifayatullah concludes.[23]

Notice how much explaining the Mufti had to do for advocating a course which entailed joint action with Hindus; notice also the basic axioms to which even such a person subscribes—a Muslim is first a Muslim, the rights of Muslims as distinct from the rights of all Indians, a non-Muslim cannot be acknowledged to be the defender of Muslim rights, and the rest.

---

22. Ibid., Volume IX, pp. 427–28.

23. Ibid., Volume IX, pp. 427–28.

The controversy over Congress vis-à-vis the Muslim League, over Jinnah vis-à-vis Gandhi continued. Mufti Kifayatullah stresses more or less the same basic points again and again. But each reiteration brings out some particular facet of the basic axioms—on occasion his emphasis is on the manifest and literal meaning of the axioms, on others he tries to fudge what has been stated explicitly—formulations of the latter kind of course were the ones upon which the Barelvis and the League-ulema pounced, they traduced them in posters and pamphlets.

A querist reports that in Jinnah's reckoning the Quran is an old outdated book, that he slights individuals who are revered in Islamic lore, that he asks for liquor at parties, that he does not observe the namaz, etc. What is the hukum about following such a man? What is the hukum about him relative to following Gandhi?

The Mufti takes no view as to the veracity of the facts but he leaves no doubt about his assessment of Jinnah: his grouse is not that Jinnah is set on a course which will break the country; his grouse is that the man is not an orthodox Muslim. I do not know the beliefs of Mr Jinnah personally, he says, therefore it is difficult to give any hukum about him. But those who bring down the honour of Hazrat Sadiq, and Hazrat Umar, who do not observe the namaz, and, characterizing the Quran as an old book, proclaim that it is not right to act on it, who partake of liquor at parties—they are not Muslims in the eyes of Muslims. Quran is the Book of Allah and the eternal law of Islam to believe in which and to act by which is the most sacred duty in Islam. To take it as the torch of guidance, and to honour and glorify it is the foremost duty of Muslims.

He presses the point: for religious leadership of Muslims, the Muslim must be an expert of religious learning and of shariah; and for their leadership in legal and constitutional matters also that Muslim is better who conforms to the norms of Shariah—each of these clauses, as is clear, in an indictment of Jinnah.

Not just that: Kifayatullah stretches the point. To fortify his position he propounds a proposition which runs in the face of what so many legists have held the Quran to specify. He says, till Mahatma Gandhi adopts Islam, till then from the religious point of view in the eyes of Muslims he remains a non-Muslim: notice that in one sense the Mufti seems to be stating a mere truism, in another sense he is stating a vital axiom, that till Mahatma Gandhi accepts Islam in the eyes of Muslims his primary identity will be that he is a non-Muslim, that when they look at him that is what they will see. In the very next sentence, however, the Mufti introduces a distinction, one which runs in the face of what the Quran as well as Hadis have been held to mean. He says that from a moral point of view a non-Muslim can be superior to and better than a bad-charactered Muslim, though from a religious point of view a Muslim is in any case better than a non-Muslim: contrast what the Mufti is saying now when he is being pressed to justify his advocating joint action under Gandhiji's leadership with what he says elsewhere—that a Muslim is better than a non-Muslim; contrast it with the fatwa in *Fatawa-i-Rahimiyyah* that to say that non-Muslims are better than Muslims because, for instance, they live up to their promises better is kufr. The Mufti continues: but this—that from a moral point of view a non-Muslim may be better than a Muslim, but that from a religious point of view a Muslim is necessarily better than a non-Muslim—is not enough to prefer the Muslim for leadership. The conditions and attributes of leadership are themselves important. And he who is superior in them can have the right to lead.[24]

I do not know the personal thoughts and beliefs of Mr Jinnah,

24. Ibid., Volume IX, pp. 430–31.

Kifayatullah avers again. But he belongs to the Shia sect. And the beliefs of the Shias are different. Some of them are such that, in spite of their being misguided and wrongdoers, they can be termed Muslims. And some are such that they cannot be termed Muslims. For instance, those who look upon Hazrat Ali as a Prophet and recipient of Divine Revelation, or those who do not take the Quran to be right and perfect, etc.—Shias have their own views about the way the Quran and Hadis were compiled after the Prophet's death, about what was included and what was left out—they are not Muslims, although they are included among the misguided sects of Islam.

As Mr Mohammed Ali Jinnah is not acquainted with Islamic rights, and as he terms some Islamic principles to be wrong and ambiguous, to take him as the defender of Islamic rights is wrong, declares the Mufti—he is writing this in November 1945.

Nor can Mr Gandhi or any other non-Muslim be acknowledged as the defender of Muslim religious rights—the reader will notice the subtlety with which Kifayatullah introduces qualifying words sometimes and drops them at others: it is 'Muslim rights' at times, 'Islamic rights' at others, 'Muslim religious rights' at still others. Muslims can defend their rights themselves, he says, and they have a responsibility to do so. The Congress is an organization which is responsible for maintaining and defending the religious rights of its members. However, to defend and look after their rights is also the task of Muslims, and it is their duty also.

A Muslim is first a Muslim, the Mufti reiterates, and thereafter a Hindustani, an Arab or an Iranian. In other words, it is incumbent upon a Muslim, he says, to keep the thought of his religion supreme above all other right and proper thoughts.

And he returns to Jinnah: Mr Jinnah is an expert in English law and English politics, because he is concerned only with these and he has studied them. Islamic politics and Islamic law are different from these. True, Mr Jinnah is included in the Muslim qaum, he says a little later. But as he is from the Shia sect and as he is bound by Western civilization, he is to be thought of as a Muslim only in a formal sense.[25]

The Urdu press prints charges against persons like Kifayatullah for helping the kafirs in their kufr. It confronts them with the ayat of the Quran in which Allah admonishes the faithful not to be with the kafirs. The question of helping the kafirs would arise only if we act in accordance with their kufr, responds Kifayatullah. As far as Muslims are concerned, he affirms, they want their independence and the superiority of their own religion. And they want to liberate the country from their opponents (that is, the British). In this the Congress is of one mind with them; therefore, they can work jointly with it.[26]

Pressed again, Kifayatullah points to the circumstance in which Muslims are placed. Foreigners will think of only their own interest, he says referring to the British. It is beyond our power to undo the fact that the Hindus are in a majority. Muslims should liberate the country and then live by coming to an agreement—with the Hindus presumably. That is why the Jamiat prefers to vote jointly with the Congress—the question at that time pertained to voting. The League has not done anything, nor is there any hope that it will do anything by opposing the government. Therefore, it is not right to support it.[27]

Muslims get taken in by the name, he says, of the Muslim

---

25. Ibid., Volume IX, pp. 432, 446.
26. Ibid., Volume IX, pp. 433–34.
27. Ibid., Volume IX, pp. 435–36.

League, and they do not see that it is a great impediment to Hindustan's Independence.[28]

Muslims should work for their religious benefit, the Mufti affirms in a compact statement of his position, not for helping any kafir. But the politics of Hindustan has become such, he says, that till Muslims and non-Muslims work together it cannot be unravelled. The Muslims alone cannot remove the British, and the non-Muslims too cannot by themselves expel them. Only by Muslims and non-Muslims working together is there any hope that they may succeed. Moreover, great benefit will accrue if the power of the British is reduced. Therefore, Muslims should adopt the way which leads to Independence. In doing so there is no pressure from Hindus, nor does it amount to working for the benefit of Hindus.[29]

But are they not kafirs and polytheists?, the critics ask. Is it right to work with kafirs and polytheists? The Hindus and the Ahl-i-Kitab are both kafirs and polytheists, Kifayatullah reminds the critics. As the material forces are these days mostly in the hands of the Ahl-i-Kitab, they are the more harmful. The critic had taken the names of several leaders of the Congress—Mahatma Gandhi, Pandit Jawaharlal Nehru, Sardar Vallabhbhai Patel, Pandit Govind Vallabh Pant, Acharya Narendra Dev, Chakravarty Rajagopalachari, Sarat Chandra Bose—and asked whether they were not Hindus. These persons which you have named are all members of the Hindu qaum, Kifayatullah concedes, and adds: one can similarly set down the names of hundreds and thousands out of the British who destroyed Muslim empires, who erased the glory and power of Muslims and are erasing it today also.[30] And so on.

These fatwas have been reproduced at length so as to

28. Ibid., Volume IX, p. 438.

29. Ibid., Volume IX, pp. 438–39.

30. Ibid., Volume IX, p. 445.

give an adequate account of the position of ulema like Mufti Kifayatullah. Note that these are the fatwas of the leading light of what would today be called the nationalist ulema: they reflect the premises, the axioms, the objectives of the ulema who supported joint action with the Congress, who endorsed participation in the Khilafat movement, in the Non-Cooperation movement, they reflect the position of the ulema who opposed the demand for Pakistan.

The first thing which becomes apparent upon reading the fatwas of these ulema is that they were always on the defensive, that they had to labour endlessly to justify their position. This was so in part because, as I.H. Qureshi stresses in his *Ulema in Politics*, they were a minority among the ulema, but even more so because the course which they were proposing ran counter to what the Quran and Hadis so manifestly prescribe at so many places.

For the latter reason, as will be evident from reading the fatwas, Kifayatullah and others could seek to justify their positions on pragmatic grounds alone.

Moreover, they too affirmed that a Muslim is first and foremost a Muslim.

They too held that his overriding objective, his 'supreme' objective is, and must be the advancement of the interests of Islam and of Muslims.

They too saw the interests of Muslims to be distinct and separate from the interests of Indians—or to use the expression they used, of Hindustanis—in general. In their reckoning too, far from a non-Muslim actually furthering and protecting these separate interests, a non-Muslim could not even be acknowledged to be the one doing so. Indeed, even a non-orthodox Muslim, one who was not adhering to the requirements of the shariah could not be acknowledged to be the defender and protector of these distinct and separate interests.

Their point was merely that the circumstances in which Muslims were placed at that time necessitated that they work jointly with one set of kafirs— the Hindus—to weaken and oust the other set of kafirs—the British. This necessity, they explained, arose from the conjunction of two factors: both the Hindus and the Ahl-i-Kitab are the enemies of Islam, they declared, but as at that time as the Ahl-i-Kitab, specifically the Christian British, were the more powerful, they constituted the greater danger to the interests of Islam and of Muslims; third, at that time Muslims could not rid the place of the British on their own—a trinity of aims which in today's circumstance would entail the opposite course.

That apart, even while urging joint action with kafirs they incessantly stressed separateness. Indeed on their reckoning joint action was justified precisely because it was the best available way, because in the given circumstances it was the only way for safeguarding that separateness. They repeatedly declared, as we have seen, that had it been possible for Muslims to safeguard their interests by their own efforts, it would indeed have been wrong to associate with kafirs even in joint action against the British.

And their opposition to the demand for Pakistan was not that Hindustan is one and should therefore remain one. They opposed the demand on the grounds that Pakistan was not going to be realized, that if attained it would confine the sway and glory of Islam to a corner of the country alone, that Muslims in the rest of India would be weakened, and that, in any case, the aim of the Muslim League was not to create a truly Islamic state.

'But they had to put the case in these terms,' runs the rationalization, 'because these were the only terms in which they could hope to carry conviction with Muslims.'

The rationalization is doubly destructive. On the one side it attributes a deep and sustained deviousness and hypocrisy to these ulema. On the other it contains within it the acknowledgement that Muslims have indeed internalized the notions about kafirs, etc., which we have encountered in the earlier chapters.

And remember these were the axioms, the objectives and premises of those who were justifying joint action, who were declaring it to be permissible for Muslims to follow the lead of Gandhiji in political matters, who were saying that Muslims may join Congress.

On their own admission they were in a minority among the ulema. The majority declared one and each of these things to be haram. As we would expect from what has been reported in the preceding chapters, Maulana Ahmad Riza Khan was an influential and representative figure of this majority. It is to his fatwas therefore that we turn.

Maulana Ahmad Riza Khan

Maulana Ahmad Riza Khan's fulminations against doing anything which entails association with kafirs, Hindus in this case, extend over more than a hundred quarto-sized pages of closely packed text. The denunciation and scorn he heaps on those who are advocating such a course are even greater than what he hurls at the course itself. Indeed, time and again he declares that those Muslims—'Muslims' is the wrong term actually for his school had issued the fatwas of kufr on the leading ulema of Deoband, etc.—who advocate such a course are greater enemies of Islam than the kafirs themselves.

His fatwas against associating with the kafirs in any way are, as we have noticed earlier, grouped under the generic heading, 'Nafrat ke Ahkam', 'The Ordinances of Hatred.'

Wishing well of Islam, the Maulana declares, consists in living within the bounds of Islam. To unite with the polytheists, to have understanding with them and the conduct of conciliation with them, to make polytheistic leaders the guides of one's religion; to take a polytheistic lecturer as the preacher for Muslims; to take him to a mosque, to make him stand higher than Muslims and have him lecture them; to have tilak put on one's forehead by polytheists; to shout 'jai' for polytheistic leaders in gatherings of polytheists; to carry the bier of a polytheist on one's shoulders and take it to the cremation grounds; to use the mosque to condole the death of a polytheist; to bare one's head in a mosque for condoling his death; to put out announcements for namaz and ask dua for him (the last three allude to the sorts of things which were done at the death of the Lokmanya); to keep the Quran and the Ramayana in one box and, venerating them equally, to carry them to a mandir together; to do these things or even anyone of these things is to cross the bounds of Islam, the Maulana declares.

He says that the polytheists pitilessly murdered Muslims over cow slaughter, they burnt them in fire, he says. To ask forgiveness for those among them who were caught and about whom the charge of murder was proven; to pass resolutions for their release; to write that we have sacrificed the entire life of Quran and Hadis on idolatry; to write that today if you persuade the Hindu brothers then you have persuaded Allah; to write that our community is striving to create a religion which shall erase the difference between kufr and Islam; to write that we want to create a religion which shall hold the Sangam and Prayag—which are the places of idol worship—to be holy places—all this is not to wish Islam well; instead, declares the Maulana, it is to slaughter Islam with a blunt knife. All these utterances and actions are kufr in the extreme, he declares.... And those who say and do such things are the enemies of Din and Allah, he says.

And among these kafirs there are gradations, Maulana Ahmad Riza Khan declares: one hard kind of basic kufr is Christianity; worse than it is Magianism; worse than that is idolatry; worse than that is Wahabiyat; and worse than all these and more wicked is Deobandiyat.... We see that unity and understanding are forged with the worst of the worst kafirs and idolaters (the *badtar-az-badtar se badtar*), the Maulana says. And asks: What unity? What understanding? Rather it is slavery, he says....and goes on to direct his fire at his favourite targets—the Wahabis and Deobandis, who were preaching unity and cooperation.[31]

'If you have to ask anything ask your *Mufti-e-Azam* and Leader,' the Maulana exclaims, alluding to Mufti-e-Azam Kifayatullah whose fatwas for unity and cooperation we have followed at length. Unity and understanding with polytheists is wholly haram, he declares, and, citing authorities, he emphasizes, conciliation of the heart with them is without doubt kufr. For the latter proposition he cites the Quranic injunction we have noted above: you shall see many among them that they befriend the kafirs, Allah says; with certainty how evil is the thing that they have devised for themselves, that Allah should prepare afflictions for them, and they shall be in eternal torment. If they had faith in Allah, Quran and the Prophet, says the Maulana referring to the ulema who were advocating joint action, then they would not maintain unity, understanding, love and conciliation with the kafirs. But the fact is that many among them have deserted the commandments of Allah, the Maulana avers. This, and another score ayats are there in which unity and understanding with kafirs have been declared to be wholly haram and kufr, the Maulana points out. The glory of Muslims, he says, is not in

31. *Fatawa-i-Rizvia*, Volume VI, pp. 3–4. We shall return to the invective against Deobandis, etc., in Chapter 11 below.

that they should heed what the non-believers say, nor does it lie in that they should fabricate arguments to appease the polytheists, in particular the Hindus.

Has Allah given you permission to do so?, he asks. Or are you out to put a stain on Allah? Or do you, without thought and comprehension, entertain doubts about Allah—for instance, that He has taken Hindus out (of the category of kafirs)? They remove the injunctions of Allah from their context, says Maulana Ahmad Riza Khan—his point is that where, for instance, Allah has used one collective word which applies to all the kafirs, the propagandists of joint action insinuate that Hindus are not included among kafirs and therefore unity and understanding with them are not haram and kufr. For such persons there is infamy in the world, warns the Maulana, and in the Hereafter great peril....

To be slaves to polytheists, to be their followers, to do what they say, to obey them in matters of importance—all this is haram, declares the Maulana, it is haram he repeats. And he recalls the warning of the Quran: O believers! among those who are on this earth, there are many such that if you heed them they shall lead you astray from the path of Allah. And he recalls the other warning: And O believers! if you heed the kafirs then, swinging you by your heels, they shall turn you away from Islam, and you shall incur the great loss.

So unity, cooperation, conciliation with kafirs, to do anything which accords a kafir— be it Gandhi or Lokmanya—a place of respect is haram.

The next step comes naturally. It is indeed an adjunct in law!

In Hanafi law, the Maulana recalls, to hold halal as haram and haram as halal is wholly kufr.... So what these worthies are advocating and doing is not just haram, it is kufr. And as usual the Maulana fortifies his ruling with citations from the *Durr-ul-Mukhtar*, from classical collections of fatwas.

To honour the kafirs and polytheists in this way is kufr, he concludes. To cry *'jai'* for them, to call strikes at their dying or going to jail, and to insist that other Muslims should join in these deeds is to be tyrannical and is also kufr.

He next takes up the question of according respect to a polytheist, be he a man as exceptional as Mahatma Gandhi. Quoting authorities, including the Quran, the Hadis, the *Durr-ul-Mukhtar*, the Maulana declares, respect is to be paid only to Allah, the Prophet and the Muslims, but the hypocrites—*munafiq*—know not. Citing the Prophet the Maulana says, he who renders respect to followers of the wrong faith has without a doubt lent a hand for the demolition of the Islamic religion. When this is the commandment in regard to one of wrong faith, what shall be the commandment for honouring a polytheist?, he asks. The Prophet has forbidden us to even shake hands with any polytheist, he says, even to refer to him by his surname (*kunniyat*), even to use words of welcome (*marhaba*) upon his arrival. These are not even very consequential things entailing great honour, they pertain to regard of a very low degree, the Maulana notes—that one should not call him by his name, one should not call him as the father of so and so, one should not say *'Aiye'* when he comes. And yet, he notes, the Hadis has forbidden Muslims from doing even these things. And these persons are asking us to cry 'jai' for him! This is a Satanic deed, the Maulana pronounces....

He turns upon the ones who have been advocating joint action. You are the ones who have incited the masses to the unity with polytheists which is haram, he fumes, you did not restrain them from such accursed deeds. In fact you made them the instruments of your evil purpose and deeds. If you had any faith in your hearts or any honour for the Faith then would you, for this unity, which is haram and kufr, be carrying the whole world on your heads, would you be jumping around from east to west all day and night, and passing such thundering resolutions in their thousands? Would you be issuing fatwas of kufr on those who do not join you in all this? Would you be soiling hundreds of columns of newspapers with them? Instead you ought to have spent a hundred times more energy in extinguishing the fire of these deeds of kufr, he declares, which you yourself had ignited. And to extinguish that fire just to save your own beards was a duty incumbent upon you. But everyone sees that you did not spare a tenth, a hundredth of the energy to do so that you are expending on perpetrating these devilish deeds. As this is what you are doing, what will you gain by concocting false excuses?, he asks. What these responsible persons did was far, far worse and wicked than the aforementioned acts of the ignorant, he says.

He turns to specific examples. Abul Kalam Azad Sahib led the *Juma* namaz at Nagpur, Maulana Ahmad Riza Khan writes. And in the khutba, instead of praising the leaders of Islam, he expressed appreciation for Gandhi, and described him to be a pious personality full of qualities worthy of appreciation. And in the gathering of thousands Mian Abdul Majid Badauni said that Allah has sent Gandhi to you as the man (of the hour). How these accursed words compare with the ignorant, uncivilized crying 'jai', exclaims the Maulana. And he continues in this vein, using the choicest epithets against those advocating joint action and cooperation with Hindus. As usual he cites the Quran, the Prophet, the *Durr-ul-Mukhtar* to fortify his fatwa.[32]

The Prophet has said that he who maintains unity with kafirs of any kind does not have faith, declares Maulana Ahmad Riza Khan. And it is clear from the ayats cited above

32. Ibid., Volume VI, pp. 10–11.

that if they—the proponents of joint action—had faith in Allah, the Prophet and the Quran they would not have observed unity with the kafirs. Citing the Quran he points out that it is stated clearly that you shall not find among the believers in Allah and the Day of Judgement any who shall be friends with those who oppose Allah and the Prophet, even if they (the latter) are their fathers, sons, brothers or dear ones. Allah be praised!

He cites the Quran again: O men of Faith! do not love even your father and brothers if they prefer kufr *to* Faith; and he among you who loves them, verily he is the truly tyrannical one. And as against this tenet of Islam, Ahmad Riza Khan says, their great leader Maulana Abul Kalam Azad tells us to love certain kinds of kafirs, he tells us that universal love is the essence of the Quran's Invitation to Truth.... Has Allah not said that those who paste a lie on Allah shall not prosper?, he asks. Let them have their little say in the world, the Maulana scoffs, for in the end for them is the great travail. Has it not been said.... O dear one, say that those who paste a calumny on Allah shall not prosper; Let them have their little say in the world. Then they have to revert to face Us; Then We shall have them taste that severe travail, the retribution for their kufr? Has it not been said.... Evil upon you. Do not paste a falsehood on Allah that He shall roast you in travail? Has it not been said.... Without a doubt only those who are kafirs concoct such calumnies? This, Ahmad Riza Khan reminds the faithful, is the fatwa of the Holy Quran itself.

He goes on reiterating the denunciation, repeating the points, citing the Quran and other authorities. And then he addresses the rationalization that there are grades of kufr and that it may be permissible to cooperate with some kinds of kafirs. Yes, he declares, if there is a difference among kafirs it is in this that the greater a person's kufr the more haram it is to deal with him. To revere evil is kufr, the more severe the evil the stricter the commandment. This shall befall the liars and calumners—that in kufr the Magians are worse than Jews and Christians; and the Hindus are worse than the Magians; and the Wahabis and apostates are worse than the Hindus. The commandments about them are progressively harsher in this very order.

The Maulana then homes in on the ones he deems to be the worst of all, that is the ones who are advocating the course which entails working together with kafirs. He says that they are kafirs by the command of the Quran itself as they contradict the Quran and deliberately alter the meaning of its words. Nor is this attempt of theirs to invert the meaning of the Quran new, he says. And he proceeds to lambast Maulana Azad in particular, charging him with perpetrating six heresies as early as 1913, the foremost among these being that the faithful should love kafirs, and that to love Muslims and kafirs is the essence of Islam.[33]

A querist states that some Muslims have made Gandhi their leader; some Maulanas have been visiting temples and have allowed Hindus to put tilak on them; they say that today to befriend Hindus is to befriend Khuda; a *dola* with Quran, Bible and Gita in it has been taken in procession; they say sacrifice of animals is not necessary; they have excused Hindus who belaboured and killed Muslims for sacrificing cows—notice that each of these 'facts' has been the butt of the fatwas of Ahmad Riza Khan himself earlier. What is the hukum about such persons?, the Maulana is asked.

To sacrifice the life of Quran and Hadis at the altar of idolatry is gross disrespect of the Quran and Hadis, and it is to accord great respect to idolatry, declares the Maulana. If this is not kufr, he says, then nothing in the world is kufr.

---

33. Ibid., Volume VI, pp. 13–14.

Alluding to an instance in which the Prophet had taken the help of a kafir to make his way in an unfamiliar place, the Maulana exclaims, where is taking a polytheist along over an unfamiliar terrain, and where is making him one's leader and guide in regard to one's faith! Can there be any comparison, he asks. If a shaikh or imam were to sit in an *ekka* and the one driving it were a kafir, does that mean that, on the ground that the shaikh or imam was sitting behind the kafir, his followers can accept the imamat of the kafir and read the namaz behind him? And that incident regarding the Prophet, the Maulana says, too is an incident of a period when the order of jihad had not yet come down (from Allah), and of a time when the practice was 'Unto you your religion and unto me mine'. But after that what was expected of Muslims regarding kafirs became progressively stricter, the Maulana points out, and eventually came the revelation for all time: O Prophet! wage *jihad* against kafirs and hypocrites.

If you draw your rule from the first incident then it is a great foolishness—if it is drawn by an ignorant man; and if it is drawn by or on the authority of an educated person then it is a crime and gross wickedness. This is false imputation on the Prophet, the Maulana proclaims. Never did the Prophet maintain any social relations with any kafir. For it is said in the Quran, He who among you maintains relations with them is one from among them. The ordinance of Allah to His Prophet was: O Prophet! wage jihad against all kafirs and hypocrites, and observe a harshness and strictness towards them.

And when did the Prophet have the occasion to keep up relations with them?, the Maulana asks. In the *Surah-Noor* revealed in Mecca it is said, The kafirs are desirous that you should be lenient to them so that they may also be lenient. He did not maintain relations with them even at that time (in Mecca). So where is the question of his doing so later?

Repentance has been demanded of one who makes a false imputation about the Prophet. It is indeed regrettable, says the Maulana, that upon a fault being pointed out in a person he should try to escape the charge by invoking the Prophet and asserting that that sort of thing had happened with him also.

Some vagrant son of an *Alim-i-Din* drinks bhang; his students object; and, to escape the charge, the son makes the false imputation, 'And did your ustad not take *charas*?' Would you stand by that kind of retort?, the Maulana implies. And where is a father and where the Prophet, he exclaims.

To say that the prohibition of kafirs from the *Masjid-i-Haram* was only for a particular time, to say that it does not hold any longer is a falsehood upon Allah. Quoting the Quran, the Maulana notes that Allah says that the polytheists (*mushrik* are najas—unclean—and that He has ruled that they should not go near the Masjid-i-Haram. To say that the prohibition was only for a particular time, to say that it does not hold any longer is a falsehood upon Allah. Similarly, to say that delegations of kafirs used to come to the Prophet is to seek to profit by a false imputation. The Maulana points out that these delegations used to come to hear the preaching of Islam or to accept Islam. Then, he asks, where is this sort of activity and where is that which those who wish Islam ill have done—those who took polytheists into the mosque with respect, who made them stand higher than Muslims, who made them their *waiz*—preacher—and leader? By that which these persons did the mosque was denigrated—and denigration of a mosque is haram, the Maulana says. And Muslims were brought into disrespect, he says, and the disrespect of Muslims is haram. And the polytheists were exalted, he says, and the exaltation of polytheists is haram.

All this was bad for Muslims, in fact it is harmful for Islam itself. One can estimate what degree of waywardness it is to do all this....

Quoting authorities, he exclaims, how ill it is for Islam that when there is non-Islamic rule, mosques should be opened for kafirs—to do so, he says, is to make way for their destruction. Especially to open them to that qaum, says the Maulana alluding to the Hindus, which in the eyes of the Quran is wholly unclean, which calls the Muslims *malechh*, and which looks upon them as equivalent to bhangis, and which, should it sell something to them, puts it in their hands from afar. That you should open mosques to their unclean bodies and have them soiled by their unclean feet—what is the Islamic logic in all this?, demands the Maulana.

And even apart from all these considerations, he asks, what can be gained from doing these things?

In the *Sahih al-Bukhari*, he recalls, we learn that during the time of the Prophet dogs used to come and go in the Prophet's Mosque. Now you yourself take dogs in the Masjid-i-Haram, in the Prophet's Mosque and in your Jama Masjid. And on Friday make two dogs sit on either side of the imam or the mimbar— that's where your argument leads, he says in a typical flourish. And when you are questioned, say, 'Did dogs not come and go into the mosque at the time of the Prophet? And so we took them, and made them sit on the mimbar. So what?' And shut your eyes, the Maulana scoffs, to the difference between their having come and gone then, and your taking them, as you have shut your eyes now.

Which eyes?, he asks. The eyes of your heart. May Khuda give you wisdom and justice! But even this is not the appropriate analogy for your work, the Maulana protests. If you make dogs sit on either side of the preacher, they won't become preachers. But you make polytheists the preachers to Muslims. Now, if you want to do what you have done, the

Maulana says, then train the dogs—so that when the imam finishes the first sermon they should begin barking and wailing in resonant voices—so that all who are outside may know that the time of seeking answers to one's prayers has arrived. In the same way, he says, in every eighth or tenth row put four or so dogs, so that they should shout at the end of takbir and they should do more in the way of preaching than the preachers.

And just quote *Sahih al-Bukhari* to the effect, 'See, in the days of the Prophet dogs used to come and go in mosques. In fact, no gain ensued from their loitering in the mosques at that time. On the other hand we have brought the dogs for the benefit of Faith, and therefore this is wholly jaiz.' Till then—your taking the dogs on the ground that they used to loiter in the time of the Prophet—was just qiyas, the Maulana says, just reasoning by analogy, but now it is an argument established on the authority of the Quran itself.

To allow tilak to be put is definitely kufr, the Maulana reiterates, and against Islam. The zunnar is after all a thread which remains covered under clothes, he points out. But this tilak is a mark, and a mark on the face, and in the face on the forehead—from where it proclaims at all times, 'We are kafirs.' Quoting authorities, the Maulana declares, the difference between Hindu and Muslim is the difference between kufr and Islam. And that, the Maulana declares, cannot be erased till the Muslim remains Muslim, and the kafir, kafir...

And they—the ones advocating joint action, cooperation—shall put together a new religion in which a Hindu does not remain a Hindu nor a Muslim a Muslim, scoffs the Maulana, parodying their proclamations of *Sarva dharma samabhava.* But as all religions other than Islam are kufr, that new, other religion shall also be kufr, nothing else, he declares.

The same goes for those who would make Prayag and

Sangam as holy as the holy places of Islam, he concludes.[34]

How come the worthies who keep chanting Ashoka's edicts at us never come across such pronouncements?

Because they look away.

To maintain unity and cooperation with polytheists; to make a polytheist one's leader out of religious necessity; to say while referring to a polytheist that he has come to purify the soil of our city; to respect a polytheist and to address him as 'Mahatma'—are these words and deeds in accordance with Islam?, the querist asks. Notice that the expressions and deeds were the kind which were urged by ulema like Kifayatullah and Abdul Bari, by Maulana Azad and others during campaigns such as Khilafat and Non-Cooperation, and for conducting the fight for freedom generally.

Unity with polytheists is a far-off proposition, declares Ahmad Riza Khan—that is absolutely haram. He cites the ayat he invokes so often: You shall not find among persons who believe in Allah and the Day of Judgement that they shall be friends with the enemies of Allah and the Prophet, even though they (the latter) be their fathers or sons or well-wishers. And he cites the other ayat we have encountered so often: He among you who befriends them is one of them. These, the Maulana emphasizes, are proofs from the Quran itself: unity and cooperation with kafirs is kufr.

O Muslims, he asks, whose fatwa is greater than the commandment of the Quran? Whose word is more truthful than that of Allah?

To make a polytheist a leader in religious matters is denigration of the Quran, the Maulana declares. A thousand ayats resonate in the Quran that they, the polytheists, are astray, they are complete strangers to the guidance, he says citing

---

34. Ibid., Volume VI, pp. 82–86. The foregoing is a precis of the Maulana's fulminations.

the Quran, like animals they are completely ignorant. In fact, even more ignorant than them is the one who makes them a leader.

The Maulana's reaction to some Muslims having used the words, 'He has come to purify the soil of our city,' is even more acerbic. The Quran, he recalls, says that polytheists are wholly unclean. And when they have adopted Hinduism, where is the doubt?, he asks. There is no doubt among the ulema that gobar is najas, unclean, and these—Hindus—are a thousand times worse than gobar. The impurity of the polytheists is clear from the Quran, he says. External impurity can be washed with a lota of water, the Maulana says turning the Kifayatullah argument on its head, but the internal impurity—the one by which Hindus and other kafirs are said by Kifayatullah, etc., to be afflicted—cannot be washed even by the sea. It can be removed only by accepting Islam.

To respect a polytheist is the gravest sin, he rules, it is to denigrate the Quran. And he invokes the Hadis: He who respects a *bid'ati,* an innovator, or a non-Muslim has helped to demolish Islam.

To join their procession is haram for other reasons also, proclaims Ahmad Riza Khan, and quotes the Prophet saying that he who joins the procession of a qaum is one of them. He invokes a second Hadis: He who increases the gathering of any qaum is one of them. He quotes a third Hadis: He who comes with a polytheist or stays with him is one and the same as him.

Similarly, he who says the 'jai' of a polytheist is a polytheist, the Maulana rules. And for this he cites yet another Hadis: When a fasiq, a reprobate is admired then the wrath of Allah shall be upon him—that is, the admirer.

And then the Maulana takes up the practice of calling Gandhiji a 'Mahatma'. 'Mahatma,' he says, means 'Great Soul,' and this, he recalls, is the appellation special to angel

Gabriel. To associate it with a polytheist is pure enmity of Allah and the Prophet.[35]

In the Quran a scale and standard have been laid down for good deeds, the Maulana declares in a related fatwa. He who wants good in the Hereafter should do good deeds accordingly—the condition, the Maulana says, is that a Muslim he must be, then his efforts shall bear fruit. About the kafirs, the Maulana recounts, the Quran says that whatever the kafirs may do, We have destroyed them, no good from the kafirs is acceptable, in fact it is unimaginable and useless; only Muslims come within the circle of those who shall get recompense for the good they do.

The Maulana nails the point with an illustration as telling as it is typical. The Quran says: Who can give the debt of goodness for Allah and He shall give double in return; for him is the recompense of honour. Can anyone say, the Maulana asks, that if a kafir gives a loan of Rs 2 without charging interest he shall be covered by this ayat? Is there a recompense of honour for him? They—the kafirs—are neither in the circle of doing good nor in the circle of remediation.

Those so-called Muslims who took help from, who entered into unity—with kafirs—in fact accepted slavery. They are busy trying to have restrictions placed on Islamic law, they are proud of accepting kufr. To respect polytheists is to strictly denigrate Islam. In the face of this the Maulana sets out the litany of deeds of 'these so-called Muslims' which he has enumerated so often earlier: the 'jai' of polytheists is shouted; they are made leaders; the life of ayats and Hadis is sacrificed at the altar of idolatry; polytheists are made guides of Muslims; they—the 'so-called Muslims' the Maulana is berating—took the corpse of the polytheist on

35. Ibid., Volume VI, pp. 91–93.

their shoulders to the cremation ground, and did dua for the peace of his soul; they put out posters for prayers to be said for his janaza— all this is kufr, the Maulana reiterates. They—the 'so-called Muslims'—he says proclaimed openly that if today you befriend Hindus you have befriended Khuda. And they have declared that if by holding on to the rope of Khuda you do not win Faith, you will at least win the world; they are out to create a religion which shall erase the difference between Hindus and Muslims, which shall make Prayag and Sangam holy.[36]

The querist asks, What do the *Ulema-i-Din* opine on the following: a meeting of the Khilafat Committee is being held in Bareilly; Maulana Mohammed Ali and Shaukat Ali and Mahatma Gandhi, etc., will be coming; the bazar has been decked up; they will be taken in a procession with great fanfare; and Muslims, Hindus, Christians, Wahabis, Shias will participate in the meeting; in this condition, should the true believers participate in the meeting, should they watch the procession or not; and is participation in such a meeting proper or is it a sin? Please give a categorical answer in terms of the Quran and the Hadis about participation in such a meeting, about giving chanda for it, etc.

Participation in such a meeting, declares the Maulana citing authorities as usual, is haram, and to watch the tamasha of that which is haram is also haram,

A maulvi or maulana who erases the difference between Muslims and kafirs, who declares Sangam and Prayag to be holy places.... cannot be a maulvi or maulana, declares Ahmad Riza Khan. It is haram to call such persons 'maulana'. Those so-called Muslims are joining (these meeting and processions) as the followers of Gandhi, he says. In the posters only his arrival is mentioned, only his services

36. Ibid., Volume VI, pp. 100–01.

and sacrifices are mentioned—the object of mentioning these is to glorify his reception. It is not the job of Muslims to dissect Hadis—that is kufr. He who participates from the heart is both outwardly and inwardly a kafir. He who participates out of necessity is not doing so by virtue of something which is a necessity according to shariah, the Maulana points out. Unless one is under a life-threatening compulsion, the 'necessity' by which one does these things shall entail that one embrace Islam again, that one do nikah again.[37]

Lambasting Maulana Abdul Bari and Firangi Mahal, Ahmad Riza Khan declares: mosques have not been made for taking kafirs to them and to call out the 'jai' of polytheists. But what shall one do, he exclaims, when their hearts have become distorted, when by becoming the slaves of polytheists they have given the go-by to all the ordinances of Allah and the Prophet?[38]

Cooperation with kafirs is wholly haram, the Maulana thunders again, whether they are *Majus*, or Jews, or Christians, or Hindus, and worst of all with the apostates. These conciliators are maintaining relations with kafirs and yet laying claim to not having conciliation. Maulana Ahmad Riza Khan likens them to a polytheist who goes on worshipping Mahadev and simultaneously goes on saying, 'Look here, polytheism is a very bad thing. Do not worship anyone other than Allah.' They hold non-cooperation with Christians jaiz, he says. The shariah has never justified this. To say that it has, the Maulana declares, is their calumny, in fact the calumny of Gandhi on the shariah. There is no duty equal to the duty to believe Allah and the Prophet to be the Truth. All other duties are inferior to this.[39]

---

37. Ibid., Volume VI, p. 174.
38. Ibid., Volume VI, p. 191.
39 Ibid., Volume VI, p. 192.

And so on.

Why do the secularists never comment on such material? Where do the *fatwas* leave the ecumenical homilies of our Sarva dharma samabhava school?

The fatwas of the 'nationalist' ulema were surprising enough: they urged joint action with kafirs on strictly pragmatic grounds, on the ground in particular that such joint action was the best, indeed the only available way to maintain separateness. But here we have fatwas which proclaim even that pragmatism to be kufr.

Notice that the person in question, the one whose leadership occasioned the fatwas was Mahatma Gandhi—a more saintly person is not likely to be available in our public life for decades and decades. And yet these were the fatwas. The cause too was as noble as a cause can be—the country's Independence. Often—as during the Khilafat movement—the cause was of direct concern to the Muslims. And yet these were the fatwas.

Notice too that while, for urging even that minimal cooperation with the kafir Hindus, an alim even of the eminence of Mufti Kifayatullah had to confine himself to pragmatic reasoning, Maulana Ahmad Riza Khan was able to justify his fatwas by citing chapter and verse from the Quran and Hadis.

For the Quran and Hadis ordain the position elaborated by Ahmad Riza Khan, and not the one the 'nationalist' ulema strained to justify.

That is the fact which our intelligentsia does not want to face.

A basic classification

A great deal in these controversies turns on whether a country is *Dar-ul-Islam*, the Land of Islam, or Dar-ul-Harb, the Land of War. If it is the latter it is obligatory for a Muslim to either wage holy war, jihad, till the place is converted into Dar-ul-Islam or emigrate from it to a land which is Dar-ul-Islam.

As the power of the British spread and dislodged Mughal rule, the ulema became more and more incensed. Shah Waliullah exhorted Ahmad Shah Abdali, the then ruler of Afghanistan, to invade India and thus restore it to Islam. The result was the Third Battle of Panipat. The long-term consequences were the opposite of what Waliullah had intended. His son, Shah Abdul Aziz (1746–1824) took up the baton. He railed against the situation which had come to prevail, one in which, as he put it, the writ of Christians mattered rather than that of the Muslim ulema. Eventually he issued a fatwa declaring Hindustan to have become Dar-ul-Harb, a land in which jihad was the obligation of every Muslim. His efforts to fan an uprising too floundered. The 1857 movement—in which on Qureshi's telling the ulema were the prime movers—also collapsed.

Muslim leaders as well as ulema now began to find reasons to proclaim that Hindustan was not Dar-ul-Harb. Sir Syed was of course in the forefront of articulating this turnabout. He declared that it was by the Will of Allah that sovereignty had been taken from Muslims and handed over to the British, that the British gave Muslims religious freedom, that they ruled with justice, ensured peace and respected the individuality and property of Muslims; and so Muslims were in duty bound to be loyal to British rule. 'It is a great mistake,' he wrote in his famous review of Hunter's *The Indian Musulmans*, 'that the country can only be either a *Dar-ul-Islam* or a *Dar-ul-Harb* in the primary signification of the words, and that there is no intermediate position. A true *Dar-ul-Islam* is a country which under no circumstances can be termed a *Dar-ul-Harb* and *vice versa*. There are, however, certain countries which, with reference to certain circumstances, can be termed Dar-ul-Islam, and with reference to others Dar-ul-Harb. Such a country is India at the present moment.' He laboured to show that the charge that the Wahabis, having recognized the country to be Dar-ul-Harb, had waged jihad was 'groundless'. On the contrary, said Sir Syed, from the very fact of India having become Dar-ul-Harb the Wahabis deemed jihad against the British government unlawful! The correct position in law, he said, is, 'If you have power, *jihad* is incumbent upon you. If you do not have power, it is unlawful.' The jihad which the Wahabis had waged had been against the Sikhs and not the British, Sir Syed insisted.[40]

Several of the ulema weighed in with arguments of their own—the arguments, as Professor Mujeeb remarked, 'a mixture of common sense, casuistry and intellectual frivolity'. The British were a legally constituted government. They allowed religious freedom. Obedience to the British could be regarded de facto as carrying out one's part of a contract—the government carrying out its part by providing security and peace. The laws of shariah were not being applied as a whole and many of them were in practice suspended—a proposition that could be taken in both senses: as laws of the shariah were not being applied as a whole even during Mughal and pre-Mughal times there was little reason to wage war if of late they had been suspended in a few more areas; alternately, the proposition could be taken in the sense that

40. Sir Syed's views on this matter are well known, and the literature on him is very considerable. For the particular sentences which have been quoted see J.M.S. Baljon, *The Reforms and Religious Ideas of Sir Sayyid Ahmed Khan*, Muhammad Ashraf, Lahore, 1958, pp. 17–18; *Writings and Speeches of Sir Syed Ahmed Khan*, Shan Mohammed (ed.), Nachiketa, Bombay, 1972, pp. 79–80; Bashir Ahmed Dar, *Religious Thought of Sayyid Ahmed Khan*, Institute of Islamic Culture, Lahore, 1971, p. 79.

even now it was only in a few areas that the laws of shariah had been suspended, in other areas they continued to be applied, and even in the former set of areas the laws had been merely 'suspended'. More ingenious was the argument that by enjoining obedience to the ruler, the shariah itself provided for its own suspension; as the British were now the rulers, the laws of the British government were now the laws of shariah. Next: shariah recognized the rule of necessity and now Muslims in India, placed as they were, had no alternative but to obey. In doing so they would not be going against the Will of Allah in any way, for had the Quran not assured, 'And God does not lay upon anyone a burden greater than he can bear?' And so on ran the rationalizations....[41]

Patently these were mere rationalizations—and the facility with which the ulema could produce arguments for one course of action, and then, as the situation changed, for its opposite was typical.

We encounter the same mixture of 'common sense, casuistry and intellectual frivolity' in the volumes of fatwas which form the subject of our survey. Maulana Ahmad Riza Khan, at all times the most insistent in applying the literal meaning of the Quran and Hadis to kafirs, takes the position that will at first sight seem surprising: he declares that Hindustan under British rule is Dar-ul-Islam! But he is only trying to ward off the consequences of taking the opposite view: a literalist, once he pronounces the place to be Dar-ul-Harb he would necessarily have to decree that the Muslims either wage jihad till the place is converted into Dar-ul-Islam or emigrate to some area which is in fact Dar-ul-Islam

---

41. M. Mujeeb, *Indian Muslims*, George Alien and Unwin, London, 1969, pp. 399–400 where he summarizes the arguments of Maulana Adul Hayy and Maulvi Nazir Ahmed.

— the former course would be suicidal, the latter would be ruinous as was proven by the Muslims who emigrated to Afghanistan in response to the exhortations of Ghulam Muhammad Aziz, alias Aziz Hindi in 1920.

Mufti Kifayatullah's fatwas jump from one position to the other from page to page.

To begin with Volume I, on page 19 the Mufti declares: It is permissible to take interest from government banks, because, governance at present being in the hands of the British, India is Dar-ul-Harb. But to deposit money in government banks wilfully and thereby render help is not proper.

On page 20 he declares: Hindustan is neither Dar-ul-Islam nor Dar-ul-Harb fully. In regard to some matters—like the observance of namaz, the celebration of Id—it is Dar-ul-Islam: presumably because there are no restrictions in observing these. In regard to others—for instance, taking interest from government banks—it is Dar-ul-Harb: a ruling of convenience surely, for if it were held that Hindustan is Dar-ul-Islam Muslims would have to be forbidden from accepting any interest. But, says the Mufti, Muslims should not get into the habit of depositing money in government banks to earn interest; however, he adds, you should not leave uncollected the interest on your deposits with government.

On pages 20–21 he declares: Hindustan is Dar-ul-Harb. But to give a fatwa in general that, therefore, it is all right for Muslims to take interest would be dangerous for Muslims he says—because then the importance of interest being haram will be drained from their minds.

Later on page 21 he declares: Because Hindustan is Dar-ul-Harb, a Muslim can take life insurance.

On pages 21–22 he says: Even if Hindustan is Dar-ul-Harb to take interest from Muslims or to take interest forcibly from non-Muslims is not proper. To take interest from non-Muslims with their consent is proper.

On page 22 he says: It is now well held that India is Dar-ul-Harb, and the fatwa is given on this basis.

Later on page 22 he again declares: It is well held that India is Dar-ul-Harb. It is therefore proper to take interest from kafirs. But because there is disagreement among the ulema about its being Dar-ul-Harb, one should exercise extreme caution in taking interest. But do take interest from the post office and spend it on the poor or give it to students.

On the next page: India is Dar-ul-Harb.

Later on page 23: That country is Dar-ul-Harb in which sovereignty lies with kafirs, who thus have the power to issue injunctions according to their will. Hindustan is definitely—*yaqinan*—Dar-ul-Harb. The duty of Muslims is that they should continue striving to convert Dar-ul-Harb into Dar-ul-Islam, and should exert to attain freedom for establishment of Islamic rule.

But on the next page: Hindustan is Dar-ul-Harb but not all indices of a country being Dar-ul-Harb are established here. Therefore, there are doubts in regard to taking interest: that is so because the ulema are not agreed on its being Dar-ul-Harb. For a place which was Dar-ul-Islam to become Dar-ul-Harb three indices are necessary: (i) no feature, no peace, no responsibility, no pardon of Dar-ul-Islam should remain; (ii) Islamic laws should not remain; (iii) link with Dar-ul-Islam should not remain.

Again on page 24: Even though Hindustan is not in its previous condition, it has not become Dar-ul-Harb. Instead its government is of a mixed kind in which Muslim members have also been included. Therefore we cannot understand the justification for taking interest.

Similarly in Volume VIII, on pages 48–49 Kifayatullah declares: For long there has been disagreement over whether Hindustan is Dar-ul-Harb or Dar-ul-Islam. Now Akbar Ali al-Sabah says it is Dar-ul-Harb. To deposit money in government banks is najaiz, but if it has been deposited, to leave interest uncollected harms Islam. Because they—the government banks—give the amount to missionaries who work against Islam, and convert people to Christianity. If we take interest and give it to the poor, there is no harm.

But on page 50 he says: the present situation is that government is with the British. Therefore, Hindustan is Dar-ul-Harb. Therefore taking interest from government banks is not najaiz. But one should not use it for oneself.

Again on page 52 he says: Muslims can have business dealings with banks because the banks are owned by *Ahl-i-Harb* who are located in Dar-ul-Harb.

Yet again on page 54: One can obtain profits from savings banks and from non-Muslims and use them for one's own expenditures. But even though Hindustan is Dar-ul-Harb it is not jaiz to take interest from Muslims.

But on page 59: There is some doubt because some ulema hold that Hindustan is Dar-ul-Islam.

The responsibility is again shifted on pages 60–61: Those who declare Hindustan to be Dar-ul-Harb and the English to be Harbis, from their standpoint there is scope for taking interest (from non-Muslims).

But on page 62: You *can* use interest received from cash certificates and post offices for personal requirements. The reason is that for both of these the government is responsible, and the government is kafir and *Harbiya.* But precaution and piety consist in using the interest money for orphans, widows and the indigent.

Again on pages 62–63: Hindustan is Dar-ul-Harb. But it is not permissible for Muslims to give interest even in Dar-ul-Harb. They should take the interest from banks, etc., and give it to the indigent, etc.

On pages 66–67: Insurance is jua and therefore najaiz. But it is permissible as this is Dar-ul-Harb—and in the case of one fatwa, also because the company is owned wholly by Harbi kafirs.

On pages 67, 69, 70, 71, 79: Insurance is jua. Precaution and piety consist in avoiding it. But as this is Dar-ul-Harb it is permissible; as in Dar-ul-Harb it is permissible for Muslims to secure advantage from kafirs even by gambling, there is no objection in taking insurance if it confers some benefit on Muslims. But even in Dar-ul-Harb it is detestable to do dealings involving interest and insurance inter se among Muslims.

On pages 72, 74–75: In one case doubts are expressed and in another case permission is denied for taking insurance. The grounds are twofold: Insurance depends on usury and gambling; second, as both Muslims and non-Muslims are shareholders in the company, taking insurance from it would amount to Muslims taking usury from Muslims.

And then on page 73 the querist asks: You along with others have been quoted as justifying insurance. Please cite the rules of shariah on which this justification is based. The Mufti replies: We have not justified setting up an insurance company. We have just said that for those ulema who say Hindustan is Dar-ul-Harb there is scope for justifying it.

Several points stand out. There is the skill. In the last case, for instance, the Mufti says that all he has said is that for those ulema who hold India to be Dar-ul-Harb there is scope for justifying the setting up of an insurance company. He doesn't say of course that among the ulema he is one who has time and again declared Hindustan to be Dar-ul-Harb.

There is also the attitude which will be familiar to all who are acquainted with communist literature and practice: one can do things to take advantage of kafirs which one cannot do vis-à-vis Muslims.

And then there is the classification itself. Whether a place is Dar-ul-Islam or Dar-ul-Harb is a basic classification. As we see, even after 1,350 years of exposition there is no agreement among the ulema on even so basic a matter.

Just as telling is the fact that such a basic matter gets entangled with mundane, even trite questions—about interest, about insurance. This entanglement is inescapable—for two reasons. First, as shariah is claimed to be a seamless web, everything comes to depend on and be related to everything else. The more basic the category—and the classification in question is indeed a foundational one—the more widespread the spheres it affects. On the other hand, there is the tug of reality. As several types of Muslims—Pathans, for instance—made a living by charging interest, as Muslims were beginning to avail of banks, post office savings schemes, as they were taking out insurance, invoking the category of Dar-ul-Harb was the way to accommodate the law to reality!

But when such a big axe is wielded or has to be wielded to swat a fly, a host of other consequences follow. If India is held to be Dar-ul-Harb—even if the purpose be to justify taking interest or insurance—it becomes the duty of every Muslim to exert to convert it to Dar-ul-Islam, including by jihad where appropriate, or to migrate from it, etc.

Yet the sledgehammer it had to be. Dar-ul-Harb one day, *Dar-ul-Aman* the next, Dar-ul-Islam for one purpose, Dar-ul-Harb for another. The controversy was never quite settled though it raged for over a hundred years—from the time of Shah Abdul Aziz to the country's Independence. On the contrary, every decade brought fresh complications. The British were Harbi kafirs. The country had to be freed from them. But the country's struggle for Independence was being led by a kafir, indeed by a kafir who was manifestly rooted in his kufr.

Moreover, the kafirs from whom the country had to be freed had begun to treat Muslims as allies. Furthermore, there was the danger that were the struggle for Independence to succeed, the faithful would be outnumbered by and be placed 'at the mercy' of the other set of kafirs. There was thus the choice of Pakistan. But the movement for that was being led by a Shia, indeed by a person who was not just a Shia but one who ostentatiously looked down upon the ulema, who did not adhere to the shariah, who said the Quran was an old book....

Even as the debate continued among the learned, the country became independent.

Independence

The argument became increasingly one-sided as more and more of the ulema gravitated towards the Muslim League and the demand for Pakistan. The 'nationalist' ulema were pushed into more and more defensive positions. Anyhow, Independence came.

Apart from those who had secured Pakistan, the reactions of everyone on the Indian side were a mixture of emotions. True, the British had to leave but the country had been divided: those were the feelings of Gandhiji and others also who had led the struggle for Independence.

Among the ulema who stayed behind there were additional reasons for ambivalence. Yes, the country had been divided, but a state—Pakistan—had been created in which Muslims were in such overwhelming majority that one could reasonably expect that it would soon be an Islamic state. But, on the other hand, while in Pakistan Muslims were in overwhelming majority, Muslims who were left behind in India were correspondingly in a minority. They were left weaker than they had been even during British rule.

Several examples can be given which speak to this ambivalence. One will suffice. It is the speech which Maulana Nanautavi, the then vice chancellor of Dar al-Ulum, Deoband, gave on the night of 15 August 1947.

It puts forth the characteristic claim: that it was the ulema 'who in fact laid the foundation-stone of this independence, and laid it at a time when the heart and mind of this country was simply devoid of the concept of liberty'—a claim akin to the claim that Ali Main, etc., habitually make that it was the Islamic invaders who brought civilization to India, that it is Islam which lifted it from the abyss of darkness to light, from oblivion and obscurity to the pinnacle of name and fame, from its parochial ambit to the family of man, etc.[42]

It puts forth the claim 'that this struggle for the independence of India had been initiated by Muslims only and they alone nurtured it.'

In it Nanautavi gives fulsome congratulations to India and also Pakistan: 'We congratulate Pakistan as Muslims and India as our native land.'

And it has anxieties about the future—now that Muslims who have been left behind are in even more of a minority.

From many points of view therefore it repays reading.

Introducing it the official historian of the Dar al-Ulum, Deoband, writes:

> The reality cannot be denied that in the struggle for the independence of India no other group can be called a rival to the proud position held by the *Ulema.* After the tumultuous revolution of 1857 this was the only party which kept the concept of independence alive in the country. Their continuous effort

42. For Ali Mian's claim—made, for instance, in the preface to the book of his father, Abdul Hai, entitled *Hindustan Islami Ahad Mein*—see Arun Shourie, *Indian Controversies, Essays on Religion in Politics*, ASA Publications, New Delhi, 1993 pp. 401–10.

and struggle at last infused the spirit of liberty in the whole nation. Hazrat Nanautavi was the greatest propagator of this concept and the outstanding preacher of this movement. It is indeed a pity that the writers of the history of this war of independence have not done justice to him for the enthusiasm with which he nurtured this concept.

As the speech throws some light on the role of the ulema, says the official history of Deoband, and as it expresses the joy that 'the group oriented and prepared for this goal (of independence) by Hazrat Nanautavi must have experienced,' it is reproducing the speech verbatim. Here it is:

* * *

Maulana Nanautavi on Independence

Elders of the nation, respectable *Ulema* and dear students of the Dar al-Ulum! The auspicious day of today will be always memorable in the history of India. A glorious and mighty empire regarding which it was admitted on all hands that the sun never set on it any time and about which an overweening and supercilious representative of this empire, namely, Gladstone himself had boasted vaingloriously in the Parliament that his empire then was so powerful that even if the sky wished to fall down upon it they would stop it on the points of their bayonets and it would not be able to cause any harm to the empire. The same empire, not due to the falling of the sky but merely due to the stirring up of a few particles from the earth is winding up so easily that history cannot offer a single example thereof! On this great revolution we offer congratulations to the whole country in general and to the old and the young in particular whose efforts and sacrifices have brought forth this sweet fruit for India.

It would be ungrateful on our part if on this occasion we do not recollect the efforts of those elders of the community who in fact laid the foundation-stone of this independence, and laid it at a time when the heart and mind of this country was simply devoid of the concept of liberty. It was the crusading party of Hazrat Shah Wali Allah's intrepid disciples which was marching in the path of this struggle for the past two hundred years not only with pen and ink but also with sword and blood. After 1857 when the English power completely dominated over the whole country, this was the lone party which kept the concept of liberty alive and at last made everyone in the country infatuated with it. According to Maulana Rasheed Ahmed Gangohi, in 1857 the greatest repository of this concept and the greatest trustee of this fervour was Maulana Muhammad Qasim. He took up sword under the leadership of his *Shaikh* Haji Imdad Allah and stepped in the path of liberty with the intention of laying down his life, but because of the difficulties of the path the chain of victory stopped at the Shamli Tehsil and could not reach Delhi and the country was deprived of independence. However, this party did not become unmindful of this idea. When Hazrat Maulana Muhammad Qasim left this world, his proper and true successor, Shaikh al-Hind Maulana Mahmud Hasan, the legitimate heir to his knowledge and views, continued the movement for freedom with his whole party.

Maulana Nanautavi

According to a statement of Jamal Pasha, the Turkish governor of Madina, what miracle was hidden in the handful of *Shaikh al-Hind*'s bones and his short *jubbah* that it took the whole Islamic world into its fold! Anyhow, the passion of these august men against the English paramountcy was neither for rank and position nor for the ministerial chairs nor for the power of any single party, but it was only for this that the oppressed country be taken out from the grasp of an oppressive nation and be entrusted, by way of rendering the due to the rightful person, to one whose trust it was, so that the word of truth be elevated.

The greatest leisure-time activity of these august men was always the same talk and anxiety as to how the yoke of the English should be thrown away from the shoulders; regarding this alone were their forecasts and spiritual revelations and about the same was their common orderliness and arrangement. One day all these elders were present in the Chhatta Mosque. In view of the English people's domination and uncommon might, Haji Sayyid Muhammad Abid said: 'The English have set their claws very deep (i.e., have stabilised their position very firmly). Let us see how will they be disrooted?' At this Maulana Muhammad Yaqub who was the first *Shaikh al-Hadith* of the Dar al-Ulum, Deoband, observed: 'Haji Sahib! What are you thinking? That time is not far off when India will be turned like a row-mat. There will be no war; on the contrary, in a state of peace and tranquillity, this country will be turned like a row-mat. At night we will sleep under their rule and will rise up in the morning in another reign.'

Maulana Nanautavi

I do not run down the daring and the valiant people of today but I also cannot back down from the conviction and claim under any circumstances that all the efforts of independence today are a building the foundation of which had been laid down by these august men and therefore I can say loudly that this struggle for the independence of India had been initiated by Muslims only and they alone nurtured it. Shah Abd al-Aziz issued a *fatwa* against the English and declared India to be a *Dar al-Harb* (Territory of War). Haji Imdad Allah and Maulana Muhammad Qasim Nanautavi used this *fatwa*; they drank this recipe of cure in a particular manner and made others also drink it. The *Shaikh al-Hind* preserved the same recipe in the form of a compound electuary and made it usable for everyone. Accordingly its use became common. In the Khilafat

Movement also though the recipe was bitter, it was used by all, and, at all events, when it began to be used commonly, the passion for freedom passed over from the Muslims to the other compatriots and they also became active, and through the indefatigable joint efforts of the Hindus and the Muslims and their sacrifices their sweet fruit is before us in the form of the independence of the country at which we extend congratulations to each other and *Maulana Nanautavi* pray for these august men who sowed the seed and the tree became so stalwart that all of us are eating its fruit today.

The independence of India is the independence of the entire Islamic world and hence gamut of our congratulations is also much wider. Both the states of India and Pakistan deserve our congratulations: we congratulate Pakistan as Muslims and India as our native land. I also cannot refrain from expressing this thought that now the Muslims have remained as an ordinary minority in India and in today's independence while they have an occasion to be extremely glad that the 200-year old paramountcy of the English has come to an end for which they were so restless, there is also an occasion to be anxious as to what would be the form of their collective life in this country? For this they should take steps from now. In the light of the holy Shariah there is only one way, that they select from amongst themselves an *Imam* (leader) and a religious chief (*amir*) for establishing their religio-legal organisation; that instead of remaining scattered the Muslim groups and sects in India unite and become one, one at the *Kalima* of Islam, and decide to pass their religio-legal life under one chief. In this one sentence alone is hidden the prolix interpretation of their collective life. The thing of foremost priority for them is to forget the past events; let us give up the system of recrimination and sarcasm and stop thinking of laying the blame at the door of each other. On the contrary, keeping the future alone in view, let us ponder over it, that to be united what can be the plans for fraternity and equality that we can put into practice today? In my opinion the chances of our being united are brighter now than ever. The parties on whom rest the bases of disputes have been turned up side down by this revolution, the fact is that they too have changed with the changing of India. Hence, now, instead of sowing the seeds of dissension by founding new parties, it is apposite, rather necessary, that we lay the foundation-stone of a single party and solve all those problems that have cropped up in the new India.[43] *Maulana Nanautavi*

* * *

Only two comments need be added to what has been said while introducing the speech. First, how does this reading of the role of Muslims—the reading that they alone kept alive the flame of liberty, that they alone sowed the seed, that they alone nurtured the movement into a 'stalwart' tree—how does this compare with the account of those very events which Sir Syed wrote? At least one of the two must be a fabrication. Second, in I.H. Qureshi's *Ulema in Politics*, written as it is from Pakistan, Shah Waliullah, Shah Abdul Aziz and the ulema in general are seen not as ones who founded and nurtured the struggle for the independence of India but as ones who founded and sustained the struggle which led eventually to the establishment of Pakistan. The ulema of Deoband, etc., are seen as the minority, renegade faction, as those who compromised their principles and honour as well as the interests of Muslims, and eventually lost out themselves.

---

43. Dar al-Ulum's journal, *Zi-qada*, October 1947; reproduced in Sayyid Mahboob Rizvi, *History of the Dar al-Ulum, Deoband*, Idara-e Ihtemam, Dar al-Ulum, Deoband, 1980, Volume I, pp. 243, 244–46.

Since Independence

The ulema thus claimed that no group had made as great a contribution to sowing the seeds of and nurturing the movement which led to Independence as the Muslims in general had and the ulema in particular had.

As always happens, the notion that they had done more than anyone else to attain an objective, that they had suffered and sacrificed more for it than anyone else was accompanied by its twin: since 1947 the ulema have been feeling, they have been the principal fount fomenting among others the feeling that Muslims in general and the ulema in particular have not received their due, that in fact they have been discriminated against, that they are actually as poorly off, if not worse off now than they were before Independence.

The fatwas of the ulema of Dar al-Ulum, Deoband, recall how the country has been Dar-ul-Harb since rulership passed from Muslims to the Sikhs, and then to the British. As to the state of affairs after 1947 they declare in their considered pronouncement as follows:

> In August 1947 the country became independent but the cruelties perpetrated on Mussalmans, and the kind of murders and bloodshed that followed Independence have no parallel in history. For this very reason the *Sheikh-al Islam,* Maulana Madani, even after Independence, called this country, on account of its state of affairs, *Dar-ul-Harb.* And some others termed it *Dar-ul-Aman,* a variant of *Dar-ul-Harb.* In any case, though the country is now free, Mussalmans and Islam have no share [in the fruits] of Independence. The life and property, dignity and honour, of a Muslim are not secure so far. And in the eyes of the government these have no value. Some special Mussalmans have of course benefited from Independence but they are in minority and this has happened in the earlier government too. The *millat-i-Islamia* continues to be unhappy. In future perhaps God would provide a solution.[44]

---

44. *Fatawa Dar al-Ulum, Deoband,* Volume XII, pp. 268–69.

A voice in the wilderness

The *Ulema* have instilled this dual image in the minds of Muslims. On the one side there is the notion that they are the crème de la crème because they are the chosen ones, because they are actually the perfected nation that Allah and the Prophet spoke about, that they are the ones who brought civilization and culture to this land, that they are the ones who ignited, nurtured, sacrificed the most for the country's struggle for freedom. And on the obverse of this is the image reflected in the fatwa of the ulema of Deoband: that they are poor, discriminated against, hunted down.

The consequence has been the politics of what Maulana Wahiduddin calls the demand-and-protest formula.[45] To even notice, much less to acknowledge that wherever they have put in the effort Muslims have done as well as others; to even notice, to say nothing of acknowledging that the blame may not lie only with others has come to be seen as betrayal of the religion and of the community.

As Maulana Wahiduddin points out, the consequences of this negativism, and of the politics and rhetoric which have flowed from it have harmed both—the country as well as Muslims. They have skewed the priorities of Muslims: instead of doing something to alleviate the real causes of their problems—their educational backwardness, for instance—they have expended their energies in wailing, and in securing symbolic 'victories' as over the Shah Bano case. The rhetoric and politics have, as the Maulana says, made Muslims

---

45. Maulana Wahiduddin Khan, *Indian Muslims, The need for a positive outlook*, Al-Risala Books, New Delhi, 1994.

as a group lose the respect of others. They have come to be seen as 'a problem group'. He contrasts that perception with the way Christians, Parsis, Sikhs—save for the early 1980s when the latter too were swept off by the same sort of politics and rhetoric—are seen, and how this has been one of the factors which has enabled these other groups to progress and prosper.

Recounting what he has seen personally—the families he has known, Muslim localities he has visited over the years—Maulana Wahiduddin observes, 'To my way of thinking, Indian Muslims have improved their lot considerably since Independence. I would go so far as to say that the condition of present-day Muslims is not that of persecution but of progress.' 'Indeed, if you make a survey of the economic and social condition of any Muslim family before and after 1947,' he writes, 'you will see that it has made remarkable progress. If in pre-Independence days, a Muslim owned a bicycle, today he owns a car. If then he had a small house, today he owns, if not a mansion, then at least a house of comfortable proportions. Where, before, he could only afford to telephone from a public booth, today he has his own telephone. Where his family had to depend on limited local opportunities, they now regularly travel and work abroad, and hold superior positions.'

Reporting the same kind of growth in regard to purely religious institutions and activities, the Maulana writes:

> Today there are lakhs of *madrasahs* spread all over the country. The old *madrasahs*, like those of Nadwatul 'Ulema in Lucknow and Darul Uloom in Deoband, were just like ordinary schools before 1947, whereas today they have expanded so much that they have more the appearance of being universities. In the neighborhood of Malegaon, a new and very big *madrasah*, the *Jamia Muhammadia*, has been established,

which completely dwarfs the old one. Hundreds of new *madrasahs* have been established all over the country, including a school for Muslim girls, the *Jamiatus Salihat* at Rampur, which is said to be the biggest *madrasah* for Muslim girls in the entire Muslim world. In fact, thousands of Islamic institutions of different kinds have been set up throughout the length and breadth of the country, and have full freedom of functioning.

He continues:

The *Tablighi Jama'at* is a Muslim religious movement headquartered in Delhi. Since 1947, its extension, too, has been exponential. In the same way, all other Muslim bodies have greatly added to their assets as well as increasing the numbers of their followers. In former times, Islamic conferences were few and far between, but nowadays, major conferences are being organized almost on a daily basis in India by Muslims. These take up different aspects of Muslims and Islam. Islamic books and journals are also being published in far greater numbers than ever before.

'What has gained momentum in India since 1947 is not, in fact, the persecution of Muslims, but yellow journalism and an exploitative leadership which sustains itself by repeated allegations of persecution,' he says. 'If there is any danger to Muslims in this country it is only from our so-called leadership, buoyed up as it is by paranoid journalism. There is no other real danger to Muslims.' 'Those who hold the reins of leadership and journalism in their hands are people of very shallow character,' he writes. 'Their only formula for boosting circulation and retaining their leadership is to create a fear psychosis among Muslims and then to exploit it. To this end, they painstakingly select negative instances from Indian Society and then, by blowing them up out of all proportion, they manage to convey the erroneous impression that Indian Muslims are the victims of prejudice and injustice.'[46]

---

46. Ibid., pp. 87, 88–90.

He blames in particular the Muslim press and Muslim intellectuals for filling the community with these feelings of negativity. 'While the Quranic "periodical" was run on positive lines,' he writes, 'the entire Muslim press of the present day is plunged in negativism.... you should, therefore, ignore difficulty, seek opportunities and avail of them. But today Muslim journalism has devoted itself entirely to the ferreting out of difficulties, mainly plots and conspiracies of others against them.' Muslim papers have sought, he writes, to correct 'what they felt were erroneous impressions (in other papers) by projecting Muslims as absolutely perfect, but ill-treated human beings'. Giving examples of the way they wrote about the Afghan *mujahidin*, the Maulana observes, 'They (the Muslim papers) act in this way because they want to prove that Muslims are entirely virtuous and innocent of all wrongdoing, and that if they appear to have shortcomings, it is because of the harsh treatment meted out to them.' He nails the point:

> To me, the Muslim press has been suffering from what I can only call quite unjustifiable self-righteousness on the part of Muslim intellectuals. It is this innate weakness which has prevented them from seeing their own shortcomings. All they can see are the plots of others behind every problem their community faces. Consequently, instead of engaging themselves in constructive activities, they spend their time inciting members of their community to protest against others.[47]

The Maulana's observation and inquiry lead him to conclusions which are in complete contrast to what that typical fatwa of Deoband we began with says and what the Muslim press shrieks out week after week. Communal riots? This is what he observes:

> A particularly dark aspect of the Muslims' existence in India

47. Ibid., pp. 73, 76–78.

seems to be communal riots. It is a fact that communal riots have taken place on a large scale in modern India over the last forty-five years and, regrettably, in some parts are still continuing. I repeat, nevertheless, that the occurrence of communal riots is not linked to the system of governance developed after Independence. It is related rather to the Muslims' own rabble-rousing leadership and yellow journalism.[48]

'Atrocities' of the police? This is what his observation leads Maulana Wahiduddin to say:

Communal violence is one of the most talked of subjects these days, and discussions thereon are dominated by the fact that the brunt of police violence has to be borne by the Muslims. 'The policemen are killers,' say Muslims. Their theme song is that the brutalities of Adolf Hitler and Chengiz Khan pale into insignificance when compared with what the police inflict on innocent Indian citizens.

At face value, this would appear to be correct. But we must pause and give greater thought to the reasons for police 'misconduct'. Why should it take place at all? If we marshal facts, we see that in every case, the situation has been aggravated more by the Muslims being easily provoked than by a desire on the part of the police to be aggressive. And it is noteworthy that wherever there is a concentration of Muslims, this oversensitiveness is very much in evidence; sooner or later, it is the Muslims themselves who have to pay dearly for it at every level.

And again:

It is clearly the Muslims who are the losers, whether at the individual or at the community level, yet they do not stop to think of the ferocity with which reprisals will be carried out when they themselves have given in to provocation, lashing

48. Ibid., p. 92.

> out at all and sundry. They think it is like aiming a blow at a domestic animal which if it reacts at all, will do so mildly and without rancour. They do not stop to consider that when they lash out in a frenzy of emotionalism, it is a savage wild beast with which they have to deal—an untamed monster, which will fight back with tooth and claw. The culminating point of their endeavour will be the inevitable backlash of police brutality.
>
> Events having shown that Muslims clash not only with Hindus, but also with the police we should now ascertain where to lay the blame. Clearly, the greatest offenders are the journalists and leaders of the Muslim community itself. After each and every riot they cannot find words enough to describe the 'brutality and savagery' of the police; in consequence, Muslim sentiments are kept perpetually on the boil. Their anger against and hatred for the police are never allowed to simmer down. As a result whenever policemen appear on the scene, they become enraged and hit out at them, trying by all possible means to humiliate them. This belligerent attitude on the part of Muslim newspapers and leaders is the root cause of the intense mutual hatred between Muslims and the police.

Shed this negativism, he exhorts the Muslims. Work hard. Educate yourselves. And you will prosper like the others. He holds up several examples. The Asian Americans are a tiny minority in the USA, he writes. Yet by dint of hard work they are today among the richest ethnic communities in the USA. Where would they have got had they kept wailing about being discriminated against, had they taken to the politics of demand and protest, to a politics of confrontation? He points to the way Hindus of the former Hyderabad state have prospered in the recent past, in spite of the marked preference which was shown to Muslims in state employment—this was because the Hindus, excluded from the state sector which was actually the stagnant sector, took to commerce and industry. He points to the example of Indian Christians and Parsis, and Sikhs.

As we saw, Maulana Wahiduddin lays the blame for the negativity in which the Muslims are mired on the Muslim press and on what he calls Muslim intellectuals. We need only add that as influential in feeding the negativity, in feeding the persecution complex among Muslims, as influential in fomenting among them the notion that the country owes them a living have been the secularist press and the secularist intellectuals; and that the original founts of the notions and attitudes the Maulana rightly nails are the ulema.

Their notions, the notions exemplified in the fatwa of Deoband that has been quoted earlier are what have got embedded into the mind of India's Muslims.

Alas! Maulana Wahiduddin's remains a voice in the wilderness.

Moreover, to put the blame on Muslim journalism and leadership is in a sense to beg the question. After all, why do Muslims prize this kind of journalism, why do they follow such leaders? The answer is in the psychology which the ulema and their fatwas have drilled into them, and, as we shall see, in the even more intractable fact that what they instil is firmly grounded in the Quran and the Hadis.

Women and Shariah

6

'Mom ki naak, balki raal ki pudiya, balki baarood ki dibiya'

'When excited a woman is a hundred times more passionate than man.... A woman is *mom ki naak,*' the (white-hot) tip of the candle, *'balki raal ki pudiya'*, in fact, a tight little packet of *raal,*[1] *'balki barood ki dibiya'*, in fact a packet of explosives. 'If she is even brought near a spark (of temptation), it will cause an explosion. She is defective in reason as well as in faith. And by nature she is crooked. And in lust a hundred times more passionate than man. When the effect of bad company ruins men permanently, what is one to say of these delicate bottles which with the slightest knock break into smithereens? This nature (of theirs) is proved from several *hadis*'[2]—That is Maulana Ahmad Riza Khan warning husbands lest they expose their wives to the company of loose women. It is not the occasion but the ulema's assessment of women per se which is of interest, for it pervades the fatwas through and through. 'For the Quran says,' declare the ulema of Deoband settling a matter to which we shall soon turn, 'the husband is the master.'

Apologists by contrast never tire of telling us that no

1. An inflammable resin.

2. *Fatawa-i-Rizvia,* Volume IX, Book I, p. 183.

religion has given as high a place to women as Islam, that no body of law has given them as many rights as the shariah. Yes, at the time of marriage, a woman is given *mehr* which in theory is hers: in fact, it is customary to have the bride renounce it on the nuptial night itself, and, as we shall see,[3] for this there is sanction from Allah Himself; and the word itself for dower—*ujoor*— is one at which humanists, to say nothing of feminists, will wince—for it means the hire paid for use of the woman.[4] Yes, a daughter is entitled to a share in the estate of the father, but it is to be half that of a son. Yes, a woman's evidence can be taken into account, but it is to count for one-half of that of a man. And so on.

These rules of shariah are not fortuitous. They follow from the view of women which is set out in the Quran and Hadis—that they are to be second to men, that their function is to obey husbands and satisfy them in every particular, that they are deficient mentally, that they are ungrateful, that a woman advancing is the devil, that a woman receding is the devil, that they shall form the majority in Hell....[5]

The point can be illustrated from many angles. We shall take up fatwas on the matter which has been in the public eye in the last few years—namely, talaq. In particular, we shall take up fatwas on Triple talaq— this became the point of considerable controversy when in 1994 the Allahabad High Court held that this power of the husband to throw the wife out by uttering one word was contrary to our laws and the Constitution. The ulema raised the familiar shout: it is a

3. Chapter 10 below.

4. Ram Swamp, *Woman In Islam*, Voice of India, New Delhi, 1994, pp. 22–23. For a similar reading of Quran, verse IV. 24—'So that ye seek them with your wealth'—and a similar reading of mehr see *Fatawa-i-Rahimiyyah*, Volume I, p. 45; the relevant fatwa— on owning and using slave women—is dicussed in Chapter 9 below.

5. Chapter 10 below.

part of the shariah, no attempt to interfere with the shariah will be allowed.

In theory, in practice

Whenever attention is drawn to the absolute and inhuman power that the Shariah gives to the husband to throw his wife out, to terrorize her into submission, the apologists say, 'That is just a smear. Allah and the Prophet have declared repeatedly that of all things, talaq is the worst.'

They have indeed.

'Allah did not make anything lawful more abominable to Him,' the Prophet is reported as saying, 'than divorce.' 'Of all the lawful acts,' he is reported to have declared, 'the most detestable to Allah is divorce.'[6]

That is all very well. But, having recounted such declarations, the apologists never explain how that which is the most detestable thing has been made so easy for the husband! For, while in theory talaq is said to be so abominable to Allah, in practice the position is entirely the opposite. The jurists repeat the counsel that divorce is something from which one should abstain. But this is just counsel. As to the power, they are unanimous: it is a power which lies with the husband, and it is untrammelled. Should the husband choose to exercise it, no one, and no consideration can save the wife. The counsel itself has the caveat invariably built into it, a caveat large enough to drive an elephant through it: you should not give talaq, the jurists say adding, except when there is need for it! In the typical instance, we read in *Durr-ul-Mukhtar,* one of the great works of Sunni jurisprudence, 'And giving of divorce is permissible, according to all (the

6. See, *Sunan Abu Dawud,* Ahmad Hasan (tr.), Kitab Bhavan, New Delhi, 1993, Volume II, pp. 585–86.

jurists) because the verses (of the Quran) *are unconditional* (in this respect). And it has been said by *Kamal*, that the most correct view is that one should abstain from it, except when there is need for it, for example, in cases of suspicion (about the character of the wife) and old age (of the wife)....'[7] and so on, each clause permitting that which the previous one had counselled against.

In theory talaq may be abominable but in practice the husband has the power—the absolute, unconditional power, a power for exercising which he is not accountable to anyone on earth—to throw the wife out by just uttering the word 'talaq'.

She is thrown out if he utters it once in each of three 'periods of purity'—that is, the period between menstruations.

She is thrown out if he utters it thrice in one go.

She is thrown out if he utters it with some adjuncts even once.

The fatwas enforce these rules with the utmost rigour. They enforce two rules in addition: the rule that, faced with such a pronouncement, the wife has no recourse at all, there is no one, no authority which can intervene to save her as wife; and the rule that once she is thrown out she is entitled to no maintenance at all, save the minimum sustenance during three menstruations, that is she is entitled to nothing at all after three months are over.[8]

---

7. Muhammad Alauddin Haskafi, *The Durr-ul-Mukhtar*, B.M. Dayal (tr.), 1913, Kitab Bhavan, New Delhi, 1992 Reprint, p. 118.

8. For the rule for instance that triple talaq pronounced at one go is valid, see as examples *Mufti Kifayatullab ke Fatawi*, Volume VI, pp. 65–66, 73–75; *Fatawa Dar al-Ulum, Deoband*, Volume IX, pp. 292 (case 313), 326 (case 371), 350–51 (case 400), 362 (case 415); *Fatawa-i-Rizvia*, Volume V, pp. 626–27, where Maulana Ahmad Riza Khan comes down heavily on a person who suggests that there is some disagreement on the matter; the rule is reiterated—for instance, at pp. 637, 638. Doubts are scotched with a firm hand. Thus, for instance, the ulema of Dar al-Ulum are asked, 'In

A woman's rights are safeguarded in many ways, the apologists say. Triple talaq is strongly frowned upon, they say. And in practice? 'By a deplorable, though, perhaps, natural, development of the Sunni law,' wrote Justice Faiz Badruddin Tyabji in his famous work, 'it is the fourth and most disapproved or sinful mode of *talaq* (that is, the Triple talaq) which seems to be the most prevalent, and in a sense, even favoured by the law....' Not only was it the most prevalent and favoured form, he noted, its effects are 'aggravated' in that talaq having been pronounced thrice, it could not but be taken to be conclusive and irrevocable.[9] That was Justice Badruddin Tyabji writing *eighty* years ago. Forty years ago, Justice Shahmiri observed that as this form of divorcing the wife is the 'least onerous for husbands, it is the most prevalent form obtaining in India.'[10] Eighty years ago... Forty years ago... And *three* years ago Professor Tahir Mahmood noted, 'For centuries the common Muslim has believed that the so-called 'Triple *talaq*' is the only 'Islamic' form of divorce...', that

---

the days of the Prophet and Abu Bakr and Umar, triple *talaq* in one sitting was counted as one *talaq*. It is Umar who made it count as three. "Zaid" (a pseudonym) says that Umar's order was not according to Shariah, but that it was political. What is the law about him who says so?' The ulema decree: 'Those Muslims who say so about Umar's *fatwa* are ignorant and misguided. Umar had enacted the order on the basis of Shariah, and how can the assertion about the consensus of the learned be correct without inquiring into its origin? It is written in *Shami*.... It is clear from this narration that Hazrat Umar had given his injunction in accordance with the Shariah. And none among the Companions objected to it at the time. Therefore this injunction is in accordance with the Shariah and those who oppose it are misguided'—*Fatawa Dar al-Ulum, Deoband,* Volume IX, p. 326 (case 371); similarly see pp. 350–51 (case 400) where the same point is reiterated.

9. Faiz Badruddin Tyabji, *Muslim Law, The Personal Law of Muslims in India and Pakistan,* 4th Edition by Muhsin Tyyibji, N.M. Tripathi, Bombay, 1968, p. 163.

10. *Amad Giri v. (Mst.) Bagha,* AIR, 1955, J and K.

'Divorce by a Muslim husband in this country (India) almost invariably means a Triple *talaq*'—with the concept of a single revocable talaq people have little acquaintance.'[11]

Yet the moment attention is drawn to this diabolic power, apologists divert the discussion by declaiming on the one hand, 'But divorce has been condemned in the strongest terms by the Prophet and by Allah,' and on the other, counting on the ignorance of their interlocutors, by insisting that, though allowed in theory, the power is seldom used.

The ulema are much more honest and staightforward. Not only do they uphold the rule that three talaqs in one breath throw out the wife, they uphold the power of the husband in other particulars as well.

Answerable to no one

To start with, the ulema repeatedly emphasize that the husband need give no reason for divorcing his wife, that he owes no one—neither the wife nor anyone else—any explanation. Here is a case ruled upon by Mufti Kifayatullah:

Zaid divorced his wife in front of a *panchayat,* and turned the

---

11. Tahir Mahmood, 'No more *"Talaq, Talaq, Talaq"* —Juristic restoration of the true Islamic law on divorce', *Islamic and Comparative Law Quarterly,* Volume XII, Number 2, Winter 1992, pp. 2, 10. Given the common background of Islam in the subcontinent it is no surprise to learn that the position in Pakistan is no different: 'The most prevalent method of exercising *Talaq al-Bidah* under the Sunni law now-a-days,' notes K.N. Ahmed in his exhaustive study, 'is to pronounce three divorces at the same time. It is not necessary that the husband should repeat the pronouncement three times in order to constitute an irrevocable divorce. The triple repetition is merely one of the many forms by which such a divorce can be effected and the same result can be obtained by any other method recognized for the purpose.' See, K.N. Ahmed, *Muslim Law of Divorce,* Karachi, 1971, Kitab Bhavan, New Delhi, 1984 Reprint, pp. 68–69.

woman out of the house. That woman then went to her brother. The brother then came (to the husband) with a *panchayat*. He asked Zaid, 'Why did you give *talaq*? '*Zaid* said, 'I am not going to keep her, and so I have given *talaq*.' Could you please say whether the *talaq* is effected on this woman?

The Mufti's ruling is categorical:

When the husband has given *talaq*, the *talaq* has happened. It is not clear how many times the husband had pronounced *talaq*. If he had given *talaq* with the words one or two, then it can be revoked.[12]

But there is no question of his having to explain his reasons to anyone. Similarly, consider the following case decided by the ulema at Deoband:

Case: A man was married at the age of nine. He lived with the woman but in his seeking for renunciation and solitude, he divorced her. The woman has no defect, nor is her honour in doubt. Is the man at fault or not? How will his renunciation be affected by the divorce? What is the law regarding divorce through a letter and when one is in solitude, that is, without witnesses?

Fatwa: There is no fault even if the divorce has been declared without any reason, although it is not good to divorce without reason. It is said in *Durr-ul-Mukhtar*.... and on this *Shami* has written.... So let it be known that in the above mentioned case if the husband has become major and given divorce, his wife stands divorced. The giver of divorce has committed no fault. His renunciation will not be affected by it. Divorce can become effective through a letter as well. It becomes effective if declared in a state of solitude (i.e., without witnesses) provided no one except the husband knows it.[13]

In a word talaq can be pronounced to the wife directly,

12. *Mufti Kifayatullah ke Fatawi*, Volume VI, pp. 83–84.

13. *Fatawa Dar al-Ulum, Deoband*, Volume IX, p. 50, case 31.

to her through others, in front of witnesses or with no witness present, orally or in writing. A husband has divorced his wife in her absence, writes the querist, and asks, has the divorce become effective? The divorce has become effective in this case, rule the ulema of Deoband, because it is not necessary that the woman be present or near at the time divorce is declared.[14] In none of the circumstances is the husband obliged to account for his decisions to anyone in any way. Far from giving a reason he does not even have to have one.

Even if in rage

So complete is the power of the husband, so terrible the effect of his word that talaq pronounced even in rage is enough to throw the wife out. This rule too is vigorously enforced by the ulema and they decree that she cannot stay in the house unless another man marries her, that second marriage is consummated, and that second husband too divorces her. As the fit of rage of the original husband is certain to bring such an extreme and humiliating consequence upon her, to what whim of his shall the wife not pander?

It is only when we read the accounts of actual instances—even though these are given in the fatwa volumes in an abbreviated form—that we can grasp how vigorously the rule is enforced, and what untold hardship and humiliation it brings upon the poor wife. As will be obvious upon reading the cases, the rage may have nothing to do with anything the wife has done or failed to do, in fact in ever so many cases set out in the books of fatwas she is nowhere on the scene. And yet the terrible consequence falls upon her. Here is a sample from

---

14. *Fatawa Dar al-Ulum, Deoband,* Volume IX, pp. 42–43.

just one collection, the fatwas of the comparatively moderate Dar-al-Ulum of Deoband:[15]

Case 30: A man quarrelled with his wife and said, 'I give you a hundred divorces.' Now the man says that he said so in a fit of anger, and had no such intention. Has the divorced become effective?

Fatwa: The Shariah does not take account of intention in divorce. Divorce becomes effective in spite of intention. It takes effect in case of anger as well. In fact it is obvious that in most cases anger is the cause of declaring divorce. The law givers have said so (p. 49).

Case 144: Zaid has sworn to this effect that Bakr's father-in-law, Umar, behaved in an ignominious manner and used words which he should not have used towards a man of status. As a result, Bakr was mad with anger so that his body started shaking. Though Bakr is well known for restraint and self-possession, he replied to Umar in the same language.... The father-in-law found faults in Bakr, and demanded divorce (for his daughter). Bakr had lost self-control. So he said, 'Divorced, divorced, divorced'.... Later on, he recovered himself, and started speaking like a sane man.... Does the divorce become effective? Maulvi Md. Shabli of Nadwah says, no, because divorce by a man out of his wits does not take place.

Fatwa: It is known that divorce is generally declared in a state of anger .... so divorce does take place due to anger.... It is therefore too difficult to annul the divorce. The law says that the wife is not legitimate for him till she is married again to him according to law (p. 117).[16]

Case 145: Bakr admits that he was mad with rage. What do you say now about the divorce?

---

15. The following representative examples are from *Fatawa Dar al-Ulum, Deoband,* Volume IX. The case number is given at the beginning and the page number is indicated at the end of each example. The last example is from Volume X.

16. The concluding words are the usual euphemism for *halalah.*

Fatwa: The *qazi* will not admit this argument, and will make the divorce effective (p. 119).

Case 153: Zaid is a pious man. But in a state of extreme rage he said his wife, 'I give you *talaq*.' The wife said she did not need divorce. Zaid became more angry and said, 'Three *talaqs*, three *talaqs*, a hundred *talaqs*.' Meanwhile, Zaid's sister came, and said to him, 'Take care, you have lost your mind.' Zaid replied, 'I have my mind all right.' When he regained self-control, he said to his sister, 'You did not ask me to take care, and I did not say that I was all right.' Zaid had no intention to divorce his wife. But two women and one man give witness that Zaid had lost his mind, his eyes were red, his *dastar* had fallen, and his hands and feet were shaking. Zaid is aware of *talaq*. Has divorce become effective?

Fatwa: The divorce has become effective. He can live with his wife only after remarrying her as per law (pp. 123–24).

Case 174: Zaid said angrily to his wife, 'One *talaq*, three *talaqs*, five *talaqs*.' Now he says he had lost his wits due to rage, and did not know what he was doing. What does the Shariah say in this case? Has the divorce taken place?

Fatwa: Zaid's wife stands divorced. Divorce is generally declared due to anger. And the legists have accepted divorce due to anger.... Zaid cannot remarry her without the proper procedure (pp. 135–36).

Case 181: Zaid divorced his wife due to her disobedience which made him angry. Is the divorce correct or not?

Fatwa: The divorce is effective. The books on law have regarded anger as a regular reason for bringing about divorce. It is also obvious that divorce in most cases is declared in a state of anger (p. 139).

Case 254: A man in a state of anger gave triple *talaq* to his wife in one moment (utterance). Does the divorce become effective? Can the marriage be restituted?

Fatwa: The divorce has become effective. That woman is now *haram* for her husband. He cannot marry her without *halalah.* Restitution is not right (p. 259).

Case 261: Zaid married Hindah. They fell out. Zaid said in anger, 'One *talaq,* two *talaqs,* three *talaqs.*' Do these words effect a divorce?

Fatwa: The divorce has become effective (p. 268).

Case 343: Zain al-Din was in a state of rage. He declared triple *talaq* on his wife. In fact, he said it five or seven times. Maulvi Abdul Rahman decided that divorce does not become effective if declared in rage. But Maulvi Khalil Rahman declared two *talaqs* and permitted their restitution without *halalah.* But Maulvi Abdul Shakoor considered it triple *talaq* and declared the divorce as effected. Whose *fatwa* is correct?

Fatwa: In this case the *fatwa* of Abdul Shakoor is correct. Zain al-Din's wife stands divorced. The other two *fatwas* are wrong. It is now illegitimate to marry them without *halalah.* Zain should separate his wife from himself (p. 311).

Case 427: A man suddenly gave eight *talaqs* to his wife. But both of them love one another, and feel helpless. I want to know if I can restitute the marriage according to the law laid down by Imam Shafi'i?

Fatwa: According to Imam Shafi'i and others the remarriage with the first husband without *halalah* is *haram.* This is in keeping with the law laid down by all schools (pp. 366–67).

Case 746: Volume 10: A man became angry in the night. He said that if she (the wife) touched his body from that day onwards, she would stand divorced. The wife lost her wits, caught hold of her husband's hand, and pleaded for forgiveness. The husband's utterance is limited to daytime. And he has no intention to divorce his wife. Has the divorce become effective?

Fatwa: Intention does not count in the law laid down by the Shariah. And in a case like this 'day' means the time when he said the words. So the divorce is effective. He cannot remarry his wife except through *halalah* (Volume X, pp. 115–16).[17]

In a drunken state

As is well known, liquor is strictly forbidden in Islam. Yet if a man who is drunk utters the word talaq thrice, the marriage is ended, and the wife is out on the street. That is, even if the husband is in a condition that is wholly prohibited, if he has got into it by doing something—imbibing liquor—which is strictly forbidden, even then the mere utterance by him of a single word thrice throws the wife out, howsoever virtuous and pious she may be, howsoever long she may have been married to the man, howsoever many children she may have borne, howsoever bereft she may be of means to look after herself. So peremptory and final is the right of the husband.

Though at times Mufti Kifayatullah relents and decrees that talaq pronounced in a state of inebriation terminates the marriage only if the husband had got intoxicated voluntarily and not if he was compelled to or beguiled into getting drunk, at others he makes no such distinction.[18] The Deoband ulema who belong to the same school decree that the wife is out in either case. A few representative cases alone can bring out the penalty which the hapless wife has to suffer because her husband got drunk.[19]

---

17. See cases 269, 273, 300, 391 in Volume IX to the same effect.

18. See for instance, *Mufti Kifayatullah ke Fatawi*, Volume VI, pp. 71–72 contrasted with pp. 72–73.

19. The following representative examples are taken from *Fatawa Dar al-Ulum, Deoband*, Volume IX. The case number is given at the beginning of the example, and the page number at the end.

Case 65: The *qazi* made Zaid marry when the latter was drunk. After two years, he gave three divorces before a gathering in a state of intoxication. After the intoxication was gone, he was very sorry, and did *taubah.* Is it legitimate for the couple to get married again?

Fatwa: If a husband divorces his wife in a state of drunkenness, the divorce becomes effective.... So if the husband has divorced her thrice, he cannot marry her again except as provided by law (that is, after she has married another man, that man has consummated the marriage, and then divorced her) (p.69).

Case 96: Zaid says *'talaq, talaq' to* his wife in a state drunkenness. He goes on saying *'talaq, talaq' as* he is beaten up by people. He asks his wife for forgiveness after three days. When he is asked as to why he divorced her, he says he is not aware of it. He had, however, uttered *'talaq'* to his wife any number of times. Does this divorce become effective? If it has become effective, which divorce is it? What is the difference between divorce (uttered) in a state of madness and that uttered in a state of drunkenness? It is written in the books that divorce given in madness does not become effective, while the one given in drunkenness does, though in both states the persons are devoid of intelligence.

Fatwa: Zaid's wife stands divorced if he has uttered *'talaq'* thrice or more times. His wife stands separated from him. He can have no contact with her. Nor can he marry her anew except according to law. But if he has uttered the word *'talaq'* twice only, he can marry her anew after *iddat.* The question, however, makes it clear that he uttered the word *'talaq'* four times—twice in his state of drunkenness, and twice when he was beaten up by people. If it is true, and if the statement is not disputed, his wife stands divorced due to three utterances. He can neither keep her nor marry her anew except according to law. And though it is not in doubt that the conditions of both madness and drunkenness are devoid of intelligence, in matters of divorce a difference is perceived. The drunken one is supposed to have his wits while the mad one is not supposed to be sane. So divorce due to madness is null and void (pp. 87–88).

Case 152: A man in a state of drunkenness addressed his wife by her name and divorced her thrice. But the man does not remember having done so. Only the woman says he said so to her, and there is no other witness. Does the divorce take place in this case?

Fatwa: Divorce declared in a state of drunkenness does become effective according to law. In the present case when she (the wife) confirms it and the man does not deny, the divorce has become effective. They cannot remain together unless they remarry according to law (p. 123).

Even if he is misled

So potent is the word of the husband that even if he is foolish enough to fall prey to deception, even if he is misled by the mistake of another person into declaring talaq, marriage is ended and the poor wife is out. The volumes of fatwas reiterate the rule time and again. Here are typical examples from the *Fatawa Dar al-Ulum, Deoband:*[20]

Case 50: I left my betrothed and married elsewhere. But in spite of this, my betrothed kept on waiting for me. Eventually, on people's persuasion, marriage preparations were made. But at the last minute he (the betrothed's father) insisted that I divorce the first wife. I was very sad and refused to do so. One day a Maulvi advised me to write the divorce on a paper so that they would be silenced. Thus time would be gained, he said, and divorce does not become effective by mere writing unless it is uttered by mouth. I believed the Maulwi's word that mere

20. *Fatawa Dar al-Ulum, Deoband,* Volume IX. The number of the case is given at the beginning and the page number at the end of the example.

writing does not effect divorce. So the Maulvi dictated and I wrote it down. Three divorces as well as the name of the wife were written. Has the divorce become effective in this case?

Fatwa: The divorce becomes effective by writing, just as it does by speaking.... that Maulvi has deceived you. The *hadis* says that divorce becomes effective even if it is uttered in fun and jest. According to the Shariah it becomes effective even if there is no intention (to divorce the wife) (p. 61).

Case 260: A Maulvi made a fool declare triple *talaq* though the wife is innocent. What is the law in this case? And what about the Maulwi?

Fatwa: The divorce has become effective. But it is bad to get a wife divorced without any reason. It is also contrary to the Sunna to say or make one say triple *talaq* at the same time. The Maulvi who did it is a bad man. But the divorce is effective. The woman is *haram* for the husband (p. 267).

The one who has been foolish or careless enough to be deceived is the husband. But it is the wife who is out on the road.[21]

---

21. The examples give the standard position. But to anticipate a point, the power of the ulema would be much reduced if they could not ordain exceptions! And so, predictably, in the same set and volume of fatwas in which these examples occur we read that a written divorce document which has been obtained by fraud does *not* effect divorce ! The case is as follows: *Case 123*: The enemies of a man conspired with a notary and registrar, made the man drink, bought a legal paper for writing a divorce deed, and got his thumb impression on the divorce register as well as on the blank document. And then these conspirators wrote on it a divorce for his married wife. Neither he nor his wife knows anything about the deed or the divorce. In short, all this amounts to a fraud. Do they stand divorced? What about the children born after this event? *Fatwa:* A divorce deed obtained by fraud does not make the divorce effective. The husband has not divorced his wife, and their children are legitimate (Ibid., Volume IX, p. 101). It is precisely in being able to rule that a case brought to them falls in the category considered in cases 50 and 260 reproduced in the text or that it falls in the category of case 123 that the power and terror of the ulema lie.

Even if the husband is ignorant

The wife is cast out even if the husband utters or writes words amounting to a divorce without understanding their full import, indeed she is out even if he does so out of complete misapprehension. Here is a typical case of the latter ruled upon by the ulema of Deoband:

> *Case 251:* A man married a woman. She fell ill after a few days. Her belly became inflated. The community came to believe that she had become pregnant before her marriage. The doctors confirmed it. So the husband gave her triple *talaq.* She should have delivered two months after the declaration of divorce, so the doctors had opined. But she did not, and it was found that she had conceived after marriage. So the whole thing was a misunderstanding. Does she stand divorced? If so, how can she return to her husband?
>
> *Fatwa:* As the husband has declared triple *talaq*, divorce has become effective. She can remarry him only by way of *halalah.*[22]

In a word, the poor bride who has had to live through the cruelty of a totally false charge must now suffer being married to a second man, being taken by that man, and being divorced by that man also before the effects of the groundless suspicion of the initial husband and his people can be undone, and she can return to the father of her child. But we must believe that the shariah accords a higher position to women than any other legal dispensation!

Even if compelled

There is indeed a peculiar harshness towards the wife. An astute and in many ways moderate man like Mufti

22. *Fatawa Dar al-Ulum, Deoband,* Volume IX, p. 262. See also Ibid., case 118, p. 99.

Kifayatullah bends to ease things for the believer: he rules, for instance, that the believer who to save his life does something that constitutes kufr or *shirk*— for instance, if he prostrates before an idol under compulsion keeping his true faith in his heart—such a person does not lose his religion. But if the man is under the same sort of compulsion to divorce his wife, and if he pronounces talaq to save his life, the wife is out.[23] The only concession Mufti Kifayatullah makes is to hold that if under compulsion the husband has only *written* the *talaq-nama* but has not spoken the words, the wife survives. Of course, if while writing them, the husband has also spoken them, or if he has spoken them though he may not have written anything, the wife is indeed out. The cases referred to him make pitiful reading. Here are a few representative ones:[24]

Case: Zaid divorced his wife under compulsion from his father. He did not want to do so. The wife too wants to return to him. She does not want to go through *halalah*. Can they be reunited?

Fatwa: If things have reached this pass the husband should obtain a *fatwa* from an *alim* who does not think that under such circumstances divorce is valid. And he should do the *nikah* again. In Hanafi law *talaq* under compulsion is effective. After three *talaqs nikah* cannot be done again without *halalah*, and a nominal *halalah* is also not complete (pp. 236–37).

Case: A man is attacked by his elder brother. And he says, 'If you want to save your life, divorce your wife thrice.' That man

23. On prostrating under compulsion see, *Mufti Kifayatullah ke Fatawi*, Volume II, pp. 207–09; and on divorce pronounced under compulsion taking full effect, see Ibid., pp. 236–40.

24. The following examples, are taken from *Mufti Kifayatullah ke Fatawi*, Volume VI. The page numbers are indicated at the end of each example.

refuses, but unsuccessfully, and to save his life he writes the *talaq* thrice on a piece of paper. And when he is writing the word *talaq* he repeatedly says, weeping, 'It is out of fear of you that I am writing this word. My heart refuses to *talaq*. I do not give *talaq* at all, I am just writing the word, and under Shariah this just cannot be divorce.' The question is: in these circumstances is the wife divorced?

Fatwa: If that man has under these circumstances just written *talaq*, and not spoken the words of *talaq* by his tongue then his wife is not divorced (pp. 237–38).

Case: Bakr's relatives came to him and said, 'Divorce your wife, or we will have nothing to do with you, and shall denounce you and defame you.' Fearing the loss of his honour, Bakr wrote, 'My wife - X, Y, Z - from my side you are divorced.' He just wrote this but did not say anything orally; nor did he in his heart intend to divorce her. Does she stand divorced?

Fatwa: If Zaid has been compelled to write this but has not repeated the words orally, then there shall be no *talaq*. And by 'compulsion' is meant that he feared for his life, or limb, or grievous hurt (pp. 238–39).

Case: My mother-in-law came over at 6 in the morning and said to me, 'Come with me.' I told her, 'I will do so. What is the work? I have just got up from sleep. Let me wash up. After that I will come. Please sit down. I will come along just now.' At this my mother-in-law answered, 'Wash up after you return, I will not sit here. Come with me straightaway.' Helplessly I accompanied my mother-in-law, and she took me to her uncle's place. There I saw that a number of men and women were gathered. I went and sat down silently and was wondering as to what the matter was. After a while all of them said to me, 'Divorce our girl.' I refused to give *talaq*. And all of them surrounded me. Compelled, I then said, 'All right, give me two days time. After that I will give *talaq*.' At that all of them said,

'Give *talaq* just now. We do not give you any time.' I said, 'All right, just give me a day's time.' This too was refused. On that I said, 'Give me an hour or two.' I asked for time again and again. But I was not given any time, and was compelled to give *talaq*. And all of them surrounded me from all sides, and made up all sorts of things, and abused my elders. I put up with all this, because I was alone, and I had no one of my own. And I had been called by fraud, saying, 'There is some urgent work.' In this state of compulsion, without heart and helpless, I wrote out what my brother-in-law dictated. Whatever he went on dictating, I wrote.

Out of fear I did not refuse to write, because my brother-in-law is stronger and more powerful than me. Moreover, there were many other men besides him. I was the only one from my family. The paper which I was forced to write by way of *talaq*, that my mother-in-law snatched away from my hands. Then, turning to the neighbours I said in a loud voice, 'I have been forced to write *talaq*. I have not written *talaq* on my own, nor have I given *talaq* by my tongue.' After that I lost consciousness, and, exhausted, did not say anything to anyone upon returning home. After that I left for my work, because my reporting time had already passed. The next day I enquired of the neighbours there, 'Do you know anything about what I have written and what has been got written from me?' Then they told me the subject matter of the letter and said, 'You were not in your senses when you were writing. We did not speak up because there would have been discord with us every day.' The matter which I was compelled to write is: 'I, Akramullah Khan son of Kifayatullah Khan, at the instance of my wife and her mother and in the presence of Abdul Hadi and Mohammed Yamin Khan, and taking my daughter, Raisa Khatoon, in my hands, do divorce my wife thrice, and expel her from being my wife....'

My wife is pregnant since three or four months, and my daughter is with her mother. And two months ago I had a quarrel with the grandmother of my wife. Now what has to be ascertained is whether *talaq* given without intention and without speaking is effective or not?

Fatwa: If this *talaq* has been got written under compulsion but has not been spoken, then the *talaq* has not taken place (pp. 239–40).

Other rulings follow the same pattern. Now, the concession of Mufti Kifayatullah—that the marriage will be saved if the talaq given under compulsion has been merely written and not spoken—is liable to help only if this rule is known to the husband, and is *not* known to his tormentors. If the latter know it too then all they have to do is to belabour him into uttering the words also !

The ulema of Deoband follow the same rule and make the same distinction. A few representative cases from the *Fatawa Dar al-Ulum, Deoband, will* bring out their statement of the law, as well as give us a glimpse of the circumstances in which the community whirls about.[25]

Case 47: A man had married a widow, but his father-in-law forced a divorce. Has the divorce become effective? And can they remain in the same marriage? Can it be done by restitution, or is it necessary (for her) to marry another man (and for him to divorce her after consummating the marriage)?

Fatwa: Divorce has become effective in this case, because divorce becomes effective even if it is forced (on the parties). If he declared only one divorce, the man can restitute his wife within the period of *iddat* without (another) marriage (ceremony). But if the period of *iddat* is over, another marriage (ceremony) is needed. A second marriage is not needed (p. 59).

---

25. The following representative cases are taken from *Fatawa Dar al-ulum, Deoband,* Volume IX. The case number is given at the beginning, and the page number at the end of each example.

Case 66: Zaid forced Umar to utter the extended triple divorce. Can the marriage be restored in any way?

Fatwa: The divorce becomes effective even if uttered under force (p. 70).

Case 77: Zaid was subjected to great violence to get him to divorce his wife Hindah. So he wrote down that he was divorcing under compulsion. He was made to write these words under the shadow of the sword. Does this divorce become effective according to law?

Fatwa: If the husband is forced to divorce due to threats and out of fear, the divorce becomes effective provided it is uttered by word of mouth. But if he is forced only to write and does not say so by word of mouth, the divorce will not be effective (p. 77).

Case 169: If a person forces someone to divorce the latter's wife, does it become effective? If it becomes effective, what is the meaning of a *hadis* in Ibn Majah which says, 'Allah, whatever my Ummah does due to ignorance or under force, may be forgiven?'

Fatwa: The divorce has become effective. There are other provisions in another *hadis* (p. 133).

Case 278: Does divorce become effective if the husband is forced to declare it? Is it necessary to say it by word of mouth? Or does it suffice to produce a deed of divorce written by someone else?

Fatwa: If the husband is forced to divorce, it becomes effective. But it is not sufficient to produce a deed written by another person (p. 276).

Case 338: People were discussing about Zaid divorcing his wife. He was forced to declare triple *talaq*. But he did not know as to who was divorced. Has divorce taken place?

Fatwa: It has taken place in this case. Because when people asked a husband to divorce his wife, he said it thrice. The context was his wife. It is the wife who is divorced (p. 309).[26]

---

26. There are other cases too to the same effect. See for instance case 96, Volume IX, pp. 86–88 given elsewhere in connection with talaq pronounced in a state of drunkenness.

The position of *Fatawa-i-Rizvia* is no different. Nikah is a mirror, declares Maulana Ahmad Riza Khan, and talaq is the rock that breaks the mirror. Whether the rock is thrown at the mirror willingly, or under compulsion, or it falls out of one's hand, the mirror shall break in all cases.[27] He too holds repeatedly that if under compulsion the words have been merely written and not spoken, *talaq* shall not take place. On the other hand, if they have been spoken, whether they have been written or not, the wife will be out.[28] The 'compulsion' which would exempt the written talaq-nama from taking effect has to be the pain or the imminent prospect of death and not mere insistence of someone.[29]

There is an exact correspondence between Mufti Kifayatullah, the Deoband ulema and Maulana Ahmad Riza Khan on the related matter of a deed of kufr or shirk which has been done under compulsion. While the words of talaq throw the wife out even if they have been uttered under compulsion, like the Mufti, Maulana Ahmad Riza Khan holds that words of *kufr* may be uttered when one is caught in a life-threatening calamity![30]

In a word, even if the husband has given in to compulsion and pronounced talaq, it is enough to end the marriage and throw the wife out. All that the persons compelling him have to do is to have him speak the words—a task that should present no great difficulty, for those who have

27. *Fatawa-i-Rizvia,* Volume V, pp. 631–32.

28. Ibid., Volume V, p. 632.

29. Ibid., Volume V, p. 632.

30. Ibid., Volume VI, p. 112.

belaboured or otherwise forced the man to an extent that he is prepared to *write out* a document declaring talaq will certainly be in a position to have him *speak out* the words.

The rationale for throwing the wife out even in these circumstances is telling. It is set out in the *Hidayah*:

> The divorce of one acting upon compulsion, from threats, is effective, according to our doctors—Shafi'i maintains that it is not effective, because a person who is compelled has no option, and no formal act of law is worthy of regard unless it be purely optional: contrary to the case of a jester, who, in mentioning divorce, acts from option, which is the cause of its validity. Our doctors, on the other hand, allege that the person here mentioned pronounces divorce under circumstances of complete competency, (maturity of age and sanity of intellect), the result of which is that the divorce takes effect equally with that of a person uncompelled, for with him necessity (namely, the necessity of separation from a wife who may be odious or disagreeable to him) is the reason of its efficiency; and the same reason applies to the divorce of a compelled person, as he is also under necessity of divorce, in order that he may be released from the apprehension of that with which he was threatened by the compeller. The foundation of this is that the man alluded to has the choice of two evils; one, the thing with which he is threatened or compelled; and the other, divorce upon compulsion; and viewing both, he makes choice of that which appears to him the easiest, namely, divorce; and this proves that he has an option, though he be not desirous that its effect should be established, or, in other words, that divorce should take place upon it; nor does this circumstance forbid the efficiency of his sentence; as in the case of a jester, that is to say, if a man pronounce a divorce in jest, it takes effect although he be not desirous that it should; and so likewise the divorce of one who is compelled.[31]

---

31. Sheikh Burhanu'd-din Ali, *The Hedaya*, Charles Hamilton (tr.), 1791, Kitab Bhavan, New Delhi, 1985 Reprint, Volume I, pp. 210–11.

The *husband* chooses 'the lesser of two evils', and the *wife* is out on the road.

Even in jest

That other circumstance mentioned by the *Hidayah*—when the husband pronounces talaq in jest—comes up in the fatwas often.

The ulema enforce the rule that talaq uttered in jest, as in anger, throws the wife out—even if she was not even present, even if the husband did not mean to throw her out.

Zaid's friend joked with Zaid about Zaid's wife, reports the querist. Zaid said in jest, 'Talaq, Talaq, Talaq'. One maulvi said that the divorce was not effective. Another said it was effective but permitted restitution. So Zaid did restitution. He did not mean 'talaq' when he said 'talaq'. He had said so in jest. Is it legitimate for Zaid to do restitution? The words aforementioned rendered Zaid's wife divorced, rule the ulema. According to shariah intention is not to be taken into account in considering the words uttered, they declare. Nor can the shariah be stretched. The context makes it clear that Zaid has said 'talaq' with regard to his wife. It is not legitimate to do restitution after uttering the word 'talaq' thrice, they declare.[32]

In another case, the querist writes:

> Umar had an English haircut. Zaid asked him to give up that hairstyle. Umar made a joke and said, 'You give up your wife.' Zaid also said in joke, 'I have given up.' Umar asked him to say the word '*talaq*' thrice. Zaid immediately uttered, '*talaq, talaq, talaq*.' He said it five or seven times. Has divorce become

---

32. *Fatawa Dar al-Ulum, Deoband,* Volume IX, pp. 42–43. Similarly, *Fatawa-i-Rizvia,* Volume V, p. 639.

effective? If so, which one? Zaid does not want to separate from his wife.

The ulema of Deoband decree:

In this case divorce has become effective. That woman has become *mughlaza bainah*. Zaid cannot remarry her without halalah.[33]

The case is typical. Two friends are engaged in banter. The matter—whether an 'English-style hair' should be retained or not—is of little moment, in any event it does not concern the marital relationship of Zaid and his wife. The wife is nowhere near the scene. But the only way she can continue in, rather return to their home is to give herself in marriage to another man, to have that man bed her, then be divorced by that second man, and thereafter be married again by Zaid of the English hairstyle.

The husband is the one who does the careless thing—of uttering a word in jest—and the wife is the one who is out on the road !

Undesirable, but nonetheless lethal

It is not necessary for the husband to divorce a wife on account of some constitutional defect she may have, rules the *Fatawa-i-Rizvia*. In fact, as far as possible one should bear the problem with patience. The Maulana cites Hadis to fortify the matter: the woman has been made from a crooked rib, the Prophet has said, to enjoy her you will have to enjoy her with her crookedness, if you attempt to straighten her she will break; if one habit of her displeases you, the Prophet has said, another might please you; what you take to be a bane, the Prophet has said, may be a boon that Allah has conferred

33. *Fatawa Dar al-Ulum, Deoband,* Volume IX, p. 339.

on you. Hence, it says, if you have to give talaq (obviously, this can be for several purposes: to make her submit on some matter, to meet the demand of someone, etc.), then give one revocable talaq alone. Giving more is a sin. You may then take her back during her *iddat*. There is no need to go through nikah again: just say, 'You are back within my nikah.'[34]

That is about as compassionate as the rulings ever get. Notice that even in this case, the power of the husband to throw the wife out is not circumscribed in any way: were he to still decide to cast her away, a castaway she would be. Nor is the provision about giving one revocable divorce going to be of much help to the poor woman: given the way our societies are, a person who has some constitutional defect is in any case going to be living in uncertainty and rejection; now subject to a divorce which the husband may or may not revoke, she is certain to be pushed further into the whirlpool of torment and repudiation.

The point is put in perspective on the very next page. If there is some doubt about a woman, the *Fatawa-i-Rizvia* rules, or if she is a sinner, or if she does not observe namaz, or if she has become old, then talaq given without detestation is proper and valid. In fact, in certain cases it is desirable to do so, says the *Fatawa-i-Rizvia.* The ulema hold, it declares, that if she does not observe namaz, then, even if he is unable to pay the dower, even then the husband should give the talaq. In certain circumstances it is proper to do so, the fatwa reiterates. For instance, if the mother and father order one to give talaq and if not doing so will upset them or if they will be put to hardship, then to give talaq is *wajib,* it is proper, even if she, the wife, is not in the wrong at all. Yes, in the Hadis it is said that talaq given without need or justification is detestable or prohibited, notes the fatwa. But if the husband

34. *Fatawa-i-Rizvia,* Volume V, p. 602.

gives it, it shall certainly be effective. His sinning and doing that which is detestable does not stop it from taking effect, it says. For instance, it is haram to give talaq during menstruation, it is disobedience of the hukum of Allah. But if it is given, it shall certainly take effect, the fatwa declares.[35]

This principle—that though a thing be undesirable, even detestable, if done it takes effect—has far-reaching consequences. Many reformers have suggested that one way to dilute the terror of talaq is to have the bridegroom agree to forego the power to throw the wife out peremptorily at the time of the marriage itself by making this a part of the marriage agreement, the *nikah-nama*. The ulema's view is to the contrary: the talaq power is Allah-given, they hold, it is inherent in the position of the husband. Thus, decrees the *Fatawa-i-Rizvia*, if a husband who had agreed not to give talaq, gives it, it shall certainly be a violation of the agreement, and therefore strictly detestable, but it shall be fully effective.[36] On the same reasoning talaq given when the wife is menstruating or when she is pregnant shall be equally effective.[37] Mufti Kifayatullah also holds that not only is a triple talaq pronounced at one go enough to terminate the marriage, the wife is out even if the pronouncement has been made during her menstruation.[38]

Enhancing the terror

A particularly cruel feature of the Islamic law on divorce is that whenever there is some doubt—for instance, if no witnesses were present when the talaq was pronounced, or

35. *Fatawa-i-Rizvia*, Volume V, pp. 603–4.

36. Ibid., Volume V, p. 604.

37. Ibid., Volume V, pp. 604, 625.

38. *Mufti Kifayatullah ke Fatawi*, Volume VI, pp. 74–75.

if the words which were used were ambiguous—the outcome turns on what the husband says ex post facto as to what his intention was at the time he uttered the expression. The wife is thus put in double-terror: the husband can throw her out at any time without even alleging a reason by just uttering one word; or he can utter one of the well-practised ambiguous expressions—her fate now depends on what he subsequently says his intention was at the time he used those words. The words having fallen from his lips, the woman knows that she can survive as wife only if, when he is questioned, he affirms that in using the words he did not intend to divorce her. She must therefore do everything he wants her to do, everything she possibly can do to make him say later that his intention was not to divorce her but something else.

This rule—that the case turns on what the husband says his intention was—is enforced by the ulema in fatwa after fatwa.

A man writes, 'I shall give her Rs 10 and two pairs of clothes regularly in a year. If I do not and create problems, then "X" can recover the dues from our property, and I shall lose claim on my wife.' He does not give even that much. And he has had no connection with his wife for four years. Is the wife free of him?, asks the querist. If he (the husband) affirms that by the words, 'I shall lose all claim on my wife,' he meant that the wife shall be divorced, rules Mufti Kifayatullah, then upon his not living up to the contract, talaq shall take effect.[39]

A husband says the words in *haalat-i-ghazab*. Subsequently he denies having said them or says that divorce is not what he meant. Is the wife out? Is the marriage ended? The outcome, rules Mufti Kifayatullah, depends on whether the husband had said the words with the intention of divorce. If

39. *Mufti Kifayatullah ke Fatawi*, Volume VI, pp. 284–85.

that was not his intention, if he says he never said the words, if witnesses testifying that he said the words are not reliable, then no divorce takes place.[40] In a word: the outcome remains in the hands of the husband—he can turn it in one direction or the other by what he says ex post facto his intention was.

A husband tells his wife not to go to the well to fetch water. She says that if she doesn't, who will fetch it? The husband says, 'If there is no one other than you to fetch water, then three talaqs on you.' If there actually is no one else, or if she actually goes and fetches water, is she out, divorced? Ask the husband what his intention was when he used the words, rules the Mufti.[41] If the intention was that if, in spite of what he had ordered, she goes to the well she would be divorced, then she is indeed divorced, if that was not the intention, then, no.

A father is forcing his son, Zaid, to marry Zainab. The son does not want to do so. While Zaid is conversing with friends, a friend says, 'But you will *have to* marry her.' Zaid says, 'If I keep her (*rakhun*), then three talaqs.' In our parts, says the querist, 'rakhun' means nikah. Is Zainab lawful to Zaid? Mufti Kifayatullah's verdict leaves everything to the ex post facto statement of the man, on what he now says his intention was when he used the word 'rakhun'. If he affirms that by 'rakhun' he meant nikah, rules the Mufti, this woman shall not be lawful to him. The Mufti's ruling means that if he has not married her, he cannot do so; if he has married her, she stands divorced. If he does not affirm that this was his meaning, then 'rakhun' shall not imply nikah, and shall not entail talaq.[42]

The other authorities enforce the rule just as sternly. If

40. Ibid., Volume VI, p. 85.
41. Ibid., Volume VI, pp. 272–73.
42. Ibid., Volume VI, p. 280.

the words he had used are not clear, the case shall depend on what the intention of the husband was, rules the *Fatawa-i-Rizvia.*[43] If the words he used are not clear, and there are no witnesses, the husband shall be asked what his intention was, it rules.[44] If there was no intention to divorce the wife then no divorce shall take place, it rules.[45] When the words used are ambiguous or unclear, the husband shall be asked: 'What did you say?' The outcome will depend on what he says, it rules.[46] A husband says, 'You are no longer of use to me, I have given you talaq'—if the husband says that he used these words so as to divorce the wife, the wife shall stand divorced, it rules.[47]

The cases show that the consequences which befall the hapless wife can hardly be imagined by a non-Muslim, specially a non-Muslim male. 'He was my husband,' writes the poor woman in the last mentioned case. 'He and I and my mother and brother used to stay in the same house. And there used to be quarrels over food and clothing. Then he used to beat me up, and used to abuse me. Then my mother and I went to the court and filed an application. And when he heard this, he said to me, 'You are no longer of use to me. And I give you talaq! Having given the talaq he came to my place. And my mother said, 'What business do you have here now? You have given talaq *to* your wife. Don't come here now.' Am I free of him?,' the poor woman asks.

'If this narrative is correct,' decrees the *Fatawa-i-Rizvia,* 'then one *talaq* has certainly taken place.' 'But the woman has not got out of the *nikah,*' it declares. 'Yes, if by the first

---

43. *Fatawa-i-Rizvia,* Volume V, p. 609.
44. Ibid., Volume V, p. 610.
45. Ibid., Volume V, p. 613.
46. Ibid., Volume V, p. 6l6.
47. Ibid., Volume V, p. 622.

expression too—'You are no longer of use to me'—he intended divorce, then two talaqs have taken place. And the woman is out of the *nikah.* The question remains, whether by these words too he intended divorce.' This depends on what he says, it rules. 'He should be asked to take an oath. If he swears that, 'By those words I did not intend *talaq*', then his statement should be accepted. And two talaqs shall not take place, and only one *rajai talaq* which the husband can revoke at will shall take place. And if during *iddat* he resumes the woman, she shall remain his wife.'[48] In a word: irrespective of the fact that the wife was being beaten and abused, irrespective of the fact that he had declared talaq, the husband can still keep her under his yoke by now saying that his intention in using the words was this and not that, and he can still 'resume' the woman—without her consent, as we shall see.

By using an ambiguous expression the husband can throw the wife into a typhoon of insecurity and terror. In giving him even greater power over the wife by making the outcome depend on what he subsequently says he intended or meant, the ulema are of course not inventing something of their own. They are following the classical position on the matter. 'A term implicative of repudiation,' explains the *Durr-ul-Mukhtar,*'.... is one that was not originally designed for it.... but is capable of expressing it....' 'Consequently by the use of ambiguous terms one is not repudiated, judicially, except when there was an intention (to divorce the wife) or circumstances show that....'[49] He can utter these ambiguous words and then, on pain of declaring subsequently that his intention was to throw her out, extract whatever he wants the wife to do.

Here is a typical instance mentioned by the Islamic jurists:

---

48. *Fatawa-i-Rizvia,* Volume V, p. 622.

49. *Durr-ul-Mukhtar,* 1992 Reprint, Kitab Bhavan, New Delhi, p. 161.

> A man says the word *Aituddi* thrice and intends a repudiation by the first and menses by the rest, he will be believed judicially, because he has intended (in his second and third repetition of the term) to use it in its original sense, but if he makes no intention thereby, i.e. by his second and third repetition of the term, three repudiations will be effected, because his intention of repudiation by the first use of the term shows the state of his mind. Two divorces will be effected if he intends by the second use of the term only to effect a repudiation, but one only will be effected if he intends to repudiate only by the third repetition of the term. And it will not be effected (at all) if by none of the three (repetitions) he meant to effect a divorce. Twenty-four different results follow from various uses of the term *Aituddi* as has been mentioned by Kamal. To these may be added one more case in which the speaker means to effect only one repudiation by every repetition of the term. In such a case one will take effect according to conscience, and three according to law.[50]

Notice both consequences: how everything turns on what the man says ex post facto he meant to denote by that single word; and notice too the alacrity of the jurists who think up twenty-four, plus one, different results from the use of that one word. Thus, if the husband uses that word, he retains inhuman power in his hand: he can declare that he meant repudiation by it and thus throw the wife out, or he can save her by affirming that he was referring not to divorce but to menses! And naturally it is the ulema who must decide which of the twenty-five pigeonholes this particular case fits into. And just as naturally, till the husband declares definitely what his intention was, and till the ulema settle upon the particular pigeonhole, the wife remains in the whirlpool of uncertainty and torment.

In fact, even words which are unambiguous can be

50. *Durr-ul-Mukhtar*, op.cit., pp. 164–65.

enlarged upon, so to say, to produce lethal effect. To continue for a moment with this classic of Islamic jurisprudence, the *Durr-ul-Mukhtar* declares, 'A man divorces his wife once after consummation, then renders that one divorce three, it is all right, just as when a man repudiates his wife with a reversible divorce and then turns it, before retracting, into absolute.' 'Similarly,' Sheikh Muhammad Alauddin continues, 'if a husband says about his wife while she is observing *iddat*, 'Apply to my wife three repudiations by this one repudiation,' or, 'I apply to her two repudiations by this one repudiation,' the effect will be as he desires.'[51] And yet we must believe, on pain of being communal, that no legal system has given a higher status to women than the shariah!

'If your mother does not come to me tonight....'

In glaring contrast to the gloss which modern apologists try to put on the matter, Islamic jurists have faithfully followed the view of women embedded in the Quran and Hadis. They have enforced the true position: that the husband has absolute power in the matter of divorce; that he need assign no reason for throwing his wife out; that he owes the wife no maintenance beyond providing her the barest minimum in the three months following his pronouncement of talaq; and that the wife has no corresponding power. The apologists make much of the fact that in certain circumstances under Islamic law the wife can divorce herself—this, they say, is a unique facility which Islamic law alone gives to the wife. But they glide over two facts about the matter: the wife acquires this power only if the husband delegates it to her; and, the moment the wife exercises this power, that is the moment she dissolves the marriage by divorcing herself she loses even the meagre rights she would

---

51. *Durr-ul-Mukhtar*, op.cit., p. 165.

otherwise have had upon the dissolution of the marriage. Far from being a facility for the wife, the practice becomes a facility *for the husband*: by driving the wife to divorce herself, the husband is not only able to rid himself of her, he is able to rid himself of anything that might otherwise have been her due.

The total inequality of the relationship is brought home by the hundreds of pages which the law books and the volumes of fatwas devote to what is called 'Conditional Divorce'. In this form the husband makes the divorce contingent upon some act or event: the moment that act or event transpires, the wife is out.

Four aspects of this form of talaq are particularly noteworthy:

- With a pronouncement of 'conditional divorce' the husband can reduce the wife to a condition of absolute and craven submission: she must either do what the husband has ordered or she is automatically and instantly thrown out;
- The husband can make the divorce contingent upon events over which the wife has absolutely no control at all;
- In determining the outcome, far from being consequential, the wife has next to no locus standi;
- The jurists go to unimaginable lengths to cater to the interests of the husband—to make the outcome depend on his ex post facto statements about what his intention was at the time he pronounced the conditional divorce, to suggest devices by which he may, if he so desires, escape the consequences of the conditions he had specified.

In addition to volumes we have been following I shall provide examples from the classic fatwas of *Fatawa-i-Qazi Khan* of Imam Fakhruddin Hasan Bin Mansoor Al-Uzjandi Al-Farghani. Along with the *Fatawa-i-Alamgiri* and the *Hidayah,* the *Fatawa-i-Qazi Khan* is among the most authoritative law books for Hanafi Sunnis—that is, for the overwhelming majority of Muslims in India. I shall list just a few representative examples from this latter work to bring home the way Islamic law is enforced between husband and wife. In each instance I shall set out the statement which the Imam lists and at the end indicate within parentheses the number of his ruling for ready reference.[52]

To begin with, the rulings of the jurists show that the husband has the total, absolute, unbridled power to tell his wife, 'Unless you do "X",' or, in the alternate, 'Unless you refrain from doing "Y",' 'you are divorced'. A mere listing of the 'X' and 'Y' which the Islamic jurists have held to cause, unless complied with, full and final divorce, a mere listing of these takes one's breath away. It shows that under the much-vaunted Islamic law of marriage and divorce, at a mere statement of the husband the wife must either reduce herself to totally submitting to the whim and fancy of the husband or stand divorced. She has absolutely no option in the matter. Indeed, once he has stated his whim or condition, the husband has no option either: he cannot ex post facto take pity or give in to the entreaties of the wife and let her stay unless she fulfils the condition he had laid down—unless she fulfils it, that is, as completely, and as fervently, and as promptly as he had specified.

A man says to his wife, 'If you step into the house, you are divorced,' and she steps into it: she stands divorced (2080).

A man says to his wife, 'If you go out of the house without my order, you are divorced,' and she steps out without his order: she is divorced (2163).

---

52. The numbers relate to the number of the English text and translations of the rulings as given in Imam Fakhruddin Hasan bin Mansoor Al-Uzjandi Al-Farghani, *Fatawa-i-Qazi Khan*, tr. and ed. by Maulvi Muhammad Yusuf Khan Bahadur and Maulvi Wilayat Husain, Kitab Bhavan, New Delhi, 1994 Reprint, Volume II; the number of the fatwa in the original Arabic text is 900 less than the number in the translated paragraph.

A man says to his wife, 'If you speak to such and such a woman (or man, or whosoever the husband specifies), you are divorced,' and she speaks to the person: she is divorced (2180).

A man in a state of intoxication summons his wife to the bedroom (the *khvabgah*) to bed her. But she tarries. The husband says, 'If you fulfil my desire then all is well. Otherwise, talaq upon you.' If, the husband having sworn an oath, the wife now or in the future does not obey his order and join him in the bed, then she is divorced. Explaining this, the commentator notes that the wife shall stand divorced even if she demurs on some future occasion, because, the reasoning goes, the husband, having expressed this desire once, must be taken to remain anxious in the future also to secure its fulfilment (2193).

A man says to his wife, 'If you pass the night except in my bosom then you are divorced thrice,' and the wife remains in his bed that night except that the husband happens not to actually take the woman in his bosom, the woman survives as wife. But if he had said, 'If you shall not come within my embrace you are divorced thrice,' and the wife remains in his bed that night but the husband happens not to actually take or keeps the woman in his embrace, she is divorced (2205).

A man says to his wife, 'If I shall put you out of temper, you are divorced,' he then strikes a child of her, and she loses her temper: does she survive as wife? Well, say the jurists, it depends. If the husband had struck the child on account of something which it is proper to correct in the child for the sake of discipline, the wife survives. The reasoning is a bit incomprehensible: 'because,' we learn, 'this is not an occasion for the woman to take offence and lose her termper; and her display of temper shall therefore not at all be heeded.' On the other hand, 'If the man has struck the child on an occasion which does not require the correction of the child for the sake of the discipline of the child, then his wife shall become divorced' (2280). What justice! Having warned the wife, the husband beats a helpless child wantonly, without the child having given any cause, the wife, if she so much as loses her temper with the husband, is out—without a pittance for maintenance, remember.

A woman is living with her husband in her father's house. The husband decides to leave for his own house and he asks the wife to come along; she demurs. He then says to the wife, 'If you shall not go with me, you are divorced thrice.' The husband then goes out of the house. Now the wife also goes out, in fact she reaches the husband's house even before him. The learned jurists hold that 'If the woman goes out so that her going out cannot be called going along with him,' then she is divorced (*2297*). That is, the wife must not just comply with the order of the husband, she must comply with the order to the letter.

A man tells his wife, 'If you do not come to my bed at once and do X,Y,Z, you are divorced,' and she tarries fearing that by complying with his wishes she might lose the time of her prayers, she is out, says the learned jurist, 'because to say prayers is quite a different act (from making preparation to comply with the husband's directions)'—she would have survived, that is, if the delay had been caused by her preparing herself for his bed, but as the delay was caused by something altogether unrelated to this—by her anxiety, in the instant case, about keeping the time of prayer—she is out. (Mercifully, in this particular case—i.e., when the delay has been caused by prayers—other jurists maintain that she will not be divorced) (2298).

The point is re-emphasized—that the wife must not just carry out the order of the husband, she must carry it out at once. A husband tells his wife that he wants to bed her. But she does not cooperate. Thereupon he tells her, 'If you do not come to the khvabgah with me, talaq on you.' If even upon this being said she does not come to the bedroom at once and instead tarries, and reaches the bedroom when his passion has subsided, she is divorced and out (2299).

A man says to his wife, 'If you ascend this stair, or put your foot on it, then you are divorced.' The wife puts one foot on the steps; then she recollects what she had been told, and turns back. She is out. Putting that one step was enough (2203).

A man says to his wife, 'Go to "X", and get back from him thing "Y", and bring it to me this instant, and if you shall not bring it this instant, you are divorced.' The wife goes to the person but is not successful in getting back the thing; she gets it back from the person the next day. She is out. 'Because,' say the jurists, 'his (the husband's) expression, 'bring it back to me this instant' is a clear (and direct) expression denoting promptness' (2319).

A drunken man strikes his wife. She goes out of the house. The husband says, 'If you shall not come back to me, you are divorced.' This happens in the afternoon. The woman returns at night. She is out. 'Because,' say the jurists, 'his oath meant promptitude' (2321).

A husband tells his wife, 'If I cause you pain, you are divorced,' and then goes and purchases for himself a female slave 'and makes *Soorryya* of her....(*Soorryya* being derived from *Sirr* which means concealment),' the wife is divorced and out. For his bringing home the female slave, say the learned jurists, is deemed 'pain' (2282).

A man tells his wife, 'If I purchase a female slave and jealousy overtakes you by reason of my purchase, then you are divorced thrice.' He then purchases the female slave. That the wife is jealous is seen from her abusive language, from her fretting. She is out. The only way she can survive as wife is that the jealousy be confined to her heart, and not show up in her word or deed (2283).

A wife is crying in her mother's house. The husband tells the mother: 'If your daughter does not go out of your house, and cries here, she is divorced.' The wife leaves the house, but later returns and cries. Does she survive as wife, or is she out? Depends, say the learned jurists. If she cries inaudibly, she survives. If others hear her cry, she is out. 'Because,' say the jurists, 'the husband only prevented her from crying in order that her cry might not be heard' (2325). The wife thus must not only bear whatever the husband inflicts on her, if she so much as cries (unless this be inaudibly) after he has told her not to do so, she is out.

Next, consider examples from the fatwas of the moderate Mufti Kifayatullah. In each of the following instances he rules that unless the wife complies with and fulfils the condition which has fallen from the lips of the husband, she stands automatically divorced:[53]

> A husband says, 'If you tell my mother this, you are divorced;' she tells his mother that; she is out (pp. 78–79).
>
> The husband says to his wife, 'If you enter the house, then you are divorced.' She enters. He explains that he did not intend divorce, that he had used the expression merely to frighten her so that she would stay away from the house. The *fatwa* is that she stands divorced (p. 280).
>
> A husband does not want his wife to wear colourful clothes. They quarrel. In the heat of the moment he says, 'If you wear colourful clothes in my presence, three talaqs on you.' She survives only if, upon wearing colourful clothes, she makes sure that she is not in the husband's presence. But if she wears them in his presence, she is out (p. 281).

---

53. The examples are from *Mufti Kifayatullah ke Fatawi*, Volume VI. The page number is indicated within parentheses after each example.

A husband tells his wife, 'If you come before your brother, you shall be *haram* for me.' If she does, she stands divorced (pp. 285–86).

A husband writes to his wife, 'If upon seeing this letter you do not at once obtain a reply from your father, three talaqs upon you,' and for whatever reason she is not able to secure the reply, she is out (pp. 313–14).

The ulema of Deoband are just as unrelenting. In each of the following circumstances, the wife is out, they rule:[54]

Case 643: A man loses his temper, asks his wife to leave his house, and says to her, 'If you show me your face, it will mean divorce,' and she appears before him (p. 55).

Case 663: Zaid says to his wife, 'If you go to your father's house, you will stand divorced,' and she goes there after her father dies. She stands divorced, decree the *Ulema,* because the father's house remains the father's house even after his death (p. 65).

Case 677: A man says to his wife, 'If you go anywhere at all out of the house, even to your parents, you will stand divorced,' and she goes to see her parents, she is out (pp. 74–75).

Case 696: A man's wife goes to attend a marriage in a relative's family. She is accompanied by her mother and blood-brother. When the husband hears of this he sends her a note in writing, 'Mrs. so and so has been my wife for five and a half years. She has gone to a stranger's house without my permission. If she does not return by such and such a time on such and such a date, I divorce her.' She returns, but is late by four days. She is out (p. 84).

But, to proceed. In the rulings of which the foregoing are representative the wife can survive by submitting herself

---

54. The examples are taken from *Fatawa Dar al-Ulum, Deoband,* Volume X. The case number is given at the beginning of the example and the page number at the end:

completely to the whims and fancies, the commands and worse of the husband. The rulings thus entail subjugation, complete subjugation, but only subjugation. At least there is *something* the wife can do—namely, submit herself completely to the husband's whims and wishes—to keep herself from being thrown out on the street. The next set of rulings entail much more—they reduce the woman to a condition of terror. For the husband may by his mere statement—a statement he may make in anger, a statement he may make just to emphasize a point, and of course a statement he may make when he in fact wants to plunge the wife into terror—the husband can make the continuance of the marriage contingent on *events over which the wife has no control whatsoever.*

In the face of the hundreds of rulings to this effect which Islam's canonical law books contain, to maintain, as the apologists do, 'No religion has given a higher place to women than Islam', is not just ludicrous, it is chicanery.

Three reasons alone explain how such assertions continue to be made, and continue to be repeated in our newspapers: first, hardly anyone among us looks up, or even knows about these rulings—although they are the very stuff of the fundamental books of Islamic jurisprudence; second, echoing, and adopting as one's own the assertions of Islam's champions is the way to be secular in India; and third, there is the power of terror—to recall that these rulings are what constitute the truth about the position of Muslim women is to open oneself to the terrorism of Islam's champions.

While reading the rulings, one should assess whether this kind of jurisprudence leaves any room for the kinds of reform that some would like to bring about by relying on 'the principles of Islamic jurisprudence' themselves. We begin again with rulings in the classic *Fatawa-i-Qazi Khan*.[55]

55. For citation and numbering see footnote 52 above.

A man is caught by thieves. They take all they find. Have you any more?, they ask. He says he does not. They then compel him to swear that if he has more his wife is thrice divorced. If it turns out that he in fact happens to have more—even if this happens to be unknown to him—the poor wife, sitting at home, having taken no part in any of this, is indeed out (2254).

A band of robbers waylays a man on a highway. They take all he has, and then put him on his oath that if he gives any information about them to anyone, his wife shall be divorced. Later passers-by approach him, and he says to them, 'There are wolves on the highway.' They understand him, and retrace their steps. The jurists declare that if by 'wolves' he really meant to alert them to the robbers, the wife, who naturally had nothing to do with either his taking the oath or with his saying anything later, is divorced. She survives only if by 'wolves' he actually meant *wolves* (2255).

A husband tells his wife, 'If you do such and thus, all my wives are divorced.' The wife does what the husband has forbidden. Not only she but also all the other wives, who had absolutely nothing to do with what the husband said or with what that particular wife subsequently did, are divorced (2264). As perfect device as can be thought of for converting the wives into a posse: all of them as a group will exert to ensure that none of them falls short in catering to the whims of the husband, lest he pronounce the conditional divorce, 'If you do not do "X" and "Y" for me, all my wives are divorced.'

A man says, 'If I abuse anyone, then my wife is divorced.' He then abuses a human corpse. The poor wife—who had nothing to do with either making the initial declaration pr with his subsequently chancing upon the corpse, is divorced (2277).

A man says to his mother, 'If you shall leave me today, my wife shall be divorced.' The mother subsequently leaves. The wife may have been entreating the mother to stay, the mother may have left because of something the *husband*, her son, has or has not done. It is the wife who stands divorced (2279).

Be she ever so innocent, a man says to his wife, 'If I accuse you of adultery, then you are divorced.' He then charges her with adultery or even addresses her as, 'O, daughter of an adultress,' she is not only humiliated, she is divorced and out (2287).

A man says to his wife, 'If I drink, you are divorced,' and he drinks (1963); 'If you have *not* stolen this, you are divorced,' and she has in fact *not* stolen the thing (2072); 'If I strike you, you are divorced,' and he strikes her; 'If I enter the house today, you are divorced,' and he does enter the house (2106); 'If I give wine to anyone, you are divorced,' and a guest arrives and he does serve wine to him (2171); a husband tells his wife, 'If I have intercourse with you, you are divorced,' and he does have intercourse with her (2173); 'If I put on this cloth, you are divorced,' and he puts on that cloth (2175); 'If I bathe on account of having done something unlawful, you are divorced,' and he does something unlawful (that is, commits adultery) and therefore bathes (2188); 'If you get sick, you are divorced,' and the woman in spite of herself falls sick (2293); 'If your menses continues tomorrow, you are divorced,' and the woman, in spite of all efforts, is still menstruating the next day (2293); 'If I ride, you are divorced,' and he rides on some animal as distinct from a human being or a wall (2310); 'If I speak falsely, you are divorced,' and he tells a lie (2311); 'If I break wind, you are divorced,' and he breaks wind (2312); 'If I commit adultery, then you are divorced,' and, on the evidence of four just witnesses or on his own admission supplemented by the evidence of two witnesses, he has committed adultery (2313); 'If I have intercourse with my slave girl, you are divorced,' and he has intercourse with the slave girl (2320); 'If I speak to so-and-so, you are divorced,' and he speaks to the person (2354)—in one and each of these circumstances the wife, though she had nothing to do with his making the declaration or with what he did subsequently, is divorced and out, without maintenance or anything else. In fact, if the husband says to the wife, 'You are divorced if', and does not care to, or forgets to even complete the sentence, she is divorced and out (2116).

In the rulings of Mufti Kifayatullah also the wife is out, without let or maintenance, for things the husband does or fails to do, because of deeds for which she is in no way responsible. In each of the following circumstances the wife is out, divorced, rules the Mufti:[56]

> The husband says, 'If I ever gamble again then my wife is divorced,' and he gambles subsequently (p. 257).
>
> The husband says, 'If I ever meet Umar again or go to him then three *talaqs* on my wife,' and he goes to Umar (p. 276).
>
> A father is forcing his son to marry a particular girl. The son is conversing with friends. A friend says, 'But you will *have to* marry her.' The son says, 'If I keep her, then three *talaqs* upon her.' As in the locality 'keep her' (*rakhun*) stands for *nikah*, if he eventually succumbs to the father and marries her, the hapless girl stands divorced (p. 280).
>
> Upset at a Hindu not being fair to them, the Muslims of an area say, 'If we cultivate the lands of this Hindu, our wives are divorced.' And they subsequently cultivate that Hindu's lands (p. 313).

The rulings of the ulema of 'India's Al-Azhar', the Dar al-

56. The examples are from *Mufti Kifayatullah ke Fatawi*, Volume VI. The page number is given within parentheses at the end of each example.

Ulum of Deoband do not show any greater concern for the hapless woman. Here are some of the representative fatwas of these learned men:[57]

Case 619: Zaid quarrels with his wife and says in a state of great rage, 'If I do "X", I have triple *talaq,*' and he does 'X' (p. 41).

Case 641: In great anger a husband says, 'Whoever does *roza* in this courtyard, will invite divorce,' and later keeps the fast of Ramzan in that courtyard (p. 54).

Case 646: Some persons are talking about *talaq*. One of them says, 'Whatever marriage I contract, they shall be divorced,' and he marries (p. 57).

Case 649: A man says to his uncle, 'If I do not take back by force the 50 rupees you owe me my wife will become *haram* for me, that is, she will stand divorced,' and neither does the uncle return the money of his own accord nor is the nephew able to recover if from him by force (p. 57).

Case 660: Zaid says, 'If I go to area "X", my wife will stand divorced,' and later buys land in area 'X' and goes there (pp. 63–64).

Case 665: A man says, 'If I have not done "X" in the past, my wife stands divorced,' and it is found that he had not done 'X' in the past (p. 67).

Case 671: Zaid quarrels with the *mullah* of the mosque. In a state of rage, the *mullah* says, 'If I work in the mosque henceforth, my wife stands divorced,' and he continues to work (p. 71).

Case 681: A man forces another to say, 'If I do not keep this secret of your's my wife will stand divorced,' and, out of helplessness, he is not able to keep the matter secret (p. 76).

Case 687: Zaid has illegitimate relations with Zainab, wife of

---

57. The examples are from *Fatawa Dar al-Ulum, Deoband,* Volume X. The number of the case is given at the beginning of the example, that of the page at the end.

Umar. Umar comes to know of this, calls Zaid and asks him why he did so. Zaid denies the charge. Umar asks him to declare that if he has in fact committed adultery with Zainab, his (Zaid's) wife will stand divorced whenever he marries. If Zaid has committed adultery or thought of doing so, rule the *Ulema*, his wife will stand divorced as soon as he marries her (p. 78).

Case 709: During a conversation Zaid says, 'If I do not murder Umar, my wife will become subject to triple divorce.' He is not able to murder Umar. The *Ulema* note that this sort of a vow for divorce is harmful, as Zaid may yet murder Umar before dying. Never the less, the wife stands divorced and re-marriage is not permissible without *halalah* (p. 94).

In the first set of conditional divorces the wife, as we saw, can stay on as wife, though only by submitting herself completely to the commands and whims of the husband. In the second set even this is of no avail: the outcome depends entirely on what the husband chooses to do, or in fact does after pronouncing the conditional divorce. But there is another set which puts the matter even more out of the reach of the wife: fatwa after fatwa pronounces that the wife must indeed be thrown out when the husband makes the continuation of the marriage contingent upon a *third* person doing something, and that *latter person* fails to or chooses not to do the thing.

In the great classic of Sunni law, the *Durr-ul-Mukhtar*, the work that is treated as gospel by so many of our authorities giving fatwas, we read: A husband says, 'If my wife's mother does not come to me tonight, my wife is divorced,' and there are witnesses who testify that, indeed, the mother did not come to him in the night, the wife is out.[58]

In the *Fatawa-i-Qazi Khan* we read of a man who accuses a woman of adultery. The husband of the woman says, 'If you do not prove her adultery today, then she is divorced

58. *Durr-ul-Mukhtar*, op. cit., p. 199.

thrice.' If the man is not able to prove the charge he has made—and he can do so only if either the wife herself confesses or he produces four eyewitnesses to the actual act—the poor wife, for absolutely no fault of her own, is out (2203).

Similarly, a man tells another person or persons, 'If you do not come to my house as guest today, my wife is with three divorces.' The other person does not come. The wife is out (2072). And so on.

The fatwas of Mufti Kifayatullah too visit the consequences of the third party doing or not doing something on the poor wife. Thus in *Mufti Kifayatullah ke Fatawi*, Volume VI, we read:

> Zaid asks his brothers for money to set himself up in business. Fearing that he will blow it up, they refuse. He says, 'If you don't give me the money then upon my wife three divorces.' And they still do not give the money. The wife, who had nothing to do with the husband asking for money, nor with the brothers not giving it, stands divorced (p. 247).

Similarly, in the fatwas of the ulema of Deoband, Volume X, we read:

> *Case* 736: At the time of going to court a man says, 'If I do not win the case, I will be subject to triple divorce.' He does not win. The wife stands divorced (pp. 110–11).

The *Fatawa-i-Rizvia* is just as merciless. A husband tells his wife, 'If you come to my house, then talaq to you'; the moment she enters the husband's house, decrees Maulana Ahmad Riza Khan, she stands divorced.[59] 'If I do not fulfil your need,' the husband tells a third party, 'then talaq on my wife,' and he fails in fulfilling the other person's need, the poor woman, who had nothing to do with the matter, is out.[60]

---

59. *Fatawa-i-Rizvia*, Volume V, p. 796.

60. Ibid., Volume V, p. 820.

Aggravating factors

The specific rulings are cruel by themselves. But they are not the end of the matter. There are several factors which make things even worse for the poor woman.

There is the Quranic view of woman, the view of her which the Prophet enunciated time and again, and which we shall take up later.[61]

There is the Islamic view of marriage. Apologists of Islam, ever so anxious to show how progressive and avant-garde and modern their religion has always been, never tire of saying: In Islam marriage is not a sacrament, it is just a contract. Woman, as we shall see when we turn to the Quran and the Hadis, is just an 'affliction' that man has to suffer; she is just a field that he may irrigate or not irrigate as it pleases him;[62] at best she is one of the things that Allah has created for him to enjoy;[63] when on top of all this marriage is but a contract specifying the terms on which he may enjoy the thing—the mehr, as Ram Swarup reminds us being literally the 'wages' or 'hire' for using the woman[64]—the

---

61. See Chapter 10 below.

62. 'O Abu Said, I have some slave-girls who are better than my wives, but I do not desire that they should all become pregnant. Shall I do *azl* (*coitus interruptus*) with them?,' asks a believer, and is told, 'They are your fields of cultivation, if you wish to irrigate them do so, or if you desire otherwise keep them dry.' (Imam Malik, *Muwatta*, Sh. Muhammad Ashraf, Lahore, 1980, Ch. 362, 1121.) And in so saying the Companion was but following the command of Allah: 'Your wives are as a tilth unto you,' Allah says in the Quran, 'So come unto your tilth when or how you will; But do some good act for your souls beforehand; And fear Allah....' (Quran 2.223).

63. 'The whole world is to be enjoyed,' the Prophet says, 'but the best thing in the world is a good woman.' *Mishkat al-Masabih*, Sh. Muhammad Ashraf, Lahore, 1975, Volume I, p. 658.

64. Ram Swarup, *Woman in Islam*, Voice of India, New Delhi, 1994, in particular, pp. 22–25. 'The Quran at several places, frankly calls dower, *ujoor*

ulema naturally visit all the consequences on the woman. The husband has but to enjoy the woman, and when he tires of her can just cast her off paying her the nominal maintenance, and the mehr which had been agreed to in the contract. And Allah, in His mercy, has not put these latter at anyonerous level. The minimum *mutah*, the consolatory gift, we learn, is one pair of clothes and the maximum is one slave or slave girl.[65] The maintenance is to be board and lodging for just three months. And while it is fashionable nowadays to fix the mehr at poetically grandiloquent levels, it is just as fixed a practice to have the wife agree to forego it on the nuptial night itself.[66]

There is another feature which is germane to the ulema themselves: they are inward-looking specialists, and, as is the wont of specialists, their concerns are arcane distinctions, the classifications and sub-classifications into which a case may fall. What shall befall the woman is no concern of theirs.

We begin with the classic, *Durr-ul-Mukhtar*.

A husband says to his wife, 'If you give birh to a male child you are divorced and if you give birth to a female child you are divorced twice.' And she gives birth to both. The jurist's concern is not the utter inhumanity of the condition, it is not the inequity of it between the son and the daughter.

(wages or hire),' he writes, 'a word quite current in that sense in India too (*ujrat*). For example, one verse in the Quran reads: 'O Prophet! Lo ! We have made lawful unto thee thy wives unto whom thou hast paid their hire.' The same term is used in verses 24 and 25 of Sura 4 too.' Ibid., pp. 22–23.

65. Imam Malik, *Muwatta*, op. cit, p. 256, f.n. 299.

66. And for this practice also the All Merciful and Considerate Allah has provided the sanction. For He has said, 'Give to the wives their dower as a free gift; but if they on their own remit a part of it, you can take it and enjoy it with cheer,' Quran, 4.4; see also Quran, 4.24 where Allah reiterates that, if after the dower has been agreed, 'You mutually agree (to vary it) there is no blame on you.'

His concern is: Which of the two—the boy or the girl—was born first? 'Now (that is, after the husband has spoken as above) she gives birth to both,' he notes, 'and it is not known which was the firstborn, according to judicial precepts she is repudiated once, but by way of precaution she should be deemed to become divorced twice, because there is the possibility of the first child being the girl.... If they both are proved to have been born as twins, three repudiations shall take place....'[67]

A husband who is as responsible for the children who are being born makes such a preposterous declaration, and these are the concerns of the learned men!

The concern is not with what shall transpire on the poor woman. The concern is whether the intonation of the husband was one rather than another, whether the expression he used was grammatically correct, whether one set of words rather than another preceded or followed the word 'talaq'. The same sort of hair-splitting occurs when the husband uses signs instead of words to throw the wife out. There is no dispute that he has the power to do so—that he can say, 'You are divorced like this,' and then raise one, two or three fingers, or, to better torment her, raise one finger, and then the second, and still later the third. The discussion among the jurists again has nothing to do with the poor wife. It has to do with the husband's fingers. Are fingers which are extended to be taken into account, or the ones which are clenched? Must the fingers be apart from each other, or can they be touching each other? What if the fingers are all touching each other, and the husband denotes the number with the palm? Such are the weighty questions which engage them.

And naturally, as jurists are involved, the answers are never simple. By the standard rulings, for instance, the fingers which

---

67. *Durr-ul-Mukhtar*, Kitab Bhavan, 1992 Reprint, op. cit., pp. 201–2.

are extended are to be counted, and not the fingers which are clenched, and the extended fingers must be apart from each other. But what if the husband indicates the number of divorces 'by keeping the back of his fingers towards the wife'? Then, rule the jurists, the rule is reversed, and 'reliance is placed on the clenched fingers, according to custom.' An even more complex situation arises when, neither the fleshy 'front' of the fingers nor their back is held towards the wife, when rather the tips of the fingers are extended towards the wife. 'Then,' rule the jurists, 'if they are extended after having been clenched, reliance is placed on those that have been extended, and if they were extended at first but have been closed afterwards, then reliance is placed on those that are closed—*Ibn-i-Kamal.*'[68] The scope for classifications and sub-classifications is even greater when, not signs but ambiguous expressions are used at or in regard to the poor wife. A single word—Aituddi— as we saw, when used by the husband may refer to repudiation of the wife or her menses. Used more than once, it may refer in the first usage to repudiations and in the subsequent usages to either repudiation or menses. And so on. Sheikh Muhammad Alauddin writes in the classic *Durr-ul-Mukhtar* that the jurists distinguish between twenty-four different results from the use of this one word. And he adds one more of his own to the list.[69]

Consider the *Fatawa-i-Qazi Khan* next. 'Whenever I shall strike you, you are divorced,' says the husband, and subsequently strikes the wife. The most arcane discussion ensues among the jurists—not about the poor wife, but about the question whether his striking her is to count for

68. On these weighty questions see for instance, *Durr-ul-Mukhtar*, op. cit., pp. 146–47.

69. Ibid., pp. 164–65. The relevant passage is reproduced above in the context of the effect of the husband using an ambiguous expression.

one pronouncement of divorce or two! A glance through the relevant fatwa will acquaint us with the concerns of the jurists. Here it is:

> And if a man says, 'whenever (or as often as) I shall strike thee, thou shall be divorced;' he then strikes her with both the hands at once (and so the striking might be held to constitute one act of striking; and the case assumed is one in which he does not strike her one after the other, because if he had done so, there would undoubtedly be two strokes, and consequently two divorces): she shall be divorced twice; but if the man strikes her with the palm of one hand (although he might strike her with the palm and the fingers), she shall not be divorced except once, although the fingers might have fallen separately (i.e., occupied several places on the body of the woman when the hand struck her); because where he strikes her with both his hands, there results a plurality of strokes as the stroke caused by each hand is a separate stroke; and there striking with both hands, is similar to the stroke by a single bunch (in which case the strokes caused would be as many in number as the number contained in the bunch); but in the second case (i.e., where the man strikes with one hand and the open palm with several fingers falls on different spaces on the body, so as to lead to the view that here also there are different strokes) the strokes are not repeated, because the principal thing by which the stroke is given (here) is the palm of the hand, and the fingers are dependent on the palm (i.e., they go and act with the palm) and therefore the strokes are not repeated.[70]

Similarly, in the 'breaking wind' case, for instance, they distinguish the case where the man breaks wind from the case in which the 'wind escapes from him without his power to control'—in the former case the wife is divorced and out, in the latter she survives. The jurists employ high reasoning:

---

70. *Fatawa-i-Qazi Khan*, Volume II, number 2083, p. 109.

in this case qiyas, the fourth pillar of Islamic jurisprudence —that is, reasoning by analogy—is brought into play. The wife, wind from whose husband has escaped without his power to control,' escapes divorce just as, reason the jurists, she would if the man had sworn. 'If I enter the house, my wife is divorced,' and then had been compelled to enter it. The purist will no doubt note that the jurists are not being altogether consistent in their reasoning: in several other instances, as we have seen, even if the pronouncement has been made under compulsion, the wife is out. But then, the moving finger writes, and having writ....

A man say to another, 'I have divorced your wife.' Now, the wife is nowhere around, she may not know the other man at all. On what does the case turn? Not on anything she may have said or done, not on anything she may say or do by way of stating her side of the case, certainly not on the wretchedness into which she will be hurled if this stranger's unsought declaration is acted upon. The case turns on what the husband says in return to that man. If he says, 'You have done well,' but says it with sarcasm, or if he says 'You have done wrong,' the wife survives. But if he says, 'You have done well, God may bless you for relieving me of the woman,' the wife is divorced and out.[71]

A husband declares 'If my eyes turn towards that which is haram, then my wife is divorced.' His eyes then alight on the face of a woman who is a stranger. The jurists hold that his oath shall not be broken, and the wife will survive. On the other hand, if the husband sees the private parts (the sharamgah) of the woman through her fine garment, or through glass or reflected in water, the wife shall stand divorced. But, rule the jurists, if the husband sees them in a

71. For this and the preceding para, Ibid., Volume II, p. 183, number 2312; p. 13, numbers 1831, 1832.

mirror, his wife shall survive as wife.[72] A husband says, 'If I am involved in doing something which is haram, then talaq on my wife.' After swearing this oath, he has intercourse with an animal. The wife is *not* divorced, rule the jurists. Because, they reason, a deed so despicable could not even have been in the imagination of the husband when he swore the oath, and so, doing it, does not involve breach of the oath ! However, they add, if the one who swears the oath is an uncouth villager who spends his time behind cattle 'then it is another matter.'[73] The wife's fate thus comes to depend on whether the deed which apparently breaches the oath could have been in the mind of the husband when he swore it, and also on what kind of a person the husband is.

A man swears he shall not kiss 'X'. He thereafter kisses X's hand or foot. What is the hukum? In this regard, the jurist tells us, there is disagreement among the *Fuqah*, the authorities on Islamic law. Some authorities, he tells us, hold that the oath shall not be broken. Others hold that if the man whose hand or foot he kissed was one on whom a beard has sprouted, his oath shall indeed be broken. Others hold that if he had sworn the oath in Persian then his oath shall not be broken unless he kisses the face of the man, and this shall be the case irrespective of whether the beard has or has not sprouted on the man kissed. But if the oath had been sworn in Arabic, the order shall be different depending on whether or not a beard has sprouted, 'And this,' says Mufti Qazi Khan, 'is the correct position.'[74] The outcome therefore depends on (i) the age of the man kissed; (ii) the part of his body that is kissed; and (iii) the language in which the original words had been uttered.

---

72. Ibid., Volume II, p. 152, number 2221.
73. Ibid., Volume II, p. 152, number 2223.
74. Ibid., Volume II, pp. 152–53, number 2225.

Another question Mufti Qazi Khan considers leads to even finer distinctions. The husband says to his wife, 'If my private parts (sharamgah) are not more beautiful than your sharamgah, talaq on you.' And the wife says, 'If my sharamgah is not more beautiful than yours, my bondage is ended.' In this regard, Mufti Qazi Khan records, Imam Muhammad has held that if, when this conversation took place, the husband and wife were standing, the wife shall prevail and the husband shall be the loser and the one whose oath would have broken. But if, when the conversation took place, the two were sitting, then the husband shall lose nothing, and the oath shall come down heavy on the wife. And the Imam spells out the reason for his ruling: the reason he says is that the wife's sharamgah is far more beautiful than the man's in the position of standing; but in the position of sitting the matter is the other way round because in that position the private parts of a woman look ugly in comparison with the private parts of a man. But, records Mufti Qazi Khan, in the event that, when the conversation took place, the husband was standing and the wife was sitting, the authority on *Fiqh*—Islamic jurisprudence—Abu Jafar says he cannot say anything definite. In this case the oaths of both should be taken as broken because the condition of effectiveness in the oath of each of them is that his or her private parts are more beautiful than those of the other. Yes, says the Mufti, in the case of dispute or objection the private parts of neither shall be deemed to be beautiful and, hence, the oaths of both shall be taken as having been broken.[75]

The questions that occupy the Fuqah, the authorities on jurisprudence. The scholarship which is expended on them. The distinctions and reasoning on which the verdicts are given. The reverence in which these authorities are held. And

75. Ibid., Volume II, pp. 167–68, number 2265.

above all, the compound of all these—the shariah—and the claim that it must be treated as Allah-given, as clear and definite, and as eternal, inviolable, unchangeable....

The counsel that to the extent possible one should not divorce a woman during her menses again has nothing to do with protecting her interests. The reason is the same one on account of which the divorced woman is prohibited from remarrying until she has completed three menstruations: the object is to preclude subsequent disputes about the paternity of a child that may be born later on. This becomes evident from considering the attitude of the jurists in the case of girls who are too young to bear children and to that of women who are too old to do so. Do the jurists require that the husband pause and reconsider? Here is the answer in *Durr-ul-Mukhtar*:

> And it is valid to divorce them, that is a woman whose menstruation has stopped on account of old age, and a minor girl, and a pregnant woman, soon after having sexual enjoyment (with them), because the prohibition (against repudiation soon after having sexual enjoyment) in case of wives subject to menstruation is due to the suspicion (or possibility) of the wife being pregnant, but this is impossible here (that is in the case of wives who are too old or too young).[76]

And when the jurists exert

Indeed, where the jurists exert, they exert the other way—that is, they do what they can to make it easier for the husband to fulfil the whim which had spurred him to make the initial declaration, or, if in the meanwhile, some other whim has supervened, to enable him to escape out of the consequences of the initial declaration. But in all cases what is being facilitated is the fulfilment of *his* whim and word—*his* initial whim and

76. *Durr-ul-Mukhtar*, op. cit., p. 120.

word, or *his* current whim and word. The jurists are quite inventive when it comes to finding a way out for the husband—Abu Hanifa, in particular, was well known for the legal dodges he could devise. Actual rulings alone can give the reader an idea of the lengths to which the jurists go, and of the person on whose behalf they go to those lengths.

A husband swears an oath that he shall not divorce his wife: he swears for instance, 'I shall never divorce "X", my newly wedded wife: if I do, all my other wives shall also be thrice divorced.' Later he changes his mind. How should he get rid of the woman and yet not be in violation of his oath? The jurists are ever so helpful, as we learn from the *Fatawa-i-Qazi Khan*: 'Then the device in this matter,' the fatwa declares, 'is that he might marry an infant who is still sucking milk (that is, a girl less than two-and-a-half years), and direct his (first) wife's sister, or his (first) wife's mother to suckle the infant wife, so that the infant wife becomes the daughter of his (first) wife's mother; the husband thus becomes one who has joined two sisters (in marriage) or has joined his wife (i.e., the infant wife) and her (the infant wife's) maternal aunt (i.e., the first wife); and therefore the marriages of both shall become invalid (and the result will be that the man gets rid of his wife and at the same time escapes from the consequences of his oath).'[77]

A husband tells his wife, 'If I shall have intercourse with you, as long as you are with me, then you are divorced thrice.' But he later wants to bed her. Our jurist suggests a way out: 'He might divorce her by way of a complete (*bain*) divorce, and then instantly marry her; he can then have intercourse with her without committing a breach (of his oath)' (2114). Now, this device is in manifest violation of what we have encountered earlier

77. *Fatawa-i-Qazi Khan*, Volume II p. 117, number 2098. The following examples are taken from *Fatawa-i-Qazi Khan*; the case number is indicated within parentheses.

—namely, the Prophet's injunction reiterated again and again in the fatwas that a man who has divorced a wife cannot remarry her unless she has been married by another man and unless that second marriage has been actually consummated. But that is precisely the point: the jurists are prepared to go ever so far to ease things for the husband; and, given their ingenuity, there can be little doubt that the jurist—who suggests the device—in this case, Mohammed, the great disciple of Abu Hanifa—when asked how his device squares with the requirement of the intervening marriage will be able to come up with a reading that harmonizes the two!

In the standard pronouncement of conditional divorce the condition must be expressed immediately after the divorce clause. But what if the husband stammers or, for some other reason, has 'heaviness of tongue', so that he is unable to complete the sentence except after an interval of time? The jurists are ever so helpful: in his case the rule shall not be binding, they rule, and his conditional divorce shall be valid (2117).

A husband tells his wife, 'If I do not have intercourse with you during the day in the midst of the market, you are thrice divorced.' He is now in a quandary. The jurist shows the way out: 'The man should carry her in a covered car (*ammari*, i.e., a litter placed on the back of the elephant or camel) and take it to the market,' and have the intercourse before the day is out (2216).

Similarly, as we have seen in part, whenever there is some doubt or ambiguity about the words which the husband had used in pronouncing the conditional or unconditional divorce, it is the word of the husband about what his intention was at the time he made the pronouncement which counts.

A husband says to his wife, 'I have given divorce to thee,' or, 'Divorce is for thee.' Was he divorcing her or was he delegating the power of divorce to her? His ex post facto statement about what his intention was is what decides the matter (1840, 1841).

A husband says to his wife, 'You are abandoned,' or, 'I have abandoned you.' Is she divorced or not? She is divorced if the husband had intended to divorce her, and not if he had not (1847).

And so also if the husband says to the wife, 'I have pledged to you your divorce,' (1849), or, 'You are not to me a wife,' (1869), or, 'Do not go out of the house without my order, because I have made a vow regarding divorce,' (1975), or, 'Go away from this place' (2009). In one and each of these and similar instances, whether the wife will survive as a wife or not turns on what the intention of the husband was, indeed on what he says his intention was. Nothing the wife may say comes into the reckoning—just as what may befall her upon being thrown out does not.

The instances can be multiplied. But in each instance the pattern is the same: the concern of the jurists is to ease the way for the husband, their concern is that the husband should not run afoul of his oath; what the wife feels about the matter, what shall transpire for her as a result of the 'device' does not figure in their discourse at all.[78]

The question whether in the particular circumstance the wife shall stand divorced or not is ever so often put alongside the question whether in the analogous circumstance a slave would be freed or not: if in those circumstances, according to some previously settled 'principle of Islamic jurisprudence',

---

78. I did come across one salutary exception though. Should a man who has divorced her try to bed her and should she have no other way to ward him off, the woman is allowed to kill him! The jurists advise that she should kill him with drugs rather than with 'an instrument of death', 'because,' they say, 'if the woman should kill him with an instrument which inflicts a wound, she shall be put to death by *qisas* (or retailation)' (2263).

the slave would be freed, the wife stands divorced; if in those circumstances the slave is to continue in bondage, the wife continues as wife. Here is a typical ruling in *Fatawa-i-Qazi Khan*:

> A man says to his wife, 'If I abuse thee, then thou art divorced'; he then says to her, 'May God not prosper thee'; she shall not be divorced; because, if he has made manumission dependent on abusing the slave, and then says to the slave, 'May God not prosper thee,' his slave shall not become free; so also in the matter of divorce (2288).

That equivalence between the wife and the slave permeates the treatise throughout.

Indeed, in several respects the position of the wife is worse than that of some other piece of the husband's property. For instance, if a husband in ignorance of the import of the words says, or is tutored to say, 'I have divorced my wife,' she is divorced and out. But if the same man in ignorance of the import of the words sells something, the sale shall be struck down as invalid and he shall not be parted from his goods (1896).[79]

That perceptual equivalence—between the wife and the slave—marks the *Durr-ul-Mukhtar* too. There is not a trace of concern for what shall pass on the wife. The concern is

---

79. The commentator notes that like the *Fatawa-i-Qazi Khan*, the authoritative *Rudd-ul-Moohtar* and *Fatawa-i-Alamgiri* state the same rule. He says that the reasons seem to be as follows: first, 'in the Arabic language the formula for divorce is the commonest form of speech,' and so ignorance of law is no excuse; second, 'the result is not so disastrous, as in the case of property: if the husband has no intention of divorce, the easiest thing for him to do is to marry again.' (See, *Fatawa-i-Qazi Khan*, op. cit., Volume II, p. 38.) The latter reason would certainly have surprised the Prophet who had made remarriage a very difficult matter, interposing as he did the humiliating requirement of halalah—the requirement that the woman first be taken in marriage by another man, that second marriage be actually consummated, and that the other man thereafter divorce the woman.

with the power of the husband, the concern is that he should not fall short of having his oath prevail. The preoccupation is with the type of conditions that the husband specified: these must concern something which may happen in the future, not something the existence of which is already known—'If the sky is above us you are divorced' thus does not end the marriage; they must be possible of fulfilment—'If the camel passes through the eye of the needle ...' is thus taken to be a statement of no account; they must be grammatically correct and complete—the expression must contain both the principal and the conditional clauses in their entirety, says Sheikh Muhammad Alauddin. But throughout he talks of the wife who is to be thrown out and the slave who is to be emancipated in one breath. Thus in describing the requirements for the conditional divorce to operate he writes,

> Another requisite is ownership—(that is, the addressor must be the owner of the addressee), it may be real ownership, as a master's saying to his slave, 'If thou doest like that, thou art free,' or it may only be presumptive, for instance a man's saying to his wife, or to a divorced wife whose *iddat* has expired, 'If thou goest away thou art divorced'....[80]

And a little later:

> Note that a contingent divorce becomes ineffectual on the husband's losing the right of lawfully enjoying the wife, but not on his losing his proprietary right over the wife. Thus if the husband pronounces three or less than three repudiations....[81]

And on the page after that:

> The loss of ownership, be it by virtue of *Nikah* or by right of property, would not nullify the oath of divorce....[82]

---

80. *Durr-ul-Mukhtar*, op.cit, p. 194.
81. Ibid., p. 196.
82. Ibid., p. 197.

And on the page after that:

> The oath of divorce becomes inoperative after the happening of the contingency, in all cases. But if the contingency happens during the continuance of the right of ownership, the wife shall become divorced and the slave shall become emancipated, but not otherwise....[83]

In the face of all this those who continue to assert, 'Shariah has safeguarded the rights of women like no other system of law has,' do so only because of their confidence that no one but them has read the texts of shariah.

But to continue with the devices that the ulema devise—one and all for the convenience of the husband.

Before marriage a man says, 'If I ever tell a lie then, whenever I marry that woman will be divorced.' He tells a lie. Marries. Is the woman divorced, asks the querist, would bedding her be adultery? Yes, rules Mufti Kifayatullah, after nikah the woman will stand divorced. But the Mufti suggests a way out for the man who had sworn never to tell a lie. The device for escaping the talaq, the Mufti says, is that Zaid, the man, should not himself do the nikah, nor should he make anyone an agent. Some other man should go through the motions of doing the nikah of Zaid with the woman. Zaid should not give his consent to this nikah by an oath, instead he should cohabit with that woman. Then this cohabitation shall become permission for nikah, and Zaid's nikah too would have taken place, and talaq too will not take place.[84] Transparently an artifice, and yet even as prudent an alim as Mufti Kifayatullah has no compunction in crafting it for the convenience of the man.

'To frighten her so that she would not beat the child and quarrel,' writes the querist, 'I said, "If you come to my house,

---

83. Ibid., p. 198.

84. *Mufti Kifayatullah ke Fatawi*, Volume VI, p. 261.

three talaqs." Then I thought, "What I have said is not what is in my heart."' Is the woman out? Is there a way for the husband to keep her without going back on his word? Mufti Kifayatullah is ingenuity itself. If she does come to the house, he rules, then three talaqs will fall on her. However, one can get around the three talaqs as follows: without her saying so, others should put her in a doli, and she should get into the doli on the asking of some one else, and others should take the doli through the doorway of the house of the husband, and there tell her to get down from the doli; then she will escape the three talaqs.[85] The reasoning here is that while the husband had said, 'If *you* come to my house....', *she* has not come, *others* have brought her! Manifestly a subterfuge. But even a sober alim does not hesitate to make it available for the husband who now says his intention was not what the words he had spoken contained. Had he wanted to get rid of her, howsoever strong the intention of the wife might have been to the contrary, howsoever strong her need to continue the marriage, no device would have sufficed to get over the triple talaqs once the husband had uttered them.

A man marries a woman in India. He leaves for another country. Six months later he wants to marry someone there. He says there that his wife and child have died during delivery. Khalid, who knows the facts, opposes him and tries to ensure that the new nikah does not take place. The man writes to Khalid, 'Do not interfere. It is a matter of life and death for me. If in spite of this you do (i.e., if in spite of this letter you continue to impede my new marriage), talaq on my wife in India.' Khalid keeps trying to stop the nikah. Does the wife in India get divorced? Yes, rules Mufti Kifayatullah. Notice that the poor woman is rotting in India, that she may or may not be a party to the efforts of Khalid.

85. Ibid., Volume VI, pp. 269–70.

She is out. Not just that, the Mufti leaves the matter even further in the hands of the husband: he says that the talaq shall be 'one revocable talaq', and the husband can revoke it during the iddat of the wife. The reason he finds for giving this further latitude to the husband is that he had said, 'We give talaq' and not, 'Talaq upon her'.[86] That bit of grammar will be little help to the poor woman: the man can just as well use the words which the Mufti would find final; on the contrary, the wife shall now be under blackmail: to get the husband to revoke the talaq she will herself have to ensure that Khalid stops his efforts!

A Hanafi says, 'If I marry, then three talaqs on the woman,' writes the querist. Can he declare himself to be a Shafi'i and marry? Mufti Kifayatullah, always reluctant to lose numbers in the fold—from Hanafis to Shafi'is, from Sunnis to Shias, and of course from Muslims to non-Muslims—does not answer the point about declaring oneself a Shafi'i, but he suggests a device of his own. Talaq will take effect if he marries, the Mufti rules. The way out is for someone else to do the *nikahfazuli* (i.e., the nominal or false nikah) without the man's permission. The man should not give his permission by any oath; rather he should give his permission by conduct—for instance, he should give mehr or commence cohabitation with the woman. Then there shall be no talaq?[87]

But the compelling need of the man overcomes the Mufti's reluctance to have a Hanafi switch to another school. Zaid's father compels him to divorce his wife. He does so, although he did not want to do so. The wife too wants to return to him. She does not want to go through the halalah. What should be done? Under Hanafi law, the Mufti writes, talaq given under compulsion takes effect. After three talaqs

86. Ibid., Volume VI, p. 309.

87. Ibid., Volume VI, pp. 301–02.

one cannot have nikah again without halalah, and a nominal halalah, that is the marriage of the wife to a second man without the man bedding her, too is not complete, he writes. But if things have reached such a pass (as described by the querist), the husband should obtain a fatwa from some alim who thinks that in such circumstances the talaq is not valid. He should then do the nikah again.[88]

A Hanafi says, 'If I marry any woman on this earth, then on her three talaqs.' But now he wants to get married. What is to be done? Under Hanafi law, rules Mufti Kifayatullah, if he marries, the woman will stand divorced. But in necessity he can marry and cohabit, the Mufti says. Then the woman should claim talaq. Then they should both make some Shafi'i alim an arbitrator. And he should give a verdict in accordance with Shafi'i rules. Then there shall be no talaq.[89]

'If I marry another woman without your permission,' a husband tells his wife, 'then three talaqs on her.' But then he wants to take another wife also. Can he? Now, if some *fazuli*—some nominal person—does his nikah with the other woman, rules the *Fatawa-i-Rizvia,* and the man does not corroborate the nikah by words, but by some action—for instance, if the second man congratulates him on the second nikah and he keeps quiet, or if he sends to that (second) woman the mehr which has been determined—then the nikah is correct, and talaq shall not take place.[90]

The examples can be multiplied. Even these few however are sufficient to show how far the ulema bend to cater to the convenience of the male. These exertions are not fortuitous. They arise from the basic position of the Quran which they recall often, namely, 'Man is master.'

88. Ibid., Volume VI, pp. 236–37.

89. Ibid., Volume VI, pp. 309–10.

90. *Fatawa-i-Rizvia,* Volume V, pp. 804–05.

The examples establish several other points also, each important in its own right.

Points to ponder

In the face of such rulings which enable a husband to so easily go back on the pledge he may have made to his wife—for instance, that he shall not take a second wife without her permission—where is the ground for the optimism of reformers who have been urging that triple talaq, polygamy, etc., can be got over by making the husband agree in the *nikah-nama* itself that he is giving up these privileges and powers?

We are often told that Islam places the greatest weight on a man suffering whatever consequences he has to but not foregoing his pledged word. That claim should be seen in the light of the fact that when a man wants to go back on his word the ulema think it right to help him do so by such patently dishonest devices.

Third, we are told that shariah is Allah-given, and therefore immutable. What kind of an immutability is it that a man who is a Hanafi can get around the relevant provision by declaring himself a Shafi'i for the moment, or by going and obtaining a fatwa from a Shafi'i alim when it suits him?

For instance, in the seventeenth-century classic *Durr-ul-Mukhtar*, Sheikh Mohammad Alauddin points out that a talaq given 'when it is to take effect on the creation of ownership—for instance by saying "Thou art divorced with my marriage"' is void. (But with a slight alteration of the words, 'On my marrying thee,' it takes effect!). He notes that Imam Muhammad, the disciple of Abu Hanifa, does not regard as valid divorces which are made contingent upon marriage, and that this view accords with the position of Imam Shafi'i, the founder of the rival school. Thus, should a husband want to escape the consequence of a declaration to this effect which he might have made, the Sheikh suggests the device we have been talking about: 'A Hanafi can, in this matter,' he decrees, 'follow the order of a Shafi'i judge, annulling the divorce, he can rather follow the order of a referee, or the *fatwa* of any honest Muslim. He can act upon two different *fatwas* in two cases.'[91] Mufti Kifayatullah, Justice Syed Ameer Ali and others urge the same sort of dodge in current rulings, and yet the insistent, aggression-laden declaration, 'The shariah is Allah-given. It cannot be deviated from .....'

Next, notice that all this gives power not just to the husband, but just as much to the ulema. For it is they alone who can certify that in this case divorce given under compulsion nevertheless takes effect or that, because it was given under compulsion, it shall not take effect. The general rule as we have seen is that divorce given in anger is as lethally effective as any other talaq. The *Fatawa-i-Rizvia* enforces this rule as stringently as other authorities.[92] But on the very pages on which marriages are terminated on this rule, we read decrees conferring greater latitude. 'If anger reaches a pitch that one loses one's sense of discrimination,' rules the *Fatawa-i-Rizvia*, 'then *talaq* shall not take place.' Whether anger had reached that pitch, it decrees, should be ascertained from witnesses, or by a statement on oath from the husband, and losing his temper to that extent should be known to be his habit. A mere claim to that effect is not enough, it says, otherwise everyone will put forth this claim and no talaq given in anger shall hold.[93] Are the witnesses reliable? Is the man's retrospective statement to be accepted? Is losing his temper to this extent his habit? Who shall decide this? Naturally the ulema!

---

91. *Durr-ul-Mukbtar*, op. cit., pp. 195–96.

92. For instance, *Fatawa-i-Rizvia*, Volume V, pp. 627–28.

93. *Fatawa-i-Rizvia*, Volume V, p. 627, also p. 630.

Three talaqs invariably end the marriage, as we have seen. All authorities enforce this rule, including the *Fatawa-i-Rizvia.* Yet we read the following. A husband pronounces talaq thrice. Is the wife out? If the husband says on oath that he did not intend divorce on two of the three pronouncements, decrees the *Fatawa-i-Rizvia,* then he shall be believed. And the talaq shall *not* take place. If he does not swear, then three talaqs shall be deemed to have taken place.[94]

To help the wife!

Even the rule that talaq pronounced by a husband when he is totally drunk can be presented as a rule that can be *of use to the wife*! As A.A.A. Fyzee, who strongly urged that the rule should be abolished by statute and who of course was far removed from this kind apologetics, recalled, 'In Turkey under the Sultans, by a well-understood convention, a wife who wanted to be rid of a dissolute husband would go before the *kazi* with two irreproachable witnesses and depose that he had divorced her when drunk, an allegation which he would not be in a position to deny.'[95]

The same can be done in regard to one of the most inhumane provisions of the shariah, namely the triple talaq rule. Thus we have Justice Faiz Badruddin Tyabji in his authoritative work observing in regard to the terrible consequences which follow upon the utterance of that one word—'talaq'— 'It is indeed possible, that Sunni jurists wished to inflict on a husband, who disregards the requirements of section 136, the penalty of rendering the divorce irrevocable; and there are

---

94. *Fatawa-i-Rizvia,* Volume V, p. 636.

95. A.A.A. Fyzee, *Outline of Muhammadan Law,* Oxford University Press, New Delhi, 1993 Reprint, p. 156.

indications that they considered it always *a favour to the wife* to relieve her of the husband!'[96]

On conditional divorce too the theory is very charitable. In theory these strict rulings have two aims, both being in the interest of the wife! The rulings, it is said, are intended to discourage, even deter husbands from laying down such conditions and making the continuance of the marriage contingent on the wives fulfilling them: the fear of losing their wives, it is said, will keep husbands from saying such things. On the other hand, should they still put out these conditions and oaths, it is said, it is just as well that the wives should be rid of them. The rule that talaq uttered in a fit of anger or drunkenness too shall cost him his wife is intended, it is said, to deter him from losing his temper, from touching liquor.

The argument can fool no one but the determined apologist. Accept for a moment the premise that as in Islam liquor is prohibited, it is legitimate to punish the man who, not only partakes of it, but takes so much of it as to get drunk. But surely it should not have been beyond the ingenuity of these jurists to devise forms of punishment which would not simultaneously inflict hardship on the wife. By proceeding on the premise that the drunken husband ought to be deprived of his wife as punishment for drinking, the jurists take a merely instrumental view of the woman. What she shall have to contend with is not among their concerns. The apologist's rationalization is that being declared free of a husband given to drink is actually a boon for the woman, and liberating her from bondage to such a husband is what the jurists intend when they maintain that talaq pronounced in a state of drunkenness shall be effective. Even though the jurists themselves do not explain their rule in this way, assume that the apologist

96. Faiz Badruddin Tyabji, *Muslim Law, The Personal Law of Muslims in India and Pakistan*, 4th Edition by Muhsin Tyyibji, N.M. Tripathi, Bombay, 1968, p. 163.

is right: assume that the object of the jurists is not only to punish the husband for his drinking but also to liberate the wife from such a wanton husband. Surely, then, the way would have been to decree that the divorce *shall* take effect, and to hold simultaneously that, as part of the punishment he must suffer for imbibing what is haram, the husband shall pay exemplary, even extortionate sums for the post-divorce maintenance of the woman. That way the husband would have been well punished for the sin of drinking: he would lose his wife, and in addition he would be saddled with a real burden in providing for her maintenance. The wife too would be twice blessed: she would be liberated from the husband, and yet she would not be out, penniless on the street. But the jurists never decree anything of the sort: they 'punish' the husband at the expense of the wife. The reason is obvious: what shall befall the wife does not enter their assessments at all.

And yet we must believe, on pain of being communal, that no system of law has guaranteed as many rights to women as shariah, that no religion is as solicitous of them as Islam.

Finally, notice that the power of the husband to decree a conditional divorce has consequences which go beyond the couple. Triple talaq is an issue of public discussion: even Pakistan and Bangladesh have declared the practice to be illegal as have many other Islamic countries; the Allahabad High Court has declared it to be violative of our Constitution and our laws. One can safely presume that Muslim women would want to be liberated from the extreme insecurity it foments as much as non-Muslim women would if the latters' husbands had been given the same power. The Muslim husband can scotch any thought his wife may have of expressing support for reform by declaring, 'If you ever question the Triple talaq rule, you will be thrice divorced.' He can go further and have her demonstrate *in favour of* her continuing to live in bondage. He can say, 'Unless you join the demonstration against the Triple talaq judgment (or the Shah Bano judgment, or whatever) on Wednesday, three talaqs on you'—and unless she joins the demonstration she is out without maintenance, without rights, without any authority from which she may seek succour.

And our editorialists will marvel at the miracle: so devoted are the women to the shariah, the editors will write, that they are out shouting that they would rather continue in servitude than allow anyone to touch it!

The sequel

The net result of the much-vaunted shariah is obvious: the woman lives in the sort of dread which a non-Muslim woman cannot even imagine, to say nothing of non-Muslim males. The husband can make her continuance subject to the most humiliating and painful conditions. He can take on other wives at will, without so much as a nominal 'By your leave'.[97] He can pronounce a revocable talaq at a whim, and 'resume' her at will.[98]

That the power to resume the wife on whom he has pronounced the talaq once or twice within the iddat period is as absolute as the power to throw her out, that in fact it is but an aspect of the power to throw her out is affirmed repeatedly by

97. Is it legitimate for a husband to contract a second marriage without the consent of the (earlier) wife?, asks the querist. It is all right for the husband to contract a second marriage without the permission of the first wife, rule the ulema of Deoband. According to shariah it is not necessary to take the wife's permission, they hold, and add in a note: 'The Quran says, "The husband is the master"' (*Fatawa Dar al-Ulum, Deoband,* Volume VII, p. 225). Is it legal for the husband to have a second marriage without the consent of the first wife?, another querist asks. It is legal, they pronounce. There is absolutely no need for consent of the first wife, they hold, adding, but it is better if the consent is there (Ibid., Volume VII, p. 225).

98. For instance, *Fatawa Dar al-Ulum, Deoband,* Volume VII, p. 225.

the ulema. The wife's consent is not needed at all, they declare.

A woman went to her parent's place without the consent of her husband, the querist reports. Her husband told her once that if she does not return that night, she would have talaq. The woman did not come back. To what sort of talaq is she subject? What right does she and her parents have in the matter? If the husband wants restitution but the woman or her parents are not willing, can he do so? Is the woman's presence needed for restitution? Is it necessary for the woman to meet him after restitution? Who is responsible for the divorce?

The woman is subject to one talaq only, decree the ulema of Deoband—the reason is implicit in what the husband had said: he had said *only once* that if you do not return this night, you will have talaq. The husband can restitute the marriage within the iddat period without the consent of the wife or her parents. He has only to utter the restitution, the ulema declare. The woman's presence is not necessary, nor is cohabitation needed—notice that if the woman had been accessible and he had resumed cohabitation with or without the woman's consent, the words need not have been uttered; the resumption of physical intimacy, as the *Hidayah* specifies, would have sufficed. The woman bears the responsibility for the talaq which the husband pronounced, rule the ulema.[99]

He may resume the woman by words which are explicit—'I revoke the talaq'—or oblique and implied; they may be uttered directly to the wife or to others—the husband may, for instance, tell others, the 'witnesses' in this case, 'I have returned to my wife.' The 'conduct' in question too can range over a vast array of familiarity and force: the talaq pronounced by the husband would stand revoked, says the *Hidayah,* if 'he has carnal connection, or takes conjugal liberties with her, such as viewing those parts of her which are

99. *Fatawa Dar al-Ulum, Deoband,* Volume IX, pp. 361–62.

usually concealed.' In doing any of this the husband is to act solely and exclusively by his will and fancy, the consent of the wife does not figure in the slightest in the transaction.

The situation is scarcely better if the husband, having thrown her out, repents, and wants the woman to continue as his wife. The ulema insist that she cannot be his wife again unless, after her iddat is over, she marries another man, unless that second marriage is actually consummated, unless that second man also divorces her, and her iddat is once again over. This is the halalah.[100] Unless the second husband consummates the marriage, the halalah is not complete, declare the ulema again and again.[101] Even if the second husband gives her talaq the woman remains haram for the first husband unless the second husband had actually consummated the marriage, they declare. All who knowingly arrange the second marriage on the understanding that it is merely to facilitate the remarriage, and on the understanding that the second marriage should not be consummated are brokers in infidelity, they declare, and the man (the original husband) and the woman are adulterer and adulteress. For all of them is the extreme torture and Fire of Hell. Those who agree to such a nikah taking place, agree not to nikah but to adultery. Muslims, they declare, are forbidden to have anything to do with them. The same decree holds for all those who maintain contacts with such persons and who take this matter lightly.[102]

The one who originally thought of arranging halalah so as to bring about a reconciliation did a meritorious thing, they say. He earns merit thereby.[103] But that is only if each of

---

100. For the steps in halalah, see for instance, *Fatawa-i-Rizvia,* Volume V, pp. 643–44.

101. For instance, *Fatawa-i-Rizvia,* Volume V, p. 658.

102. Ibid., Volume V, p. 639.

103. Ibid., Volume V, p. 645.

the prescribed steps is followed strictly, and only if there is no understanding at the outset that the second marriage is being done only to enable the couple to remarry. If the provisions are short-circuited, the ulema warn, the woman should be compulsorily removed from the husband, and both should be completely boycotted by the community as well as by anyone who is in contact with them.[104] It is improper and a sin to make a condition during nikah that the woman will be divorced in a few days for halalah, and a curse has come down in the Hadis on the one who entertains such a condition, declare the ulema.[105]

The ulema of Deoband are just as unrelenting. Here are typical rulings:

> *Case 414:* If in keeping with an agreement, the second husband of a woman divorces her without having cohabited with her, is it proper *halalah* or not? Or is cohabitation compulsory for *halalah*?
>
> *Fatwa:*. If the second husband divorces her without cohabiting with her, she does not become *halal* for the first husband.[106]
>
> *Case 419:* A man divorces his wife who marries another man and he divorces her also without cohabiting with her. Will remarriage to the first husband be legitimate?
>
> *Fatwa: Halalah* means cohabiting with the second husband.[107]

The mandatory requirement—that though she might have been cast out in a fit of rage, or drunkenness, under total misapprehension or whatever, the wife must become

---

104. *Fatawa-i-Rizvia,* Volume V, p. 645.

105. Ibid., Volume V, p. 645. Though, as noted earlier, it is all right if the thought is in his heart, they say in one case, in fact a reward is to be expected for doing so.

106. *Fatawa Dar-al-Ulum, Deoband,* Volume IX, pp. 361–62.

107. Ibid., Volume IX p. 366.

another man's wife, that that second man must bed her, and then divorce her, before she can return to her original home, her children and her husband—that requirement entails untold suffering and humiliation on the poor woman. The fear that she will have to go through that suffering and humiliation unless she keeps her husband satisfied in all respects and at every moment, that fear naturally reduces her to a condition of abject slavery: the more she loves her home and children, the more of a slave she must become. Nor need the second marriage and its consummation spell the end of her suffering and humiliation, for the practice is manifestly open to much abuse. Consider the following case set out and ruled upon by the ulema of Deoband:

> *Case 407:* Niamat Khan gave triple *talaq* in one sitting to his wife, Gabro, under orders of a court in the Hindu State and due to pressure from his clan. After two-three days, on being persuaded by some persons, he said in the presence of some Hindus that he would take back his wife at the proper time. The couple by word of mouth reached a compromise after three-four months. After some time the clan also advised remarriage. As the woman had been divorced and had not married another man, she was married to Mangal Khan on the condition that he would divorce her immediately after marriage. But after the marriage Mangal Khan said that he would not divorce her immediately, but after a few days. Next, he refused to divorce her. The woman does not want to be Mangal Khan's wife. Now the question arises whether the divorce given earlier by Niamat Khan is legitimate or not, whether Mangal Khan's marriage is right or wrong, and what is the implication of Mangal Khan saying that he will divorce her after a few days? The woman says that she does not want to be Mangal Khan's wife. As a result she has not gone to Mangal Khan, nor cohabited with him. What is the way so that she may be separated or divorced?
>
> *Fatwa:* Niamat Khan's triple *talaq* in the first instance has

> become effective, and he cannot marry her again without *halalah.* His intention for restitution of marriage has no meaning. Mangal Khan stands properly married. Unless he cohabits with her and then divorces her and the period of iddat passes, Niamat Khan cannot marry her legitimately. Suppose Mangal Khan divorces her without sexual intercourse with her, she will not become *halal* for Niamat Khan. Mangal Khan's statement that he will divorce her or divorce her after a few days, does not effect divorce. The woman's statement that she does not want to be Mangal Khan's wife, after she has married him, is nonsense. It does not make any difference to the marriage. And a married woman retains no right to live separately after she has married. She cannot get away from her husband without divorce, nor marry another man. The only way for Niamat Khan to marry her is that Mangal Khan cohabits with her and then divorces her.[108]

We read of cases of that kind from Mughal days to our own times.

Thus, a procedure which does not just inflict suffering and humiliation on the wife, a procedure which is manifestly misused—and manifestly so to the further suffering and humiliation of the wife.

Only one word need be added: that is the law not just in the fatwas of the ulema, that is the law as recognized and enforced by our courts. They too have insisted that there must be a second marriage, that the second marriage must be actually consummated, and that the second husband must divorce the woman, and only then can she again become the wife of the original husband.

In particular, the courts have held that

- Remarriage shall not create a presumption of validity; there must be proof of the intermediate marriage, and of that intermediate marriage having been consummated; in

108. *Fatawa Dar al-Ulum, Deoband,* Volume IX, pp. 356–57.

particular, if the husband divorced the wife, repented and resumed living with her without halalah, the children who are born subsequently shall be illegitimate offspring;

- For purposes of halalah, 'valid retirement' is *not* sufficient; 'when the husband and wife are alone together under circumstances which present no legal, moral or physical impediment to marital intercourse,' explains the standard textbook, 'they are said to be in "valid retirement"'; as regards dower, establishment of paternity, observance of iddat, maintenance during iddat, etc., 'valid retirement' carries the same weight as consummation; but for halalah it is *not* enough, there must be actual consummation.[109]

That is not just the shariah as enforced by the fatwas. As our governments have not acted upon the directive of the Constitution to enact a Uniform Civil Code, that is the law of secular India enforced by our courts!

---

109. See for instance, *Mulla's Principles of Mahomedan Law*, 18th edition, by M. Hidayatullah and Arshad Hidayatullah, N.M. Tripathi, Bombay, 1977, Sections 257 and 336, pp. 286, 354; and A.A.A. Fyzee, *Outlines of Muhammadan* Law, Oxford University Press, 4th edition, New Delhi, 1993, pp. 157–58; and the cases cited by them, in particular *Rashid Ahmad v. Anisa Khatun* and *Hayat Khatun v. Abdulla Khan.*

Shariah and Power

7

Shariah as Power

The 'Triple *talaq*' 'is the heretical or irregular mode of divorce,' Syed Ameer Ali wrote over a hundred years ago in his famous *Muhammadan Law*, 'which was introduced in the second century of the Mahommedan era. It was then that the Omeyyade monarchs, finding that the checks imposed by the Prophet on the facility of repudiation interfered with the indulgence of their caprice, endeavoured to find an escape from the strictness of the law, and found in the pliability of the jurists a loophole to effect their purpose.'[1]

In his recent work, *The Rights of Women in Islam*, Asghar Ali Engineer makes the circumstance more specific and vivid. He writes, 'The question arises as to why Hazrat 'Umar, the second Caliph, enforced *talaq-i-battah* (the "Triple *talaq*"), Muhammad Husain Haykal, the noted Egyptian Islamic scholar, says that it was done in view of the extraordinary conditions prevailing at the time. During wars of conquest many women from Syria, Egypt and other places were captured and brought to Madinah. They were fair complexioned and beautiful and the Arabs were tempted to marry them. But these women were not used to living with co-wives and

1. Syed Ameer Ali, *Muhammadan Law*, Kitab Bhavan, New Delhi, 1986 Reprint, Volume II, p. 435.

often made a condition that the men divorce their former wives thrice so that they could not be taken back. Little did they know that according to the Quran and the Sunna three divorces were treated only as one divorce. The Arabs would pronounce three divorces to satisfy these Syrian and other women but later took their former wives back, giving rise to innumerable disputes. To overcome these difficulties, Hazrat 'Umar thought it fit to enforce three divorces in one sitting as an irrevocable divorce. Since then this form of divorce has become an integral part of Islamic *shari'ah* among the Sunni Muslims. It is widely practised throughout the Islamic world....'[2]

In a recent essay Tahir Mahmood goes even further: on his reckoning the Triple talaq is not just a rule which the Islamic jurists formulated to help women be rid of undesirable husbands, it is a rule which the jurists came to recognize and accept *at the initiative of the aggrieved women!* 'This simple but meaningful reform introduced by the Prophet got corrupted in the course of time,' he writes, recounting that the Prophet's pronouncements constituted a deterrent to husbands and that they put limits on what a husband could do. 'In fits of anger husbands began pronouncing on their wives "three divorces at a time". *And married women, sick of their tyrant husbands, in a bid to get rid of them, insisted that "three divorces at a time" should be given the effect of third-time divorce* so as to instantly divorce the marriage. *To help wives in distress,* most jurists of the time agreed.'[3]

---

2. Asghar Ali Engineer, *The Rights of Women in Islam*, Sterling, New Delhi, pp. 125–26.

3. Tahir Mahmood, 'No more *"Talaq, Talaq, Talaq"*—Juristic Restoration of the true Islamic law on divorce', *Islamic and Comparative Law Quarterly*, Volume XIII, Number 2, Winter 1992, pp. 1–12, at p. 2. In a typical gloss Tahir Mahmood goes on to argue that the Triple talaq rule is actually

Expedients become the eternal shariah

In either event two distinct points are evident. The first is that the 'rule' was an expedient which was given the aura of legitimacy to deal with specific circumstances: the desire of the Umayyad monarchs to 'indulge their caprice' as judged by Syed Ameer Ali, or, in the alternate construction favoured by Asghar Ali Engineer, to deprive the wayward Arabs of the trick they were playing to secure the 'fair complexioned and beautiful women' who had been captured in the campaigns. The second is that over the centuries the expedient became, and is today in India, law. Indeed it is unshakable law—for it is taken to be part of the shariah, and the shariah, having been proclaimed to be a pillar of Islam, is not to be touched.

There are several reasons that account for the latter result but, confining ourselves to judicial matters alone, one rule deserves mention even in a cursory survey. The overriding aim of the British rulers was not to improve the condition of Indians. It was, entirely understandably, to consolidate and perpetuate British rule. Giving occasion to the controllers of different communities to incite their followers was therefore the last thing they wanted to do, specially after the jolt of 1857. In regard to personal laws of different communities therefore they adopted three rules: let each community's affairs be

---

a *misunderstanding* of the true position in Islamic law. Some misunderstanding which can last 1,350 years! And that in spite of the Prophet's declaration that his people—the Muslim ummah—shall never agree upon an error! Tahir Mahmood puts the blame for perpetuating this 'misunderstanding' on to authors of books on Muslim law written *in English!* Ignoring for the purpose the fact that the classic texts—written in Arabic!—the *Muwatta* of Imam Malik, and the *Hidayah* of Sheikh Burhanu'd-Din Ali contain as clear an enunciation of the Triple talaq rule as any textbook in English. As does the *Fatawa-i-Alamgiri*. But a 'misunderstanding' it becomes and one perpetuated by authors of books in English!

settled in accordance with the laws it has been following, howsoever regressive and unjust these may be; second, until and unless there is a clear and overwhelming demand from the controllers of a community to amend some provision of that law, do not try to amend it; third, and this is the rule that entailed the consequence we are looking at, in deciding what the law of the community is on a particular matter do not go back to the original sources—the Quran and the Sunna of the Prophet in the present instance—just follow what the jurists and commentators of that community have been saying.

But to a large extent these jurists had just been devising and then legitimizing expedients of the 'Triple talaq' kind. By the rules of self-denial that the British courts adopted these expedients therefore became law. And today confront us, and shackle the poor Muslims, as unalterable shariah.

Twenty years ago in an important essay Danial Latifi—who was later to argue the case for Shah Bano—gave a telling example. The Quran (2.241) explicitly says, 'Those of you who die leaving surviving widows shall bequeath to their widows provisions for a year without (their) being turned out.' In direct contravention to this the compendium of Islamic law, the *Hidayah,* states, 'Maintenance is not due to a woman after her husband's decease...' The *Imamia* goes even further to say, 'A widow has no right to maintenance even though she be pregnant.' As Danial Latifi noted, when the matter went to the Privy Council (in *Aga Mahomed v. Koolsom Bee Bee* in 1897) it refused to give effect to the injunction of the Quran. '(We) do not care to speculate on the mode in which the text quoted from the Quran, which is to be found in Sura II verses 240–2, is to be reconciled with the law as laid down in the *Hedaya* and by the author of the passage quoted from Ballie's *Imamia,*' the Judicial Committee of the Privy Council recorded. 'But it would be wrong for the Court on a point of this kind to attempt to put their own construction on the Quran in opposition to the express ruling of commentators of such great antiquity and high authority.' As Latifi noted, the Privy Council reiterated the same rule of self-denial, a rule really of British convenience, in 1903 in *Baqar AH Khan*'s case. It observed:

> We think it would be extremely dangerous to accept as a general principle that new rules of law are to be introduced because they seem to lawyers of the present day to follow logically from ancient texts, however authoritative, when the ancient doctors of the law have not themselves drawn those conclusions.[4]

After 1947 that rule of convenience became the lament of helplessness. Thus for instance in 1955 in *Amad Giri v. (Mst.) Bagba*, Justice Shahmiri, as we have seen, observed that the 'Triple *talaq*' is the most prevalent form obtaining in India. Any change in this respect cannot be brought about by the judicial interpretation. If there is a general desire among the Muslims to "revert to the pristine purity of Islam" how such changes in the present state of Muslim law can be brought about, in the words of late Sir Syed Ameer Ali "whether by a general synod of Muslim doctors or by the direct action of the legislatures it is impossible to say."'

The result? Even the most inhumane accretions to what was already the heavily skewed world view of the Prophet's time cannot be touched, simply because a society accustomed to inequity and the domination of males ensured that such humane possibilities as there might have been in some pronouncements of the Quran or the Prophet were not enforced in the past. And every attempt to enforce them—by

4. On the foregoing, Danial Latifi, 'Change and the Muslim law', in *Islamic Law in Modern India*, The Indian Law Institute, New Delhi, 1972, pp. 99–113.

the Supreme Court in the Shah Bano case in regard to maintenance, by Justice Tilhari in the matter of the 'Triple Divorce'—is denounced as an assault on Islam.

In denouncing these judgments what is it that the fundamentalists cite? They cite the Privy Council's ruling of 1897 that the courts shall not look at the Quran or the Sunna of the Prophet, that instead the courts shall go only by what the commentators have held!

Fundamentalists relying of all things on the British Privy Council to prevent bringing to fruition, of all things, the humaneness and equality which they themselves say are the essence of the Quran and of the exhortations of the Prophet! And this in the name of safeguarding the shariah which they themselves maintain is contained in and derived from the same Quran and the same Sunna of the Prophet!

Eternal shariah is overridden by expedients

The 'Triple talaq', we are told, was an expedient. By processes that we have seen it has become immutable law. The opposite is just as true of what is presented to us as the shariah today: namely, that what was to be eternal, unchangeable law has been reduced to a nullity by expedients.

Next to the Quran, Muslims venerate no document as much as they venerate the Prophet's 'Last Sermon'. In these final instructions the Prophet reiterated, 'All usury is hereby declared unlawful (literally, cancelled).... God has decreed that there shall be no usury....' To set an example he announced that the interest which was due to his own uncle —Abbas b. Abd al-Muttalib—was forthwith given up. But Islamic banks and banks in Islamic countries, no less than other banks elsewhere, charge interest for the loans they give and pay interest to Muslim depositors, the latter take the interest as decidedly as any non-Muslim would. Scores of legal fictions have been devised from the earliest time, and are in use to this day in Pakistan for instance, by which the debtor pays and the creditor receives interest—but in such a way that it may be called something else. To take one typical device, the borrower who needs a loan does not just pledge some goods as security, he 'sells' them to the lender (for instance, the bank). And at the same moment he repurchases them from the lender at a higher price. The difference between the price at which he 'sold' the goods and the price at which he 'buys' them back is assumed to be the *profit* of the bank. It just so happens that the differences in the prices are so calculated as to correspond to what the amount would have been had the bank charged interest! This device or dodge, Schacht informs us, had come to prevail in Medina itself as early as in the time of Imam Malik—that is, within a century of the Prophet's Last Sermon.[5] It prevails in Pakistan today. There is just one notional difference: in Imam Malik's time the 'goods' that were 'sold' and 'repurchased' were slaves; today they are goods of an ordinary kind. But the expedient is exactly the same.

Liquor is strictly forbidden, in the Quran and by the Prophet. It has been declared to be an abomination, to be the 'mother of all vile things'. Yet, as Goldziher wrote, from the very beginning a veritable discipline has been in place to devise ways around the prohibition. The authorities have held that it is not liquor which is forbidden, but strong liquor; that it is not strong liquor which is forbidden, but getting drunk on strong liquor; that it is not wine in general, to say nothing of liquor other than wine which is forbidden, only wine made from grapes.... And sure enough, the jurists have unearthed sanction for such easement from within the Quran

5. Joseph Schacht, *An Introduction to Islamic Law*, Oxford, 1964, pp. 78–82.

itself: for the Quran (5.93), they point out, has said, 'Those who believe and do good works are not regarded as sinful on account of what they ate as long as they place their trust in God, believe, and do good works.'[6]

The charge of adultery, the Quran (24.4, 11–12) lays down, must be established on the evidence of four eyewitnesses to the actual act. But judgments—and the subsequent stoning to death—have not waited for that standard of evidence to be met. Similarly, the law of inheritance is a very important constituent of the Shariah. Verses 4.11–14 and 4.176 of the Quran specify the shares which fall to heirs upon the death of a man. But the proportions specified are not adhered to, they *cannot* be adhered to—for the simple reason that the shares specified (that is, fractions of one) add up to more than the total (that is, one).[7]

The examples can be multiplied. The point is that just as what were mere expedients have become law, what was clearly and unambiguously law eternal—in that it was specified in the Quran itself—has been circumvented throughout by expedients.

The shariah as we know it today is less a listing from the Quran, it is more an accumulation of such expedients. And yet everyone—Muslim as much as non-Muslim—is put on the defensive by it being shouted at him that the shariah is Allah-given, and therefore eternal and unalterable.

The plea of reformers

From the very beginning—from the Mutazilah who

---

6. Ignaz Goldziher, *Introduction to Islamic Theology and Law*, Princeton, 1981, pp. 57–63; the German original was printed in 1910,

7. For details see Arun Shourie, *Indian Controversies, Essays on Religion in Politics*, op. cit., pp. 207–09, 357–58.

maintained that everything be put to the test of reason as that too was a divinely given faculty and therefore as important a source of faith as revelation—to reformers of our own times, many have wailed against this attitude. We have already seen what Sir Syed, Iqbal, Maulana Azad had to say on the matter—how they sought to distinguish between Din and shariah, the sorts of apertures they sought to create through which Muslim society could be liberated from the confines of received Muslim law. Reformers like Hamid Dalwai and his associates in the Muslim Satyashodhak Mandal urged the wholesale replacement of the shariah—they did so in a forthright manner and on the basis of truly secular principles.

A useful way to assess what the ulema maintain in regard to the shariah is to first recall what reformers who have reflected on the plight of Muslims have been driven to conclude. Even a brief glance at it will show up the assertions of the ulema for what they are, it will also bare the objectives which impel the ulema in making those assertions.

To set the stage I will recall briefly the work of two scholars, both of whom have been well known in our times.

Asaf A.A. Fyzee was a distinguished scholar, author of the well-known *Outlines of Muhammadan Law*, the seventh print of the fourth edition of which was published by the Oxford University Press in 1993. His succinct book, a gem of lucidity and courage, *A Modern Approach to Islam*, (Asia, 1963, Oxford, 1981) glows with the passion to salvage Muslims, and just as much with exasperation at what has been made of the shariah, and through that of Muslim society by the ulema.

'It must be realized,' he wrote, 'that religious practices have become soulless ritual; that large number of decent Muslims have ceased to find solace or consolation in the traditional forms of prayer and fasting; that good books on religion are not being written for modern times; that women are treated badly, economically and morally, and that political rights are denied to them even in fairly advanced countries by the *fatwas* of reactionary *Ulema*; that Muslims, even where they constitute the majority in a country, are often economically poor, educationally backward, spiritually bankrupt and insist on "safeguards"; that the beneficial laws of early Islam have in many instances fallen behind the times; and that the futile attempt to plant an Islamic theocracy in any modern state or fashion life after the pattern of early Islam is doomed to failure.' And therefore 'the time for heart-searching has come. Islam must be reinterpreted, or else its traditional form may be lost beyond retrieve.'

The very laws which we are considering as an illustration—those of marriage and divorce—and which the controllers of Muslim society make such a fetish of, those very laws Fyzee held up as exemplifying the ossification, and the consequences of that ossification.

'The law of marriage in Islam, with certain important reservations, is beneficial to women; and so is the law of inheritance,' he wrote and asked, 'Why is it that almost everywhere in Islamic countries women have been denied rights by custom over immovable property? That is so in India, Indonesia, Egypt, Persia, and North Africa. And what is more disturbing is that not only is woman denied her Koranic rights but she is considered *inferior* to man and not fit for certain political rights. Travel in Muslim countries demonstrates the painful fact that woman is considered the plaything of man and seldom a life-companion, co-worker, or helpmate. It is not enough to brush this aside by saying that a particular practice is un-Islamic or contrary to the spirit of Islam. It is necessary to face facts, to go to the root of the matter, to give up inequitable interpretations, and to re-educate the people.' And he gave the telling example: 'The Koranic verse (IV. 34): *Men are in charge of women, because God hath made one of them to excel the other* should be reinterpreted as purely local and applicable only for the time being. Its wider application should be reconsidered; and it may be possible to construe it as a rule of social conduct which was restricted to conditions existing in Arabia at the time of the Prophet, and as being no longer applicable in modern life.'

'The greatest gift of the modern world to man is freedom,' Fyzee wrote, '—freedom to think, freedom to speak, freedom to act.' And in contrast what does Islam do, he asked, and answered, 'It closes the Gate of Interpretation. It lays down that legists and jurisconsults are to be divided into certain categories and no freedom of thought is allowed.' And in the very next sentence he pinpointed the root of the trouble: 'Iqbal and Abdur Rahim amongst recent Indian writers have rebelled against this doctrine, and yet none ventures to face the wrath of the *Ulema*.' So, the ulema rule. And what is their condition? Here is Fyzee's answer: 'Some ten years ago (the essay was written in 1959), there were disturbances in Pakistan and an inquiry was instituted. The Chief Justice of Pakistan questioned several *Ulema* regarding Islam and its essential tenets; and according to his analysis, some of the *Ulema* were, in the opinion of their fellow-*Ulema*, unbelievers. Such is the degree to which fossilization of thought has taken place in our faith. Islam, in its orthodox interpretation, has lost the resilience needed for adaptation to modern thought and modern life.'

He drew attention to the changes that were taking place by the day, and in country after country. He showed how regulations made for one period, for one country were wholly unsuitable for another time and place. Pointing to the way provisions of the shariah itself had changed drastically over the years and across countries, pointing to the certainty that even more radical and even more rapid changes would be required in the coming decades, he stressed:

> Such gradual modifications, even of the rules of Shariah do not destroy the essential truth of the faith of Islam. On a truer and deeper examination of the matter, it will be found that certain portions of the Shariah constitute only an outer crust which enclose a kernel—the central core of Islam—which can be preserved intact only by re-interpretation and restatement in every age and in every epoch of civilization. The responsibility to determine afresh what are the durable and what the changeable elements in Islam rests on us at the present time. The conventional theology of the *Ulema* does not satisfy the minds and the outlook of the present century. A re-examination, re-interpretation, reformulation and restatement of the essential principles of Islam is a vital necessity of our age.

Accordingly he urged three things. First, he urged, the corpus of Muslim law ought to be re-examined by asking the following questions in relation to each legal doctrine and rule: (i) What was the condition of society in relation to that doctrine prior to Islam?; (ii) What rule did the Prophet lay down?—that question itself is certain to winnow out much of what passes for the shariah today; (iii) What was the result of such legislation?; (iv) Today, after thirteen centuries, how is the rule interpreted in diverse countries in which Islam subsists?; (v) Can we not, always keeping the spirit of Islam before us, mould the rules of law so that healthy reforms can be carried out?

'It is the writer's conviction,' he wrote, 'that gradually all individual and personal laws, based upon ancient principles governing the social life of the community, will either be abolished or so modified as to bring them within a general scheme of laws applicable to all persons, regardless of religious differences....' From this assessment flowed his second proposal: 'What we have to face,' he wrote, 'is that a Muslim living in a secular or a modern state must have the freedom and independence to obey fresh laws; and new legal norms, whether related to the Shariah or not, will have to be formulated. It is becoming increasingly clear that something good and legal may be entirely outside the rule of Shariah, just as, surprisingly enough, some rules which are unjust and indefensible may be within the orbit of acts permitted by the Shariah. I refer to some rules in the Hanafi law of *talaq* (divorce) in India, to take a simple example.'

Fyzee's third proposal gets to the heart of the matter. 'My solution,' Fyzee wrote, 'is (a) to define religion and law in terms of twentieth century thought, (b) to distinguish between religion and law in Islam, and (c) to interpret Islam on this basis and give a fresh meaning to the faith of Islam. If by this analysis some elements that we have regarded as part of the essence of Islam have to be modified, or given up altogether, then we have to face the consequences. If, on the other hand, belief in the innermost core can be preserved and strengthened, the operation although painful will produce health and vigour in an anaemic body which is languishing without a fresh ideal to guide it.'

'It is necessary to add,' Fyzee declared, 'that true Islam cannot thrive without freedom of thought in every single matter, in every single doctrine, in every single dogma.' And he nailed what had to be said, and to whom: 'It must be asserted firmly,' he wrote, 'no matter what the *Ulema* say, that he who sincerely affirms that he is a Muslim, is a Muslim; no one has the right to question his beliefs and no one has the right to excommunicate him. That dread weapon, the *fatwa* of *takfir*, is a ridiculous anachronism. It recoils on the author, without admonishing or reforming the errant soul.

Belief is a matter of conscience, and this is the age which recognizes freedom of conscience in matters of faith. What may be said after proper analysis is that a certain person's opinions are wrong, but not that "he is a Kafir."'[7a]

Next, recall an essay of Tahir Mahmood. Now a Professor of Law at Delhi University, he too has authored a standard work on Islamic law. He edits one of the principal journals on Islamic law. And he has been much sought after by governments, by traditionalists as well as by the press whenever controversies over Shah Bano, etc., have erupted.

The essay, 'Progressive Codification of Muslim Personal Law', was his contribution to The Indian Law Institute's, *Islamic Law in Modern India* referred to above. After a survey of the manner in which Muslim law had come into being—its origins in miscellaneous incidents, the effect of diverse times and places—Mahmood remarked, 'The existence of so many schools of Muslim law in India and, more than that, the insistence by the followers of each of these schools to stick exclusively to the doctrines of their own school, lead to the conclusion that what is applicable in India under the banner of "Muslim personal law" cannot be equated with the revealed or inspired tenets of the Islamic religion. Its major portions are rather based on the verdicts and opinions of particular Muslim jurists, who lived in different periods of history and in different social conditions.'

Furthermore, given these miscellaneous and dated origins, Mahmood emphasized, 'It is palpably inconceivable that none of these traditional legal principles has lost even an iota of its original rationale and utility, even after the expiry of tens of centuries. Also the possibility of some of these principles having unconsciously deviated from their revealed base, if any, cannot itself be ruled out. The fact is that certain

---

7a. A.A.A. Fyzee, *A Modern Approach to Islam*, Oxford University Press, Delhi, 1981, pp. 82–83, 87–88, 103–08.

aspects of the presently prevailing Muslim personal law in India have outlived their utility and do need a reconsideration.' Giving several examples, he asked, 'Which of the following features of the Muslim personal law can be claimed to be based on the intention of the Almighty Law-giver or considered superb in the context of the present social conditions?'

Among his examples were two that bear on the law we have been considering: '(i) Man's uncontrolled freedom to contract a bigamous marriage, without informing his first wife about it, irrespective of whether he really needs another woman or can equitably maintain the co-wives satisfying, in any degree, the demands of the Quran from a polygamous husband; the only relief available to a wife unwilling to share her marital house with another woman being to seek termination of her own marriage in the court by proving that the husband is unable (or neglects) to fulfil the Quranic requirement of equal justice.' (And that aperture, we should add, is available to the woman only by the grace of the Dissolution of Muslim Marriages Act which the legislatures in British India passed in 1939.) '(ii) Sudden termination of long married life under the so-called "triple divorce in a single sitting formula" (pronounced in the words "I divorce you thrice", or by a triple repetition of "I divorce you")—even if resorted to unconsciously or under the effect of a momentary provocation, intoxication or duress—leaving no room for remarriage unless marital relation (actually consummated) between the woman and a third person is interposed.'

'It is unwise for the Muslims of India,' Tahir Mahmood pointed out, 'to shut their eyes to the tremendous progress in the fields of personal law and succession made in a major part of the world of Islam. A unified, codified and modernized law of personal status is now the order of the day in a large number of countries where Muslims constitute overwhelming majorities. In India, the Muslims have to live in the company of a dominant non-Muslim majority and other co-minorities, all of whom are now governed by largely modernized and codified personal laws. How can they afford to insist on an absolutely undisturbed continuance of their classical and uncodified personal law? And if they do so it would be to their own sheer detriment.'

'To insist that the Muslim personal law prevailing in India should be preserved as it is amounts to insisting on the retention of certain legal rigidities, social inequalities, uncalled for discrepancies and undesirable hardships,' he stressed, and asked, 'Do these features, one may ask, behove the followers of that great religion that was Islam?'

'It is claimed that Islam was the emancipator of women,' he recalled. 'It liberated Eve from man's oppression and gave her a legal status which was denied by most of the pre-Islamic civilizations. The personal law of Islam conferred on women right to hold and dispose of property, right to inheritance, right to make free marital choice and right to seek divorce. By virtue of these unprecedented features, the religion of Muslims claimed to be the pioneer of feminism. Now, after Islam has completed a life of over thirteen centuries, further progress in the fields of women's rights and equality of sexes has been made in all parts of the globe. And this course of progress has been joined, to varying extent, also by what represents a major portion of the Muslim world. Why are, then, the Muslims of India lagging behind?'

Mahmood's denunciation of what had become the standard assertions of the traditionalists was indeed vigorous. He said, 'Equating the Muslim personal law, in its present local state, to the Quran and Hadith, describing it as a wholly revealed or inspired law, and declaring that not an iota of the existing principles can be changed, only exposes the ignorance of Islamic values, Islamic religion and Islamic jurisprudence. Attempting to distort facts about the recent reform of personal law in the Muslim countries cannot do any good. Throwing mud on those who have progressive tendencies and talk of reform of the Muslim personal law, or making contemptuous remarks about their sincerity and wisdom, cannot help either. Instead of trying to conceal the realities, the Muslims must face them. If after having been practised in India in an uncontrolled way for tens of centuries, the Muslim personal law is found being misused and misapplied and consequently lagging behind the social progress in the country, there is nothing in it to be ashamed of. Instead of being stubborn or obstinate about it, the situation has to be duly appreciated, and made good.... It is no sensible argument that any reform of the Muslim personal law would amount to interference in religious freedom and affect the cultural identity of Muslims. If the Muslim personal law is codified and reformed—men are restrained from pronouncing a divorce arbitrarily, women's rights in family life are enlarged, and orphaned grandchildren of a deceased Muslim are allowed to share the latter's heritage along with other heirs—how is the religious freedom or cultural identity of Muslims going to be affected?.... It is irrelevant for cultural identity whether a Muslim can torture his first wife by contracting a bigamous marriage against her wishes and without necessity, or a wife can tease her husband throughout his life by exploiting his inability to pay dower. These and the other drawbacks in the existing personal law cannot be considered essential ingredients of the Muslim culture....'

Well put, and true to the dot. Five years later Tahir Mahmood elaborated these notions in a full-scale book. He established with a wealth of evidence how what is called shariah had never been outside the jurisdiction of the state;

how it had been changed ever so often; how it was being changed ever so often; how it was being changed even as he was writing in one "Islamic country" after another. He established how it *needed to* be changed in several particulars. He showed how wholly baseless was the notion which had been planted into the minds of Muslim masses here—that the shariah was divinely ordained like the Quran. He urged the state to stop administering all personal laws which were based on religion. He urged Muslims to take the lead in having the state live up to its constitutional obligations and enacting a Common Civil Code.[8]

Ten years later he published *Personal Law in Islamic Countries*. In it he detailed the changes which had been made in personal laws from countries in North Africa to Indonesia. The data established again that Islamic personal law was a product of and squarely within the purview of ordinary legislation. It also demonstrated how the features of personal law which are declared by the ulema here to be sacrosanct and immutable have been recognized to be repressive and retrograde, and have therefore been replaced in one Islamic country after another.[9]

The journal he edits, *Islamic and Comparative Law Quarterly*, has continued to provide information about further changes which are being made in the 'eternal' and 'immutable' Shariah in country after country.

Such are the conclusions to which reformer after reformer has been led for a hundred years, such are the data that strikes them. And now listen to the ulema.

---

8. Tahir Mahmood, *Muslim Personal Law, Role of the State in the Subcontinent*, Vikas, New Delhi, 1977.

9. Tahir Mahmood, *Personal Law in Islamic Countries, History, Text and Comparative Analysis*, Academy of Law and Religion, New Delhi, 1987.

The ulema on the shariah

To give precedence to a rule of customary law over shariah is kufr, rule the ulema.[10] Where the state does not allow us to conduct affairs in accordance with shariah—for instance in regard to criminal and political laws—there Muslims are helpless, *majboor.* But not to follow shariah even on matters on which the state has given us the freedom to do so would be kufr. One must abide by the shariah even if one can do so only in regard to a few matters. The argument used by those who hold the contrary and who give precedence to rules of custom over shariah, that argument is just an excuse they use. Such persons are not just definitely sinners, there is doubt about their Islam, Mufti Kifayatullah declares. These persons should at once do taubah from such conduct and lower their heads in obedience before the religion of Allah and the Prophet.[11]

To even say, 'What is shariah? Does anyone go by shariah today?', is kufr, declares the *Fatawa-i-Rizvia.* Even if the words have been uttered to taunt others, they constitute a grave sin.[12]

To say, 'We do not recognize shariah, we go by custom,' is kufr, it declares.[13] 'Unity processions' are being taken out to bring Hindus and Muslims together. The ulema issue a fatwa prohibiting Muslims from joining processions of polytheists. A man says, 'Issuing a fatwa not to join processions of polytheists, etc., is sheer *lathbazi.*' The utterance is reported to the ulema. The utterance constitutes denigration of

---

10. For instance, *Mufti Kifayatullah ke Fatawi,* Volume I, pp. 31, 36; Volume IX, pp. 264–65.

11. *Mufti Kifayatullah ke Fatawi,* Volume IX, pp. 275–76, for a similar ruling see *Fatawa Dar al-Ulum, Deoband,* Volume XII, p. 346, case 20.

12. *Fatawa-i-Rizvia,* Volume VI, p. 114.

13. Ibid., Volume VI, pp. 159, 171.

shariah, the *Fatawa-i-Rizvia* rules, and denigration of shariah is kufr. The man's wife is free of his nikah.[14]

The force with which obedience to, indeed obeisance to the shariah is enforced by the ulema is best gleaned by glancing through a few fatwas of the ulema on the cases referred to them. Here are a few rulings pronounced by the ulema of Deoband:[15]

> *Case 85:* Some people got together to settle a quarrel. One party insulted the Shariah by saying that it did not care for the Shariah and preferred a decree by the *panchayat* instead. It also said that it did not need an Islam which imposed such restrictions, and that it thought the customs of the clan more sacred than the Shariah. Are people who have such beliefs and utter such words, Muslims? Should there be a new confession of faith, and new marriage by them or not?
>
> *Fatwa:* People who said these words have become *Kafirs*. They should confess the faith anew and do their marriage again. They should do *taubah* and seek forgiveness. It is not proper to have dealings with them till they do these things (pp. 383–84).
>
> *Case 110:* Firman Ali and Mehdi Khan said publicly in a gathering that they did not care for the law of the Holy Shariah. What is the law in respect of such persons? Should *namaz* be done after their death? Should people have dealings with them?
>
> *Fatwa:* No doubt such an utterance is *kufr*. Such a person is not qualified to sit with the Muslims. What can be a greater offence than for a Muslim to say such insulting words about the Shariah of Islam? Such daredevilry creates permanent degradation and annihilation in the Hereafter. Let Allah keep the Muslims steadfast. But in the present instance the utterance is of a mixed sort. So care should be taken before they are declared

---

14. *Fatawa-i-Rizvia*, Volume VI, p. 95.

15. The cases are from *Fatawa Dar al-Ulum, Deoband*, Volume XII. The number of the case is given at the beginning, and the page numbers are given within parentheses at the end of each example.

Kafirs. We should stop short of making a Muslim a *Kafir* so long as some doubt remains and he can retract (p. 402).

Case 114: Umaru wants to distribute his property among his children during his life-time, and says he does not care for the Shariah. Does he stand excommunicated from Islam or not? Is his marriage null and void or not?

Fatwa: Umaru stands excommunicated from Islam on account of this utterance. His wife stands divorced. He can marry her again after confessing the faith anew (p. 405).

Case 121: Two persons had a dispute. One of them said, 'Let us settle it according the *Shariah-i-Muhammadi*.' The other said that he was not prepared to accept such a settlement, and that custom should prevail. What is the law in respect of a person who denies the Shariah?

Fatwa: This is *kufr*. That man should do *taubah*, confess the faith again, and remarry (p. 411).

Case 149: A man said, 'I do not accept a settlement according to Shariah, Shariah is nothing.' Has he become an apostate or not? Is it legitimate to have dealings with him?

Fatwa: This is *kufr* no doubt (p. 425).

To say, 'I am prepared to live in hell, you are welcome to heaven,' is kufr, the ulema declare.[16] He who says, 'I shall die the same death as the Hindus,' is an apostate, they declare.[17]

To question *ijma* (consensus) or taqlid (literal adherence) is kufr, they declare.[18] Running down an Alim-i-Din makes one a hypocrite, they declare.[19] Not to believe in *Fiqh* is kufr, they declare.[20] He who does not accept *Fiqh* is Satan, they declare.[21]

---

16. *Fatawa Dar al-Ulum, Deoband*, Volume XII, p. 437.
17. Ibid., Volume XII, p. 434.
18. *Fatawa-i-Rizvia*, Volume VI, pp. 35–36.
19. Ibid., Volume VI, p. 79.
20. Ibid., Volume VI, p. 124.
21. Ibid., Volume XI, p. 106.

And, remember, one single deed of kufr makes one a kafir, they warn. Citing the Quran and Hadis, they declare that he who does a thousand Islamic things but one of kufr is a kafir. If one puts one drop of urine in ninety-nine drops of rose water, they declare, all of it becomes urine.[22] And, remember, they declare citing the Quran, all transgressions can be pardoned and be expiated for, but not kufr.[23]

He who so much as asks, 'Is everything in the Quran correct?,' is definitely guilty of kufr.[24] He who says that he would rather go by the way of his forefathers than by a Hadis has uttered words of kufr.[25] He who debates polemically with the ulema about the articles of Faith—be these about the centrality of shariah or even about such questions as *taqdir*, fate, and the torment in the grave—is guilty of kufr.[26] He who denies the authority of the *Fatawa-i-Alamgiri* and other fatwa collections is guilty of denigrating the Ulema-i-Din. He who denies the miracles of the prophets is a Kafir murtad and is to be denounced forever.[27]

And should the ulema send down such a declaration on one, the consequences are horrendous, indeed a non-Muslim can scarcely imagine them. No one from the community—not even one's closest relatives—can maintain any sort of relationship or contact with the person. His marriage stands dissolved

---

22. 'And the religion of these *Kbabees*,' Maulana Ahmad Riza Khan continues with his customary vigour, 'is that if in 99 *tolas* of urine there is one *tola* of rose-water, it is all rose-water. It is *paak*, drink it.' *Fatawa-i-Rizvia*, Volume VI, p. 95.

23. *Fatawa-i-Rizvia*, Volume X, p. 9.

24. Ibid., Volume VI, p. 181.

25. *Fatawa Dar al-Ulum, Deoband*, Volume XII, p. 430, case 159.

26. Ibid., Volume XII, p. 426, case 152.

27. *Fatawa-i-Rizvia*, Volume VI, p. 52.

—his wife and children are immediately out of his reach. And so on. In the final instance the ulema can pronounce one to be an apostate, to be one who, having accepted Islam, has reverted to some non-Islamic way. And the penalty for that is death—in the Quran and Hadis, of course, but also in the volumes of fatwas which are the staple of the community today.

Islam ordains that an apostate should be kept in confinement for three days and that, if he refuses to return to Islam, he should be killed, notes the querist, and asks, what sort of justice is this? Entering the religion of Islam and apostatizing after that is open revolt, declare the ulema of the institution we are told is one of the prides of India. This brings great harm, they declare. Law books deal with the matter in detail. If he does not reconfess Islam, they declare, he should be killed.[28]

Doubt, questioning border kufr

Not only is the Quran to be obeyed to the letter, the ulema alone have the competence to state what the Quran means. They cite for this claim the command of the Quran itself for non-alims: Ask the alim, the ulema recall the Quran as saying, not the one following whom pleases your heart.[29]

And when the ulema have declared what the shariah requires in a particular case, the fatwa must be obeyed to the dot; for to deny the authority of the fatwas is to denigrate the Ulema-i-Din, declares Maulana Ahmad Riza Khan.[30] It is to disobey the shariah, one of the essential pillars of Islam.

As usual, Mufti Kifayatullah moderates the mandate a bit, but just a bit. The ulema gave a fatwa in accordance with the Quran and Hadis, the querist reports. A Muslim said, 'I do not

---

28. *Fatawa Dar al-Ulum, Deoband,* Volume XII, p. 438, case 175.
29. *Fatawa-i-Rizvia,* Volume IX, Book II, p. 140.
30. Ibid., Volume VI, p. 52.

accept such a fatwa.' Does he remain in Islam? If there is an Islamic government, does he deserve *qatl*, execution? What is the order for him when the government is one of kafirs?

If the fatwa is correct and, knowing that it is in accordance with the shariah, he refuses to heed it, then his refusal to abide by the fatwa is certainly kufr, rules Mufti Kifayatullah. And if there is no scope for investigating the ground for his refusal or for delaying the matter, then the man deserves qatl, execution. In Hindustan the corresponding hukum is that no Muslim should keep any sort of contact with such a person. However, the Mufti cautions, as a decree to this effect can only be given after deep inquiry, unless such a person has been presented before the ulema and the matter has been thoroughly inquired into, it is not proper for Muslims to severe contacts with him.

So, the requirement is careful inquiry. But if the inquiry establishes that he has knowingly disobeyed the fatwa, the rule is qatl in case an Islamic government is in power, and total severance of all contacts in case a government of kafirs is in power.

The Mufti makes a further distinction. Refusal to obey a fatwa can be of two kinds, he says: one may refuse to obey knowing that the fatwa is in accordance with the shariah: this kind of refusal is kufr, and the consequences follow; the other kind is that one may believe that the fatwa is not in accordance with the shariah—refusal of this sort is not disobedience of the shariah, it is disobedience only of that particular fatwa. If this fatwa was about an essential element of religion then it shall amount to disobedience of shariah, and thus be kufr; on the other hand, if the fatwa was about some incidental matter, then the disobedience shall not be kufr.[31]

On the face of it that is of course a much more flexible view than that of the other authorities. But who is to decide

31. *Mufti Kifayatullah ke Fatawi*, Volume I, pp. 37–38.

whether a particular fatwa deals with an essential or an incidental matter? The ulema of course!

Consider a question that will not seem 'essential' to most persons: keeping a beard or, to be precise, poking fun at someone who keeps a beard, be this only by addressing him as 'Uncle'. Not the essence of religion one would think, certainly not essential to any spiritual quest one would think. But the question sends the ulema into quite a rage and calls forth a long, emphatic fatwa.

The points we have been considering are so well blended in it that it is worth reading the query and the ulema's response in full: the triviality of the question; the ulema's obsession with externals, with the uniform so to say; their insistence on literal adherence to the Sunna; their denunciation of any departure from what has been laid down. Here is the exchange.

* * *

Regulation regarding criticism of the beard

Q. By Grace of God I am wearing a beard but my friends poke fun at me and put me to shame by calling me 'uncle', and giving me different titles. Some say that it does not look good on my face and advise me to shave it off. They vex me like this. So what should I do? Will I be guilty if I shave it off?

A. Alas! the time has come of which the True Reporter (pbuh.!) had given intelligence. One day the Holy Prophet (pbuh.!), addressing the noble Companions (r.a.!), said: 'What will be your condition when your young men will become immoral and sinful (*fasiq wa fajir*)?' The Companions asked, 'O Prophet of Allah! Is it going to be so?' He said: 'Yes; rather more severe than this.' Then he said: 'What will be your condition when you will become an obstruction against good works and will bid for evil?' The Companions asked, 'O

Prophet of Allah ! Will it happen like that?' He said: 'Certainly, more severe than this.' Then he said: 'What will be your condition when you will begin to consider righteous acts an evil and evil works to be good?' (JF.). Aren't all these things happening today?

The people shave off their beards and propagate for shaving it; not only this, they consider shaving it better and wearing it bad! Let alone the young men, even old men, opposing the Holy Prophet's Sunna by shaving off their beards, are openly becoming immoral.

Fatawa -i- Rahimiyyah

The Holy Prophet (pbuh.!) has said: 'Don't pluck your white hair. The Mussalman who becomes old in the state of Islam, God Most High gives him the merit (*thavab*) of a good work for each white hair and pardons him, and on the Day of Judgement these white hair will be a light for him.'

(*Abu D.*, vol. ii, p. 225)

It is stated in another *hadith* that God Most High feeleth ashamed of inflicting torture upon an old man. Good Heavens! The Holy Lord feeleth ashamed of punishing the old man for his sins but the old man, by shaving his beard to hide his age, does not feel ashamed of becoming an artificial young man!

The Holy Prophet (pbuh.!) has said: 'Among young men the best is he who tries to resemble the old and among the old the worst is he who tries to look like young men.'

(*Kanz.*, vol. viii, p. 129)

The beard is an Islamic and national sign and is a thing of adornment for man. The hymn (*tasbeeti*) of some angels is: 'Holy is the Being Who adorned men with beard and women with braid.'

(*Al-Haditb*)

The Holy Prophet (pbuh.!) wore a beard and insisted upon the *ummah* to wear a beard. To adopt his practice and to acknowledge his order and decision sincerely is a condition for faith (*iman*), because in legal terminology Islam means to comply with the divine commandments in accordance with the true Prophet's instruction—to obey God according tc one's own liking and intelligence is not Islam but it is infidelity (*kufr*). Hemstitch:

'Egotism and opinionatedness is infidelity in this religion.'

God Most High says: 'But nay, by the Lord, they will not believe in (truth) until they make thee judge of what is in dispute between them and find within themselves no dislike of that which thou decides, and submit with full submission' (IV: 65). In the commentary upon this verse it is reported from Hazrat Imam Jafar Sadiq that if a people worship God and acquit themselves of all the obligations like prayer, fasting, *hajj and zakat* but if they say, by way of an objection, about any act of the Holy Prophet as to why he did like this or that, or they feel any dislike in their hearts about any of his orders, their acts of fasting and prayer notwithstanding, they are in the order of infidels and polytheists.

Fatawa -i- Rahimiyyah

(*Taf. RM.*, vol. v, p. 65).

The case of a Muslim and a Jew was submitted to the Prophetic Court. After investigating into the matter, the Holy Prophet (pbuh.!) decided in favour of the Jew. The Muslim did not agree with this decision and took the matter to Hazrat Umar Farouq. Hazrat Umar, after hearing the case, decided that the plaintiff had become an apostate, and, accordingly, got him beheaded and said that this was the correct decision for one who did not agree with the Holy Prophet's decision.

It was a matter of procedure and law that he who deviated from the Holy Prophet's decision and considered a person other than the Holy Prophet (pbuh.!) to be more just was an apostate and infidel and if he professed Islam, it was sheer hypocrisy. Besides this, the reality is that, when God Most High raised Muhammad the Prophet of Allah as the paragon of all perfections and virtues and announced that 'verily in the messenger of Allah ye have a good example' (XXXIII: 21), a perfection is that which may be a reflection of the prophetic perfections and a virtue is one which may be a sample of the Holy Prophet's virtues. The noble Companions (r.a.!) used to understand this philosophy of beauty and perfection fully; accordingly, not only in devotions did they follow the prophetic *sunnahs* and mould their own habits according to the prophetic mould, but they also gave his ordinary hints the status of orders and the compliance thereof they considered a great good fortune. For instance, once the Holy Prophet (pbuh.!) ascended the pulpit and told the audience: 'Sit down, sit down.' Now see an example as to how this order was carried out:

Fatawa -i- Rahimiyyah

Hazrat Abd Allah ibn Masud was near the door. The moment this order reached his ears, he sat down. When the Holy Prophet (pbuh.!) called him forward, he got up and went there.

When the intelligences of the refractoriness and apostasy of Arab tribes began to reach Madina after the Holy Prophet's demise, the noble Companions counselled to Hazrat Siddiq-e Akbar (r.a.!) that it was not advisable in such a crisis to send the army to Syria, for it was just possible that the rebellious and apostate tribes, finding Madina vacant, might launch an attack on the city. Hazrat Siddiq replied: 'By the Being in Whose hands is my life! If Madina is so vacated that I am alone left here and wild beasts and dogs pounce upon and devour me, even then I will send Usamah (who was the commander-in-chief of this army) on this expedition on which the Holy Prophet (pbuh.!) was sending him.'

(*Ibn Asakir*, etc.)

Such was the concern of the first caliph, Siddiq-e Akbar. Of an ordinary Companion there is an incident that the Holy Prophet took off from his finger a gold ring and threw it away, saying: Man deliberately keeps in his hand a live charcoal. When the

Holy Prophet (pbuh.!) had gone away, someone asked the Companion to pick it up and use it for some other purpose, but the Companion replied: 'No, no. By God! I can never pick that up which the Holy Prophet (pbuh.!) has thrown away.'

(*Muslim* with ref. to *Miskhat*, p. 378.)

Hazrat Abu Zer Ghifari was irrigating his field. Some people came thither and by their feet the dike of the furrow was broken and water began to flow out. When Abu Zer saw the water being wasted, he at once sat down and then lay down in the same mud. Those who were present there were much amazed and asked Abu Zer about this queer behaviour. Abu Zer replied: 'I was angered by these people's carelessness but at the same time I remembered the Holy Prophet's advice that if one feels angry, one should sit down and even then if anger does not subside one should lie down. So I complied with this precious advice.' That is, he neither cared for his body and the clothes nor worried about the people's laughter and making fun of him. The compliance of the Holy Prophet's auspicious hint has precedence over all things; vis-à-vis which all else is naught.

Fatawa -i- Rahimiyyah

Once Hazrat Umar Farouq, having put on clean clothes, was going for the Friday prayer. *En route*, a spout of water mixed with the blood of a slaughtered hen fell upon him from the eaves of the house of Hazrat Abbas. He came home, changed clothes and ordered the eaves to be removed from the passage. When his order had been carried out, Hazrat Abbas incidentally told him that this eaves had been put there by the Holy Prophet (pbuh.!). No sooner Hazrat Umar heard this than he got up and went to the eaves. As there was no ladder, he himself bent down and beseeched Hazrat Abbas to stand up on his bent back and refix the eaves at the same place where the Illustrious Master, the Beloved of God (pbuh.!) had fixed it.

This was the noble Companions' (r.a.!) respect. Wherever the eaves was but since it had been fixed there by the Holy

Prophet (pbuh.!) and though it had been removed from there unknowingly, the expiation for removing it was that causing Hazrat Abbas to stand on his own back, it was refixed at its original place; whereas the other sense of respect is of our young men and many old men that they insist upon keeping no trace of either the mustache or the beard—the beard which our Holy Prophet (pbuh.!) always wore and insisted upon the Muslim to grow beard and clip the mustache. Could there be greater disrespect and audacity than this? However, the wearing of beard is the Sunna of all the prophets (pbut.!); the beard is an Islamic sign, the symbol of nobleness and augustness, the discriminator between the young and the old, and a complement for the masculine face. To shave the beard is a devilish act and is to mar the God-given appearance; to consider the shaving of beard good is antagonism and counteraction vis-à-vis the Holy Prophet's Sunna.

Fatawa -i- Rahimiyyah

(God forfend!)

In the world-renowned book of *Fiqh*, the *Hedaya* (vol. iv, p. 571) is stated: 'The beard in its time (i.e., when it begins to grow) is the cause of handsomeness and adornment, which is completely lost on shaving it.' It is stated in the *Bahr al-Ra'iq* also: 'In its time the beard is a thing of beauty.' In support the following *hadith* has been adduced as argument that the daily recitation of a band of angels of God is: 'Holy is the Being Who adorned men with beard and women with pigtails and braid.' (*Tuk. Bahr.*, vol. viii, p. 331). Another tradition is to the effect that when the angels take an oath, they say: 'By the Being Who adorned man with beard!'

If one has true love for the Holy Prophet (pbuh.!), then each and every practice and habit of his should be beloved, for each manner of the beloved is loveworthy; dislike (God forfend!) towards it is a sign of want of love. One who shaves the beard tramples the Holy Prophet's Sunna; how can he be a true lover? How well has someone put it:

You claim to have love for the Prophet of Allah and at the same time also disobey his order. What a strange thing it is! If you had really had his love in your heart and you were true in your claim of love, then you would never have been insubordinate, and would have loved all his actions and manners.

Whenever Majnu passed through Layla's lane, he would kiss the walls and say:

When I pass through Layla's lane, I kiss this wall as well as that;
the great love in my heart is not for the lanes but for
one who resides here.

Fatawa -i- Rahimiyyah

An august man says:

I am proud of my eyes that they have seen thee. I sacrifice myself over my feet that they have reached thy lane. Every moment do I plant kisses on my hand that, catching thine skirt, it has pulled thee towards myself.

It is stated in the *Mathnavi* that a beloved asked her lover: 'Thou hast toured many cities. Which is the best of them?' The lover answered: 'The city where resides my beloved.'

One feels sorry that they claim love for God and the Prophet whereas in practice they hate beard! The Beloved of the Lord of the Worlds and the Sovereign of the Here and the Hereafter (pbuh.!) has said: 'The claim of love is not reliable as long as the believer's desire is not subordinate to my instruction' (*Mishkat*); that is the desire and yearning of the heart should be the same which is the Holy Prophet's instruction and Sunna. Repeatedly has he said: 'One who does not follow my Sunna is not mine'; 'One who follows the practices of others is not one of us'; 'One who turns one's face from my method is not of my community'; 'One who wasted my Sunna, for such an one my intercession is unlawful'.

Once Imam Abu Yusuf was narrating the *hadith*: 'The Holy

Prophet used to like pumpkin.' One of the disciples blundered out, 'But I don't like it.' The Imam was so provoked at this insolence that he drew out his sword and said: 'Recant and repent, otherwise I'll kill you.'

In Madina it escaped out from the tongue of a confirmed saint (*sahib-e-nishat*, having spiritual relation with God) that the curd of Syria or India is better than the curd of Madina. The Holy Prophet (pbuh.!) told him in dream: 'Go away from here and live at the place where the curd is good.'

Fatawa -i- Rahimiyyah

Imam Rabbani says that all the *sunnahs* have been approved by the Lord of the Worlds whereas all things contrary to the Sunna have been approved by Satan.

(*MIR*, vol.i, p. 255)

You ask me what you should do? My brother-in-Islam! To give up the truth, discomposed by the censure and taunting of the slaves of desire, is Abu Talib's wont. At the time of his death the Holy Prophet (pbuh.!) told him: 'Uncle ! Please say, "There is no God but Allah" once'. Abu Talib replied: 'You have proffered to me a religion which I consider superior to all the other religions of the world. Had I had no fear of the people's censure and taunting, you would have found me brave in accepting the truth.'

The long and short of it is that to forsake the truth for the people's sneer and reproach is Abu Talib's way; and to stick to truth unflinchingly, without caring a rap for the criticism of the whole world, is the Sunna of the crusader of Islam, Hazrat Huzaifa b. Yaman. He was in a journey. While dining a morsel fell down from his auspicious hand. Cleaning it he began to put it into his mouth. The Persians were watching. The attendant told him *sotto voce*: 'Sir, please don't do like this. These Persians consider the eating of a fallen morsel out of etiquette and look down upon such persons.' He replied: 'Should I give up the Sunna of my beloved Prophet (pbuh.!) for the sake of these fools?'

This is faith; this is the reliance on the Holy Prophet's being the most superior among all the prophets and on his teachings to be the most perfect teachings! The attendant feels impressed by the Persians' culture and Huzaifa b. Yaman feels proud of his holy friend's (pbuh.!) culture. He calls every man foolish who does not consider the Holy Prophet (pbuh.!) to be a perfect teacher and is not enamoured of his culture.

So you should not shave your beard; if you act upon the remarks of your foolish friends, you will become guilty. The Holy Lord has instructed his Apostle (pbuh.!): 'And now have We set thee (O Muhammad) on a clear road of (Our) commandment; so follow it, and follow not the whims of those who know not.' *Fatawa -i- Rahimiyyah*

(XLV: 18). Finis. VAKB.[32]

Questioning quelled

And anyone who expresses the slightest doubt on any of this—on the authority that the ulema say is theirs, on the centrality of shariah, on what the ulema say the shariah is—the ulema put down with a heavy hand.

There is for instance the manifest anomaly: talaq is declared to be the most abominable of things in the eyes of Allah, and yet it has been made so very easy. The anomaly has continued to trouble scholars and laymen alike. How do the ulema deal with the question? They just stamp out the doubt. A single exchange included in the *Fatawa-i-Rahimiyyah* will suffice to recall the doubt that assails laypersons, and also to show the way the authorities squelch the doubter and the doubt.

The querist recalls the fatwa which had been given. In his rendering it had read:

32. *Fatawa-i-Rahimiyyah*, Volume II, pp. 319–25.

In our Hanafi *mazhab* (rite) it is an innovation and an unlawful act to pronounce three divorces collectively at a time. (After reproducing some *hadis*, it is written), it is proved from the said *hadis* that the divorce is accomplished.

The querist then asks:

In the understanding of ignorant masses like us it is illegal that a matter which involves disobedience to God, which makes mockery of the Divine Book, which has been frowned upon by the Prophet and which Hazrat Abu Hanifa himself has called unlawful, becomes proper (*ja'iz*) and the divorce is accomplished. How is it possible? According to the Holy Quran, drinking and usury are also unlawful but no divine has said that though these works are unlawful and involve disobedience to God, they are also proper. Why do then the jurisconsults issue a ruling for the propriety of divorce?

A perfectly justifiable, even obvious question. But now see how the ulema deal with the querist and his query. The authority concerned first sets down some Hadis and obiter from law books like the *Fatawa-i-Alamgiri* to the effect that the triple divorce indeed ends the marriage. Next, he administers a stern admonition: laymen ought to stay clear of the subtleties of law, he declares, they should leave these to the experts. His admonition is indeed worth reading to see the assertions by which, and the fervour with which clerics safeguard their monopoly of 'knowledge', and thereby their hold over the community. Here is the admonition the *Fatawa-i-Rahimiyyah* administers:

When the critic and reviewer is not a scholar and has not studied the Quran, *hadith, Fiqh,* principles of *Tafsir* and other religious sciences nor is he in touch with these sciences, he should not dabble and interfere in religious matters and such delicate problems.

Maulana Ashraf Ali Thanvi remarks about such persons: 'The educated men of today are so arrogant that by learning English they consider themselves to be scholars of religion also and give opinion about legal matters, too. Let alone the poor *moulvis*, they reject even the Prophet's statements' (*Mohasin-e Islam*, p. 49).

Imam Ghazzali says: 'It is a duty of the common masses of Muslims that after embracing faith (*iman*) and Islam they should engage themselves in devotions and their own vocations and should not meddle in religious matters which they should leave to the charge of the religious scholars. The disputation of a layman in religious academic matters is more harmful and dangerous than adultery and thieving, because if the man who does not have insight in and mature understanding of the religious sciences, debates and discusses about God and the propositions of His religion, he may, it is just possible, form an opinion which may (in effect) be infidelity (*kufr*) and he may not perceive that what he understands is infidelity. He is like a man who does not know swimming and yet casts his boat in the sea' (*Ihya*).

The common Muslim masses should know the religious regulations and act upon them but they should not entangle themselves in their subtleties. It is stated in a noble *hadith* that a man came to the Holy Prophet (pbuh.!) and requested him to explain to him academic subtleties. The Holy Prophet first asked him certain questions: 1) Have you acquired gnosis (*marifa*)? 2) How many rights of God have you discharged? 3) Do you have knowledge of death? 4) Have you prepared for death? Then, at the end, he said: 'So go away. First strengthen the foundation and then come so that I may tell you about academic subtleties' (*JBI*, p. 133). In short, meddling in matters academic is not the common men's fare.'[33]

---

33. *Fatawa-i-Rahimiyyah*, Volume II, pp. 107–10. As we shall see in Chapter 9 below, the same sort of admonition is administered to the querist who asks how it is just for the lawgivers to hold that a man may bed his slave woman without nikah.

And the fatwa adds a third argument. It isn't all that incongruous for a thing to be sinful and abominable, it declares and for it to yet have effect. And to prove the point it gives a list of examples. The list is as telling as it is long:

- (i) *Zihar* (to make one's wife unlawful for oneself like one's mother) is legally forbidden; some *Ulema* have called it a grave sin. The Quran has called it: 'They indeed utter an ill word and a lie' (LVII: 2) but *Zihar is* accomplished and, one has to expiate for it. (Holy Quran).
- (ii) To make one marry for *halalah* (legitimization) with a condition is impermissible (*na-ja'iz*) and liable to execration, but the marriage is correct.
- (iii) Cohabitation during the menstrual period is unlawful (*haram*), but it is sufficient to accomplish *halalah*.
- (iv) It is unlawful to go on pilgrimage with unlawful money but the pilgrimage is accomplished (though it is unacceptable to God).
- (v) It is unlawful for a woman to go on pilgrimage without her husband or a *mahram*, but the pilgrimage is accomplished.
- (vi) It is impermissible—it is a sin—for a traveller to say four *rak'ahs* of prayer instead of two but the prayer is accomplished (provided he may have performed *qa'da* at the second *rak'ah*), although it is necessary to be reperformed.
- (vii) It is abominable to use Zamzam water for purification after easing oneself (*istinja*)—according to some, it is unlawful—but purification is accomplished.
- (viii) It is unlawful to bathe in a mosque after copulation but the bath is accomplished.
- (ix) It is unlawful to copy the Quran in a state of uncleanness but whatever has been copied is Quran and its reading deserves recompense (*thavab*) and showing disrespect to it is unlawful.
- (x) Adultery is unlawful, but from this unlawful act the honour of matrimonial alliance is established. The purpose is that everything has an effect; when that thing happens, it inevitably produces its effect. An act may be performed rightly or

wrongly, but its result will be there; for instance, to kill calculatedly is unlawful but the act of killing is inevitably accomplished.

(xi) To commit suicide by taking poison is unlawful but one is naturally killed.

(xii) Similarly, it is unlawful to pronounce three divorces at a time but the divorce is accomplished; i.e., the marriage runs on rocks and the woman becomes irreversibly divorced (*mughalizah*) and cannot be taken back in wedlock without *halalah*.

Now, if one does not understand, whose fault is it? Hemstitch: 'Is it any fault of the sun if the bat cannot see during daylight?'[34]

The list is scarcely in answer. After all, the question could be asked the other way round: as these things are sinful and disapproved of, why does Allah, who is All-powerful after all, not arrange affairs in such a way as to render each of them ineffective? But our authorities do not ask the question. And if a layman does they are bound to revert to the admonition they had handed out in the first instance—namely, that laymen should keep off the subtleties of religion and law! And should the layman persist in 'polemical disputation' in spite of their explanation, their admonition, their warning, he will be guilty of fanning doubts about the Holy Shariah, he would be guilty of insulting the Ulema-i-Din. The question will then not be the merits or otherwise of Triple talaq. The question will be the man's kufr.

Why is it that while witnesses are needed at the time of contracting marriage, they are not deemed necessary at the time of divorce?, asks the anxious querist. Why is it that divorce takes effect even when the grounds for it are insignificant? 'That is what the Shariah ordains,' rule the ulema of our al-Azhar, the Dar al-Ulum at Deoband—'that is, a

34. For the foregoing exchanges, *Fatawa-i-Rahimiyyah*, Volume II, pp. 107–11.

marriage is not effective without witnesses while this condition does not apply to divorce.' 'And,' they declare, 'we are bound to follow what is laid down in the Shariah. Finding faults with it (the Shariah) is not permitted. A proclamation is necessary for marriage so that it can be distinguished from an illegitimate affair. Divorce needs no such distinction.'[35] And that is that.

The querist asks a perfectly legitimate and straightforward question about sacrificing animals: the Quran, he recalls, declares that the flesh and blood of the animal do not reach Allah, what reaches Allah is your piety; as this is the case, why is sacrificing animals necessary? Instead of answering the question, the *Fatawa-i-Rizvia* seeks to drown the man in scorn and to condemn him by association. To deny the efficacy of sacrifice is meanness, it declares. The Hindus are irritated by the sacrifice of the cow only. This person has exceeded them in this thing—for he denies sacrifice all together....[36]

To ask a question without necessity, *bezarurat,* is haram, declares the *Fatawa-i-Rizvia.* A person who asks such questions is a condemnable fasiq, a sinner, it declares. It is a sin to make such a one imam. The namaz behind him of all—the learned as well as the ignorant—is detestable.[37]

Ambiguity as power

Notice how the mere utterance of words which call the shariah in question becomes kufr. Notice the extreme penalty for even uttering such words. Notice also how the prospect that one's words may be reported to the ulema or that such words may be attributed to one puts one in dread of the community, it makes the entire lay community a sort of ubiquitous

35. *Fatawa Dar al-Ulum, Deoband,* Volume IX, p. 89.

36. *Fatawa-i-Rizvia,* Volume VI, pp. 52–53.

37. Ibid., Volume III, p. 250

Thought-Police, roving and listening on behalf of the ulema. Notice that it lies with the ulema wholly and solely to declare a man to be guilty of kufr, to have become a kafir, to have become an apostate, and it becomes the duty of the entire community to ensure that the penalties which have been prescribed for the crime are indeed carried out on the person.

This gross and absolute power accrues to the ulema from one source: they are the interpreters and enforcers of the shariah. This is why, in contrast to the reformers, the ulema insist that the shariah is Din, that to doubt that it is so is itself kufr, that to doubt those who maintain that, namely the ulema, too is kufr, and so on in an infinite regress.

But we would miss the extent of their power if we stopped there. Their power comes not just from the fact that they have had the community deify shariah, it comes also from the fact that the shariah is ambiguous, from the fact that when a case comes before them the ulema can use the shariah as readily to yield one result as to yield its opposite.

It is to this feature that we shall turn, and we shall revert to the law on divorce as an illustration. The survey will show:

- how completely hollow is the claim that the shariah is a clear and definite code;
- how completely hollow is the claim that it is an eternal and immutable code.

The survey will show how easy it is for the ulema to pluck one Hadis rather than the other, to invoke one 'principle of Islamic jurisprudence' rather than another and how this is at the heart of the power they wield. It will then become evident why to our very day the ulema not only fight back every attempt to replace religion-based personal laws by a Common Civil Code, but also why they fight back every attempt to codify the shariah itself.

For their power shall be impaired not just when the shariah is replaced by a Common Civil Code. It shall be impaired when the shariah is codified in clear and unambiguous rules.

Are three THREE?

How often we are told that the shariah—having been spelled out by Allah—is an eternal and immutable code, that it is a clear and definite code. Even this little detail—whether a husband has the power to throw his wife out by uttering one word—shows that the code is neither immutable nor definite.

That the rule has changed over time is evident from what Islamic historians and jurists record about the way the Prophet had disapproved of multiple talaq pronouncements at one go and yet how over time that way of ridding oneself of wives became the method most frequently used for casting wives away. The debates among the jurists over the centuries about the exact words by which, and over the manner of repeating them by which a wife may be thrown out illustrate how indefinite shariah is as a code, how tenuous is its foundation, how, on vital as well as elementary particulars, its provisions rest on little more than hair-splitting, and that too of the most arcane kind.

Is the wife out once the husband has pronounced the word 'talaq' thrice in one go? Is she out if he has pronounced it not in one go but on different occasions during the same 'period of purity', that is in the same interval between the wife's menstrual courses? What if he has had intercourse with her during that 'period of purity'? Is the talaq to take effect if it has been pronounced during the time she is in her menstrual course? The pronouncements in any of these forms or under any of these circumstances are 'unorthodox', they are 'disapproved', according to the Hanafi school, but they suffice to end the marriage. The Hanbali school regards them as 'sinful', but effective. The Shafi'i school regards them as 'forbidden', but still enough to terminate the marriage. The Maliki school, on the other hand, holds that the pronouncement of talaq would end the marriage if, and only if the wife is in 'a state of purity', only if the husband has not had intercourse with her in that particular 'period of purity', and only if 'talaq' has been pronounced no more than once at a time. Among the Shias too the pronouncements are void and totally ineffective if they are made at the same time, if the wife is pregnant or if she is menstruating, or if, though talaq is pronounced when the wife is in a 'period of purity', the husband has had intercourse with her during that period.

Sure enough, each school has 'a principle of Islamic jurisprudence', plus a Hadis to cite in support of its position. In declaring such talaqs to be void the Malikis and Shias point to the sudden and grave anger with which the Prophet had reacted upon being told that a follower had divorced his wife by pronouncing three divorces at the same time—the Prophet had stood up and declared that the man was making a plaything of the Quran even while the Messenger was amidst them; they point to the Prophet making Ibn Umar take back his wife and telling him that, if after taking her back he still wanted to be rid of her, he should divorce her in the proper manner. The Hanafis, Shafi'is and Hanbalis, recalling the same incident, point to the fact that while the Prophet showed his disapproval of this form of divorce, he did not forbid it.

Is three ONE?

To start with the most elementary case: *If a husband pronounces talaq once but says he intended three divorces, shall it count for one pronouncement and thus be a revocable divorce, or three pronouncements and thus be irrevocable?*

Imam Shafi'i, Imam Malik, Ishaq b. Rahwaih, Abu Ubaid and Urwah b. al-Zubair, each a name to reckon with in Islamic jurisprudence, we are informed, maintain that the one pronouncement shall count for three. On the other hand, we are informed, equally hoary authorities, Abu Hanifa, Sufiyan al-Thawri, al-Awzai and Ahmad maintain that the one pronouncement shall count for one.[38]

If the talaq is pronounced thrice in one go, or during one period of purity, does it count for one pronouncement and thereby remain revocable, or does it count for three and thereby become irrevocable? Ibn Rushd, Ibn Abbas, Ibn Ishaq and several others hold that the three count for one pronouncement only. Abu Hanifa, Imam Malik and several others hold that they count for three.

Those who hold 'Three-is-one' point to the Quran: nowhere, they say, does it say that three divorces pronounced at one go are to count for three divorces and thus be final. Those who hold 'Three-are-three, and thus final' also point to the Quran: nowhere, they say, does it say that three divorces pronounced at one time are to count for one and thus be revocable.

As usual the dispute turns on one word. Allah says that a man may divorce his wife twice and then either retain her on honourable terms or let her go in kindness, that if he divorces her a third time she becomes unlawful to him unless she marries another man, who then also divorces her, etc. (Quran, 2.229 and 230). The 'Three-is-one' jurists say that Allah is not speaking of pronouncing the divorce *twice* or *thrice* (that is, uttering the word one after the other) but of pronouncing it two *times* or three *times* (that is, uttering it after intervals), and that therefore when the word is uttered

38. See *Sunan Abu Dawud*, Ahmad Hasan (tr.), Kitab Bhavan, New Delhi, 1993, Volume II, p. 594, footnote 1528.

in succession without intervals the utterances count for only one pronouncement. The 'Three-is-three' jurists say this is sophistry, and they point to the same verses. Allah is not saying that the utterances must be interspersed with intervals of any specified length, they point out. He is specifying the number alone—that is, whether the word has been pronounced twice (verse 2.229) or thrice (verse 2.230). The difference between 'twice' and 'two *times*', between 'thrice' and 'three *times*', they say, is that between 'half a dozen' and 'six'. Even when the word 'talaq' is uttered 'thrice in one breath' or 'thrice during one period of purity', it is being uttered three *times*: one utterance follows the preceding one, the utterances are not—they *cannot* be—simultaneous.

The scheme of Allah, say the 'Three-is-one' jurists, is to provide the husband the opportunity to repent, to reconsider, to retain the wife. That is evident from verse 2.229, they say, for Allah says, 'Divorce is twice; then honourable retention or setting free kindly....' Now, if three pronouncements made at one go are taken to throw the wife out irrevocably then, they say, the right which Allah had conferred upon the husband, the right to retain the wife upon reconsideration, is extinguished; if the three pronouncements are taken to end the marriage then the scheme of Allah—of providing the husband an occasion to pause and reconsider what he is doing—is set at naught. The others maintain that Allah's scheme is contained not in one verse, 2.229, taken by itself, but in the four verses—2.228 to 231—taken together. True, they say, Allah has given the husband an opportunity to repent and reconsider, but the husband has this opportunity up to the moment he pronounces talaq only twice; once he utters the word a third time, the opportunity is over, and the woman is put beyond his reach.

The controversy is compounded by the next verse

(Quran, 2.231). In it Allah says: 'When you divorce women, and they fulfil the term of their (*'Iddat*), either take them back on equitable terms or set them free on equitable terms....' Those who maintain that three pronouncements count for only one point out that here the words, 'When you divorce women' clearly relate to three pronouncements of talaq, and that, hence, by this verse the right of the husband to take back his wife remains even after he has pronounced talaq thrice, and till the time her iddat is over, that is he can decide to revoke his pronouncement any time till she has completed three menstruations after he had pronounced talaq. The 'Three-is-three, and irrevocable' jurists infer quite a different rule from this verse. The verse (2.231), they maintain, is to be read in association with the two verses which precede it. This particular verse does not confer a general right to retain the wife after having divorced her conclusively, they say, it merely relates to one way in which a husband who has pronounced talaq twice may retain the wife: if, after he has divorced her twice, he has intercourse with the wife before she has completed three menstrual periods, the talaq is abrogated; if the three menstruations are over, and he has still not either revoked the talaq explicitly or done so implicitly by resuming marital relations with her, the marriage is ended.

Here is a representative 'Three-is-one' reading of verse 2.231:

> The verse explicitly provides that when *'Idda'* is about to be completed then retention in an honourable way is possible, that is the wife can honourably be retained before completion of *'Idda'*.
>
> The question is that before the completion of *'Idda'* who can take away this right of retention which has been given by Allah to men? If there is any explicit commandment to the contrary, the question is solved but if there is none it will mean that there exists the right of retention for a man before divorcing on

> the third occasion during the period of *'Idda'*. *Therefore the right of retention remains even after three divorces have been given on a single occasion.* In other words the third divorce becomes effective only after two revocable divorces have been given separately, not at a time. Allah has given man the choice to give divorces separately as is obvious from *'Al*-Talaq-*Marratan*. Hence when the right of combining divorces has not been given at all, how can three divorces given on a single occasion have any legal effect?[39]

The reader would have noticed the non sequitur, and how the critical assertion—'Therefore the right of retention remains even after three divorces have been given on a single occasion'—makes its way into the presentation. But then such is logic in such matters.

On the other hand, here is Yusuf Ali on the same verse:

> If the man takes back his wife after two divorces, he must do so only on equitable terms, i.e., he must not put pressure on the woman to prejudice her rights in any way, and they must lead clean and honourable lives, respecting each other's personalities. There are here two conditional clauses: (1) when ye divorce women, and (2) when they fulfil their *'Iddat;* followed by two consequential clauses, (3) take them back on equitable terms, or (4) set them free with kindness. *The first is connected with the third and the second with the fourth.* Therefore if the husband wishes to resume the marital relations, he need not wait for *'Iddat*. But if he does not so wish, she is free to marry someone else after *'Iddat.*[40]

There is the assertion again—the portion which has been italicized, the one in which Yusuf Ali relates the first

39 Firasat Ali and Furqan Ahmed, *Divorce in Mohammedan Law*, Deep and Deep Publications, New Delhi, 1983, pp. 46–47.

40. Abdullah Yusuf Ali, *The Meaning of the Glorious* Quran, Dar Al-Kitab al-Masri, Cairo, 1934, Volume I, p. 91.

clause to the third and the second to the fourth. It could just as well have been maintained, for instance, that the two conditions which the verse has specified are to be both fulfilled conjointly, and thereupon one or the other course which the verse specifies—of resuming to live on equitable terms or parting with kindness—is to be adopted.

Theories are read in

We can by now see that there are three distinct features which give ulema the ambiguity they need. These features are:

- The verses of the Quran are not arranged chronologically;
- They are not arranged or grouped by subject;
- There are not universally accepted rules about the proper way of reading the verses—for instance, whether a verse is to be read by itself or in association with other verses which, though occurring in other parts of the Quran, bear upon the same subject.

It has thus become possible for the authorities to not just read their own view of the matter into a verse, it has become customary for them to join their reading of the matter to the verse itself while presenting the latter for the lay public. In fact often even when two authorities are more or less of the same view, one will make bold to go even further in interpolating his reading into the text. Consider the very verses —2.229 and 230—the different constructions put on which we have been discussing. Yusuf Ali presents verse 2.229 thus:

A divorce is only
Permissible twice; after that,
The parties should either hold
Together on equitable terms,
Or separate with kindness....

Nothing is suggested to the reader about whether there need or need not be any intervals between the pronouncements.

Maulana Azad presents the same verse as follows:

> A return to each other is permissible even after divorce has been pronounced twice (in two successive months). Thereafter two ways are open before the husbands—an honourable retention or a graceful parting (after the pronouncement of divorce for the third time in the third month) ....

Notice the words which have been added by the Maulana within parentheses. The same sort of difference occurs in presenting the next verse. Yusuf Ali renders verse 2.230 as follows:

> So if a husband
> Divorces his wife (irrevocably),
> He cannot after that,
> Remarry her until
> After she has married
> Another husband and
> He has divorced her....

The parenthesis alerts the reader to the fact that the word 'irrevocably' has been supplied by Yusuf Ali to bring out what he takes to be the correct meaning of the verse. Even with this addition, however, latitude remains: for the question as to what would make the pronouncement 'irrevocable' remains open. Do three pronouncements in one go make the divorce 'irrevocable'? Does the pronouncement, 'I divorce you irrevocably', make the divorce 'irrevocable' though it be just a single pronouncement? Does an ex post facto statement by the husband about what his intention was when he pronounced talaq—'Yes, I meant it to be irrevocable'—make it irre-vocable, irrespective of the number of times he had pronounced 'talaq', irrespective of whether he had pronounced 'talaq' thrice in one go or with intervals? The questions remain open.

Now see how Maulana Azad presents the same lines:

> But if a man (does not reclaim the woman after the pronouncement of the divorce twice, and) pronounces divorce for the third time (in the third month), then divorce becomes absolute....

A particular view is now presented as the definitive law: a divorce is now irrevocable only when the talaq is pronounced three times, once each in three successive 'periods of purity', and if after the first two pronouncements the husband has not resumed marital relations with the wife.

The way the next few lines of the verse are presented also shows how what each thinks ought to be the way of ordering things finds its way into the plain text, and thereby becomes a statement of law. Once the man has divorced the wife 'irrevocably', Yusuf Ali renders Allah as saying,

> He cannot after that
> Remarry her until
> After she has married
> Another husband and
> He has divorced her.

And what if this sequence has been gone through? On Yusuf Ali's rendering Allah says,

> In that case there is
> No blame on either of them
> If they reunite, provided
> They feel that they
> Can keep the limits
> Ordained by God....

Maulana Azad has Allah speaking to a significantly different emphasis:

> Thereafter it is not lawful for him to take her again until she shall have married another; and if this another man to whom she is married also divorces her, and the woman cares to come back to the first husband, then there shall be no blame on them if they return to each other, trusting that they will keep within the bounds set by God....

Of course the condition specified in Yusuf Ali's rendering—that the two desire to be reunited—contains the condition specified in Maulana Azad's rendering—that the woman cares to return to her first husband—but the difference in the emphasis is evident: Allah's concern in the latter rendering is much more decidedly weighted in the direction of the woman's view of the matter than it is in Yusuf Ali's presentation.

Or consider inheritance. A man dies. Does his brother have a share in his estate. Allah's verdict is set out in Verse 4.12. Abdullah Yusuf Ali renders the relevant lines as follows:

> If the man or woman
> Whose inheritance is in question,
> Has left *neither ascendants nor descendants*
> But has left a brother
> Or a sister, each one of the two gets a sixth; but if more
> Than two, they share in a third....

Maulana Azad renders the same lines as follows:

> And if the man or the woman who leaveth the heritage have *neither parents living nor children* but hath a brother or sister, either shall have a sixth, and if more than one, they shall have alike in a third....

Notice how much more restrictive Maulana Azad's rendering is than Abdullah Yusuf Ali's: '*parents*' instead of '*ascendants*', '*children*' instead of '*descendants*'.

And now see the 'Rampur' rendering of the Quran—the one which, being in Urdu and Hindi is used most widely in north India—puts the lines:

Aur agar aise mard ya aurat ki miras ho, jiske na baap ho, na beta, magar uske bhai ya bahan ho, to unme se har ek ka chhata hissa aur agar ek se ziada hon to sab ek-tihayi mein sharik honge....

Where Yusuf Ali reads 'ascendants' and Maulana Azad reads 'parents', Maulana Fath Muhamad sees only baap, that is 'father'. Where Yusuf Ali reads 'descendants' and Maulana Azad reads 'children', Maulana Fath Muhamad sees only 'beta', that is 'son' ![41]

To revert to our question. Imagine that the man who has died is survived by a daughter. As there is neither baap, father, nor beta, on Maulana Fath Muhamad's rendering the daughter must part with one-third of the estate to her uncles and aunts. On Maulana Azad's rendering, she does not—as she is covered by the term 'children'.

If the man has been survived by a granddaughter alone, on the renderings on both Maulana Fath Muhamad and Maulana Azad the girl has to part with one-thid of the estate to her grand-uncles and grand-aunts. But on Yusuf Ali's rendering, she does not—as she is a 'descendant' !

The differing consequences were described to me graphically by one of the most prominent Muslim women leaders in India. Her father died. This lady and her sister were the only ones to survive him. The uncle arrived carrying the Quran *Majid*—claiming his sixth on the ground that his brother, the girls' father, had not been survived either by the baap, father, or beta, son. They were able to save themselves

41. Compare, Abdullah Yusuf Ali, *The Meaning of the Glorious* Quran, Dar Al-Kitab Al-Masri, Cairo, Volume I, p. 182; Maulana Abul Kalam Azad, *The Tarjuman al-Quran*, Syed Abdul Latif (tr.), Volume II, pp. 215–16; and *Quran Majid,* Arabic Text with Hindi translation by Muhamad Faruq Khan and Urdu translation by Maulana Fath Muhamad, Maktaba al Hasnat, Rampur, 6th edition, 1976, p. 223.

only by confronting him with Yusuf Ali's *'ascendants'* or *'descendants'*!

The girls were lucky—the uncle did not know that Yusuf Ali himself was not as certain about the critical word as the girls made out ! In his note to the use of the word 'descendants' Yusuf Ali says:

> The word in Arabic is *Kalalat,* which is so construed usually. But it was nowhere defined authoritatively in the lifetime of the Apostle. This is one of the three terms about which Hazrat Umar wished that the Apostle had defined them in his lifetime, the other two being *Khilafat,* and *riba* (usury) ....

And these divergences are standard: recall the way words were put into Allah's mouth to justify the slaughter of cows.

The Hadis

The latitude which the Hadis afford is even wider: some Hadis occur in some collections and not in others; even when the same Hadis occurs, all too often the exact words differ from collection to collection; some Hadis are found reliable by some jurists and rejected as unreliable by others; and there is no agreement on the relevance of the particular Hadis to whatever is the question at hand—for instance, in our case the question whether or not three pronouncements of talaq in one go end the marriage.

Imam Muslim for instance records Ibn Abbas, a Companion of the Prophet and the source of many Hadis, as saying that in the time of the Prophet, as well as during the Caliphate of Abu Bakr and the first two years of the Caliphate of Umar, three pronouncements of talaq were taken to be only one pronouncement. Thus the three amounted to only a revocable divorce. It was only Umar who later decreed that three pronouncements, whether given at one sitting or after intervals, shall count for three, and thus irrevocably end the marriage. Ibn Abbas reported that Umar had done this when he saw that husbands 'have begun to hasten in the matter in which they are required to observe respite'. That is Hadis number 3491 in *Sahih Muslim*. Number 3492 reiterates the substance of the preceding one, though now we learn that three counted for one up to the third year of Umar's Caliphate. But the very next Hadis has the same Ibn Abbas reporting that actually Umar reversed the decision later and allowed people to treat the three pronouncements they had uttered in one breath as one![42] In Hadis number 3491 and 3492 Umar is pictured as seeing that husbands are being too free in pronouncing divorces, and therefore to deter them from doing so, and as punishment for those who in spite of his admonition continue to do so, he decrees that three pronouncements shall count for three. In Hadis number 3493 also Umar is pictured as noticing that husbands are being too free in pronouncing divorces, but he now comes to the opposite conclusion: as enforcing the rule, 'Three is three' inflicts too harsh a punishment for rashness, he is pictured as allowing them to count 'Three as one'!

In any event, these three Hadis recorded one after another in one single collection establish three things: (i) that during the time of the Prophet, during the Caliphate of Abu Bakr, and during the first two years of the Caliphate of Umar three pronouncements were taken to count for only one, and to thus amount to just a revocable divorce; (ii) that in the second or third year of his Caliphate, Umar enforced the rule that three pronouncements shall count for three, and thus end the marriage irrevocably; (iii) that subsequently he reversed this

42. See, *Sahih Muslim*, Abdul Hamid Siddiqui (tr.), Kitab Bhavan, New Delhi, 1978, Volume II, p. 759.

decision and allowed husbands to count three pronouncements as being just one revocable pronouncement.

In other collections[43] the third step is missing, and Umar is shown as having continued to enforce the rule that three pronouncements, though made in a single breath, shall in fact count as three ! These collections leave us with the first two 'facts' alone: namely, that (i) during the time of the Prophet, the Caliphate of Abu Bakr and the first two years of the Caliphate of Umar, three pronouncements were taken to be one; and that (ii) from Umar's second or third year the three were made to count for three.

The two 'facts' together justify jurists on both sides of the question! Those who maintain 'Three-is-one', take as their norm the fact that *that* is how the pronouncements were counted during the time of the Prophet himself. They say that Umar's ruling was an 'innovation', that it was an expedient devised to deal with a particular evil prevalent at a particular time and not a universal rule applicable for all time.

The others—the Hanafis for instance—maintain that when Umar formulated the 'Three-is-three' rule a large number of the Prophet's Companions were alive. Had Umar's rule been at variance with what the Prophet held to be proper, they would have objected and kept Umar from enforcing the rule. As they did not do so, the 'Three-is-three' rule must be taken to have been arrived at by ijma, that is by consensus among the Companions of the Prophet, and thus to be binding.

This difference of opinion leaves us with one 'fact' alone—namely, Ibn Abbas's statement that during the time of the Prophet three pronouncements counted for one. Alas! Even on this there is no agreement. As against the statement of Ibn

---

43. See, for instance, *Sunan Abu Dawud*, Ahmad Hasan (tr.), Kitab Bhavan, New Delhi, 1993, Volume II, pp. 586–88.

Abbas, al-Hasan relates that Abdullah b. Umar made one pronouncement of divorce against his wife while she was in her menses. His intention was to make the remaining two pronouncements in the ensuing 'periods of purity'. When he reported to the Prophet that he had pronounced talaq during the wife's menses, the Prophet made him take the wife back. Once he had done so the Prophet told Ibn Umar, 'Now when your wife is purified you have the right to divorce her or keep her.' Then comes the point crucial to the question at hand. Ibn Umar thereupon asked the Prophet, 'Tell me, Prophet of Allah, if I had completed the three pronouncements, would it in that case be proper and permissible for me to return to my wife?' The Prophet said, 'No, the divorce then would have become complete and irrevocable but you would have incurred sin for pronouncing divorce not in the proper way.'[44]

As against Ibn Abbas's account by which during the Prophet's time three pronouncements were taken to amount to only one, here the Prophet is saying that had Ibn Umar actually pronounced talaq thrice, the marriage would have been at an end irrevocably.

The other set of jurists doesn't of course give up that easily. While the context of the Hadis seems to imply that Ibn

---

44. *Sahih Muslim,* Volume II, footnote 1933, pp. 759–60. Though Ibn Umar was commanded to take back his wife, the pronouncement of talaq he had made against his wife during her menses was not declared to be void. It was taken to count for one pronouncement: *Sahih Al-Bukhari,* Volume VII, pp.130, 133. Also *Sahih Muslim,* Volume II, pp. 755–58. In *Sunan Abu Dawud* in one Hadis one pronouncement during the wife's menses is reported to have been counted as one. In the very next Hadis the husband is reported as saying, 'He (the Prophet) returned her to me and did not count it (the pronouncement) anything'. See, *Sunan Abu Dawud,* Ahmad Hasan (tr.), Kitab Bhavan, New Delhi, 1993, Volume II, Hadis, 2179, 2180; pp. 587–88.

Umar was asking what the consequence would have been if he had pronounced three talaqs instead of one at the time he had made that one pronouncement, those who would have three count as one insist that what Ibn Umar was asking was not, 'What if I had pronounced three divorces in one breath instead of pronouncing talaq once on that occasion?,' but, 'What if I had gone through with my plan of pronouncing the remaining two talaqs in the succeeding two periods of purity?'

But if Ibn Umar had gone through and pronounced talaq thrice after intervals, where would have been the occasion for the Prophet to say, '..... but you would have incurred sin for pronouncing divorce not in the proper way?' For in that case the talaq would have been pronounced 'in the proper way'.

That shows, say the 'Three-is-three' jurists, that the question was about three pronouncements, made at one go. On the contrary, say the 'Three-is-one' jurists, that disapproval refers to the fact that, though Ibn Umar would have completed the prescription of making three pronouncements after intervals, the first pronouncement had been made when the wife was in her menses, an occasion when it should not be made. It is this irregularity which the Prophet had in mind in his remark, they say.

And so on. Thus, even when just a simple Hadis is in question, the controversies are endless.

Nor is that all. As against the incident involving Abdullah b. Umar, the 'Three-is-one' set of jurists cite the incident of Rukanah. It is recorded by Abu Dawud as follows:

> Rukanah b. Abd Yazid divorced his wife absolutely. Thereupon he reported the matter to the Prophet. The Prophet asked him: 'What did you intend?' Rukanah said: 'A single utterance of divorce.' The Prophet asked: 'Did you swear by Allah?'

Rukanah replied, 'I swore by Allah.' Whereupon the Prophet declared 'It stands as you intended.'[45]

Notice that in this instance the husband had divorced his wife 'absolutely', that is, to use the words we find in Trimizi, he had pronounced the 'final and decisive divorce' against his wife—that could mean either one pronouncement of talaq with the additional words specifying that it was final, or three pronouncements. Nevertheless, ask the 'Three-is-one' jurists, what view did the Prophet take of it? He declared that the outcome would depend on what the man had intended—that is, it would depend not on whether the man had declared his pronouncement to be final, nor on whether he had made the divorce final and decisive by repeating the word thrice; rather the outcome would depend on what he says ex post facto his intention was at the time he pronounced the 'final and decisive divorce'.

It is now the turn of the jurists of the other view not to be taken in that easily. They declare this Hadis to be a 'weak' one, to be unreliable and hence not to be taken into account.[46]

That is not much trouble, for the 'Three-is-one' jurists produce the Hadis involving the father, Abd Yazid, of Rukanah. In this instance the Prophet did not make the matter rest on the ex post facto statement of the husband about what his intention had been when he had pronounced talaq: he just declared the wife to be lawful for the husband though he had

45. *Sunan Abu Dawud*, Volume II, Hadis 2200–02, pp. 595–96. Alas! The restoration by the Prophet did not save the poor woman. For we learn in *Sunan Abu Dawud* that the man divorced her a second time in the time of Umar and a third time in the time of Usman! See, *Sunan Abu Dawud*, Volume II, p. 595, Hadis 2200.

46. For the version of the Hadis in Tirmizi and the view that it is 'weak', see Firasat Ali and Furqan Ahmed, *Divorce in Mohammedan Law, The law of 'Triple Divorce'*, Deep and Deep Publications, New Delhi, 1983, pp. 53–54.

divorced her irrevocably. That, say our jurists, certainly means that three pronouncements must count for one.

> Abd Yazid divorced his wife, the mother of Abu Rukanah and his brother, and he married instead a woman of the tribe Muzainah. But that latter lady went to the Prophet and said, 'He is of no use to me except that he is as useful to me as a hair,' and so saying she pulled out a hair from her head [— her way, it would seem, of indicating that Abd Yazid was impotent]. The Prophet became furious. He pointed to the resemblances that Rukanah and his brothers bore to their father. How could Abd Yazid be impotent in that case? The Prophet then commanded Abd Yazid: 'Divorce her.' He did so. The Prophet then said: 'Take your wife, the mother of Rukanah and his brothers, back in marriage.' The man said, 'I have divorced her by three pronouncements, Apostle of Allah.' The Prophet concluded, 'I know; take her back,' and recalled the verse in the Quran, 'O Prophet, when you divorce women, divorce them at their appointed periods.'[47]

Conclusive, you might say. But the Hanafis remain unconvinced. And continue with the strict rule given in the *Hidayah*.

It is one Hadis against another. It is the word of one set of jurists on one Hadis against the word of another set on that very Hadis.

More than enough scope therefore for the fatwa to go either way on any given case.

The law books

With the Quran and the Hadis themselves yielding such wide latitude, the law books render the freedom for the

47. *Sunan Abu Dawud*, Volume II, Hadis 2191, p. 591. In another version, Abd Yazid is said to have divorced his wife 'irrevocably', not specifically by pronouncing talaq thrice.

ulema to decide a thing one way rather than another well-nigh complete.

A man says to his wife, 'Your divorce is obligatory on me,' or that it is 'binding (*lazim*) on me,' or that it is 'established (*sabit*) on me,' or that it is 'compulsory on me'. Is she divorced or not? This is typical of the situations considered in the law books, and here is the typical passage about it from the commentator of *Fatawa-i-Qazi Khan*:

> A man says to his wife, 'Thy divorce is obligatory on me (that is, it is obligatory on me to divorce thee),' or binding (*lazim*) on me,' or 'established on me,' or 'compulsory on me'; some of the learned lawyers have said that in each of these cases one reversible divorce is caused, if the husband has had intercourse with her (for in the case of the wife with whom there has been no intercourse, even a reversible divorce is tantamount to a complete divorce), whether the husband has any intention or not; and some of them have said no divorce shall be caused, even if the husband intends a divorce by those words; and some of them have said that there exists a difference of opinion, and that according to Aboo Haneefa, on whom be peace, divorce shall be caused by every one of those expressions, and that according to Mahomed, on whom be peace, divorce shall be caused if the husband makes use of the expression *lazim* or binding; and that according to Aboo Yusoof, on whom be peace, it is necessary for the husband to intend divorce in each of these (and in that case divorce shall be caused in each of these cases); and Sudur-i-Shuheed has said in the Book on Oaths, in his work called the *Shurah-ool Mookhtasur*, that the correct principle is, that in none of these cases shall divorce be caused according to Aboo Haneefa, on whom be peace; and he says in his work called the *Wakiat* that divorce shall be caused in each of these cases: and the lawyer Aboo Jaffer, on whom be peace, says that if the husband makes use of the expression *Wajib* or obligatory, divorce shall be caused on

> account of popular recognition; and that if he makes use of the expression *Sabit* that is established, or *Furz* that is compulsory, or *lazim* that is binding, divorce shall not be caused on account of the absence of popular recognition of these words in the sense of divorce.[48]

A man says to his wife, 'You are not to me a wife,' or 'I am not a husband for you.' Is she divorced or not? The commentator of *Fatawa-i-Qazi Khan* explains:

> Aboo Haneefa, on whom be peace, says, if the husband intends to cause divorce, divorce shall be caused, otherwise not; but his disciples have said, no divorce shall be caused even if he has an intention.[49]

And what if the divorce has been pronounced by a slip of the tongue? Again, the answers range all the way:

> And if a man intends to say one thing, but by a slip of the tongue he uses expressions of vow (or *Nuzar*, ...) or divorce, or emancipation; then the lawyer Aboo Jaffer, on whom be peace, says, that in the case of a vow, the subject-matter of the vow becomes obligatory on him, without any difference of opinion; and in case of divorce or emancipation, according to the view taken by Mahomed, on whom be peace, the divorce or emancipation shall be caused; but Aboo Yusoof, on whom be peace, says, that divorce shall not be caused as between the man and his God (although the *Kazee* must decree the divorce), but emancipation shall take effect (both as between him and his God and also as far as the *Kazee* is concerned) and what is reported from Aboo Haneefa, on whom be peace, is the reverse of this, and that divorce shall be caused, but emancipation shall not: but from the sayings of Aboo Haneefa, on whom be peace, what is obvious is that is that the divorce and emancipation shall

48. *Fatawa-i-Qazi Khan*, Kitab Bhavan, New Delhi, 1994 Reprint, Volume II, para 1845, pp. 16–17.

49. Ibid., Volume II, para 1869, p. 25.

> (both) take effect, in accordance with the view of Mahomed, on whom be peace.[50]

And so on indefinitely. The effect of all this will be obvious: when you take a problem to them, the ulema can facilitate your way or thwart it by invoking one authority rather than the other. Simultaneously they, joined this time by the apologist, will insist that we, in particular the non-Muslims, must never cease to believe that the shariah is a clear and definite code, that it is a divinely ordained, and therefore an eternal and unchanging code!

Does 'and' make three THREE?

There are further subdivisions among the jurists, and, as K.N. Ahmed explains, much seems to turn on whether or not the word '*and*' has been used while repeating the talaq. A husband may say, for instance, 'I divorce you, and I divorce you, divorce you,' or he may say, 'I divorce you, divorce you, divorce you.' According to the Hanafi school the marriage is ended in both cases. According to the Maliki school, in the former case the three pronouncements count as three and the wife is out. In the latter case, according to the Malikis, further inquiries are in order. If the husband had added a condition to the thrice repeated talaq—as in, 'If you step out of the house, you are divorced, divorced, divorced'—his explanation of what he intended shall be taken at face value: if he says that he repeated the pronouncement only to emphasize the point, the divorce shall not be final, and he will be allowed to revoke it; if he says that he really intended it to be final, it shall indeed be final. On the other hand, if he had just repeated the pronouncement

50. Ibid., Volume II, para 1899, pp. 42–43.

without making the talaq contingent on some event, his explanation shall *not* be considered—the three pronouncements shall count as three and the marriage shall be finished.

The Hanbali school makes subdivisions of an even finer kind—they depend in part on whether the word 'and' was used or not, in part on what the intention of the husband was, and in part on whether the marriage has been consummated or not. If the marriage has *not* been consummated, the word *'and'* has *not* been used, and the husband avers that he used the second and third repetitions only to emphasize the first, the wife survives as wife. If the marriage has been consummated, the wife is out even though *'and'* was not used, and the husband says that he did not intend to make the divorce final. If the word *'and'* was used, the matter shall turn on what the intention of the husband was: if it was to pronounce an irrevocable divorce, the divorce shall be final forthwith; if the repetitions were merely to emphasize the point, the divorce shall not be final whether the marriage has been consummated or not.

Under the Shafi'i school the matter turns not on whether a word like *'and'* was used or not but on whether the marriage has been consummated or not. If it has not been consummated, the three repetitions—with or without the *'and'*—count as one. If it has been consummated, the matter turns on what the husband says was his intention: if he says that he really did intend an irrevocable divorce, or if he says that he did not really have any definite intention, the wife shall indeed be cast away; if he says that by repeating the word he merely meant to emphasize the point, the marriage shall survive, whether the *'and'* had or had not been used.

And so on. And for each step and each position, the jurists have 'principles', Hadis, and logic. Notice that such hair-splitting increases the power of the clerics and the 'theological' seminaries to the point of making them the indispensable and final arbiters in determining the consequences of private acts. Correspondingly, the subdivisions increase further the power of the husband. Even in the elementary case, he can shout 'talaq' once and throw the wife into a state of extreme insecurity; he can repeat the word a second time, throw her into a state of absolute terror and then, having made her submit to his will and whim, he can 'revoke' the divorce. But now he can go further. He can pronounce the word a third time too, numb the woman into complete submission, and still not lose hold of her—for much will turn on what he says his intention was: the wife is thus even more at his mercy.[51]

And the differences among authorities and the minute subdivisions they have crafted redouble the power of the ulema: when the case comes to them they can invoke this authority or that, they can put it in a pigeonhole which saves the wife or in one by which she is cast away.

The same sorts of divergences are to be seen on other circumstances that attend the pronouncements.

Bhang vs. liquor

Does talaq pronounced in a state of intoxication throw out the wife? Well, the matter turns first of all on the substance by taking which the husband has got intoxicated. If it is hemp (bhang) then, hold several jurists as well as law books like *Fatawa-i-Qazi Khan*, the pronouncement does *not* end the marriage. They give two sorts of reasons for this view: they reason first that, while liquor is prohibited by Islam and therefore a man consuming it ought to be made to

51. For a handy listing of the canonical authorities on the foregoing positions, see K.N. Ahmed, *Muslim Divorce Law*, Karachi, 1971, Kitab Bhavan, New Delhi, 1984 Reprint, pp. 85–92.

suffer the consequences of his action, bhang is not prohibited and so such a severe punishment—of the man losing his wife—should not be visited upon him; second, they reason that as a divorce pronounced by a man bereft of understanding—a minor, a lunatic—is not effective, talaq pronounced by a man who has temporarily lost his understanding because of bhang is not to be given effect to. But other law books—*Fatawa-i-Alamgiri* being the foremost—argue the opposite: consumption of bhang too has become so widespread, they say, that it too needs to be discouraged and therefore, divorce pronounced under its influence, exactly like that under the influence of liquor, is to be final. Another law book—*Al-Bahr Al-Raiq*—goes in for finer differentiation: if bhang has been taken for pleasure, the divorce is effective; if it has been taken as a medicine, it is not.

What if the husband is intoxicated not from bhang, but from liquor? Does talaq pronounced in that state throw out the wife? The law varies over the entire spectrum—from 'No, never,' through 'Depends,' to 'Yes, invariably'—and the distinctions which the Islamic jurists make are fine as can be.

In the orthodox view as stated, for instance, in *Fatawa-i-Alamgiri,* talaq pronounced by a man who is under the influence of liquor *does* end the marriage, and for two reasons: the talaq has been pronounced and a pronouncement is a pronouncement; moreover, it has been pronounced upon partaking that which is forbidden, that which is sinful. The talaq must therefore be given effect to because the husband decreed it, and also to punish the husband for the sin of consuming liquor.

But jurists are seldom ones to give a ruling without making fine distinctions. So they make the result contingent upon (i) whether the liquor was consumed voluntarily, or under compulsion, or under necessity (for instance, for medicinal purposes); (ii) whether the man had got only mildly intoxicated or he had got so drunk as to have lost his understanding; (iii) whether the drink had been made from substances liquor from which is prohibited, or from other substances; (iv) whether the drink had fermented to such a degree as to fall in the prohibited category. And so on.

Each of these contingencies is further subdivided by the jurists, and the benchmarks that are used for each criterion differ from jurist to jurist. For instance, even Abu Hanifa allowed that talaq pronounced by a man who had lost his understanding ought not to end the marriage. But, he laid down, a man must be taken to have been out of his understanding only when he could not at that time distinguish between the sky and land. Divorces pronounced short of this state must be given effect to. His principal disciples—Abu Yusuf and Muhammad—whose rulings are ever so often given precedence over those of Abu Hanifa, gave a more lenient criterion: the husband must be taken to be not responsible for his actions, and hence his divorce is not to be acted upon, if he is not able to control his speech. A subsequent legist—Ibn al-Humam—carried even that criterion—of whether the man was in control of his speech—further, for, once we accept the Abu Yusuf-Muhammad criterion, the question of degree must be settled: how much of the man's speech must be irrational before he can be said to have said things which ought not to be acted upon? If on the occasion he pronounced talaq 'the greater part' of his speech was rational and only a small part 'wild and meaningless', the jurist held, the man must be assumed to have been in possession of his understanding and the talaq he pronounced must take effect. If not, the talaq is void. We have only to pursue the question to the next step—'What shall be the signs by which we should assess whether 'the greater part' of the husband's speech was coherent or not?'—to see that the trail is far from ended, nor therefore are the occasions for differences among these jurists.

Not only do the rulings of the four schools differ on these points—a fact which knocks out the claim that the shariah is a clear and definite code—the leading jurists changed their opinions as time passed—a fact that knocks out the other claim which is made on behalf of shariah, namely that it is immutable and eternal.

As K.N. Ahmed notes, the *Fatawa-i-Alamgiri* decrees that whether the husband is sober or drunk, whether he is only a little intoxicated or dead drunk, and irrespective of the substance which has caused the intoxication, once the talaq is pronounced, the marriage is ended and the wife is out. Abu Hanifa, the founder of the Hanafi school, declares that the marriage is ended unless, as we have seen, the husband is so drunk that he cannot distinguish between the sky and the earth. Abu Yusuf and Muhammad, his greatest disciples and authorities who are revered as much by the Hanafis as Abu Hanifa, decree that the talaq shall not be effective if at the moment of pronouncing it the husband is not able to exercise control over his speech. So, there are differences among the Hanafis themselves. Under the Maliki school the talaq is not effective if the man is under the influence of alcohol and is not able to distinguish between right and wrong—a criterion wholly different from, and much more obtuse than the ones prescribed by Abu Hanifa, Abu Yusuf and Muhammad. Imam Shafi'i, the founder of the Shafi'i school, initially decreed that a divorce pronounced by a man under the influence of liquor is void. Later he decreed the opposite—the talaq would be effective, he said. Some jurists of his school and some of its law books cling to his initial verdict, others to the later one. The founder of the Hanbali school, Ahmad b. Hanbal, initially decreed that talaq pronounced by a man who is under the influence of liquor to the extent that he does not know what he is talking about is void. Subsequently he expressed different opinions on different occasions, ultimately, as Ahmed records, holding that the matter was too complicated as there had been no agreement even among the Companions of the Prophet, and so each case must be decided on merits.

Again, there is no dearth of Hadis, there is no dearth of 'principles of Islamic jurisprudence' to back up each of the contrary decrees. Scores and scores of examples can be given. But just one will suffice to illustrate both—the differences in opinion and the changes in them over time on the specific question we are considering, and also the sorts of 'reasons' and analogies by which debates among the jurists proceed. Citing authorities at each step, Ahmed writes:

> Shafi'i expressed different views at different times. At first he held that a divorce pronounced when one has temporarily lost one's reason is not valid and is ineffective. He based this view on the ground that the drink might have produced delirium or inflammation of the brain to such an extent as to make him devoid of reasoning faculties. He justifies this opinion on the ground that the divorce pronounced by a minor is not effective because he does not possess understanding and the same rule shall apply here. His second ground is that divorce under the influence of *bhang* (hemp) is not effective and there is no difference in the use of *bhang* and of a fermented liquor as both produce the same result, namely, temporary loss of reason. The third reason is that apostasy under the influence of drink is not permitted and the same rule shall apply here. The Hanafis have explained that Allah has permitted divorce and there is no exception in the case of a divorce given under the influence of drink. In (the) case (of) a divorce by a minor or a lunatic, it is not effective for want of understanding. They have not violated any rule of Muslim law, but in (the) case of drinking the husband has been guilty of an offence and so his divorce shall be held effective by way of punishment. The use of *bhang* is not an offence and so it (the rule that a divorce

> pronounced under the influence of *bhang* shall not take effect) has no application here. The case of apostasy is also inapplicable because there an attempt is made to save him (the husband) from renunciation of Islam while here the husband has to be punished to discourage drinking. Without entering into the merits of these statements, it is to be stated that Shafi'i subsequently changed his opinion and held divorce given under the influence of wine to be effective....[52]

Not only may the alim thus choose between authorities, he can facilitate the wish of the husband by relying on one ruling of an authority or thwart it by invoking some other ruling of that same authority!

Compulsion as choice

Or consider another question. *Does talaq pronounced by a husband under compulsion or duress end the marriage?* The Hanafi school holds that even such a talaq ends the marriage—in contrast to the question about talaq pronounced in an intoxicated state, there is no scope for manoeuvre on this matter as Abu Hanifa and the two disciples, Abu Yusuf and Muhammad, are in agreement on the point. But the other three main Sunni schools—Maliki, Shafi'i and Hanbali—hold that divorce pronounced under compulsion is void, as do the Shias.

Again, each has his Hadis and his 'principle of Islamic jurisprudence.' The Hanafis hold that even when a man is under compulsion, in pronouncing talaq he is in fact exercising a choice, and so the talaq is as effective as any other. Were a father to tell a son, 'I will throw you out unless you throw out your wife,' or were an enemy to tell him, 'I will kill you unless you throw out your wife,' say Abu Hanifa and the other jurists, it is not that the husband has no choice. Even

52. Ibid., pp. 48–49.

when he is decreeing a talaq under such pressure or compulsion, the husband is exercising a choice—between the comforts of staying on in his father's house and his wife in the former case, between his life and his wife in the latter. They press the analogy further. Consider the case of a man who is not under pressure or compulsion of these sorts, the jurists say. When and why does he pronounce talaq? He does so *under necessity*, they note. The wife has become so odious and repugnant to him, they say, that *out of necessity* he casts her out. The essential point, they stress, is that he is acting *out of necessity.* Well, they say, that is exactly what the man faced with, say, a threat to his life is doing: he too is acting *out of necessity.* Thus, they decree, the two talaqs are completely at par and equally potent in ending the marriage.[53]

Imam Shafi'i and the others have their own 'principles of Islamic jurisprudence' for the opposite view. They say that a person who is compelled has, by definition, no option, and no act is worthy of having legal consequences which is not purely optional. And they cite several Hadis to buttress their view: Allah, they recall the Prophet saying, shall not hold a Muslim responsible for things he did or neglected to do by mistake, or out of forgetfulness, or under duress; Aisha, they recall, said, 'I heard the Messenger of Allah say, "There is no divorce and no emancipation (of slaves) by force."'[54]

And we learn from no less an authority than Imam Malik's *Muwatta* that this is the law that was administered by the highest personages in the earliest years of Islam. Here is the account:

---

53. Recall the reasoning in the *Hidayah* on the point cited earlier in Chapter 6.

54. For instance, *Sunan Abu Dawud,* Ahmed Hasan (tr.), Kitab Bhavan, New Delhi, 1993, Hadis, 2188, Volume II, p. 590. The words as given by Abu Dawud are: 'There is no divorce or emancipation in case of constraint or duress (*ghalaq*)'. Abu Dawud said, 'I think *ghalaq* means anger.'

> Thabit Ahnaf married Umm Walad of 'Abd al-Rahman b. Zaid b. Khattab. He said, ' 'Abd Allah b. 'Abd al-Rahman b. Zadi b. Khattab sent for me, and I went to him. I saw lashes, two iron fetters and two slaves who were made to sit by. He said to me: Divorce this Umm Walad, otherwise I will beat you and severely punish you. I said: If it is so, I give her *talaq* a thousand times. He said: When I left the place, I met 'Abd Allah b. 'Umar on his way to Mecca and narrated all this to him. Abd Allah b. 'Umar was furious and said: This is not a divorce and she is not forbidden to you; return to your family. Thabit said: My heart did not feel satisfied and I went to 'Abd Allah b. Zubair at Mecca. 'Abd Allah b. Zubair was at the time the Governor of Mecca. I informed him of what had taken place and told him also what 'Abd Allah b. 'Umar had said to me. 'Abd Allah b. Zubair said to me: Verily, that woman has not become forbidden to you. Go to your family. He also wrote to Jabir b. Aswad Zuhri, the administrator of Medina, ordering him to chastise 'Abd Allah b. 'Abd al-Rahman and deliver the wife of of Thabit Ahnaf to him. When I returned to Medina, Safiyyah, the wife of 'Abd Allah b. 'Umar, sent my wife to me, clothed and adorned. On instructions from 'Abd Allah b. 'Umar, I arranged a *walimah* feast and invited 'Abd Allah b. 'Umar and he came.[55]

If the ulema want to help a man who has pronounced talaq under compulsion to retain his wife, they can invoke this Hadis and the words of the Prophet, 'There is no divorce and no emancipation (of slaves) by force.' If they want to thwart the husband they can cite the rule laid down in the *Hidayah*.

Incidentally, by the axium that they should leave these things alone, our courts do not look at these Hadis and jurists. Instead they opt for convenience and follow the orthodox Hanafi position as stated in the *Hidayah* and in the fatwas. And

55. Imam Malik, *Muwatta*, Sh. Muhammad Ashraf, Lahore, 1980, Ch. 357, Hadis 1199, pp. 263–64.

so in the view taken by our courts, whether the talaq is pronounced by a husband compelled or by one uncompelled, the wife is cast out. The consequences moved Justice Ameer Ali to urge the sort of escape we have encountered earlier. He wrote:

> Supposing a Hanafi, under the influence of threat and strong coercion pronounces a *talaq* against his wife, and on receiving his freedom of action, disavows the validity of his act, and places himself under the Shafe'i rules to escape the results of the *talaq*, there can be little doubt that he would be justified in doing so, and the repudiation he had pronounced would be invalidated.[56]

With a husband pronouncing talaq as a Hanafi, and then escaping the consequences by proclaiming himself to be a Shafi'ite, and such devices being urged by such eminent men of law, the shariah must still be regarded as a sacrosanct, unchangeable, Allah-given code!

Which 'principle' shall prevail!

The 'principle of Islamic jurisprudence' which underlies the non-Hanafi position in regard to talaq pronounced under compulsion is that regard must be had to what the *intention* of the husband was when he pronounced the talaq. Did he *really* want to get rid of his wife—that, these jurists say, is the real question. They cite in support of their view the saying of the Prophet: 'The deeds are evaluated *according to one's intentions,* and everyone will receive the reward of *what he has intended.*'[57] And they draw an analogy. On

56. Syed Ameer Ali, *Muhammadan Law*, 1908, 1986 Reprint, Kitab Bhavan, New Delhi, Volume, II, p. 443.

57. *Sahih Al-Bukhart*, Islamic University, Medina Al-Munawwara, Kazi Publications, Lahore, 1979, Volume VII, p. 144. For statements to this effect of Al-Hasan and Az-Zuhri, see Ibid., Volume VII, pp. 145,146. Also, *Sunan Abu Dawud*, Volume II, Hadis 2195–96, pp. 593–94, to the same effect.

what basis is it decided, they ask, whether three pronouncements of talaq in a single sitting shall count for *three,* and thus result in a final, irrevocable divorce, or as one only? The matter is settled by ascertaining from the husband *what his intention* was: if he pronounced the talaq just once but intended it to be final and irrevocable, the wife is out; similarly if he uttered talaq thrice and intended three to mean *three,* the wife is cast out; on the other hand, if he pronounced talaq the second and third time merely to impart emphasis to the first pronouncement, the three pronouncements are to count for one only. The same regard, they reason, should be shown for *the intention of the husband* when he pronounces talaq under compulsion. As he did not really want to throw his wife out but pronounced talaq only to save his life, the marriage should not be dissolved, they say.

But just see what happens at the hands of these very jurists to this very criterion—of the husband's intention—in other circumstances.

What if a man, not really intending to cast his wife away, utters talaq in jest? The same Imam Shafi'i who held that talaq pronounced under compulsion shall be void, holds that talaq even if it has been uttered in jest must be given effect to. Now the 'principle' of looking at the man's intention is put aside, and another 'principle' is invoked. This is the 'principle' of option: where the man is under duress or extreme pressure he does not have an option, reasons Shafi'i, and hence what he says or does in that case must not be taken to have legal consequences; the man speaking in jest certainly acts of his own free will and so what he says must be given effect to, even though, by definition, he did not seriously intend what he said. And, naturally, there is a Hadis to fortify this ruling also—the Prophet is reported to have said: 'There are three things which, whether undertaken seriously or in jest, are treated as serious: marriage, divorce, and taking back a wife (after a divorce which is not final).'[58]

A telling case

This rule leads to telling results, as was brought out by a recent, and much publicized case in Pakistan. In a serial broadcast over Pakistan television the man playing the part of the husband pronounced talaq against the woman who was playing the part of his wife. Unfortunately, the lady who was acting the part of the wife was in fact the wife in real life of the man who was acting the husband. The clerics pounced, and declared that their marriage had indeed been dissolved as a result of the talaq pronouncement, and that, this having happened, the only way in which the husband could reclaim his wife was for her to first marry another man, for that marriage to be actually consummated, for the second husband to divorce the wife, and then for the original husband and wife to marry again. That the man had no intention of divorcing the woman was totally immaterial to the question, they ruled. No step could be skipped, they ruled, in particular the intermediate step of the wife getting married to another man and consummating that marriage could not be skipped. And they certainly had the Hadis to buttress their edict. We read in *Sahih Al-Bukhari*:

> Narrated 'Aisha: The wife of Rifa'a Al-Qurazi came to Allah's Apostle and said, 'O Allah's Apostle! Rifa'a divorced me irrevocably. After him I married 'Abdur-Rahman bin Az-Zubair Al-Qurazi who proved to be impotent.' Allah's Apostle said to her, 'Perhaps you

58. *Sunan Abu Dawud*, Volume II, Hadis 2189, p. 590.

want to return to Rifa'a? Nay (you cannot return to Rifa'a) until you and 'Abdur-Rahman consummate your marriage.'[59]

The Prophet reiterated the rule on yet another occasion:

Narrated 'Aisha: A man divorced his wife thrice (by expressing his decision to divorce her thrice), then she married another man who also divorced her. The Prophet was asked if she could legally many the first husband (or not). The Prophet replied, 'No, she cannot marry the first husband unless the second husband consummates his marriage with her just as the first husband had done.'[60]

Yet another Hadis in *Sahih Al-Bukhari* goes on to specify what consummation actually means:

Narrated 'Aisha: A man divorced his wife and she married another man who proved to be impotent and divorced her. She could not get her satisfaction from him, and after a while he divorced her. Then she came to the Prophet and said, 'O Allah's Apostle! My first husband divorced me and then I married another man who entered upon me to consummate his marriage but he proved to be impotent and did not approach me except once during which he benefited nothing from me. Can I re-marry my first husband in this case?' Allah's Apostle said, 'It is unlawful to many your first husband till the other husband consummates his marriage with you.'[61]

---

59. *Sahih Al-Bukhari*, Volume VII, p. 136. A little later the same incident is reported in another Hadis in the following words: 'Narrated 'Aisha: Rifa'a Al-Qurazi married a lady and then divorced her whereupon she married another man. She came to the Prophet and said that her new husband did not approach her, and that he was completely impotent. The Prophet said (to her), 'No (you cannot remarry your first husband) till you taste the second husband and he tastes you (i.e., till he consummates his marriage with you)'. Ibid., Volume VII, p. 182.

60. Ibid., Volume VII, p. 136. For similar Hadis, Imam Malik, *Muwatta*, Sh. Muhammad Ashraf, Lahore, 1980, Ch. 317, pp. 234–35.

61. *Sahih Al-Bukhari*, Volume VII, p. 139. Abu Dawud reports to the same effect: 'Aisha said: the Apostle of Allah (m.p.b.u.h.) was asked

Notice that in these cases the intention is clear. In the first instance—that is in the case of the wife of Rifa'a Al-Qurazi—the circumstance, the impotence of the second husband, makes the fulfilment of the rule impossible, and yet the Prophet reiterated the requirement: before the original couple can be reunited, the wife must be married to a second man, *that* second marriage must actually be consummated, the second husband must then divorce the wife, and only then can she and the original husband be reunited. Notice that the 'principle' of going by what the intention of the husband was is set aside by the 'principle' that to discourage husbands from divorcing their wives lightly (and to discourage wives from annoying their husbands to the point that the latter divorce them) the two ought to be punished. Now, when the Prophet insisted that each step must be adhered to even in circumstances in which the crucial step—of the second marriage being actually consummated—was beyond the realm of possibility, how could the actor husband and his actress wife be allowed to escape the consequences of the talaq pronounced during the TV serial?

Notice that for *both* positions 'principles', sayings and decisions of the Prophet are available: on the one hand, there are sayings to the effect that persons shall be called to account according to their intentions, that things done or left undone by inadvertence, forgetfulness or by mistake shall be overlooked; and, on the other, there are decisions in which the Prophet visits terrible and swift punishment by looking at the face value of the deed alone.

---

about a man who divorced his wife three times, and she married another who entered upon her, but divorced her before having intercourse with her, whether she was lawful for the first husband. She (Aisha) said: The Prophet (m.p.b.u.h.) replied: She is not lawful for the first (husband) until she tastes the honey of the other;' *Sunan Abu Dawud*, Volume II, Hadis 2302, p. 629.

The same cleavage among jurists and law books persists in regard to other circumstances also which may have attended upon the pronouncement of talaq.

Does a talaq pronounced by a husband subjected to fraud end the marriage? For instance, upon being informed wrongly that his wife has been unfaithful to him a husband may pronounce the talaq; is the wife out, even if on inquiry the allegation against her turns out to be false? Yes, say the Hanafis. No, say several of the others. And the reasoning of each set is similar to what it was in the case of a husband acting under compulsion: the husband had the option to be taken in by the allegation or not, he had the option of not reacting to the allegation at once and awaiting the results of an inquiry, but he chose to utter the words, and, so, the moving finger having writ, not all thy piety nor wit...., say the Hanafis.

What if the man is ignorant of the implication of the words and yet utters them or is led to utter them—and remember the words do not have to definitely spell out that the wife is cast aside—what then? The marriage is ended say the Hanafis, and the wife has no recourse. It is *not* ended say the Hanbalis. It is *not* ended say the Shafi'is. It is *not* ended say the Shias. And in noting the Hanafi rule remember that the words may be ever so elliptical: to take just one of scores and scores of examples which have been listed in the law books, how many would know that saying 'Thy rope is on thy hump' will end the marriage? And yet Hazrat Umar himself ruled that even those words ended the marriage as we learn from Imam Malik.[62]

But can we who are reviewing the matter be any more definite that such words end the marriage than the ignorant husband? Not if we go by the law books ! Take the expression,

---

62. Imam Malik, *Muwatta*, Sh. Muhammad Ashraf, Lahore, 1980, Ch. 332, p. 246.

'Your affairs are in your hands'—quite innocuous, indeed words that a husband who is, say, encouraging his wife to stand on her own, to pursue her career say, might use. Al-Hasan narrates a tradition by which these innocuous words amount to a divorce of *three* pronouncements. Umar, Ibn Masud and others on the other hand hold that they will amount to a *single* pronouncement, as do Sufyan and Abu Hanifa. Uthman b. Affan and Zaid b. Thabit, on the third hand, maintain that the outcome depends on the decision of the *wife*, and that is what Imam Malik too holds.[63] From three, to one, to the decision of the wife....

Notice that as the subject of our present concern is the triple talaq alone, the examples have been confined to this little fragment alone. Similar examples can be compiled from almost every other aspect of the law of divorce, and of course from the law relating to other matters—adoption, inheritance, *waqfs*.

Power, and its perpetuation

Two features would by now be obvious: (1) far from being a clear and definite code, the shariah is ambiguous; (2) it is ambiguous on the entire spectrum of issues.

Two operational consequences follow: (1) this ambiguity is one of the bases for the unrivalled power of the ulema; (2) the ulema therefore sabotage every effort to codify the shariah as zealously as they fight back every effort to replace it by a modern code common to all.

As we have seen, the general rule is that talaq given in anger is as lethally effective as any other talaq. The *Fatawa-i-Rizvia* enforces this rule as stringently as other authorities.[64]

63. *Sunan Abu Dawud*, Volume II, Hadis 2198, pp. 594–95. See in particular the comment of Professor Ahmed Hasan in footnote 1531.

64. For instance, *Fatawa-i-Rizvia*, Volume V, pp. 627–28.

But, as we saw, on the very pages on which marriages are terminated on this rule, we read decrees conferring greater latitude. 'If anger reaches a pitch that one loses one's sense of discrimination,' rules the *Fatawa-i-Rizvia*, 'then *talaq* shall not take place.' Whether anger had reached that pitch, it decrees, should be ascertained from the pitch, it should be ascertained from witnesses, or by a statement on oath from the husband, and losing his temper to that extent should be known to be his habit. A mere claim to that effect is not enough, it says, otherwise everyone will put forth this claim and no talaq given in anger shall hold.[65] Are the witnesses reliable? Is the man's retrospective statement to be accepted? Is losing his temper to this extent his habit? Who shall decide this? Naturally the ulema!

The standard position is that three talaqs invariably end the marriage, as we have seen. All authorities enforce this rule, including the *Fatawa-i-Rizvia.* Yet we read the following. A husband pronounces talaq thrice. Is the wife out? If the husband says on oath that he did not intend divorce on two of the three pronouncements, decrees the *Fatawa-i-Rizvia*, then he shall be believed. And the talaq shall *not* take place. If he does not swear, then three talaqs shall be deemed to have taken place.[66]

Zaid told his wife, 'If you enter the house, talaq.' He avers that he did not intend talaq, that he spoke the words only to frighten her. She enters the house. Is she divorced?, asks the anxious querist. Yes, rules Mufti Kifayatullah.[67]

The very next case on the very same page yields the opposite result. The husband says that to frighten the wife he said, 'If you go to the house of Khalid, then our relationship

---

65. *Fatawa-i-Rizvia,* Volume V, p. 627, also p. 630.

66. Ibid., Volume V, p. 636.

67. *Mufti Kifayatullah ke Fatawi,* Volume VI, p. 280.

will end.' She goes to Khalid's house surreptitiously. But the husband says that he had not intended either talaq or separation, that he had spoken the words only to frighten the wife. Does she stand divorced? No, rules Mufti Kifayatullah—because the husband did not intend talaq and because the word 'talaq' had not been used.[68]

And so on. Notice that such decisions occur cheek by jowl in the formal compilations of the fatwas. These are the 'model' cases so to say. And these are decisions of the superior, appellate authorities. Even these model cases in these model collections of the judgments of the higher authorities show how much latitude, and thereby how much power the ulema have carved up for themselves.

Ambiguity has thus become of the essence of the shariah. That ambiguity and the shariah itself are necessary, not for Islam but for the ulema. Moreover, the shariah has become the fulcrum of the politics and ideology of separateness which the ulema, and Muslim politicians have fostered—that ideology of separateness is one limb of their power, the other is the insecurity which they deliberately and ceaselessly stoke in the lay Muslim. For stoking that insecurity also the shariah comes in handy. For, as we have seen, given the totalitarian claim of Islam—the claim that the totality of life falls within its regulatory purview—everything can be said to be a part of shariah; thereby every development—every step of the state for instance—can be made the occasion for working up a rage in the Muslims: 'They are encroaching on shariah, and thus attacking Islam.'

'Defending' the shariah in this way becomes one of the main objects, and at the same time one of the main instruments of the ulema. They make no bones about it. Indeed, they

68. Ibid., Volume VI, p. 280.

look upon and present their activities 'on behalf of the shariah' as one of their hallmarks.

'It is clearly known from the past history of the Dar al-Ulum, Deoband, that its sphere of activity has not remained confined to mere educational field,' states the official history of the institution. It continues:

> Since Islam is a complete code for both religious and secular life, it provides a permanent programme not only for the Hereafter but also the worldly life. Islam is such a charming amalgam of the rationalism and traditionalism of its commandments, spiritualism and materialism, individualism and socialism, devotions and social life, human rapport and divine connections that it invites hearts to accept it by satisfying them with argument and proof along with the healthy traditions of the human intellect. It is for this reason that the Muslims' attachment to Islam has been naturally so strong. Accordingly, whenever Islam or the Muslims were attacked or any religious or political necessity arose for the Muslims, the elders of the Dar al-Ulum, Deoband, rose to the occasion and left no stone unturned in fulfilling the said necessity or in defending Islam or the Muslims.

Notice how the notions—Islam, shariah, political action—have been fused. History recounts how the ulema of this 'educational institution' took the initiative in 1917 to ensure that the constitutional reforms which were being contemplated at the time did not touch on Muslim personal law; indeed how they proposed steps to reverse the integrative measures which had been taken by the British: they proposed that a separate Department of Justice (*qaza*) be established to enforce Muslim personal law, that as that law can be enforced by Muslim officials alone, '*qazis* ought to be selected and appointed from amongst the *Ahl-e-Sunnah wal-Jama'ah*', and that a separate post of *Sheikh al-Islam* should be created 'for the protection, supervision and administration of Muslims' practices, mosques, *madrasahs*, tombs, pious foundations, hospices and other religious public works.'

It narrates how the ulema strove in 1929 to ensure that it was the shariah which was taken as the basis for regulating Muslim waqfs.

And how they mobilized Muslim public opinion against the Sarda Act—which sought to prescribe that girls ought not to be married before the age of fourteen years and boys not before the age of eighteen; for this matter, the official history says, 'was in itself a permanent part of the personal law.'

Then the ulema mobilized opinion against the legislation which was introduced in UP to abolish zamindari—this time the ground was that the proposed legislation affected the lands of endowments also, and 'this too was a basic part of the personal law.'

And then of course when the proposal came up for a Common Civil code, it 'being against the religious law, it was challenged by the Dar al-Ulum with all the force at its command.'

In 1972 there was the proposal to ensure that Muslim husbands who threw out their wives too would have to pay maintenance like husbands belonging to other communities. The official history gives a glowing account of the way this 'educational institution' mobilized first the ulema and then Muslims in general, and defeated this attempt. It recalls how the authorities of the institution wrote papers, mobilized signatures, convened meetings and seminars, forged 'a collective legal response', and eventually stirred up the Muslim masses. The campaign culminated in an All India Personal Law convention in Bombay in December 1972. Of the results and significance of the convention, the official history of this 'educational institution' says:

> As much as this Convention, in respect of the gathering and representation of the various schools of thought of the Indian

> Muslims was out of the common, to that extent Allah Most High also made it successful. From amongst the different religious schools of thought and classes of Indian Muslims there had remained no class whose prominent *Ulema* and top-ranking men might not have gathered at the platform of this Convention. This Convention, and in other words, the Muslims of all the schools of thought in India, proclaimed unanimously through their resolution that they could under no circumstances tolerate any change and amendment in the Muslim Personal Law, which is an integral part of the Islamic Shari'ah. This unanimous voice affected both the country and the government, and through this Convention, due to the unity of the Kalima, all the Muslims of India were united, which was an unparalleled situation in the history of India.

The significance and results were not limited to defeating the proposed amendment. As the history of Dar al-Ulum records:

> This was the first occasion after the Khilafat Movement that the Muslims of India, of every school of thought, uniting and gathering at one platform, gave proof of their Islamic unity and solidarity. Thereafter the second great meeting of the All-India Muslim Personal Law Board was held at Hyderabad....
>
> While defending the Personal Law and saving it from amendment, the basic purpose of the Bombay Convention was to declare it on behalf of the learned men and the intelligentsia belonging to all the schools of thought in India that the Indian Muslims of every shade of opinion and school of thought can neither relinquish their Personal Law under any circumstances nor can tolerate any kind of change or amendment and alteration in it nor are they ready to accept any such law that may affect even a small portion of their Personal Law. In other words, the Muslims are not ready to annihilate their social and cultural characteristics and distinctions on which the edifice of their communal existence is standing and their distinct legal and communal pre-eminence rests.[69]

---

69. On the foregoing, Sayyid Mehboob Rizvi, *History of the Dar al-Ulum Deoband*, Idara-e Ihtemam, Dar al-Ulum, Deoband, 1980, Volume II, pp. 308–13.

The same technology, and the same 'success' were repeated in 1985 over the Shah Bano case. The same minatory voices were raised against Justice Tilhari's judgment against the Triple talaq and the judgment of Justices Kuldip Singh and Sahay against fraudulent conversions in which they had once again urged that steps be taken to enact a Common Civil code. In each instance the cry was 'Assault on Islam'. In each instance the instrument and the effect was political. And in each instance the mobilization as well as the results fortified the ideology of separateness, the *dens ex machina* of the ulema.

But it would be a job done only in half if the ulema stopped at 'defending' the shariah. For as we have seen their power rests not only on the shariah, but on the shariah remaining ambiguous and uncodified. The sequel to their victory on the Shah Bano campaign illustrates how resourcefully the ulema guard this source of their power as well. Tahir Mahmood who was much involved in the negotiations over the bill to overturn the Shah Bano verdict, later reported:

> During the campaign for this Act leaders of the Muslim community had agreed to get prepared by experts a comprehensive draft-code of Muslim law for the country, to be submitted to Parliament for enactment. A committee of theologians and legal practitioners was appointed in 1987 for this purpose by the All India Muslim Personal Law Board. Until now the committee having its headquarters at Phulwari Sharief near Patna in Bihar could, however, do nothing more than producing a few booklets in Urdu detailing the principles of Hanafi law—ignoring the fact that what they have come out with is far from being a draft-Code and that in a country where followers of at least four different

> schools of Muslim law (Hanafi, Shafi'i, Ja'fari and Isma'ili) live, Hanafi law can never be accepted as the only legal code for the entire community. Theirs has been an exercise in futility—while in the absence of any Code worth the name, the courts and other interpreters and appliers of the law continue to rely on unauthentic, sometimes faulty, textbooks and recorded precedents....[70]

And yet our liberals make-believe that the ulema can be beguiled into giving up this essential source of their power by dialoguing!

70. Tahir Mahmood, 'Muslim Law', in *Annual Survey of Indian Law,* The Indian Law Institute, New Delhi, 1989, pp. 227–39, at p. 227.

Their World

8

Yet it moves not!

As is well known, according to Quranic cosmology the earth is flat, a circular disk, stretched out like a carpet (Quran, 13.3; 15.19; 78.6), Allah has put mountains on it, like paperweights, 'lest it shake with you' and driven them in as pegs (Quran, 16.16; 37.6–10; 67.5). The earth is fixed stationary. Seven 'planets' revolve round it, in the following order: the Moon, Mercury, Venus, Sun, Mars, Jupiter, and Saturn. The sun, moon, etc., move round the earth in a circular motion, 'like a handmill' (*Sahih al-Bukhari*, IV, Book 54.4). At sunset, says the Prophet, the sun goes and prostrates itself under the Throne of Allah, and next morning it takes Allah's permission to rise again. This permission is granted but, as the Quran (36.38) says, Allah has decreed a fixed time for which the sun will be allowed to go on its round around the earth. A day shall come, as the Prophet explains, when 'it will be about to prostrate itself but its prostration will not be accepted, and it will seek permission to go on its course, but it will not be permitted, but it will be ordered to return whence it has come and so it will rise in the West' (*Sahih al-Bukhari*, IV, Book 54.4).

Beyond these 'planets' lie the stars: they too are fixed, stationary. As Allah explains (Quran, 16.16; 37.6–10; 67.5), He has created them for three purposes: as lamps to decorate the sky, as missiles with which to hit and drive away the devils, and as signs to guide travellers (*Sahih al-Bukhari*, IV, Book 54.3).

The ulema insist that each of these averments is literally true, and that is but logical—these being the statements of Allah and of the Prophet. Thus, for instance, commenting on the verse and the Hadis in volumes published in the year 1979 scholars of the Islamic University, Medina Al-Munawwara, say, '... in our limited knowledge of geography, it is well known that the Sun is going round the Earth continuously on its fixed course without stopping, as fixed by Almighty Allah its Creator....'[1]

The dissemination of information about the finding of science has strained the credulity of the faithful. For hundreds of years now the earth, for instance, has been known to go around the sun, and not vice versa. The stars too are known not to be stationary. How is that information to be reconciled with Quranic lore?

Can the matter be resolved in the following way, asks a querist: can we assume that when the Quran speaks of the earth and the heavens (that is, the firmament with stars beyond those seven 'planets') being stationary, it allows for movement in a fixed plane? Are they 'stationary' in the sense that they do not move out of a plane which has been fixed for them?

That the question has to be asked in the *twentieth* century speaks to the state of affairs. That it is asked not of a scientist, but of a religious authority, speaks to it even more. That the question is an effort to fit what has become common knowledge—that the earth and stars are not stationary—on to the procrustean bed of medieval lore speaks still more.

---

1. *Sahih al-Bukhari*, Kazi Publications, Lahore, 1979, Volume VI, p. 309, note 1.

But it is the fatwa on the matter which speaks most of all to the way things are.

Each body floats in a particular sky, the *Fatawa-i-Rizvia* says. The Islamic question is whether both the earth and the heavens are stationary or whether they move, begins the *Fatawa-i-Rizvia.* The question is an empirical one, but to the Maulana it appears as an *Islamic* one, and, quite correctly, as we shall see. Each body floats in a particular sky, declares the *Fatawa-i-Rizvia,* as a fish in water. As Allah says 'each (just) swims along in (its own, that is its appointed) orbit' (Quran, 36.40). Without a doubt Allah holds the earth and the heavens so that they do not move, and if they move who other than Allah can stop them? Only He who knows and is forgiving....

The *Fatawa-i-Rizvia* declares that the Prophet understood these ayats to completely deny all movement, so much so that he declared the rotation of a body on its axis even as it remained stationary at the same place to be *zawal,* to be movement which the Quran had denied altogether. The *Fatawa-i-Rizvia* emphasizes, reiterates, re-emphasizes this position for the next *sixteen* quarto-sized pages of closely packed text. It cites authorities, it cites lexicographical works, works on the meaning of Arabic words, but never any scrap on science.

The entire argument turns on the meaning of one word—zawal. In connection with the earth and the stars the Quran has denied, negated zawal, the fatwa says, and zawal means *any* movement, the *slightest* movement. Rotating on an axis while being 'stationary at one place', would still be movement. Movement on a fixed plane as suggested by the querist would be movement nonetheless. As all movement has been declared to be excluded by the Quran in relation to these bodies, the *Fatawa-i-Rizvia* asks, how can rotation, how can movement on a fixed plane be taking place?

That is the decree in short. The 'reasoning' is lexicological.

Imam Abu Malik and Hazrat Abdullah ibn Abbas have explained zawal to be the least movement, the absolute absence of movement, and who knows the Arabic language, who understands the Quran better than these two, asks the *Fatawa-i-Rizvia.* Allama Nizamuddin Hasan, it recalls, has explained the verse as follows: Allah holds the earth and the heavens lest they shift from their appointed centre.... Then follow explications of each Arabic word.... *markaz,* the word Hasan has used, means the centre where one is stationed, states the fatwa, it means *gadna,* as in to drive a peg into the earth, it means *jamana,* to fix, to root—that is, the verse means that the earth and the heavens do not budge from the place in which they have been driven, in which they have been fixed.

The fatwa moves on to cite another ayat, and what another authority, Imam Fakhruddin Razi has explained its meaning to be. And then observes: only that has to be taken to be the meaning of the Holy Quran which these authorities have taken it to be. How can it be halal for any Muslim to take a meaning contrary to these authorities, to take a meaning which conforms to what is found in Christian science? Quoting another injunction from the Quran—that 'he should make his abode in Hell'—the fatwa exclaims, 'And this (the contention of Christian science about the earth and stars moving) will be even worse than that (for which the Quran has pronounced that ordinance).' It goes on citing authorities to the same effect. It cites the Prophet to the effect that we should go by the meanings as they have been set out by these authorities. And pronounces: The greatness of the meaning we have taken (namely, that the expression used in the Quran negates all movement altogether) is proven by the aforesaid authorities, it is proven by the *Tab'in,* by the *Sahaba-Karam,* by the injunctions of the Prophet. And, it declares, we shall hereafter cite several ayats from Allah, and hundreds of Hadis, the consensus of the ummah as well as the admissions of the *mujtahid kabir* which will provide further proof about the meaning of the verse, and about the earth and heavens being absolutely still.

Can you, it asks the querist, show the meaning you have taken to have been put forward by any *Sahabi*, any *T'abbi*, any imam, any commentary, or, leave these aside, can you show it to have been given even in any ordinary Islamic book? Namely that the ayat means that the earth revolves around the sun?

That Allah holds it only to the extent that it should not go outside the orbit, that He has allowed it to move within this—never can you give any evidence of this from any Islamic journal, paper, or note, declares the fatwa. The only evidence you can provide is from Christian science. Now you can decide, it says, whether the meaning of the Quran should be taken to be that (which has been accepted by all Islamic authorities) or this (which the querist has put forward and for which there is no evidence except in Christian science).

What is there on which one cannot fabricate an interpretation!, the *Fatawa-i-Rizvia* scoffs. So much so that the Qadiyani kafir, it says, fabricated the interpretation on *Khatm-ul-Nabiyan* itself—the interpretation that the zenith of prophethood ended on him (the Qadiyani kafir), and that there is no prophet like him. Nanautavi (a leading maulana, and a beacon of the Dar al-Ulum, Deoband) concocted that he himself is a prophet of sorts.... and that if there were to be a prophet after him even that would not be contrary to the prophethood having ended (with the Seal of Prophets, Muhammad). So much so that some polytheist can read an interpretation even into *la illaha il Allah* (There is no one worthy of worship except Allah) to the effect that there is no God equal to Allah though there can be many smaller than Him, as it is in the Hadis....*Dard nahin magar aankh ka dard, pareshani nahin magar karz ki pareshani,* there is no pain save the pain of the eye, there is no anxiety save anxiety of debt....

One should not be content with such constructions, warns the fatwa; instead one should lay one's head at the feet of the construction which is well recognized. And the position which is celebrated and popular among all the Muslims is the one in which Muslims should put their faith. Allah has made you staunch and steady Sunnis, it exhorts.

Remember what the question was: do the earth and stars move? The reasoning is about a word in the Quran; about what the authorities have held that word to mean; about whether any *Islamic* authority has asserted the meaning to be something else; about whether the proof of the proposition is not to be found solely in Christian science; about whether as staunch Mussalmans they should put their faith in what Christian science says or in what the consensus has been among all Muslims....

Do you know by what the Rafazis (the Shias), who were not apostates earlier, became Rafazis?, asks Maulana Ahmad Riza Khan. Were they deniers of Allah, or of the Quran, or of the Prophet, or of the Day of Judgement, etc.—that is of the necessities of the Faith? Not at all. The reason is that they did not honour the *Sahaba-Karam....* To put one's defective comprehension at par with the words of the Prophet is barbarity, the fatwa declares. It is as if an ignorant, uncivilized oaf should compare himself to a man of wisdom.... What a way of honouring the lovers (of the Prophet), specially Abdullah ibn Masood, it would be if we thought that what they took the Quran to mean was wrong, and what we take as the meaning is correct. I give you unto Allah, the Maulana exclaims, that such peril should never come near your heart!

He then proceeds, as he says, to 'submit a bit of detail'.

Zawal, he says, is *sarkana,* to shift, *hatna,* to move, *jana,* to go, *harkat karna,* to stir, *badalna,* to change. And he cites Arabic works and passages in which the word has been used in senses such as these, and remarks: see, zawal is used to imply movement, and the Great Quran negates movement of the heavens and the earth. Therefore, he concludes, the movement of the heavens and of the earth have both become false.

Next, on the same sort of reasoning, the Maulana says, zawal is jana, to go, and badalna, to change. To move on an axis or to move in an orbit are both movement. Therefore both have been negated. Therefore neither takes place.

Citations from several other Arabic works lead the Maulana to equate zawal with restlessness, and restlessness, he points out, is the opposite of rest, and to be at rest is to be at peace. Therefore, he says, zawal is the opposite of being at peace, and every movement is in every sense zawal. And the Great Quran negates the movement of the heavens and earth in every way.

After further confirmations of the same sort he turns to verses and passages in which zawal has been used in the context of mountains. They are fixed to a particular place, they do not have the power of movement. If a mountain were to shift a finger-width, it would just move a bit, it would not go rolling about all over the world. That little shift would in fact confirm us in the knowledge that it is stationary.... It is only when the Day of Judgement comes that the mountains will be in zawal.

Several lemmas later, that consideration leads to a discussion of what 'collapse' implies, what 'to be uprooted' implies. And after all that lexicology the Maulana reaches the same conclusion: zawal is movement of any kind, hence movement of all kinds has been negated by the Great Quran.

Next comes a dilation on what it means to be 'at rest', what *rokna,* to stop, *thamna,* to bring to a halt, *band karna,* to shut down, mean. It has been said that Allah holds, that

He has stopped the heavens and earth. It has not been said that He holds them in their orbits; it has not been said that planes have been determined for the earth and the stars and that it has been provided that they should not move out of those planes. To add such clauses, declares the Maulana, would be to add clauses of one's own to the word of Allah. It would be to give on one's own some special construction to what has been said in the Great Quran. And this is not proper at all.

In fact, says the Maulana, one of the wide gates to degradation is that we should on our own stuff meanings into the words of Allah, that we should advance contrived meanings instead of relying on the plain meaning. All this from one who had no compunction about putting words in the mouth of Allah to justify cow slaughter!

From the Hadis also we learn, he reminds us, that Allah is doubtless holding the heavens and the earth, for if they were to move, who shall stop them? These words have been reported by persons who themselves heard the Prophet himself speak them. See, says the Maulana, all these Companions took the least movement to be zawal, and negated it. They condemned those who held that the earth and heavens move, and held these notions to be akin to the notions of the Jews. Could they not have thought up that orbits or planes have been appointed for the heavens and the earth, and that for them to move in these orbits would not be zawal? But their 'blessed reasoning' did not go towards this false construction. Nor could it. In fact it saw the falsehood of such a construction—and this had to be, for Allah has declared the complete negation of all movement, and not merely the negation of movement away from some orbit or plane. They did not tack additions on to the word of Allah.

Now, Kab, a Companion, did say that the heavens rotate around an axis. Contradicting him the Prophet said, Kab has said something wrong. It would be foolish to infer from this that the earth moves because the Prophet contradicted only the assertion that the heavens rotate. There was no occasion for him to contradict the assertion that the earth moves because Kab did not claim it does, says the Maulana, quite plausibly. Kab had said the heavens move. Jews too hold that the earth is stationary. Before 1530 when Copernicus put out his bid'at—the pejorative for 'innovation'—the Christians too held the earth to be stationary. And thus only 'The heavens move on an axis' was said in the presence of the Prophet. Why would the Prophet condemn what was not stated before him?, the Maulana asks. Who had said that the earth moves on its axis that the Prophet should have denied it?, he asks, adding that if anyone had said that the earth moves on its axis, the Prophet would have condemned that also on the basis of the same ayat. Read the ayat, admonishes the Maulana, it says the same thing about both—the heavens and the earth.

It is as if Allah were to say: I saw eleven stars and the sun and moon prostrate before Me. And an alim were to talk of the prostration of the sun. Hearing him someone were to get up and deny that the moon prostrated before Allah on the ground that the alim had talked about the prostration of the sun only, that he had not said anything about the moon, that he had remained silent. What shall we say about such a man?, asks the Maulana.

Now you will see, the Maulana declares, that they—those who hold that the heavens and earth move—have no option but to shut their eyes to what the Prophet, to what the Companions, in fact to what the Quran says. And to do so, he reminds all, is to put oneself up for the great loss, and may Allah save you, me, and the entire *Ahl-i-Sunnat, Amin,* he prays.

The argument thus far has been: the earth and the heavens

are stationary because the Quran negates zawal—that is, any and every kind and degree of movement—in regard to them. The Maulana next approaches the matter from the other side—the sun is said to have zawal. What kind of a movement does it have that zawal is attributed to it?

That the sun moves is clear from the Quran, from the Hadis, it is accepted by all, the fatwa notes. Does it move out of its appointed orbit at the time that its zawal *is* spoken of? No. Yet it is said to have zawal. If all that mattered was not leaving its appointed orbit, the same would have been said about the earth also. But in this case zawal has been negated. It follows therefore, says the Maulana, that the earth does not move at all. Now, if you were to say that the sun moves all the time, yet why is it not said to have zawal at all times and to have it only when it is declining, if you were to say this that would be the height of ignorance, declares the Maulana, and proceeds to give several analogies of words which are used for one thing though not for the other, even though the latter does the same thing. The Maulana continues to dissect words.

He then goes on to those who hold that night and day, as well as the time of day occur because of the rotation of the earth. This is their belief, thunders the Maulana, and it is a calumny upon the Quran. What to say of Muslims, he says, if you talk to even the people of Beirut, etc., who admit of the movement of earth and whose language is Arabic, they call time *waqt* zawal, and they call the sundial *mizula*—that is a device to measure *the movement of the sun*, and yet if you ask them does the sun rotate, they shall say 'No, instead the earth,' though the earth does not leave its orbit or axis. Hence, the Maulana says to the querist, neither the opponents nor the supporters accept your proposition. He recalls how people use expressions involving the word zawal a thousand times, and asks the querist to ponder how he himself uses the expression. Now be just, he says, and remember, belief in the word of the Quran is mandatory.

He sets out eight ayats. He next alludes to the Hadis. There are thousands of expressions, he says, about the sun rising, setting, moving across, rising, declining—all of which testify that the earth is absolutely stationary. The persons who oppose the view about the earth being stationary themselves admit, he says, that mere rising and setting are not zawal— in other words the full movement around the earth is what is meant. From these considerations it is established, he says, that day and night are caused by the movement of the sun and not by that of the earth.

Therefore, he remarks, it is established that the arrogance of science is false and stands rejected. The daily movement of the sun from which come rising and setting, and zawal—these would not take place but for its going round the earth, he says. Therefore, he concludes further, from the Quran, from the Hadis, as well as from the ijma of the ummah it is proved that the sun goes round the earth and not the earth round the sun. Therefore, it is not possible that the earth should go round the sun and that the sun should be at the centre of the earth's orbit. Therefore, from the ayat, it is established that both the rotation and revolution of the earth are false.

The argument continues in this way. Therefore, he says, it is a duty incumbent upon a Muslim that he should establish belief in the movement of the sun and the stationarity of the earth. He proceeds to quote authorities and translations and says: it is evident that if, by false supposition, the earth were moving then neither would the residents be able to sleep nor would there be any breeze at summer time. If the earth moved, the Maulana says after presenting further allusions, then at all times its movement would cause violent earthquakes and intense hurricanes, no man or beast could live on it.

The arguments that you have copied from English books, he says, are from books in which there is no name worth the name. All of them are just hot air. For these problems, he tells the querist, you shall find answers to all those arguments in my book...., Chapter IV.... specially in those eight lines which I have written at the beginning itself—namely that the Europeans do not really know the method of argument, they do not know how a claim is established, their prejudices which they present as arguments are just *illatein*, bad habits. From those defects—in the European way of argumentation—the just and intelligent understand that these arguments do not go beyond those prejudices. And for an honest Sunni Mussalman believer, the Maulana declares, a single consideration should be enough: how can any argument contrary to the words of the Quran, of the Prophet and of the ijma of the ummah stand?

Even if one were to suppose that at this moment we do not comprehend its truth—of what has been stated in the Quran, etc.—even then without doubt the Quran, the Hadis and the ijma of the ummah are true—this, Allah be praised, is the glory of Islam, proclaims the Maulana.

Science shall not be Muslim in this way—that is by putting ayats and Hadis aside on Islamic questions and making them accord with science. By Allah, were this way to be adopted then Islam would have accepted science, not science Islam. Sciences shall be Muslim in this—that on whichever Islamic question Islam is opposed, on all of them it should project the Islamic position, and the arguments of science should be rejected and trodden under foot. At every point through affirmations of science itself it is the Islamic position which should be brought to the fore. Thus will science come to heel, declares the Maulana.

And for a scientific thinker like you, the Maulana encourages the querist, to do this is not difficult.....[2]

The object, method and test of reasoning

Though the foregoing is but a summary of the extensive and emphatic fatwa on the question, it will give an idea of how firmly the minds of the ulema are rooted in the Quran, and therefore in the state in which knowledge was in the immediate circle of the Prophet fourteen hundred years ago. The fatwa is also instructive as it gives us a glimpse into the mode of reasoning of the ulema, a mode of which they are manifestly proud—witness the scorn of Maulana Ahmad Riza Khan for the Europeans who, in his considered view, do not know the method of scholarly argumentation, who do not know the methods by which a proposition is established, who advance their prejudices as arguments.

Recall that the question was whether the Quran's affirmation that the heavens and earth are stationary can be reconciled with what is now known by assuming that the stationarity it speaks of refers to these bodies remaining in planes or orbits which Allah has determined for them.

To the Maulana the basic question—whether the heavens and earth move—appears as an *Islamic* question.

That question is to be settled not be empirical investigation and deductions from observation of actual phenomena but by looking up what the Quran says on it.

That leads to a dissection of what one word means which the Quran has used in the relevant verse.

That leads to determining whether anyone can be said to know Arabic and the Quran better than two personages he names.

---

2. *Fatawa-i-Rizvia*, Volume XII, pp. 273–89.

That leads to an inquiry of the senses in which others who know Arabic have used the word.

The question now becomes what the consensus on the matter has been among Muslims, and for this the senses in which the word is employed in popular usage are examined.

The point is sought to be nailed by inquiring whether what is being proposed is found in any *Islamic* book, or only in the books of Christians.

Instead of studying the heavens and earth, we are taught how perverse and distorted interpretations can be put on everything. And how what is being done amounts to calumny upon the Holy Book because what is being proposed is nothing but adding clauses to the Word of God.

And then the ringing conclusion: the duty incumbent upon a Muslim is to make science accept Islam, not Islam science—in practical terms it means that he must stand by and 'prove' that what has been said even about empirical phenomena in the Quran, Hadis, etc., is true and what science claims to have found is false, unless it accords with the Quran and Hadis!

Earthquakes and famines

'What are the causes of earthquakes?,' asks the querist, adding, 'Kindly explicate from the *shara'i* point of view.'

The *Fatawa-i-Rahimiyyah* gives the ulema's answer. It is as follows:

> Allah Most High hath created veins in the earth and hath given them into the hands of angels. Wherever the burden of sins increases and Allah Most High wants to scourge the people there, He orders the angels and the angel of that place pulls the vein (i.e., the vein of that region) and the earth there trembles and there occurs the earthquake. (Verily, Allah knoweth best!)
>
> There occurred an earthquake during the Holy Prophet's

(*Sall-allaho alaihe wa sallam!*) auspicious time. Addressing the Companions, he said, 'Your Lord wants you to repent; so, repent.' Anyhow, it is known from Hadiths that excess of sins is the cause of earthquake and repentance for sins is the means of deliverance. (May Allah protect us and unto Him we repent!)

An earthquake occurred during Hazrat Umar Faruq's auspicious period. Addressing the people he said, 'There is some particular sin which is being committed. O people! Repent! I say on oath that if the earthquake occurred again, I will not live here.'

Hazrat 'Ayesha (*Razi Allah anba*!) was asked about the occurrence. She said: 'When adultery, liquor, dancing and music come into vogue (lit., become the taste of the people), Divine Jealousy (*ghayrat*) is stirred. If the people forswear at an ordinary warning, well and good, otherwise buildings are razed down and lofty constructions are turned into heaps of dust.'

She was further asked: 'Is an earthquake a punishment?' 'A blessing for the true believers (*muminiri*),' she said, 'and a punishment for the infidels.'

Hazrat Umar bin Abd al-Aziz (*Razi Allah anha*!) during his caliphate, wrote a Mandate (*firman*) and sent it to his dominions, to the effect that this earthquake is such a thing whereby Lord Most Holy expresses His wrath over His slaves and demands repentance (for sins) from them. At that time the people should sincerely repent, give up wrong-doing and give alms and *sadqahs* abundantly, and if it is not abominable time should engage themselves in supererogatory prayers. And the following Invocations of Prophet Adam, Prophet Noah and Prophet Jonah (Yunus), respectively, as well as other invocations should be recited....

For further details, see Hazrat Ashraf Ali Thanvi's *Akhbar-e Zalzalah*. Finis. Verily, Allah knoweth best![3]

---

3. *Fatawa-i-Rahimiyyah*, Volume III, pp. 187–88.

All this in volumes published in the 1980s! In volumes greatly hailed for their erudition, for the wealth of information they provide!

And what, pray, is the cause of scanty rainfall and famine?, the ulema are asked. Their considered, and manifestly well-researched reply is as follows:

> The cause of drought and famine consists in the infringement of divine commandments and our own misdeeds; particularly adultery, destruction of others' rights, lack of helping the indigent and the needy, to give short weight; these are the real causes of famine. It is stated in a *hadith* that those who give short weight and measure, they are involved in famine, severity of death and the oppression of rulers. It is reported in another *hadith*: 'The people among whom adultery becomes common are involved in famine.'
>
> Maulana Rum says in his *Mathnavi*:
>
> 'The cloud does not come on account of the refusal to pay *zakat*; and plague spreads in the world due to adultery.'
>
> It is reported from Hazrat Abu Sufyan that he says that he received news that the Children of Israil were involved in drought for seven years, so much so that they ate up their dead and their own children. They used to go to the mountains and lament before their Lord and supplicate. Then the Lord Most High sent a message to their prophets that He would not accept their invocations nor would pity those of them who lamented until they discharged the dues of others. So they discharged the dues and then rains came.
>
> (*Majalis, majlis* 45, p. 272)
>
> Sayyid Abd al-Qadir Jilani says:
>
> It is related that once the Bani Israil were involved in famine. They gathered together and came to a prophet and said: 'Please tell us that work wherewith God may be pleased so that we may perform it and it may become the cause of the

removal of this calamity.' The prophet asked God Most High about such a work, and message was sent to him to tell the people that they should please the poor; if they pleased the poor, God would be pleased with them and if they did not do so, God, too, would remain displeased with them.

So, hearken O intelligent men! You always keep the poor displeased and yet desire divine pleasure? You will never attain His pleasure; on every side you are under His displeasure!

(*F. Yaz.*, Trans. of *Al-Fath.*, m. 38, p. 257)[4]

Notice again that the matter is settled not by looking up some book on meteorology but by looking up what Rumi said, what Abu Sufyan said, what a prophet told the Bani Israil.

Nor is the point confined to the sort of books the ulema turn to for an answer. The point is that even if they looked up the book on meteorology but it contained something which went contrary to the Prophet's explanation for droughts, the ulema would be duty-bound to reject what the book said, to denounce it, to keep the faithful from believing it, they would be duty-bound, as Maulana Ahmad Riza Khan puts it, to ensure that meteorology, like every other science, is brought to heel, that it sheds its 'arrogance' and submits to Islam.

The sown field

Agronomy meets the same fate as astronomy and meteorology. 'Every year, for the last so many years, my sown field is ruined; it yields no crop,' laments a faithful querist. 'Either the seeds rot or the field is visited by natural calamities. So please show me some way whereby the sown field may remain safe.'

The ulema do not send him to the local agronomist. They prescribe the remedy in shariah:

4. *Fatawa-i-Rahimiyyah,* Volume II, pp. 327–28.

Before the sowing operation, make ablution and say two *rak'ahs* of prayer at the edge of the field, and then, after reciting the *Durud Sharif*, recite this invocation with extreme humility before Allah:

.....'O Allah! I am your weak slave. I entrust this work unto You. Preserve it and return it to me and create abundance in it for me.'

Recite the *Durud Sharif again*. It is hoped that Allah, by the blessing of this invocation, will preserve it from all misfortunes and calamities and will create abundance in it. Thereafter, when the crop is ready, the measurer, having made ablution, should start measuring facing the Qiblah, and after having given from it the poor men's due, again say two *rak'ahs* of prayer and recite the following invocation:

....'O my Lord ! I sowed few seeds and You gave me abundantly. Now make it a food of obedience and not of disobedience and make me a grateful slave.'

It is stated in a noble *hadith*: 'A slave is deprived of providence on account of his sins.' (Narrator: Ahmed). Hence it is required of man that remaining away from acts of disobedience to Allah, which incur His wrath, he should do works that win his pleasure and place trust in Him. Then the Holy Allah says, 'And whoso keepeth his duty to Allah, Allah will appoint a way out for him, and will provide for him from (a quarter) whence he hath no expectation. And whosoever putteth his trust in Allah, He will suffice him.' (*Surah* LXV *At*-Talaq 2,3).[5]

Iblis, djinn and other spirits

Nor is it merely that the mental world of the ulema is filled with such notions about stars, the earth, and natural phenomena. These are notions that filled the medieval world, but they were not the only notions. As every student

5. *Fatawa-i-Rahimiyyah*, Volume I, pp. 88–89.

of the Quran and Hadis knows, at every turn these contain accounts of the doings of Satan, of djinns, of spirits of various kinds. As in regard to natural phenomena, therefore, the fatwas contain reference after reference to the mischief and evil of these entities: events are attributed to them, cures and antidotes are prescribed against their design.

Every set of fatwas as we have noted earlier prescribes the mandatory sequence in which and the things with which a believer is to clean himself or herself after urinating or defecating. These are the fatwas relating to the well-known istinja. As we saw, the ulema decree that 'to dry the *istinja* everything which costs nothing and can absorb the liquid and moisture, and cleans the place' can be used, 'whether it is the ball of mud, *dbela*, or stone, or soil, or old cloth, the earth, or a wall—all are equal.'[6]

That it is all right for a person who has urinated or defecated to use a wall to clean himself will be the first surprise, but he may do so, say the ulema, and they know best.[7]

But I am on the other point. 'Yes, bone or coal or a baked brick or *thikri* (the broken shards of a pitcher) should not be used,' they decree. If anyone else thought it necessary to prescribe a rule such as this, I suppose he would deem it sufficient to point to the common-sense consideration that were one to use a piece of bone or brick, etc., he would most likely injure himself. But that sort of argument is neither necessary nor sufficient for the ulema. They say one should not use these things because the *Durr-ul-Mukhtar*, the seventeenth-century work, says one should not, and they proceed to quote it at length.

Why a piece of bone must not be used is explained as follows:

---

6. *Fatawa-i-Rizvia*, Volume II, p. 143.

7. Using the wall to clean oneself is sanctioned elsewhere also, for instance, Ibid., Volume II, pp. 156–57.

> A delegation of *djinn* came before the Prophet, and asked for food for themselves and for their animals. They were told, 'For you is every bone over which the Name of Allah has been recited, that is it should be the bone of a *halal* animal... In your hands it will be as wholesome as it was when flesh was on it. (That is, when you find the bone without flesh it shall be with flesh.) And all droppings shall be food for your animals.' Then the men were told, 'Do not do *istinja* with bones and droppings because these are the foods of your brothers.'[8]

Thus, the believer must use three balls of dried earth, say, and not a piece of bone to wipe himself because were he to use the bone he would be depriving the djinn of their food. How do we know that bones are the food for djinn? Because the Prophet told a delegation of djinn that they are.

Now, it may be that this was the sort of thing which was believed 1,350 years ago and that the Prophet merely shared what was, after all, a common belief. Or it may be that he knew that this was just folklore but nevertheless put his prohibition in these terms for he felt that, given the state of ignorance of the people, the way to have them desist from using pieces of bone and thereby hurting themselves was to put it in terms of djinn, etc. But for the ulema, as he said that bones are the food of djinn, they are the food of djinn. And anyone who does not believe them to be so is asserting that what the Prophet said was wrong. Therefore, he is a non-believer—a kafir or an apostate. In either case he is out of Islam.

The weighty questions

From the heavens to the earth, from the world of the Devil and djinn to the world of day-to-day life, the same mindset comes through in the fatwas, the same mode of reasoning.

8. *Fatawa-i-Rizvia,* Volume II, p. 145.

Going through a few of the fatwas will acquaint us with the weighty questions over which these learned men expend their time and scholarship; with the mode of reasoning by which they seek to establish their propositions; and, just as important, with the inner state of the much vaunted shariah. For the claim, remember, is not just that the shariah is the divinely ordained code, and therefore an eternal, unchangeable code. The claim also is that it is a seamless code—that not one bit of it can be altered without sundering the whole. The claim also is that the shariah is a definite code—that Allah Himself has and Islamic jurisconsults over the centuries have set down unambiguous rules of conduct on every point.

A fatwa from the recent and highly lauded work, *Fatawa-i-Rahimiyyah,* will suffice to illustrate the weighty questions that preoccupy the jurists, and the flavour of the discourse among them. It will also enable us to assess the claim that the shariah is a clear and definite code. The weighty question is:

> Has Maulana Rasheed Ahmed Gangohi written that the eating of the flesh of the crow is permitted?

Maulana Gangohi, as you will recall, was the co-founder of our Al-Azhar, the Dar al-Ulum at Deoband, and took over as the chief patron and guide of the institution upon the death of Maulana Nanautavi. Precisely because he was a pillar of Deoband, Maulana Gangohi was the butt of derision for the Barelvis. The question has obviously been asked in that spirit, and is answered with that background in mind. The *Fatawa-i-Rahimiyyah* declares:

> Maulana Rasheed Ahmed Gungohi has only repeated what the Hanafite jurisconsults have written all along; the enemies deliberately vilify him. Vide Maulana Gungohi's *fatwa* and *fatwa* of the Chief Mufti of Mecca, Abdallah b. Abbas b. Siddiq which is in support of it.
>
> (*Vide TR.*, Vol. i, p. 178)

N.B.: This answer should be read after noting the fact that the same regulation which applies to one who calls an unlawful thing lawful also applies to one who calls a lawful thing unlawful.

The crow is called *kawwa* in Urdu, *zagh* in Persian and *ghurab* in Arabic (*Lugbat-e Kishori*). Crows are of several species: some lawful and some unlawful. However, this is a secondary problem (*mas'ala*). There are many an animal regarding which there is difference of opinion among the Imams. For instance, iguana (*goh*), according to Imam Abu Hanifa, is unlawful, whereas Imam Shafi'i calls it lawful. The badger is unlawful but according to Imam Shafi'i it is lawful. (*TR.*, vol. i, p. 178). Some call the bat lawful and some, unlawful, (p. 290). According to some the horse is unlawful and according to some it is lawful. The fox is lawful according to the Shafi'ite whereas the Hanafite consider it otherwise. The water-frog, according to Imam Shafi'i is lawful but Imam Abu Hanifa calls it unlawful. Even between Imam Abu Hanifa and his two famous disciples there is difference of opinion as regards some animals being permissible or impermissible, abominable or non-abominable. Similarly there is difference of opinion among the jurisconsults as regards the crow.

Fatawa -i- Rahimiyyah

Our Hanafite jurisconsults (mbut.!) write that the crow is of three kinds. (Some jurisconsults have stated more than three kinds.)

One is that which eats carrion; this is unlawful. The second eats grain; this is lawful. The third eats both carrion and grain and is called *'Aq'aq'*; this, too, according to Imam Abu Hanifa, is lawful because it is like the cock which eats both carrion and grain. But according to Imam Abu Yusuf this third kind is abominable because it mostly eats carrion. However, Imam Abu Hanifa's *mazhab* (rite) is the most proper (*ahaqq*). (ZSK.; Tuk. Bahr., vol. i, p. 172; *M. Anh.*, vol. iv, p. 514; *ZU*, pp. 429–30; *F. JR*, vol. iii, p. 143; *F. Qazi*, vol. iv, p. 151; *Al-Dwar.*, vol. i, p. 171).

> It is stated in the *Fatawa Alamgiri* (vol. v, p. 289): 'The crow that eats grain and like things is unanimously lawful.' (*Vide BS.*, vol. v, p. 39; *KB.*, p. 218; *Quduri*, p. 226; *DM & S.*, vol. v, p. 268; *Sha waq.*, vol. iv, p. 337; *S. Siraj*, p. 87; *Hedaya*, vol. iv, p. 425; *EQJ.*, vol. iii, p. 268).
>
> From these jurisprudential traditions it is proved that certain kinds of crows are lawful and some unlawful. The very word 'crow' seems to be the Bareilvis' *bete noir*; the very mention of it provokes them and, calling all kinds of crows unlawful, they oppose and prove the majority of jurisconsults to be in the wrong. What is the meaning of maligning Maulana Gangohi only when he, too, like other jurisconsults, considers some crows lawful and some unlawful?
>
> *Fatawa -i- Rahimiyyah*
>
> I can emphatically say that he has not written contrary to other jurisconsults. Even if he had committed a mistake, he did not deserve to be cursed, for to err is human. No less a book than the *Fatawa Alamgiri* states the owl to be lawful, whereas the fact is that it is unlawful. (Vol. v, p. 290). May Allah save us from suspicion! Amen, O Lord of the worlds ![9]

Notice the question, whether the flesh of a crow is halal or haram—hardly a matter of earth-shaking importance. Notice the scholarship which has gone into the matter: clearly the authorities have been addressing the question for over a thousand years. Notice that, in spite of such intensive effort spread over ten centuries they have not been able to come to any agreement on the matter. On the contrary, the controversy goes on. Notice too the passions which this little question ignites among the learned—the traducing of Maulana Gangohi by the Barelvis, the impassioned defence by the Deobandis. All over the flesh of a crow!

---

9. *Fatawa-i-Rahimtyyah*, Volume II, pp. 183–85.

The droppings of the crow

As much scholarship is expended upon, and the controversies are as fierce about the beeth of a crow as about its flesh.

'What is the ruling of the Ulema-i-Din about the droppings of a crow?,' asks the querist. 'If they fall into a well, does the well remain pure or does it get defiled?'

In regard to the beeth of creatures whose flesh is not to be eaten, rule the ulema of Ahl-i-Hadis, there are different views in *Fiqh*—'*Fiqh*', explains the *Dictionary of Islam*, is 'the dogmatic theology of the Muslims. Works on Mohammedan law, whether civil or religious...;' so the question about the beeth of a crow is to be settled as a matter of dogmatic theology. If your clothes get sullied by the droppings of such a creature, prayer while wearing them is permissible according to Imam Abu Hanifa and Imam Abu Yusuf, the fatwa states, but according to Imam Muhammad prayer while wearing them is *not* permissible.

There are differences of opinion on the underlying principle also: according to some scholars, explain the ulema of the Ahl-i-Hadis, the difference of opinion is based on a question of purity and impurity—in other words the slightest soiling renders the cloth impure; whereas according to other scholars the question is to be settled in the light of the quantum of beeth. And it is the latter which is correct.

There is a further difference. As is well known, one of the most important principles in Islamic jurisprudence—one which, because of its potency, requires the most judicious application—is the Rule of Necessity. This heavy armour is brought into play to settle this business about the beeth of the crow. Imam Muhammad, the Ahl-i-Hadis ulema recall, says that impurity depends on the necessity behind it: from this he concludes that to pray while continuing to wear clothes which have been soiled by the beeth of the crow is not permissible because there is no necessity which ties one down to saying one's prayers in those clothes alone. But from the same rule—the Rule of Necessity—other ulema come to the opposite conclusion. It is a matter involving helplessness, the Ahl-i-Hadis ulema cite them as ruling: the birds drop their beeth from the sky and it is difficult for a person to dodge them; and so prayer in those clothes is permissible.

The ulema next take up the question of the beeth falling into a utensil. Here too, they record, there is a difference of opinion among the jurists. Karkhi, they report, says that according to the sheikhs the droppings of a bird are not by themselves impure. Imam Muhammad holds them to be impure. But even on that last statement obviously there is no unanimity: Hindwani, the ulema report, says that according to Imam Sahib the droppings are slightly impure, whereas the Companions say that they are dirty.

Thus far the disagreement seemed to be between the Companions and Imam Sahib—the former holding that the droppings are not impure, and the latter holding, according to some, that they are entirely impure, and, according to others, that they are only slightly impure. But a fresh complication arises. The Ahl-i-Hadis ulema tell us that according to the great jurist Sheikh Qazi Khan, whom we have encountered at length earlier, the Companions' verdict is not that the droppings are *not* impure but that they *are* impure, and that if they fall into a small quantity of water they defile it. On the other hand, according to Karkhi, the Companions do not hold the water to be defiled. The authorities who take the middle position agree with Karkhi, report the ulema. Furthermore, Allama Tehtavi, the ulema tell us, says that if the droppings of birds whose flesh is haram fall into a well, the well would not be defiled. And, they add, Mukhtar too says the same thing and so does Jalbi.

Hence, they conclude with more finality than their narration warrants, according to the injunctions of all the three scholars the water remains clean.[10]

The question. The eminence of the scholars who have brought their learning to bear upon it. The juristic principles they have deployed. The difference over the import of those principles. The differences among the primary authorities. The differences among the secondary authorities over what a primary authority has said.

Nor are matters settled by holding that the droppings of the birds which are halal do not defile the water whereas droppings of the birds which are haram defile it. For one thing, upon seeing the droppings one has then to ascertain whether they come from a bird which is halal or haram. For another, that question itself is far from being settled: as we have seen, the jurists and scholars have the widest differences possible on which birds are halal and which are haram.

Dogs versus cats

Dogs and cats, the reasons for the contrary views which have been taken about them since the times of the Prophet, the difference between the saliva of one and the saliva of the other, between the saliva and the body of one—each of these topics occasions fatwas upon fatwas. Notice again that there is never even the suggestion that the matter be settled by asking doctors or pathologists, or by submitting the saliva or flesh to some analysts. The answer turns on which alim said what.

'There is great turmoil in Bhagiadi,' reports the anxious

10. *Fatawa Ahl-i-Hadis,* Volume I, p. 19.

querist to Maulana Maulvi Hafiz Abdullah of Ahl-i-Hadis. 'The Wahabis are of the opinion that food a bit of which a dog has eaten is clean. A maulvi has given the injunction that water in a utensil from which a dog has drunk remains paak. It has given rise to a dispute which might lead to a fight. Please give a considered reply. Both the parties have accepted you as judge.'

Notice that the question is looked upon as a *religious* question—and given the frequency with which similar questions concerning dogs come up in the canonical works of shariah, it *is* a religious question—and the answer is accordingly sought from a *religious* authority.

Now study the answer.

Abu Huraira (a Companion of the Prophet, and the source of a very large number of the Hadis) has related a tradition, says the Maulana, that Rasul Allah had pronounced that when a dog touches a utensil by his mouth, the utensil can be made paak after being washed seven times, the first time it should be scrubbed with earth. Imam Muslim has also confirmed this. And in another tradition in Muslim it is stated: whatever is in the utensil, throw it away. This Hadis shows, the Maulana points out, that what has been defiled by having been eaten by a dog is defiled—as the utensil becomes defiled and there are specific instructions to purify the utensil by washing it seven times, it shows that whatever was contained in the utensil also becomes defiled. That is why, says the Maulana, the instruction is to throw it away. It also shows, he says, that the flesh of a dog is unclean because his saliva defiles, and the saliva comes out of the flesh.

If the maulvi has given the injunction that the food that remains after a dog has eaten part of it is pure, the Maulana says, he must not have knowledge of this Hadis. How can this (the maulvi's ruling) be the religion of the followers of Hadis—because their religion must depend on the Holy

Quran and the Hadis, not upon independent opinions. Many people, specially the party from Bareilly, the Maulana warns, are trying to bring the Ahl-i-Hadis into disrepute. Some details are given in....[11]

In brief: a dog's saliva is unclean, and 'as saliva comes out of the flesh' the flesh too is unclean according to the ulema of Ahl-i-Hadis.

By contrast, a utensil which has been licked by a cat does *not* become napaak, declare the ulema of Ahl-i-Hadis. It is another matter, they say, if you do not feel like eating from it, you may not. If you feel like cleaning it, clean it. But it is not at par with *kute ka jutha*, they declare. On the contrary, it is clear from the Hadis that if something has been eaten from a dish by a cat, what remains is not napaak.[12]

The dog per se

In any event, to get back to the dog itself, as food touched by a dog's mouth is defiled, what if the dog actually falls into a well? This question turns up again and again, and leads the ulema to devote a great deal of erudition and energy to settling it.

The ulema take a common-sense position: if the dog falls in but the water does not change colour, taste or odour, it remains paak, they hold. That seems to be a handy, common-sense rule of thumb. But naturally that rule does not hold in the eyes of the ulema because some chemical analysis has shown that, when one cannot get the water analysed, it is safe to proceed by this ready reckoner. The rule holds because there is a Hadis to that effect.

Not quite, though: the fact is that there is a Hadis to that effect according to *some* of the ulema.

---

11. *Fatawa Ahl-i-Hadis,* Volume I, p. 21.
12. Ibid., Volume I, p. 26.

If water has not changed its colour or taste or odour, then the water is pure, declare the ulema of Ahl-i-Hadis. That is so, they say, because the Prophet said that water is pure and nothing can pollute it. And he also said that if it changes colour, taste or odour then it is polluted.

That makes two Hadis. But as the very next sentences reveal, there is no agreement.

The Hadis—that is, the first one, that water is pure and nothing can pollute it—has been termed weak by Abu Hatim, note the Ahl-i-Hadis ulema. But 'from the other point of view it is proven,' they declare. And on the latter part of the second Hadis—that if the colour, etc., have changed, the water is polluted—there is consensus among jurists. Therefore, they rule, the former is also fortified.

In the next paragraph though, the Ahl-i-Hadis choose to be less careful than the actual Hadis. The Prophet has said, they note, that if the water in question (into which the dog has fallen) is *ten matka*s or more then it is not polluted if the colour, taste, odour have not changed. The Ahl-i-Hadis rule that if it is less than *five matka*s then, even if the colour, etc., have not changed, it is polluted.

They turn next to the well. The *Hidayah* has said, they begin, that if a goat, a person or a dog falls and dies in the well, the entire water in it must be taken out. The basis for this rule is telling: the *Hidayah,* the Ahl-i-Hadis report, prescribed this rule because Ibn Abbas and Ibn Zubair had given this very fatwa when a *hupshi* fell in the Zamzam and died. But for several reasons this hukum is not *qabile taslim,* it is not worthy of being followed, say the Ahl-i-Hadis. First because it is based on a fatwa of Ibn Abbas and Ibn Zubair, and that fatwa is defective in many ways. Its chain of transmission is weak. It is written in the *Hidayah* that the chain of transmission is weak because it snaps, and that is so because Ibn Sirin did not meet Ibn Abbas. Some of the arguments in the Hadis are also weak, the Ahl-i-Hadis say, though they do not specify what they have in mind. Even if one accepts the Hadis, they say, one cannot take *hujjat* or support from it. Even if one takes the verdict of a Companion as valid support, it cannot be a substitute for a fully reliable tradition. After citing opinions and counter-opinions of authorities, the fatwa declares that in view of the reasons given above the fatwa of Ibn Abbas is not worthy of acceptance. On the same grounds, say the Ahl-i-Hadis, the verdict of the *Hidayah* too cannot be accepted.

It is very strange, they say, that the Hanafis call the water of such a well impure, and yet they call unpolluted the water which is a hundredth of this, and in which filth is more than this (than the quantum of filth, that is, which would be in the well upon a goat, or a person or dog falling and dying in it). It is said in the *Fatawa-i-Alamgiri,* they recount, that if during the rains there is filth and faecal matter in the *parnala,* the drain-pipe, and the rainwater is flowing down touching it, the test is that if more than half of it is touching the filth, faecal matter, etc., then it is napaak, but if less than half is touching the filth, etc., then the water is paak; and if the dirt is scattered about on the roof and rainwater, having fallen on it, flows down then that water is paak. God bless them! What a finding! The reason which has been given for this (for holding that the water is paak) is that it is running water. Moreover, the Ahl-i-Hadis point out, Hafiz ibn Hajr writes that Behaqi has quoted Ibn Ainiya who says that he stayed in Mecca for seventy years and did not hear the hupshi-*wali* Hadis from any young or old person, nor did he hear the story about the water being taken out of Zamzam. Imam Shafi'i, the Ahl-i-Hadis note, says that even if this incident is correct—namely, that water was actually taken out of Zamzam—it is possible that some impurity may have occurred (other than what is supposed to have occurred because of the hupshi falling in) and the water may have been taken out for cleaning the well for that reason.[13]

Recall what the question was: what is the hukum about the water of the well into which a *bakri* or person or dog has fallen and died? Neither is the question asked, nor is it answered with respect to a particular well, on a particular occasion when a specific thing has fallen into it. The question and answer set out a general principle: it is this which determines what has to be done in each particular situation. And that general principle is deduced not from any fact gleaned from the condition of the water in question, but from what was done 1,350 years ago. And the point turns on different views about whether that incident took place, on conjectures about the occurrence which could have accounted for the incident, on the fact that even if that decision was taken—of emptying out the water in Zamzam—it was taken by Companions of the Prophet and not by the Prophet himself.

Just as there is no end to differences among authorities, there is no end to distinctions. Notice that the foregoing discussion concerned inter alia the dog falling into the well. And the water turned out to be paak.

For the purist that would be a decision of convenience: as is well known, while the body of a dog is intrinsically paak—that is, it is paak unless some filth is apparent on it—its saliva is intrinsically napaak. It is on account of this distinction that Mufti Kifayatullah, for instance, rules that while one may keep a dog for purposes of security of grain, of crops, for shikar, it is not permissible to keep a dog as a pet. The Mufti is at pains to explain the reasons for the distinction.

13. *Fatawa Ahl-i-Hadis,* Volume I, pp. 11–14.

He says that the dog's dry body is paak; that even if it is wet with water which is itself paak it remains paak. But its saliva is napaak, he says, and if that saliva touches the body or clothes of a man then that person or his clothes, as the case may be, become napaak. If the dog sits on the floor, bed or chair, the Mufti points out, it is possible that its saliva may touch these, and if a person sits on the floor, bed or chair then it is possible that the dog's saliva having touched these, the man's body and clothes too shall become napaak. To touch the Holy Quran or observe the namaz in this condition would be wrong. Those who play with dogs cannot keep their bodies and clothes free from the saliva of dogs. Hence the verdict: a dog must not be kept as a pet but it may be kept for security of the crop, of grain, for shikar.[14] But presumably the dog that falls into the well falls in saliva and all. Yet the water is decreed to be paak. The same goes for using the dog for shikar. What about the duck for instance, which, upon being shot, falls into the pond and is retrieved and brought back by the dog in his jaws? Is it not touched by the dog's saliva?

These weighty questions, the subtle distinctions which can tilt the verdict one way or the other—these are the warp and woof of fatwas. They are also what give the ulema great power. For, as we saw in regard to the fatwas on talaq, had the rules been clear cut, laypersons could have themselves looked up the manuals. It is the fact that at every turn the matter can be made to go one way or the other which compels the layperson to turn to the ulema, and gives the ulema their enormous power.

Chhipkalis and two kinds of frogs

If a chhipkali falls into the well then how much water is

---

14. *Mufti Kifayatullah ke Fatawi*, Volume IX, pp. 263–64.

to be taken out, and, if it gets bloated or bursts in it, should all the water be taken out?, asks the querist. A chhipkali does not have dam-e-sayal, says Mufti Kifayatullah, therefore its bursting or getting bloated will not pollute the water. The reason for this is also given very clearly in the law books: that though those animals which do not have dam-e-sayal are haram, they are not napaak—for instance the fly or *jheengar.* If these fall into water or soup and die, the water and soup do not become napaak.[15] The same holds for the water of a well in which a frog has died. As the frog does not have dam-e-sayal, rules the Mufti, the water does not become napaak.[16]

The Deoband ulema set out a more detailed fatwa, and bring us to the source of the distinction. A frog has been taken out of the well, the querist asks, but we do not know whether it is *barri* or *bahri*—that is, whether it lives on land or in water. Nor do we know whether it as dam-e-sayal or not. What is the hukum about the water? The ulema of Deoband decree: In the *Durr-ul-Mukhtar* it is written that that frog which does not have skin between the legs is from land, and there is dam-e-sayal in it. And therefore by its dying in the water, the water becomes impure. And by the dying of a water frog the water shall not become polluted. The ulema provide a rule of thumb: whether there is dam-e-sayal or not can be ascertained by seeing whether it (the frog) is large or small.[17]

Four points stand out: such questions are referred to religious authorities; they settle them by looking up the actual case or, if that is not available, an analogical case in a book written in the seventeenth century; the application of the rule sometimes requires empirical verification: in the instance of the

15. *Mufti Kifayatullah ke Fatawi,* Volume II, pp. 275–76.
16. Ibid., Volume II, p. 280.
17. *Fatawa Dar al-Ulum, Deoband,* Volume I, p. 206.

frog, for example, whether or not there is skin between the legs; next, there is sometimes a rule of thumb to go by.

And finally there are of course the fine distinctions, the subtleties which only an alim trained in Islamic law and Islamic science knows how to apply. Not everyone for instance would know that a passage in *Durr-ul-Mukhtar* dealing with the case of sick goat can settle the matter in regard to a hen grabbed out of the mouth of a cat. Similarly, going by the strong denunciations of liquor and swine in the Quran and Hadis, a layperson would think that trading in intoxicants, and of course in pigs would be forbidden. But that is not so, rules Mufti Kifayatullah: trade in liquor and pigs alone in prohibited; trade in ganja, charas and cocaine is jaiz.[18] Even that is not the end of the matter. As we have seen, whether talaq pronounced under the influence of liquor, for instance, shall take effect or not comes to depend on *the substance from which* the particular liquor was made.[19]

A typical dispute

One set of fatwas after another takes up the question: 'Is it permissible to urinate while standing?' A person who comes fresh to fatwas, and to the shariah will be quite bewildered at the passion which is expended on this trivial matter. The fatwas on it give one a glimpse both of the method of reasoning—the heavy reliance on texts of hundreds of years ago, in this case, the Hadis—and of the quandary into which this method inevitably lands one.

It is permissible to pass urine while standing, decree the Ahl-i-Hadis, if you can ensure that no drop of urine falls on you. It has been said in the Holy Hadis that the Prophet had himself

---

18. *Mufti Kifayatullah ke Fatatui*, Volume IX, p. 115.

19. Chapter 7 above.

passed urine while standing, they record. Most of the commentators on the Hadis are in agreement over this—that is, on the Hadis in which it is reported that the Prophet passed urine while standing. The ulema cite the authorities one should read on the matter.

The next querist asks the same question the other way round: please cite the Hadis which forbid one from passing urine while standing, he says. The Prophet forbade Umar from passing urine while standing, the Ahl-i-Hadis answer. But they add: this Hadis is weak—we shall soon see how others look upon it, and what consequences follow. Even though the Prophet passed urine once while standing, it was not his habit to do so, the Ahl-i-Hadis now concede, modifying the emphasis they had employed in their preceding fatwa. And they cite in support of their altered emphasis, the observation of Aisha: 'If someone says the Prophet used to pass urine while standing, do not accept the statement. He used to pass urine while sitting.' The Ahl-i-Hadis list the authorities for the two Hadis— the one involving Umar and the other Aisha, they note which Hadis is the weak one, they rule on the relative weight to be attached to a Hadis based on an act and to one based on an utterance.[20]

The ulema of Deoband are much more emphatic. To urinate while standing without justification is prohibited and detestable, they declare. And the Prophet's urinating while standing happened only once—and that was because of justification and necessity, they declare. Moreover, they say, the Prophet has himself prohibited urinating while standing. Hazrat Umar has stated, they recall: 'Once upon seeing me urinating while standing, the Prophet said, "O, Umar, do not urinate while standing!" Then after that I never urinated while standing.'[21]

20. *Fatawa Ahl-i-Hadis,* Volume I, p. 42.

21. *Fatawa Dar al-Ulum, Deoband,* Volume I, pp. 376–77.

The matter takes up four quarto-sized pages of tightly packed text in the *Fatawa-i-Rizvia.* Recall that in their first fatwa the Ahl-i-Hadis had ruled that it is permissible to urinate while standing, and on the basis of a Hadis they had said that the Prophet had himself urinated while standing. Maulana Ahmad Riza Khan comes down like an avalanche on such pleading. In the process he cites four Hadis which he terms 'reliable', among these is the very one which the Ahl-i-Hadis characterize as 'weak'. He takes up the contentions of various other authorities and gives detailed refutations for each—so important is the issue, and so intense the debates on it.

The fatwa illustrates the method of reasoning as well as the earnestness which goes into the debates over such questions. It will repay study.

Urinating while standing is detrimental in four ways, declares the Maulana.

First, drops of urine may fall on the body and the clothes, thus rendering the body and the clothes unclean, and this would have happened for serving no need at all. This is prohibited (haram). To fortify the postion the Maulana cites authorities including the *Durr-ul-Mukhtar.*

Second, the drops of urine invite the torments of the grave. The Maulana recalls that the Prophet of Allah said, 'Avoid (being polluted by) urine, because quite often it occasions the torment of the grave.' The Prophet saw two persons being tormented in the grave. He observed, 'One of them did not screen himself while passing his urine, the other was a back-biter.'

Third, urinating while standing amounts to uncovering oneself to passers-by or other people who may be present. The thighs provide a cover when one sits down (to urinate), and one is naked when one stands up. This invites anathema (*laanat*). The *Ilahi Hadis* says, 'Anathema on him who seesit (the male member), and anathema on him who shows it.'

Fourth, declares the Maulana, this is the way of the Christians and it behoves them. Those who take to this habit these days, are accursed and invite torment. To nail the point the Maulana quotes the Quran and the Hadis.

There are many traditions which regard this sort of activity as opposed to and in disobedience of the Prophet's Sunna, the Maulana declares, and proceeds to cite some of them.

Tradition No. I: Imams Ahmad, Tirmizi and Nasai as well as the *Sahih* of Ibn Haban quote Aisha who said, 'He who says that the Prophet urinated while standing, is not to be deemed truthful. He never urinated except when sitting.' Imam Tirmizi says, 'Of all the traditions on this subject, the one from Aisha is the best and the most correct.' The same tradition is found in *Sahih Abu Awanah* and *Mustadrak-i-Hakim* in the following words, 'Ever since the Quran was sent to the Holy Prophet, he never urinated while standing.'

Tradition No. II: Bazar says in his *Musnad,* on the authority of *Sahih Buridah,* that the Prophet said, 'Three things count as disregard (*jaf*) and disrespect: that a man urinates while standing, that he wipes away sweat from his brow while doing *namaz,* that he blows his breath (on the floor) while doing prostration (*sajdah*).' Again the Maulana cites other authorities who have endorsed this position.

Tradition No. III: Tirmizi and Ibn Majah and Behaqi cite Umar Faruq who said, 'The Prophet saw me urinating while standing. He said, 'Do not urinate while standing.' I never did it again after that day.'

Tradition No. IV: Ibn Majah and Behaqi cite Jabir who said, 'The Prophet has forbidden urinating while standing.' Imam Khatimal-Hafaz says that this tradition is correct.

What remains, Maulana Ahmad Riza Khan notes, is the tradition from Khadifah which says, 'The Prophet went up a dung-heap, and urinated there while standing.' Many theologians and scholars have countered it in many ways, declares the Maulana.

First, this tradition stands abrogated in view of the tradition from Aisha, as is accepted by Imam Abu Awanah in his *Sahih*, and by Ibn Shahin in *Kitab al-Sunnah*.

Second, he says, the Prophet had a wound in his side at that time, and could not sit down. This is related by Abu Huraira and accepted by Hakim Wadar Qatin and Behaqi.

Third, there was no place there for sitting because of dirt, declares the Maulana. Imam Abd al-Azim Zaki al-Din Manzari supports this fact.

Fourth, the dung-heap was so graded that the Prophet could not sit (anywhere on it), he says. This interpretation has been followed by Abahri and others.

Fifth, the sacred back of the Prophet had an ache in it, and this act is a curative in the eyes of Arabs. This interpretation is from Imam Shafi'i and Imam Ahmad. Forty physicians agree that to do like that while standing cures seventy ailments. Other reasons follow.

It may be that the Prophet urinated once while standing, the Maulana avers. But, he declares, the authentic tradition says that after the Quran started coming to the Prophet, he always urinated while sitting, till the end of his life. The authentic tradition also proves that the Prophet regarded urinating while standing as disrespectful and bad-mannered. There are any number of traditions in support of the Prophet prohibiting this way of urinating, he declares. These traditions alone should be regarded as proper. The particular should not be hailed in the face of the general.

Moreover, *Nafs-i-Hadis* explains that the heap was pretty high and graded, and below it the ground was so soft on account of dung that there was no chance of drops falling (on his body or his clothes). In front of him there was a wall.

The dung-heap was in an isolated place, not on the main road. And he had made Khadifah stand at his back, so that this side too was covered. It shows that he did not like his sacred behind to be seen. And what he did only once in his life was with these precautions.

Do these modern ones want to follow only this instance?, the Maulana demands, and exclaims, 'Good God! What should we say about them and their uncivilized acts! On top of it, they are trying to find support in a sacred tradition !'[22]

The question. The scholarship and time expended on it. The minute dissection of an incident. The vehemence the matter evokes.

Only one word need be added. The matter has not just doctrinal but immediate practical consequences. Surely, it is only their ignorance of the relevant Hadis and of these fatwas which has kept our secularists from proclaiming the standard public urinal to be a conspiracy to make the believers act in contravention of the Sunna.

The importance of Hadis

But we are on the method of reasoning. Notice the importance such a question has. Notice the difficulty, in fact, if one is to be true to the Faith, the impossibility of doing things in ways which differ from the way the Prophet did them, be they ever so removed from matters of Faith as others would understand the term. Now, the way of the Prophet, the Sunna is to be gleaned from the Hadis.

Therefore, when a question arises as to what one should do, and how one should do it, and there is a Hadis on the matter, the Hadis settles it. There is no way around this. But

---

22. On the foregoing, *Fatawa-i-Rizvia*, Volume II, pp. 146–51.

it leads to great difficulties ever so often. A single example will suffice.

There is a tradition which occurs in *Sahih Muslim* and other Hadis books in varying words but with the same meaning, writes the querist. The Prophet is reported to have said, 'Islam will always be there and it will have twelve Caliphs.' The following questions arise, he writes:

1. What are the names of these twelve?
2. Will all the twelve be good persons or will some of them be good and others bad? If the latter statement applies to them, was this detail provided by the Prophet or by some other ulema?
3. Have all the twelve already ascended the throne, or are some of them still to come?
4. This tradition has occasioned a problem among the Shias. They say that Islam will not come to an end till all the twelve Caliphs have appeared and the count is complete. Now, if the Caliphs have already appeared and the count has been completed, is anything of Islam left in the world in terms of this tradition?
5. *Sharih-Fiqah-Akbar* of Mulla Ali Qari gives on page 82 or some other pages the names of the twelves Caliphs. Are they correct or incorrect?

You will see the point of the questions at once. For even if we take only the Sunni count, there had already been almost a hundred Caliphs by 1924 when the Caliphate was abolished. When the Prophet had said twelve, how is one to account for a hundred? That is not the only problem the Hadis lands the believer in, as we shall see in a moment. But it is an obvious problem: how to square a hundred into twelve?

One cannot doubt that when the Prophet has said there shall be *twelve* Caliphs there shall be *twelve,* and *only twelve*

Caliphs. On the other hand, there had already been over eight times that number.

Notice the somersaults and evasions which even so resourceful a polemicist as Maulana Ahmad Riza Khan has to execute. He declares: the fact is that whatever Allah or the Prophet has said about the hidden (secret) things, is true for sure. And there is no way of believing what they have not told, because the hidden cannot be known unless made known by Allah or the Prophet. So this tradition has been under discussion since the days of the Tab'in. Mahalab said, 'I have found no one who could tell me the full intent of this tradition.' Imam Qazi Ayaz Maliki, after mentioning many implications of this tradition from *Sahih Muslim*, said, 'There may be other meanings of this tradition and Allah alone knows the intention of His Prophet.' Imam Ibn al Jozi writes in *Kashf al-Mushkal* 'I have searched for years the meaning of this tradition. I consulted whatever books I thought would have the meaning. I questioned the scholars of my time. But I am not satisfied as regards the meaning. How can I be satisfied? The details which Allah and the Prophet do not provide about the hidden, how can we be definite about those details? Of course, people speculate.' But nothing can be believed for sure. All that can be said for sure is that some signs are found in that tradition about the twelve Caliphs. Those of them who possess those signs will be Muslim for all practical purposes though not for purpose of belief, and those who do not will be false (Caliphs). The signs are as follows: 1) all of them will be Quraish sheikhs; 2) all of them will be kings and lords of lands according to various compilations of Hadis; 3) Islam will become powerful in their times; 4) their times will be peaceful; 5) they will be backed by consensus of the ummah, that is rulers and believers will accept them as lords and true Caliphs; 6–7) they will act on the tenets and teachings of Din, and only one of them will rule at a time.

Those who have speculated have not consulted all the Hadis collections, and have drawn conclusions from some stray sentence, the Maulana declares. For instance, Abul Hasan Manavi has concluded that there will be twelve Caliphs at the same time. He has depended on a single word in *Sahih al-Bukhari*. If you look at other words, the Maulana says, you wonder how such conflict and consensus can go together, how can Islam be powerful, dominant, stable and well established under such conditions? Ali Qari's statement that the twelve should be counted from Abu Bakr to the last of the Ummayads is baseless. The dirty one, Yazid, has also been included among them, though the reign of that devil has nothing to do with the power of the Din or peace. A study of the various traditions would not have permitted this statement if only twelve reigns were to be taken into account. The fact remains that that devil (Yazid) martyred the Prophet's own grandson, Hussain, simply because the latter refused to pay him homage. He was a man who ruined the honour of daughters and sisters. He drank wine. He gave up namaz. So this interpretation is baseless. The tradition says nowhere that they—the Caliphs—will follow one another without any interval.

Eight of them have already happened—Abu Bakr, Umar, Usman, Ali, Hasan, Muawiya, Abdullah bin Zubair, and Umar bin Abdul Aziz. Another is sure to come—Imam Mahdi. Allah and the Prophet know about the other three. It is a thousand wonders that one of them, namely, Abdullah bin Zubair, a Companion as well as the son of a Companion, a just imam, a nephew of the Prophet himself, and a grandson of Abu Bakr, is not included (in the count) but that dirty devil (Yazid) is included. When in fact the *Amir al-Mu'minin*, Umar bin Abdul Aziz, had whipped that man twenty times. Let alone Abdullah bin Zubair, even Ali has not been included in this count because the period of his Caliphate was brief. But Walid has been included, the man who had put up the Holy Quran against a wall and perforated it with arrows.

Such baseless and meaningless statements have no authenticity, declares the Maulana. It (the list given) is only the folly of a stupid scholar, he concludes.[23]

A clear saying of the Prophet: there shall be twelve Caliphs. A clear fact: there have been almost a hundred.

Mountains of scholarship and labour expended on the matter by the ulema.

No agreement on what the figure twelve means: Twelve at one time? Twelve in a row one following the other, or one following the other after intervals of undefined length? Twelve individuals or twelve dynasties?

No agreement on who the twelve are.

No agreement on whether they have all come and gone, or whether some are still to come.

The ultimate explanation of the ulema? That only Allah and the Prophet know what the Prophet meant.

And remember what the question was—the number of Caliphs. A simple question. A basic question. And yet this is the state of the answers.

The problem is not in the Hadis. It is simple and straightforward. The problem is in the insistence that hundred must somehow become twelve. It is in the basic stance, expressed in the opening sentences of the fatwa: 'The fact is that whatever Allah or the Prophet has said about the hidden things is true for sure. And there is no way of believing what they have not told, because the hidden cannot be known unless made known by Allah or the Prophet.'

That this Hadis relates to some secret, hidden thing is

---

23. *Fatawa-i-Rizvia,* Volume XI, pp. 57–59.

itself a twist: the Caliphate was an open, very visible institution; it becomes a 'hidden thing' only because the number 'twelve' has to be explained away.

And 'twelve' is not the only problem with the Hadis, There is another clause in the Hadis in *Sahih Muslim* which the querist omitted. That also leads to somersaults and evasions of the same kind.

In the Hadis the Prophet says: 'This religion will continue to remain powerful and dominant until there have been twelve Caliphs.' Adding, 'All of them shall be from the Quraish.'

Apart from the question of their being only twelve, how is one to explain the fact that not all the Caliphs have been from that one tribe, Quraish? Second, how is one to square the fact that here the Prophet was placing persons from his own tribe above other believers with the claim that Islam is the one religion in which all believers are strictly equal?

'The question whether the Caliphate is the privilege of the Quraish,' writes the editor and translator of *Sahih Muslim*, 'is one of those debatable issues over which there has been a good deal of difference of opinion amongst the scholars.' Some say that a Caliph must necessarily be a Quraish, he notes, others that a man from among the Quraish is only to be preferred if he has all the other qualifications required for being the Caliph.

The scholar quotes another tradition of the Prophet in which the Prophet says, 'The Caliphate will remain with the Quraish and those who would contend with them would be overthrown on their faces, *so long as they would establish the* Din.' He quotes yet another Hadis in which the Prophet says, 'The Caliphs would be amongst the Quraish *so long as they would rule with justice, fulfil their promises and treat (their people) mercifully*'—words that are wise counsel but that are vastly different from, 'This religion shall continue to remain powerful and dominant until there have been twelve

Caliphs. *All of them will be from the Quraish.'*

Similarly, that the Prophet in a sense anointed his own tribe for this, the highest office, is explained away: he chose them only for that time and place, it is explained, because at that time and place they were the best equipped to carry on the institution. Ibn Khaldun is quoted, Shah Waliullah is quoted to fortify the assertion.[24]

And yet, hundred must be made into twelve, 'Quraish' must be made to include non-Quraishites.

For how can a believer, and least of all an alim acknowledge that something the Prophet said is not absolutely and literally true?

Nor is it a question merely of one's personal faith. It is a question of the glory of the Faith. For the entire Faith rests on the word of the Prophet.

That is why Maulana Ahmad Riza Khan is only being true to the Faith when, as we saw at the beginning of the chapter, he says that the glory of Islam consists in having science bend to it, not in its bending to science. What holds for science holds a fortiori for mere historical 'facts'—of whether there have been a hundred Caliphs or twelve.

---

24. For the Hadis and these efforts to explain it away, *Sahih Muslim*, Kitab Bhavan, New Delhi, 1978, Volume III, pp. 1009–12.

9

A closed, self-perpetuating circle

The earth is stationary. The sun revolves around it. The stars are stationary, hung as lamps by Allah to guide travellers, and to stone the Devil. To believe anything contrary to all this is to betray The Faith. Men are the masters. Each may keep up to four wives *at a time* and as many concubines 'as the right hand holds'. The wives are fields which the husband may or may not 'irrigate' as he will. The husband can bind them to obeying his merest whim on pain of being divorced. If he is still not satisfied, he can throw them out with one word. Upon being thrown out they are to be entitled to bare sustenance—but only for three months, and nothing at all beyond that. To see any inequity in this, to demand anything more for the women is to question the wisdom of Allah, it is to strike at Islam. To urinate while standing, to fail to do istinja in the prescribed way, to fail to believe that the saliva of a dog is napaak and his body paak—these are grave sins. To ask for the well-being of a kafir, be he ever so saintly, even upon his death, to fail to believe that a Muslim, be he ever so sinful, is better than a kafir, be the latter ever so virtuous, is kufr itself.

Such is the mindset of the ulema. It pervades their rulings on all aspects of life.

Education

Education is central to advancement—of the country, of the individual. But the ulema have fought hard and long against what most today would consider education. For them religious education must take priority over modern, technical education. Only those subjects are to be studied, only that knowledge is to be imparted which strengthens one's faith—in practical terms, only those subjects are to be studied, only that knowledge pursued which confirms one in the belief that whatever is written in the Quran and Hadis, whatever has been put out by the ulema over the centuries is true and the acme of wisdom as well as perfection. The education of women, in particular their being awakened to new values, their being trained for new professions, their being awakened to their rights—all this is anathema; it is held to be injurious to them, in fact it is declared to be the way to disrupting society and undermining Islam.

The results are before us—in the lower levels of education among Muslims, in particular among Muslim women, and in Muslims falling behind as a consequence in the professions.

True to form, our secularists blame non-Muslims for Muslims falling behind. But the ulema are the ones who have kept the community tied to maktabs and madrasahs, the ulema are the ones who have dinned into its mind the notion that opting for modern education is to walk away from, to walk against Islam.

Maulana Wahiduddin Khan puts the problem well. In his *Indian Muslims, Need for a Positive Outlook,* to which we have referred earlier, he writes:

> Up till now Muslims have tended to attribute their problems to prejudice and discrimination and to waste the better part of

their time and energy in railing against offenders who often exist only in their own imaginations. What I have to say is simply that it is high time they changed their way of thinking and devoted themselves whole-heartedly to the processes of self-reconstruction.

Our world—let us face it—is one of stiff competition and the race of life between individuals and communities is unending. The real problem of Muslims is that, at this point in their history, they have been left behind by other communities, particularly in the field of education and economic development. The major part of the 'discrimination and atrocities' that Muslims are facing in this country are, in actual fact, the consequences of their own backwardness, which they misguidedly wish to blame on others.

Maulana Wahiduddin Khan

The solution to their problem does not lie in protest. It lies, quite simply, in greater application, diligence and tenacity of purpose....

One notable instance of this very strange psychology was their response to the setting up in Calcutta of the first medical college in India by Lord William Bentinck in 1835. Because of their hatred of the English 'usurpers and conspirators', the Muslims led a procession through the streets to protest against the opening of this college, and demanded that it be closed. There then ensued the strange spectacle of other communities thronging to seek admission, while Muslims clamoured for its closure. By adopting this negative stance, Muslims lagged more than 100 years behind other communities in medical science.

This event is symbolic of the causes of the Muslim dilemma in the world of today. And there is no sign of any abatement of this general negativism. Surely they must one day realize that the prejudice and discrimination which they so loudly decry would rapidly disappear if they were simply to apply themselves with the utmost dedication in the academic and economic fields. In this way they would remove the obstacle of

> their own backwardness, and, with that, the stigma of intellectual and social inferiority. This accomplished, they would be able, as an updated and self-rehabilitated community, to stand shoulder to shoulder with the most advanced nations of the world.[1]

The Maulana refrains from specifying the group which has done most to foment the negativism he so rightly criticizes. The fact is that even more than the political leaders of Muslims and the Muslim journalists he criticizes elsewhere in the book, it is the ulema who have done so, as the slightest acquaintance with the fatwas shows.

It is a duty to save oneself from that in the college and in education which is against the shariah, declares the *Fatawa-i-Rizvia*, but not from that which is not against the shariah.[2] That latter proviso is little help for, as we have seen, once one has catered for the notions and practices and laws which the ulema declare to be intrinsic and unalterable parts of shariah, there is little left. And this consequence becomes apparent soon.

Which knowledge should one obtain?, asks the querist. The first duty is to obtain that knowledge which enables one to fulfil the obligations of faith, that knowledge by which one is made secure in his Sunni Islam, declares the *Fatawa-i-Rizvia*. Next, one should obtain knowledge about the proper way of observing namaz, Ramzan, of meeting one's obligations of zakat, of maintaining the distinctions between haram and halal. These are the topics which are emphasized in the Hadis, it recalls.

There are some disciplines which should not be acquired, the *Fatawa-i-Rizvia* declares, in that they are false

---

1. Maulana Wahiduddin Khan, *Indian Muslims, Need for a Positive Outlook*, Al Risala Books, New Delhi, 1994, pp. 43–44.

2. *Fatawa-i-Rizvia*, Volume VI, p. 171.

and useless and condemnable. As examples it cites philosophy and *najum* (astrology). There is no harm in learning arts and crafts, it says, as these do not harm one's faith. But philosophy is haram, it says, and harmful to Islam. The things that are taught in philosophy are ignorance, in fact they are worse than ignorance, it declares.

Is that knowledge proper, it asks, which the Prophet left aside? Or that knowledge which is of the Greek kafirs?

In the same way, it declares, that knowledge in which there is denial of the existence of heavens, in which there is denial of the contradiction of the movement of stars, etc., in which there are all these notions of the kafirs in opposition to the shariah—all such knowledge is like astrology, the *Fatawa-i-Rizvia* declares, and is haram and condemnable. Moreover, knowledge of mathematics and geography beyond what is necessary too is included in the worthless, it says. The Prophet says knowledge is of three kinds: knowledge of Quran, knowledge of Hadis and knowledge of things which in action are akin to them (as if, says the compiler, he is pointing to knowledge of ijma, consensus, and of reasoning by analogy)—and whatever is other than these is all useless.[3]

Clearly, 'philosophy' here is a generic term meant to cover any and every discipline which would cause a person to apply the tools of rational examination to what has been stated in the Quran or Hadis, or indeed by the ulema. Excluded too are all empirical sciences the findings of which would lead one to question the notions enunciated in the Quran and Hadis, etc. As the *Fatawa-i-Rizvia* explains a little later, to read science, etc. to acquire those arts and skills and read their books in which there is denial of the heavens, of the revolution of the sun, etc. (around the earth), in general the education of *kufriyat* are all haram.

3. *Fatawa-i-Rizvia*, Volume IX, Book I, pp. 16–17.

Moreover, it is also haram to read with the intention of acquiring some job which is itself haram or which assists that which is haram. It is jaiz only to read proper subjects for acquiring proper jobs. Even in these cases, the *Fatawa-i-Rizvia* reminds us of the overriding condition: in pursuing these subjects it is necessary that there should be no effect on one's obligations under Islam, on one's Muslim character and form; it is necessary while acquiring knowledge in these subjects that one remain steady in one's Islamic beliefs and ways—the education and occupation which ensure these beliefs and ways are jaiz.[4]

The point is emphasized repeatedly. Is it right to learn English, the querist asks. To read English or anything else which engenders doubt in regard to The Faith, to read anything from which esteem for the Ulema-i-Din is lowered in one's heart is haram, declares the *Fatawa-i-Rizvia.* And if in response one were to say, 'What do the ulema know?,' one would be lowering the honour of the ulema, and doing so is kufr, it declares.[5]

Is it right to read English?, the Maulana is asked again. If a Muslim reads it like Christians, he warns, then he shall attain recompense accordingly. If it is learnt for worldly purposes alone, he says, then there is no harm, just as Islam permits mathematics and geography. This concession must of course be read with his earlier warnings—that worldly purposes must subserve Islam, that in particular they must only be those which Islam approves, that mathematics, geography, etc., beyond what is necessary are useless. Moreover, if after learning English, the person loses himself in that sort of learning and forgets the knowledge of Faith, then that learning is

4. Ibid., Volume IX, Book II, p. 190.

5. Ibid., Volume VI, p. 24.

haram, declares *Fatawa-i-Rizvia.* Similarly, it is not right to read those books which contain false beliefs of Christians—for instance, which contain denials of the existence of heavens, etc.[6]

The *Fatawa-i-Rahimiyyah* too pronounces upon the matter at length—that while establishing schools for worldly sciences and arts is meritorious, religious education must take precedence over 'profane education'; that 'the education of schools and colleges is also contrary and antagonistic to Islamic deeds, Islamic characteristics and Islamic culture.' 'If the Muslim children remain deprived of and weak in Islamic education,' it declares, 'they will certainly be affected by the noxious education of schools and colleges and antagonistic atmosphere and society, with the result that they will become averse to Islamic beliefs and characteristics and, God forbid, irreligious.' It cites Maulana Gilani to the effect that, given the doubts and scepticism which they have blown among Muslim masses, it would have been better if modern educational institutions had never been established; it cites Mufti Maulana Abdul Hai Kafletvi Surti to the effect that in point of fact secular education is already leading Muslims into losing 'the estimable virtue of conforming to the Shariah'. It declares that there are many others to set up institutions for profane education, and 'We, on our part, should strengthen our weak religious institutions which are the citadels of protecting Islam, and increase their number; it is necessary to have orthodox schools attached to each mosque and in each and every locality and lane.' The fatwa, though longer than the ones we have been citing, is worth reading. It is a moderate one as these things go, but the approach, the underlying premises are clear enough. And the number of modern authorities it cites shows how widely the point of view is held.

6. Ibid., Volume IX, Book I, p. 99.

'Is it permissible and a good work to establish schools for learning profane sciences, Gujarati, English, etc., and starting classes for teaching technology, or not?,' the querist asks. The ulema respond:

* * *

> To establish schools where Gujarati, English and other worldly sciences and arts are taught and to start classes for technological instruction which may be helpful in earning lawful livelihood is, no doubt, permissible and is a good act, worthy of recompense and merit; but religious education and helping orthodox schools should be given priority.
>
> 'You may fondly prosper in the college and frisk and gambol in the park; it's meet you fly in the balloon and swing in the sky; but from this humble servant remember only one precept: "Forget not Allah's and your own reality!"'
>
> Turning the back to religious instruction, leaving religious schools in precarious position, and to engage in profane education is not a good work; on the contrary, it is tantamount to displeasing Allah. It is stated in the Quran:
>
> 'But ye prefer the life of the world although the Hereafter is better and more lasting' (*Surah A'la*, LXXXVII: 16, 17).
>
> Primarily, the children may be given correct and systematic instruction about the Quran and be acquainted adequately with the legal directives and requirements of religion; the picture of Islam may be so firmly impressed upon their mind that their Islamic sentiments and feelings of faith may become indelible and lasting in order that no power may be able to cool their fervour or change their practical ability. The education of schools and colleges is also contrary and antagonistic to Islamic deeds, Islamic characteristics and Islamic culture. If the Muslim children remain deprived of and weak in Islamic education, they

will certainly be affected by the noxious education of schools and colleges and antagonistic atmosphere and society, with the result that they will become averse to Islamic beliefs and characteristics and, God forbid, irreligious. Hence, if religion is dear, one ought to be orthodox and firm in it, though it may result in some worldly loss. The correct well-wishing for one's children and the community lies in this that one cares more for the improvement of their religious beliefs and welfare in the Hereafter than their secular betterment. The *Majalisu'l-Abrar* says: 'A man's best friend is he who endeavours for the betterment of his life in the Hereafter though it may incur some worldly loss for the man; and his enemy is he who strives to damage his future life (in the Hereafter) though there may be some worldly gain in it for him' (*majlis* 85, p. 500).

Fatawa-i-Rahimiyyah

Hence it is a duty of the children's guardian to be more careful about the religious betterment of their wards than for their mundane betterment. The parents have a great responsibility. The Quran says: 'O ye who believe! Ward off from yourselves and your families a Fire....' (*Surah Tehreem* LXVI: 6). If you are remiss in it, you will be asked for it in the Divine Court. The Holy Prophet has said: 'Remember! Each one of you is a supervisor and a shepherd: each one of you will be asked about his charges' (*Bukhari & Muslim*). Another *hadith* says: 'Every child is born in the nature of Islam, but its parents make of him a Jew or a Christian or a Gabr.'

Maulana Ashraf 'Ali Thanvi has written an exemplary and instructive story which he had heard from Gwalior that a man had given English education to his son from his very childhood and had spent a lot of money over it. He had also sent him to London to acquire higher degrees. On his return from there the boy fell ill. When he was about to die, the father, sitting near his pillow, began to weep, saying, 'Ah son ! I had spent twenty to twenty-five thousand rupees on your education but I did not even see the fruit of my labour.' The boy opened his eyes and said, 'Dear father! Why do you weep now? You will weep when you see me going to Hell in after-life, because, you, by spending 20–25 thousand rupees, have arranged for my being thrown into Hell; you've bought Hell for me with all this money, because you kept me quite blank in religious instruction. Now I see that all my knowledge is useless. The angels of death are about to come. By spending so much money over me you've not acted as a friend but as a foe' (*W'azu'l Huda wal-Maghfirah*, p. 33).

Fatawa -i- Rahimiyyah

Such is the consequence of being deprived of religious instruction on account of engagement in profane education! Hence Maulana Gilani says: 'Although from the financial point of view, the condition of the students of modern educational institutions may look better, a majority of them has, by its own behaviour in respect of Islam, proved that for Islam their non-existence was better than their existence. The sparks of the type of doubts and scepticism blown by them among the Muslim masses, and the ineffable things and undesirable acts which they committed in the scorning and detraction of Islamic beliefs and actions have made them deserve the said verdict that the non-existence of these degenerate sons of Islam was certainly better than their existence' (*Al-Furqan, Ifadat-e Gilani*, p. 188).

Such is the pathetic result of showing negligence and carelessness towards Islamic education!

A great august man of Gujarat, Mufti Maulana 'Abdu'l Hai Kafletvi Surti had, fifty years ago, openly evidenced before the community: 'Of course, this education has affected a majority of Muslims at least to the extent that the estimable virtue of conforming to the religious law (*shari'a*) that it had it has lost. Neither did the warmth of faith (*iman*) remain in such Muslims' hearts nor any Islamic sign (beard) on their faces. They advise other Muslims to unite but they themselves oppose the Muslims in appearance and dress' (*Nasim us'-Saba*, p. 3).

The late 'Allamah Iqbal expresses his thought in a poem entitled *Firdaus men Ek Mukalima*—'A Dialogue in Paradise'—thus:

> The Invisible Voice told me that one day Sa'di of Shiraz addressed Hali in Paradise thus: 'Tell me something about the condition of the Indian Muslim. Is he still away from his destination or busy in making efforts? Has he still in his veins the warmth of religion—he whose heat of voice once burned the sky?' Hali was moved by the Shaykh's words; crying, he began to say, 'O master of miracle! When the aged sky turned the page of time, a voice
>
> *Fatawa-i-Rahimiyyah*
>
> was heard saying, "You'll receive honour through education"; but from this education has come shakiness in belief. The world was gained but the bird of religion flew away. If religion is there, aims also can be lofty; the youth's nature is world-conquering, earth-traversing. But if the foundation of the garden-wall is shaken, it's obvious that it is the beginning of the end of the garden. Since it was not irrigated from the Zamzam of the nation (*millat*), the new generation is showing attitudes of atheism. But please don't mention this in the presence of the King of Yathrib lest the Indian Muslims consider me a tale-bearer.'

'Dates cannot be obtained from the thorn that we planted; brocade-silk cannot be had from the wool that we yarned.'

This proves that the real cause of degeneration lies in being deprived of religious instruction or in being weak in it. Hence even as cholera inoculation is required as a protective measure against contagious air, religious instruction is intensely required along with modern profane education, and so provision for this ought to be given priority. Maulana Ashraf Ali Thanvi says: 'Muslims do not have orderliness at all. If English education is taken after studying religious books, the apprehension of the corruption of beliefs is lessened; but when there is no knowledge regarding one's religious beliefs, it often results in degeneration' (*Malfuzat*, vol. v, p. 436).

So, more attention should be paid to religious knowledge in these times than to secular education. There are many other people to establish schools for profane education and to run classes for technical arts and crafts; the government itself sponsors these. We, on our part, should strengthen our weak religious institutions which are the citadels for protecting Islam, and increase their number; it is necessary to have orthodox schools attached to each mosque and in each and every locality and lane. Maulana Thanvi says: 'There is not the least doubt in it that the existence of religious schools at this time is a great boon, anything superior to which is unimaginable, for the Muslims; if there is any means of sustaining Islam in the present day world, it is these orthodox schools' (*Huququ'l Ilm*, p. 51).

Fatawa -i- Rahimiyyah

Maulana Gilani put it like this: 'The truth is that while, on the one hand, children were being snatched from the laps of their Muslim parents to be admitted into contemporary schools and universities and the culturists were culturing in their (the students') young hearts and minds the heretical germs of refractoriness and arrogance, of atheism and apostasy, there were, on the other hand, vis-à-vis the modern schools, these our conservative (lit. cave-like) orthodox schools, which made a successful attempt in keeping clean a part, however small, of the future generations of Muslims from the impurities of faith and morality' (*Al-Furqan, Ifadat-e Gilani*, p. 188).

Hence it is necessary to precede and surpass others in financial sacrifice for sustaining, strengthening and increasing the number of such religious institutions. Hazrat Mujaddid Alf-e Thani says: 'The greatest virtue is this that one may endeavour to spread the religious law (*Shariah*) and to revive any of its laws, particularly at a time when religious practices may have become obliterated. The spending of millions of rupees in the way of Allah is not equal to the propagation of one religious regulation (*mas'ala*). There is a lofty rank for the spending of those sums of money which are meant to support the religious law and to preach religion: to spend one pice with this intention is like spending a lakh of rupees with another intention' (*Maktubat-e imam-e Rabbani*, vol. i, *maktub* 48, pp. 66–67).[7]

* * *

The strictures against 'profane', modern education are pressed even more emphatically in regard to the education of Muslim women. There is no harm if a woman learns enough to be able to sign her name or write the address on her letter to her husband in English, says the *Fatawa-i-Rahimiyyah*. But, 'It is not permissible to send girls to schools and colleges for acquiring higher education and academic degrees,' it says, 'for there is more harm than benefit in it'—and to nail the matter the fatwa invokes a line from the Quran, 'The sin of them is greater than their usefulness' (2.219), a line which could scarcely have been spoken by Allah with modern schools and colleges in mind.

It cites Akbar Allahabadi, Maulana Mahmudul Hasan, Maulana Ashraf Ali Thanvi, W.W. Hunter, Sir Syed, Iqbal, even Gandhiji, and others to the effect that modern education leads Muslims to scoff at Islamic beliefs and ways, that it leads them to hurl 'atheistic effronteries' at their co-religionists, and, the fatwa declares, it is far better that Muslims remain ignorant than that they take in such education. It invokes Maulana Thanvi: 'It is a billion times better to be useless and remain in orthodox Islamic schools than to be busy in learning English; for though there may be no ability and accomplishment, religious beliefs at least will not be corrupted, there will at least be love for men of religious knowledge.

7. *Fatawa-i-Rahimiyyah*, Volume I, pp. 36–40.

Although one may get the job of a mosque-sweeper, it is better than attaining proficiency in English and becoming lawyers, barristers, etc., whereby one's beliefs may get corrupted, faith may become shaky and effrontery may be committed in respect of Allah, the Prophet (pbuh.!), the Companions (Abph.!) and other religious elders which is these days very common, rather a necessary consequence of English education. The above-mentioned preference is quite clear to a lover of religion; yes, one who is not grieved by losing religion, he may say whatever he likes.' It cites with approval Maulana Thanvi's admonition to a father who was in a quandary whether or not to admit his sons to Aligarh College lest their religion be ruined: 'What Allah wills will happen but among the apparent causes this admission (to the College) is a powerful cause of ruination (of religion), and hence admission of paralysis (into their bodies) is better than this admission to the college, for in the latter there is harm to their religion whereas in the former there is harm to the body only; of these two diseases the real one is that which is caused by the college atmosphere.' It cites with approval the Maulana's reaction to a person who informed him that Kashmiri Muslims would now be able to give up working as sweepers as arrangements were being made for their education: 'If the scavenger's occupation were given up, this occupation in English education would be worse than that. So far there was only external uncleanliness, now there would be internal uncleanliness instead. I have often marked that this education corrupts belief.'

Such consequences are inherent in the type of education itself, the fatwa's argument runs: 'Dates cannot be obtained from the thorn that we planted; brocade-silk cannot be had from the wool that we yarned.' Not to save oneself from these inevitable consequences would be to go against the shariah. For, the fatwa reminds us, 'It is a rule of the Shariah that it is necessary to remain away from destruction and save oneself from evil.'

But that is just about modern education in general. Modern education being given to girls is condemnable on two additional grounds as well: first, the atmosphere of the schools and colleges itself will corrupt them—they are to be kept away from these institutions just as they were kept from going to mosques by Umar; second, women are particularly susceptible to corruption.

The passages in this and the subsequent fatwa are worth reading in full as they give us a glimpse of both—the ulema's hostility to modern education as well as their view of women. Here they are:

> In ablution (*wuzu*) and ritual bathing (*ghusl*), gargling is an act of Sunna, but it is forbidden for a faster for the fear that water may glide down the throat; similarly, running the fingers through the hair (of head and beard) is an act of Sunna, but it is abominable (*Makruh*) to do so during the state of *ahram* (unstitched pilgrimage uniform) for the fear that some hair may get broken.
>
> During the propitious time of the Holy Prophet (pbuh.!) womenfolk enjoyed the permission of saying congregational prayers in the mosque, but soon afterwards, due to apprehension of corruption, Caliph 'Umar Farouq (Abph.!) prevented them from coming to the mosque, and Hazrat Ayesha (Abph.!), supporting this decision, observed: 'Had the Holy Prophet (pbuh.!) witnessed this condition which Hazrat 'Umar has seen, he, too, would not have granted you the permission to say prayers in the mosque' (*Abu Da'ud*, Vol. 1, p. 91).
>
> As per this ruling, when it became impermissible (*na-ja'iz*) for women to say congregational prayers in the mosque, how can it be permissible (*ja'iz*) then, for fear of religious harm, to send girls to colleges for higher education? In other words, it is

> impermissible to give an education which adversely affects one's faith and religion and becomes a means of adopting unIslamic culture, morals and habits; it is impermissible for all, whether girls or boys. However, a distinction can be made that since girls, by reason of their nature, are more susceptible to bad influence and, from the point of view of religion, are not liable to shoulder economic responsibility, they should be kept aloof from English education—they should not come in contact even with the atomsphere prevailing in schools and colleges; but the boys, provided they are well-grounded in the basic beliefs and principles of religion and promise to stick staunchly to Islamic culture, morals and habits, have, no doubt, scope to acquire as many English degrees as they like; as Akbar Allahabadi has well put it:
>
> *Fatawa -i- Rahimiyyah*
>
>> You may fondly prosper in the college and swagger in the park; it's meet you fly in the balloons and swing in the sky; but from this humble servant remember only one precept: 'Forget not Allah's and your own reality.'
>
> But, in the present age, this guarantee seems quite impractical. If there is no certainty that they will firmly stick to Islamic beliefs, culture and morality and there is not full satisfaction of security against evil influence and unhealthy atmosphere, then it is necessary to protect the children from the aforesaid education and culture even as they are guarded from fatal diseases and deleterious climate.

'The parents who send their daughters to college are the enemies of their daughters, not their friends,' the *Fatawa-i-Rahimiyyah* declares, citing authorities to the effect that the friend is one who prepares one for the Hereafter, though doing so may inflict worldly loss. 'There is no doubt,' it declares, 'that a collegiate girl becomes extremely free, *purdahless*, immodest and shameless. This is the general consequence of English education and college atmosphere.' And 'A girl who loses modesty loses everything,' it says, citing the Hadis, 'Modesty and faith—they are inseparable companions; when either of them is taken away, the other too goes away.'

'Now it can be decided easily,' it states, 'whether the parents who send their daughters to colleges are their friends or foes. For the parents the Quranic instruction is this: "Ward off from yourselves and your families a Fire..." (LXVI.6), while the parents are continuing to throw their children into Hell and yet claim that they love them!' 'The sole responsibility for children's spoiling lies upon the parents,' it declares.

And then the fatwa comes to three intertwined reasons for keeping women from colleges: women are particularly susceptible to corruption; the dresses they will wear, the atmosphere in which they will move will suck them into the whirlpool of faithlessness and immodesty; and, corrupted themselves, they will entice others, that is men, into corruption. To buttress these propositions, the fatwa invokes no less an authority than the Prophet himself. This is how it puts the admonitions:

> The sole responsibility for children's spoiling lies upon the parents; it is in their hands to make or mar the children's lives. What the children would become depends upon the type of training and education they are given. It is stated in a *hadith*: 'Every child is born with an upright nature (i.e., he has had ample capability for imbibing the religion of Islam) but his parents (through education and training) make of him a Jew or Christian or a Gabr' (*Mishkat,* p. 21). Admitted that a girl reading in a college can progress in worldly affairs but from the point of view of the Hereafter, she would surely be in loss. Hence, according to (Allah) 'the sin of them is greater than their usefulness' (*Surah, The Cow,* II: 219), a work entailing loss shall be unlawful (*haram*) and forbidden (*mamnu*). The Holy Prophet's assertion is: 'He who is involved in the love of the world will be in loss as regards the Hereafter, and he who is always engaged in the love of the Hereafter will be in loss

from the worldly point of view; hence prefer the lasting (the Hereafter) over the perishable (the world).' Hazrat Salman Farsi has said: 'When a man develops disinclination towards worldly affairs, his heart is illuminated with wisdom and his limbs assist him in devotions to Allah; hence one should give preference to the lasting object (the Hereafter) over the ephemeral thing (the world)' (*Minhaj-u'l-A'bidin*).

If a girl is not come of age but is adolescent, yet she is liable to be considered major. It is not permissible (*ja'iz*) for her to stir out without a veil. It is stated in a *hadith*: 'The woman comes in the form of Satan and goes in the form of Satan' (*Mishkat*, p. 268). The purport of the *hadith* is that even as Satan insinuates evil suggestions, looking at a woman too causes evil thoughts and corruption. Another *hadith* says: 'The woman is a thing (i.e., even as hidable things are hidden, the woman too should be hidden, and even as it is bad for hidable parts to remain open it is bad for a woman to be unveiled and to wander); when she stirs out, Satan sets about in ambush for her,' (and thinks out to involve her in sin). And it has been stated in a *hadith*: 'Allah's curses be upon him who looks (licentiously at a woman), as also upon her who is so looked at' (*Mishkat*, pp. 269–70). Another *hadith* says: 'The eyes fornicate—their fornication is seeing; the ears fornicate—their fornication is hearing; the tongue fornicates—its fornication is talking; and the hands also fornicate—their fornication is grasping' (*Muslim*, Vol.II, p. 336).

Fatawa -i- Rahimyyah

When a girl goes about unveiled, she will face all these prohibitions and by contravening these she will be committing sins at every step, involving others too in them. When there is the injunction for the holy wives and holy daughters (Abpt.!) of the Prophet (pbuh.!): 'And stay in your houses,' and when for some physical or legal need they have to go out they have been ordered 'to draw their cloaks round them (when they go abroad)' (*Surah, The Clans* XXXIII: 33 & 59, respectively);

> then how can there be permission for the common women to go about unveiled? When a major or adolescent girl is not permitted to go to a mosque for congregational prayers, how can she have the permission to go to a college? And then in a dress which is as good as wearing no dress at all? One *hadith* says: 'There are many women who are ostensibly dressed but are, in fact, naked; they are experts in inclining to others and in attracting others to themselves.' Further, they have been warned of the punishment that 'such women will not only be deprived of Paradise but also its fragrance.' Nowadays college girls wear so tight and body-clasping clothes that it becomes difficult for them to sit down and get up; their limbs become visible externally. How can it be permissible to come, in such clothes and such fashionable dress, before strangers? The Holy Prophet (pbuh.!) has said: 'The man who sets his eyes on the back of a woman and looks at her clothes in such a way as to see the thickness of her bones (i.e., the shape and curves of her body), he will not be able to smell the fragrance of Paradise.' It can be understood from this *hadith* that the seeing of clothes in such a way as to have a view of the shape of the body is forbidden, though the cloth may be so thick that the skin may not be visible (*Shami*, vol. v, p. 321).[8]
>
> *Fatawa-i-Rahimiyyah*

As always, Mufti Kifayatullah expresses the point moderately. As always, he urges a via media. But his prescription too is not liable to help those who want to place Muslims at par with others.

To attain knowledge is one of the duties of Islam, he opines, and that duty is not confined to men. The Prophet himself taught shariah to women, the Mufti recounts. The Prophet delivered the khutba again so that the women could hear him. Therefore, he says, there is no distinction between men and women—as far as religious knowledge is concerned.

---

8. On the foregoing, *Fatawa-i-Rahimiyyah*, Volume I, pp. 17–25.

But for women to mix freely with others is not desirable, he says. The Prophet, he recalls, said that it is better for women to observe their namaz at home than in a public place. And purdah must be observed. Moreover, one should not give such freedom to women that they imbibe the habits and ways of European women, and desert Islamic values.

If the Muslim qaum progresses by leaving aside Islamic laws and values, the Mufti declares, then it will not be progress of Islam and of the Muslim nation. By Allah!, those who deviate from this ummah shall never progress by adopting Western ways; they shall not progress unless they accept Muslim civilizational norms.

The Mufti accordingly suggests a via media: it is in accordance with shariah to open institutions for female education and for girls to go to them to acquire that knowledge and those arts which have been prescribed by Islam. Therefore, he urges that there be madrasahs for women, that there be schools for girls exclusively, and that such ways be devised to get them to these places and back as would ensure that there is no disturbance. Teachers for them ought to be carefully selected and supervised. The women must observe purdah, covering every part except hands and feet. Their dress must ensure Muslim modesty.

In view of this perspective the Mufti prescribes that in these madrasahs and special schools women be imparted knowledge of their religion, of shariah, of etiquette, social conduct, livelihood, occupation and *hunar*: knowledge in these things, he says, should be imparted in accordance with shariah and the aptitude of the women.

It is the duty of the father to compel children to learn their duties in accordance with the shariah, he stresses, and, if necessary, to punish them to ensure this.

The sorts of things he has in mind when he talks of livelihood and occupation become clearer a few pages later. For women to go out of their houses without necessity, to join processions of or mix with men, to mix with strangers without the restraints of formality, he declares, will not only destroy femininity but also Islamic civilization.

Should women be taught anything beyond the Quran?, the Mufti is asked. He says that they should be taught to read and write, and arithmetic, Urdu, skills, cooking, sewing, embroidery, etc. There is no harm in their being taught these things, the Mufti says, but of course they must observe purdah, and their capabilities to learn these things ought to be kept in mind.[9]

Not quite the agenda which is liable to lift either Muslims in general or Muslim women. And of the lot these are the progressive fatwas.

All other aspects of life too

Thus, on the one hand we have the complaint that Muslims are poor and backward; we have the diagnosis that this is so mainly because they have lagged behind in acquiring modern education and technological skills. On the other hand we have the evidence of the fatwas: the ulema are the ones who for a hundred and fifty years have vehemently and unremittingly admonished Muslims to 'save themselves' from the evil of modern education, who have proclaimed again and again that it is far better for Muslims to be 'worthless', to lose out on worldly advantage than for them to forfeit the Hereafter, to forfeit Paradise and even 'the fragrance of Paradise' by falling for modern education and thereby—inevitably,

9. On the preceding, *Mufti Kifayatullah ke Fatawi*, Volume II, pp. 29–44, 47.

necessarily—deserting Islamic values and ways. They are the ones who have dinned into Muslims the notion that Muslim women in particular must be saved from the guiles of modern education.

And yet it is the rest of India, and, by the secularists, the Hindus in particular who are held responsible for Muslims not having acquired modern education!

The fatwas on education are but one of an entire genus. To every aspect of change, to every new development the attitude of the ulema is the same: they react with what the Americans call the IRI—the Instant Rejection Instinct.

Interest of course must never be taken or given. Therefore one must not work in banks, as they charge interest. To deposit money in banks is to assist in sin. One must not work in or be members of cooperatives. One must not be a writer of stamp papers or deeds notifying transactions which involve interest.

One must not take out insurance as that is a form of gambling. For the same reason one must not work in an insurance company.

One must not buy or sell shares of companies. One must not work even in an Islamic educational institution which has deposited its corpus in a bank and pays salaries out of the interest it earns.

One must not take Western medicines as they contain alcohol.

If one listens to the radio it must be only to hear desirable speeches, that is those which fortify one's faith in Islam and one's adherence to Islamic values.

One must not have any paintings or photographs of living things in one's home. One must not have oneself photographed. One must not work in a camera shop. One must not play musical instruments or sing songs at weddings as the kafirs do. Accordingly one must not work in bands....[10]

A fair-sized volume can be filled with such examples and the fatwas on them. Two will suffice to illustrate the mindset which leads the ulema, and through their influence the community, to confront the future resolutely facing the past.

Birth control

Birth control is denounced repeatedly—on the ground that it would be to deny the bounty that Allah has prepared for one, that it would be to defy the prohibition by the Prophet, that it would be to kill the child that is in the sperm.

The querist asks: How is it to go in for tubectomy? What is the regulation regarding it in health and sickness? Some people take recourse to it on account of poverty. Is it permissible?

The ulema declare:

---

10. For examples of the general position, and the rare voice of pragmatism, see the following:

On interest: *Fatawa-i-Rizvia,* Volume VI, pp. 75, 78; *Fatawa-i- Rahimiyyah,* Volume III, pp. 155–58; Volume II, pp. 158, 160–79.

On writing stamp papers: *Mufti Kifayatullah ke Fatawi,* Volume VII, pp. 376–77.

On deposits in banks: *Fatawa-i- Rahimiyyah,* Volume II, p. 163.

On working in a bank: *Fatawa-i- Rahimiyyah,* Volume II, pp. 162–63; *Mufti Kifayatullah ke Fatawi,* Volume VIII, p. 50.

On insurance: *Mufti Kifayatullah ke Fatawi,* Volume VIII, pp. 66–79; *Fatawa-i- Rahimiyyah,* Volume II, pp. 159, 165–67.

On cooperatives: *Mufti Kifayatullah ke Fatawi,* Volume VIII, p. 52.

On buying and selling shares: *Mufti Kifayatullah ke Fatawi,* pp. 108–9.

On photographs: *Mufti Kifayatullah ke Fatawi,* Volume IX, pp. 233–35, 238–40, 242–45; *Fatawa-i-Rizvia,* Volume IX, Book I, pp. 71–72.

On musical instruments and singing in marriages: *Mufti Kifayatullah ke Fatawi,* Volume IX, pp. 264–66.

On working in bands: *Fatawa-i-Rizvia,* Volume IX, Book I, p. 72.

If need be, then, as long as the excuse lasts, one can use contraceptive methods, but, frankly speaking, it is sheer ingratitude for divine bounty that one gets oneself deprived of offspring through tubectomy without a legal excuse. The Holy Prophet (pbuh!) has said: 'Contract marriage with women who love more and beget more children so that on account of your multitudinousness on the Day of Judgement I may take pride in your number vis-à-vis the other *ummahs*' (*Mishkat*). God is the Provider; He will provide for you as well as your children. The children's provider is God, not we. He who supplied nourishment in the mother's womb, He will provide it after birth also. The list of livelihood the offspring bring with them from the mother's womb and they will receive their quota according to the same. Why should then one entertain such thoughts? The Divine Commandment is:

> 'And that ye slay not your children because of penury—We provide for you and for them' (6:151).

At another place it has been said:

> 'Slay not your children, fearing a [fall to poverty]; We shall provide for them and for you' (17:31).

Hence, on account of an ordinary excuse, it is not permitted. However, if the woman, due to unsound health, cannot carry through the difficulties of pregnancy and there may be danger to her life, and there is no other go excepting a tubectomy, provided it is advised by an able and orthodox Muslim *hakim* or an honest and experienced Muslim doctor, then it can be availed of.

Another querist writes, 'Nowadays, we, railway servants, are forced to practice birth-control; we are told not to procreate. Either husband or wife, it is insisted, should undergo an operation; the husband is particularly forced to undergo vasectomy. In case of our refusal, every method is used to harass us and we are deprived of advance monetary help, medical aid and medicines from the railway doctor during our sickness. Many such methods are used to harry and pester us with the result that some, in sheer desperation, yield to vasectomy; because when we refuse and resist, the service becomes a torture and when the aforesaid facilities are denied us, our hardships multiply. What should we do under such circumstances? What are the *Ulema*'s thoughts in this connection? Can we treat the said conditions as helplessness or not and will it be proper if, considering it a helpless situation, we go in for vasectomy? When we tell them that it is against our religion, they tell us not to bring in religion in this matter. What should we do? Kindly explain fully.'

The ulema declare:

> No doubt children are a great gift of God. The Holy Prophet (pbuh.!) has said: 'Contract marriage with women who love more and beget more children so that on account of your multitudinousness on the Day of Judgement I may take pride in your number vis-à-vis the other *ummahs*.'
>
> To undergo vasectomy or tubectomy and be deprived of the means of procreation forever just to preserve one's service or to avail of its facilities is indeed ingratitude for divine gift, and legally impermissible (*na-ja'iz*) and forbidden (*haram*). It is reported in a *hadith* that certain Companions, in order to save themselves from sins and wordly worries and to engage themselves in devotions, expressed the wish to get themselves castrated. The Holy Prophet (pbuh.!) did not permit it and recited the Quranic verse:
>
>> 'O ye who believe ! Fobid not the good things which Allah hath made lawful for you, and transgress not. Lo! Allah loveth not transgressors' (V. 87). (*Bukh.*, vol. ii, p.759).
>
> It is conclusively proved from this that castration, that is, the discontinuance of procreation artificially is unlawful (*haram*) according to the explicit verse of the Quran also and is included in transgression from the limits fixed by God. Hence an

operation that discontinues procreation is unanimously unlawful (UQ, vol. xx, p. 72). And the jurisconsults have said: 'Castration of men is forbidden' (*haram*). (DM & S., vol. v, p. 342).

A *hadith* says: 'To submit to creatures by disobeying God is impermissible.' Hence, in answer to 'Don't bring religion in this matter', all should say unanimously and in unison unequivocally: 'First religion, then service.' God is the provider of livelihood. He says in the Quran:

Fatawa -i- Rahimiyyah

> 'And there is not a beast in the earth but the sustenance thereof dependeth on Allah'
>
> (XI: 6)

At another place He says:

> 'And how many an animal is there that beareth not its own provision! Allah provideth for it and for you.'
>
> (XXIX: 60)

And:

> 'And whosoever keepeth his duty to Allah, Allah will appoint a way out for him, and will provide for him from (a quarter) whence he hath no expectation. And whosoever putteth his trust in Allah, He will suffice him.'
>
> (LXV: 2–3)

And:

> 'And that ye slay not your children because of penury—We provide for you and for them.'
>
> (VI: 151).

And:

> 'Slay not your children, fearing a fall to poverty.We shall provide for them and for you.'
>
> (XVII: 31)

It is reported in a *hadith* that Hazrat Umar says that he heard the Holy Prophet (pbuh.!) saying: 'No doubt, if you put your trust in God as much as He deserveth to be trusted, He will provide for you livelihood even as He does for the birds that go out hungry in the morning and return satiated in the evening.'

(*Mishkat, p.* 452)

The illustrious Shaykh Sa'di has said:

> 'O Benevolent One Who keepeth the fire-worshipper and the Christian provided from Thine Invisible Treasure! Where wilt Thou, Who art so affectionate to Thine enemies, deprive Thine friends?'

It is said that when a crow-chic comes out from the egg, its feathers and downs are white. Its parents think that it is not their offspring for it must have been black like themselves and so they do not feed it as long as its hair and feathers do not become black. In the meanwhile God provides it sustenance: when it opens its bill, small insects flying in the air reach it and become its food. When God Almighty provides sustenance to the downy hatching, will He not send it down to His faithful servants? Will He starve you to death? Never. As a poet has said:

> 'Worry not about livelihood and shut not the leaves of the book because God fills the mother's breast even before the child sees the light. So wonderfully is the sustenance supplied.'

Notice that tubectomy and vasectomy are not opposed on the ground that these are radical or invasive or 'unnatural' methods, but because they are methods for regulating births. The ulema look down just as sternly upon, say, coitus interruptus, and for the same reason. The ulema declare:

> When the Companions asked the Holy Prophet (*Sallallaho Aliaihe wa sallam*!) about *coitus interruptus* (*'azl*), he said: 'This is like burying a live child.' And this is the same which has been described in the Quranic verse: 'And when the girl-child that was buried alive is asked' (LXXXI) (Vide *Muslim Sharif*, vol. i, p. 466; *Mishkat Sharif*, p. 276).
>
> In *Path al-Mulhim Sharh-e Sahih-e Muslim,* Allamah Shabbir Ahmed Usmani quotes that Qazi has written that the Holy

> Prophet (*Sallallaho Aliaihe wa sallam*!) has determined *coitus interruptus* 'a hidden burial', that is, to waste the seed which Allah Most High had prepared for procreation is like infanticide and burying the child alive. The result is the same: the only difference is that it is not buried alive openly and hence it has been called hidden (vol.iii, p. 518). There is a *hadith* in the *Bukhari Sharif* to the effect that when the Companions, on account of their zest of engaging in devotions and in order to avoid sins and for remaining aloof from relations, expressed the desire to get themselves castrated, the Holy Prophet (*Sallallaho alaihe wa sallam*!) did not allow them and adduced the Quranic verse, 'O ye who believe: Forbid not the good things which Allah hath made lawful for you, and transgress not. Lo! Allah loveth not transgressors' (V: 87), in proof.
>
> Even as the Holy Prophet (*Sallallaho Alaihe wa sallam*!) has, by this verse, determined castration to be unlawful, it is obvious that the termination of propagation under the family planning scheme will also be included under this order (*'Umadat al-Qari Sharh-e Sahih-e Bukhari*, vol. ii, p. 72). Finis.[11]

And yet when it is suggested that Islam is opposed to, or is used to oppose family planning, the secularists jump and charge, 'That is just communalist propaganda of the Hindu fundamentalists!'

Slave women

Or take an even more regressive institution—slavery. It was common in seventh-century Arabia. It was one of the hallmarks of Islamic rule in India.[12] The rights of the master

---

11. On the three preceding fatwas on birth control, *Fatawa-i-Raihimiyyah*, Volume II, pp. 192–95; Volume III, pp. 199–200.

12. K.S. Lal, *Muslim Slave System in Medieval India*, Aditya Prakashan, New Delhi, 1994.

over his slaves form an important part of shariah. The use one may make of concubines and slave women forms the subject of Hadis. Slavery, retaining concubines—all these things have Allah's approval in the Quran.

But that was 1,350 years ago. How do the ulema view the institution in this day and age?

As is customary on all questions, if there is something owning up to which would be somewhat dishonourable today the ulema maintain that it is a 'pre-Islamic institution,' and that it is Islam which humanized it and formed dykes to prevent its misuse. When questions are asked about the degrading and wholly inequitable place of women in the shariah, the reply is that actually the shariah improved the position of women from what it was in pre-Islamic Arabia. That it froze it there is sought to be covered, to pluck Lenin's phrase, with a shroud of angry words. That women were not as oppressed in non-Islamic societies—India before Islamic rule, for instance—that they may not have been as oppressed even in pre-Islamic Arabia—recall, as Ram Swarup observes, the position of Khadija herself; she was a substantial trader in her own right, among whose employees was the Prophet himself before he married her[13]—all such considerations are sought to be dismissed as the propaganda of Islam-baiters.

So also with slavery. It was a pre-Islamic institution, observe the ulema. Islam humanized it. Islam exhorted believers to treat their slaves well. It made the manumission of slaves an act that earns the believer merit with Allah, they stress. They list examples of Muslim eminences who freed slaves: 'The Holy Prophet himself freed 63 slaves,' the *Fatawa-i-Rahimiyyah* points out, 'Hazrat Abu Bakr freed 63; Abdur Rahman b. Auf, 30,000; Hakim b. Huzam, 100; Hazrat

---

13. Ram Swarup, *Woman in Islam,* Voice of India, New Delhi, 1994, pp. 2–3.

Abbas, 70; Hazrat Uthman used to manumit one slave every Friday and would say that he would free any slave who offered prayers with awfulness and humility; Hazrat Ayesha freed 69 salves; Abdullah b. Umar freed 100; and Hazrat Zul Kilah Himayari manumitted 8000 in one day only.' Assume the figures to be true. Quite apart from the fact that before they could have been set free, the slaves had been taken, kept and used as slaves, how do these paltry numbers compare with the hordes who were enslaved in the name of Islam in countries such as India, the hugeness of whose number Islamic historians used to hold up as a mark of Islam's might, indeed as proof of its being Allah's anointed religion? That is not the sort of question which is taken up by the ulema these days.

Having pasted the responsibility for the institution of slavery on to pre-Islamic times and having granted the credit for humanizing the institution to Islam, the ulema take up the remaining queries:

(2) A slave woman is lawful for her master without nikah ceremony. Why? What is the wisdom in it?
(3) Can one own a slave woman in the present times or not?
(4) If a Muslim wishes to have a female slave, is it necessary for her to be a Muslim, or can he have a non-Muslim one also?
(5) How many woman slaves were owned (by one man) in old times and how many can be owned now?
(6) Is purdah necessary for a woman slave or not? What is the reason if it is necessary, and why so if it is not?
(7) Are the woman slave's children free or slaves?
(8) Do the woman slave and her children inherit their master's wealth or not?

The ulema begin by first stamping on the querist for

seeking to inquire into the wisdom of the rule of shariah that a man may bed a slave woman without marrying her. They say:

> It is necessary for the Muslims to know the legal regulation about every affair but not necessary to know the wisdom and expediency of such regulation, for to know its wisdom is not the work of every person. Hence it is wrong to be after knowing the wisdom of every matter. To make action dependent on knowing the wisdom is contumacy and to consider the matter, on not knowing its wisdom, as against wisdom and expediency is deviation (from virtue). If one fails to understand the wisdom of certain matter, one should consider it the fault of his perception, for a legal regulation is never contrary to wisdom—the fault is in one's own understanding. Once it rained, at which a saintly person exclaimed: 'O God! What an opportune rain it is !' From the Invisible Realm a Voice said, 'Tell Us when did We cause an inopportune rain?' The saintly man heard this Voice. He thought that he had committed an affront in respect of God, and with this realisation he fainted. In short, a religious legal regulation is never devoid of expediency. A slave-girl is lawful for her master without marriage—this, too, is full of expediency and wisdom. What can we understand? The Quran has decided for us: 'And of knowledge ye have been vouchsafed but little' (*Surah* XV, *Bani Israel*: 85).

Having made the general point, they turn helpful and explain the wisdom of the rule. It turns out that the freedom given to the master to bed the slave women without going through the trouble of marrying them is something which actually *benefits the slave women*! This is how they put the point:

> If the legislator (pbuh.!) had prescribed marriage as necessary for the lawfulness of coition with slave women, the latter themselves would have faced great difficulties. It is stated in the glorious Quran that the Most High Allah intends facility for you and does not wish to put you to hardship and trouble: 'Allah

desireth for you ease; He desireth not hardship for you' (II: 185). May it be remembered that the prescription in the religious law of a slave woman's being lawful for her master is not with a bad intent and purpose; on the contrary, it is due to wishing well for the slave woman and for social and cultural good.

The point is fortified by that hoary principle of Islamic jurisprudence, qiyas, reasoning by analogy. The ulema set out the analogy—which will seem striking to the reader for reasons other than the ones which the ulema had in mind:

> A slave woman does not need marriage for the reason that the Shariah has made the possession of a slave woman the substitute of marriage-ceremony and the legal permit for coition with her. Even as the establishment of the marriage contract through 'affirmation and consent' (*ijah wa qubul*) and the obtaining of the right of reaping advantage (the right of sexual congress with wife) are merely due to legal credence, the gaining of the right of enjoyment by reason of possessing a slave woman is also due to legal credence. Hence there remains no scope for doubt and suspicion, legally and rationally, in its being permissible.
>
> *Fatawa -i- Rahimiyyah*
>
> It will not be out of place to clarify that the forms of credence are different for different things. For example, slaughtering with the recitation: *Bismillah, Allah-o Akbar*—(In the name of Allah, Allah is greatest)—is a necessary condition for the lawfulness of the meat of the goats, other animals and birds; without such slaughtering it is not lawful, whereas there is no such condition (of slaughtering) for the fish to be lawful which can be eaten without slaughtering. To be in possession of a fish and to be its owner is a substitute for its slaughter, though both the kinds of animals are animate, the condition of slaughter applies to one and not to the other. Then, if marriage be a condition for a free woman and not for a slave-woman—to possess whom may be considered equivalent to marriage—what is contrary to reason in it?

> Now the question why an owned slave-woman is lawful without marriage, why there is no condition of 'affirming and consent' and marriage in her case. The answer, firstly, is that it is not required at all. That is, there is 'affirming and consent' in marriage (*nikah*) for the reason that a particular type of benefit to which one has no right one may obtain the right thereof legally. In the case in question when one becomes owner, through purchase and ownership, of the whole slave-woman and all rights concerning her, one has also become owner of the benefit which is obtained through marriage. So, now marriage is absolutely superfluous and unnecessary. Secondly, the divine directive regarding marriage is: 'So that ye seek them with your wealth' (IV: 24), i.e, in consideration of the women's honour the Divine Book has stipulated that they should be offered some wealth which is called 'dower-money' (*mahr*). Now, if a slave-girl is married to another man, this money (*mahr*) will be taken by the slave-girl's owner; but if the slave-girl is married to her own master, the question would be: Who will offer the dower-money and who will receive it? A slave-girl, as long as she is a slave, remains deprived of the right of property; she cannot be owner of anything. Whatever she has got belongs to her master. Now, should she take dower-money from the master and return it to him, and should the master be the payer as well as the payee? This is a joke of sorts; it cannot be a canon of law and regulation.

And there is the reason, believe it or not, of the moral needs of the slave woman! If the master were not allowed to bed slave women without marrying them, the ulema explain, the slave women would be at a great disadvantage. Being slaves the women will have difficulty in finding husbands; not having husbands they will commit lechery and debauchery. Hence the rule *to help them*—that their master can bed them without marrying them! As the ulema put it:

> There were in it other difficulties as well on account of which the condition of marriage was unwise; for instance, the slave-girl is not equal in status to a free woman and as such it would be difficult for her to have a husband which could result in lechery, called 'an abomination' and 'debauchery' by Allah's Book, repugnant to God and the worst of habits. Hence the Shariah proposed this form which, though, as it is, is not like marriage but, by reason of its result, creates in it the virtue of marriage, because after the slave-girl's bearing a child the owner's ownership becomes defective, that is, it is then not permissible to sell her. She then becomes the mother of her master's children, a mistress of the house and as good as the owner's wife; she will become free after her master's death; she cannot be given to the heirs nor can she be sold.

In their reckoning the difficulty is not in the institution of enslaving women but in the fact that these days slave girls are not easy to come by legally. The ulema say:

> It is difficult to come by slave-girls in the present times, for the conditions required for lawful slave-girls are difficult to obtain now, and hence one cannot have and keep a slave-girl. If the custom of slave-girls obtains anywhere, it is not reliable without legal inquiry and to cohabit with them without marriage is not permissible. 'Allamah Shami writes: 'In our times the slave women secured as booty are not lawful slave women and copulation with them is not permissible because it is certain that the division of the booty is not done as it ought to be done, and hence the rightful claimants' (the recipients of the 1/5 share—*khums*—and the rest of the warriors') rights are ignored (and thus *de jure* possession is not proved for any slave woman)' (*Shami*, vol. ii, p. 396). Lawful slave women are those who, having been captured in war and crusade (*jihad*), may have been included in the booty, and the *amir*, that is the Caliph of the Muslims or his vicegerent, after having brought them from the territory of war (*daru'l-harb*) to the

> land of Islam (*daru'l-Islam*), may have distributed them according to the law of the Shariah. Prior to her being brought to the land of Islam and distribution by the *amir*, the slave woman is not lawful for anyone, although the *imam* or the cornmander-in-chief may have announced that the captor of a slave woman will be her master, yet she shall not be lawful for the captor and victor before bringing her to the land of Islam. Where do these laws obtain anywhere in the period? According to the Islamic law of holy war the rule is that 1/5 part of wealth captured as booty from the enemy should be set aside to be given to the needy and the indigent like orphans and widows and the remaining four parts should be divided among the victorious soldiers; as long as the booty is not brought to the country, that is, the land of Islam, its division is not valid, and so long as it is not divided, it is joint property on which all have a claim; however, after the *amir* has divided it, the share of each will be lawful for the recipient. Even as a girl becomes lawful for the man with whom her guardian marries her and not before marriage, the *amir* is the slave woman's guardian and whomever he makes her master for him she becomes lawful with certain conditions. If the master then sells her or gifts her away to anyone, she becomes lawful for the buyer or the recipient of the gift, as the case may be. Similarly, if a slave woman has continued being transferred from one inheritor to another she is even now a legal slave woman and the owner can keep her. But where is found such a slave woman today? Apparently such slave woman does not exist in the present times at least.

That is the lament, not the institution of enslaving women.

The ulema set out other points of law also in regard to slave women:

> A slave-girl of any race and any religion can be owned but coition is permissible with only that who is a Muslim or a scripturary (Jew or Christian); copulation with a polytheist, i.e., an idol-worshipping slave-girl is not permissible.

> One may, as per his strength and status, keep as many legal slave-girls as he likes, for there is no restriction on number, but the rules for having slave-girls are very delicate and they should be kept in mind. For example, if one has copulated with a slave-girl, then it is not permissible to have sexual relations with her near relatives (like sister, mother's sister, father's sister, sister's daughter, brothers' daughter, etc.), although such related women be his property; sexual congress with them is as impermissible as in the case of marriage.
>
> Strict veiling, as in case of free women, has not been prescribed for slave women for whom it is necessary to serve her master; she has to perform domestic and out-door chores, and hence the Shariah has not enjoined upon her, like free women, to observe purdah.
>
> A slave woman's progeny from her master's seed shall be deemed free (*Al-Jauharatun' Nayyarah*, vol. ii, p. 188).
>
> A slave woman does not become heir to her master's property, but the master's children (begot through her) shall be heirs.[14]

And all this in volumes published in the 1980s! In volumes which, as we have seen, Ali Mian and others hail for the erudition and guidance they contain!

The schizophrenia

Notice the schizophrenia. On the one hand we are told day in and day out that no religion has placed as high a value on learning as Islam—how many times we are reminded of the Prophet's saying that one must seek knowledge wherever it is to be found, travelling even to China if necessary. On the

14. On the foregoing fatwa, *Fatawa-i-Rahimiyyah*, Volume I, pp. 40–47.

other hand, we have the ulema stamping out every bud of rationalism, scotching every inclination to acquire modern education. We are told day in day out that Islam is the one religion which is most open to science, which embraces technology and change. On the other hand there is the insistence on taqlid, there is the most vehement denunciation of innovation, of thinking for oneself, there is, as we have seen, the premise that the glory of Islam consists in having science bend to it, that the duty of Muslim thinkers is to ensure that whenever it departs from the notions which Islamic thinkers, in particular the Prophet had put forth 1,350 years ago, it retraces its steps and accepts the Islamic notions. We are reminded day in and day out of the achievements of Avicenna (Ibn Sina) and Al Ghazzali. But we are not told why there has been so little science in the Islamic world since Avicenna. Nor are we told that the one achievement of Al Ghazzali which has lasted is that he killed off all independent, rational inquiry within Islam—specially about Islam itself.

On the one hand we have the claim that no religion has given as high a status to women, no religion has done as much for their liberation and well-being as Islam. And on the other we are given expositions on how the permission for a Muslim male to keep as many slave women as he can afford, on how the permission for him to bed them without marrying them are actually rules to benefit the women.

The ulema do not see the schizophrenia. The lay Muslim knows that he better not see it. The secularist insists that no one else see it.

Proximate reasons

The ulema are not just anti-change. They are antediluvian. With them the question whether Satan can take on the appearance of the Prophet; the question whether the dead shall rise from their graves naked or in a shroud; the question of the exact amount of time left till the Day of Judgement; the question whether the sun which shall rise on the Day of Judgement shall be the same as our day-to-day sun; the question whether angels take possession of the souls of men and Allah of the souls of animals; the question whether the heavens exist; the question whether a soul is made 2,000 years before the body; the question whether the interrogation in the grave of a Muslim shall be conducted in Arabic or Syriac—these and similar questions are live issues. They are issues on which enormous amounts of scholarship is expended. They are issues over which grave controversies arise.[15]

What explains this mindset? Is there a way out?

The proximate explanation of course is the world in which the ulema are weaned—the closed, medieval world of the 'Centres of Islamic Learning'. These centres prepare them for the past. They prepare them for the Arabia of the past. They prepare them for continuing, spreading, enforcing in India what they have been taught was Islam in the Arabia of the past.

To this day the syllabus of most of them is almost entirely based on the *Dars-i-Nizami*—the syllabus devised by Mulla Nizamuddin in the early years of the eighteenth century. Arabic language, cantillation, Arabic literature, *Tafsir*— exegesis of the Quran, Hadis, *Fiqh*, Islamic religious philosophy, Arabic poetry and prose, etc.—are the subjects which the students learn for six to ten years.

At the trend-setting institution, the Dar al-Ulum, Deoband, the founders had from the beginning reduced even further

---

15. On the language of interrogation in the grave, *Fatawa-i-Rahimiyyah*, Volume I, p. 16. On the rest, *Fatawa-i-Rizvia*, Volume XI, pp. 17, 18, 20–21, 99. Scores and scores of examples can be given to illustrate the point.

the residual readings on logic and philosophy which were found in *Dars-i-Nizami*—Maulana Rashid Ahmad Gangohi pronounced these subjects to be 'useless', indeed to be subjects the pursuit of which led one into the snares of heresy and ratiocination; the institution had been set up in a sense to counter what the ulema considered was the baneful tilt towards analysis and examination which had crept in, it was set up to carry forward Shah Waliullah's vision—of relying primarily on the Quran and Hadis. But even that was only true in a restricted sense—in that everything was made to revolve around and be traced back to the Quran and Hadis: there was not a trace in the curricula or in the products of that robustness and independence which, howsoever repugnant one may find his views to be, one finds in Shah Waliullah. More than that, Deoband has throughout persisted in its hostility to both—rational disciplines in general, and to empirical sciences in particular; to everything, that is, which might lead its wards to think for themselves.

The discourse that Maulana Nanautavi gave in 1873 setting out the reasons why the Dar al-Ulum was going to keep modern sciences out is still regarded as all that needs to be said on the matter: that because education in modern sciences is growing in any case with the establishment of government schools at an unprecedented scale; that because traditional, religious sciences are the ones which have fallen into neglect; that because the mental training which a student will acquire in learning these latter subjects will enable him to learn modern sciences swiftly should he choose later on to pursue them—Deoband shall consciously concentrate on 'religious sciences'.[16] 'There is no arrangement here at all for

16. For the text of the address, Sayyid Mahboob Rizvi, *History of the Dar al-Ulum, Deoband*, Idara-e Ihtemam, Dar al-Ulum, Deoband, 1980, Volume I, pp. 130–32; also Volume II, pp. 211–13. Writing over a hundred years later,

the teaching of the worldly science,' Nanautavi reiterated two years later. 'The answer (to the objection that these subjects are missing) firstly is that there ought to be a treatment of the disease. To take medicine for a disease which is not there is useless. The crack in the wall should be filled in; it is necessary to fill the kiln. What is it but foolishness to be anxious about the brick that has not fallen down? Of what earthly use are the government schools? If the profane sciences are not being taught there, what else is done?'[17]

The disease, the crack in the wall, the brick which has fallen into neglect—this is the neglect of 'religious sciences'. The revival, indeed survival of the community depends on training students in these 'sciences'—those were the diagnosis and prescription a century ago; they remain so today. And commentators wail over the lack of modern education among Muslims!

The effect that the exclusive focus on such subjects has is compounded by the fact that the subjects are taught through books written hundreds of years ago. A survey by the Khuda Bakhsh Oriental Public Library of books in use in the madrasahs turned up just one solitary book written in the twentieth century. The other eighty had all been written from a hundred to twelve hundred years ago. Thus when we hear that 'Jurisprudence' and 'Principles of Jurisprudence' are being taught, for instance, we should remember first that the jurisprudence in question is just 'Islamic jurisprudence'—the graduate from this system is certain to be wholly

---

the official historian of the Dar al-Ulum refers to the discourse as 'a very crucial and momentous address in which the necessity and significance of the establishment of the Dar ul-Ulum and its curriculum have been discussed with great perspicaciousness and insight....', See, *History of the Dar al-Ulum, Deoband,* op. cit, Volume I, p. 130.

17. *History of the Dar al-Ulum, Deoband,* op. cit., Volume II, p. 213.

ignorant of modern developments in law outside 'Islamic jurisprudence'; second, that even in regard to 'Islamic jurisprudence' he is more than likely to be ignorant of modern developments in this jurisprudence even in Islamic countries—for the books that are used for instructing him date from four hundred to a thousand years ago.

Logic and philosophy too have seen substantial developments in the last three hundred years. *Mantiq wa Falsafa* is certainly a subject in several of the 'Centres of Islamic Learning'. But, as a glance at the books being used for instruction in it will show, the graduate is certain to be wholly ignorant of developments in Western philosophy, of the results of the application of new analytical tools in these disciplines, of the developments which have occurred in these fields because of association with other disciplines—mathematics and the rest, and most of all of the developments which have occurred in them because of the interface with technology—the effects of logic and control systems on each other, for instance. As in the case of jurisprudence, so also in logic and philosophy—learning at these 'Centres of Islamic Learning' consists in mugging up and reproducing books written 150 to 750 years ago, and those too only by Muslim authors. And on top of this is the fact that taqlid—strict adherence to things written by the learned—has been the order of the day since Al-Ghazzali (AD 1058–1111); and then there is the fact that the doors of Ijtihad, of interpreting the texts, were formally closed a thousand years ago—on the ground that all points had already been clarified and that, in any case, the levels of piety had fallen so low that there were no men left who were qualified enough to exercise the right to interpret the texts; and then, as we have seen, there is the heavy hand with which the ulema come down on the slightest hint of bid'at, of innovation. The teaching of *Mantiq wa Falsafa*, of logic and philosophy, is thus not what a reader trained in the Western system might assume it to be—a device to equip the student to think for himself. On the contrary, it is yet another device for deepening the grooves along which alone the mind must move.

Nor should the presence of 'modern' subjects in the curricula of a few of the institutions mislead one. For instance, 'mathematics' is taught. But what is taught is hardly 'mathematics'—instruction is confined to the simplest arithmetical operations, those needed, for instance, for determining the shares of heirs in an estate.

And there is the deep predilection. To take an example, among the subjects which are taught in the third year of the eight-year course at Dar al-Ulum at Deoband is 'Contemporary Subjects'. This includes *Tarikh-e Hind*, the History of India, '*from the regime of Sultan Mahmud Ghaznavi till A.D. 1947*', specifies the official account of Deoband. The second head is *Tarikh-e Islam*, the History of Islam, which includes histories of the first rightly guided Caliphs, the Umayyad and Abbassid dynasties, and the history of the Turkish sultans. The third component is 'Municipalities (Elementary Civics)'. Then comes geography. This is divided in two parts: 'Geography of the Arab peninsula and other Islamic countries', and 'World geography (regionwise)'.

Is an institution the Indian history course of which covers only the period from the raids of Mahmud Ghaznavi to 1947, the geography course of which focuses on the Arabian peninsula, an institution of and for India?

The methods of instruction too remain primitive: rote, regurgitation, reproduction. In fact until just twenty years ago, instruction was not even subject-wise but book-wise: it was only in 1971 that teaching at Deoband came to be classified by subjects rather than by books.

The sole purpose for which the institutions strive, the entire objective of the syllabi in them is the furtherance of, and evangelization for Islam. The institutions continue to be closely connected with tabligh—formally the movement to 'spread the Word'. in fact the movement to secure converts and to exorcise all syncretistic practices. In several institutions the graduate having completed his studies must spend a certain time—often up to two years—in tabligh work before he gets his degree. 'Refutation' of the other 'false' religions is of course an element of tabligh. From the early decades of the twentieth century Sanskrit began to be taught for this purpose in Deoband, for instance, and Sanskrit teachers were appointed in the Department of Preaching ![18]

As the ulema have been weaned on this kind of instruction for centuries, as the 'Centres of Learning' have been producing graduates who in turn have been becoming teachers in the same centres of learning for 150 years, an institutional inertia has by now set in. The controllers of these institutions, the teachers in them fight back every proposal for changing the syllabus because they themselves would be put out of eminence, if not out of jobs, were the syllabus to be changed in any real sense.

Observer after observer surveying the evolution of these

---

18. As usual the responsibility is put on the other person! The official history of Deoband says that this had to be done to counter the baneful activities of the Arya Samaj! The Kashi Vishwanath temple had to be destroyed because Aurangzeb heard that a Rajput princess had been raped! India had to be partitioned because Muslims were persecuted under the Congress ministries in 1937! That conversion is an essential element of Islam, predating Arya Samaj by 1,250 years, that temples and idols were being smashed and converted into mosques long before Aurangzeb—from the Prophet's takeover of the Kaba itself—that no Muslim historian mentions the yarn about the rape of the Rajput princess, that the movement for separation pre-dated the Congress ministries by half a century, that the accounts of atrocities on Muslims, like the Pirpur Report, have been shown up to be wholesale and deliberate concoctions—makes no difference to the charge. The responsibility is always that of the infidel!

institutions remarks on the doggedness with which the institutions have resisted change. Here is Professor Mujeeb:

> In course of time it became apparent that the absence of coordination of any kind between religious and secular education was creating a deep rift in the Indian Muslim community. Some of the *'ulama* felt the need of an institution where both types of education could be imparted side by side. To give practical shape to this idea, the *Majlis-i-Nadwah-al'*ulama was constituted in 1892, and the Dar-al 'Ulama established two years later. But even those *'ulama* who had sponsored the idea could not, when the time came, agree to providing for education in English and other secular subjects in the *Nadwah.* They succeeded in burking the issue for a number of years, agreeing, when cornered, to introduce a revised syllabus, but later evading it. Even in 1905, when Maulana Shibli Nu'mani became the Education Secretary, and ordered the teaching of English, nothing was done for three years. The *'ulama* had, in fact, conscientious scruples about spending money collected for religious education on the teaching of secular subjects. In 1908, the U.P. Government sanctioned a grant-in-aid for the provision of secular education in the *Nadwah,* and English began to be taught up to the matriculation standard. In the same year, Hindi and Sanskrit were also introduced, and a pandit was appointed to teach them. But after a few years, when Maulana Shibli left the *Nadwah,* the classes were closed. Since then, the syllabus has been revised several times and is now about as near the *Dars-i-Nizami* as it was in the beginning.

M. Mujeeb

It is apparent from a glance at the syllabus during all the five periods that there was no material change in the approach to education, except that during the last two periods the syllabus was expanded to include texts published later, and give the student a wider knowledge of the old subjects. As the chances of the graduates from the *madrasahs* getting employment under the government diminished rapidly, the expansion of the syllabus may have been due to a desire to make education itself more worthwhile. The addition of *munazirah* (theological disputation) to the subjects in the fifth period shows that orthodoxy was on the defensive, but there is hardly any change that indicates awareness of contemporary conditions. Orthodoxy protected itself by seeking isolation from the outside world, and by attempting to keep those who recognized its prerogatives aloof from contemporary knowledge. It inculcated, through its education, a suspicion and supercilious disdain for systems of ideas based on the relativity of truth, and refused to consider the implications of scientific discoveries and technical inventions.[19]

And here is Professor Aziz Ahmad:

The manifesto of the Nadwat al-'ulama' aimed at the advancement of theological studies, the development of a consensus of theological opinion, the minimization of differences in the theological views, the rehabilitation of ethics and a general reform of Muslim society, without any involvement in politics. Rashid Rida was invited to visit the school, and since then it remained sensitive to the intellectual speculations of the *al-Manar* group in Egypt. The school was conceived as having a middle position between the extreme conservatism of Deoband and the modernity of Aligarh, but soon it developed conservative contours of its own and its product became generally indistinguishable from that of Deoband in theological and intellectual outlook.[20]

Indeed the tug of the same conservatism has drowned all 'modernity' out of Sir Syed's child, the Aligarh Muslim University, the same tug has drowned it in the Jamia Millia Islamia. As far as religion is concerned, as far as 'issues affecting

19. M. Mujeeb, *The Indian Muslims*, George Allen and Unwin, London, 1969, pp. 409–10.

20. Aziz Ahmad, *An Intellectual History of Islam in India, Islamic Surveys*, VII. Edinburgh University Press, 1969, p. 59.

Muslims' are concerned these institutions toe more or less the same line as the seminaries. The few in them who would look at these issues from either a national or a modern perspective are perpetually set upon. By now they are few, they are isolated, they are thoroughly on the defensive.

By contrast the mosques, madrasahs, maktabs, seminaries, 'Centres of Islamic Learning' constitute a vast and intricately interlinked network. The numbers themselves are vast: by Maulana Wahiduddin's reckoning there are about 350,000 mosques in India; a large proportion of them have madrasahs attached to them; there are about a thousand seminaries; tabligh centres too number in the thousands.

The seminaries and centres spawn many of their kind: the official history of the Deoband Dar al-Ulum estimates that Deoband by itself has established close to 9,000 schools in different parts of the country. And these numerous institutions are interlinked. The training, the texts which the functionaries are liable to need, for instance, the casebooks on law, the volumes of fatwas—the doctrine, the line on an issue, all come from the seminaries. The products of these 'Centres of Islamic Learning' form the core of organizations such as Jamaat-i-Islami and Jamiat-ul-Ulama, as well as of revivalist movements such as the Tablighi Jamaat. They are the ones who directly man and guide, train and influence those who man madrasahs and mosques, as well as those who function as lay preachers.

The ulema, their institutions, their wards thus form a vast but closed circle, a circle looking inwards, a circle looking to the past, a circle looking to what they have been taught a particular region in the Middle East was in the past.

But it is not just that the ulema and their wards form a closed, inward-looking group. They form a self-perpetuating, self-multiplying group. One of the consequences of the syllabus which is followed, of the methods of instruction which are adopted, and even more of the atmosphere in which these institutions are enveloped, is that the products of these institutions are completely unfit to secure jobs in any modern occupation. All they can do is to be propagandists, and to go back to work in these very 'centres of learning'. And all they can do there is to produce more of their type. The consequences are lethal.

The group goes on reproducing and enlarging itself, but in addition it is a group which is constantly assailed by fears that changes taking place in the rest of the world are doing it out of business. Thus, even as it is a very strong group in terms of the hold it has on the Muslims, it is a frightened and insecure group vis-à-vis time and the rest of the world. It is this insecurity which it sows and multiplies in the entire Muslim community, and that insecurity in turn has grave consequences for the country at large.

But none of this can be talked about. Were the fears which are fanned among Muslims to be attributed to the true causes—that is, to the strength and orientation of the fundamentalists, and even more so, as we shall see, to the basic premises of Islam—the secularists are bound to pounce on the explanation as being nothing but another miasma conjured by the communalists.

Indeed, the weakness of society and of the state – which has been dressed up as secularism – has itself become another impediment to change. For instance, in most Islamic countries the old madrasah system has been replaced by modern educational institutions. Any suggestion that this should be done in India also is bound to be set upon with the charge that it is yet another device of the Hindus to swallow up Islam. With the growth of terrorist and sectarian violence in Pakistan, the Pakistan government announced in early 1995 that it would restrict and regulate foreign funds flowing to

'Centres of Islamic Learning', madrasahs, etc. There has been ample evidence in the past that rivalries among the patrons of these institutions—of Iran and Iraq during their ruinous war, for instance, of Kuwait, Saudi Arabia, etc., on one side and Iraq on the other during the Gulf crisis—led to the exacerbation of hostilities between fundamentalists and between sectarian groups within Pakistan. Quite clearly the same rival sources of patronage have had a good bit to do with escalating the Shia-Sunni violence in Pakistan today. Therefore the Pakistan government was entirely in the right to decide to regulate and restrict the flow of funds from foreign patrons to these institutions within Pakistan. Now, there is more than ample evidence of the manner in which the Rabita of Saudi Arabia, the ISI of Pakistan and other agencies have been patronizing these so-called centres of Islamic learning within India. Intelligence reports allude to the links and the uses to which they have been put. But should an effort or law be made to restrict and regulate the flow of foreign funds to these institutions, the secularists are bound to yell, 'Foul'. And the state is bound to retreat.

We thus have a vast network, a strongly interlinked network extending over thousands of institutions throughout India. The products of this system are not equipped to face the modern world. In fact their training makes them unfit for jobs in modern professions. They are equipped only for one purpose and that is to produce persons in their own mould for the same network. Second, not only is this a self-perpetuating group, the rest of society and the state have developed an entire ideology which keeps them from even an attempt to open up this group to modernization. How can the result be any other than that this powerful group spreads antediluvian notions in the entire Muslim community?

But it is not just a question of the network and its syllabus.

It is not a malaise that can be overcome just by the remedy which is so often proffered—namely, that the syllabus of these institutions should be 'modernized'.

The proposal is a non-starter to begin with. Little has come of such proposals in the past, little is liable to come of them now. The ulema have successfully resisted every effort to change the syllabus and content, and even more so the viewpoint for hundreds of years. And have those who peddle this nostrum of modernizing the syllabus ever tried to spell out what alternative syllabus they would propose which would be justifiable within the parameters of the ulema's Islam?

These considerations by themselves tell us that there can be little hope from this quarter. But the problem is a more basic one and no superficial 'modernization' of the syllabus, even if it were possible, can alleviate it.

It is to this point that we shall now turn.

Quran and Hadis

10

A fundamental difficulty

In 1989 the geopolitical world turned upside down—the communist states collapsed one after the other. For seventy years they had been held up as exemplars: of efficiency, of equity, of justice. Unemployment had been abolished in them, it was said. There was no divorce, no alcoholism—these were diseases of the ailing, about-to-collapse capitalist West, it was said. The environment was well cared for. A new man had been created. There was no crime. That is what we were fed, day in and day out.

The collapse of the communist states lifted the lid.

In India the falsehoods about those states had been propagated with the utmost vehemence. Communists and their fellow-travellers were everywhere in universities, and in the press. Anyone who raised a doubt about the conditions in those countries was traduced as a capitalist stooge, as an agent of the CIA. He was blacklisted—from the press, from academia.

One would assume that the collapse of the communist states, that the facts which became common knowledge about what life had been under that system would have occasioned a complete re-examination of what these journals and university departments had been pouring out. The newspapers and journals adopted the simplest solution: they just looked the other way. They just erased from memory the falsehoods they had been printing right till 1989; not once did they analyse what they had been purveying.

As for the facts which were now obvious—which were being printed all over the world, which any cub reporter and photographer could have verified for himself by visiting the countries—the newspapers and journals just ignored them. Though among the most numerous in the world, though among the freest, Indian papers published next to nothing of what became known about eastern Europe and the former Soviet Union.

Universities like the Jawaharlal Nehru University (JNU) went one better: they too ignored the facts that were now known to all, but they did not just forget what they had been teaching in the past. They continued it, as if nothing had happened. Years have passed. There has been no change in the syllabus, no change in the readings which the students are prescribed.

The consequence is obvious: teachers at the universities continue to produce clones of themselves, and the graduates enter the media, the civil services, the universities and continue to regurgitate the old 'analyses'.

And the causes are obvious too. The university professors select who shall be the new teachers in their departments. They set the examination papers, they examine the answer books—their preconceptions turn the students: to do well in the examinations the latter must mug up the texts which those professors esteem, they must judge events and policies through spectacles which the examiners approve. The teachers in turn have invested countless hours in that particular standpoint—not just hours, their entire careers have been built on that standpoint—the book or two they might have written, in the dozen odd articles they may have published they would have done little more than 'apply' that standpoint to this 'concrete situation' or that. Nor is it just the intellectual capital they have invested in those texts and that standpoint, there is enormous psychological investment too. They would have formed friendships, and broken them around the 'ideological issues' which had broken through over the years as they sought to fit the world and its events to that ideological bed.

So, that small, tight, closed world is their only world. Even when events as cataclysmic as the collapse of an entire system—their system—take place, they just go on reciting the old dogma, they just go on with the old subjects, the old textbooks.

That is the position in regard to universities which have been in existence for just a few decades, in regard to an ideology which had been in power for just seventy years. That is the position in universities and in papers and journals which function in an open society, a society in which they have to necessarily interact a good deal with the rest of society.

With this recent experience in mind, consider the world of the 'Centres of Islamic Learning'. An ideology which was in power for not seventy but a thousand years. An ideology which sanctioned not just verbal terrorism—as in the case the Indian Left—but physical terrorism. An ideology that enforced conformity not just by peer-group pressure—and even this can be potent enough: recall the conformity in the numerous, multifarious and free Indian papers—but in addition by pressure deployed by the state, and parastatal squads. Institutions in which the ulema selected who shall teach alongside them, who shall study, institutions in which they alone determined what shall be taught, through which texts. A network far, far more extensive, far, far better knit than the network of Leftist academics and journalists, and a network consisting of institutions which do not need even to interact with the rest of Indian society—which, for instance, can get the funds and 'inspiration' they may need in much greater measure from Saudi Arabia and Iran than from within India.

Is it any surprise then that when even departments at the JNU have not changed their syllabi and reading-lists, the ulema have successfully fought back every attempt to 'modernize' their eighteenth-century syllabi?

That is one point: those who say that the way out is to 'modernize the syllabus' of the madrasahs, etc., of the Dar al-Ulum at Deoband and the Nadwah at Lucknow do not reckon with even the threshold obstacle—institutional inertia.

But there is a much graver difficulty than this one—a difficulty which cannot be got over by 'modernizing the syllabus,' in fact a difficulty that strictly limits the extent to which the syllabus, the teaching methods, etc., can be 'modernized'.

Hindus, Christians and the rest

We bewail the way the ulema characterize kafirs, the non-believers—Christians, Jews, the Hindus in particular. But the Quran characterizes them no differently.

'They are the worst of creatures,' it proclaims. They shall be in hellfire, to dwell therein for ever, it proclaims (Quran, 98.6). It ascribes the most evil intentions to them.

They are the cause of 'tumult and oppression', it declares. They prevent access to the path of Allah, it declares. They deny Allah, it declares. It ordains slaughtering them as the lesser evil, because, it declares, 'Tumult and oppression are worse than slaughter.' 'Nor will they cease fighting you,' it warns the faithful, 'until they turn you back from your faith if they can' (Quran, 2.217). 'They but wish that you should reject Faith, as they do,' it declares, 'and thus be on the same footing (as them),'

> But take not friends
> From their ranks
> Until they flee
> In the way of God
> (From what is forbidden).
> But if they turn renegades,
> Seize them and slay them
> Wherever you find them;
> And (in any case) take
> No friends or helpers
> From their ranks.....
>
> (Quran, 4.89)

except those, it adds, who enter into a covenant with you, and give up their ways!

'The unbelievers spend their wealth to hinder (men) from the path of Allah,' the Quran warns, adding, 'and so they will continue to spend.'

'In the end they will have (only) regrets and sighs,' the Quran assures the believers. At length they will be overcome:

> And the unbelievers will be
> Gathered together to Hell;
> In order that Allah may separate
> The impure from the pure,
> Put the impure, one on another,
> Heap them together, and cast them
> Into Hell....
>
> (Quran, 8.36–37)

'Strongest among men in enmity to the believers,' the Quran warns, 'you will find the Jews and Pagans' (Quran, 5.85)—a warning that apologists and secularists can scarcely explain away. 'And nearest among them in love to the believers,' it says, 'will you find those who say, "We are Christians": because amongst these are men devoted to learning, and men who have renounced the world, and they are not arrogant' (Quran 5.85).

Sir Syed used to quote that last ayat frequently after the defeats of 1857. It is little help. For one thing, the ayat can scarcely be of any comfort to Hindus, nor to those who want to portray Islam as the religion of peace and tolerance, as the faith which respects all other faiths—for Hindus are among the 'pagans' covered by the very first words of the ayat. But even for Christians that ayat can provide little comfort. For the Quran warns:

> O ye who believe!
> Take not the Jews
> And the Christians
> For your friends and protectors:
> They are but friends and protectors
> To each other. And he
> Amongst you that turns to them
> (For friendship) is of them.
> Verily Allah guideth not
> A people unjust.
>
> (Quran, 5.54)

'Never will the Jews or the Christians be satisfied' with you, Allah warns the Muslims, 'unless you follow their form of religion.... Were you to follow their desires after the knowledge which has reached you, then would you find neither Protector nor Helper against Allah' (Quran, 2.120). They conceal the testimony they have from Allah, it declares (Quran, 2.140).

They have perverted the Message Allah sent them, the Quran declares, they have breached the Covenant (Quran,

5.14). They have perverted what Jesus himself told them, declares the Quran, for he told them to worship Allah, not him (Quran, 5.119). They are forever bent on deceit, it declares (Quran, 5.14). They falsely claim that earlier prophets were Jews or Christians when in fact all of them were Muslims (Quran, at several places, for instance, 2.140). They try to lead you astray (Quran, 3.69). They 'clothe Truth with falsehood, and conceal the Truth' (Quran, 3.70, 71).

Their very beliefs are blasphemy upon Allah, upon the Prophet. They 'blaspheme' Allah by saying that Christ is God (Quran, 4.171; 5.19, 75, 78; 9.30–31; 43.57–59, 63–64). They blaspheme Allah by saying that Jesus is the Son of God (Quran, 5.76; 9.30; 19.35)—and Allah's Curse is upon them for saying so (Quran, 9.30; 10.68–70; 4.171–72). They most certainly blaspheme Allah by saying He is, not one, but a Trinity (Quran, 4.171–72; 5.76–77).

They are 'contentious people' (Quran, 43.58). Christ was just an apostle, he was 'no more than a servant (of Allah)' (Quran, 5.78; 43.59).

The conclusion thus is inevitable: if they accept the Quran and its teaching and repudiate their falsified faith, well and good; otherwise, fight them you must as you must fight the other unbelievers, you must fight them until they are subdued, and acknowledge that they are subdued, declares, not some alim, but Allah Himself.

'Those who believe (in the Quran), and those who follow the Jewish (scriptures), and the Christians and the Sabians,' Allah declares, 'and who believe in Allah, and the Last Day, and work righteousness, shall have their reward with their Lord: on them shall be no fear, nor shall they grieve' (Quran 2.62; reiterated at 5.72). But if they do not own up to a belief in the Quran and its teachings, that is if they do not repudiate Christianity and become Muslims:

Fight those who believe not
In Allah nor the Last Day,
Nor hold that forbidden
Which has been forbidden
By Allah and His Apostle,
Nor acknowledge the Religion
Of Truth (even if they are)
Of the People of the Book,
Until they pay the *jizya*
With willing submission
And feel themselves subdued.

(Quran, 9.29)

That is not the command of Mufti Kifayatullah or Maulana Ahmad Riza Khan, but of Allah Himself.

And will they listen at last? On the contrary, declares Allah: the very fact that the Revelation has been sent to you, the Prophet and the believers, is going to make them even more obstinate in their blasphemous beliefs and in their opposition to you, He declares:

Say: 'O People of the Book!
You have no ground
To stand upon unless
You stand fast by the Law,
The Gospel, and all the revelation
That has come to you from Your Lord.'

But in fact:

It is the revelation
That comes to you from
Your Lord, that *increaseth* in most
Of them their obstinate
Rebellion and blasphemy.
But sorrow thou not
Over (these) people without Faith.

(Quran, 5.71)

The Christians are no better thus than the other non-believers, and the believers have no option but to fight them as they must fight the other non-believers. And that is Allah's reckoning, not that of some alim.

'If they were to get the better of you,' warns the Quran, 'they would behave to you as enemies, and stretch forth their hands and their tongues against you for evil; And they desire that you reject the Truth' (Quran, 60.2). Therefore, Allah reiterates, 'Take not My enemies and yours as friends, offering them (your) love even though they have rejected the Truth that has come to you, and have (on the contrary) driven out the Prophet and yourselves (from your homes) (simply) because you believe in Allah your Lord....' Do not take them as friends, 'holding secret converse of love (and friendship) with them: for I know full well all that you conceal and all that you reveal. And any of you that does this has strayed from the Straight Path' (Quran, 60.1). 'O, you who believe,' Allah warns again, 'Turn not (for friendship) to people on whom is the wrath of Allah. Of the Hereafter they are already in despair, just as the unbelievers are in despair about those (buried) in graves' (Quran, 60.13). What is it that believers seek in befriending unbelievers rather than believers?, Allah asks. 'Is it honour they seek among them?'— that is, they cannot get any spiritual advantage in any case from being friends with non-believers? Is it then some worldly advantage they seek?, Allah asks, and answers: 'Nay—all honour is with Allah' (Quran, 4.139). Thus, believers are certain to get nothing by being friends with non-believers except perdition in the Hereafter and dishonour in the world here.

We bewail at the way the ulema picture Hindus and the rest in the fatwas—that they are congenially and incorrigibly filthy. But is it just a fatwa or a *Durr-ul-Mukhtar* which declares that they are so?

The Quran declares,

> O, you who believe! Truly
> The pagans are unclean.....
>
> (Quran 9.28)

We look askance at the denunciations which were heaped on Muslims who sought peace for the soul of Lokmanya Tilak upon his death, on Muslims who thanked Allah for sparing the life of Gandhiji as he battled through his fast for Hindu-Muslim unity and who prayed that he live long, but it is the Quran which declares:

> It is not fitting
> For the Prophet and those
> Who believe, that they should
> Pray for forgiveness
> For pagans, even though
> They be of kin, after it is
> Clear to them that they
> Are companions of the Fire.
>
> (Quran, 9.113)

It is the Quran which declares of the true believers,

> Nor do they ever pray
> For any of them that dies,
> Nor stand at his grave;
> For they rejected Allah
> and His Apostle, and died
> In a state of perverse rebellion.
>
> (Quran, 9.84)

We look askance at the ulema as they heap scorn and worse at the gods and goddesses of Hindus. But it is the Quran which declares again and again that these gods of the pagans and polytheists are false, that they are nothing but 'fuel for Hell'—that is, they are things which raise further the torment to which the polytheists will be put in Hell:

> Verily you, (Unbelievers),
> And the (false) gods that
> You worship besides Allah,
> Are (but) fuel for Hell!
> To it will you (surely) come!
> If these had been gods,
> They would not have got there!
> But each one will abide therein.
> There, sobbing will be
> Their lot, nor will they
> There hear (aught else).
>
> (Quran, 21.98–100)

We are incredulous when Maulana Mohammed Ali declares, 'However pure Mr Gandhi's character may be, he must appear to me from the point of view of religion inferior to any Mussalman, even though he be without character.' But it is Allah Himself who declares to the believers,

> You are the best
> Of Peoples, evolved
> For mankind,
> Enjoining what is right
> Forbidding what is wrong,
> And believing in Allah.
> If only the People of the Book
> Had faith, it were best
> For them: among them
> Are some who have faith,
> But most of them
> Are perverted transgressors.
>
> (Quran, 3.110)

And poor Gandhiji wasn't even among the People of the

Book! We are incredulous when Maulana Ahmad Riza Khan declares that no good a kafir may do is acceptable to Allah. But it is Allah Himself who says of those 'as join gods with God'—that is polytheists—and Hindus are surely polytheists —

> The works
> Of such bear no fruit;
> In Fire shall they dwell.
>
> (Quran, 9.17)

And again:

> They!—
> Their works are fruitless
> In this world and in the Hereafter,
> And they will lose
> (All spiritual good).
>
> (Quran, 9.69)

And yet again:

> Do the Unbelievers think
> That they can take
> My servants as protectors
> Besides Me? Verily We
> Have prepared Hell
> For the Unbelievers
> For (their) entertainment.
> Say: 'Shall we tell you
> Of those who lose most
> in respect of their deeds?
> Those whose efforts have
> Been wasted in this life,
> While they thought that
> They were acquiring good
> By their works?'

They are those who deny
The Signs of their Lord
And the fact of their
Having to meet Him
(In the Hereafter): vain
Will be their works,
Nor shall We, on the Day
Of Judgement, give them
Any weight.

That is their reward,
Hell; because they rejected
Faith, And took My signs
And My Messengers
By way of jest.

(Quran. 18.102–06)

And then again:

Woe to each sinful
Dealer in Falsehoods:
He hears the Signs
of Allah rehearsed to him,
Yet is obstinate and lofty,
As if he had not
Heard them: then announce
To him a Penalty Grievous!
And when he learns
Something of Our Signs,

He takes them in jest:
For such there will be
A humiliating Penalty.
In front of them is
Hell: and of no profit
To them is anything
They may have earned,
Nor any protectors they
May have taken to themselves

Besides Allah: for them
Is a tremendous Penalty.

(Quran, 45.7–10)

And for the n'th time:

O' ye who believe!
If ye will aid
(The cause of) Allah,
He will aid you,
And plant your feet firmly.

But those who reject Allah,
For them is destruction,
And Allah will render
Their deeds astray
(From their mark).

That is because they
Hate the Revelation of Allah;
So He has made
Their deeds fruitless.

Do they not travel
Through the earth, and see
What was the End
Of those before them
(Who did evil)?
Allah brought utter destruction
On them, and similar
(Fates await) those who
Reject Allah.

That is because Allah
Is the Protector of those
Who believe, but
Those who reject Allah
Have no protector.

(Quran, 47.7–11)

Do we not have it on the authority of Aisha herself that when she asked the Prophet whether any of the good deeds that a relative of hers had done—feeding the poor, etc.—would be of any avail to him, the Prophet said, 'It would be of no avail to him as he did not ever say: "O my Lord, pardon my sins on the Day of resurrection"'?[1]

Is it not the Prophet who affirms that only the believers shall enter Paradise?[2]

Do the ulema then concoct anything on their own when they proclaim that no good a kafir does, that no good a Gandhi or a Ramakrishna Paramahamsa or a Raman Maharshi does is acceptable to God?

Are the ulema to be faulted for double standards, when it is Allah Himself who says:

> Lo! Those who love that slander should be spread concerning those who believe, theirs will be a painful punishment in the world and the Hereafter.
>
> (Quran, 24.19)

It is not some sundry alim but the Prophet who has declared, 'Allah will cover up the defects (faults) on the Day of Judgement of him who screens the faults of the others in this world.'[3] It is not some graduate of Deoband, it is the Prophet himself who says, 'He who sees something which should be kept hidden and concels it will be like one who has brought to life a girl buried alive.'[4]

---

1. *Sahih Muslim* Volume I, pp. 139–40; see also, ibid, pp. 18–19.

2. Ibid., Volume I, p. 37.

3. Imam Muslim in the chapter, 'Concealing faults of the Muslims', in *Riyad as-Salihin,* Volume I, 1988 edition, Kazi Publications, Lahore, pp. 174–75.

4. *Sunan Abu Dawud,* Kitab Bhavan, New Delhi 1993, Volume III, pp. 1362–63. Reproducing the Hadis under the heading 'Concealing the faults of a Muslim', the editor/translator says, 'It means that if a Muslim sees the fault of a Muslim, he should conceal it. He will be rewarded for it by Allah.' Ibid., Volume III, pp. 1362–63.

It is not some sundry alim but the Prophet who declares that in contrast to the Muslim the Kafir is congenitally avaricious: 'A believer eats in one intestine (if satisfied with a little food), and a *Kafir* or a hypocrite eats in seven intestines (eats too much).'[5] It is not from some outdated, easily replaceable textbook that the rule that a Muslim shall not be killed for killing a Kafir originates, it originates from the Prophet himself.[6]

Is it not the Prophet himself who says that polytheism is the gravest sin, that it is worse than killing your child, that it is worse than committing adultery with the wife of your neighbour?[7] As the punishment for the latter itself is death by stoning, what is the appropriate punishment for a sin so much greater than it?

We are surprised at the unabashedness with which the ulema deploy double standards as between believers and non-believers, at the way they declare non-believers to be unclean and believers to be clean—dead or alive; at the way they shout and scream at even the slightest obstruction in what they say are their religious practices and simultaneously declare that it is but right for the rulers to expel non-believers from Arabia—it is not just right but a duty for rulers of Islamic states to prohibit practices associated with religions other than Islam; at the certainty with which they insist that the punishment of a sinning Muslim shall only be temporary while every non-believer shall roast in Hell eternally.

But it is not some sundry alim, it is Allah who declares non-believers to be inherently unclean, it is the Prophet who declares that a Muslim is never defiled.[8] It is not some sundry

5. *Sahih al-Bukhari*, Volume I, p. 232.

6. For instance, *Sahih al-Bukhari*, Volume IX, pp. 37–38.

7. *Sahih Muslim*, Volume I, pp. 50–55. Also *Sahih al-Bukhari*, Volume VI, pp. 269–70.

8. For instance, *Sahih Muslim*, Volume I, pp. 203–04.

alim, it is Allah who declares that Islam must spread everywhere, it is the Prophet who declares that all polytheists must be expelled from Arabia.[9] It is the Prophet who certifies that Allah shall create room in Paradise for every Muslim by evicting such Christians or Jews as may have found place there and dispatching them to Hell: it is he who declares, 'When it will be the Day of Resurrection Allah would deliver to every Muslim a Jew or a Christian and say: that is your rescue from Hell-fire;' it is the Prophet who declares, 'No Muslim would die but Allah would admit in his stead a Jew or a Christian in Hell-fire;' it is the Prophet who declares, 'There would come people amongst the Muslims on the Day of Resurrection with sins as heavy as a mountain, and Allah would forgive them and He would place in their stead the Jews and the Christians.'[10]

We were put off by the fatwas of the ulema in which they admonish the Muslim to make sure to put down the kafir, even in so small a matter as the ordinary greetings which are exchanged when we chance to meet each other. But it is not some ordinary alim, it is the Prophet who commands, 'Do not salute the Jews and Christians before they salute you and when you meet anyone of them on the roads, force him to go to the narrowest part of it.'[11]

Nor is the fact that these unbelievers reject the Truth, that they put their faith in false gods accidental. Allah says that He has Himself led them astray. No one—no believer, no prophet, not even *the* Prophet—can help them. In fact, Allah says, He has deliberately put them—complete with their obstinate unbelief, their scheming and treachery—in the way of the believers so as to test the latter. There can be

---

9. For instance, *Sunan Abu Dawud*, Volume II, pp. 860–61.

10. For instance, *Sahih Muslim*, Volume IV, p. 1444.

11. *Riyad as-Salihin*, Volume I, p. 531.

only one operational conclusion from that: the believers will have to fight them, they must fight them—till the unbelievers submit and thereby Islam reigns, or they are exterminated and thereby Islam reigns.

'Would you guide those, whom Allah has thrown out of the way?,' Allah asks. 'For those whom Allah has thrown out of the Way, never shall you find the Way' (Quran, 4.88). 'And those whom Allah leaves to stray, no one can guide,' He proclaims again (Quran, 13.33).

And yet again:

It is he whom Allah guides,
That is on true guidance;
But he whom He leaves
Astray—for such wilt thou
Find no protector besides Him.
On the Day of Judgement
We shall gather them together,
Prone on their faces,
Blind, dumb, and deaf:

Their abode will be Hell:
Every time it shows abatement,
We shall increase for them
The fierceness of the Fire.
That is their recompense,
Because they reject Our signs.

(Quran, 17.07, 98)

And then again:

Say, 'I do but warn you
According to Revelation.'
But the deaf will not hear
The call, (even) when
They are warned!

(Quran, 21.45)

And yet again:

Or have they a god
Other than Allah?
Exalted is Allah
Far above the things
They associate with Him!
Were they to see
A piece of the sky
Falling (on them), they
Would (only) say: 'Clouds
Gathered in heaps!'
So leave them alone
Until they encounter
That Day of theirs,
Wherein they shall (perforce)
Swoon (with terror),
The Day when their plotting
Will avail them nothing
And no help shall be Given them.

(Quran, 52.43–46)

And yet again:

They reject (the warning)
And follow their (own) lusts
But every matter has
Its appointed time.
There have already come
To them Recitals wherein
There is (enough) to check (them),
Mature wisdom—but
(The preaching of) Warners
Profits them not.
Therefore, (O' Prophet,)
Turn away from them.
The Day that the Caller

Will call (them)
To a terrible affair,
They will come forth —
Their eyes humbled —
From (their) graves, (torpid)
Like locusts scattered abroad,
Hastening with eyes transfixed
Towards the Caller !
'Hard is this Day,'
The unbelievers will say.

(Quran, 54.3–8)

In a word, the unbelievers, the apostates, the hypocrites have all been set on the road of unbelief and thence of perdition by Allah Himself. They are not going to heed the Truth. They are going to persist in their wrong. Indeed, as we saw earlier, the fact that the Revelation has now been given through the Prophet, and through him to the believers, is going to make them even more obstinate in their rebellion and blasphemy.

One part of Allah's counsel therefore is: leave them to their fate, waste neither your efforts nor your sighs on them, I shall gather them up and cast them in the blazing Fire, I shall roast them in it. They shall then cry out that they were wrong, that they accept the Revelation, says Allah again and again, but it shall be too late. They shall have to endure the torment for ever.

But that is just one part of the counsel. Take no friends from their ranks, Allah declares, unless they accept the way of Allah, 'But if they turn renegades, seize them and slay them wherever you find them' (Quran, 4.89). There will be those among them who will wish to gain your confidence and that of your people, Allah warns. 'If they withdraw not from you nor give you (guarantees) of peace besides restraining their hands,' commands Allah, 'seize them and slay them wherever you get them' (Quran, 4.91).

Thus, the command is simplicity itself: if the unbelievers accept Islam, well and good, do not punish them for their past unbelief; if they don't, slay them till Islam is established everywhere:

> Say to the Unbelievers,
> If (now) they desist (from unbelief),
> Their past would be forgiven them
> But if they persist, the punishment
> Of those before them is already
> (A matter of warning for them).
> And fight them on
> Until there is no more
> Tumult or oppression,
> And there prevail
> Justice and faith in Allah
> Altogether and everywhere;
> But if they cease, verily Allah
> Doth see all that they do.
> If they refuse, be sure
> That Allah is your Protector —
> The Best to protect
> And the best to help.
>
> (Quran, 8.38–40)

Those pagans who submit to you, who honour their treaties and alliances, who, in short, see the Light, fulfil your obligations towards them, Allah says, with reference to the immunity which was declared for four months—a sort of grace period which was given to the pagans to accept the Message of the Prophet:

> But when the forbidden months
> Are past, then fight and slay
> The pagans wherever you find them,
> And seize them, beleaguer them,
> And lie in wait for them

In every stratagem (of war);
But if they repent,
And establish regular prayers
And practice regular charity,
Then open the way for them....

(Quran, 9.5)

That counsel is repeated: if they repent, if they establish namaz and zakat, in a word if they adopt Islam, forgive them; if they don't, seize them, beleaguer them, slay them. The prospect of their living up to their commitments of course remains remote:

How can there be a league
Before Allah and His Apostle,
With the pagans, except those
With whom you made a treaty
Near the Sacred Mosque?
As long as these stand true
To you, stand you true to them;
For God does love the righteous.

How (can there be such a league),
Seeing that if they get an advantage
Over you, they respect not
In you the ties either of kinship
Or of covenant? With (fair words
From) their mouths they entice you,
But their hearts are averse
From you; and most of them
Are rebellious and wicked.
The signs of Allah they have sold
For a miserable price,
And (many) have they hindered
From His way: evil indeed
Are the deeds they have done.

(Quran, 9.7–9)

And again:

O' Prophet ! strive hard against
The Unbelievers and the Hypocrites
And be firm against them.
Their abode is Hell,—
An evil refuge indeed.

(Quran. 9.73)

And it is not for nothing that Allah puts these unbelievers in the path of the believers:

Therefore, when you meet
The unbelievers (in fight),
Smite at their necks;
At length, when you have
Thoroughly subdued them,
Bind a bond
Firmly (on them): thereafter
(Is the time for) either
Generosity or ransom:
Until the war lays down
Its burdens. Thus (are you
Commanded): but if it
Had been Allah's Will,
He could certainly have exacted
Retribution from them (Himself).
But (He lets you fight)
In order to test you,
Some with others.
But those who are slain
In the way of Allah —
He will never let
Their deeds be lost.
Soon He will guide them
And improve their condition.
And admit them to

The Garden which He
Has announced for them.

(Quran, 47.4–6.)

Therefore, proclaims Allah:

Fighting is prescribed
Upon you, and ye dislike it.
But it is possible
That ye dislike a thing
Which is good for you,
And that ye love a thing
Which is bad for you.
But Allah knoweth,
And ye know not.

(Quran, 2.216)

And therefore,

Go ye forth, (whether equipped)
Lightly or heavily, and strive
And struggle, with your goods
And your persons, in the Cause
Of Allah. That is best
For you, if ye (but) knew.

(Quran, 9.41)

Those commands to seize, to beleaguer, to slay the unbelievers and hypocrites and apostates; those certifications of their evil intent; those promises of Paradise for ones who die fighting the enemies of Allah and Islam—these are not the commands, assessments and promises of the ulema; they are not gleaned from some secondary books; they are the commands, assessments, promises of Allah Himself as set down by Him in the Quran itself.

Imam Bukhari, Imam Muslim and the other compilers of the Hadis devote entire 'Books' to recording how the Messenger of Allah followed these commands. The injunctions are thus twice reinforced. '*Jihad* in the way of Allah! *Jihad* in the way of Allah,' we hear the Prophet proclaim, is what 'elevates the position of a man in Paradise to a grade one hundred (higher) and the elevation between one grade and the other is equal to the height of the heaven from the earth' ....[12] 'I love to fight in the way of Allah,' he declares, 'and be killed.' to fight and again be killed, and to fight again and be killed.'[13] He declares that if only he had the means, or his fellow believers themselves had the means, he would equip all of them for jihad. 'Who is the best of men?,' the Prophet is asked. 'A man who fights in the way of Allah spending his wealth and staking his life,' he affirms.[14] Every injury to an unbeliever tots up merit for the faithful, the traditions recall Allah saying.[15] 'A man came to Allah's Apostle,' the Hadis records, 'and said, "Instruct me to such a deed as equals jihad (in reward)." He replied, "I do not find such a deed."'[16]

Jihad against the opponents of Islam is ordained for eternity: 'A section of my community will continue to fight for the right and overcome their opponents till the last of them fight with the Antichrist,' the Prophet declares.[17] In particular the polytheists are to be fought till they submit to and accept Islam: the Prophet says, 'I am commanded to fight with the polytheists (the "men", in an alternative version) till they testify

---

12. *Sahih Muslim,* Vol. III, p. 1046; *Sahih al-Bukhari,* Vol. IV, pp. 39–40.

13. *Sahih Muslim,* Volume III, pp. 1043–44.

14. *Sahih Muslim,* Volume III, pp. 1048–49.

15. *Sahih al-Bukhari,* Volume IV, pp. 50–51.

16. Ibid., Volume IV, p. 36.

17. *Sunan Abu Dawud,* Volume II, pp. 686–87. 'This does not refer to any particular section of the Muslim community,' explains the editor/translator. 'This includes all those who strive gallantly to promote the cause of Islam. They may be warriors, scholars, preachers, teachers, doctors of Islamic law and doctors of tradition (*hadis*).' Ibid., p. 687.

that there is no god but Allah, and that Muhammad is His servant and His Apostle, face out *qibla* (direction of prayer), eat what we slaughter, and pray like us. When they do that, their life and property are unlawful for us except what is due to them. They will have the same rights as Muslims have, and have the same responsibilities as the Muslims have.'[18] The man who kills the infidel, even the one who kills a wounded infidel, shall have the right to retain what he has taken from the man he killed—that booty will not be subject to the one-fifth deduction customary for booty in general. He shall of course also get in addition his share of the general spoils.[19]

The Quran and Hadis give glowing accounts of the rewards that accrue from jihad—booty in this world (this apparently had not been legal at that time, Allah and the Prophet made it so) and Paradise in the next. 'Allah has purchased from the believers their persons and their assets,' proclaims Allah. 'For them in return is Paradise. They fight in the cause of Allah, and slay and are slain; He has made a promise binding on Him, mentioned in the Torah and the Gospel and the Quran; and who is more faithful to the covenant than Allah? Then rejoice over the bargain which you have made. That is the achievement supreme' (Quran, 9.111).

And again:

O' you who believe!,
Shall I lead you
To a bargain that will
Save you from
A grievous penalty

18. *Sunan Abu Dawud*, Volume II, pp. 729–30.

19. Ibid., Volume II, pp. 756–58.

That you believe in Allah
And His Messenger, and that
You strive (your utmost)
In the Cause of Allah,
With your property
And your persons:
That will be best for you,
If you but knew!

He will forgive
Your sins, and admit you
To Gardens, beneath which
Rivers flow, and to beautiful
Mansions in Gardens
Of Eternity: that is indeed
The Supreme Achievement
And another (favour
Will He bestow), which you
Do love—Help from Allah
And a speedy victory.
So give the Glad Tidings
To the believers.

(Quran, 61.10–13).

The Prophet is just as eloquent in describing the boons that accrue from jihad.

Fighting even once in jihad, says the Prophet, brings rewards greater than all this world and all that is in it.[20] No one who dies and receives some good from Allah in the Hereafter would ever want to return to this world, the Prophet says, even if he were offered the whole world and all that is in it as an inducement, except for the one who has been martyred in jihad. So great will be the honour which he will receive

---

20. *Sahih Muslim,* Volume III, pp. 1045–49; *Sahih al-Bukhari,* Volume IV, p.41.

from Allah that he will desire to return to this world again and be killed ten times in the cause.[21]

Indeed, everything a believer does towards and as part of jihad earns merit with Allah. Thus we have the Prophet saying, 'If somebody keeps a horse in Allah's Cause motivated by his faith in Allah and his belief in His Promise, then he will be rewarded on the Day of Resurrection for what the horse has eaten or drunk and for its dung and urine.'[22] Whatever wrong a Muslim may have done, once he kills an infidel the Muslim ensures that he shall never be in Hell, for in the Hadis entitled, 'Excellence of killing an infidel', the Prophet says, 'An infidel and the one who killed him will never be brought together in Hell.'[23] The one who dies while waging jihad or subsequently of an injury sustained in jihad is a martyr and is guaranteed Paradise.[24] Every martyr acquires the power to intercede with Allah for up to seventy of his relatives.[25]

'A seal is put over the actions of every dead man,' says the Prophet, 'except one who is on the frontier in Allah's path because his deeds will be made to go on increasing for him till the Day of Resurrection, and he will be safe from the trials of the grave.'[26] 'Paradise becomes incumbent for a Muslim who fights for the cause of Allah as long as the time

21. *Shahi Muslim*, Volume III, p. 1045; *Sahih al-Bukhari*, Volume IV, p. 42.

22. *Sahih al-Bukhari*, Volume IV, p. 72.

23. *Sunan Abu Dawud*, Volume II, p. 690. The editor/translator explains: 'This means that a person who kills an infidel while fighting in Allah's path (i.e., *Jihad*) will have his sins remitted and forgiven, and will, therefore, go to Paradise. The infidel will inevitably go to Hell. Therefore a man who killed an infidel will not be brought together in Hell with him.' Ibid., p. 690.

24. *Sunan Abu Dawud*, Volume II, p. 691. Also Ibid., pp. 698–99.

25. Ibid., Volume II, p. 699.

26. Abu Dawud and Tirmizi, in *Riyad as-Salihin*, Volume II, p. 197.

between two milkings of a she-camel (that is, for the shortest time),' the Prophet assures. 'He who received a wound or a bruise in the cause of Allah will appear on the Day of Resurrection as fresh as possible, its colour will be just like that of saffron and its fragrance will be similar to that of musk.'[27] Hence the Prophet's unambiguous, emphatic command: 'Fight against the polytheists with your properties, lives and tongues.'[28]

As the duty is an overriding one all means are permissible. 'War is stratagem,' the Prophet says, 'War is deceit.'[29] Thus one may lie, one may kill the enemy while he is asleep, one may kill him by tricking him.[30]

The *Fatawa-i-Alamgiri*—the great compendium of extracts from the works of the authorizes on Hanafi law compiled on the orders of Aurabgzeb—lays down that jihad is the noblest of professions. The compendium most frequently relied upon in India is of course the *Hidayah* of Sheikh Burhanu'd-din Ali (d. AD 1198). It restates Allah's injunction to 'slay the infidels,' and recalls the Prophet's words, 'War is permanently established till the Day of Judgement.'

It sets aside all pretence about jihad being defensive. 'The destruction of the sword is incurred by the infidels', it lays down, 'although they be not the first aggressors, as appears from the various passages in the sacred writings, which are generally received to this effect.'

One should normally invite the infidels to embrace Islam before attacking them, it says, 'but yet if he (the Mussalman) do attack them before thus inviting them, and slay them, and take their property, neither fine, expiation nor atonement are

27. Abu Dawud and Tirmizi, in *Riyad as-Salihin*, Volume II, p. 199.

28. Abu Dawud in *Riyad as-Salihin*, Volume II, pp. 217–18.

29. *Sahih Muslim*, Volume III, pp. 945 versus 990–91; *Sahih al-Bukhari*, Volume IV, pp. 166–67; *Sunan Abu Dawud*, Volume II, p. 728.

30. For example, *Sahih al-Bukhari*, Volume IV, pp. 164–65, 167–68.

due, because that which protects (namely, Islam), does not exist in them, nor are they under protection by place (namely, the Mussalman territory), and the mere prohibition of the act is not sufficient to sanction the exaction either of fine, or of atonement or property; in the same manner as the slaying of the women or infant children of infidels is forbidden; but if, notwithstanding, a person were to slay such, he is not liable to a fine.'

If they do not surrender to Islam, if they do not pay the capitation tax, invoking Allah,

> the Mussalmans must then, with God's assistance, attack the infidels with all manner of war-like engines (as the Prophet did by the people of Tayeef), and must also set fire to their habitations (in the same manner as the Prophet fired Baweera), and must inundate them with water, and tear up their plantations, and tread down their grain; because by these means they will become weakened, and their resolution will fail, and their force be broken; these means are therefore all sanctioned by the Law.

Women, children and the disabled should not be slain, it says, 'But yet if any of these persons be killed in war, or if a woman be a queen or a chief, in this case it is allowable to slay them, they being qualified (i.e., being in a position) to molest the servants of God. So also, if such persons as the above should attempt to fight, they may be slain, for the purpose of removing evil, and because fighting renders slaying allowable.'

Peace may be made when advisable, it says, or broken when necessary, giving the infidels due notice, unless they act perfidiously, in which case they may be attacked without warning.

All movable property of the infidels must be confiscated. As for the rest, it says, affairs should be so arranged that 'the inhabitants are merely the cultivators of the soil on behalf of the

Mussalmans, as performing all the labour, in the various modes of tillage, on their account, without their (i.e., the Mussalmans) being subjected to any of the trouble or expense attending it.'

As for the prisoners, it lays down, 'The *Imam*, with respect to captives, has it in his choice to slay them, because the Prophet put captives to death and also because slaying them terminates wickedness—or, if he choose, he may make them slaves, because by enslaving them the evil of them is remedied, at the same time that Mussalmans reap an advantage; or if he please he may release them so as to make them free men or Zimmis....' The idolaters of Arabia or apostates are not to be released. They should be killed. In any case, they should not be allowed to return to their country, 'as this would be strengthening the infidels against the Mussalman.'

He who converts to Islam should not be killed. He should not however be sent to his country. He can retain his liberty, the property that is 'in his hands' and his infant children. But his lands, his wife, her foetus, his adult children, etc., all become public property, says the law book.[31]

Thus, is the problem merely that of updating the text books that are used in the 'Centres of Islamic Learning'?

Moreover, are the apologists right when they try to explain away the verses on jihad by saying that jihad merely means to wage war inside one's being to overcome the evil tendencies in oneself? Do the verses of the Quran, do the Hadis in which the Prophet explicates those verses refer to such inner striving?

The verses are clear as can be. The Hadis are clear as can be. And those who heard the Prophet had not the slightest

---

31. Sheikh Burhanu'd-din Ali, *The Hedaya*, Charles Hamilton (tr.), Kitab Bhavan, Delhi, 1985 Reprint, Volume II, pp. 140–256.

doubt about the import of what he meant. Muslim's *Sahih* relates a typical incident: 'Jabir (Allah be pleased with him) reported that a man asked the Messenger of Allah: Tell me where shall I be if I am killed fighting in the way of Allah? He replied: In Paradise. The man threw away afar dates which he had in his hand, jumped into the battle and fought on till he was killed.'[32] And yet the apologists insist that in spite of what Allah says so explicitly, so emphatically and so often, in spite of what the Prophet reiterates so explicitly, so emphatically and so often, in spite of the fact that the meaning of what he was saying was so evident to his Companions, in spite of the way they acted in response to his command and exhortation, and in spite of the fact that such action on their part invited nothing but warm approbation from the Prophet, in spite of all this for the apologists 'jihad in the way of Allah' refers to inner striving against the evil tendencies in our inner beings! And if you don't believe them, you are an Islam-baiter !

Allah's singular concern

We are astonished at the single-minded concern of the ulema—their obsession with the aggrandisement of Islam, their obsession with stamping out, with doing in all 'rivals' to Islam and Allah, their frenzied preoccupation in ensuring that no Muslim retains any residual regard, to say nothing of veneration for any entity other than 'Allah'—intolerance, verbal and physical terrorism, organized violence, regarding non-believers as congenitally inferior, all these flow from this basic, foundational premise.

As every reader of the Quran knows, Allah's overriding concern is that we worship Him, and none but Him: 'For Allah hath said, Take not to yourselves two gods—for He

---

32. For this and similar responses, *Sahih Muslim,* Volume III, pp. 1052–54.

is one God: Me, therefore! yea, Me revere,' 'All in the Heavens and in the Earth is His! His due unceasing service! Will ye then fear any other than Allah?' (Quran, 16.51–52).

Indeed, Allah categorically states that nothing is of greater concern to Him than this, that every one pay obeisance, to Him, and Him alone:

> O ye to whom the scriptures have been given [He declares] believe in what We have sent down confirmatory of the Scripture which is in your hands, ere We efface your features, and twist your head round backward, or curse you as we cursed the sabbath-breakers; and the command of God was carried into effect.
>
> *Verily, Allah will not forgive the union of other gods with Himself: But other than this He will forgive to whom He pleaseth....* (Quran, 4.50–55).

He goes to the most extraordinary lengths to remind us of His power and glory. Thus, for instance, He visits afflictions on a people to humble them; next He sends them a prophet so that they may believe in him; and when they don't believe in the prophet (and this too, it must be remembered, happens by His decree) He wreaks the most terrible vengeance on them. A single passage will suffice to give us a glimpse of His obsession in the matter and of the extraordinary lengths to which He goes to have that obsession prevail:

> *Nor did We ever send a Prophet to any city without afflicting its people with adversity and trouble,* that haply they might humble them....
>
> Then changed We their ill for good, until they waxed wealthy and said, 'Of old did troubles and blessing befall our fathers.' Therefore did We seize upon them suddenly when they were unaware....
>
> But *if that the people of these cities had believed and feared Us,* We would surely have laid open to them blessings, out of the

> Heaven and the Earth: but they treated Our signs as lies, and *We took vengeance on them for their deeds....*
>
> Were the people therefore of these cities secure that Our wrath would not *light upon them by night while they were slumbering?....* Were the people of those cities secure that our wrath would not *light on them in broad day, while they were disporting themselves?....*
>
> Did they therefore deem themselves secure from the deep counsel [i.e., the stratagem] of God? *But none deem themselves secure from the deep counsel of God, save those who perish. Is it not proved to them who inherit this land after its ancient occupants, that if We please We can smite them for their sins and put a seal upon their hearts, that they hearken not?* We will tell thee the stories of these cities. Their apostles came to them with clear proofs of their mission; but they would not believe in what they had before treated as imposture—*Thus does Allah seal up the hearts of the unbelievers.* And We found not of their covenant in most of them; but We found most of them to be perverse (Quran, 7.92–100).

It is of course not evident why Allah, who is Self-sufficient in all respects, is so concerned that this puny little man, on this puny little earth, in this puny little solar system, in this little bit of the universe acknowledge His greatness. And even if this is His one concern, surely He—all-powerful, omniscient, as He is—can find an easier way of having man acknowledge His greatness. Why does He not instil the veneration directly rather than by adopting these circuitous and painful routes—of springing His wrath by night, while the poor man is slumbering, and springing it in broad day, while he is disporting?

There is no answer in the Quran any more than there is in the Old Testament, the 'Jealous God' of which is a direct predecessor of Allah in this regard.

In keeping with this singular concern of Allah, the purpose

of almost everything He does is to ensure that we recognize and acknowledge His power. Thus, for instance, He says that He creates the heavens, earth, clouds, lightning, plants, beasts and everything else as 'signs' so that we, His creatures may see that He is All Powerful, that He alone is the creator, that He has no associates, no equals, no offspring and as a manifestation too of His munificence so that we may partake of His creation (Quran, 2.157–60; 6.99). He rescues the Israelites from drowning so that those who are to come afterwards may know the things He can do (Quran, 10.90.2). 'I have not created djinn and men,' He declares, 'but that they should worship Me; I require not sustenance from them, neither I require that they feed Me' (Quran, 51.6)—that is, Allah is self-sufficient, needing neither food nor any other kind of sustenance from us, yet He creates us; He does so for one purpose, for one purpose alone: so that He may be worshipped.

Allah has created animals too for that singular purpose—that we should use them to glorify Him by sacrificing them in His Name, that upon eating them we may be reminded of His munificence. Thus Allah says,

> To every people did We
> Appoint rites (of sacrifice),
> That they might celebrate
> The name of Allah over
> The sustenance He gave them
> From animals (fit for food)....
> The sacrificial camels
> We have made for you
> As among the Symbols from
> Allah: in them is (much)
> Good for you: then pronounce
> The name of Allah over them
> As they line up (for sacrifice):
> When they are down

On their sides (after slaughter),
Eat ye thereof, and feed
Such as (beg not but)
Live in contentment,
And such as beg
With due humility: thus have
We made animals subject
To you, that ye
May be grateful.
It is not their meat
Nor their blood, that reaches
Allah: it is your peity
That reaches Him: He
Has thus made them subject
To you, that ye may glorify
Allah for His guidance to you:....

(Quran, 22.34–37)

That is an odd conception: a being who is so obsessed with having everyone acknowledge that He is all-powerful, that He alone is powerful, that He is excellent, that He alone is excellent, a being who throws good things our way so that we may thank Him, who ensnares us in evil and then punishes us so that we may not forget His power and wrath. The poor camels too He has created just so that we may slaughter them in His name, and so that upon eating them we may be reminded how kind He is to have provided us their meat.

There is a slight sublimation in 22.37 above: 'It is not their meat nor their blood that reaches Allah,' Allah tells the faithful. Why not have the piety reach Him directly? Why has it to be reached to Him through the agency of slaughtering a living being?

There is no answer of course, it is just His policy.

Women

We are left aghast at the ulema's view of women, at the sternness with which the ulema trample upon their dignity, their rights, at the way the ulema enforce medieval rules: up to four wives at a time, triple talaq, conditional talaq, talaq without even alleging a reason, no maintenance at all beyond three months, halalah. But is the problem here just that their textbooks have not been updated?

It is not some sundry ulema who say, but Allah who says:

> Your wives are
> As a tilth unto you;
> So approach your tilth
> When or how you will....
>
> (Quran, 2.223)

The wife is just tilth for man?[33]

---

33. The verse does proceed to say:

But do some good act
For your souls beforehand.

What the 'some good act', however, is will not bring much relief to the women. As I have mentioned in *Indian Controversies*, in explaining the verse the traditions narrate: 'Jews used to say: "If one has sexual intercourse with his wife from the back, then she will deliver a squint-eyed child." So this verse was revealed....' (*Sahih al-Bukhari*, Volume VI, p. 39). The act for the good of one's soul that is to be done is not specified in the Quran. One possibility is suggested by the traditions. The Prophet says, 'If anyone of you on having sexual relations with his wife said (and he must say it before starting), *"Bismillah, Allahumma Jannibni-sh-Shaitan wa Jannibni-sh-Shaitan ma razaqtana* (i.e., In the name of Allah ! Protect me from Satan and protect what you bestow upon us (i.e., an offspring) from Satan," and if it is destined that they should have a child then Satan will never be able to harm that offspiring' (*Sabih al-Bukhari*, Volume I, p. 105 and Volume VII, p. 70). The probability that this is the sort of counsel which is intended by the verse about the act one must do before 'going into one's field' is reinforced by another tradition. The prophet Solomon, son of the prophet

'And women shall have rights similar to the rights against them according to what is equitable,' Allah says, only to add, 'But men have a degree over them' (Quran, 2.228). That remains the basic view. For instance, Allah declares again:

> Men are the managers of the affairs of women for that Allah has preferred in bounty one of them over another, and for that they have expended of their property. Righteous women are therefore obedient, guarding the secret for Allah's guarding. And those you fear may be rebellious, admonish; banish them to their couches; and beat them. If they then obey you, look not for any way against them; Allah is All-high, All-great.
>
> (Quran, 4.34)

That is why a man is allowed up to four wives at a time plus as many captive girls 'that your right hand possesses' (Quran, 4.3). That is why while a dower is to be specified for the wife which is to be her's, there is an escape hatch: 'And give the women (on marriage) their dower as a free gift; but if they, of their own good pleasure, remit any part of it to you, take it and enjoy it with right good cheer' (Quran, 4.4).[34]

Is it any surprise to learn that, while it is fashionable nowadays to fix the mehr at poetically grandiloquent levels, it is just as common a practice to have the wife forego it on the nuptial night itself?

David, we are told, said: 'Tonight I will go round (i.e., have sexual relations with) one hundred women (my wives) everyone of whom will deliver a male child who will fight in Allah's Cause.' But Solomon did not say the words and forgot to say them. Then he had sexual relations with them but none of them delivered any child except one who delivered a half person. The Prophet said, 'If Solomon had said: "If Allah will," Allah would have fulfilled his (aforestated) desire and that saying would have made him more hopeful' (*Sahih al-Bukhari,* Volume VII, p. 122–23).

34. See also Quran, 4.24 where Allah reiterates that if after the dower has been agreed 'you mutually agree (to vary it) there is no blame on you.'

It is because of the basic assessment of the relative place of men and women—'Men are in charge of women, because Allah hath made them to excel the other'—that, while a daughter is to have a share in the property of her father, her share is to be one-half that of a son (Quran, 2.11; 4.12, 175).

It is for the same reason that when a husband wants to take back the wife he has thrown out, say, in a fit of anger the poor woman is put through the repugnant and humiliating halalah—not by the orders of the ulema, but by the command of Allah (Quran, 2.230).

Believers are told, 'A believer must not bear enmity against a believing woman; if he dislikes one of her characteristics he will be pleased with another.' And while the formulation would scarcely be of comfort to those who insist that Islam gives a higher place to women than other religions, the counsel given elsewhere can at least be seen as counsel for moderation: 'Treat women kindly,' the believers are told, 'they are like captives in your hands. [You have no claims on them except that] in case they are guilty of open indecency you may leave them alone in their beds and inflict slight punishment. If they are obedient to you, do not have recourse to anything else against them. You have your rights over your wives and they have rights over you. Your right is that they shall not permit anyone you dislike to enter your home, and their right is that you treat them well in the matter of food and clothing.' Believers are told, 'The believers who show the most perfect faith are those who have the best disposition, and the best of you are those who are best to their wives.'[35]

But they are also told:

- By Him in whose hand my soul is (that is, Allah), if

35. Muslim and Tirmizi, respectively; see, *Riyad as-Salihin,* Volume I, Kazi Publications, Lahore, 1988 Reprint, p. 199.

any woman who has been called to come to her husband's bed refuses, He who is in heaven is displeased with her till the husband is pleased with her;

- When a man calls his wife to satisfy his desire she must go to him even if she is occupied at the oven;
- If I were to command anyone to make prostration before another I would command women to prostrate themselves before their husbands, because of the special right over them given to the husbands by Allah;
- Woman has been created from a rib and will in no way be straight for you; so if you enjoy her you will do so while crookedness remains in her; but if you attempt to straighten her you will break her, breaking her being divorcing her;
- A man will not be asked about why he beat his wife;
- Worship your Lord and honour your brother. If I were to order anyone to prostrate himself before another, I would order a woman to prostrate herself before her husband; and if he were to order her to convey stones from a yellow mountain to a black one, or from a black mountain to a white one, it would be incumbent on her to do so.

And who is the one who says these things? And the following?

- If a woman dies in a state when her husband is pleased with her, she will enter Paradise;
- No woman annoys her husband without his wives among the large-eyed maidens (of Paradise) saying: 'You must not annoy him. Allah curse you ! He is only a passing guest with you and is about to leave you to come to us.'
- If a man invites his wife to sleep with him and she refuses to come to him, then the angels send their curses on her till morning.

- When a young man explains that his wife 'keeps on fasting and I am a young man who cannot contain himself,' who is it who orders, 'A woman may fast only with her husband's permission?'

Not some sundry alim, whose textbook we can replace by the book of some more recent author. Those are the declarations and commands of the Prophet himself.[36]

It is the Prophet who declares, 'After me I have not left any affliction more harmful to men than women.'[37] It is the Prophet who says that upon touring Heaven and Hell he saw that women are the ones who constitute the majority in Hell.[38] And that is not because they are less pious than men but because they are ungrateful to their husbands: 'Then I saw the (Hell) Fire,' the Prophet says, 'and I have never before seen such a horrible sight as that, and I saw that the majority of its dwellers were women.' The people asked: 'O' Allah's Apostle! What is the reason for that?' He replied, 'Because of their ungratefulness.' He was asked, 'Do they disbelieve in Allah (are they ungrateful to Allah)?' He replied, 'They are not thankful to their husbands and are ungrateful for the favours done to them. Even if you do good to them all your life, when she sees some harshness from you [at another place the words are, "and then she sees something in you (not to her liking")] she will say, "I have never seen any good from you."'[39]

---

36. *Mishkat al-Masabih,* Book XIII, Chapter 11, pp. 688–94; similarly, *Sunan Abu Dawud,* Volume II, p. 574; *Sahih al-Bukhari,* Volume VII, p. 93; *Riyad-* Volume I, pp. 197–205; Ibid. Volume II, pp. 449–50.

37. *Sahih Al-Bukhari,* Volume VII, p. 22; *Sahih Muslim,* Volume IV, pp. 1431–32.

38. *Sahih Al-Bukhari,* Volume I, p. 29; Volume VII, pp. 94–96; *Sahih Muslim,* Volume IV, pp. 1431–32.

39. *Sahih Al-Bukhari,* Volume VII, pp. 95–96.

In addition to women counting for half of men in inheritance, the evidence of two women is to equal the evidence of one man—'This,' says the Prophet in relation to the latter, 'is because of the deficiency of a woman's mind.'[40]

It is not just some sundry alim who sees women as being one of the things Allah has created for man to enjoy. It is the Prophet who declares: 'The whole world is to be enjoyed but the best thing in the world is a good woman.'[41] They are also temptresses that one has to beware: 'Whenever a man is alone with a woman,' the Prophet says, 'the devil makes a third.' 'Do not visit women whose husbands are away from home,' he says, 'for the devil circulates in you like your blood.'[42] And wives are seen as objects into whom one should expend one's passion when thus tempted by other women. 'A woman advances in the form of a devil and retires in the form of a devil,' the Prophet says. 'When one of you is charmed by a woman and she affects your heart he should go to his wife and have intercourse with her, for that will repel what he is feeling.' The point is reiterated in another tradition in which the Prophet, after a personal incident, says, 'If any man sees a woman who charms him, he should go to his wife, for she has the same kind of thing as the other woman.'[43]

Men are exhorted to look after their wives. But it is in the Hadis themselves that women also emerge in the conventional, medieval way, as pots to vent one's passion in: 'Young men,' counsels the Prophet, 'those of you who can support a wife should marry, for it keeps you from looking at strange women and preserves you from immorality; but

---

40. Ibid., Volume III, p. 502.
41. *Mishkat al-Masabih*, Volume I, p. 658.
42. Ibid., Volume I, p. 663.
43. Ibid., Volume I, p. 662.

those who cannot should devote themselves to fasting, for it is a means of suppressing sexual desire.'[44]

And as vehicles of procreation, and that too for the glory of the Prophet and the strength of his ummah. A man comes to the Prophet saying that his wife is good and beautiful and he loves her, but that she produces no children. The Prophet tells him to divorce her forthwith, saying, 'Marry women who are loving and very prolific, for I shall outnumber the peoples by you.'[45]

The Quranic concept of women being a man's tilth, his field that he may go into when or how he will, finds many echoes in the traditions, sometimes literally. The question is put, 'O' Abu Said, I have some slave-girls who are better than my wives, but I do not desire that they should all become pregnant. Shall I do *azl* (*coitus interruptus*) with them?' And, not some sundry alim but the Prophet's Companion answers, 'They are your fields of cultivation, if you wish to irrigate them do so, or if you desire otherwise, keep them dry.'[46]

It is not just some sundry alim but the Prophet who when asked about the rights of a woman over her husband puts them at a very modest level. Approach your tilth when or how you will, he says echoing the words of Allah, but give her food when you take food, clothe her when you clothe yourself, do not revile her. Beyond that there is a difference in the narrations. Some Hadis enumerate no more. Some record the Prophet adding, 'Do not strike her on the face,' while others record his adding, 'and do not beat them.'

But the latter version is immediately followed by the Hadis 'On beating women'. The matter went to and fro during the life of the Prophet but the outcome can provide little

44. Ibid., Volume I, p. 662.

45. Ibid., Volume I, p. 658.

46. Imam Malik, *Muwatta*, Muhammad Ashraf, Lahore, 1980, p. 269, Hadis 1221.

solace to those who would have us believe that no religion has provided as many rights to women as Islam. A Hadis records that once the Prophet said, 'Do not beat Allah's handmaidens.' But when Hazrat Umar came to him and said, 'Women have become emboldened towards their husbands,' the Prophet gave permission to beat them. Then, the Hadis records, many women came round to the family of the Prophet complaining against their husbands. 'So the Apostle of Allah (may peace be upon him) said,' concludes the Hadis, '"Many women have gone round Muhammad's family complaining against their husbands. They are not the best among you."' And that Hadis is followed immediately by the Hadis we have encountered earlier: 'A man,' declares the Prophet, 'will not be asked as to why he beat his wife.'[47] That is the declaration of the Prophet, not of some ordinary alim.

It is not some sundry alim but Al-Ghazzali himself who tells us that 'merit has one thousand components, only one of which is attributable to women, while nine hundred and ninety-nine are attributable to men.' It is the view not of some sundry alim but of this, the most influential of Islam's theologians and philosophers that for Eve's disobedience and the moral depravity of womankind Allah has punished women in eighteen different ways, which include menstruation, pregnancy, the pain of childbirth, separation from her parents and marriage to a stranger, the liability to be divorced and her inability to divorce, the fact that it is lawful for a man to marry four wives while she has to be content with one husband, that her testimony counts for just one half of the testimony of a man, that her share in property shall be half that of her brother, and so on.[48]

47. On the foregoing, *Sunan Abu Dawud*, Volume II, pp. 574–75.

48. Cited in Ram Swarup, *Woman in Islam*, Voice of India, New Delhi, 1994, pp. 4–5.

Can the problem be got over, then, merely by substituting some textbooks at Deoband?

Stars and the rest

We are bewildered at the vehemence with which the *Fatawa-i-Rizvia* insists that the sun moves round the earth. But it is in *Sahih al-Bukhari* that we learn that the sun and moon move in a circle 'like the handmill'.[49] It is in *Sahih al-Bukhari* that we learn that stars have been created for three purposes: 'as decoration on the sky, as missiles to hit the devils, and as signs to guide travellers. So, if anybody tries to find a different interpretation, he is mistaken and just wastes his efforts and troubles himself with what is beyond his limited knowledge.'[50] And the basis for these affirmations is not some sundry text on astronomy but the Quran itself. For Allah Himself tells the faithful that He has created 'the stars (as beacons) for you, that you may guide yourselves, with their help, through the dark spaces of land and sea' (Quran, 6.97). It is Allah Himself who affirms that the bright shooting stars, the 'flaming fire', the shooting stars with 'piercing brightness' are hurled to pursue the Evil one 'that gains a hearing by stealth' (Quran, 15.18, 37.10).

We are amused when *Fatawa-i-Rahimiyyah* says that the way to protect a field is to recite an invocation. But the canonical collections of Hadis are the ones which prescribe invocations for all sorts of occasions: upon going to bed, upon sleeping on the right side, upon awakening in the middle of the night, upon going to the lavatory, upon encountering difficult moments, upon ascending a high place,

---

49. *Sahih al-Bukhari*, Volume IV, p. 282.

50. 'For example,' explain the scholars of the Islamic University, Al-Medina Al-Munawwara, 'to send a man over the stars or moon, etc., is just wasting of money and energy;' *Sahih al-Bukhari*, Volume IV, p. 282.

upon descending into a valley, upon having sexual intercourse, for seeking refuge from being overpowered, for seeking refuge from afflictions, for seeking refuge from debt, for increasing one's wealth, for increasing the number of offspring.[51]

We think it odd that the ulema repeat medieval notions about diseases and their treatment gathered from texts of the thirteenth century. But it is the Prophet who declares that fever is from the heat of Hell and that therefore one should abate it by sprinkling water.[52] It is the Prophet who certifies that the effect of the evil eye is a fact, and that the spell of the evil eye may be broken by using a spell.[53] It is the Prophet who states in several Hadis that the poisonous bites of snakes and scorpions are to be treated with invocations.[54] It is the Prophet who tells us that the way to eliminate the disease which may come from a fly falling into some food or liquid in a vessel is to dip the entire fly into it before throwing away the fly, for 'in one of its wings there is a disease and in the other there is healing, that is the treatment of the disease.'[55]

We are baffled at the insistence of the ulema on istinja: using balls of mud, pebbles, etc., to clean oneself after urinating or defecating. But it is the Prophet who prescribes this method of cleaning oneself, specifying that three or more pebbles be used, that the right hand not be used, etc.—the fatwas merely reiterate these points.[56]

---

51. See, for instance, Book 75 in *Sahih al-Bukhari*, Volume VIII, pp. 211–81.

52. *Sahih al-Bukhari*, Volume VII, pp. 416–17.

53. Ibid., Volume VII, pp. 426–27.

54. Ibid., Volume VII, p. 427.

55. Ibid., Volume VII, pp. 452–53; also Volume IV, p. 338. The scholars of the Islamic University, Al-Medina al-Munawwara, say that findings of microbiologists confirm this prescription; Ibid., Volume VII, p. 453.

56. *Sahih al-Bukhari*, Volume I, pp. 111,114; *Sahih Muslim*, Volume I, pp. 160–61; *Sunan Abu Dawud*, Volume I, pp. 8–10.

We find it incomprehensible that the ulema should be so stern in demanding that one must not either urinate or drink water while standing. But it is the Prophet who attached great importance to both matters, as several Hadis testify.

Halalah—the insistence that a woman who has been divorced by a husband pronouncing 'talaq' even in a fit of anger must get herself married to some other man, have that marriage consummated and have herself divorced by that second husband before her original husband can take her back as his wife—seems to us a procedure that inflicts cruel humiliation on the poor woman. But the procedure is prescribed by Allah in the Quran, it is what the Prophet enforced.[57]

We think it cruel that though she was in her seventies, that though she was indigent, that though she had been married to her husband for forty-five years and had borne him five children, the ulema insisted that Shah Bano was not entitled to any maintenance at all once her prosperous lawyer of a husband threw her out by uttering one word—'talaq'. But it is the Prophet who declared in case after case that the divorced woman is entitled to no maintenance.[58]

Comprehensiveness

We are surprised, and a little abashed when we see the types of subjects on which fatwas are sought and issued. But this genre of fatwas is just the continuation of the genus: the canonical collections of Hadis themselves contain Hadis upon Hadis on similar topics. One has just to look at the heads of Hadis collections, under the *Kitab al-Taharah,* The Book of Purification, to see that this is so. The *Sunan Abu Dawud*

57. Quran, 2.230; *Sahih al-Bukhari,* Volume VII, pp. 181–82; *Sunan Abu Dawud,* Volume II, p. 629.

58. For instance, *Sahih Muslim,* Volume II, pp. 769–73.

begins with this 'Book'. It contains Hadis on 145 topics. The topics are as follows:

* * *

Sunan Abu Dawud

Observing privacy while relieving oneself; One should seek soft ground for urination; What should a man utter while entering the privy; Disapproval of facing the Qiblah while relieving oneself; Permission to face the Qiblah at the time of relieving oneself; How to uncover the private parts of the body; Disapproval of conversation in the privy; Return of salutation at the time or urination; One may remember Allah without purification; Entering the privy with a ring in the hand on which is inscribed the name of Allah; Safeguarding oneself from urine; Urinating while one is standing; A man may urinate in a vessel at night and keep it with him; Places where urinating is prohibited; Urinating in the bath; Prohibition to urinate in a hole; What a man should utter when he comes out of the privy; Disapproval of touching the penis with the right hand while purifying; Taking cover at the time of relieving oneself; Things with which cleaning after easing oneself is forbidden; Cleaning with stones; Performing ablution after relieving oneself; Cleansing with water after relieving oneself; Wiping one's hand on the ground after easing; The tooth-stick; How to use the tooth-stick; Using other's tooth-stick; The washing of the tooth-stick; Using tooth-stick is one of the characteristics of *Fitrah* (nature); Using the tooth-stick after getting up during the night; Ablution is obligatory for prayer; A man may renew the ablution without defilement; Things that pollute water; On the well called *Buda'ah;* The water left over after bath is not defiled; Urinating in stagnant water; Performing ablution with water left over after a dog has drunk of it; The left-over of a cat; permissibility of performing ablution with the water left over by a woman; Prohibition of washing with the water left over by the male or the female; Performing ablution with sea water; Performing ablution with *Nibidh;* Can a man offer prayer while he is feeling the call of nature; The quantity of water that is desirable for ablution; Exceeding the limits in ablution; Performing ablution in full; Performing ablution with a brass vessel; The utterance of *Bismillah* in the beginning of ablution; A man who puts his hand in the utensil before washing it; Description of the Prophet's (may peace be upon him) ablution; Washing the limbs in ablution three times; Washing the limbs in ablution twice; Washing the limbs in ablution once; Distinction between rinsing the mouth and snuffing up water; Ejecting mucus after snuffing up water; Making the water go through the beard by inserting fingers; Wiping over the turban; Washing the foot; Wiping over the shoes; The limit for wiping over the shoes; Wiping over the stockings; How to wipe over the socks; Sprinkling water on private parts of the body after ablution; What a man should say after ablution; Offering various prayers with the same ablution; Leaving any spot dry in ablution; A man who is sure of purification but doubts that something has rendered it invalid; Ablution does not become void by kissing a woman; By touching the penis ablution becomes void; Ablution is not necessary after touching the penis; Performing ablution after eating the flesh of camel; Performing ablution after touching the flesh of an animal or washing it is not necessary; Performing ablution is not necessary after touching a carcase; The performing of ablution is not essential when one takes something cooked with the help of fire; Strictness in performing ablution after eating anything cooked with the help of fire; Rinsing the mouth after drinking milk; Rinsing the mouth after drinking milk is not necessary; Performing ablution is necessary because of bleeding; Performing ablution after awaking from sleep; A man who treads on unclean place; On the breach of ablution during prayer; On prostatic fluid (*Madhi*); On mutual contact and eating with a menstruating woman; Bathing is obligatory after sexual intercourse with seminal emission; A person with sexual defilement may repeat intercourse without taking a bath; Desirability

Sunan Abu Dawud

of performing ablution after intercourse if one desires to repeat it; Permissibility of sleeping before taking a bath for a person who is sexually defiled; A person who is sexually defiled is permitted to eat anything before washing; Desirability of performing ablution for a person who is sexually defiled before eating or sleeping; A person who is sexually defiled may postpone washing; On reciting the Qur'an by a person who is defiled; Permissibility to shake hands with a person who is sexually defiled; A person who is sexually defiled is prohibited to enter the Mosque; About a person

Sunan Abu Dawud

who is sexually defiled and leads the people in prayer in forgetfulness; Washing is necessary if a man finds moisture (on his clothes) due to sexual dream after awaking from sleep; Pertaining to a woman who sees what a man sees (in his sexual dream); Quantity of water sufficient for bath; On taking a bath because of sexual defilement; Performing ablution after taking a bath is not necessary; Should a woman undo her plaited hair at the time of taking a bath; A man who is sexually defiled may wash his head with marshmallow; Flow of the fluid between man and woman; Eating with a menstruating woman and association with her; It is permissible for a menstruating woman to get something from the mosque; A menstruating woman should not complete the abandoned prayers after purification; On cohabitation with a menstruating woman; It is permissible for a man to do anything with his wife while she is menstruating except sexual intercourse; Pertaining to the woman who has a prolonged flow of blood, and about one who said that she should abandon prayer for the number of days she used to menstruate; The woman who has a prolonged flow of blood should not abandon prayer when her menstrual period is finished; The woman suffering from a prolonged flow of blood should not abandon prayer when her menstrual period is finished; The woman suffering from a prolonged flow of blood should abandon prayer when menstruation begins; Reports stating that the woman suffering from prolonged flow of

Sunan Abu Dawud

blood should take a bath for every prayer; The view that a woman who has prolonged flow of blood should combine the two prayers and take a bath only once for them; The view that the woman having flow of blood should take a bath once when purified from her menses; The view that the woman having a flow of blood should take a bath at the time of the noon prayer; The view that the woman having a flow of blood should take a bath only once every day and not at the time of the noon prayers; The view that the woman having a prolonged flow of blood should wash during menstrual period; The view that the woman having a flow of blood should perform ablution for every prayer; The view that the woman having a prolonged flow of blood should perform ablution only when it becomes void and not for every prayer; The Shariah law about the woman who sees yellowness after purification; The husband is allowed to cohabit with his wife who has a prolonged flow of blood; The law of Shari'ah pertaining to the woman who has a bleeding after delivery (puerperal hemorrhage); On washing the blood of menstruation and bathing after it; *Tayammum*; performing *tayammum* while one is at home; A person who is sexually defiled may perform *tayammum*; If a person who is sexually defiled fears cold, should he perform *tayammum*; A person suffering from smallpox may perform *tayammum*; If a person prays on its right time after performing *tayammum*, and he finds water while the time of prayer remains (what should he do?); On taking a bath on Friday; Concession for abandoning bath on Friday; The infidel who embraces Islam should take a bath; Should a menstruating woman wash her clothes that she was wearing during her menstrual period; Offering prayer in the clothes in which one has sexual intercourse with one's wife; Offering prayer in the waist-wrappers of women; Concession of prayer in the clothes of women; The law of Shari'ah about the clothes if they are smeared with semen; How to clean the clothes smeared with the urine of a child; The earth smeared with urine; The earth is pure when it becomes dry; On the border of the clothes being smeared with impurity; On the shoe being smeared with impurity; On repeating prayer offered in an impure garment; Dropping of saliva on the clothes.

* * *

And these are the contents of just the opening 'Book' of one collection of Hadis, the *Sunan Abu Dawud*. Other 'Books' in that collection for instance have Hadis, inter alia, on the following topics:

* * *

Sunan Abu Dawud

Spreading gravel in the mosque; On sweeping in the mosque;....On strict prohibition of women from attending prayer in the mosque; On running for praying;.... On the *imam* who reads the prayer sitting; If one of the two persons acts as *imam* for the other, where should both stand; If there are three persons (in congregational prayer) how they should stand;....On adequacy of clothes for validity of prayer; On a man who ties the cloth over his nape and then prays; On a man who prays in a single piece of cloth one part of which lies over the other person; On a man who prays in a single shirt; If the cloth is tight, it should be used as a wrapper; On trailing the garment during prayer; In how many garments should a woman pray; On a woman who prays without wearing a veil; On saying prayer upon the sheets of cloth of women; On a man who prays tying the back knot of his hair; On praying in sandals; When a person who is going to pray takes off his sandals, where he should place them; On praying on a small mat; On praying on a mat; On a person who prostrates on his cloth; On straightening the rows; ...On the view that if a woman passes in front of the worshipper, she does not cut off the prayer; On the view that if a donkey passes in front of the worshipper, it does not cut off the prayer; On the view that the passing of a dog in front of a worshipper does not cut off the prayer; On the view that the passing of anything in front of the worshipper does not cut off the prayer;.... On making a sign during prayers; On removing pebbles during prayer; On putting hands on the waist during prayer; on resting on a staff during prayer; ... On the side to which one should turn after finishing the prayer;.... On which the hour is on Friday at which a prayer is accepted by Allah; On the excellence of Friday;.... On estimating the fruit on trees;....On the creatures which can be killed by the pilgrim in the sacred site; On eating the flesh of same by a pilgrim who is wearing *ihram*; On killing locusts by a person who is wearing *ihram;* On wearing the mantle under one's right armpit with the end over one's left shoulder;... On marrying virgins; On prohibition of marrying women who do not give birth to children;.... On a man who has sexual intercourse with his wife before giving her something; On what should be said to a bridegroom after his marriage; On a man who marries a woman whom he finds pregnant; On division of time among one's wives;.... On having intercourse with female captives of war; On having intercourse with a menstruating woman and lying with her; On expatiation for cohabitation with a menstruating woman; On withdrawing the penis while cohabiting with one's wife; On the disapproval of spreading the secrets of intercourse to others;.... On a man who hears the call of prayer while he has a vessel in his hand;.... On the use of a tooth-stick by a man who is fasting; On whether a man who is fasting can pour water over his head due to thirst and snuff water abundantly to his nostrils;.... On a man who is fasting and has nocturnal emission during Ramzan; On a man who is fasting applying collyrium at time of sleeping; On intentional vomiting by a man who is fasting, On kissing by a man who is fasting; On a man who swallows the saliva while he is fasting; On a man who is fasting during the month of Ramzan and gets up in the morning sexually defiled; On the expiation by a man who has sexual intercourse with his wife during Ramzan;.... On the

Sunan Abu Dawud

disapproval of clipping the forelocks and tails of horses; On colours which are appreciable in a horse; On whether a mare can be called horse;.... On hanging bells in the necks of horses and camels;....On the prohibition of making asses cover mares to beget mules;.... On having a dog for hunting and some other purposes; On eating the part cut off of an animal while it is alive;.... On the earnings of slave girls;....On taking hire for a stallion's covering;.... On the sale of a cat; On payment for dogs; On payment for wine and dead meat;.... On prohibition of wine;.... On the drink made from mixing of various kinds of dates or dates and raisins; On drink made from unripe dates; On the drink made from honey; On drinking while standing; On drinking from the mouth of a water-skin; On drinking by inverting the heads of skin-vessels; On drinking from the broken place of a cup; On sipping water with the mouth;.... On what should be said while drinking milk;.... On eating while reclining; On eating from the top of the dish; On eating with the right hand; On eating meat; On eating pumpkin;.... On eating horse-flesh; On eating hare; On eating lizard; On eating the flesh of bustard; On eating insects and little creatures of the land;.... On eating the hyena;.... On eating the flesh of domestic asses; On eating locusts;.... On the falling of a mouse in clarified butter; On the falling of a fly in one's food; On wiping hands with a handkerchief;.... On dates on which it is commendable to get oneself cupped;.... On a charm for one who is possessed;.... On the command for the use of collyrium;.... On hanging amulets; On spells; On how a spell should be used; On medicine for making women fat;.... On wearing silk;.... On garments dyed in yellow colour,.... green colour,.... red colour; On a concession in wearing red clothes; ....On opening the buttons of the collar; On the extent to which one should wear the lower garment;.... On wearing sandals;.... On using perfume; On setting the hair right; On the dye for women; On adding false hair;.... On a woman who uses perfume when she goes out; On parting the

Sunan Abu Dawud

hair; On the extent to which the hair should hang; On growing long hair;... On clipping the moustaches; On plucking out grey hair; On hair dye,... black dye,... yellow dye;.... On the signs of the Last Hour;.... On the coming forth of the *Dajjal* (Antichrist); On *Al-Jassasahr*, the spy of the *Dajjal*, a beast which is to seek for news to take to the *Dajjal* (Antichrist);.... On sitting partly in the shade and partly in the sun; On sitting in a circle; On sitting in the middle of a circle; On how a man should sit;.... On a man who sits cross-legged;.... On placing one leg over the other while lying on the back;.... On playing with dolls;.... On the prohibition of playing backgammon; On playing with pigeons;.... On yawning; On sneezing; On the response to the one who sneezes; On how many times one should respond to the one who sneezes; On how one should invoke blessing on a *dhimmi* (a protected non-Muslim) when he sneezes; On a man who sneezes and does not praise Allah; On a man who lies on his stomach; On sleeping on the roof of a house with no stone palisade; On sleeping in a state of purification; On which side one should face while sleeping; On what a man should say while going to sleep; On what a man should say when he is alarmed while asleep at night; On glorifying Allah at the time of going to bed; On what one should say in the morning; On what a man should say when he sights the new moon; On what a man should say when he goes out of his house; On what a man should say when he goes into his house; On what a man should say when a stormy wind blows; On rain; On cocks and beasts; On the braying of asses and the barking of dogs;.... On killing snakes,.... geckos, ... ants, ... frogs; On throwing pebbles; On circumcision of girls; On the walking of women with men in the road;....

Sunan Abu Dawud

* * *

The contents speak for themselves. We need only note that the Prophet's guidance has been considered necessary even on such subjects. That, the guidance having been provided, if one does not act according to it even on such matters one is guilty of the great sin—that is, of defying the explicit command and example of the Prophet. That a community which has been weaned on the dogma that even on such matters it needs the guidance of a Prophet has had all capacity for thinking for itself drained out of it. That a community drained in this way is ripe for picking by the ulema.

But to proceed: the *Sahih Muslim* sets out Hadis upon Hadis, inter alia, on matters such as the following:

* * *

> While cleaning the nose and using pebbles to clean oneself after defecation, the odd number is preferable;....Purging of sins with ablution water;.... The tooth-stick; how to cleanse oneself after relieving oneself;.... Instructions pertaining to the licking of a dog;.... Pertaining to the urine of a suckling babe, and how it is to be washed away; Washing away of the semen from die garment and its scraping; The impurity of the blood of menses and its washing; An entire series on menstruation: lying above the waist-wrapper with one in menstmation; The menstruating woman is permitted to wash the hair of her husband, comb his hair, and her left-over is clean, and one is permitted to recline in her lap and recite the Quran; Washing the face and hands after getting up from sleep; ... Bathing is obligatory for a woman after experiencing orgasm in a dream;.... Bathing after sexual intercourse or seminal emission; The quantity of water which is desirable for a bath because of sexual intercourse; Bathing of the male and female with one vessel in the same condition and washing of one of them with the left-over of the other; .... Law of Shariah pertaining to the plaited hair of the woman who takes a bath; The desirability of using musk at the spot of blood while bathing after menstruation;.... Emission of semen makes bath obligatory; Abrogation of (the command that) bath is obligatory (only) because of seminal emission and

> instead contact of the circumcised parts makes bath obligatory;.... What should be uttered while entering the privy;.... There is no harm in observing fast if one is *junbi* even after dawn; Sexual intercourse is completely forbidden during the day in the month of Ramzan;.... Hunting with the help of trained dogs;.... Pertaining to eating the flesh of the domestic ass,.... horse,.... lizard,.... locusts;.... disapproval of drinking water while standing; Permissibility of drinking Zamzam water while standing; It is repugnant to breathe in a vessel and appreciable to breathe three times outside the vessel in the course of drinking; It is desirable to circulate water or milk (in an assembly) from the right-hand side of the one who serves; The merit of licking the fingers after taking food and wiping the dish (with fingers) and eating of the fallen mouthful after removing the dirt sticking to it;.... Permissibility of eating soup and the merit of eating pumpkin;.... Eating cucumber with dates;.... Pertaining to the wearing of sandals;.... It is prohibited to lie down on one's back and place one's foot upon the other; Permissibility of placing one foot upon the other while lying;.... It is prohibited to play chess; Pertaining to the interpretation of dreams;.... The majority in Paradise would consist of the poor, pious persons and the majority of the denizens of hell would consist of women, and the trial by means of women;.... Description of the Day of Judgement, Paradise and Hell;.... The feast for the inhabitants of Paradise;....The splitting up of the moon;....The non-believers will be made to crawl on their faces; Several *hadis* describing a tree in Paradise, a river in Paradise, a street in Paradise, the tent in which the inmates of Paradise will be housed; Description of Hell and the intensity of its heat and torments;.... Sneezing and the disapproval of yawning....
>
> *Sahih Muslim*

* * *

Again, the contents speak for themselves. In addition to what has been said earlier, we need note just three things in brief. Along with the Quran, the Hadis are the very basis of the much vaunted Shariah. Second, there is no basis for holding that the Hadis on some matters—say, divorce—are more important or are to be adhered to more strictly or are more reliable than the Hadis on other matters—say, the explanation for sneezing or yawning, the geography of Paradise or the meteorology of Hell: as all originate from the Prophet, if one doubts them on one matter one doubts them on others as well. And third: as will be evident, in dealing with the sorts of subjects which at first occasioned surprise in us, the ulema in their fatwas are only following the precedent of the Prophet and the Companions; indeed in case after case, when a question is asked the fatwa faithfully reproduces the exact words of the Prophet on the matter.

Being more voluminous than the rest, the most revered among the Hadis collections, *Sahih al-Bukhari*, has a far greater number of Hadis on matters of the same sort of gravity, for instance:

* * *

Sahih al-Bukhari

What to say when entering the lavatory; Providing water in lavatories; The direction to face when defecating or urinating; On women answering the call of nature; Defecating in the houses; Washing the private parts after answering the call; The hand one should use for cleaning the private parts; The right hand not to be used to hold the private parts; The right hand not to be used to hold the private part while urinating; Cleaning the private parts with stones; Cleaning the private parts with dung; how an odd number of stones should be used to clean the private parts; The side of the body from which one should start while washing;....Passing urine while sitting or standing; Washing out semen with water; Spots not completely removed;.... Repeating sexual intercourse without bathing; Washing away emotional urethral discharge;.... Remembering in the mosque that one is *junub*;.... Women having a wet dream; A Muslim does not become impure; Going out of a person while he is in *junub*; a *junub* staying home only with ablution; *Junub* performing only ablution before sleeping; If male and female organs come in close contact; Washing away a woman's discharge; An entire Book on menses—a menstruating woman washing the husband's head and combing his hair; Leaning on menstruating wife while reciting the Quran; Fondling a menstruating wife—and so on and on;.... An entire series on bargains—on goods which have been paid for but will be delivered later, on renting, on transference of debt, on agriculture, on distribution of water....; 199 'chapters', on *jihad*; 41 'chapters' on distributing the booty taken in war;.... Description of the gates of Paradise, of the gates of Hell; On the 'intense blackness' of the irises of *houries* and the 'intense whiteness' of the sclerotic coat of their eyes;.... Marrying several women; Marrying virgins; Marrying matrons;.... Not to marry more than four wives at a time;.... Beating the tambourine during the *Nikah*;....Consummating the marriage before going on a campaign; Consummating marriage with a girl of nine years; Consummating marriage on a journey; Consummating marriage during the day; The curtains, bedding, etc. designed for women;.... What a man should say on having sexual intercourse; Several on the wedding banquet.... a meal of trotters;....A woman should not fast except with the husband's consent; Deserting her husband's bed;.... On women constituting the majority in Hell, because they are ungrateful to their husbands;.... 'beat them' (lightly); *Coitus interruptus*; To draw lots among wives; The wife giving up her turn to another wife; difficulty of dealing justly between women; Marrying a virgin after having had a matron; Taking one bath only after having had sexual intercourse with all the wives; Sexual relations with all the wives in one day; Taking the permission of all the wives; Loving some wives more than others;.... Women going out for their needs;.... 'I will go round to all my wives tonight';.... Eating what is nearer you; Eating with the right hand and beginning other things from the right side;.... Roasted

> meat; Dried yoghurt;....Eating a foreleg;.... Handing something across a dining table; Snake cucumber and fresh dates;.... Eating two dates at a time;....To lick and suck fingers before washing; ....A pet dog; ....The eating of locusts;.... The meat of chicken.... horse flesh, ... donkey flesh,.... the rabbit; If a mouse falls into butter; 16 'chapters' on slaughtering for sacrifice to Allah; 31 'chapters' on drinks; 22 'chapters' on patients, 58 on medicine; 103 'chapters' on dress:.... Dragging one's garment without conceit; To tuck up or roll up one's clothes; The part of the garment hanging below the ankles; Dragging one's garment out of conceit;.... The wearing of shirts; The pocket of a shirt;.... trousers; turbans;.... Green clothes; White clothes;.... while putting on shoes one should start with the right foot; While taking off shoes one should take off the left one first; The sandal with two straps;.... Cutting short the moustache; Clipping nails; Leaving the beard; Grey hair; Dyeing the hair; Curly hair;.... Parting the hair; .... Combing one's hair; Menstruating wife combing the hair of her husband; Start combing from the right side;....What to say on going to bed;.... Putting the right hand under the right cheek; Sleeping on the right side;.... On going to the lavatory; On getting up in the morning;.... Invocations against epidemics and disease;.... Invocation upon having sexual intercourse;.... Invocation against pagans; Invocation in favour of pagans; 53 'chapters' on emotions, 15 on Divine foreordainment, 33 on oaths and vows; 32 'chapters' on blood money .... a tooth for a tooth;....Not to kill a Muslim for killing a *Kafir*-,.... 48 'chapters' assigning meaning to dreams, 29 on afflictions to come—*Ad-Dajjal* (Antichrist'), Gog and Magog....

* * *

In the subjects they deal with, in the message they convey, in the mind they create, what a contrast the Hadis are to, say, the discourses of the Buddha!

Second, it the Shariah is a seamless web, as the ulema insist it is, so that not a thread of it can be plucked without the whole coming apart, knowledge transmitted by the Prophet is all the more so: the Shariah, after all, has in addition to what Allah said (which is set out in the Quran) and what the Prophet said (which is set out in the Hadis) the interpretations, etc., of ordinary mortals; but what is contained in the Hadis is knowledge and data certified by the Prophet himself. So every word is true, literally and absolutely so. There is no litmus by which one can say, 'We'll believe him on X, Y and Z; but on A, B and C what he said is superseded by what has become known since.'

Two points emerge from juxtaposing the volumes of Hadis and the volumes of fatwas.

Glancing through even the mere contents of the Hadis volumes shows that in issuing their fatwas the ulema follow the Hadis most faithfully. They expend a large part of their energies and scholarship on questions of the same kind. The other side of the coin is to be seen in the attitude of the community: it is to the ulema that it turns for deciding questions of even this kind.

Concerns

Nor is it just a matter of the sorts of topics which are dealt with. On the topics themselves the nature of the concerns is the same. We were surprised at the extent to which the fatwas on prayer, fasting, pilgrimage dealt with externals, for instance. But the hundreds and hundreds of Hadis which deal with these topics are concerned with little other than the externals. We were surprised that the ulema should be so emphatic about using balls of earth and pebbles to clean oneself after urinating or defecating. But they are only reiterating the command of the Prophet. We were surprised, and a bit amused that among the reasons Maulana Ahmad Riza Khan should give for not using toilet paper is that the Christians do so. But then that was the Prophet's mode of reasoning too.

On one thing after another the Prophet's edict was to do the opposite of what the non-believers did. Indeed his criterion for deciding what ought to be done or how a particular thing ought to be done was to determine what the non-believers did or how they did it, and to then prescribe the opposite.

The pagans of the time kept their moustaches and cut their beards. Accordingly the Prophet said, 'Do the opposite of what the idolaters do; take out the moustaches and grow the beards.'[59] He prescribed that believers should tie their turbans on their caps saying that 'this is the difference between ourselves and the idolaters.'[60] He forbade believers from lining their clothes with silk and from putting silk over their shoulders saying that doing these things was the way of Ajamis. (Ajamis are non-Arabs, particularly people to the East of Iraq.)[61] He ordered Muslims, 'Do away with the (white) hair of old age,' and added, 'Do not be like the Jews.'[62] He chanced upon a child, Anas bin Malik. The child had two plaits of hair. The Prophet put his hand on the child's head, blessed it, and told the guardians, 'Either shave them or cut them away.' The reason? 'This is the way of the Jews.'[63] The reason on account of which he forbade Muslims from wearing saffron clothes was the same: 'These are the clothes (usually worn by) the non-believers, so do not wear them,' he told a Companion when he saw him in clothes dyed saffron. In another version of the Hadis, the Prophet upon seeing the Companion clad in saffron clothes first mocked him,

---

59. *Sahih Muslim Sharif*, Volume I, p. 389.

60. *Mishkat Sharif* ,Volume II, Rabbani Book Depot, Delhi, n.d., Hadis 4144/32, p. 150.

61. Ibid., Hadis 4158/46, p. 153

62. Ibid., Hadis 4256/37, p. 169.

63. Ibid., Hadis 4683/64, pp. 175–76.

'Has you mother ordered you to do so?' The Companion at once promised to wash them. The Prophet said, 'Burn them.'[64]

The Prophet was asked about food eaten by Christians. He replied, 'Let no such thing come to your mind as is like that of the Christians.'[65] 'Do not slice meat with a knife,' he ordered, 'because that is what the Ajamis (Iranians) do, instead bite it with your teeth—that is very pleasant.'[66]

The Jews and the Christians of the time did not dye their hair. The Prophet ordered: 'The Jews and the Christians do not dye their hair. You do the opposite.'[67] The editor/translator of the Hadis collection adds in parentheses, 'For the simple reason that opposing the *Kafirs* is necessary for doing better things.' And then softens the rule a bit by adding, 'A Muslim should always act according to this rule. He should accept the better and wiser course. If that is opposed to the way of the *Kafirs*, it is all the better.'[68] I suppose one has to settle for the small mercy!

The same criterion settled other matters—from how one should deal with women who were menstruating to what one should do at the death of a person. When a woman was in menses, we learn in the *Sunan Nasai Sharif*, the Jews did not let her eat or drink with them; nor did they dwell in the same house as her. What should we do about them?, the Companion asked the Prophet. Allah thereupon sent down the well known verse, 'They ask you about menstruation....' (Quran, 2.222). The Prophet ordered, as usual, the course opposite to what the non-believers were doing. He ordered

---

64. *Sahih Muslim*, Volume III, Hadis 5173–78, p. 1146.

65. *Mishkat Sharif*, Volume II, Hadis 3908/24, p. 105.

66. Ibid., Hadis 4029/52, p. 126.

67. *Sunan Nasai Sharif*, Allama Wahiduz Zaman (tr.), Aiteqad Publishing House, Delhi, 1986, Volume III, Hadis 5074, p. 433; see also Hadis 5246, p. 477.

68. *Sahih al-Bukhari Sharif*, Volume III, Hadis 520, p. 319.

the Companion to let the women in menses eat and drink with them and to live in the same house with them. They could do anything with them, he decreed, except have sexual intercourse with them.[69]

What held for food, for the way food ought be eaten, for dress, for women who were having their menses, held too for how one ought to conduct oneself. The Prophet came bending on a stick, narrates a Companion. Those present stood up in his honour. The Prophet said, 'Do not stand up as the Ajamis (Iranians) do for honouring particular persons.'[70]

A Jew died. His people were weeping. The Prophet saw them. He said that the dead suffer torment in the grave if his people weep over his depth. He therefore forbade believers from weeping audibly over their dead.[71] Similarly, whenever the Prophet accompanied a bier he would not sit down till the bier was lowered into the grave. One day a learned Jew happened to pass by. Addressing the Prophet he exclaimed, 'O, Muhammad, we also do the same.' The Prophet at once sat down and told the Companions, 'Do the opposite of what they do.'[72]

Similary, Sulaiman mentioned to the Prophet that the Taurat states that it is propitious to do ablution after eating. The Prophet observed that it was propitious to do ablutions both before and after eating. By the next Hadis, one may eschew it before eating: the Prophet comes out of the lavatory; people ask him if water is to be brought to him for ablution; he says that he has been ordered to do it only before standing for *namaz*.[73] In another Hadis Sulaiman is reported

69. *Sunan Nasai Sharif*, Volume I, Hadis 291, p. 97.

70. *Mishkat Sharif*, Volume II, Hadis 4493/6, p. 219.

71. *Jama Tirmizi*, Allama Badi al-Zaman (tr.), Aitqad Publishing House, Delhi, 1983, Volume I, p. 371.

72. Ibid., Volume I, p. 376.

73. Ibid., Volume I, pp. 667–68.

as telling the Prophet that he had read in the Taurat about doing wuzu after meals and sought his ruling. The Prophet then prescribed wuzu both before and after meals.[74]

The exact same criterion settled what one would consider are strictly religious observances. As is well known, when the Prophet and his Companions first came to Medina he directed that they bow towards Jerusalem in their prayers that is Jerusalem was prescribed as the Qiblah. Jewish holidays and festival days were adopted and prescribed for the faithful. Once the power of the Prophet had been consolidated the faithful were commanded to stop bowing towards Jerusalem and to bow towards the Kaba in Mecca instead. Other changes followed the same pattern.

The Prophet's wife, Aisha related that the Quraish used to fast on the day of Ashura (the tenth day of Muharram). The Prophet used to do so also. He kept to this practice after migrating to Medina also and asked the believers to do the same. But soon enough he shifted the obligatory fasting to Ramzan. It was no longer obligatory to fast at Ashura.[75]

Only death prevented a further change, it seems. In the *Sunan Abu Dawud* we learn that the Prophet used to keep a fast on Ashura, the tenth day of Muharram and had ordered the Companions to do so also. The Companions pointed out that this day was the same one which the Jews and Christians honoured. The Prophet then observed that if he remained alive at the end of that year he would observe the fast on the ninth day. But, notes the Hadis, before the year ended he passed away.[76]

Both the morning meal and the breaking of the fast were devised so as to set the Muslims apart from the Jews and

---

74. *Mishkat Sharif*, Volume II, Hadis 4023/46, p. 125.

75. *Jama Tirmizi*, Volume I, p. 291.

76. *Sunan Abu Dawud Sharif*, Volume II, Hadis 673, p. 268.

Christians, and the Prophet was at pains to make sure that the followers saw them as such. Pointing to the *sahri,* the morning meal, he remarked, 'This is the difference between our way of fasting and that of the People of the Book—the eating of *sahri.*'[77] His admonition regarding the ending of the fasts—about the *Iftar*—was couched in the same vein and was to the same effect. He decleard: 'The Din will prevail so long as people hurry in ending the fast, because the Jews and the Christians delay the *Iftar.*'[78]

What held for fasting held equally for the details of prayer. When Muslims came to Medina, they used to get together for namaz by making a guess about the time. Nobody called them to prayer. It was proposed that they be called to prayer by a flag being raised. Then someone suggested, 'Why not have a horn like the Jews?' The Prophet did not like the suggestion, we learn in the books of Hadis, 'because it meant action like the Jews and the Prophet did not like similarity with the People of the Book in matters of Faith.' Thereupon someone suggested the bell. The Prophet rejected that proposal also saying, 'This is what the Christians do.' He then ordered Bilal to call out the azan.[79]

The infidels were in his mind while prescribing the time of namaz too. He said: 'Do the morning *namaz* before the sun rises because it rises between the horns of Satan when the infidels do prostrations to it.... Wait for the evening *namaz* till the sun has set because it sets between the two

---

77. *Sunan Nasai Sharif,* Volume II, Hadis 2170, p. 51.

78. *Sunan Abu Dawud Sharif,* Volume II, Hadis 581, p. 237.

79. *Sunan Abu Dawud Sharif,* Volume I, Hadis 495, pp. 212–13. The translator comments: 'This *hadis* has been interpreted by some people as a prohibition of keeping any similarities with the Jews and Christians.' To the same effect see *Jama Tirmizi,* Volume I, pp. 114–15, *Sahih al-Bukhari Sharif,* Maulana Akhtar Shahjahanpuri (tr.), Delhi, 1984, Volume I, Hadis 393, p. 290.

horns of Satan when the infidels do prostrations to it...'[80] The infidels were just as much in his mind when he prescribed the dress for namaz: he declared, 'He among you who has two pieces of cloth should wear them both for doing *namaz*. If he has only one cloth, he should use it as a *tahband* and not let it hang as the Jews do.' He added, 'Do the opposite of what the Jews do. They do not do *namaz* with shoes and socks on.'[81]

Why did he prescribe Friday as the day for special prayers: 'We are the last to appear in the world,' he explained, 'but we will be the first on the Day of Judgement. It is a small matter that they got the Book earlier and we got it later. This (Friday) is the day He (Allah) had made prayers obligatory on them but they disobeyed and Allah instructed us regarding the day, so those people follow after us (that is, they pray on Saturday and Sunday after we have prayed on Friday).' He said, 'Allah has led the earlier people away from Friday. The Jews chose Saturday and the Christians plumped for Sunday. Then Allah created us and told us about Friday. Now Friday comes first, then Saturday, and then Sunday. So the Jews and Christians will follow after us on the Last Day.....'[82]

And so also on the rites of the hajj pilgrimage. 'Urwah relates that I read the verse (Quran, 2.158) to Aisha,' we are told in the Hadis, 'and said that it does not matter if I run or not between Safa and Marwah. Aisha said 'You are talking nonsense. People did not run between Safa and Marwah during the days of Ignorance but considered it a sin. When

---

80. *Sahih Muslim Sharif*, Volume II, p. 299.

81. *Sunan Abu Dawud Sharif*, Volume I, Hadis 633, p. 264; and ibid., Hadis 647, p. 269.

82. *Sahih Muslim Sharif*, Volume II, p. 318; *Sunan Ibn Majah*, Volume I, Hadis 1131, p. 313; *Sahih al-Bukhari Sharif*, Volume. I, Hadis 557, p. 371.

Islam came and the Quran was revealed, this verse was made known and the Prophet ran between Safa and Marwah and we ran with him and it become the Sunna.'[83] What was the reason for leaving the Madhdalfah during hajj? 'We were standing in the Madhdalfah,' we learn in the Hadis. 'Umar bin Khattab said, 'The idolaters did not leave it before the sun rose. They used to start after sunshine had brightened the hill of Sabir.' The Prophet did the opposite. Umar left the place before sunrise....'[84]

On one thing after the other the criterion of conduct was: What is it that the non-believers do? You do the opposite. How do they do this particular thing? You do it in the opposite way. Are the ulema at fault when they also adopt that kind of reasoning and issue fatwas accordingly?

Dated notions

The notions which underlay many of the fatwas surprised us by their outlandishness. But the Hadis—the source of Muslim law, lore and learning next only to the Quran—contain notions which are just as quaint.

'When any of you eats,' says the Prophet, 'he should eat with his right hand, and when he drinks, he should drink with his right hand, for the devil eats with his left hand and drinks with his left hand'[85]—a specific bit of information about the Devil.

---

83. *Sunan Nasai Sharif,* Volume II, Hadis 2972, p. 296; *Sahih Muslim,* Volume II, pp. 644–46.

84. *Sunan Ibn Majah,* Volume II, Hadis 239, p. 233; *Sahih al-Bukhari Sharif,* Volume I, Hadis 1571, p. 620.

85. *Sunan Abu Dawud,* Volume III, p. 1065; and *Riyad as-Salihin,* Volume II, pp. 384, 392. See *Riyad as-Salihin,* Volume I, pp. 458–60 for several Hadis which set out the emphasis the Prophet placed on using the right hand, and on beginning everything—combing the hair, cutting it, wearing shoes, bathing, performing ablution, wearing clothes—from the right side.

We were surprised that the ulema should expend their energy to decide what the language will be—whether it shall be Arabic or Syriac—in which a person will be questioned in his grave. But the inquisition in the grave is a very live topic in the Hadis. The Prophet explains how the dead man, when his friends leave him, shall hear the beat of their sandals; how two angels will come and question him: Who is your Lord?, they will ask; What is your religion?, they will ask; the Prophet explains that upon the man declaring his allegiance to Allah, the Prophet and Islam, bedding and clothes shall be sent down for him from Paradise; that, on the other hand, for the infidel 'some of its (Hell's) heat and pestilential wind will come to him, and his grave will become restricted so his ribs will be pressed together;' that a being who is blind and dumb will then be placed in charge of the infidel, he shall have a sledgehammer such that if a mountain were stuck with it, it would become dust; then he will give the infidel 'a blow with it which will be heard by everything between the east and the west except by men and djinn, and he will become dust....'[86]

Anyone surprised at the fatwas would be equally surprised to learn that—amidst all His preoccupations—'Allah likes sneezing and dislikes yawning.' The reader may not be surprised at being urged to hold his hand over his mouth while yawning, but he *will* be surprised at the reason on account of which he must do so: he must hold his hand over his mouth while yawning, the Prophet says, 'for the devil enters' him through his mouth while he yawns.[87] Indeed yawning per se is said to be from the devil.[88]

---

88. *Sahih Muslim,* Volume IV, p. 1540.

86. *Sunan Abu Dawud,* Volume III, pp. 1329–31.

87. *Sunan Abu Dawud,* Volume III, pp. 1397. Also *Sahih Muslim,* Volume IV, pp.1539–40.

He will also be surprised to learn that there is the most vital of distinctions between a cock crowing and an ass braying: 'When you hear the cocks crowing,' the Prophet declares, 'ask Allah for some of His grace, for they have seen an angel; but when you hear an ass braying, seek refuge in Allah from the devil, for it has seen the devil.'[89]

'When any of you wakes up from sleep and performs ablution,' the Prophet says, 'he must clean his nose three times'—there is no problem with that simple rule of hygiene, but the reason will occasion surprise: 'for,' declares the Prophet, 'the devil spends the night in the interior of his nose.'[90]

Good dreams come from Allah, the Prophet declares, bad dreams are from Satan. The remedy he proposes is as specific as it is surprising: 'So when one of you sees a bad dream which he does not like, he should spit on his left side thrice and seek refuge with Allah from its evil, then it will not harm him.'[91]

There are descriptions of a tree in Paradise 'under which a rider of swift horse will not be able to cover the distance from one end to another in one hundred years'. There are descriptions of a street, of a river in Paradise, of 'the tent of a single-hollowed pearl of which the breadth or length will be sixty miles,' of the layers of apartments in Paradise each as distant from the others as planets from the earth. There are descriptions of the 'intense blackness' of the irises of houris and the 'intense whiteness' of the white of their eyes, of their being 'sixty cubits tall', of their skin and flesh being transparent so that 'the marrow of their shanks would glimmer beneath the flesh.' Each man shall be given two of these as his wives.

---

89. *Sunan Abu Dawud,* Volume III, pp. 1414–15.

90. *Sahih Muslim,* Volume 1, p. 153.

91. *Sahih Muslim,* Volume IV, pp. 1223–24. Also *Sahih al-Bukhari,* Volume IX, pp. 105, 111.

The Prophet certifies that in Paradise the faithful 'suffer no toil, nor shall they ever be ejected from there;' 'There they shall be served in dishes and cups of gold. There they will find all that the soul desires and the eyes cherish;' 'There you shall have abundant fruit, enough for you to eat;' there 'the righteous will be lodged in a place of peace, amongst gardens and springs. They shall wear fine silk and heavy brocade, and sit face to face... And We shall wed them to maidens having wide lustrous eyes....' They will suffer no death, nor illness, nor ageing: the last by a special device, for, 'In Paradise there is a market to which the people will come every week ("Friday"). The northern wind will blow and scatter fragrance on their faces and clothes and it will enhance their beauty and loveliness. They will then return to their families (of the maidens having "wide lustrous eyes") having been increased in beauty and loveliness....'

'The inhabitants will eat and drink in Paradise, but they will not have to pass excrement, to blow noses or to urinate,' the Prophet certifies. 'Their food will be digested producing belch which will give out a smell like that of musk...;' '....Their combs will be of gold and their perspiration will give out smell like that of musk;' 'Their fire-places send forth the fragrance of aloes .....;' They shall live in bliss, reclining on couches; 'They shall be given to drink a pure beverage securely sealed with musk and tempered with the water of Tasnim, a spring from which the chosen ones will drink ...;' and of course they will have the bliss of being able to see the face of Allah 'as you are seeing this moon'....

There are corresponding descriptions of the intensity of the fire in Hell, of its inhabitants. And of *Ad-Dajjal*, the Antichrist: that 'he is one-eyed while Allah is not,' that he has a huge body, a red complexion, that he is blind in one eye, that the other eye protrudes like a grape, that he will have with him fire which will seem water and water which will seem fire, and between his eyes will be written the word 'kafir'; he will encamp near Medina and then Medina will shake thrice whereupon every kafir and every Hypocrite will go out of Medina towards him, but Ad-Dajjal will not be able to enter Medina as each of its seven gates will be protected by two angels....[92]

If these notions pervaded some medieval text book, one could get over them by replacing that book by something contemporary. But when these are knowledge stated by the Prophet, when they are facts certified by the Prophet, can updating of textbooks get over them? All the more so when there is no rule by which one can assert that the knowledge and opinions set out by the Prophet on one set of subjects—inheritance, talaq, etc.—are on a different footing than the knowledge and opinions set out by him on other subjects—Antichrist, the Last Hour, the Day of Judgement, questioning in the grave, jihad, the shapes of houris, the Fire of Hell, whether one shall only eat and drink in Paradise and not have to urinate and defecate.... They are a seamless whole. As we saw, the accounts of the latter are as specific as of the former, they are as definite. If one doubts what the Prophet has set out in regard to them, there is no rule to stop one from doubting what he has specified on any other matter.

Dialogue, discourse

We look askance at the ulema when they scotch rational dialogue. But it is not some sundry alim, it is Allah who says,

> When thou seest men
> Engaged in vain discourse
> About Our signs, turn

---

92. For instance, *Sahih al-Bukhari*, Volume IX, pp. 182–86; *Sahih Muslim*, Volume IV, pp. 1476–92; *Riyad as-Salihin*, Volume II, pp. 542–50.

Away from them unless
They turn to a different
Theme....

(Quran, 6.68)

It is Allah Himself who repeats the admonition:

Already has He sent you
Word in the Book, that when
You hear the Signs of Allah
Held in defiance and ridicule,
You are not to sit with them
Unless they turn to a different
Theme: if you did, you would be
Like them. For God will
Collect the hypocrites and those
Who defy Faith—all in Hell.

(Quran, 4.140)

All who have seen how Christianity has been liberated from dogma would chafe at the fatwas by which the ulema stamp out inquiry and questioning. But what will they do when Allah Himself declares:

O you who believe!
Ask not questions
About things which
If made plain to you
May cause you trouble.
But if you ask about things
When the Quran is being
Revealed, they will be
Made plain to you....

(Quran, 5.104)

And as the revelation of the Quran was completed over 1,350 years ago, the time for asking questions is clearly over. What will they say when it is the Prophet himself who forbids one from 'persistent questioning'?[93] What will they do when it is the Prophet himself, and not some ordinary alim, who asks the believers to do as they have been told, and who warns, 'verily the people before you went to their doom because they had put too many questions to their Prophets and then disagreed with their teachings?'[94]

It is the Prophet who warns people from trying to discover the meaning behind 'the allegorical verses' of the Quran. And how much is shut out by that rule one cannot be certain—for, as the editor of the *Sahih Muslim* records, 'There is a good deal of difference amongst scholars as to which verses or words of the Quran are allegorical.' We saw earlier that confronted with the task of showing how the fact that there have been a hundred Caliphs squares with the Prophet's declaration that there will be only twelve, the *Fatawa-i-Rizvia* holds that the declaration even about the number of Caliphs relates to a hidden matter.

It is the Prophet who, upon hearing two persons arguing about a verse, grows angry and exclaims, 'Verily, the (peoples) before you were ruined because of their disputation in the Book.' It is the Prophet who dubs persons who enter into disputations about the meanings of the Word of God 'the most despicable amongst persons in the eyes of Allah'. It is the Prophet who warns, 'Ruined were those who indulged in hair-splitting,' and repeats the warning thrice.[95] It is the Prophet who admonishes the faithful, 'I enjoin you to fear Allah, to hear and obey even if he (the ruler) be a Negro slave. Because whoso among you shall live after me shall soon see much discord, you shall then hold fast to my

93. *Sahih Muslim,* Volume III, pp. 929–30; also *Riyad as-Salihin,* Volume I, pp. 117–23.

94. *Sahih Muslim,* Volume IV, pp. 1256–58.

95. On the preceding, *Sahih Muslim,* Volume IV, pp. 1402–3.

example and the example of the rightly guided Caliphs who come after me. Adhere to it and hold them firm with teeth. Beware of new things because every novelty is innovation, and every innovation is misleading.'[96]

It is not the ulema, it is Allah who declares,

> Nothing have We omitted from the Book (of Our decrees).
>
> (Quran, 6.38)

In accordance with that premise, it is not some alim, it is the Prophet who declares, 'If anyone introduces into his faith something that does not belong to it, he is a reprobate.' In warning the faithful against innovations, it is about the Prophet that a Companion recounts, 'While the Messenger of Allah was delivering a sermon, his eyes turned red, his tone became loud and he flew into a passion as if he was alerting us against an army of the foe. He said, "The enemy is about to attack you in the morning and the enemy is advancing against you in the evening." He further said, "My annunciation (as Prophet) and the advent of Doomsday are in juxtaposition with one another as my two fingers"—and he would hold up his forefinger and middle fingei together. He used to point out: the best discourse is the Book of Allah and the best example is the example of Muhammad; the worst practice is the invention of new elements in the faith and every innovation is misguidance....'[97]

Are the ulema then concocting something of their own when they inveigh against those who think of attending interdenominational meetings where religious issues are discussed? Are they concocting something of their own when they inveigh against even the slightest impulse to examine verses of the Quran, the Hadis, and, by extension, the rulings of the ulema?

---

96. Abu Dawud and Tirmizi in *Riyad as-Salihin,* Volume I, p. 119.
97. Muslim in *Riyad as-Salihin,* Volume I, pp. 127–28.

In a word: the problem is not one that can be got over merely by updating the textbooks which are in use at 'the Centres of Islamic Learning'. A textbook or two may be replaced. But how can the Quran and Hadis be got around?

Is there no way out then?

Our World

11

To give history a helping hand

It is of the very essence of a totalitarian ideology that it enforces its right to regulate the totality of life. The Quran, the Hadis, the fatwas represent one continuous endeavour in this respect: they aim at controlling every single aspect of life.

As we have seen this comprehensiveness is one of the main pillars of the power of the ulema. But that very comprehensiveness becomes one of the reasons for the eventual collapse of such systems. At first it is not just a mark of the power of the ideology and the system, it is its actual power: for, even while he is engaged in the most private acts, the adherent has to go by what the ideology or system lays down. The adherent himself is so conditioned that, when engaging in that private act, he feels it necessary—out of 'faith' at times, out of prudence at others—to first ascertain what the official prescription is about how that thing ought to be done. But by encompassing everything the ideology also lays itself open on every front. Thus in the end when a man just urinates while standing he is in a deep sense subverting the ideology itself.

The individual is departing from the Sunna of the Prophet in that particular of course. But in fact he is doing much more. When the norm that he must adhere to the Sunna of the Prophet has been dinned into him so strenuously, the point that bores into his mind as he stands urinating is not just that he is urinating in one posture rather than another, but that he is departing from the Sunna. Guilt and fear erupt naturally—guilt at departing from the clear directive of the Prophet, and fear that someone might notice that he is doing so and that he might then have to suffer the consequences. When, in spite of the guilt and the fear, he persists in doing that private act in that way, he gets into the mode of, into the habit of disregarding the Sunna in general. Every condom becomes a rapier subverting Papal authority, every public urinal a saw undercutting the authority of the Hadis and the Shariah.

The comprehensiveness boomerangs in another way also. That every aspect of life is covered by the Shariah is the fount of the ulema's power. But that also means that differences can arise over the minutest matter. Moreover, as every matter is a matter of religion, and as in the *Ulema*'s world view religion is more important than life itself, every disagreement becomes *a disagreement over religion.* Every difference of opinion thus becomes *a religious dispute.* If an alim were spotted to be urinating while standing, if he were to be charged not to be doing istinja with the odd number of stones, if he were seen to be using his left hand while eating or tying his turban, if he were to be seen wearing a pyjama which extended beyond his ankles, in the eyes of the ulema he would be wilfully spurning the clearest instructions of the Prophet. He would be guilty not just of deviant conduct on some small, peripheral matter, but of defiant conduct, of rebellion against the Faith. The ulema would naturally ask: 'Unless he is checked on these matters will he not start disregarding the Shariah on other matters? And then, 'Unless he is checked, will others not act likewise?' And finally, 'What will be left of the Faith then?'

And in a sense it is a religious question. When the authority and example of the Prophet have been vested with absolute supremacy, when they have been made the be-all and end-all of the Faith, then for what reason can the man be disregarding the clear instruction of the Prophet except for a religious reason? What is his deviation except a conscious, premeditated subversion, even repudiation of the religion?

But when every departure is a deviation for a religious reason, a disagreement is bound to become a dispute, variance is bound to end in schism.

We thus have two reasons for hope. First, as the totalitarian ideology of the shariah has laid itself open on every front, as it has vested the conduct and remarks of the Prophet with total finality, the normal evolution of life even in the most peripheral areas is bound to lead people to disregard the Shariah in practice, and thereby to get into the habit of disregarding it in general. Muslims pay and receive interest today. They wear clothes which violate the norms prescribed by the ulema. They take photographs and have their photographs taken. They act in films and see films. They have TVs in their homes. Their youth attend modern schools and colleges. They use contraceptives. All of them are not engaged perpetually in waging jihad.... In a word, life itself is the corrosive which is eating away at this totalitarian ideology, as it has at other such ideologies.

Second, the ulema split, and divide into warring factions. One reason as we have seen is germane to the ideology: the smallest difference on the most peripheral and trivial matter quickly becomes, in fairness it *is* a difference over fundamentals. The other reason is germane to the ulema. Their whole pursuit is power. For them, as for the communist parties for instance, ideology is an instrument for acquiring power and aggrandizing it. To a faction of the ulema the rival is not just the one who has influence over the kafirs, the more immediate rival, and therefore the one demanding more urgent attention is the other faction of ulema. Differences of opinion thus become disputes over dogma, and the disputes become bitter and shrill as they are weapons of dominion.

The tussles for dominion are doubly destructive. They divide the ulema, they pit factions against factions and, as we shall see, during the fights the factions say such things about other factions, they expose such facts about other factions that the ulema as a whole are discredited. Second, each faction argues its case by citing verses and texts—the Quran, the Hadis. The ease with which each faction is able to conjure verses and texts to its aid convinces even the believer that the verses and texts are so diverse, or so pliable that they can justify any and every position. His reverence for the texts splinters. Moreover, as the factions twist and invoke some verses and texts and gloss over others in what are manifestly tussles for dominion, the believer too sees that the verses and texts are mere *instruments*—for securing worldly, profane power. The ideology starts as a Revelation from on high. The factions use it as an instrument for aggrandisement. The believer comes to see that it is but an instrument.

The ulema on each other

You wouldn't think that the question whether the saliva of a cat is clean or unclean is a question of great moment. But it caused the gravest controversies between two great jurists—Qazi Shihabuddin Daulatabadi and Sheikh Abul Fatah Jaunpuri—so much so that, as Professor Mujeeb notes, 'the two abused and cursed each other.'[1]

During the congregational prayer may one say, Amin (the equivalent of Amen) loudly after *Surah-ul-Fatiha*? May one raise one's hands up to one's ears at the commencement

1. M. Mujeeb, *The Indian Muslims*, George Allen and Unwin, London, 1969, pp. 76–77.

of some *rukus* during *salat*, prayers? Of what significance can such questions be in relation to the inner quest? But these are the very questions which have led to the most virulent dissensions among the ulema during the last two hundred years in the subcontinent. Qureshi's detailed and laudatory study, ulema *in Politics*, contains several examples of the fierce controversies which have raged over such issues, and much lament over the consequence such issues have had in dividing the ulema and the ummah. A single example will illustrate the ferocity with which the issues are joined, how they get entwined with the struggles for domination, indeed how, having started as disputes over ritual, they become instruments in the struggles for domination. Recounting the career of that important early nineteenth-century evangelist-fundamentalist, Sayyid Ahmed Shahid, and of his associate, Shah Isma'il, Qureshi writes:

> The people were staunch and to them little points in rituals were of fundamental importance. Shah Isma'il Shahid had adopted some points of the Shafi'i *fiqh* in prayers like *raf'u yadain*, raising the hands up to the ears in the midst of prayers at the change of some postures. This created so much mischief that the Saiyid had to assert publicly that the Mujahidin were staunch Hanafis. This was true, because Shah Isma'il also called himself a Hanafi subject to conclusions arrived at by personal inquiry. This deviation was so close to *ghair taqlid* (non-conformity with established belief) that the common man could not understand the difference. Indeed when carried further, it did create the sect *Ghair Muquallids* or *Ahl-i-hadith*. The Saiyid himself was moderate in these matters, and he successfully persuaded Shah Isma'il to conform to the prevailing norms. These differences created opposition even in the more sophisticated (circles in) India. Among the Pathans it created a most explosive situation. Though Saiyid's intervention was successful with Shah Isma'il and his small group of followers,

some of the more extremist adherents of non-conformity to the Hanafi ritual, did not give up their practices. One of these had even to be expelled, but the Saiyid could do little more in a matter of religious conviction. The local chiefs had received a *mahdar* which bore seals of many *Ulema* alleging that the Saiyid was a British agent and had been sent to collect information about the area. He was ostensibly leading a *Jihad* but in fact his purpose was to corrupt the faith of the people. He had invented a new religion which did not believe in any saint or man of spiritual greatness. Then there was an appeal that the recipients should combine together to destroy the Saiyid and his followers before they were able to indulge in any further mischief.

I.H. Qureshi

The first allegation was palpably false, but the other had a germ of truth in it in so far as the Saiyid did hold and preach that reverence for saints should not be so immoderate as to compromise belief in monotheism. He, therefore, considered many practices smacking of saint worship as un-Islamic. In this context the simple people considered aberrations of many of the Mujahidun from the normal Hanafi practices as heresy. The allegations became exaggerated in the popular mind so that the Saiyid had to contradict the charge of heresy in his letter to some leading *Ulema* of Peshawar. It seems that the allegations had snowballed enormously and Shah Ismail also had to address leading *Ulema* of the locality twice, refuting the charges of a similar nature. The rumours in general circulation accused the Saiyid of being such a great heretic that he did not follow any moral code and went to the extent of justifying unlawful pleasures. This was totally false because the Saiyid and his followers were known for the purity and austerity of their lives. They were men who had given up their home and hearth for a religious purpose; they had been attracted to the Saiyid because he preached adherence to the code of Islam and the utmost sacrifice in its cause; some of them had been men of means and were now content to live most frugally, sometimes

> going hungry and doing menial chores for the upkeep of the camp. It is obvious that the slanderous campaign must have originated from the Sikhs, but it found credence because of minor differences that had been introduced in the ritual. Another reason of the discontent of the tribesmen was that the Saiyid had to appoint officers mostly from amongst men who had come from India, not because of any discrimination, but because of the lack of such persons among the locals....[2]

How urgent and all-consuming the question whether one may raise one's hands up to one's ears becomes, how it gets intertwined with the pursuit of power and spheres of dominance.

The Barelvis maintain that when one hears the name of the Prophet in the call to prayer one should kiss one's thumbs and put them to one's eyes. They maintain that this induces visions of the Prophet. The others declare this to be a heretical practice.

The Barelvis set great store by the *auliya*, the sheikhs, and pirs. They maintain that these personages continue to exist not just as entities of the spirit but in a bodily sense also after death, and that therefore they continue to have the power to render help of various kinds—on Friday nights, in particular, the powers of these deceased personages are particularly potent (on those nights even the ordinary dead can talk to us, they maintain). The Barelvis therefore set great store in visiting the graves of pirs, in seeking help from or through them, in observing days and anniversaries associated with them—in particular the *giyarvin* and urs of Shah Abdul

---

2. I.H. Qureshi, *Ulema in Politics*, Karachi, 1972, Renaissance Publishing House, New Delhi, Reprint 1985, pp. 150–52. For similar examples of the esoteric matters over which the ulema split and quarrelled and for Qureshi's anguish at the consequences this had for Muslims see in addition, pp. 116, 171–72, 174, 218, 222–24.

Qadir and Shah Barkatullah, in making offerings for the fulfilment of some particular goal or wish. They also prescribe specific practices: keeping a white chicken, drawing blood on Saturdays, driving four nails into the corner of one's house to keep out evil djinn...[3]

The others condemn these as vestiges of pagan, specifically Hindu practices. They condemn them as forms of that deadliest of sins—polytheism. They condemn them as bid'at, heretical innovations, as shirk, idolatry and polytheism, as kufr, infidelity. They declare these practices to be grounds for being expelled from the pale of Islam.

Of course one can seek help from entities other than Allah, rules Mufti Kifayatullah—but only as the indigent may ask for food from the rich, as a patient may ask the physician for medicine, as the subject asks for protection from the ruler. But one must not ask for such help from the dead, he continues. One may seek help only from Allah: all one can do in the case of the dead is to ask them to commend one's case to Allah so that one may be given a place in *jannat*, etc., There are two restrictions, therefore: one must seek help only from Allah; second, one must seek such help only for one's 'spiritual good'—a place in jannat, etc., being enumerated as a 'spiritual good'—not for any worldly gain, like health or offspring, etc. If a person belonging to a circle or sect, the Mufti rules, were to ask even the head of that circle or sect for help, he too would be out of Islam. The Mufti reiterates this position over several pages, buttressing the point by citing authorities.[4]

---

3. For a fine and succinct account, Barbara Daly Metcalf, *Islamic Revival in British India: Deoband, 1860–1900,* Princeton University Press, Princeton,1982, pp. 296–314.

4. On the foregoing, see *Mufti Kifayatullah ke Fatawi,* Volume IX, pp. 20–23, 106, 265–66, 269, 503.

Whereas the Barelvis allow local customs to be continued unless there is an express prohibition against them in the Quran, etc., Mufti Kifayatullah insists that all customs and practices smacking of Hinduism must be jettisoned.[5]

In a comprehensive fatwa that has many allusions to practices which the Barelvis encouraged or condoned, Mufti Kifayatullah declares that while it is permissible to visit the graves of elders, to make offerings at them is najaiz and bid'at. To make offerings to Allah alone is jaiz, he declares, to make them to anyone other than Allah is haram. Often, for seeking some boon people take offerings of various kinds to the graves of auliya, the Mufti notes—offerings of cash, candles, essence of *zaitun*, sweets, chaddars, goats, chicken, etc. Let it be known that all these are false and haram, the Mufti declares. He rejects the contention that these offerings are in fact offerings for the public as they will be distributed among the public: offerings are worship, he declares, and worship cannot be for any public.

One must not do *sajda* at graves, the Mufti rules. And there is no distinction between doing sajda merely out of respect for the deceased person and doing it out of *ibadat*, worship. The former is indistinguishable from the latter. Therefore, people should be taught not to do sajda to anyone but Allah, so that they may refrain from this practice altogether.

If the intention of making the offerings is not to participate in some ritual but to obtain blessings, then making them is jaiz, he says. But there is a condition, he declares: they should not be made at graves but at one's own house or some other place; and, with proper deference, they should be given to the helpless and the poor, and the blessings that would ensue should also be distributed.

---

5. For instance, *Mufti Kifayatullah ke Fatawi*, Volume IX, Chapter III.

It is of course proper, indeed it is admirable to honour and to love and follow an elder with the idea that he is a pious and obedient servant of Allah, the Mufti says. But to honour an elder in the belief that he is an efficacious intercessor, to recount miracles of his which are not proven and are in fact far from reason and contrary to the shariah, to ask the elder to fulfil one's wishes, to resolve 'I shall donate 'X' if 'Y' happens,' to make offerings at his grave, to attribute divine powers to him and seek to prove these—all these things are haram, they are *pir-parasti*, and are reckoned among the beliefs and deeds of polytheism, declares Mufti Kifayatullah.

If one beseeches someone other than Allah thinking that he shall fulfil our wish, then that is polytheism. However, if one asks a person for a thing which he has—as, night and day, a son seeks from his father, a wife from her husband, the indigent from the one who has—then that is not polytheism, because through them the thing can be obtained.... Whenever you ask, ask of Allah; whatever you want, want of Allah, declares the Mufti.

It is najaiz to offer flowers or to light lamps, if the intention is to secure access and proximity to these persons as ones who would confer the boon one seeks.

To make offerings at graves is haram, he declares. And to eat that which has been offered at graves is haram.

To offer flowers, to drape chaddars, to light incense at graves is to offer nazar, and to offer nazar to entities other than Allah is wholly impermissible, rules the Mufti. At the least, if these offerings are not nazar, they are wasteful, and on that count haram, he declares.

It is impermissible and bid'at to insist on observing *som daham, chehlum* and to think that they are in accordance with the shariah, he says.

The same hukum holds for observing the eleventh,

the fortieth, the *urs*—to commemorate a name, to fix a date for commemoration is bid'at, the Mufti declares: recall the emphasis Maulana Ahmad Riza Khan placed on observing the eleventh day in commemoration of Shah Qadir Khan.

Is it jaiz to observe urs at graves, asks the querist, is it jaiz to hold readings of the Quran at graves, to commemorate the person by singing qawwalis at the grave? The practice of urs as it is current is makruh, detestable and bid'at, a heretical innovation, declares the Mufti. The other practices mentioned are najaiz and inappropriate, he declares.

The authorities of shariah have not appointed any day or date for obtaining blessings, nor held it necessary, the Mufti rules:[6] again, recall Ahmad Riza Khan's affirmation that Friday nights are particularly efficacious as the powers of saints, etc. to fulfil one's wishes are particularly strong at that time.

Are the Hindus polytheists or not?, the Mufti is asked. Yes, he declares. But he takes the opportunity to encompass many more than those who are formally Hindus in the category. Yes, he declares, those who worship entities other than Allah, or who take many entities to be Khuda, or *who ascribe divine powers to auliya*, all of them are polytheists.[7]

The ulema of Dar al-Ulum, Deoband are just as emphatic. They declare lighting lamps at graves and putting covers on them to be prohibited and detestable. They stress repeatedly that neither to gain a boon nor as thanks is it right to make offerings or offer *gilaf*s and chaddars at the graves of pirs or others—indeed it is illegitimate, haram, and a cardinal sin to do so. To pray to a pir for a boon, to give offerings at his

---

6. *Mufti Kifayatullah ke Fatawi*, Volume IX, pp. 49–51; see also p. 105 where also the Mufti rules that it is haram to make offerings at graves, and that the observance of the eleventh, of urs, of the fortieth and general *dhoom-dhaam* at graves are all bid'at.

7. *Mufti Kifayatullah ke Fatawi*, Volume IX, p. 423.

grave as thanks to him, to perambulate around and prostrate at the grave, to light lamps and burn incense there, to put up flags, etc., at the graves—all these are worship of *ghair* Allah, they declare, and as such are haram. They are *shirkiya* and *kufriya*, the ulema declare. One should pray and prostrate only to Allah; even if one has said, 'If "X" happens I shall make "Y" offering to pir "Z",' one should distribute the amount or object among the needy and requite the benefit of doing so to the pir. Observing the urs of the pir, holding majlis for Imam Husain, observing the giyarvin or any other date associated with a pir, celebrating the birthday of the Prophet himself, laments on the martyrdom day of Hasan and Husain—each of these comes in for censure. Like Mufti Kifayatullah, the ulema of Deoband also declare that there is no difference between doing sajda at the graves of pirs to honour the pir and doing it to worship or pray to the pir. The two are indistinguishable, they declare, so the practice is to be shunned altogether.[8]

Incidentally, notice where the innocence of our secularists takes them! Every urs of Nizamuddin Auliya or Muinuddin Chisti, every death anniversary of Fakhrudin Ali Ahmed or Maulana Azad is for them a photo opportunity. They troop ostentatiously to the graves of these personages, go through the gestures as the fatiha is read, and drape chaddars, etc., over the graves. But all this is idolatry, it is contrary to the strictest prohibition, not just of the fatwas but of the Prophet himself! As he lay dying the Prophet warned Muslims against the practice of Jews and Christians—the practice of venerating the graves of their prophets. He called down the curse of Allah on them and the practice: 'May Allah curse the Jews and Christians for they built the places of worship at the

---

8. *Fatawa Dar al-Ulum, Deoband*, Volume III, p. 106; Volume XII, pp. 102, 124, 126, 135–43, 153–54, 160–62, 359–60, 382, 385.

graves of their prophets,' he declared. He forbade Muslims from building any structure over the grave, he forbade them from even plastering it.[9] Our friends, however, can't forgo the photo opportunity !

But to return to our main concern: notice that the fatwas of Mufti Kifayatullah, of the Dar al-Ulum, Deoband, etc., denounce the very practices which the Barelvis prescribe. Notice also that in themselves the practices are quite harmless: they can hardly be seen to be very important either way to one's inner search, nor can they be reckoned as significant in relation to any great trans-personal worldly purpose. And yet in a moment we shall see what happens as a sequel to disagreements over such trifling matters of ritual.

If a person reciting the *Kalima teeba* (the Confession of Islam) joins the names of the honoured companions to that of the Prophet, asks the querist, for instance if he reads, '*La Ilah il Illah, Abu Bakr, Umar, Usman, Ali, and Muhammad Rasul Allah,*' will he be a kafir or a sinner?

The ulema of Deoband decree: it is stated in the law books that if in some statement there are ninety-nine grounds of kufr but one ground for Islam, and even if the latter is weak, the Mufti should focus on that one ground. And even if because of those ninety-nine the scales incline towards kufr, the Mufti should make concessions towards the Muslim and should not give the fatwa of kufr. However, they say, these sorts of statements create apprehension of kufr, and one should be cautious in the future.[10]

The *Fatawa-i-Rizvia* descends on such permissiveness with an avalanche of scorn. It quotes the Quran and Hadis as declaring: he who does a thousand Islamic deeds and one

---

9. *Sahih al-Bukhari,* Volume I, p. 255; *Sunan Abu Dawud,* Volume II, pp. 916–17.

10. *Fatawa Dar al-Ulum, Deoband,* Volume XII, pp. 381–82.

deed of kufr is a kafir. It denounces the contrary view—the view we have just seen the ulema of Deoband articulate—with a typical analogy: if one puts one drop of urine in ninety-nine drops of rose water, all of it becomes urine, it declares; but the religion of these *khabis*, it declares, is that if in ninety-nine *tolas* of urine there is one tola of rose water, it is all rose water; it is paak, drink it.[11]

There are differences over truly esoteric matters also—matters which are even further removed from our existence and affairs, which in fact are matters that cannot be settled by argument or proof or reason.

Can Allah lie? Surely that is not a question of any practical significance: whether lying is or is not among His capacities is not going to affect our existence and affairs. But it is the question which has ignited ferocious, indeed, as we shall see, abusive controversy. The Ahl-i-Hadis and others reason that Allah is omnipotent, that there is nothing, doing which is beyond His power; hence, He *can* lie; of course He does not do so; but that He *can*, on that there can be no doubt. Maulana Ahmad Riza Khan lampoons not only the Ahl-i-Hadis but their Khuda for this; and denounces them for raising the question, declaring that they do so only to split the community. Lampooning the Deobandis, ridiculing their Khuda, flaunting the inconsistencies in which they tie themselves, in a typical passage the *Fatawa-i-Rizvia* proclaims: And such is the reality of that knowledge which he (the Deobandi Khuda) gave to his companion (Satan)—and bestowing which he called his great benediction, and which he conferred as a great favour—that every lunatic and beast has it. Yes, the Deobandi Khuda is such that to call him All-powerful is false from the very consideration that to attribute power over all things is on all counts false, or else if he too had all

11. *Fatawa-i-Rizvia*, Volume VI, p. 95.

power then possibly he would not remain Khuda. And if what he has is only some power, then what is his uniqueness, for every lunatic and every beast has some power. The Deobandi Khuda is one who chose as his foremost Prophet one who did not have the comprehension to understand his Word. His comprehension was just of ordinary folk, and this limitation of his was evident to all wise men. And even then this Deobandi Khuda did not keep him from this absurd blunder, possibly he (the Deobandi Khuda) did not understand his own Word himself, for he can be ignorant too. The Deobandi Khuda is such that, just as to count six others as the seals of prophets is to add lustre to *the* Seal of the prophets, in the same way to call him the sole Allah is to rob from his glory. His great glory is in this that he is the Khuda of many Khudas. Is such a one Khuda?...[12]

Is there a 'Light of Muhammad' apart from the Prophet, Muhammad? Has it existed from the beginning of creation? Did it act as an intermediary in creation? Yes, yes, yes, insist the Barelvis, like the Trinitarians. To maintain that *Noor-i-Muhammad* has existed from the beginning of creation is to strike at the cardinal principal of Islam, the oneness, the indivisibility, the unity of Allah, declare the Ahl-i-Hadis and others.

Did the Prophet have unique knowledge of the unknown, did he know everything about everything unknown? Yes, insist the Barelvis, who lay special emphasis on the uniqueness of the Prophet—holding, as they do, that the world was created to vindicate the glory of the Prophet. No, he did not have knowledge in general about the unknown, declare the Ahl-i-Hadis and others. His knowledge about the unknown was confined to the specific aspects of the unknown which Allah enabled him to glimpse from time to time.

12. *Fatawa-i-Rizvia,* Volume I, pp. 746–47.

And so on.

As Lenin would have said: these are controversies over the colour of the Devil, over whether he is green or yellow. They are literally so.

And they have been vicious, as even a small sampling of the fatwas will show.

'Jahannum ke kutte'

'And among these *Kafirs* too there are gradations,' declares the *Fatawa-i-Rizvia* in its *Nafrat ke Ahkam*, the *Ordinances of Hatred*. 'One hard kind of basic kufr is Christianity; worse than it is Magianism; worse than that is idolatry; worse than that is Wahabiyat; and worse than all these and more wicked is Deobandiyat.'

Denouncing them for their view that Muslims should work together with Hindus—even though they were urging this for attaining strictly Muslim objectives—Maulana Ahmad Riza Khan dubs Deobandis to be *badtar-az-badtar-se-badtar*—worse than the worst of the worse. If your hatred had been what Allah has prescribed hatred should be, and you had hated evil deeds one degree, you would have hated idolaters a lakh degrees, he declares, and if you had hated idolaters a lakh degrees, then you would have hated Deobandis a crore degrees, the Maulana declares.[13]

They are apostates, he declares, far worse than the *asli* kafirs—the ones who refuse Islam and are kafirs from the very beginning, that is the atheists, polytheists, fire-worshippers, Jews and Christians. And among the apostates, the Deobandis and Wahabiyas are the worst of all—because they dress up as Muslims and deceive Muslims.[14]

---

13. *Fatawa-i-Rizvia*, Volume VI, pp. 3–4.
14. Ibid., Volume VI, p. 55.

The *Fatawa-i-Rizvia* declares the Deobandis, Ahl-i-Hadis, etc., to be 'barking falsehoods', to be swearing false oaths, to be kafirs, to be apostates, to be bid'atis, to be *jahannumi*, the dwellers of Hell, to be *jahannum ke kutte*, the dogs of Hell. To call them the equivalent of Kharijis and Shias, it declares, is to be cruel to the latter.[15]

The *Fatawa-i-Rizvia* declares the Ahl-i-Hadis, the Wahabis and of course the Shias to be guilty of kufr on several counts: they do not go by the four imams on whom there is a consensus, they denounce taqlid as 'shirk'. These beliefs are a denial of the Quran, of the Hadis, of the ijma, consensus, of the ummah, and all that is kufr, it says. The Ahl-i-Hadis are accordingly out of the circle of Islam, it declares. He who refuses the consensus on these matters pains Allah and the Rasul, and such a one is accursed. Fire, Fire for him, the sinner, it curses. The wayward—and it is correct to call the Ahl-i-Hadis 'wayward' it declares—are the dogs of Hell, it says, and that too dogs of the worst kind; they are worse than dogs, worse than pigs, they are the dogs of ones who are worse than pigs....[16]

Accusing the Wahabis of regarding the Turks to be no better than the Christians, the *Fatawa-i-Rizvia* declares that knowing someone to be a Wahabi and yet to not take him to be a kafir is itself kufr. To say nothing of such a person being a Sunni, he is not even a Muslim, it declares. Namaz should not be observed behind one who doubts the kufr of the Wahabis, it decrees.[17] The heat of Fire on the deceit of the Wahabis, it curses.[18] They call Muslims polytheists, it says; according to them all—from the Companions to Shah

15. *Fatawa-i-Rizvia*, Volume VI, pp. 88–91.
16. Ibid., Volume VI, pp. 35, 70.
17. Ibid., Volume VI, pp. 5, 80, 81.
18. Ibid., Volume XI, p. 200.

Waliullah—are polytheists, it declares. As one who calls a Muslim a 'kafir' is a kafir, they are kafirs, declares the *Fatawa-i-Rizvia,* which itself calls several groups of Muslims Kafirs![19]

Similarly, the Deobandis are kafirs, the *Fatawa-i-Rizvia* declares, and he who doubts that they are kafirs is also a kafir.[20]

The books and beliefs of the Deobandis are worse than those of the Hindus, it declares.[21] But it makes a concession, prescribing a limit to what the true believer may do with their writings. The limit the fatwa draws and the reason the fatwa gives for it speak for themselves.

'What is the opinion of the learned ulema as to whether the papers written by Ashraf Ali Deobandi are valid or not, and whether one should act on their magazines or use them for istinja and throw them away?', asks the querist, and adds: these magazines are worse than logic chopping. '*Bait* at the hands of Ashraf Ali is absolutely *haram,* whether we do so directly or by writing,' declares the *Fatawa-i-Rizvia.* 'Not only this, the learned ones have unanimously held that he who, having come to know what they (the Deobandis) say, has any doubt about their *kufr* is himself a *Kafir.* All the books of Ashraf Ali and of all who hold the Deobandi beliefs, including the books of logic and even the Book of Philosophy, are worse than the religious books of the Hindus.' 'Because,' it continues, 'the danger of Muslims being corrupted by seeing the books of the Hindus is not as great as the danger from seeing these books.' 'To look them up is certainly *haram,*' it says.

'But,' it adds, 'that one should do *istinja* with their pages, is too much.' And it specifies the reason for this concession:

---

19. Ibid., Volume XII, pp. 110–12.
20. Ibid., Volume VI, pp. 81–82; Volume IX, Book II, pp. 313–14.
21. Ibid., Volume I, p. 152.

'Respect for (religious) words is incumbent, not for their books: the books contain mention of Allah and the Prophet also, by which they deceive the people. An Imam passed by some young men who had written the name of Abu Jahl on a target, and were practising archery on it. The Imam restrained them from doing so. When he passed by that way again he saw that they had removed the letters of Abu Jahl's name, and were shooting arrows at it (the remaining paper). He said, "I had not asked you to respect the name Abu Jahl, but to respect the letters."[22] In others words, while what is written by the Deobandis is worse than worthless, because of the paper on which it is printed, we should not use it for istinja.

Namaz behind the Deobandis, Ahl-i-Hadis and others is false, it declares. Indeed, namaz behind even one who has studied in a madrasah run by Deobandis is *batil*, false. When a querist recalls fatwas in which it is stated that one should go by the conduct of a person and not by conjectures about his inner beliefs and seeks thereby to justify observing namaz behind a person who might have gone to madrasahs of Deobandis, the *Fatawa-i-Rizvia* descends like a ton of bricks. This fatwa (to which the querist had referred) is absolutely wrong, it declares. In it they have sought to evade the real issue and they have just jotted down irrelevant traditions. The ones who have signed it are ones who are of the Deobandi persuasion, or do not hold the Deobandis to be kafirs. They will of course want to say this, it declares, although the ulema have unanimously given the fatwa that Gangohi, Nanautavi, and Thanwi are all apostates. And it has been stated in *Durr-ul-Mukhtar*, the *Fatawa-i-Rizvia* records, that he who doubts their kufr is himself a kafir.

To claim to believe in the ones who follow the Sunna or to call oneself to be a Hanafi, or to call oneself a believer

22. *Fatawa-i-Rizvia*, Volume II, p. 152.

in *Tawhid* (*the* oneness of Allah), and the prophethood and the superiority of Din and miracles means nothing—which of these do the Wahabis and Deobandis not acknowledge? And yet they are kafirs. And such kafirs are they, declares the *Fatwa-i-Rizvia*, that anyone who has doubts about their kufr is himself a kafir. In fact, even Qadiyanis believe in these four things, it says, and in addition they call themselves the followers of Abu Hanifa. Is their kufr lifted by these assertions?

Undoubtedly the shariah lays emphasis on what is evident, it says, only to add, and what is evident is that a person shall not take religious instruction from the ones whom he knows to be kafirs and apostates. The analogy of schools and *pathshalas* is ignorance, it declares. Does anyone go to pandits and padris to study Quran, Hadis and *Fiqh*? And even suppose—wrongly—that if a person who studies from the Wahabis does not incline towards their beliefs and knows them to be kafirs and apostates, even then to make them one's teachers amounts at least to granting them respect. And the ulema have pronounced that anyone who shows respect to a Magian or calls him a teacher becomes a kafir. It is stated in *Durr-ul-Mukhtar*... When this is the position for merely showing respect or just calling such a one a teacher, how shall it be to actually respect and to actually take such a one as teacher?

Without a doubt, such a person is not qualified to be an imam. No one who has respect for the Faith shall make such a person imam, nor shall he read the namaz behind such a person. Yes, one who takes faith to be a mere plaything can do what he likes. May Allah grant guidance to Muslims so that they do not waste their namaz, the fatwa concludes.[23]

---

23. *Fatawa-i-Rizvia,* Volume III, p. 246; also Volume III, p. 265 where the same points are reiterated and we are told that everyone—except the wholly jungli— knows the nature of the Deobandis and Wahabis, and that they are kafirs; also at Volume XI, p. 73.

Predictably, in Maulana Ahmad Riza Khan's reckoning the Shias are not Muslims at all.[24] Their 'mosques' are not mosques[25]—and remember, as Mir Baqi and his descendants, the *mutwallis* of the mosque were Shias, the 'Babri masjid' was a Shia mosque. Animals sacrificed by them, meat from their places are all haram.[26] One must not maintain any connection, not even contact with them. Those among the Rafazis and others of wrong faith whose bid'at has reached the limits of kufr are apostates, declares the *Fatawa-i-Rizvia.* The believer must have no relations with them—not even the kind he may have with zimmi kafirs. It is incumbent on Muslims that in all matters—eating, drinking, sitting, etc.—they should take them as they would swine, commands the *Fatawa-i-Rizvia*: even for those among them whose bid'at has not reached that limit, believers must refrain absolutely from having any friendship with or affection for them....; barring extreme necessity or helplessness do not associate with them either, it declares: the affection of the ones of wrong faith is *aag*, fire, association with them is *naag*, a serpent, and both shall destroy faith.[27] One must refrain from associating with them, from going to their functions, from doing anything which accords them praise. It cites the Quran: Do not associate with the *zalim*, the tyrant, lest the Fire of Hell consume you. What arguments are needed for this?, the Maulana asks. Their conduct speaks for itself.[28]

But the matter does not end with the Shias. Just as namaz behind Deobandis, Ahl-i-Hadis, etc., is false and infructuous, animals sacrificed by them are impure, they are

24. Repeatedly, for instance, *Fatawa-i-Rizvia*, Volume VI, p. 81; Ibid., Volume IX, Book II, p. 119.

25. Ibid., Volume VI, pp. 428–29; Ibid., Volume IX, Book II, p. 125.

26. Repeatedly, for instance, Ibid., Volume VIII, p. 329.

27. Ibid., Volume IX, Book I, p. 79.

28. Ibid., Volume IX, Book I, p. 176.

polluted, *murdar*, and meat sent by a Deobandi, even if it has been brought over by a Muslim, is polluted. To eat meat from the places of Wahabis, Shias, Bohras, Ismailis, is haram.[29]

Indeed, one must have no connection or contact with them: all relationships and contact with Deobandis, Wahabis, Ahl-i-Hadis is haram. To sit near them is haram; to greet them is haram; to listen to and talk with them is haram; to visit them if they are sick is haram; to bathe their body if they die is haram; to read namaz at their demise is haram; to bury them in the graveyard of Muslims is haram; to visit their graves is haram; to pray for the peace of their soul is haram.

The fatwa cites the Quran to drive home the point: If Satan forgets you, you remember him. Do not sit near these zalims. Do not associate with these sinners, that the fires of Hell shall engulf you. The Prophet said, 'Run from them'—then what degree of kufr it shall be to take them to be Alim-i-Din, the Maulana asks, and prays, May Allah save us from all these *khabi*s...May they (the believers) run from the shadow of these enemies. Upon seeing them may blood run in his (the believer's) eyes.... Shall *Qayamat* not descend upon one who maintains relations with such calumners?....[30]

Returning to the charge again, the *Fatawa-i-Rizvia* declares that the Deobandis, in particular their leaders—Maulvi Qasim Nanautavi, Rashid Ahmed Gangohi, and their 'Peshwa', Ashraf Ali Thanwi—must be dealt with in the way the Hadis says bid'atis and the bad-mazhab, those of wrong faith ought to be dealt with. And it cites a series of Hadis to specify what this way is. The Prophet, it records, has said:

---

29. Ibid., Volume VIII, p. 332.

30. Ibid., Volume VI, pp. 88–89.

- Stay far from them, keep them far from you, lest they lead you astray, lest they throw you in tumult;
- If they fall ill, do not go to inquire after them; if they die, do not join their funeral; when you meet them, do not greet them; do not sit near them; do not drink water with them; do not eat with them; do not intermarry with them;
- Do not read namaz at their death;
- Do not read namaz with them;
- I am disgusted with them, I have nothing to do with them. Jihad is upon them as it is upon the kafirs;
- Whenever you see any one of wrong faith (bad-mazhab), be bitter and harsh towards him. Allah considers every one of wrong faith to be His enemy. None of them shall be able to cross the bridge of *Sarat*, but will be torn to pieces and fall into the Fire as flies and spiders do;
- He who honours one of wrong faith helps in demolishing Islam.

The fatwa declares that there are several other Hadis also to the same effect. It then proceeds to quote ancillary authorities to buttress its ruling.

When shariah has prescribed such hatred for them, and has narrated such ill of them, it asks, is it not the religious duty of Muslims that they keep them from entering mosques? And that they sever all connections with them, specially with such among them in whose hands is the work of Muslims, in whom the Muslims believe and upon whom they look with respect?

The ulema have issued the fatwa of kufr against the three, it notes, Thanwi, Gangohi, Nanautavi—the very originators, the reader will recall, and pillars of the Dar al-Ulum, Deoband:[31]

31. *Fatawa-i-Rizvia,* Volume VI, pp. 103–04.

But even severing all relations with such kafirs and apostates is not enough, the *Fatawa-i-Rizvia* declares repeatedly. It is the religious duty of every true believer to expose the Deobandis, Wahabis, etc., and to narrate their evils, it declares.

The ulema of Deoband are kafirs, it declares in a typical *fatwa*. Those who harbour doubts in this regard are themselves kafirs. The beliefs of the Deoband ulema are manifestly kufr. It is typical of the deniers (of the Truth) that they try to escape the charge to save their lives. But for the believers enmity towards the enemies of Allah and the Prophet is a duty.... He who calls the Deobandis 'kafirs' is not guilty of any wrong, it declares, because Allah has commanded that a kafir be called a 'kafir'.... If there is some opportune reason for a person to evade calling kafirs 'kafirs'— a reason connected with the needs of Din and only to the extent of those needs—then he, though not a kafir, is a sinner. But if he really thinks that to call a kafir a 'kafir' is wrong and contrary to civilized etiquette, then he puts a blemish on the Holy Quran, it declares, and to put a blemish on the Holy Quran is kufr.[32]

Similarly, it is a duty to narrate the evil of the Wahabis, it declares repeatedly. Citing the Prophet the *Fatawa-i-Rizvia* asks: Are you shy of calling the *fajir* evil? When and how will the people recognize him (if you keep silent)? Testify to his evil so that the people may save themselves from him....[33]

On the other hand, the querist asks Mufti Kifayatullah: how is the pir who calls the ulema of Deoband kafirs to be regarded? Is it jaiz to become his disciples? He is a fasiq, a reprobate, declares the Mufti. Following him is not jaiz.[34]

---

32. *Fatawa-i-Rizvia*, Volume IX, Book II, pp. 313–14.
33. Ibid., Volume III, p. 251.
34. *Mufti Kifayatullah ke Fatawi*, Volume IX, p. 269.

Inevitable

The examples can be multiplied many times over—the denunciations of the ulema of Deoband, of the Ahl-i-Hadis, etc., by the Barelvis alone will fill a thick volume. The denunciations by all of them of the Qadiyanis, the Ismailis, and of course the Shias would fill equally substantial volumes. But the principal conclusions will be clear by now:

- While there is incessant talk of the Islamic ummah, *this* is the condition of the guides of and the learned among that ummah;
- Each set charges the other with the same sort of offences: in the eyes of each set the practices and beliefs of the others are heretical innovations, several of them are kufr.

These disputes, as we have seen, are inevitable, inescapable. They flow as necessities from:

- The claim of Islam to regulate every aspect of life;
- The consequence of this claim, namely that every matter thus becomes a matter of religion;
- As the contest is about dominion over the flock, all issues become weapons in the struggle for power.

Even the venom and malevolence which we see in the fatwas are a necessary, inevitable feature: as religion is everything, the deviance of the other on some detail of private conduct or ritual is not deviance on that little detail, it is defiance of the command of Allah, and Allah Himself has prescribed and His Prophet has prescribed how the one who, having accepted Islam, defies His command or the Prophet's is to be dealt with.

Islamic revolutions therefore devour their proponents just as rapidly as those of other totalitarian ideologies. Islamic sects split as rapidly as other totalitarian sects.

In a word, just as the comprehensiveness of the ideology boomerangs, the fervour which is its hallmark boomerangs.

The world of today

The third reason for hope stems from the world of today—more precisely, from the fact that the content of the ulema's ideology is so totally inappropriate to the world of today.

How can their notions about the earth and the sun, about the universe, about disease and medicine withstand the growth of modern knowledge? Even more important: how can their fundamental premise—that the glory of Islam is not in bending to modern science but in making science bend to the 'Islamic position' on every question—survive?

How long can they go on enforcing a legal and social order so manifestly iniquitous to women at a time when satellite television brings information about the rest of the world right into the homes even of the faithful?

Even in states which are Islamic how long can they go on enforcing a legal and social order so manifestly iniquitous to non-believers, an order the basic premise of which is the double standard between believers and kafirs? How long will they be able to continue to do so in a world in which what is being done in a country to minorities becomes known the world over within hours, in a world in which the concern for human rights grows by the year?

There is finally an even more consequential dissonance between the world and the ideology of the ulema. The ideology is premised not just on the belief that believers are eternally separate from, and eternally superior to non-believers. It is premised on eternal hostility between the two. Fanaticism and terrorism, aggression are inevitable results of this world view. Accordingly, the ideology makes it well-nigh impossible for Muslims to live peaceably in societies in which Muslims are just one of several communities. Indeed, it makes it impossible for an Islamic state to live peaceably in a world where there are non-Islamic states also. The ulema of course hold fast to that ideology today. But their doing so has deep consequences both within the multi-religious societies in which the Muslims live, and in other countries: their aggressiveness has fomented a deep reaction among the Hindus in India for instance; and their 'wars of liberation', their terrorism are waking even Europe and the US to the danger which the ideology constitutes.

Given time, therefore, the ideology will undercut itself as surely as Marxism-Leninism did. But to wait for it to do so will inflict incalculable suffering on the country as well as on the Muslims themselves. To pluck a phrase of Lenin: we must give history a helping hand.

We must, the Muslim liberal in particular must master the canonical texts; and having done so, we must not go on pleading for 'the doors of ijtihad' to be opened, we should formulate and put out the interpretations ourselves.

Next, we should broadcast the arguments and recall the canonical authorities which have been urged by persons whom even the fundamentalists cannot disregard.

We should show up the consequences which the stance and the politics of the fundamentalists and the ulema visit upon the country, the consequences these have already brought upon the Muslims—their remaining uneducated and therefore poor, their getting isolated, and the mighty reaction which those stances and that politics have ignited among the Hindus.

We should, in particular the Muslim liberal should speak the whole truth about the condition of Muslim society—for instance about the plight of women within it. And not flinch from tracing it back to its roots—the texts, the laws, the ways of thinking.

We should document the social practice of the ulema and of the fundamentalist politicians—what they have made of the waqfs for instance, and the use to which they have put the funds that come from abroad, who gets them and what they make of them.

We should document what the ulema, etc., have been saying and decreeing on religious issues themselves—the fatwas which have emanated from them, for instance, certainly lead one to doubt that they merit the authority which is reposed in them, and to question the pride of place which is accorded to them.

We should show how utterly false is the propaganda of the fundamentalists. 'The judgment goes against Article 25 which guarantees freedom of religion,' they said in the case of Shah Bano, they say now in the case of Justice Tilhari. In fact, Article 25 makes freedom of religion subject to public order, morality and health and the other provisions of the Fundamental Rights part of the Constitution—the right to equality and the rest—all of which are violated by the talaq-power. The same article specifically provides that nothing in regard to freedom of religion shall affect the power of the state to make any law to regulate or restrict, inter alia, any secular activity of any religious group, nor to provide for social welfare and reform. 'But no such law can be passed because of the Shariat Act of 1937,' they say. It isn't just that if that Act restricts the power of the state in ways not permitted by the Constitution then that provision of the Act is ultra vires and void.' The fact is that the Shariat Act imposes no restriction of the sort at all. As I have pointed out earlier in *A Secular Agenda* the original bill provided, 'Notwithstanding any custom or usage *or law* to the contrary' in matters like marriage and divorce, where the parties are Muslim, shariah shall apply. But the words 'or *law*' were specifically dropped, and so since 1937 the Act has only said, 'Notwithstanding any custom or usage to the contrary.... the Shariat shall apply.' Wherever there is a law to the contrary, *it is the law which is to prevail.* That is so manifestly the position. And yet the denunciation proceeds, 'It violates Articles 25, it is contrary to the Shariat Act.' The liberal must nail these gross misrepresentations, so that the poor and ignorant masses are not further misled and inflamed.

We must, in particular the Muslim liberal must take the consistently secular position on every matter—that is the only way to confront the fundamentalists, it is the surest way to bring home the alternate viewpoint to the community. To take an obvious example: *hukam-namas*, fatwas and the rest which impinge on the civil rights of a person are manifestly a criminal infringement of law; we should show them up as such; and join others in demanding that anyone who seeks to trample upon the rights of others by using hukam-namas or fatwas should be brought to book under the law. Similarly, we must expose, and work to thwart concessions by our opportunist politicians which are meant to appease, and will in the end strengthen the grip of these reactionary elements—the new amendments to the Waqf Act are a ready case at hand.

We must devise and support plans for the modernization of the community—for educating Muslim women for instance, for equipping workers in traditional industries so that they can move into the new, growth industries; the Muslim liberal in particular must teach the community to judge leaders by what they are doing to help in this process, rather than by seeing who is most vociferous in shouting 'Islam in danger'.

There is a further point which is specially relevant to the Muslim liberal: he must join hands with liberals irrespective of their religion to strengthen the institutions in the proper working of which the security and prosperity of all sections of our people lie.

Hardly any of the tasks can be accomplished by the Muslim liberals alone. For each of them they need to join hands with the liberals of all communities in India. The ulema-fundamentalists have retained their hold by keeping not just the poor and ignorant Muslims isolated from the rest of India, but, through their verbal terrorism, by keeping the Muslim liberal isolated—from ordinary Muslims on the one hand, and from other liberals on the other. The way to loosen the ulema's grip, the only way to counter their organizational resources is for Muslim liberals to join hands with liberals across the board. And, instead of trying to convince the ulema, instead of going on appealing to the ulema to enter into a dialogue, to turn one's back to them.

Recall the resolution against Triple talaq which the Muslim Intelligentsia Meet sent to the Muslim Personal Law Board in 1993, the fate of which was set out in Chapter 1.

So: projects which even as they address specific reforms have as their running aim the nailing of fundamentalists, projects accomplished in open and vigorous cooperation with liberals of all traditions—that should be the agenda, that should be the modus operandi.

The sorts of steps which have been listed above are necessary, and I have little doubt that even they will go a considerable distance towards liberating Muslims from the vice of reactionary elements. But it is not going to be enough to counter the ulema, and their networks, or to show up their syllabi. As we have seen, what they proclaim, and regurgitate, and enforce is what the Quran and Hadis prescribe. Therefore, to really break the vice, liberals, and liberal Muslims in particular must examine and exhume the millenarian claims of Islam: the claims that there is only one truth, that it has been revealed finally to only one man, that it is enshrined in only one Book, that that Book is very difficult to comprehend, that the select few alone know its inner meaning, that therefore it is everyone's duty to heed them, just as it is the duty of the select to make sure that everyone heeds them. In a word, the basic texts themselves have to be opened to examination.

It is when liberals took apart these claims and texts of Christianity that Christians were liberated from the thrall of the Church. It is because the communist parties and their fellow-travellers were able to prevent these claims from being examined in the case of Marxism-Leninism that people in the Soviet Union and eastern Europe could not be liberated. Till the whole thing collapsed.

But to wait that long in the present case would be to condemn the vast majority of Indian Muslims to continue in their present condition. And it would be to open our country to being torn asunder.

12

'But who reads the Fatwas?'

'I just don't believe they will have said this.'

That would be the initial response of many friends when in some discussion I would recall what the fatwas on the matter had held.

And when I produced the fatwas, the friends would jump and say, *'But who reads the fatwas?'*

One might as well ask, 'But who reads *Supreme Court Reports* or the *Labour Law Journal?'* The answer obviously is: judges do, lawyers do, litigants do. Similarly, the ulema who enforce the shariah read the fatwas, the community which follows the shariah does, in any event it regulates its life in accordance with the substance contained in the fatwas.

'But these are old fatwas.'

On the contrary, the fatwas on which this study is based are fatwas which are current. And, as has been shown in Chapter 10, the notions which they articulate, the commands which they enforce are what have been set out in the Quran and Hadis themselves. Instead of trying to wish away this enormous amount of evidence, why not try the shorter route: Why not try and secure a fatwa from one of the recognized authorities—say, the Dar al-Ulum at Deoband—which counters or goes contrary to the fatwas which have been cited here?

'But who follows these fatwas in practice?'

For one thing, the tallest among Muslims—Iqbal, Maulana Azad, Dr Zakir Hussain, as we saw—had to heed them, indeed the mere apprehension that fatwas might be issued against them was sufficient to have these high personages bend and offer explanations for and in effect retract what they had written or done.

'But that is just the thing: when these big persons say or write something, the ulema take notice and kick up a storm. But the ordinary Muslim goes about his life completely oblivious of the mullahs'—this at a seminar in Delhi from a leading Muslim scholar.

How self-serving can one get! It is not necessary for the ulema to go round hunting down the ordinary Muslim in his hovel, it is enough to make a Maulana Azad or Dr Zakir Hussain take due account of what they say. When he sees that even such major figures are defenceless against the ulema, the ordinary fellow will not dare to act without heed to the ulema's diktat on the matter. The compilations of fatwas themselves nail the point: they show that it is the ordinary Muslim who turns to the ulema day in and day out for rulings on how to conduct his life. Not just that. Ever so often the requests for fatwas are in the form of one Muslim reporting what another has said or done and asking the ulema for their injunction in the matter. In other words, it is not just that ordinary Muslims believe that they must turn to the ulema for the fatwa, vis-à-vis each other, the ordinary Muslims constitute a vigilant, and at times diabolic Thought Police. They tell on each other to the ulema. And thereby they strengthen the grip of the ulema on the entire community.

In any event, if no one follows the fatwas, what is all this hullabaloo about the shariah being untouchable, what is all this noise that Muslim personal law must never be touched? After all, the fatwas are the shariah in action.

Disregard the fatwas for the sake of argument. The premises on which the fatwas are based, the propositions, which they contain still remain. What about these? As we have seen, they are rooted in the Quran and the Sunna of the Prophet. Is the argument then that no Muslim reads the Quran and the Hadis also? That no Muslim lives by them either?

What an irony it is. 'These books are sacred'—that is the refrain about the Quran and the Hadis compilations. Until you reproduce them. Then the apologist exclaims, 'But who reads them?' Indeed, as happened in the case of Ram Swarup's pioneering study, *Understanding Islam through Hadis*, then the demand is that the book reproducing them be banned!

'But the ulema are not the entire Muslim community.'

Of course, they are not. But they are the cutting edge. They have the networks, the financial and other resources, and the legitimacy which no other group in the community has. When an issue erupts, the matter at once becomes one that has to be settled by reference to the texts. And, as we have seen, the texts are on the side of the ulema. For all these reasons, while they are not the entire community, they have an inordinate influence on the course events take. We must believe, after all, that most of the Muslims who stayed back in India were not for the partition of the country. But could they prevent it? Similarly, it is true that common folk in the Maghreb and the Middle East are adopting modern mores and modern gadgets. Yet the direction of events is not being determined by this large, amorphous mass: it is being determined by a minority—those who are fired by the world view of the Quran and the Hadis. It is for this reason that the mindset of the ulema has a significance which far exceeds their numbers: and the fatwas reveal that mindset.

'Arrey bhai, but why don't you write on Hindu fatwas?,'—that from a prominent intellectual who carries a haloed name.

There is nothing like the fatwa among Hindus—but surely even our intellectuals know that. The point of such admonitions is different. In this view of the matter, a Hindu should stay clear of writing on Islam. Rather, that if he writes about matters Islamic or Muslim, he should only pen Hosannas—'the religion of tolerance, equality....'—he should only write books 'understanding', that is *explaining away* the 'Muslim mind'. At the least, if he just *has* to allude to some unfortunate drawback in it, he must attribute it to some special time and place and exculpate Islam from it! Even more important, he must make sure that he 'balances' his remark about that point in Islam with denunciation about something in Hinduism, *anything*—the caste system, dowry deaths, looking upon foreigners as malechh, at least sati if nothing else fits the bill!

'But, you see, as you have written on the question, they will just dismiss it, "O, that fellow," they will say, "He is biased against Islam"'— this from another intellectual, indeed a prominent manager of intellectuals in Delhi.

But, pray, why don't you and your associates take up such subjects yourselves? Why don't the liberals among Muslims? On your own reckoning the findings would then carry weight among Muslims.

He didn't answer the first question. On the second, he was quite impassioned: *'But, you know how any Muslim who writes on such a subject has to suffer. Look at "X"'*—he named a Muslim scholar—*'Remember how much he had to suffer.'*

Such a person does not pause to reflect that his indignant observation —*'....you know how any Muslim who writes on such a subject has to suffer'*— contains a vital clue: why is a Christian writing about Christianity today, why is anyone writing on Hinduism not put to that kind of suffering? Does that not tell us something about Islam, and those who have authority in it? Why can our intellectuals not get themselves to speak out what that feature of Islam is?

As for the second point—about how little support 'X' got when he was under attack—it so happens that there is only one section which did *not* stand up to support him: namely, the Marxist-secularist intellectuals! And for the obvious reason: the man was being attacked by a rabble instigated by fundamentalists, he was being pilloried and threatened in the name of Islam—standing up on his behalf would have stained the secular credentials of these intellectuals!

In any case, look at the operational implication of such observations: the liberal Muslims will not take up such subjects because they will be put to great suffering if they did so; the non-Muslim 'liberal' will not take them up because he is so busy writing about federalism, about decentralization, about global disarmament; therefore, no one else should take them up either!

'But not one of the Muslims I know lives the kind of life which the fatwas you cite dictate. Not one of them has those attitudes. They fare just like you and me'—several friends responded this way.

For that matter, that is true of the Muslims I know also. In general the persons we know happen to be from our own social circle—they are therefore more or less 'like you and me', for our social circle consists of persons who are more or less like us. But our social circle is not the community. In particular, the ones who are in our social circle are not the cutting edge among Muslims, they are not the ones who determine the direction the community takes on vital issues. Quite the contrary, the Muslims who are like 'you and me' are the ones who are on the receiving end among Muslims, they are forever being set upon. What is more, within the community they are on the defensive. They are on the defensive not just on specific issues, but generally, one might almost say psychologically. Vis-à-vis the community they are on the defensive, most of all in regard to matters Islamic—faced by the ulema they are virtually apologetic for not being Islamic enough. Far from being the community, far from being the ones to determine the direction the community shall take, the Muslims 'you and I' know are looked upon, and they look upon themselves as the Uncle Toms of the community.

But there is an even more important distinction: we should not confuse Muslims, specially the Muslims 'you and I' know with Islam. Even the ulema in a country like India have to temper their conduct in view of the fact that they have to function in a non-Islamic environment. How wrong it would have been, in fact how totally wrong it was to take communism to be just the communists 'you and I' knew writ large. The communists we knew, specially the fellow-travellers we knew were 'just like you and me'. Not only were they far from being the cutting edge in the communist parties, these parties themselves were not a true indicator of what communism actually was. For instance they could not dispose of recalcitrants within their own ranks the way Stalin and Mao and the other communist rulers did: the fact that they were operating in an open, free political system forced them to be more humane. To see what communism actually was, therefore, one had to see the ideal that the canonical texts of Marxism-Leninism-Maoism contained, one had to see the mindset they created, the conduct they rationalized. To see what it was in practice one had to see what the communists did when they were liberated from the ropes which a non-communist society tied around them, one had to see what the communists did when they were in power.

Exactly so with Islam. We should go not by the Muslims 'you and I' know but by the canonical texts, by the ulema and by what the ulema and Islamic rulers do when they are in power.

'But by publishing these you are fomenting animosities between communities and groups.'

But the fatwas are in circulation already. They are available in book shops around the mosques. Indeed, they are looked upon as the high literature of the community. The volumes I have used are purchased and read by large numbers. They condition their minds. All that this book does is to analyse them. And this book is in English: the original volumes are in Urdu—the language which is much more accessible to the masses whose minds the fatwas are designed to mould.

'I find all this deeply offensive, it is humiliating'— that was one of the rising Marxist stars from one of our leading universities reacting to an allusion I had made to a fatwa at a seminar in Delhi.

As Lenin might have asked: Offensive to whom? Humiliating to whom?

To the secularists alone. To those who want to hide this primary information.

And the reason has nothing to do with shielding the sensibilities of Muslims: the Muslims already know what the fatwas contain; they chafe at the tyranny the ulema impose upon the community; they know the consequences the ulema's hold has, and their politics has for the community. Who is it who in his book recalls Imam Ghazzali declaring, 'The *ulama* are the physicians, but these days they are themselves confined to the sick-bed, and are unable to cure others'?—not a Hindu but a Muslim commentator. Who is it who recalls Shah Waliullah's characterization as being apposite to the ulema of today:

> I ask the descendants of the Spiritual Guides who have occupied their seats without deserving them: Why have you turned Religion into a play-thing of your prejudices and whims? And why have you all abandoned the way of life which was ordained and taught by Allah through His Apostle Muhammad (May Allah's peace be upon him)? Each of you has become a self-centered Leader and is inviting the people to himself. Each of you regards himself as rightly-guided and a Mehdi; whereas he has lost the right way and is leading others also astray. We cannot approve of the behaviour and attitude of those who seek to enlist the allegiance of the people for the sake of worldly gains and interests, or who acquire knowledge in order to fulfil and meet their mundane desires, or who call the people to themselves and demand of them to serve their lusts and selfishness. They are indeed all dacoits and impostors and liars; they have deceived themselves and are now deceiving others.

Not a Hindu but a Muslim author.

Who writes, 'These baneful *ulama,* who are virtually the Agents of Doom for the community, cannot help the Muslims to come out of the past, live in the present, and face the future'? Not a Hindu but a Muslim commentator. After a searching analysis who concludes, 'It appears that in earlier times, the proportion of *Mulla-e Haq* (the virtuous *Mulla*) was considerably larger than that of the *Mulla-e Soo* (the vicious *Mullah,* while in recent times the proportion has been drastically reversed, the *Mulla-e Soo* preponderating in high numbers within the Muslim society, while the *Mulla-e Huq* are few in number and are rarely seen'? Not a Hindu, but a concerned and anguished Muslim commentator. Who declares that while they foment communalism in the community saying it is necessary for 'protection of Islam', 'the underlying motive is personal gain in money, power and social prestige'? Not a Hindu but a Muslim commentator. Who writes that, faced with rising prices and the higher incomes of those with equivalent secular education, the ulema 'stoop to lower levels of honesty and morality, and are unfit to provide moral and religious guidance to the Muslim Society'? Not a Hindu, but a Muslim commentator. Who writes that by splitting hair in regard to rituals and creed they aggravate the 'duels' between sects and groups in villages? Not a Hindu but a Muslim commentator. Who is it that writes,

> The private lives of many of these ulama and of some of the Shariah Amirs in India are tainted with calumny and slander in the matter of marriage and divorce. There are many ulama who are recipients of secret funds, un-accounted for grants and Financial Assistance. Many of the ulama have been involved in communal riots and convicted and jailed. While the Muslim Community was suffering under a multitude of Political, Economic and Educational handicaps, the ulama, without paying heed to the basic grievances of the Community, got themselves involved in an affair of much less importance, namely, against the Supreme Court Judgement in the Shah Bano Case. This unwise venture was undertaken for the sake of Political gains though a false show of religious issue was maintained. The conduct of the ulama involved was far from honesty and wisdom.

Not some Hindu fundamentalist but an anguished Muslim observer. Who sets out the way the ulema ingratiated themselves into the inner circles of the rulers and then 'they took undue advantage of the Ruler's whims and fancies whenever occasions arose. They would then incite the Rulers to humiliate many a great savant of Islam on false or flimsy grounds'? Who records, 'Sometimes the *Fasiq* ulama would provoke the Rulers to pass orders of severe punishment, torture or imprisonment on grounds of heresy against the spiritual leaders. In such cases the intriguing ulama cunningly remained in the background to pull wires from behind the scene of activity'? To illustrate the charge who tracks down to the intrigues of the ulema the flogging and imprisonment of

Imam Abu Hanifa, the flogging of Imam Malik, the torture and imprisonment of Imam Hanbal, the tormenting and near fatal assault on Imam Nasai, the life imprisonment of Hafiz ibn Tamiyah and suggests that these attitudes and techniques continue? Not some Hindu fundamentalist, instead a concerned Muslim scholar. Who is it who to show what the ulema are doing recalls the warning of the Prophet:

> Their *ulama* shall be the worst people under the Heaven, and mischief will begin from them, and will revert to them.

Who, anguished by the consequences they are inflicting upon the Muslims, recalls the Prophet's forecast that the ulema born among the latter-day ummah will be the first to fill jahannum, Hell? Again, a Muslim observer.[1]

So, who is offended? Who is humiliated by the fatwas being reproduced and analysed?

It is the secularist. And the reason is manifest. He has no answer in the face of this evidence, in the face of the express and emphatic commands of the Quran and the Prophet, in the face of the repeated and absolutely explicit declarations contained in the fatwas. He has no evidence with which to counter these. But when what they say is brought out on the table, he cannot sustain his inverted 'secularism'. As long as these things are confined to Urdu they do not inconvenience him in his circle. But the moment they are out in English he is pinned.

And so he feigns offence! What is the answer? To go on setting out the facts. To go on analysing them. In the faith that abuse shall not bury evidence. In the faith that ideas are seeds, that they shall take root.

---

1. On the foregoing, Al-Haj Moinuddin Ahmed, ulama, *The Boon and Bane of Islamic Society*, Kitab Bhavan, New Delhi, 1990; the passages cited are taken from pp. 4, 79–88, 91, 104–05; the subtitle notwithstanding, the book has little to say about the boons which the ulema of the kind I have dealt with hold out for the community.

Epilogue

Epilogue or reasons for hope, but work to be done

The querist asks—

But first a word about the manner in which what they ask is set out in the following pages: so that nothing may be lost in translation, so to say, the questions and answers, including their spellings and grammar, are given exactly as they appear in the official website of the Darul Ifta, Dar-al Ulum, Deoband.[1] To get back to the querist, he asks,

> I would like to refer to book Fadaail-e-Hajj (English version) by Shaykh al Hadeeth Maulana Mohammad Zakariyya published by Kutub Khana Faizi Lahore, Pakistan, on Section 9; Manners of *Ziarat*, story no 9, a story about Syed Ahmad Rifaee (*rahmatullahi alaih*) which perform a *hajj* and *ziarah rasulullah* grave. On the grave, he recited a couple of poem. After that, the sacred hand of *rasulullah* came out of the grave and the syed kissed it. It is said that the occasion is witnessed by 90,000 people. My question, 1. can I trust the story because as what I knew, dead people

1. http://darulifta-deoband.org/ The citations the authorities invoke have been omitted as they do not add to the declarations of the Deoband ulema. In some cases, the relevance of the citations is so obscure as to be almost invisible.

> cannot at any circumstances be brought alive. So, can dead people become alive?[2] The 90,000 witnessess is also seem superflous as can people with that huge number see the hand of *rasulullah* comes out from the grave and kissed by the *syaikh*? To me, the story is merely sufism in nature which laypeople like me could potentially misunderstood about the story and brought forward false story to other. Only Allah knows best.

The ulema of the Dar-al Ulum, Deoband, the institution that is often referred to as the al-Azhar of the East', answer as follows:

> Answer: 23583
> Jul 28, 2010
> (Fatwa: 1118/L=306/tl=1431)
> This event does not belong to *tasawwuf* (mysticism), rather the people saw the holy hand coming out of the blessed grave with their naked eyes. It is proved that the dead can be alive with the permission of Allah. The book *"Tazkira Shah Abdur Rahim Dehlavi ...,"* published from Al-Furqan Lucknow, contains a booklet with the title *"Murdon Ki Zindon Se Ham Kalami."* In this booklet, Hadhrat Maulana Manzoor Nomani ... has substantially proved in detail that the dead can talk to those who are alive. For details, study the same.
> Allah (*Subhana Wa Ta'ala*) (Mighty and Great) knows Best
> Darul Ifta,
> Darul Uloom Deoband[2]

That is not a fatwa issued in the middle ages. It was issued on 28 July 2010. Two points are worthy of notice here: what the ulema of this high authority regard as fact, and what they regard as proof of that fact. That something is written in a book to the effect that 90,000 persons witnessed the hand

---

2. http://darulifta-deoband.org/showuserview.do?function=answerView&all=en&id=23583&limit=1&idxpg=0&qry=%3Cc%3EFAB%3C%2F c%3E%3Cs%3EIAP%3C%2Fs%3E%3Cl%3Een%3C%2Fl%3E

rise out of the grave 1,400 years ago is both necessary and sufficient for them to maintain that the hand did indeed rise out of the grave; that a booklet written by Maulana Manzoor Nomani says that the dead can talk to the living establishes that they can indeed talk.

'Do animals go to heaven?' asks another querist, this time all the way from the United Kingdom. The ulema have no doubt that there is a heaven—for that is written in the Quran, and because the Prophet himself journeyed to it, where, as is well known, he met Moses and Jesus who implored him to convert them to Islam. And they have evidence about the animals too. And what is this evidence? As they put the matter,

> The author of book *al-Ashbah* has written with the reference of *Mustatrif* that only five animal will enter paradise: (1) the dog of People of Cave (2) the ram of Hazrat Ismail (Alaihis Salam) (3) She-camel of Hazrat Saleh (Alaihis Salam) (4) the donkey of Hazrat Uzair (Alaihis Salam) (5) the Buraq of Hazrat Muhammad (Peace Be Upon Him) ...
> Some authors have mentioned ten animals, out of which the first four are those mentioned above and remaining six are: (1) She-camel of the Prophet (PBUH) (2) the calf of Hazrat Ibrahim (Alaihis Salam) (3) the cow of Hazrat Musa (Alaihis Salam) (4) the fish of Hazrat Yunus (Alaihis Salam) (5) the ant of Hazrat Sulaiman (Alaihis Salam) (6) the hoopoe (hudhud) of Bilqees ...[3]

'Oh my Beloved Brother in Islam/ Dear learned Shaiekh/ *Assala-mu-Alaikum,*' writes a teacher in a high school in New York. 'Recently I was talking to a Muslim Brother and in our conversation we came accross a question which is, "what language will be after death of mankind or what language will be that pople will speak, either with Angels or Allah

3. Darul Ifta, Dar-al Ulum, Deoband, 8 July 2007; Answer 680; Fatwa 300=294/M. Henceforth only the date, the answer number, and the fatwa number as they appear on the website of the Darul Ifta, Deoband, are given.

[swt] to mankind." 2nd question is that "Is Arabic Language Allah [swt]'s language." I am grateful if you would Answer from Quran and Hadith citation please. I am in New York High school teacher, In USA. Please make *du'ah* for me.'

'Arabic will be the language of people after death,' declare the ulema.

> They will reply to the questions of angels in Arabic. Allah Almighty will also talk to the people in Arabic language. It is in Hadith that the language of people in Paradise will be Arabic ...
> And it is in Durr-e-Mukhtar ...
> (2)Yes, Arabic language is the language of Allah Almighty; hence Allah Almighty has spoken it, as it is in mentioned in Sharh Al-Fiqh Al-Akbar ...[4]

A believer in the United Kingdom is in search for answers to equally vexed questions. '1-I have heard that when a babys born a *shaitan* is also born and the *shaitan* stays with that person untill he dies is this true and what is the reference?' he writes. '2-If the above is true then when the person dies then does the *shaitan* who was with the person also die as well or does the *shaitan* go by someone else?'

The ulema answer with becoming gravity and satisfaction, and also modesty:

> You are right. Every man is born with a jinn companion who accompanies him till death ...
> We could not find whether this satan dies after the person or goes anywhere else, but it is reported from scholars that if a dead is buried after reciting the verse ... the satan companion is also buried with him.[5]

Another querist is worried: Will cutting hair and/or nails on Saturday cause vitiligo? Is going to a doctor on a Thursday

4. 21 June 2008; Answer number 4099; Fatwa number 230/230=M/1429.
5. 16 August 2009; Answer number 14984; Fatwa number 1182/978=/ 1430.

very bad? Is travelling on Wednesday good? The ulema give a nuanced verdict:

> They are not proved from Shariyah. They belong to superstitions and mistakes of people. However, it is proved by some hadith that whoever cuts nails on Friday Almighty Allah not only keeps him safe from calamity and misfortune till next Friday but three more days i.e. upto ten days as well. Cutting nails with teeth is said to be the cause of leprosy.[6]

The fatwas issued in response to such queries give us a glimpse of one of the root causes of two, indeed twin, fundamental problems. For the ulema as well as the community they have weaned, that something is said in the Quran or narrated in the Hadis, that something has been asserted by a person whose chief claim to being an authority on matters ranging from the mundane to the entirely unknown was that he could invoke a verse from the Quran or recall an apposite Hadis or, indeed, cite the passage from the work of someone like himself—each of these is sufficient as proof of an assertion. The other side of this feature is that the liberal is always on the defensive. He would proceed by evidence—as it is understood in, say, empirical sciences. But he has no way to discount a proposition if his interlocutor can invoke the Quran or some old authority in its support.

The third difficulty for the community, and therefore for the rest of the world, is also in evidence in such pronouncements: the mind of the ulema remains rooted so far in the past as to be incomprehensible.

That is not all. For there is the other side to the coin—the mind of the followers whom they have weaned.

---

6. 21 December 2009; Answer number 16736; Fatwa number 1996/1587/D=1430.

Religious questions?

An anxious querist residing in Canada asks:

> My question is that I pronounced one talaq to my wife as an intention of *talaq-e-raja't* that I will make *ruju* with her until end of three menses but at the same time I decided not to inform her about my intention. Before completing three months I showed her my private part through Skype video and also I saw her breast (not her private part). Unfortunately, I could not make *ruju* with her in first three menses due to her bad behavior. After 6 months she told me that "the *ruju* already happened when we saw each other through Skype". My question is that is it true whatever she said? In fact, I too had the intention of *ruju* when I was showing her my private part as I mentioned above but I was in doubt about the validity of Skype camera whether Shariahh considers it a real showing or not. Please satisfy me whether I have to make fresh *nikah* with her to make *ruju* or I have already made it as my wife says?

Skype or no Skype, the ulema are unyielding. They declare,

> Your *raja't* was not complete as per the Shariahh merely by showing your private parts to your wife and seeing your wife's breast through Skype videos. It is necessary to have new *nikah* in order to reestablish the marital life with her after the *iddah* is over.[7]

The fact that the husband pronounced talaq; that he did not inform his wife about his intention—such features will not be a surprise in the light of what we have seen of fatwas on divorce in the earlier parts of this study. Perhaps the ingenious use of a new technology to resume marital relations may be a bit of a novelty. But the main point that has far-reaching consequences is a different one. That point is the kind of questions that both the community and the ulema

---

7. 18 October 2011; Answer number 35074; Fatwa number 1759/1416/ B=1432.

regard as being matters that are strictly religious and, therefore, require the verdict of religious authorities.

As we saw in Chapter 2 above, 'All of Life', religious authorities claim that they have the right to regulate the totality of life. The laity submits to this claim. Nor is this a feature of some bygone era. The fatwa we just read through dates from October 2011.

The liberal has no recourse. For both—the claim of the religious authorities as well as the submission by the laity—are firmly grounded in the very foundations of the religion.

To this day, as the questions they send in and the urgency with which they demand decisions from the ulema show, believer after believer is driven to distraction by those capricious droplets—of urine, of 'pre-coital liquid', of semen—and those infernal jets of trapped wind.

'Can we pray behind the Imam who uses tissue paper regularly after feces (human feces) or urination because I am presently in China and find no water in the lavatory of Masjid,' asks a devotee. 'People use tissue paper which is the general practice here. Is it ok?'[8] '... After awakening, if there is some *mazi* (pre-coital fluid) but we are sure that there is no wet dream and *mazi* is due to any other reason for example erection in night or early morning which occurred while thinking some erotic matter,' asks another anxious believer. 'Is there any requirement of *ghusl* (bath) (*fardh/wajib*) (obligatory/desireable)? For example, while sleeping and dreaming erotic dream *mazi* (pre-coital fluid) has come out but you had got up before ejaculation of semen (*mani*). In general, I want to know in any cases while sleeping or awakening if we are sure that ejaculation of semen (*mani*)

---

8. 3 October 2011. In this section, only the date of the corresponding fatwa is given—that will be enough to indicate the contemporariness of the queries and of the pronouncements of the ulema.

does not take place but *mazi* has come out due to any other reason, then whether we need bath (*ghusl*) or not?'[9] 'I want to know that how we should settle down the seat of w.c in toilet. Is it right to sit facing our backside toward QUIBLA/ west in the toilet? ...'[10] 'It is mentioned that do not use your right hand during *istinja*. [*Bahisti zewar*] What does it mean,' asks a puzzled believer. 'Either do not hold your private parts with your right hand or do not hold stone with your right hand? Or do not use your right hand at all during *istinja*. We generally hold our private parts with left hand and stone with right hand. Are we correct?'[11]

Questions follow questions follow questions about droplets of urine. After passing urine, say the believers, we follow the prescription of wiping and washing ourselves and then of walking a while near the place where we urinated to ensure that there is no residual urine that we need to pass. But soon, after we have left the place, we feel that a few droplets have oozed out. Have we to go through the prescribed procedures again? Will our prayer said in that condition be accepted by Allah? Must we change our underwear every time this happens? Must we change all our clothes?

An even more intractable problem erupts for believers who are residing in non-Islamic countries. Our religion mandates that we must urinate sitting down. But here all the toilets are Western-style ...

Most of us will not be able to fathom the anxiety which that droplet produces:

> *Hazraath e Ulema Ikram, Assalamualaikum Warahmatullahi Wabarakatuh.* 1. I am facing a problem with my *taharah*, often I

9. 20 June 2011.
10. 16 May 2011.
11. 27 April 2011.

> hesitate to pass urine because of this. After passing urine, I try my best to see to it that the last drop of urine is out, then wash with water, after this I walk for a short while on the place where I stand, again wash with water and come out. I use only the INDIAN toilet. After coming out I find some small drops of urine passing out, if I wash it with water, there will be a pressure to pass urine again. Because of this reasons my Prayers (*Namaz*) have been missing. I am really ashamed to narrate my problem personally to an AALIM, because looking at my face they would be shocked to hear such problems from me, as I ALHAMDULLIALAH have a big beard and wear Sunna'h cap always ... [12]

An equally troubled believer beseeches:

> *AssalamoAlykum* the toilet water is high and lots of splashing occurs i try to guard my self as much as i can but usually when i urinate tiny particles splash back onto me when i do *istinja* for urinating, i am forced to also clean my back passage because that is where the urine splashes usually fall. my question is, when i do *istinjaa*, the water i use for *istinjaa* falls to the bottom of the toilet (which has already been flushed so the water in it is not dirty) and water splashes back on me. Would that water be *najis*? Since i heard if the water's smell/taste doesent change, it is pure. the water in the toilet doesent seem to change, so is the water splashing back pure? I try my best but there is no way possible to guard against such splashes. I often have to resort to taking showers, either from urine splashing, or water used for *istinjaa* splashing. Please help me because i have been praying lately with *istinja* water splashing back and i try to avoid *waswas* (uncertainty) and try my best but some things i can not control, and Allah says he will not put on us a burden we can not handle. Please help me. Almighty Allah will reward you! [13]

The same problems foment the same degree of anxiety in the case of droplets of semen and other fluids. What if the droplets have come out because of a dream? What if I have

12. 3 June 2011.
13. 29 November 2010.

been able to rush to the toilet before the discharge? What if the droplets have dried?

What about menstruating women? How are the days to be counted if the bleeding is interrupted in the middle of the period? Can the woman touch the Quran during these days? Can she, without touching the Quran, recite ayats she knows by heart? Can she pray for a deceased relative? Can she touch books of rules? Can she read? Can she cut her nails? The queries are as numerous as they are anxious and urgent. The rulings are conclusive—grounded in the same deep and earnest scholarship that we have encountered throughout.

Intercourse naturally begets even more penetrating queries. Is it mandatory to bathe immediately after intercourse or can one wait till the morning? Has the bath to be from head to toe? What kind of contact with my wife— kissing her cheeks or lips, for instance, just stroking her private parts without full intercourse—make a bath mandatory? Will Allah heed my prayer if I have not bathed? In addition to having a bath, have we to change our clothes as well as the bed sheet and blanket? What of the woman who reaches orgasm but does not have a discharge? What about masturbation? The variations are many:

> *Assalamu alaikum,* is it necessary to have *gusal* before having sex for conception. I mean I have come to know that if I wish to conceive and have sex twice in the same night I have to perform *gusal* in between please help.[14]
>
> I am a Male and My name is Rehmatullah. I have a problem that sometimes i discharges liquid from penis when I had a feeling of sex and drops of liquid comes out. This continues happens and I faces same situation more than one time in 5 to 10 mins. I have a question that whether I have to perform *gushal* after each discharge. Second thing that piece of cloth on which discharge dropped will be *"paak"* after washing that part only with water or need to change the cloth.[15]

---

14. 18 August 2008.
15. 5 June 2010.

From the length of the beard to inadvertently seeing the parts of bodies seeing which is forbidden; to using a toothbrush; to cutting pubic hair; to shaving the hair on one's chest, legs and arms; to allowing the doctor to clean the spot at which he is going to give us an injection; to cleaning one's throat and nose thrice; to using tissue paper for wiping oneself after defecation instead, as we have seen earlier, of what has been insisted upon hitherto—pebbles and balls of earth; to using polythene so that that damned droplet does not render one's clothes napaak; to trapped wind escaping one during prayer

> *Salam,* it is good to sleep in wuzu (ablution). I do my wuzu and go to sleep. I read the three *quls* (fragments of Quranic verses) and then *ayat kursi* (a Quranic verse to ward off fear) and when I lay down to sleep I feel to fart (pass the air). Do I have to do my *wozo* again if I fart or the first *wozo* was enough. I will get the reward all night or not?[16]
> If a person has to pass air but keeps it in because of him being in *salat* but then feels a bubble or a very small quantity has passed which does not give of smell or does not feel like the normal passing of air. Does this person invalidates his *salah* or abolition and must he repeat all the *salah* made in such condition.[17]

> I have a problem performing each salat without passing gas during it. When I do *sajda* then get up, gas is slightly passed so easily that many times I am in doubt whether it was gas or just my suspicion. This is happening because of weakness in the muscles after childbirth. So I have to keep performing *wudhu,* and sometimes there is not enough time for this. What should I do?[18]

to having a shower instead of bathing from a bucket; to standing while bathing rather than sitting; to whether one should kill black dogs and those of other colours—as they are

---

16. 1 December 2008.
17. 19 January 2008.
18. 4 April 2007.

Shaitan ... each and every one of these questions is taken to be—both by the faithful and by the clerics—a matter on which the decision must rest with religious authorities. The only way for the reader to get a feel of the subject is to go through the fatwas themselves.19

Now, this is not accidental. On the contrary, the insistence that Islam, and in practice that means those who speak in its name, shall regulate every aspect of the life of the believer is a central feature of such ideologies. One of the senses in which they are 'totalitarian' is in their insistence that they shall regulate the totality of life.

Nor is the insistence confined to clerics operating out of India. The difference is that in a plural society like India, the ulema do not have the force of the state behind them. In Iran when they decree, as they did in June 2010, that no one shall keep dogs as pets, when they follow this up, as they did in August 2010, with a fatwa banning advertisements that promote food and other items for pets, especially cats and dogs; when the Saudi authorities decree that no woman shall drive a car, when they decree prohibitions against music ... they are able to *enforce* their edicts.

That is a difference, of course, but only if one condition is fulfilled—the laity should not have become self-enforcers. No external agency is needed to enforce these rulings once the faithful have *internalized* the belief that their fatwas just have to be obeyed, that not obeying them is a betrayal of faith.

---

19. There is one convenient way to see at least a few of them: just go to the official website of the Darul Ifta, Darul Uloom, Deoband, and study the 4,864 fatwas that they have put up for the convenience of English-speaking believers and readers. The incidental advantage of doing so is that this set has been selected by the Deoband authorities themselves. From within this set, as a sample, he can peruse the 229 queries and edicts that are set out in the section on *Taharah*, purity, on the website.

Enforced or internalized, the consequence of the ideology underlying these dictates is as immediate as it is grave. Conditioned to look to the religious authorities for guidance on even these matters, the faithful are easily steered by those authorities on matters that reach far beyond laving and the like.

Even so, the questions as well as the edicts would already have given a glimpse of the first two reasons for hope:

- The ulema as well as so much of the laity are so preoccupied with sticking to the minutiae of rituals, and the rituals are just so many that, given the pace of modern life, they will just not be able to keep observing the rituals in detail. And once the process starts, the slide is steep—in this case, the slide towards liberation from formalism.
- Life gallops ahead. Minds so out of sync with change—whether the minds be of the edict givers or of those obeying the edicts—are bound to lose all potency.

We have but to study fatwas

The twenty-first century

As is well known, ever since the days of the Prophet, there is the strictest prohibition in Islam against representation of living beings, in particular of human figures. But the television shows men and women. So, is it permissible to have a television set in our home or to watch it?

The querist is in a bind:

> *Assalaamualeikum* brothers, I am in bit trouble, I have TV at my home and I have stop watching it. My family members watch and I am insisting them from last six months to remove it and I am telling

> them the disadvantages of it but they are not listening to me. And I am going to get marry within few months and I don't want my wife to watch TV. So please advice me what to do. *Zakaak-allah*.

The ulema have a solution:

> Call reliable Ulema to your house and arrange their speeches. Also, study books written about the evils of television.[20]

But what about using television and other visual media for a good purpose—like propagating Islam and bringing people into its fold? a seeker asks. After all, so many preachers are using it to spread the teachings of Islam, and to answer the queries of Muslims. The ulema are unyielding, though they couch their pronouncement as if it is conditioned by what television has become 'in present time':

> In present time, television has become an instrument of entertainment and fun as well as a hub of sins and transgressions. Therefore, our elder *Ulema* do not allow using television for religious purpose as well.[21]

The mention of Saudi Arabia and what the clerics there are doing sparks some prudence. The querist writes that he

---

20. Darul Ifta, Darul Uloom, Deoband, 22 July 2008; Answer number 6344; Fatwa number 1252/1058=B/1429. Henceforth, unless specified otherwise, the fatwas are of the Darul Ifta, Deoband.

21. 4 August 2008; Answer number 6514; Fatwa number 808/742=L-1429. In the fatwa they had issued on 8 December the previous year, they had been more categorical: television is being used as a device for entertainment and enjoyment, they had declared; it is used mostly for 'unlawful and prohibited things'. Why then do we watch hajj on television? Khalid Rashid Firangi Mahali had asked? The Deoband clerics themselves are no strangers to television and videos, he had pointed out: they often come on it for debates. (Cf, *The Telegraph*, Kolkata, 20 December 2007.) In fact, we can today go to YouTube and see videos of their eminent teachers giving discourses to large gatherings of students and fellow ulema, videos taken not secretly but openly with cameras in the view of all, including the leading lights responsible for such edicts.

has seen videos that have been shot in Riyadh for 'Islamic propagation'. Is shooting videos for this purpose permissible? What about videos of marriages and similar functions? The ulema respond,

> Making video films of marriage functions is obviously impermissible. But, as far as the video of Islamic propagation programmes in Riyadh is concerned, we are not aware of it. Please, contact the Ulema of that office and whatever reply they give to your question send a copy of it to us also.[22]

What about using the Internet then? The fatwa has at least the virtue of consistency:

> It is allowed to use the Internet forum if it is according to Shariah. If there is online discussion (by writing) then there is no problem, even if there is a woman at another end. But, if there are pictures or voice of women, then it will not be allowed even if it has only Islamic contents. So, it is allowed to use Internet in itself provided that there is no picture of living being and voice of women.[23]

Forget the view they have of women—to which we shall turn in a moment—what is the view they have of men? That they are so deprived and frustrated that the mere voice of a woman will send them dripping?

Indeed, that does seem to be the case. A querist writes from South Africa:

> *assalamu alaykum w.w mufti shab* My quistion is here in south africa they is radio station called radio islam and it is very beneficial for evry one. but my qustion is on that radio station evry hour women read out the news is that permissible? it is permissible for ger mahram man to listen to here voise? because thru out the world 1000 of litsener and many of them ger mahram (strangers)? so plz

22. 15 April 2007; Answer number 148; Fatwa number 561/H=367/H.
23. 8 April 2007; Answer number 122; Fatwa number 245/N=241/N.

replay me with answerd as soon as possible is it permisseble for women to broadcast on radio whey she is not invoved with man or camera? please please replay me soon i'm waiting for your replay. *salam*

The mind of the ulema and the conception they have of the nature of Muslim men and women are firmly grounded in the shariah:

Women have been prohibited to speak loudly, read out something in melody and talk softly. The scholars of Fiqh say that voice of a woman is also *satr* (to be covered, kept private, in seclusion). That is why women have been stopped to call Azan and recite *talbia* loudly in Hajj. Yes, in cases of necessity, they can talk as they can have some words with a doctor etc. However, without any need, it is not right for women to broadcast news at radio stations as well it is not permissible for non-*Mahram* men to hear their voice without a need.[24]

The good woman

A puzzled and manifestly anxious woman from Pakistan writes:

A/salam i wanna know how to be a good wife, infact i recently married n i m confuse n bit afraid wether i m fulfilling the rights of him or not?

The learned ulema, often referred in our media as 'the learned divines', of Deoband declare,

Hadhrat Abu Hurairah (may Allah bestow grace on him) narrates that the Messenger of Allah (Peace be Upon Him) was asked who among the woman is the best. He replied: One who pleases her husband when he sees her, obeys him when he orders and does nothing against his wishes in herself and his property (Sunan Nasai).

---

24. 5 August, 2008; Answer number 5722; Fatwa number 442/442=M1429.

> In order to be good wife, you should know what rights you owe to your husband. In this regard, *Tuhfa Dulhan* and *Huqooquz Zaujain* are good books, get it from any book depot and study them repeatedly.[25]

Not just authoritative, irrefutable—as that really is what the Prophet had laid down.

We are harangued that Muslims have got left behind in education, and that this is the root of the disadvantages from which they suffer. We have seen earlier who it is who has kept them from modern education. Universities, IITs, IIMs and other institutions of higher learning are being opened. In them, young men and women attend classes together. Is this permissible? What about *deeni* classes—classes for religious instruction in which boys and girls who have reached puberty are taught together, and to which they have to travel together in vans? From what age must the children be separated in classes and in transport vehicles? Here is what the ulema deem forbidden:

> (1)It is unlawful for women to meet non-*Mahram* men without *Hijab* or mix with them ...
> The co-education system of colleges and universities is having a number of evils; therefore it is undoubtedly unlawful.
> (2) Such *deeni* class which co-educates grownup boys and girls is unIslamic and attending such class is not allowed.
> (3) It is ordained to separate the bed of girls and boys when they reach ten years of their age. This implies that the boys and girls can learn together maximum to the age of ten years.[26]

To enable girls to attend schools and to ensure that they are not harassed or teased on the way, several state

---

25. 18 February 2009; Answer number 10950; Fatwa number 221/169=L/1430.

26. 2 July 2007; Answer number 481; Fatwa number 202/L.

governments have started distributing cycles free to girl students. May a girl ride the cycle? The ulema's edict:

> It may be allowable in childhood as play and game, but after 9 of age (sic) when she is mature and starts attracting gaze of non-*mahram* men, cycling is not lawful for her.[27]

What is the consequence of such a prohibition on the ability of girls to attend schools when these are a few kilometres away? And yet, if one goes by our secularists' discourse, it is the rest of us who are responsible for keeping Muslims, in particular Muslim women from getting educated.

All right, maybe a little girl of ten should not ride a bicycle as that will arouse men—on a cycle they will be seeing her whole body, after all. What about a car? May a woman drive a car? After all, most of her body will not be visible to those crazed men. Can she travel in the car driven by a driver? In either event, how far may she travel? The ulema lay down the prohibitions again and again. She may go 'to nearby places without a *mahram*, observing *hijab*, provided there is no fear of *fitna (evil/mischief)*,' they declare. But for a journey she must be accompanied by a relative. In any case, driving a car is not allowed. In another case, the ulema insist that a woman cannot travel even with female siblings. She must not travel more than 48 miles without a mahram relative.[28] In yet another case, the ulema hold that she can travel 78 kilometres, but in no case can she travel with a non-mahram driver 'since she will be in privacy with a non-mahram'.[29]

---

27. http://islamopediaonline.org/fatwa/deoband-seminary-issuesfatwa-against-adoloscent-girls-riding-bicycles. Posted 21 July 2010.

28. Answer number 30182; Fatwa number 511/308/D=1432.

29. 9 November 2008 and 14 July 2009; Answer numbers 8668 and 13592; Fatwa numbers 1414/1183=L/1429 and 1109/1066=D/1430.

An especially poignant case comes up. A lady writes from Canada. The lady's parents are in India. They are old, one of them is ailing. Her husband is working and cannot get leave. May she travel alone from Canada to India to see her parents? The ulema are uncompromising: 'As per the shariah,' they declare, 'she is not allowed to travel such a long distance alone only for seeing her parents, it is prohibited.'[30]

No bicycle. No driving a car. No travel without a related male. May she take up a job? If so, what kind of a job?

The position of the ulema, whom so many of our secularists address with high epithets, is that in normal circumstances, women should *not* take up jobs. The querist inquires:

> *As salamu alaikum,* I would like to know if it is permissible for a Muslimah to work as a translator for the tribunal. *JazakAllah* (Allah have mercy).

The ulema declare:

> It is not a good thing for women to do jobs in offices. They will have to face strange men (non-*mahram*) though in veil. She will have to talk and deal with each other (sic) which are the things of *fitna* (evils). A father is committed to provide maintenance to his daughter and a husband is asked to provide maintenance to his wife. So, there is no need for women to do jobs which always pose harms and mischief.

In a related case, the ulema are asked, 'Can Muslim women in India do Government or private jobs? Shall their salary be *halal* or *haram* or prohibited?' 'It is unlawful for Muslim women to do job in government or private institutions where men and women work together and women have to

30. Answer number 14595; Fatwa number 1585/1260=H/1430.

talk with men frankly and without veil,' decree the ulema. The fatwa by the Saudi clerics against women working as cashiers, etc., came as a surprise? Here is what is being prescribed not in Saudi Arabia but in India, just a few hundred miles from Delhi.

If the circumstances leave no alternative, the ulema relent a bit—for instance, and I am just citing the cases that are pronounced upon in the sample on the website of the Darul Ifta, Deoband, if the woman is a widow and there is no one else who will take care of her and her children; if the earnings of the husband are not enough to maintain the family—then the woman may work *provided*: she wears the full hijab at work; fulfils the requirements of shariah; does not mingle with or talk to non-related men 'unnecessarily'; and goes out of her home after obtaining permission from her husband.[31]

Talk of the most vital segment of Muslim population in India remaining bereft of the wherewithal to compete in the world—that is, modern education! Talk of a section of the population not sharing in the fruits of development! But, if you go by what our secularists declaim, the fault for all this lies with the rest of us, in particular with the majority, that is the Hindus.

Some mercies

And yet one must be thankful for some mercies: in India, Muslim women do not live in a country in which the ulema have the power to enforce their decrees. In Saudi Arabia, in

---

31. Dates 4 April 2010, 26 July 2008, 11 September 2007, 2 November 2008, 26 April 2009 respectively; Answer numbers 5405, 21031, 1044, 8618, 12326; Fatwa numbers 577/381/L=1431, 691/636=D1429, 721/721=J, 1347/1135=L1429, 824/688=D/1430.

Pakistan since 1977 when Zia ul Haq promulgated the Hudood Ordinances, in Iran since the Khomeini revolution, that power derives from and is conjoint with the power of the state. In a nominally secular state—like Bangladesh—it comes from the inability of the state to enforce its nominal commitment to the primacy of secular laws and institutions.

In either event, the results are tragic. Several of the horrid cases have been much written about. Adultery and rape figured prominently in Zia's Hudood Ordinances. For adultery, there had to be four, reliable, adult, Muslim, male eyewitnesses to actual, physical penetration—the stated purpose was to protect persons from being falsely accused. In several cases of women, in particular single, unmarried women, who had been raped and had become pregnant, the requisite eyewitnesses could not be produced. But their pregnancy was proof positive that they had had illegal sexual relations. And so, while they had been victims of rape, they became the accused—accused of *zina*, adultery: their charge that they had been raped became a confession of their having had illegal intercourse; and the fact that they were pregnant became proof positive. In a typical case, fifteen-year-old Jehan Mina was raped by two of her male relatives. She became pregnant. She was sentenced to 100 lashes. A higher court, out of 'charity', reduced the sentence to ten lashes. Thirteen-year-old Safia Bibi was blind. She was employed as a maid. Her employer and his son raped her. She became pregnant. The rapists went scot-free. She was sentenced to three years in prison, and thirty lashes—the flogging was limited to thirty lashes, the court said, out of leniency for her being blind. The case became a cause célèbre. Asma Jehangir, Hina Jilani and other human rights activists mounted a vigorous challenge. Pakistan's Federal Court set the judgment aside—though it concurred that the evidence against the father and son was insufficient. And young Safia survived. But cases that are just as baseless and just as weighed against women, and the extreme fear they generate, have continued—under 'laws' that range from rape to divorce to blasphemy. At one time, it was reported that almost 70 to 80 per cent of undertrials languishing in Pakistan's jails were women who had been charged with offences of this kind.[32]

---

32. In an interview with Damien Carrick in April 2008, one of Pakistan's intrepid fighters, the distinguished lawyer, Hina Jilani, described the consequences of Zia's laws, and of the uses to which they were put:

> *Damien Carrick:* So what, hundreds, thousands of women were ending up in jail?
>
> *Hina Jilani:* Thousands ended up in jail but not, of course, as many were ever punished.
>
> *Damien Carrick:* So were rape victims charged with adultery or fornication?
>
> *Hina Jilani:* Not all of them, but yes, a good measure of them were. But the major issue also was that women who were charged with adultery, and a lot of them were charged under that because the law made it very easy for people to target women for different reasons. So women who were inheriting something after their parents had died, or father had died, other relatives wanted them out of the way so they'd use an accusation of adultery to put her behind bars for years.
>
> Husbands who had problems with their wives, who eventually had decided to leave them, would charge whoever they took shelter with, accusing them of having extramarital relations with the wife, so the wife was sent to jail. Custody and guardianship of children, women's assertion of that kind of right, a lot of things happened, but also major issue here was when women asserted their right of choice in marriage, their own parents charged them with adultery and sent them to prisons. Thousands of women went through that process. Not many were tried because, as I said, the system itself was so faulty and so deficient that they never ended up in trials. But that again showed another aspect of the injustice, that you could detain women for longer periods of time. Even bails were denied to women, and it's a funny thing that for many years bails ...

In Bangladesh, with the gallop towards Islamization, the rapid spread of Tablighi Jamaat, the ever-widening reach and influence of fundamentalist organizations like the Hizb-ut-Tahrir and the Hizb-ut-Tauhid, Shariah Committees sprang up in several parts of the country. Fatwas became ever more frequent. They were often issued by the local mullahs in rural areas, and ever so often the victims were women who had in fact been victims of violence, rape and the rest. On 1 January 2001, the high court issued a verdict declaring fatwas ultra vires, and affirming that under the Bangladesh Constitution, the courts alone had the power to decide all questions relating to legal interpretations of shariah and all other laws. Fatwas, in particular, the court ruled, and punishments meted out under them were illegal. Riots broke out. Seven died. The Supreme Court stayed the high court judgment.

Around 500 women are reported to have been subjected to flogging since then as a result of fatwas having been issued against them. In July 2010 again the high court ruled that extrajudicial punishments are illegal, including those being meted out in the wake of fatwas. In December 2010, a woman accused of sleeping with her stepson was whipped forty times as the result of a fatwa. She died as a consequence. In February 2011, as she returned from an outdoor toilet, a fourteen-year-old girl, Hina, was gagged, beaten and then

---

> ... were denied to women by courts that said that these women can only step out of prison if they are taken over by a member of their family, and these were the families who had actually been responsible for sending them to the prison in the first place ...'

Hina Jilani was at the time the Special Representative for Human Rights Defenders of the UN Secretary General. Cf, Conversation of Damien Carrick with Hina Jilani, ABC Radio National, Law Report, 8 April 2008. www.abc.net.au/rn/lawreport/stories/2008/2209518.htm

raped by a cousin near the latter's house. The wife of the cousin, hearing the commotion, came rushing out and dragged Hina into the house. Hina was beaten black and blue to unconsciousness. The wife of the cousin complained to the Village Council—it had the local ulema as its members—that Hina had been having an illicit affair with her husband. Hina's father was not allowed to speak. She herself was barely conscious. The Village Council, including the local clerics, held Hina as well as her assaulter guilty. Hina was sentenced to be flogged 101 times, the assaulter to be flogged 201 times. Conveniently, the latter was to be lashed by his father. He 'escaped' after a few strokes. Hina's flogging commenced with full force. By the time she had been lashed seventy-odd times, she collapsed. Six days later, she died.

The post-mortem was as convenient as such things are in our parts. It recorded no injuries, and concluded that Hina had committed suicide. Her parents and human rights' activists agitated. Her body was exhumed. Severe injuries were all too apparent. The high court began proceedings against the doctors, as well as against the Village Council personnel, including the clerics for ignoring its earlier verdict against extrajudicial punishments.

In March 2011, the Supreme Court at last took up the appeal that had been filed against the high court judgment of 2001 against fatwas. It lifted the ban that had been in existence for a decade (there had been a ban on fatwas, yes, in fact!), and declared that fatwas were legal, but that punishment could not be meted out because of them. In its majesty, it invited Islamic scholars to submit their views on fatwas, on the punishments that are meted out as a result, etc. The law taking its majestic course ...

The last word on such sequences was given by Hina's father—he had had to carry her to the verandah for the proceedings in which she was condemned to be flogged. *The Guardian* quoted him as saying:

> I am not educated. I don't know what the court laws are. But I know that if I don't listen to the elders, we would be outcast. None of my daughters could marry, no one would even look at us. If I had known that it would be them who would be punished, not me, then I would have tried to stop it.[33]

Which government in today's world that allows such dictates to stand will be able to defend itself? The fact that the world is getting knit closer by the month ensures that no country can remain an island unto itself, and eventually the controllers of no community will be able to continue to insist that they shall do as they please with members of the community—they will not be able to maintain this stance whether they claim their mandate from texts and proclamations of religion or on grounds such as national sovereignty.

History gets a helping hand—in fact, two hands reach out to speed it up, and in them lies hope.

The unreasonable, fortified though it is by the highest authorities, becomes the indefensible

In Egypt as elsewhere, clerics had maintained time and

---

33. Hina's case was reported widely. For instance, see http://www.guardian.co.uk/world/2011/feb/04/bangladeshi-girlwhipping-fatwa;http://articles.cnn.com/2011-03-29/world/bangladesh.lashing.death_1_alya_lashes_elders?_s=PM:WORLD;http://wwwaolnews.com/2011/02/03bangladeshi-girl-dies-after-publicflogging/;http://www.hudson-ny.org/1959/bangladesh-supreme-court-fatwas;http://web1.globalpost.com/dispatch/news/regions/asia-pacific/110330/hena-begum-teenager-flogging-bangladesh

again that those who died in road accidents or in mishaps at sea while travelling were martyrs and as such would go straight to heaven. Apart from the fact that, high religious authorities having certified this to be the case, they must obviously have had direct evidence of the deceased being in heaven, the rulings had been a source of solace to the surviving relatives. In 2007, there was a sudden jolt. Some Egyptians were trying to reach Europe. The vessel capsized. Twenty-six of them drowned. The tragedy shook the country. The ruling party—of the then president, Hosni Mubarak—was in session. The rulers had made ambiguous statements about those who were leaving Egypt in search of better prospects and thus depriving the country of their labour and talents—there was nothing the matter with Egypt's economy that warranted emigrating, they had maintained. Even as the country was mourning the deaths, even as the relatives were waiting at the Cairo airport for the bodies, the country's Grand Mufti, Sheikh Ali Gomaa, issued a fatwa: no, the twenty-six were *not* martyrs. They had left the country for more money. Hence, they were propelled by greed, and journeys motivated by greed could not be taken to be 'striving in the way of Allah'.

There was an outcry—among the relatives, among the liberals, among the general public. The outcry led one of the world's most renowned centres of Islamic learning, the al Azhar to set up a committee to examine the ruling. The committee held that the fatwa was 'abhorrent', that it was something that 'even the Devil himself had not thought of.' Allah has commanded us to travel to the four corners of the world for earning a living. Hence, those who die in their quest for good jobs *are* martyrs. The Grand Mufti retracted. He had not issued any fatwa, he now claimed. All that had happened was that, after a lecture that he had delivered at the university, a student had asked him a question and he had only stated his opinion. It is the press that was responsible: it had misreported what had been said and in which context.[34]

Soon, this great centre of Islamic learning was to get entangled in an even more consequential, and more prolonged fracas. As is well known, all through the ages the highest authorities of Islam have repeatedly held that no Muslim woman is to be alone or, even if she is accompanied by other women, bereft of full hijab with a man except those of her immediate family—the two of them are not to be alone even in the open to say nothing of a closed room or of the woman regularly going to a place where she is commonly interacting with unrelated men. What then is to be done when, as is now sometimes the case, a Muslim woman works in an office where there are men also—for instance, when there are men working on the same floor, often in the same hall?

In 2007, not 1007 but 2007, this urgent question came up before Dr Ezzat Attiya. He was the head of one of the most important departments, the Hadith Department, of that crown of Islamic learning, al-Azhar in Cairo. He went strictly by the Quran and the Hadis, and issued the requisite fatwa laying out the solution.

The root of the problem lies in the fact that the woman and the men are not related, he reasoned. The solution, therefore, is to establish a relationship, and not just any relationship. The relationship must approximate that of a mother and a child whom she has suckled. This can be established by the woman having every male in the office or the floor drink milk from her breasts. He elaborated the edict

34. http://www.asiaone.com/News/The%2BStraits%2BTimes/Story/A1Story20071122-37907.html

in an interview with *Al-Watani Al-Yawm*, the official weekly of the then ruling party of Egypt. 'The religious ruling that appears in the Prophet's conduct [*sunnah*],' he explained, 'confirms that breastfeeding allows a man and a woman to be together in private, even if they are not family and if the woman did not nurse the man in his infancy, before he was weaned—providing that their being together serves some purpose, religious or secular ...'

He was on solid ground in this. For, we learn in a Hadis handed down by none other than Aisha herself that the problem had arisen in the case of the son whom Abu Hudhaifa had adopted. The adopted son was an adult—'with a beard'. In the normal course, he would be in the house when Abu Hudhaifa's wife would be present. Even if others were present, the question remained of whether the lady must remain in full hijab when this young man was in the house. On the directions of the Prophet, the problem was solved by Abu Hudhaifa's wife letting the young bearded man suckle at her breasts. 'The fact that the *hadith* regarding breastfeeding of an adult is inconceivable to the mind does not make it invalid,' Dr Attiya explained. 'This is a reliable *hadith,* and rejecting it is tantamount to rejecting Allah's Messenger and questioning the Prophet's tradition.'

The Hadis is set out, to take just one instance, in the *Sahih Muslim* as follows:

> Aisha (Allah be pleased with her) reported that Salim, the freed slave of Abu Hudhaifa, lived with him and his family in their house. She (i.e., the daughter of Suhail came to Allah's Apostle [may peace be upon him] and said: Salim has attained as men attain, and he understands what they understand, and he enters our house freely. I, however, perceive that something (rankles; in similar Hadis the word used is 'disgusts') in the heart of Abu Hudhaifa, whereupon Allah's Apostle (may peace be upon him) said to her: Suckle him and you would become unlawful for him, and (the rankling) which

> Abu Hudhaifa feels in his heart will disappear. She returned and said: So I suckled him, and what (was there) in the heart of Abu Hudhaifa disappeared.[35]

That solution having been set out so unambiguously and so authoritatively, Dr Attiya reiterated that the woman must directly breastfeed the men. Pumping out some milk and other such indirect methods are less desirable, he ruled. In fact, before pumping can be used as an alternative, he said, doctors and religious authorities have to determine whether the composition of the milk so produced is the same as the composition of the milk obtained by putting one's mouth directly to the breasts.

Dr Attiya added an auxiliary requirement, and proposed a widening of the circle of women whose breasts may be offered—in allowing the latter relaxation he was clearly violating his own ruling and going beyond what the Hadis had set out. The additional requirement he laid down was that the fact that the woman has breastfed the man must be officially documented in writing. And the relief? 'The important point,' he said, 'is that the man and the woman must be related through breastfeeding. [This can also be achieved] by means of the man's mother or sister suckling the woman, or by means of the woman's mother or sister suckling the man, since [all of these eventualities] turn them into brother and sister.'

And there is 'logic' to the solution, he declared. Breastfeeding an adult man will turn 'the bestial relationship' between the men on the floor and the woman into a religious one based on religious duties.

Even though the learned doctor was on firm ground, after

35. *Sahih Muslim,* Abdul Hamid Siddiqi (tr.), Volume II, pp. 741–43, Hadis numbers 3425–28.

all he was the head of the Hadith Department at the most prestigious centre of Islamic learning, and he had the Hadis in which to ground his solution, a furore ensued. Al-Azhar was compelled to appoint a committee to review his fatwa. The committee held against him. He recanted. Even so, he was removed from his post.

Two facts conclude the matter. First, the recantation that Dr Attiya issued in a sense reinforced the authenticity of his edict. 'My statements on the issue of breastfeeding an adult,' Dr Attiya wrote in his recantation, 'were based on the Imams Ibn Hazm, Ibn Taymiyya, Ibn Al-Qayyim, Al-Shawkani and Amin Khattab [Al-Subki], and on the conclusions I drew from the statements of Ibn Hajar [Al-Askalani].' As conclusive a list of authorities as anyone could ask for, and please do not miss the high and earnest scholarship that had gone into the fatwa—after all, the good Doctor had not just located the pertinent Hadis, he had looked up the treatises of all these authorities on Islamic law and lore. 'However,' he continued, 'I hold that only the breastfeeding of an infant creates a family relationship [that prohibits marriage between the parties and allows them to be together], as the four Imams [the founders of the four Sunni legal schools] said, while the [act of] breastfeeding a grown man [mentioned in the *hadis*] was a [specific] incident that came to serve a [specific] purpose, and the fatwa I issued was based solely on my personal interpretation. Based on what I have learned with my brothers the religious scholars, I apologize for my earlier [statements] and retract my opinion, which contradicts [the norms accepted] by the public.'

In the event, he was removed from his position. But, and that is the second fact, he was reinstated within the year on the orders of the Cairo Administrative Court![36]

---

36. A host of papers and journals of the time reported the fatwa and its sequel. For convenience of the reader, I have taken the aforementioned

The controversy and embarrassment had but to abate, and an even higher authority issued the fatwa again. In March 2009, a seventy-five-year-old widow, Khamisa Mohammed Sawadi, was ordered to be lashed forty times and to spend six months in prison in Saudi Arabia. Her crime? Two men were found in her house when she was alone. They had come to deliver bread. The pleas of innocence were rejected. In addition to the punishment that had been decreed for the poor widow, they too were sentenced to receive punishment: forty lashes and four months of imprisonment in one case, and sixty lashes and six months of prison in the other. The matter of women and men being alone, therefore, remained much in the public mind. Moreover, King Abdullah had begun taking the first, admittedly tiny steps towards reform. Women had been allowed to take up a few types of jobs—for instance, to work as cashiers in stores. That raised the problem in a way that could not be ignored—after all, the cashiers would in the normal course now come in contact with men who were not related to them.

In 2010, Sheikh Abdul Mohsin Bin Nasser Al-Obeikan was asked for his ruling on the matter. The Sheikh was the much celebrated imam of the Masjid Al-Haram, the Grand Mosque of Mecca. Apart from the fact that he occupied such high office, the Sheikh was looked up to for his sonorous recitations of the Quran and because he was the first black man to have reached that high position. In addition, he was advisor to both the Royal Court as well as the Ministry of Justice. He fully endorsed the fatwa that Dr Ezzat Attiya had

---

... facts from two easily accessible websites: *The Middle East Media Research Institute, Inquiry and Analysis Series, Number 355*, 25 May, 2007, http:// www.memri.org/report/en/print2215.html; and http:// www.jihadwatch.org/2009/05/breastfeeding-fatwa-sheikh-back-at-alazhar, 23 May, 2009. See also, http://the memriblog.org/blog_personal/en/ 16533.html, 18 May 2009.

issued—with one emendation. The woman must give milk to male colleagues, acquaintances or any males with whom she comes in regular contact, he ruled. But she need not necessarily do so by offering her breast to the men. She could extract the milk from her breast, and the men could drink it in a cup.

No, not at all, thundered an equally high authority, Sheikh Abu Ishaq Al Huwaini. The woman must suckle the men directly from her breast. And she must do so for five 'fulfilling' sessions.[37]

Women were indignant. They took to the new media, the Internet, text messages and meetings to pour derision at the religious authorities that had issued the fatwas. For one thing, these worthies know nothing about women, the women said. Is every woman lactating all the time? 'Do they even know men?' asked another lady. 'Having taken a few tugs at the breasts of their colleague on the floor, will they be *less* or *more* excited when they chance upon her next?' The women poured ridicule. We are not allowed to drive a car. Hence, we have perforce to use drivers. They are not related to us. And yet, once in the car, we are in an enclosed space with them. Are we to offer them our breasts? And what happens when we are doing so, and our husband arrives on the scene? Intrepid women decided to put the fatwa to work. As, in view of the fatwa, they said, we have no choice but to offer our breasts to our drivers, we should be afforded the more sensible alternative—we should be permitted to drive cars ourselves[38] ...

---

37. Reporting on this with evident delight, editors of *Swerve Left* noted, 'For those of us who have endured slappings and indignant nays when we've proposed this to the women with whom we are in contact daily, it's a relief to see support from conservative Saudi clerics.' http://swerveleft, blogspot.com/2010/06/latest-fatwa.html

38. Gulfnews.com, 20 June 2010, 'Saudi women use fatwa in driving bid'.

The matter did not end. On the contrary. As part of his efforts to introduce reforms, in 2009, King Abdullah had inaugurated a university in which young men and women were studying together. In February 2010, Sheikh Abdul Rahman al-Barrak, reputed to be 'the leading independent authority of Wahabism', issued a fatwa decreeing death for those who were promoting *ikhtilat*—the impermissible mixing of sexes. This makes it possible for the parties to see what is forbidden and to engage in exchanges that are forbidden, the fatwa declared, and 'All this leads to whatever ensues.' 'Whoever allows this mixing allows what is forbidden,' the Sheikh decreed, 'and whoever allows them is an infidel and this means defection from Islam.' 'Either he retracts,' the fatwa read, 'or he must be killed because he disavows and does not observe the Shariah.' Furthermore, 'Anyone who accepts that his daughter, sister or wife works with men or attends mixed-gender schooling cares little about his honour and this is a type of pimping,' it held.[39]

The fatwa was volubly opposed in countries like Kuwait. One form of protest against it caught the eye and ear of large numbers. *Sha'ir Al-Milyon* is a hugely popular television poetry contest. Broadcast out of Abu Dhabi, it is watched keenly across the Middle East. A lady, Hissa Halal, opposed and parodied Sheikh Rahman's fatwa in verse. The panel of judges vaulted her over 14,000 contestants into the semi-finals, and was reported to have been 'fulsome in its praise for Halal's verses', saying that she had 'bravely addressed a

39. Neeraj Gangal, 'Saudi cleric's fatwa urges death for coeducation', 26 February 2010, http://www.arabianbusiness.com/saudi-cleric-s-fatwa-urges-death-for-coeducation-78813.html. And Reuters in *Al-Arabiya News*, 28 February 2011. Reuters added that in 2008 the Sheikh had issued a fatwa pronouncing the death sentence on two writers for writing an article that questioned the Islamic view that Christians and Jews are unbelievers.

public concern, a concern of the *ummah* in the current times, and which is an important and sensitive topic'.[40]

A remedy for the 'chaos'

Such draconian fatwas opposing even mild reforms illustrated what many came to call 'the fatwa chaos'. A typical dispute erupted in July 2010. Sheikh Al-Obeikan, the imam of the Masjid al-Haram of Mecca whom we have encountered earlier, issued a fatwa decreeing that singing and music are not un-Islamic. 'There is no clear text or ruling in Islam that singing and music are prohibited,' he pronounced. As all kinds of music, save some folk music, are forbidden in Saudi Arabia, a furore broke out. Other clerics stoutly denounced Al-Obeikan's ruling. He took a step back, saying that he had not endorsed any and every kind of music, only 'decent music with decent words'. Sheikh Abdul Rahman Al-Saudais compared him to a conman selling counterfeit goods. Sheikh Abdul Aziz Al-Sheikh, the Grand Mufti of the kingdom, warned that those who were issuing such fatwas would be subjected to serious reprisals. He demanded that such persons be stopped—just as fake doctors are prevented from treating patients so such unqualified persons should not be allowed to issue fatwas ...[41]

The 'chaos' had been swelling for a long time, and, time and again, the fatwas had brought discomfiture to the royals themselves. Soon after 9/11, in September 2001, Sheikh Hamoud bin Oqla Al-Shuabi, an eighty-year-old blind religious authority had issued a fatwa expelling King Fahd and his entire—30,000 strong—family from Islam. He had charged

40. 'Sheikh Al-Barrak's "death fatwa" shot down in verse', 9 March 2010, www.saudigazette.com.sa/index.cfm?method=home.recon&contentID

41. *Al Arabiya News*, 1 July 2010.

them with what is in Islam one of the gravest of crimes, that of helping infidels—in this case, the US—in their war against Islam. The Sheikh 'is no lonely firebrand', *The Economist* reported at the time. 'He is a prominent scholar who once taught law to the Saudi Chief Justice.' 'Now from his home in Burayda in Nejd province, the Kingdom's Wahabi bastion, he has become the standard-bearer of Saudi Arabia's turbulent prelates,' it continued. 'When the royal family sought retraction of his fatwa, other religious scholars added their voice, including some mainstream preachers.' The Sheikh scorned the overtures, and stuck to his fatwa, telling the authorities that came to question him, 'Whoever backs the infidel against Muslims is considered an infidel.' And right too. *The Economist* recalled that the Wahabi manifesto, *Tawhid*, 'which is compulsory study in schools', specifies that one form of apostasy is 'support for the pagan by hand, tongue or money. As Allah has said, never support the infidels.' The fatwa was of the gravest import as the Saudi rulers derive a very large proportion of their legitimacy from the Wahabi clerics.[42] In a word, the recent fatwas were exacerbating a problem that had been festering for long.

Come mid-August 2010, and King Abdullah decreed that henceforth only the—officially appointed and recognized—Committee on Scholarly Work and Ifta shall issue fatwas. It would function under the twenty-one-member Council of Senior Ulema. 'We have noticed some excesses that we cannot tolerate,' the royal decree stated, 'and it is our legal duty to stand up to these with the strength and resolve to preserve the religion, the dearest of our belongings.'[43] The best

---

42. 'Dissent in Saudi Arabia, The fatwa against the royal family', *The Economist*, 11 October 2001, http://www.economist.com/node/313971.

43. Liz Leslie, 'Saudi Arabia aims to curb excessive fatwas', 19 August 2010, http://muslimvoices.org/fatwas-issued-appointed-clerics-saudi-arabia

known religious authorities continued issuing fatwas. And the officially appointed committee and council reiterated their version of Islam time and again. Soon after being constituted, the council denounced the practice of bringing or sending flowers to patients in hospitals. This is a foreign custom, it decreed, and 'imitates Allah's adversaries'.[44] In little time, the bodies were at odds with the king who had selected and appointed them. A quarter had not passed since the royal decree giving it a monopoly over issuing fatwas, and the very body that the king had anointed issued a fatwa squarely blocking the king. Over 60,000 young women undergraduates were reported to be looking for jobs in Saudi Arabia. The king set out a list of jobs, manifestly the most restricted of restricted lists, that such women could take up— they could work as cashiers, receptionists and beauticians, for instance. In his own case, he had even appointed a lady as a deputy minister for education. These jobs are impermissible, the new fatwa declared, as in them women have to mix with men who are not related to them. Women must confine themselves to decent work at places at which they cannot be tempted by men or tempt them, these authorities ruled. The fatwa was signed by the Grand Mufti of the kingdom, Sheikh Abdul Aziz Al-Sheikh and six other members of the committee.

The problem soon enveloped other spheres. In 2009, the Grand Mufti declared that it was permissible for girls of ten or above to be married by their fathers. The Saudi government tried to limit the age at which girls so young could be married. But there was not just a statement of the Prophet on the matter; there was his example to contend with. And in the Quran itself—in expounding the procedures for divorce,

---

44.http://www.theblaze.com/stories/glut-of-fatwas-spurs-saudi-kingto-impose-curbs/

maintenance and remarriage, for instance—Allah decrees that the limit is three menstrual courses for those who are menstruating as well as for those who aren't—an expression that is taken to cover not just women who have stopped having periods but also prepubescent girls.[45] Sheikh Saleh Al-Fawzan, a member of that committee and council, issued a fatwa denouncing this effort and declared in a minatory tone that no one could mistake, 'Those who are calling for a minimum age for marriage should fear God and not violate His laws or try to legislate things that God did not permit [them to legislate].' Invoking the example of the Prophet, and citing the Quran, the fatwa declared that fathers could marry off their daughters even if they were in a cradle. There is only one caution, it said. The husbands are not permitted to have sex with the little girls 'unless they [the little girls] are capable of being placed beneath and bearing the weight of the man'. The Sheikh cited the example of the Prophet who had married Aisha when the latter was six years old, but had not consummated the marriage till she was nine.[46]

The royal decree notwithstanding, independent religious figures have continued issuing fatwas and other sorts of edicts. Women have continued to be a special focus of their scrutiny and censure. For long, women have had to drape themselves in full-length burqas, and to hide their eyes behind a veil. By 2008, even this turned out not to be enough. That year, Sheikh Muhammad Al Habadan decreed that, in addition to wearing a burqa and veil, women, when they go out of their houses, must cover one eye completely with

45. Quran, 55.4.

46. Angus McDowall and Summer Sad, 'Cleric fights Saudi bid to ban child marriages', 29 July 2011, http://online.wsj.com/article/SB10001424053111903635604576472011907391364.html

cloth. 'Revealing both eyes behind the veil is likely to encourage women to put make-up on and accentuate their eyes,' he ruled. 'This is corrupt behaviour which conflicts with Islamic principles.' He did allow one, fleeting exception: when she is out shopping and has to inspect an item, a woman can remove the cloth 'for a limited period of time,' he ruled.[47]

Three years is an eon. The committee for the Promotion of Virtue and Prevention of Vice is a much feared body in Saudi Arabia. And justly so. In 2002, a school in Mecca caught fire. Young girls trapped in the burning buildings were trying to rush out. The personnel of the committee prevented them from coming out—they were not wearing the mandatory head cover. Fifteen girls perished as a consequence. Outrages of this kind have taught everyone to steer clear of members of this organization.

It so happened that one of the members of this powerful organization was walking down a street in November 2011. He chanced to see a woman who was walking with her husband. Her eyes aroused the committee worthy. An altercation ensued. The husband suffered two stab wounds. And on whom did the blame fall? On the poor woman's eyes. So, steps were taken to pass a law to make it mandatory for women with attractive eyes to cover, not just one of the eyes but both of them.[48]

Exasperating? No doubt. And yet, even in these instances, green shoots of hope are visible.

---

47. Smadar Peri, 'Fatwa: Saudi women must cover one eye', ynetnews.com, 10 June 2008, http://www.ynetnews.com/articles/0,7340, L-3605914,00.html

48.http://www.dailymail.co.uk/news/article-2063143/Saudi-women-attractive-eyes-forced-cover-resolution-passed.html. For similar accounts see, for instance, http://ndtv.com/article/world/saudi-women-with-twmpting-eyes-may-be-forced-to-cover-them-151370?pfrom=home-otherstories

Intrepid groups, new instruments

First and foremost, the very ones who have been the focus of many of these outlandish decrees—women—are standing up. They are admittedly few, but they are intrepid. And they are pushing back with the most formidable of weapons—mockery, humour: the Saudi women who decided to use the breastfeeding edict to push the case for being allowed to drive; the poetess who punctured the fatwa of the formidable Sheikh Abdul Rahman al-Barrak ...

For them as well for others a new instrument is available—the new media: Internet, television, sheer physical mobility. These new developments, of course, make it easier for the ulema to spread their message and ideology, no doubt—the proliferation of channels through which the sheikhs and maulanas broadcast their edicts day in and day out is a constant reminder; the way terrorists have used the channels to spread their message and even their operational messages is an even more forbidding reminder. But, equally, one has just to glance through the reactions that their pronouncements evoke to see how these very media give voice to the targets of the sheikhs' and maulanas' creed. Apart from the speed at which these victims can send their darts flying across the world, the new instruments—the Internet, in particular—provide anonymity.

The foregoing examples point to other reasons also for hope.

Symbiotic relationships, and how they turn into a rope

Even in recent times, in every Islamic country there has been a symbiotic relationship between rulers and the religious authorities. In Egypt, even in recent times—that is, since the revolution of President Nasser in 1952—all governments have ensured that the two authorities that could issue fatwas—al-Azhar and the Darul Ifta of the Ministry of Justice—remained under government control: rulers are the ones who chose who shall man the principal posts in these organizations. In Saudi Arabia, of course, the two—the House of Saud and the religious sheikhs—have been literally intertwined: the religious authorities have provided legitimacy to the rulers, and, in their turn, the rulers have not just permitted but enabled the Wahabi sheikhs to enforce their edicts at home and to export their ideology. In the last few years, as we have seen, the king has decreed that fatwas can be issued only by the committee and council each of whose members the government has selected.

The appointees have strained to help the rulers. In Egypt, criticism of President Hosni Mubarak and his son, Gamal, became shriller by the year. In 2007, several journalists were jailed for setting out facts about members of President Mubarak's circle. The criticism became even shriller. The Grand Imam of al-Azhar, Sheikh Mohammed Sayed Tantawi, who had been chosen by Mubarak in 1996, stepped forth. He issued fatwas—in October and November 2007—to the effect that anyone, in particular journalists, who spread 'rumours' about the president's health, as well as anyone who 'slandered' the president in regard to passing on his office as an inheritance to his son are to be lashed eighty times. The fatwas sparked a vigorous debate. Tantawi felt compelled to hold a press conference in which 'with tears in his eyes' he maintained that there had been no political pressure on him to issue the fatwas.[49]

A few protestors took to the streets. The police were dragging a lady away—this happened in November 2007.

---

49. *Al-Ahram Weekly On-line*, 15–21 November 2007, Issue 871.

Her sister-in-law, Reda Shehata, pleaded with them not to take the lady away. The police flung the woman into their vehicle. Reda Shehata clung to the front of the vehicle. The officer ordered the driver to start the vehicle. Reda lost hold, and was crushed to death. People, and not just those who had witnessed the scene, were angered. The Grand Mufti, Ali Gomaa, who like Tantawi had been appointed by the Mubarak regime, stepped forth to help the regime's forces deal with demonstrators and the like. Drivers of vehicles that ran over and killed persons who were 'deliberately standing still' in the face of an oncoming vehicle were not responsible for the deaths—the deaths had clearly occurred from the intention of the victims to commit suicide.

The fatwa ignited anger. Have these personages ever issued fatwas against corruption, rigging of elections, cronyism? the people demanded. The Grand Mufti was forced to plead that he had not issued the fatwa in question ...

The religious authorities strained to shield the rulers who had appointed them. They issued their fatwas, but that only stoked anger. The fatwa-givers had to retract. That showed them to be not just lackeys but also to be less formidable than they had seemed to be. The net effect was that they undermined both the rulers and themselves. And now that the rulers whom they had tried to shield have been swept aside!

True, the religious sheikhs have options. It was of the very essence of the technique of ruling of the despots who have been toppled that during their long reign they left no institution standing. Their ouster has, therefore, left a vacuum. The only groups that managed to survive are those that operated secretly, like the Muslim Brotherhood. As a result, the only groups that can swiftly start operations as an organized force are those that are committed to as 'pure' a version of Islam as the fatwa-givers. Hence, the symbiosis can be re-established in an even more virulent form.

But that would only mean that the cycle would commence again. The clerics will strain to be of use to the new, 'purer' rulers. Seeing how useful and willing these worthies are, the new rulers will, with a roughness befitting revolutionaries, accept their services. As the new regimes fail to deliver, the rulers will turn even more to these religious authorities for legitimacy. In the end, the two will undermine their legitimacy together.

Invoking Allah and the Prophet to squelch petitions and demonstrations ...

But even where regimes and rulers have not been swept aside, the decrees of the religious authorities avail the rulers less and less. As the Arab Spring unfolded, a few whiffs reached Saudi Arabia also. Individuals and groups began using the Internet to urge each other. A woman drove her car. A man immolated himself ... That highest of religious bodies, the Council of Senior Ulema, every member of which had been appointed by the regime, issued a minatory fatwa. It is worth spending a little time reading through it as the fatwa illustrates how religious authorities and rulers in Islamic countries remain intertwined even today. The idiom, and the ease with which phrases from the Quran and the Hadis are plucked to legitimize a position convenient to the rulers and those buttressing them are just as instructive. First the fatwa, and then the reasons for hope.

> Praise be to Allah, Lord of the worlds. Greetings and peace be upon His honest servant and Messenger and upon his family and companions. Indeed Allah Almighty took a covenant from the scholars to make a clear statement (about truth) as He said in his glorious book: "And remember God took a covenant from the People of the Book, to make it known and clear to mankind, and not to hide it" (*Al-Imran*: 187). He also said, "Those who conceal the

clear (Signs) We have sent down, and the Guidance, after We have made it clear for the People of the Book, on them shall be God's curse, and the curse of those entitled to curse" (*Al-Baqarah*: 159).

Notice how defensive the sheikhs who have been appointed to this supreme council are: they are saying here that they have no alternative but to speak against the tumult that is sweeping regimes off their feet; and they are driven to invoke verses which clearly have little to do with a few handpicked appointees speaking up.

It is necessary for the scholars to make statement in times of strife and crises, the like of what is happening these days in various parts of the world. The Council of Senior Scholars prays to Allah Almighty for all Muslims, rulers and ruled alike to maintain the safety, stability and loyalty to the truth. The Council praises Allah Almighty for what He has bestowed upon the Kingdom of Saudi Arabia with unity of words and action on the basis of the book of Allah and tradition of the Messenger, under the wise leadership of legitimate allegiance. May Allah prolong its success and correct it constantly. May Allah guard for us this blessing and complete it.

The trigger-words start appearing: 'strife and crises' contrasted with 'the safety, stability and loyalty to the truth'; the blessing that has been bestowed of 'unity of words and action on the basis of the book of Allah and tradition of the Messenger, under the wise leadership of legitimate allegiance'—'unity of words and action', 'wise leadership', 'legitimate allegiance'; and the blessing has been bestowed, not on Saudi Arabia, not on the people of Saudi Arabia but on 'the Kingdom of Saudi Arabia'.

(Protection of the community is of the greatest principles of Islam. It is ... what Allah commanded in His Holy Book and condemned whoever abandoned it. Allah Almighty says: "And hold fast, all together, by the rope which God [stretches out for you], and be not divided among yourselves; and remember with gratitude God's favour on you; for ye were enemies and He joined your hearts in love, so that by His Grace, ye became brethren; and ye were on the brink of the pit of Fire, and He saved you from it. Thus doth God make His Signs clear to you: That ye may be guided" [*Al-Imran*: 103]. ("Be not like those who are divided amongst themselves and fall into disputations after receiving Clear Signs: For them is a dreadful penalty" [*Al-Imran*: 105]). ("As for those who divide their religion and break up into sects, thou hast no part in them in the least: their affair is with God: He will in the end tell them the truth of all that they did" [*Al-Ana'am*: 159]). (This is the principle of protection of the community which the Prophet commanded upon all citizens, common and elites alike as he said: "Allah's hand is with communion" [narrated by Tirmidhi]. He also said: "[He] who held back the hand from obedience, will meet Allah on the Day of Resurrection without any justification for himself, and who died without the pledge of allegiance on his neck have met a death of ignorance" [narrated by Muslim]. He again said: "He who wanted [to] separate affairs of this nation who are unified, you should kill him with sword whoever he is" [narrated by Muslim]...

Whenever a passage is cited from the Quran or the Hadis which the apologists find inconvenient or embarrassing, their standard response is, 'But you are quoting out of context.' Reading the phrases that this supreme Council of Senior Ulema, who would maintain that the context in which these were spoken related to the rulers of the moment, to say nothing of the House of Saud which currently rules Saudi Arabia?

The council gives up all indirection:

Indeed Allah Almighty bestowed upon this country unification in its leadership based on the light of the guidance of the Book and the tradition. Neither foreign influences nor parties who have various motivations can separate them as exemplified in the Quran: "in repentance to Him, and fear Him: establish regular prayers, and be not ye among those who join gods with Allah. Those who split up their Religion, and become (mere) sects, each party rejoicing in that which is with itself" (*Al-Rum*: 31-32). The Kingdom has maintained its Islamic identity with progress and prosperity and obtained it with legal secular means. It has been the great blessing of Allah upon citizens of this country, rulers and ruled alike, that He honoured them with the service to two noble shrines which, by praise and grace of Allah, receive full care of the government of the Kingdom of Saudi Arabia in order to implement the command of Allah: "Remember We made the House a place of assembly for men and a place of safety; and take ye the station of Abraham as a place of prayer; and We covenanted with Abraham and Isma'il that they should sanctify My House for those who compass it round, or use it as a retreat, or bow, or prostrate themselves (therein in prayer)" (*Al-Baqarah*: 125). The Kingdom has won a special priority in the Islamic world because of this service for it is the direction of the worship for Muslims and the land of the two shrines. Muslims come from all directions to perform the pilgrimage in the season of Hajj and (during the) whole year for Umrah and visiting.

And then the operational handle for the rulers to use 'all means' to quell 'all means' that their adversaries may try to use—from petitions to demonstrations, whatever.

The Council of Senior Scholars, with the blessing of loyalty to guidance of the Book and tradition and under wise leadership, hereby calls all people to utilize all means that increase the cohesion, strengthen intimacy, and warn against all means contrary to this. Taking this opportunity, the Council affirms the necessity of mutual advice, understanding and cooperation in righteousness and piety, and in prohibition of evil and hostility. It warns against injustice, oppression, and despis[ing] of the truth, as it warns also from deviated intellectual trends and partisanship. This nation in this country is one group committed to the tradition of the pious Salaf and their followers and to the footsteps of Imams in the past and present ...

The Council considers this advice as having a high religious value, for the Prophet said: "the religion is advice". When asked to whom, he said: "to Allah, His Book, His Prophet, Imams of the Muslim and common folk" (narrated by Muslim). It is certainly applicable to the guardians (in charge of Muslim affairs). The Prophet said: "Allah is pleased with you for three things: to worship Him without joining anyone with Him, to hold fast the rope of Allah without division and to give advice to whom Allah has entrusted your affairs" (narrated by Imam Ahmad).

Therefore the Council hereby reaffirms that the only reform and council (sic) that has its legitimacy is that which may bring welfare and avert the evil, whereas it is illegal to issue statements and take signatures for the purposes of intimidation and inciting the strife.

And who will decide whether the effort to obtain signatures on a petition or to issue a mere statement is 'for the purposes of intimidation and inciting the strife'? Naturally, the guardians of the two noble shrines—the current rulers who chose the senior ulema—and the guardians of the religion—the senior ulema themselves.

That is contrary to what Allah Almighty commanded in His words: "When there comes to them some matter of public safety or fear, they divulge it. If they had only referred it to the Messenger, or to those charged with authority among them, the proper investigators would have tested it from them (direct). Were it not for the Grace and Mercy of Allah unto you, all but a few of you would have fallen into the clutches of Satan" (*An Nisa*: 83).

As an exercise, the reader really should look at that much vaunted 'context'—the context in which this revelation was received and try and figure out how that matches the use to which the senior ulema are putting it.

Since the Kingdom of Saudi Arabia is based on the Qur'an, Sunnah, the pledge of allegiance, and the necessity of unity and loyalty, then reform should not be by demonstrations and other means and methods that give rise to unrest and divide the community. This is what is affirmed by scholars of this country in the past and present to prohibit these methods and warn against them.

'The pledge of allegiance, and the necessity of unity and loyalty'—in fact, it has been held time and again by Islamic legists that the duty of allegiance ceases as, among other things, the ruler becomes heedless of the interest of his wards. Notice too the juxtaposition of the words that follow— 'then reform should not be by demonstrations and other means and methods that give rise to unrest and divide the community.' That is, 'demonstrations and other means and methods' are conjoined with, they are taken to necessarily 'give rise to unrest and divide the community'. Hence,

> The Council affirms prohibition of the demonstrations in this country and the legal method which realizes the welfare without causing destruction rests on mutual advice. It is what was practiced by the Prophet (peace be upon him) and followed by his companions and their followers.
>
> The Council affirms the mandate of legislative, inspective and executive institutions

Pause for a moment, we know that 'executive' institutions include the police and armed forces, but what does that unfamiliar addition—'inspective'—encompass? Does it include intelligence agencies? Does it include that committee for the Promotion of Virtue and Suppression of Vice?

> to carrying out their duties as stipulated by state regulations and instructions for the governors.

That is, whatever these agencies do is legitimate so long as it is in accordance with what has been 'stipulated by state regulations and instructions for the governors', and, naturally, the regulations and instructions shall be so crafted by the state that whatever they do turns out to be legitimate!

> We pray to Allah Almighty to protect our country and all Muslim countries from all evils ... Guide us to the path of peace, show us the truth and enable us to follow it. Show us the falsehood and help us to avoid it. Guide the misguided Muslims, for Allah is the only one

responsible for the leadership of the guardians upon which the welfare of the people and country rests. He is the only guardian and the powerful. May Allah bless our Prophet Muhammad, his family and companions ...[50]

How handy, the senior ulema.

But four things stand out—each a reason for hope.

First, those who oppose rulers experience no greater difficulty in invoking verses from the Quran and sayings of the Prophet—we just encountered Sheikh Hamoud bin Oqla Al-Shuabi who expelled the king and his entire family from Islam for supporting the infidels in their war against Islam.

Second, the clerics are even more orthodox and unbending than the rulers so that, as we saw, when the rulers think it prudent—in the interest of the same stability and unity about which the senior ulema are so concerned—or when they have a change of heart and initiate some reforms, these very clerics seek to block them. So, deriving legitimacy from them is literally a double-edged sword.

Third, there is a genuine dilemma here. If the religious sheikhs are left unbridled, a host of persons and institutions acquire and in fact exercise the right and authority to issue fatwas. The country becomes 'a fatwa factory'—the expression has been used both in Egypt and Pakistan by thinkers to describe what has come to transpire in those countries.[51] If, on the other hand, as successive governments

---

50. A fatwa from the Council of Senior Scholars in the kingdom of Saudi Arabia warning against mass demonstrations; posted 3 October 2011. Website URL: Asharq al awsat News Organization. http:// islamopediaonline.org/ fatwa/fatwa-council-senior-scholars-kingdomsaudi-arabia—warning-against-mass-demonstrations

51. Countries in which Muslims form the overwhelming majority are, of course, not the only ones in which 'fatwa factories' mushroom. Countries within Europe in which there has been a substantial influx of Muslims, the ulema have strained hard to ensure that Muslims maintain a separate

have done in Egypt and Saudi Arabia, an effort is made to regulate the issuing of fatwas, the fatwa-giving authorities come to be known as handles of the rulers. They lose legitimacy, and, thereafter, are not able to shore up the waning strength of the rulers.

Finally, as we have seen in the case of Egypt, while clerics and the rulers who appoint and then invoke them, are able to bolster each other when affairs are manageable, when the descent starts, their being associated with each other becomes a rope tying them to each other.

An even stronger reason for hope

Almost since the day the country was founded, the worst

... identity, an identity that will set them apart from the general population of those countries both in their own eyes and in the eyes of the others. That is at the root of the insistence, for example, on the headscarf or the hijab in general. The dress clearly sets them apart from the general population. If the country agrees to allow them the freedom to enforce their edict on the Muslim immigrants, they have established their primacy. If it does not, they can allege discrimination. Apart from having the Muslims internalize the belief that Muslims everywhere are under siege, the clerics have been issuing fatwas and preaching at every possible opportunity that the shariah must have primacy over the normal, secular laws of the country and that it must govern all aspects of the life of the Muslims—including their relationships with non-Muslims—and with every institution— including the State. A network of organizations has sprung up to broadcast and instill such beliefs, and one of the instruments they most frequently deploy is the fatwa. The Federation of Islamic Organizations in Europe is based in Brussels. It has 30 affiliates. One of these is The European Council of Fatwa Research, headquartered in Ireland. In France, the portmanteau organization is the UOIF, the Union of French Islamic Organizations; in Germany, the ZMD, the Central Council of Muslims; in Norway, the IRN, the Islamic Council of Norway; in Sweden, the Swedish Fatwa Council. Many such organizations are closely intertwined with the Muslim Brotherhood. Cf, Soren Kern, 'Europe's fatwa factories', http://www.hudson-ny.org/1857/europe-fatwa-factories, 3 February 2011.

charge that can be hurled at anyone in Pakistan has been that she or he is an Ahmediya. Ahmediyas are forbidden to call themselves Muslims. They are forbidden to designate their place of worship as a mosque. They are forbidden from having any signs or boards or carvings or neon lights, etc., on their buildings which proclaim their faith in the Quran—they must not display even a calendar inside their shop or structure with a Quranic verse. They have been convicted for doing the namaz in the open. They have been convicted for holding a prayer meeting in a private home. They have been convicted because their wedding card had *Bismillah-ir-Rahman-i-Raheem*—In the name of Allah, the Most Beneficent, the Most Merciful—and *Nahmaduhu wa Nusalle Ala Rasul-i-hil Karim*—We invoke the blessings of Allah and our eminent Prophet—printed on it. Women have been set upon for wearing a dupatta that has some expression printed on it which is used by Muslims—say, 'Allah be praised', or something venerating the Prophet—for wearing a ring that had a verse from the Quran inscribed on it. Shopkeepers have been thrown into prison for five years because their cash receipts bore the Islamic expression, *'In the name of Allah the Beneficent, the Merciful'*. They have been sentenced because they wore a badge on which was inscribed the sacred kalima. They are forbidden from even greeting each other or other Muslims with expressions that are customarily used by Muslims, *Assalam-o-Alaikum* or *Inshallah*. Such expressions are in essence a copyrighted trademark of Islam, the majority judgment of the Pakistan Supreme Court held in 1993, and, therefore, apart from everything else, the use of such expressions by the Ahmediyas violates the Trademark Act of 1940! In any case, any and every fundamental right has to be subject to the injunctions of Islam, the Court held. For them to recite the kalima, or any of the other expressions connected with Islam is to publicly defile the name of the Prophet, and so it is blasphemy. They are forbidden from offering the janaza prayer at funerals of their deceased. They are, of course, forbidden from preaching their faith—*even to their own children.* They are not even to distribute food to the needy on any special day connected with Islam, lest such an activity 'directly or indirectly incite and injure the religious feelings of Muslims'. They are not to give courses in their educational institutions purporting to teach 'Islamic Studies' or 'The Holy Quran'. Hundreds and hundreds of them have been picked up, beaten black and blue by the police, and charged with blasphemy.

And all this has been done with the imprimatur of the Pakistan Supreme Court. The very use of Islamic expressions and signs, the very performance of Islamic rituals by the Ahmediyas, the court has ruled, 'is enough to make a Muslim lose control of himself'. 'Can then anyone blame a Muslim if he loses control on hearing, reading, or seeing such blasphemous material as has been produced by Mirza Sahib,' the Supreme Court asked while upholding the constitutional amendment and alluding to the writings of the initiator of the Ahmediya sect. 'If an Ahmedi is allowed by the administration or the law to display or chant in public the *Shar'i Islam*, it is like creating a Rushdi' (sic) out of him. Can the administration in that case guarantee his life, liberty and property, and if so at what cost?' In a sense, therefore, the prohibitions are in the interest and for the security of the offenders themselves, the Ahmediyas.

The most effective foreign minister that Pakistan has ever had, the suave and formidable Zafarullah Khan, was hounded and pilloried on the charge that he was an Ahmediya. The only Pakistani who has won the Nobel Prize—the physicist, Abdus Salam—had in effect to spend his life in exile in Trieste, as he was an Ahmediya.

In 1953, Pakistan, the Pakistani part of Punjab in particular, was rocked by riots. Clerics harangued the people about conspiracies that, they said, were being hatched by the Ahmediyas. They harangued mobs asserting that these perfidious creatures were out to destroy Islam. They demanded that the government pass laws declaring Ahmediyas to be non-Muslims. Mobs rampaged cities and villages hunting for Ahmediyas, destroying their homes, breaking down their mosques.[52] The government set up a commission to inquire into the riots. It was headed by Justice Muhammad Munir. The report of that commission remains one of the very best reports produced in the subcontinent since the two countries became independent.

Two findings of the Munir Commission—and these were extensively documented in the form of verbatim statements of the most prominent Pakistani maulanas of the time—are of particular interest to our study. The commission found that none of the Islamic authorities was able to agree with any of the others on who is a Muslim. Second, each of the sects that these worthies represented had proclaimed the other sects to be kafirs, apostates and the rest. After setting out verbatim pages and pages of definitions of a 'Muslim' given by the highest religious authorities of the time in Pakistan, the

---

52. In 1974, the Constitution of Pakistan was amended, and a provision was added formally excommunicating Ahmediyas from Islam. Ten years later, Zia ul Haq promulgated a Martial Law Ordinance making it a criminal offence for Ahmediyas to engage in Islamic rituals, to use Islamic terms or to 'pose' as Muslims. The burden of proof was placed on the accused. When the Ahmediyas approached the Pakistan Supreme Court on the ground that these restrictions and laws violated the right guaranteed under the constitution—the freedom to practise one's religion—the court rejected their plea on the ground that the practice of their right would disturb public order as it would ignite the hostility of the majority which considered their beliefs offensive to Islam!

commission concluded—and that conclusion is as true today as it was sixty years ago and is a potent reason for hope—as follows:

> Keeping in view the several definitions given by the *Ulema*, need we make any comment except that no two learned divines are agreed on this fundamental. If we attempt our own definition as each learned divine has done and that definition differs from that given by all others, we unanimously go out of the fold of Islam. And if we adopt the definition given by anyone of the *Ulema*, we remain Muslims according to the view of that *alim* but *kafirs* according to the definition of every one else.[53]

Nor was this discord over the definition of a Muslim just an academic disagreement. It had an immediate and fatal operational consequence. For in the eye of each authority every other authority and the sect he represented automatically became apostates. And the punishment for apostasy, the commission emphasized was just one—death.

> According to this doctrine, [on which, the Commission noted, there was near-unanimity among the *Ulema*] Chaudhri Zafarullah Khan, if he has not inherited his present religious beliefs but has voluntarily elected to be an Ahmadi, must be put to death. And the same fate should befall Deobandis and Wahabis, including Maulana Muhammad Shafi Deobandi, Member, Board of Talimat-i-Islami attached to the Constituent Assembly of Pakistan, and Maulana Daud Ghaznavi, if Maulana Abul Hasanat Sayyad Muhammad Ahmad Qadri or Mirza Raza Ahmad Khan Barelvi, or anyone of the numerous *Ulema* who are shown perched on every leaf of a beautiful tree in the *fatwa*, Ex. D.E. 14, were the head of such Islamic State. And if Maulana Muhammad Shafi Deobandi were the head of the State, he would exclude those who have pronounced Deobandis as *kafirs* from the pale of Islam and inflict on them the

53. *Report of the Court of Inquiry constituted under Punjab Act II of 1954 to enquire into the Punjab Disturbances of 1953*, Superintendent, Government Printing, Lahore, Punjab, 1954, p. 218.

> death penalty if they come within the definition of *murtadd*, namely, if they have changed and not inherited their religious views.
>
> ... According to Shias all Sunnis are *kafirs*, and Ahl-i-Quran, namely persons who consider *hadith* to be unreliable and therefore not binding, are unanimously *kafirs*, and so are all independent thinkers. The net result of all this is that neither Shias nor Sunnis nor Deobandis nor Ahl-i-Hadith nor Barelvis are Muslims and any change from one view to another must be accompanied in an Islamic State with the penalty of death if the Government of the State is in the hands of the party which considers the other party to be *kafirs*. And it does not require much imagination to judge the consequences of this doctrine when it is remembered that no two *Ulema* have agreed before us as to the definition of a Muslim. If the constituents of each of the definitions given by the *Ulema* are given effect to, and subjected to the rule of 'combination and permutation' and the form of the charge in the inquisition's sentence on Galileo is adopted *mutatis mutandis* as a model, the grounds on which a person may be indicted for apostasy will be too numerous to count.[54]

Over the years, Hanafis, Ahl-i-Hadis, Deobandis, Barelvis, Shias, each of the Sufi orders—one and all have had fatwas issued declaring them to be kafirs and apostates, deserving death. And ever so many of the most honoured figures of each sect have been individually pronounced to be kafirs and apostates by the best-known and authoritative figures of other sects. From Sir Syed Ahmed Khan to Maulana Maudoodi to Muhammed Ali Jinnah, one and all have been pronounced kafirs by authoritative fatwas.

This feature got accentuated as Pakistan became more and more Islamic. From Sir Mohammed Iqbal to his acolyte, Ghulam Ahmad Pervez, one of the most respected and pious Islamic scholars of post-independence Pakistan, a very long

54. Ibid., pp. 218–19.

list of eminent thinkers, reformers, poets have been declared to be kafirs.[55]

The trend has only got accelerated in recent times. Musharraf, Zardari, the former information minister Sherry Rahman, the former tourism minister Nilofar Bakhtiar, the minister for minority affairs Shahbaz Bhatti, even the army and the ISI have been declared kafirs and apostates, and *wajib e qatl*, deserving death. As the Munir Commission had forecast, the grounds have been varied and numerous: from advocating changes in the blasphemy law; to being embraced by an infidel after a successful parachute jump; to helping the infidels—Americans—in their war against Islam.

This feature—of detecting deviations by others and therefore excommunicating them—is not peculiar to Islam, of course. It is an unvarying fixture of all fundamentalist ideologies—consider the purges under every communist regime. Ever so often, the custodians of the ideology are so obsessed with their version that they cannot but denounce the slightest departure as a repudiation of the faith. Equally often, jostling for power and primacy are dressed up in an ideological garb: periods and episodes in Islam's religious history compare very well with purges under Stalin and Mao. In either event, this penchant for denouncing each other, and, of course, doing much more than merely denouncing would be considerable relief to genuine non-believers, so to say, for it keeps the faithful busy with each other. But it isn't entirely so, and for one obvious reason: while they are obsessed with each other's deviations, all the sects and their

---

55. One of the comprehensive listing of such fatwas declaring others to be kafirs was published by Ghulam Ahmad Pervez in his influential monthly journal, *Tolu-e-Islam*—The Resurgence of Islam—in 1969. He often wailed against the fact that 'The *mullahs* have hijacked Islam.' In turn, he was denounced both before and after publication of the article, by the mullahs as a heretic, an apostate, a kafir.

controllers are one in regard to the genuine kafirs. One has only to see the rhetoric of Islamist groups of Pakistan against the *Amriki-Yehudi-Hindu* conspiracies to know that this is so, and to gauge the consequences this commonality can have for the rest of us.

Other religions

Clerics across the Islamic spectrum remain firm in their belief that those who have not embraced Islam are worse than being merely inferior. They are perverse—for how can anyone not adopt the Message after Allah has revealed it?

To discern the potential inherent in an ideology, one must look what its adherents do where and when they are in power—to get a measure of what communism does in practice, one must look at the Soviet Union under Stalin, to China under Mao, not at what the communists do and say when they have to operate in a plural, democratic country like India. So also with the ideology of the fatwa-givers. Look at what they are laying down in Saudi Arabia in the case of Sunni Islam and in Iran in the case of Shia Islam. Look at what the great authorities lay down about other religions in *these* countries. That is where you will see things in true relief.

And you will see it on every question—from what a life is worth to what consideration women of another religion are worth. In Saudi Arabia, if a person, say a male, is killed in an accident—on the road, in a fire, by murder—the maximum compensation that is reported to be generally admissible varies *fifteen to sixteen times* depending on the person's religion. For a Muslim, the *diyya,* the compensation in lieu of death is 100,000 Saudi Riyals. For a Christian or a Jew, it is half that amount—50,000 Saudi Riyals. For a Hindu, Buddhist, Jain, etc., it is 6,666 Saudi Riyals![56]

56.http://knowing-Islamic-doctrines.blogspot.com/2010/05/koransays-muslims-and-non-muslims-are.html

Or consider the attitude that high religious authorities mandate towards women of other religions. In 2010, not 1010, Muslim male students studying in universities in the West said that they were aroused by Western women wearing seductive clothes, and sought guidance about what they should do. Sheikh Adil Al-Obeikan, the imam of Haram Al-Sharif, the Grand Mosque of Mecca, whom we have encountered earlier, issued a fatwa—the fatwa was put on the Saudi-owned website, Al Arabiya.net on 16 July 2010. The fatwa declared that the students could marry Western girls with the intention of divorcing them when they are done with the girls or when they are returning home. Not just that: they could marry these girls without telling them of their intention ...[57]

We keep intoning, *Ishwar Allah Tero Naam* ... The ulema scorn ecumenism. 'Concept of ecumenism in Islam?' asks the querist from Pakistan of the ulema of Deoband. 'Such an ecumenism in which one has to call right as wrong and truth as false,' the ulema declare in their fatwa, 'is deplorable according to Islam.'[58] Living in a plural society, they are tactful not to spell out which ecumenism it is in which they would not have to acknowledge that other religions too may be valid paths to God and personal growth.

57. The fatwa incensed groups in the West, and also a candid discussion of the kinds of marriage that the shariah sanctions—the mutah marriage which is contracted for a specified time, one that may be as short as an hour, and does not require a divorce at the end of that period; the *urfa* marriage, one that does not entail a formal contract and gives women no rights; the *misyaf* or tourism marriage; the *misyar* marriage in which the woman 'voluntarily' gives up her rights ...See, for instance, http://londonprogressivejournal.com/article/735/saudi-sheik'sobsession-with-sex-fatwas by Iqbal Tamimi.

58. Darul Ifta, Deoband, 21 July 2010; Answer number 22522; Fatwa number 872/693/D

What about propagating and preaching one's religion? As is well known, propagating a religion other than Islam and preaching it in an Islamic country is just not permissible. Think of Saudi Arabia, but not just Saudi Arabia. Think what happens to those who even in private practise some religion other than Islam in Pakistan—think of the way the blasphemy charge is fabricated, and the persons are hounded. But Muslim clerics and preachers and organizations like the Tablighi Jamaat must have the fullest freedom in every country—in particular, the non-Islamic countries—to spread their message and to convert people to their religion. And for an obvious reason, the ulema reason: doing so is an essential ingredient of their faith, a peremptory duty of the community as well as of each individual Muslim according to his capacity. So, any restriction on their doing so will ipso facto be a curtailment of their right to practise their religion. *'Daawat ka kaam karna kya farz-e-ain hai?'* asks the querist. 'Learning religion is obligatory on every Muslim (individually) while preaching the religion is the collective obligation of the Muslim community,' the ulema state in their fatwa. 'Its importance will increase as per the need and one will be asked to discharge this duty as per his ability. So, every Muslim should discharge this duty as per his power and scope.'[59]

The mandatory requirement is made sharper in the ensuing fatwa. The querist has heard contradictory counsel. He observes,

> *Assalamualaikum* WR WB I have heard from some Muslim brothers that da'wah to Muslims is compulsory but not to non-Muslims (at present) since Muslims themselves have become irreligious. But some Muslims say that both are compulsory. What is the correct ruling?

---

59. 14 June 2008; Answer number 4278; Fatwa number 331/331=M/1429. Unless specified otherwise, the fatwas are of Darul Ifta, Deoband.

The fatwa is categorical:

> It is necessary to invite non-Muslims as well to *Eiman*. Muslims are invited to make them know Islamic rulings and do good deeds so that their beliefs may be stronger and they get rewards in the Hereafter and save themselves from the Hell. While, the purpose of preaching to non-Muslims is to inspire them towards Islam and make them embrace Islam. It is essential to preach both the groups. Those saying that it is not compulsory to preach non-Muslims are not right to say this. Allah (*Subhana Wa Ta'ala*) knows Best.[60]

In response to another query—this one from distant Guyana—the ulema of Deoband affirm that tabligh has always been *fardh* on the ulema of ummah. The Quran and Hadis contain proofs of this. And this is an obligation that has to be discharged as a duty. It is not just an opportunity Allah has held out so as to earn a reward from Him.[61]

Transpose the dicta to preachers of other religions plying their identical duty in an Islamic country—the most sagacious and pious though the preachers be—and assess how the authorities there would react to these claims. Does the answer require much guessing? No? That shows not just that the ulema believe in double standards as a principle, as a norm that flows naturally from the fact that their religion alone is true. It shows that the rest have internalized the fact that it is natural for the ulema to believe in double standards and for Islamic authorities to enforce them.

One consequence is that the *Ulema* require that believers strictly desist from any and every syncretistic practice. They insist that those practices be followed that clearly set the Muslim apart from the rest.

60. 11 August 2008; Answer number 6200; Fatwa number 1055/1000=D/1429.

61. 18 June 2011; Answer number 32440; Fatwa number 935/781/B=1432.

An anxious lady from Mauritius says that she believes that wearing the veil is a duty. But she feels awkward doing so as no one else in her surroundings wears it. Second, have I to wear the *niqab* all the time, even in family gatherings, or only when I go out or am in the presence of non-mahram, non-related men?

The ulema are minatory:

> The Shariah ruling does not depend on someone's willingness and denial. The non-*mahram* relatives especially brother of husband among in-laws was regarded as 'death' in *hadith*. Therefore, you should try to observe complete *hijab* and repent to Allah earnestly for shortcomings occurring in this regard. Keep yourself restrained to define the status of any Shariah matter; since it may lead one to the pit of disbelief and it sometimes results in devastation in this world and the Hereafter. May Allah protect us all![62]

A believer from India asks whether it is permissible to sing and play musical instruments at weddings, and to put on haldi and mehndi as these are customary rituals in India. Second, he says that a skin problem has left ugly marks on his leg, 'so I wear pants below my ankle because if I don't then people keep looking at my feet and this causes embarrassment.' He assures the ulema that he will revert to wearing pants above his ankles as soon as he gets well. Is this all right?

'Singing and playing musical instrument is haram,' the ulema warn. Haldi and mehndi may be applied within the limits prescribed by the shariah. As for wearing pants that reach below the ankles, just because of the skin condition and the marks, it is not allowed to wear the pajama or pant below the ankle 'since it [the marks], does not attract the attention of people generally and second if it is so [that is, if the marks do

62. 18 August 2009; Answer number 15187; Fatwa number 1796/322=TH/1430.

attract the attention of the people in general] and causes embarrassment then you can wear socks.'[63]

Is it permissible to celebrate someone's birthday? asks an anxious believer as one of his Muslim friends does so. Notice the reason that the ulema give for forbidding this practice:

> The custom of celebrating birthday has been invented by the Europeans. There is no room in Islam for such nonsense. The *Hadith* says ... (One will be counted among those whose resemblance he adopts). Whose birthday is greater than that of the Prophet (Peace Be Upon Him)? but the Prophet (Peace Be Upon Him) did neither celebrate his birthday nor he ordered the same. Celebrating birthday is not proved by the *Sahaba,* their successors and pious people of *Ummah.*[64]

Every single practice that smacks of 'innovation' or which has the trace of having been adopted from local customs must be jettisoned—that has been the norm. 'I am from Gujarat,' writes a querist. Here in Rajkot, people 'make lighting decoration in the month of Muharram. They call it *roshni.* 'Is it okay to do this lighting decoration?' 'According to Islam, this practice (of lighting and decoration) is *haram* and a sin,' declare the ulema.[65]

Blissful ignorance

Incidentally, pronouncements of this kind illustrate the utter ignorance of our secularist poseurs! The birthday of the Prophet has been declared to be a national holiday in India.

---

63. 14 August 2008; Answer number 6957; Fatwa number 1758/1354=H/1429.

64. 15 September 2008; Answer number 7563; Fatwa number 923/923=M/1429.

65. 6 January 2011; Answer number 28895; Fatwa number 167/124/H=1432.

Going to the graves of Muslim saints, even of fatwa-givers like Maulana Ahmed Riza Khan, sending chaddars for being draped over the graves, attending urs at the graves, are de rigueur as emblems of one's secularism. And what do the ulema say about these practices?

'Chaadar *poshi* on *mazaar* is right or wrong?' asks a believer. 'Should we go to mazaars of saints like Nizamuddin and Moinuddin Chishti Rahmatullah?' The ulema are categorical:

> *Chaadar poshi* (covering grave with sheet) is innovation (*bidaa'h*) and thus unlawful ... There is nothing wrong in visiting to the graves of pious people, but one should go there according to *sunnah* and return after *fatiha* and *isaal-e-sawab* (conveying the reward). It is *haram* to invoke their mercy in ones needs.[66]

To light a lamp at the asking of one's non-Muslim employer; to eat meat served by a Christian; to buy meat imported from non-Muslim countries—are all haram, the ulema pronounce.

A few months have but to pass and the ulema are using stronger expressions to dissuade the faithful from visiting the dargahs. 'Should we go to a dargah or not?' asks a querist from India. 'If one visits a *dargah* according to *sunnah* it is allowable. However, now-a-days the shrines of Auliya (saints) have turned into dens of innovations, so it is better not to go there.'[67]

A devotee from Australia asks a series of questions. Is it right or wrong to celebrate urs? How is it to feed the needy on an urs? Are the shahid alive in their graves or can one speak

---

66. 24 November 2007; Answer number 2104; Fatwa number 540/540=L.

67. 23 July 2010; Answer number 23792; Fatwa number 1088/825/L=1431.

of them as dead? The ulema of Deoband are as uncompromising as they are faithful to the received injunctions. They declare:

> Celebrating *urs* is innovation and unlawful. Celebrating *urs* is not proved from the Prophet (PBUH), his companions and their successors. The scholars of *Fiqh* have regarded it *bidah* (innovation) in the light of a hadith ...
>
> (2) One should avoid feeding at the time of urs in particular; since it is resemblance to the innovators which has been prohibited. If one wants to do *isal-e-thawab* one should feed the poor without fixing any date or give something in charity.
> (3) Those who are killed in the path of Allah i.e. real *shaheed*, only they should be called *shaheed*. The Quran clearly mentions about the *shaheeds* that they are alive and they should not be called dead ...
>
> But, those who are called *shaheed* only by rule, they will not be called so.[68]

The disdain for and prohibition of innovations. The unlawfulness of the urs celebrations at which our secularists strain to be seen. The belief that because the Quran or Hadis say that martyrs are alive in their graves, they *are* alive.

'All right, we are wrong to go to urs of savants. But what about the Prophet? What about occasions—the Milad-un-Nabi—at which ballads and verses in honour of the Prophet himself are rendered, and where the cry goes up, *Ya Nabi, Ya Nabi?*' asks an anxious devotee from Kenya explaining the quandary in which he is. 'I personally do not believe that the Prophet is present on such occasions,' he says, 'but perhaps the others do have such a belief. Some say that we have to use our discretion, our wisdom and join such persons so that, Inshallah, they will listen to us in future. On the other hand,

68. Answer number 10415; Fatwa number 160/166=D/1430.

they take our joining them at such functions to be proof of the fact that they are right. In particular, what about an alim joining such occasions?'

'People and *Ulema* in particular should shun totally from attending programmes wherein innovations and anti-*sunnah* customs are committed and should excuse with wisdom and justifiable reasons,' the ulema of Deoband pronounce.[69]

Thus, the secularists show up at urs celebrations; they send chaddars to drape over graves—making sure that they are photographed by the media as their chaddar sets of; they show up at graves; and go through the gestures—hands raised, eyes upturned—that someone has taught them are proper for such occasions and places. At the same time, they also visit and pay obeisance to ulema and institutions like Deoband that roundly condemn such practices and programmes! The latter too play their part: they declaim such practices and functions, and at the same time accept homage from persons who organize and turn up at such functions and sites! A compact, not just ignorance. But perhaps the reasoning on both sides is that, as the devotee from Kenya put it, 'we have to use our discretion, our wisdom and join such persons so that, Inshallah, they will listen to us in future.'

And what about the Taj Mahal? It is a grave, after all, and the grave is elaborately done up and decorated. Hence, it is worthy of censure. But it is also the diamond of Islamic architecture. What should one's attitude towards it be? A querist asks,

> Is it Islamic to Celebrate the Urs of Deads? Also is It Islamic to Build Shrine over the Graves of Muslims? What will be opinion of Shariat in Concern to the Taj Mahal at Agra? This also a Shrine Over the Graves. Is this Monument Islamic?

---

69. 14 June 2008; Answer number 5150; Fatwa number 854/1182=H/1429.

The answers are clear-cut—till the end, when we have to resort to inference.

> (1) It is not allowed to celebrate the *urs* of the dead ...
> (2) It [to build a shrine over the graves of Muslims] is also not allowed ...
>
> The above text clearly says that it is prohibited to build *mazar* (a shrine or a mausoleum).[70]

The Taj is a mausoleum, and, hence, prohibited in Islam. But it is also an acme of Islamic architecture, and so to disown it would be to disown a priceless treasure, a monument which is often held up as an example of the culture and civilization and art that Islam brought to India. And so, prudence dictates that the question whether it is an Islamic monument be left in the air. And so it is!

The sensibilities of others, India, cows and the rest

As we have noticed in the text already, this insistence on differentiation—doing things in ways, wearing clothes that clearly set one apart from the rest—leads to the ideology of separatism, and that to the fact of separation. There is some glacial shift, of course—the plural society in which the ulema of Deoband must function dictates that one has only to contrast their pronouncements with those of 'Deobandi' clerics of Pakistan to see the weight that the nature of India imposes. To take an example, in their writings the ulema speak freely of kafirs, apostates and the rest—after all, in doing so they are just following the path shown by the Quran and the Hadis. But to the face of a kafir? In public? The ulema relent a tiny bit! 'Can a kafir be called kafir?' asks a querist.

---

70. 19 November 2007; Answer number 2009; Fatwa number 516/516=L.

'There is no wrong in saying *kafir* to a *kafir* if he does not dislike it, but it is wrong if he dislikes ...'

Only to add, 'Yes, it can be called in case of need.'[71] How apt a chimera that Arthur Koestler had conceived! He had always been fascinated by hybrid creatures, he wrote, and, among his creations his favourite had been the mimophant— a hybrid of the frail mimosa and the weighty elephant. We are as shy and vulnerable as the delicate mimosa where our own feelings are concerned, he wrote, and give as little thought to the matter while trampling like an elephant on the feelings of others.

The mandate to slaughter cows that we have encountered earlier affords a glimpse into the tussle that wages in the mind of the ulema. We have seen one of the figures to whom all and sundry paid obeisance, Maulana Abul Hasan Ali Nadwi, declare that slaughtering cows is a great Islamic practice in India; that it may not be a great Islamic practice in other countries, but in India, because the cow is worshipped, slaughtering it is a great Islamic practice.[72] So, it was great news for the principal paper in Uttar Pradesh, the *Dainik Jagran,* when it could report that the head of the Darul Ifta at Dar-al Ulum, Deoband, Mufti Habibur Rahman Sahib, had issued a fatwa declaring that sacrificing cows, selling beef and eating beef were haram.[73] Others picked up the news. A Pakistani cleric weighed in: the head of the Darul Ifta wa Al-Qazzath of the Jamaat-ud-Dawa, Mufti Abdul Rehman Al Rehmani, demanded that Deoband withdraw the fatwa. Slaughtering cows and selling and eating their meat are permissible according to the shariah, he pointed out. He said

71. 3 February 2008; Answer number 2758; Fatwa number 39/39=J.

72. Ibid., pp. 155–56.

73. *Dainik Jagran,* 26 April 2008.

that 'according to Islamic education the cow is a major cause of idolism and polytheism. And if Mufti Habibur Rahman tells Indian Muslims to comply with Indian law, then the coming generations of Muslims in India will be involved in Hindu beliefs.' The Pakistani cleric invoked the example of the Prophet: the Prophet had preached his Message even in secret and had not allowed the hostility of the Quraish to deter him. He said that if Muslims in the largest democratic, secular country, India, feared to practise their religion, 'the peace of the whole world will be in danger.'[74] The Dar-al Ulum immediately issued a refutation. The news report about the fatwa is 'baseless and false', a press release from the Office of the Mohtamim of the institution quoted the Mufti as saying. He had never issued such a fatwa, the Mufti said. Slaughtering cows and eating and selling beef are permissible. But in states where slaughtering cows is banned, Muslims slaughter cows and eat and sell beef surreptitiously—*this* is what is wrong in the eyes of the shariah. He roundly blamed the media for such habitual misrepresentation.[75]

What about jihad? Secularists internalize and repeat ad nauseam 'Jihad is the internal struggle that each of us has to wage against the lower tendencies in us.' That such an assertion flatly contradicts what and the occasions on which Allah and the Prophet spoke of jihad is, of course, beyond their ken or interest. What do the Indian ulema say here, in the twenty-first century, in an India plagued by sponsored terrorism and separatist violence? The Tablighi Jamaat people say that

---

74.http://www.thaindian.com/newsportal/india-news/pak-cleric-asks-indian-counterpart-to-withdraw-fatwa-on-cow-slaughter.7May 2008. ANI.

75.http://www.darululoom-deoband.com/english/news/shownews.php?id=6

the highest form of jihad is against the *naafs*, and it is called *jihad-e-akbar*, reports a querist from Bangladesh and asks, 'Is this correct?' The ulema declare:

> The highest type of *Jihad* which is known is to wage war against the enemies of Islam in order to raise the words of Allah in which a *Mujahid* scarifies his life and wealth. It is also *Jihad* to keep the self suppressed, controlled and going against its will on the path of Shariah. According to the Sufis, it is *Jihad-e-Akbar* is (*sic*) to struggle for reforming the self and enlightening the heart ...[76]

'Among the Sufis'—they are more honoured among non-Muslims than among most hues of *ulema.*

What about India? Is it the land of war, the Dar-ul-Harb, in which and against which one must wage jihad, or, if that is not possible, from which one must migrate to a Dar-ul-Islam, the Land of Peace? The answer is nuanced:

> In the present situation India is not *Darul Harb* (the land of war) but instead it is the *Darul Aman* (land of peace) and *Darul Muahida* (land of truce).[77]

A considerable advance over what used to be the standard pronouncement even twenty years ago. But notice, 'In the present situation'—the rest are on notice, in a word. And 'the Land

76. 24 July 2008; Answer number 5877; Fatwa number 1295/1101=B1429.

77. The compiler explains: 'According to Islamic jurisprudence *Darul Harb* means that *jihad* can be waged there because of its non-Muslim population, and *Darul Aman* is where *jihad* is not waged due to Islamic existence in rule or due to an existing truce or armistice with the ruling government which is why the fatwa authors consider India *Darul Muahida,* or land of truce.' http://islamopediaonline.org/cite/7243. Fatwa posted on 22 April 2010. The site invites us to read the full fatwa at http://www.darulifta-deoband.com/index.jsp. For the month during which I have been trying to access this particular site, I get only the notice, 'Due to technical issues website is down. We are working on it. Thank you for your patience while we hustle to get this work done.'

of Truce'—a truce is between not just separate but hostile parties! But even so, an advance.[78]

And then, of course, we have Ghalib: *Dard kaa had se guzarnaa hai davaa ho jaanaa* ... The terrorists have induced formulations that argumentations by liberals could never have brought about.

What liberals could not have accomplished

Since the early 1980s, terrorism by persons acting in the name of Islam has overtaken all other forms of terror. So

78. The ulema often affirm that Islam does not respect territorial divisions between countries, that Muslims all over the world constitute one ummah. What would the ulema in India then say about the following incident reported at length by the Middle East Media Research Institute? The Taliban leader Maulana Sufi Muhammad observed that the movement in Kashmir is not jihad as it does not seek to institute shariah in Kashmir. That reason could bring little comfort for us in India. But the even more significant fact is that the statement had but to become known, and a host of prominent Islamic authorities came down on him for the assertion. Here is how the MEMRI website reported their pronouncements:

> *Al-Qaradhawi:* 'Kashmir Is Part of the Muslim Ummah, And The Whole Muslim Community Is Like One Body.'
>
> Criticizing Sufi Muhammad's statement, Dr Yousef Al-Qaradhawi said that the Kashmiris are fighting *jihad* against the Indian Army.
>
> He added: 'Kashmir is part of the Muslim *ummah*, and the whole Muslim community is like one body, and it is its duty to help the Kashmiris to obtain freedom from the Indian aggression.'
>
> *Al-Sudayyis:* Muslims Should Do Their Part 'To Bring the Kashmiris Out of the Indian Despotism and Autocracy.'
>
> Sheikh Abd Al-Sudayyis said that Muslims must do their part 'to bring the Kashmiris out of the Indian despotism and autocracy, and [Muslims] should join hands with Kashmiris in this crucial situation'.

much so that for many 'Islam' and 'terrorism' have become hyphenated. The sixty-three killed in attacks on the US embassy in April 1983; the attack on American barracks in Beirut in October that year killing over 300; the bombings in Mumbai in March 1993 leaving over 250 dead and thrice that number injured; the killings of eighty-five Jews in Buenos Aires in July 1994; 1995: the bombings in the Paris Metro; the murder of almost

---

He added, 'The Indian Army launched genocide by killing innocent children and by raping women; mosques were being demolished and they wanted to impose the secular and blasphemous system in Kashmir'.

Palestinian-Kuwaiti Sheikh Ahmad Al-Qattan: Waging Jihad Against India Is 'Absolutely Lawful'.

Palestinian-Kuwaiti religious scholar Sheikh Ahmad Al-Qattan said that waging *jihad* against India is absolutely lawful under Islamic *shari'a,* and also accused the Indian army of launching genocide by killing children and women in Kashmir,[4] quoting Koranic verses that instruct Muslim believers to wage Jihad.

Sheikh Abdullah Al-Sabil: Kashmiris Are Waging *Jihad* in Kashmir and Fighting the Enemies of Islam.

Sheikh Muhammad bin Abdallah Al-sabil, an imam at the Kaaba, declared in his Friday sermon that India had snatched religious freedom from the Muslims and Kashmiris, and that Kashmiris are waging *jihad* in Kashmir and fighting against the enemies of Islam.

Endnotes:

[1] www.sananews.com.pk, Pakistan, May 5 and May 8 2009; photo dailymuslims.com.

[2] For more on Sheikh Al-Qaradhawi, see MEMRI TV page for him at http://www.memritv.org/subject/en/589.htm

[3] For more on Sheikh Al-Sudayyis, see MEMRI Special Dispatch No. No. 939 "Friday Sermon By Leading Saudi Imam Al-Sudayyis in Mecca: 'Oh Allah, Liberate Our Al-Aqsa Mosque...Punish the Occupying Zionists and Their Supporters Among The Corrupt Infidels... Oh Allah, Scatter and Disperse Them,'" "July 21, 2005, http://www.memri.org/report/en/0/0/0/0/0/0/1419.htm.

[4] For more on Sheikh Ahmad Qattan, see MEMRI TV page for him at http://www.memritv.org/subject/en/784.htm.

seventy tourists at Luxor in November 1997; the thirteen simultaneous explosions in Coimbatore in February 1998; the 224 killed in attacks on US embassies in Nairobi and Dar es Salam in August 1998; the explosions across Moscow and other Russian cities in September 1999 that left over 300 dead; 9/11 2001 that took the lives of over 3,000 in New York; December the same year—the attack on our Parliament; October 2002: the siege of the theatre in Moscow; October 2002: the over 200 killed in Bali; November 2003: the attack at the HSBC offices in Istanbul; March 2004: 191 killed and nearly 1,500 injured on trains in and around Madrid; the explosions in Riyadh in April 2004; September 2004: the siege of schoolchildren and others in Beslan, Russia; the fifty-three killed in the London Underground in July 2005; the sixty-five killed at Sharm al-Sheikh; three months later, the series of explosions in Delhi leaving sixty dead; July 2006: seven bombs across Mumbai, over 200 dead; the explosions at over twenty sites across Ahmedabad in July 2008; September 2008: bombings across Delhi again; the attacks on the Sankat Mochan temple in Varanasi, the Akshardham temple in Ahmedabad ...; the siege and killings in Mumbai in November 2008 leaving 174 dead; the hundreds killed in Iraq, across Pakistan, across Afghanistan, in Israel ...

The series is as long as it has been lethal. No wonder, for many across the world, 'Islam' and 'terrorism' became synonyms. That gave what was for millions their most cherished treasure, Islam, a bad name. It made Muslims living in Europe, the US and other places feel that they were being looked upon with suspicion, indeed with hostility. In several cases, the regimes that were being targeted—in Saudi Arabia, for instance, in Egypt—were ones with which the senior ulema of the country were closely allied. And clearly, the hundreds who were getting killed had done nothing to harm or question the truth of Islam.

Several of the dramatic instances spurred some of the major authorities of Islam to issue statements, press releases, and eventually fatwas condemning wanton violence against innocents. Ayatollah Ali Khamenei, the supreme religious arbiter in Iran; Abdulaziz bin Abdallah Al-Ashaykh, the Chief Mufti of Saudi Arabia; Shiekh Muhammad Syyed Tantawi, the Grand Sheikh of the mosque at al-Azhar, and Ali Gomaa, the Grand Mufti of Egypt, both of whom we have encountered earlier; Sheikh Yusuf al-Qaradhawi of Qatar, whom we just saw declare the killings in Kashmir to be a legitimate, Islamic jihad; the Council of Senior Ulema of Saudi Arabia some of whose edicts we have studied; groups of Muslim leaders and those associated with mosques in the UK; some of the councils in Europe and the US that had been issuing fatwas…all of them stepped forth and condemned the killings of innocent persons. They affirmed that killing even one innocent person was so abhorrent to Islam that one who does so is as guilty as he would be if he had killed all of humanity. That such terrorism is an injustice, that Islam would never countenance or tolerate it, that it is a gross crime, a heinous one and a sinful act. That it foments harm and corruption on earth. That Islam forbids all violence. That killing of children is no jihad. That those who kill innocents have become apostates as they have violated Allah's prohibition. That suicide bombings are vehemently prohibited. That the assailants are spurred by perverted, un-Islamic ideology. That such criminals are no martyrs. That Islam enjoins upon Muslims that they obey the laws of the country in which they are residing . .

In May 2008, the Dar-al Ulum at Deoband itself issued a fatwa. Signed by the Grand Mufti, Habibur Rehman, whom we have encountered in regard to slaughtering cows or not, and two of his colleagues, the fatwa incorporated many of the themes that had been stressed by other authorities. The fatwa declared:

> Islam is a religion of Peace and Harmony. In Islam, creating social discord or disorder, breach of peace, rioting, bloodshed, pillage or plunder and killing of innocent persons anywhere in the world are *all* considered most inhuman crimes. The Quran clearly states that the killing of (even) one innocent person is equivalent to the massacre of all humankind while saving one life is equivalent to the rescue of all humankind. The extent of Islam's emphasis on peace can be seen from the fact that even while granting the right of self-defense to the oppressed, it insists that no excess be committed in retribution and strictly forbids the targeting of any innocent person. The Prophet (PUBH) insisted that even in a war human rights must be fully respected. Islam teaches us that *all* the creatures of Allah are like one family and whoever treats this family of Allah with compassion and mercy would be loved the most by Allah. It is a basic principle of Islam that you assist each other in the pursuit of good and righteous causes and you *do not cooperate* with *anyone* for committing sin or oppression. It is evident from the clear guidelines given in the Holy Quran that the allegation of terrorism against a religion like Islam which enjoins world peace is nothing but a lie. In fact, Islam was born to wipe out all kinds of terrorism and to spread the message of global peace.

The fatwa was followed by a big rally in Delhi—it was said to have been attended by over five lakh Muslims. All present took an 'oath of allegiance': 'We are bound by the fatwa of Dar-al Ulum Deoband and undertake that we shall condemn terrorism and spread Islam's message of global peace.' Ziauddin Sardar, the prominent scholar, hailed the fatwa and the pledge. 'The beginning of the end of the war on terror has started,' he wrote. The fatwa followed as it was by an oath of allegiance is 'canny and unparalleled in history'.[79]

---

79. *New Statesman*, UK, 19 June 2008.

In a word, there are reasons for hope. But we cannot leave things to work themselves out on their own—that may take too long, and, as we have seen in the case of terrorism and the time it took the ulema to react, in a world packed ever tighter together great harm may be inflicted in the meanwhile. Hence, we must 'give history a helping hand.'

A few lessons

- On ever so many matters, the world view of the ulema remains what it has always been.
- There is little leeway for changing it as it is firmly grounded in the twin pillars of Islam, the Quran and the Sunna.
- Often, pressures from within the community are enough to ensure that the laity does as they decree. Power and, therefore, the ability of the clerics to inflict hardship are greatest where and when they are allied to the rulers.
- Ever so often, in Islamic history as well as today, there has been a symbiotic relationship the between the rulers and the clergy.
- Even then, tensions and on occasion open conflict have arisen between the two—rulers have had to accommodate the realities of their time while clerics have insisted on remaining rooted in what Allah has prescribed and the Prophet exemplified.
- These tensions between rulers and their legitimizers as well as disagreements among the clerics—and disagreements between them almost invariably end up being pushed to the extreme—are an opportunity for liberals and for laity: each set can move ahead through the crevices. But this does not happen automatically.

Nor can the few and beleaguered liberals within the community hack their way alone through the crevices. Others should come to their aid—through scholarly examination of the claims and pronouncements of the ulema most of all.

- The ability of rulers and clerics to bolster each other has waned when the rulers have become less legitimate and as life has advanced beyond seventh-century Arabia.
- The invariable ossification of regimes rooted in ideologies and life itself are the great corroders. And so everyone and every development, which takes matters beyond the old confines, helps. Every ruler who grabs legitimacy by setting himself up as the enforcer of some purer version of the ideology—a Zia ul Haq— and eventually leads his countrymen into the rut of stagnation; and, on the other end, every artist who paints the representation of a living being; every actress and actor who appears on TV and in the movies; every progressive person who opens up new opportunities for education—in particular, for girls; everyone who advances new technologies of communication and study; every Muslim woman who takes up a job or, indeed as we have seen, drives a car; every blogger who punctures the ulema's mighty pronouncements with a pin is dealing a mighty blow for liberation.
- Every Muslim in India must remember how lucky she or he is to be living in a country whose traditions are pluralistic and inclusive. She and he must, therefore, bear in mind that any conduct or demand that sets off a reaction in the majority community—'We too must take on the elements of being an exclusivist ideology'—undermines their own future.

- In the meanwhile, liberals should open their eyes. Before genuflecting to some 'renowned alim', someone holding high religious office at al-Azhar, some Grand Mufti of some kingdom or mosque, our liberals and rulers should first ascertain what the gentleman stands for.
- Even more important, liberals—for they are the chief obfuscators in India today—should study the high literature of those on whose behalf they declaim. They should look squarely at the mind which that literature reveals, the mind of the ulema. They should see the mind the ulema seek to foment in the community, and weigh the consequences that shall come about for the entire country should the ulema succeed. They must shed apologia, political correctness, wishful thinking. In a word, the liberals must face the facts, and not lull the country to sleep, on the supposition that no one really heeds what the ulema are proclaiming.
- Terrorists have triggered a more candid and truthful discourse in the West about the ideologies from which they derive legitimacy for their message. In India, that has not been the case at all. That is not because the consequences of that ideology are any the less lethal for us—the country was divided on that ideology; terrorists strike and kill at will; the entire machinery of Pakistan is set on India in the name of religion. The reason that even these depredations have not led to any meaningful discourse is plain and simple intellectual cowardice. This is what has to be overcome first and foremost.
- Nor should one despair of the violence that extreme versions of the ideology may trigger. It sets off a reaction—in terms of counter-violence as well as perceptions. And, as we have just seen, these as much

as their common humanity induce even the ulema to stand up against such violence and hatred.

- When such ideologies take up arms, they have to be defeated, and defeated decisively by arms. But that is never enough. Two further things are necessary.
- The ideology must be defeated ideologically.
- Those who stand by another set of values must do better, they must succeed in spite of what those weaned on the ulema's notions—that itself will trigger a re-examination eventually. As the Spanish proverb has it, 'Living well is the best revenge.'

Basic Texts and Index

Basic texts which have been referred to frequently

Quran

Abdullah Yusuf All, *The Meaning of the Glorious Quran, Text, Translation and Commentary,* Volumes I and II, Dar Al-Kitab al-Masri, Cairo, Dar Al-Kitab Allubnani, Beirut.

Maulana Abul Kalam Azad, *The Tarfuman al-Quran,* Volumes I to III, edited and rendered into English by Syed Abdul Latif, Dr Syed Abdul Latif Trust for Quranic and other Cultural Studies, Hyderabad, 1967.

Hadis

Sahih Al-Bukhari, Volumes I to IX, Muhammad Muhsin Khan (tr.), Islamic University, Al-Medina Al-Munawwara, Kazi Publications, Lahore, 1976 to 1979.

Al-Jame Al-Sahih Al-Bukhari Sharif, Volumes I to III, Maulana Akhtar Shahjahanpuri (tr.), Aiteqad Publishing House, New Delhi, 1984.

Sahih Muslim, Volumes I to IV, Abdul Hamid Siddiqi (tr.), Kitab Bhavan, New Delhi, 1978.

Sahih Muslim Sharif, Volume I to III, Allama Wahiduz Zaman (tr.), Aiteqad Publishing House, New Delhi, 1986.

Sunan Abu Dawud, Volumes I to III, Ahmad Hasan (tr.), Kitab Bhavan, New Delhi, 1993.

Sunan-e Abu Dawud, Volumes I to III, Allama Wahiduz Zaman (tr.), Aiteqad Publishing House, New Delhi, 1985.

Sunan Nasai Sharif, Volumes I to III, Allama Wahid al-Zaman (tr.), Aiteqad Publishing House, Suiwalan, New Delhi, 1986.

Sunan Ibn Majah, Volumes I and II, Abdul Hakim Khan Akhtar Shahjahanpuri (tr.), Aiteqad Publishing House, Suiwalan, New Delhi, 1986.

Imam Malik, Muwatta, Muhammad Rahimuddjn (tr.), Muhammad Ashraf, Lahore, 1980.

Mishkat Al-Masabih, Volumes I and II, James Robson (tr.) Muhammad Ashraf, Lahore, 1975.

Mishkat Sharif, Volumes I and II, Imam Waliuddin Muhammad bin Abdullah al-Khatib al-Umari, Maulana Muhammad Umar Bastavi (ed.), Rabbani Book Depot, Delhi.

Imam Yahya bin Sharaf-ud-Din An-Nawawi, *Riyad As-Salihin,* Volumes I and II, Abdur Rahman Shad (tr.), Kazi Publications, Lahore, 1988.

Fatwas

Imam Fukhruddin Hasan bin Mansoor Al-Uzjandi Al-Farghani, *Fatawa-i-Qazi Khan,* Volumes I and II, Maulvi Yusuf Khan Bahadur and Maulvi Wilayat Husain (trs & eds), Kitab Bhavan, New Delhi, 1994.

Ala Hazrat Imam Ahmad Raza Qadri Barelvi, *Fatawa Rizviyyah,* Volumes I to XII, Raza Academy, Bombay, 1994.

Kifayat-ul-Muftj, Mufti-e-Azam Kifayatullah ke Fatawa, Volumes I to IX, Hafiz al-Rahman Wasaf (compiler), Jadid Barqi Press, Delhi, 1982 to 1987.

Fatawa Dar al-Ulum, Deoband, Volumes I to XII, under the guidance of Mufti-e-Azam Arif ba-Allah Hazrat Maulana Mufti Aziz al-Rahman Sahib Usmani, Mufti Awwal Dar al-Ulum, compiled by Maulana Muhammad Zafiruddin Sahib, Dar al-Ulum, Deoband, 1981 to 1985.

Fatawa Ulama-i-Hadis, Volumes I to IV, Abul Hasnat Ali Muhammad Saiyyidi, Maktaba Maulana Sanaullah Amritsari Academy, Nai Sarak, Delhi, 1981 to 1989.

Mufti Sayyid Abdur Rahim Lajpuri Randeri, *Fatawa-i-Rahimiyyah,* Volumes I to III, M.H.F.H. Quraishi (tr.), Maktaba Rahimiyyah, Rander, Gujarat, 1975 to 1982.

Index

Volumes of fatwas and authorities issuing them are referred to throughout the book. Their names have not been included in the Index. Their fatwas on a topic will be found under the appropriate subject heading.